Y0-BRS-601

County Government in North Carolina

Fourth Edition
1998

Edited by

A. Fleming Bell, II, and
Warren Jake Wicker

INSTITUTE *of* GOVERNMENT
The University of North Carolina at Chapel Hill

NEW HANOVER COUNTY
PUBLIC LIBRARY
201 CHESTNUT STREET
WILMINGTON, N C 28401

THE INSTITUTE OF GOVERNMENT of The University of North Carolina at Chapel Hill is devoted to teaching, research, and consultation in state and local government.

Since 1931 the Institute has conducted schools and short courses for city, county, and state officials. Through monographs, guidebooks, bulletins, and periodicals, the research findings of the Institute are made available to public officials throughout the state.

Each day that the General Assembly is in session, the Institute's *Daily Bulletin* reports on the Assembly's activities for members of the legislature and other state and local officials who need to follow the course of legislation.

Over the years the Institute has served as the research agency for numerous study commissions of the state and local governments.

Michael R. Smith, DIRECTOR
Thomas H. Thornburg, ASSOCIATE DIRECTOR FOR PROGRAMS
Patricia A. Langelier, ASSOCIATE DIRECTOR FOR PLANNING AND OPERATIONS
Ann C. Simpson, ASSOCIATE DIRECTOR FOR DEVELOPMENT

FACULTY

Gregory S. Allison
Stephen Allred
David N. Ammons
A. Fleming Bell, II
Maureen M. Berner
Frayda S. Bluestein
Mark F. Botts
Joan G. Brannon
Anita R. Brown-Graham
William A. Campbell
Margaret S. Carlson
Stevens H. Clarke
Anne S. Davidson
Anne M. Dellinger

James C. Drennan
Richard D. Ducker
Robert L. Farb
Joseph S. Ferrell
Susan Leigh Flinspach
L. Lynnette Fuller
Milton S. Heath, Jr.
Cheryl Daniels Howell
Joseph E. Hunt
Kurt J. Jenne
Robert P. Joyce
David M. Lawrence
Charles D. Liner

Ben F. Loeb, Jr.
Janet Mason
Laurie L. Mesibov
Jill D. Moore
David W. Owens
John Rubin
John L. Saxon
John B. Stephens
A. John Vogt
Richard Whisnant
Gordon P. Whitaker
Michael L. Williamson
(on leave)

© 1999
INSTITUTE OF GOVERNMENT
The University of North Carolina at Chapel Hill
∞ This publication is printed on permanent, acid-free paper
in compliance with the North Carolina General Statutes.
Printed in the United States of America
03 02 01 00 99   5 4 3 2 1
ISBN 1-56011-331-6 (paperback)
ISBN 1-56011-345-6 (hardback)
♻ Printed on recycled paper.

Contents

II   County Revenues and Finance

III   General County Government Functions

Preface

North Carolina is a land of contrasts. Its topography ranges from the lush green wilderness of the Smoky, Black, and Nantahala mountains, to the rolling hills of the Piedmont, to the flat fields and lowlands of the Coastal Plain, to shallow sounds and seemingly endless miles of barrier island beaches. The places where its people live, play, and work are also diverse—from the surging traffic and towering skyscrapers of its metropolitan areas, to smaller cities that mirror the problems and opportunities of their larger cousins, to towns where everyone still knows most everyone, to rural areas where communities are measured in square miles instead of city blocks.

Despite these contrasts, all North Carolinians have certain things in common. One of these is the fact that they are county residents. In appearance and characteristics, these counties vary as widely as the state of which they are a part. Their size ranges from Chowan's 173 square miles to Robeson's and Sampson's nearly 1,000; their population ranges from Tyrrell's 3,671 inhabitants to Mecklenburg's 593,514 (certified state population estimates as of July 1996). Their natural resources and features differ widely. Their economies may be based on agriculture or research or manufacturing. Yet, while they vary in many ways, more important are the similarities in the roles played by all 100 counties.

First and most fundamentally, counties provide identity. The beginnings of North Carolina's division into counties date from the earliest colonial days, and many of its people still derive their sense of place to a large extent from their residence in a particular county. If you ask Tar

Heels where they are from, they are as likely to mention a county name as that of a city or community.

Counties also give shape to the state's political life. Election campaigns for county offices—from commissioner to register of deeds to sheriff to school board member—are often colorful political events. Citizens vote in precincts that are subdivisions of counties, and their ballot-casting is supervised by a county board of elections. Historically, members of the state legislature were elected from districts that did not cross county lines. While in recent decades considerations of federal voting rights laws have overridden the historical boundary line purity, members are still known in the General Assembly in connection with the counties from which they come.

People depend on their county government to carry out or provide money for many of the programs that touch them most directly: schools, courts, social services, and public health activities, for example. County as well as municipal employees inspect new buildings, lay water and sewer lines, and operate recreation programs and landfills.

Many of the rules that govern our lives are written at the county level—from health regulations for swimming pools to zoning, subdivision, and animal-control ordinances for areas outside municipal jurisdiction. Counties determine the tax value of property and maintain the records that determine land ownership and define legal status and relationships.

The government of counties has become increasingly sophisticated in recent decades, as the demands placed on them have continued to grow. For example, there has been a strong trend toward professional administration; all 100 counties now have a full-time manager or chief administrative official. County government officials have also become effective at expressing their concerns at the state and federal levels: both the North Carolina Association of County Commissioners and the National Association of Counties are articulate advocates for county interests.

Each county government generally acts in one of two capacities in carrying out its varied functions. First, as a subdivision of the state, it serves as the state's agent in administering—and to some extent, funding—statewide programs. Second, as a local government, it makes rules and administers programs to meet the needs of the people of a particular area. Knowledge of the differences in these two roles is important in understanding county government structure.

Counties were originally established as state administrative and political subdivisions, used to achieve state goals. While the government responsibilities of the state have changed over the years, this role of the county has been retained. Typically, governmental programs are operated statewide whenever a need is perceived for a service to be offered to all the citizens. Counties are often left with relatively little discretion concerning goals or service levels for such programs, and funding is often provided primarily by the state from statewide revenues such as income taxes.

The funding and administration of the public schools, one of the largest programs in the budget of a county, is a prime example of the county's role as state agent. In the 1995–96 fiscal year, state revenues paid 83.5 percent of the cost of instructional programs in public schools and 68.6 percent of total public school costs. Also, the majority of decisions concerning curriculum, salaries, and even purchasing of supplies for local schools are made or controlled at the state level. Similarly, social services programs consume a large portion of counties' budgets, yet they receive the bulk of their funding from the federal and state governments. Most social services programs, while locally administered, are subject to substantial state and federal regulation, although some additional local flexibility has been introduced in recent years.

A number of autonomous and semiautonomous local boards are involved with state programs at the county level: boards of elections and education, for example. This arrangement sometimes results in divergent views on the part of the officials involved. Those on the state level may find it useful to deal with local boards that specialize in and presumably understand the issues and problems in particular areas of statewide concern. Boards of county commissioners, on the other hand, may view an arrangement that does not give them direct oversight of certain programs as cumbersome and inefficient, and they may dislike providing money to organizations over which they have little influence.

In contrast to their role as state agent, counties also serve as local governments for the people in a particular part of the state. Indeed, about 50 percent of North Carolinians look to the county as their only general-purpose local government. Counties often serve the citizens of both incorporated and unincorporated areas, and increasingly provide services that closely parallel those offered by municipalities. The state's growth in recent years has been predominately in the areas surrounding its towns and cities, and the county has emerged as a logical unit of government to provide services for and to answer the concerns of residents of these urbanizing areas, often in cooperation with municipalities.

This is the fourth edition of *County Government in North Carolina*. Previous versions were published by the Institute of Government in 1989 (third edition, A. Fleming Bell, II, editor), and in 1979 (second edition),

1975 (revised edition), 1969 (supplement to first edition), and 1968 (first edition), all edited by Joseph S. Ferrell. Students of county government may also be interested in *County Government and Administration in North Carolina*, by Paul Woodford Wager, published in 1928 by The University of North Carolina Press.

This book is designed to help the reader understand both what counties do and how they go about doing it. It is intended primarily to meet the needs of county elected officials and administrators in North Carolina. It will also be of interest to citizens and students who need to understand how county government works in the Tar Heel State. Consisting of four parts and thirty-four chapters, it proceeds from consideration of across-the-board organizational and financial concerns to discussions of specific functional areas. The table of contents lists chapter subjects and authors. A detailed list of topics covered in each chapter is given on the chapter's first page.

Part I begins with a general discussion of county government and the responsibilities of county commissioners, followed by consideration of county management issues and the use of performance measurement in managing county functions. Legal liabilities with which counties and their officials must be concerned are the next subject, after which we turn to the roles of two officials who work closely with the board of commissioners: the county attorney and the clerk to the board. Part I concludes by examining county responsibilities for public records management and access, the role of interlocal cooperation in meeting county needs, and city-county consolidation.

Part II examines financial matters in some detail, including revenue sources, property taxation, budget preparation and enactment, capital budgeting and finance, and fiscal control and cash management.

The role of the county as local government is a primary focus of Part III. General functions such as personnel administration, purchasing and contracting (including conflicts of interest), and property acquisition and disposal are considered here. We also devote attention to planning, land use, and physical development, and community development, housing, and economic development. Operation of water and sewer systems and other public enterprises and the management of park and recreation programs conclude this part.

Part IV is devoted primarily to the variety of county government functions that involve other boards and agencies. The county's role as agent of the state is clearly seen in some of the activities discussed in the fourteen chapters of this section.

Reference is made throughout the volume to pertinent provisions of the North Carolina General Statutes (abbreviated as "G.S." or "N.C. Gen. Stat.") and to relevant court decisions. A section on where to obtain further assistance may be found at the end of the book, and lists of suggested readings accompany each chapter.

Nearly all of the chapters were prepared by Institute of Government faculty members who specialize in the subject matter concerned. We hope that this book will serve as a useful text and reference for those who work with and for North Carolina counties and that it will provide students of government with an important tool in understanding the role and significance of county government for the people of this state.

A. FLEMING BELL, II
Professor of Public Law and Government

WARREN JAKE WICKER
Gladys Hall Coates Professor Emeritus
of Public Law and Government

Chapel Hill
Fall 1998

I
Organization and Responsibilities of County Government

1 Counties and County Governance

Joseph S. Ferrell

Contents

Joseph S. Ferrell is an Institute of Government faculty member whose fields of interest include general county government and the legal aspects of property tax listing and assessing.

A Brief History

From 1776 to 1868

Like its neighboring colonies, pre-Revolutionary North Carolina relied heavily on the county for local government purposes. Justices of the peace, as a body or court, administered the county's affairs. They were men of standing, often men of substance, and were generally leaders in their communities. Independence from England brought no wrenching changes to the system. In the early days of North Carolina's statehood, the justices were appointed by the governor to serve at the pleasure of the governor, but in making his appointments the governor relied on recommendations from the General Assembly. Thus, as a matter of practical politics, the members of the legislature from a given county had a powerful voice in the selection of its justices of the peace and therefore in its government.

As a group, the justices in a county formed a body known as the Court of Pleas and Quarter Sessions. Any three justices sitting together constituted a quorum for transacting business. The common practice was for the justices to meet each January, select a chair,[1] and then elect five of their number to hold the regular sessions of the court for the year. At first the court appointed the sheriff, the coroner, and the constables. Later, these offices were made elective—the sheriff and coroner from the county at large and the constables from captains' districts (militia-mustering areas). The justices were also responsible for appointing a clerk of court, register of deeds, county attorney, county trustee (treasurer), surveyor, and overseers or wardens of the poor.

The Court of Pleas and Quarter Sessions had a dual task. Although called a court—and it did perform judicial functions—the body also had administrative duties. Thus the justices were responsible for assessing and levying taxes; establishing and maintaining roads, bridges, and ferries; granting licenses to taverns and controlling the prices charged for food; and the erection and control of mills. Through their powers of appointment, they supervised the work of law enforcement officers, administrative officers of the court, the surveyor, and the wardens of the poor. Taxes were collected by the sheriff.

In its judicial capacity, the Court of Pleas and Quarter Sessions heard civil cases (except those assigned by law to a single justice or to a higher court); it was responsible for probate, dower, guardianships, and the administration of estates; and it had jurisdiction in minor criminal cases.

The county itself was a single political unit. There were no townships, and the Court of Pleas and Quarter Sessions exerted strong control over county affairs through its appointive and administrative powers. It should, however, be emphasized that the voters had no direct control over the court (since it was appointed by the legislature) and thus no such control over county government. This was the situation until the end of the Civil War (1861–65).

From 1868 to 1876

When the North Carolina Constitution was rewritten in 1868, its drafters—many of whom were acquainted with local government systems in other parts of the country—devised a new and apparently more democratic plan of organization for the counties. It strongly resembled the plans used in Pennsylvania and Ohio.

Although the position of justice of the peace was retained, the old Court of Pleas and Quarter Sessions was eliminated. Its judicial responsibilities were divided between the justices of the peace and the superior court. Its administrative work was assigned to a board of commissioners, composed of five members elected by the voters of the county at large.

The commissioners were made responsible for public buildings, schools, roads, and bridges, as well as for the financial affairs of the county, including taxation. The wide appointive powers of the Court of Pleas and Quarter Sessions were not transferred to the board of commissioners. Instead, the voters of the county elected the sheriff, coroner, clerk of court, register of deeds, surveyor, and treasurer. The sheriff continued to serve as tax collector.

Each county was divided into townships—a distinct innovation in North Carolina—and the voters of each township elected two justices of the peace and a clerk who together served as the township's governing body. Under the county commissioners' supervision, this board was responsible for roads and bridges and for assessing property for taxation. Each township also elected a constable and a three-member school committee.

This long-ballot system with numerous separately elected officials favored the newly formed Republican party, whose support was gathered from the newly enfranchised African Americans, most of whom had been slaves only three years before; from native whites of small means who had opposed secession and remained loyal to the Union throughout the Civil War; and from a relatively small number of prominent citizens who believed that the state's shattered fortunes could be recovered only through cooperation and understanding between the races as well as accommodation with the dominant national political party. This new long-ballot system seriously undermined the political power of the landowners, professionals, and merchants who had dominated state government—and thus local government under the old system—for nearly a century. Although most of these people were disenfranchised by the Fourteenth Amendment to the United States Constitution because they had "engaged in insurrection or rebellion against the United States, or given aid or comfort to the enemies thereof" by actively supporting the Confederacy, they formed the Conservative party, a new political group devoted to restoring as much of the pre-war social and governmental system as was possible under the circumstances. The new system of county government created by the constitution of 1868 became one of their major targets.

Constitutional Changes of 1875

Seven years after the constitution of 1868 established the county commissioners and township systems, political control shifted to the Conservatives. By convention in 1875, the constitution was amended to authorize the General Assembly to modify the plan of county government established in 1868, and the legislature was quick to exercise its authority. The 1877 General Assembly stripped the townships of their powers. They were retained as convenient administrative subdivisions, primarily for road building and maintenance purposes, but they were no longer distinct units of local government with their own elected governing boards. More importantly, the General Assembly returned to the old system of appointing justices of the peace by special act of the legislature, which meant in practice that justices were chosen by the county's legislative delegation. The most powerful tools of government—the powers to tax and to conduct elections—were handed over to the justices. The boards of county commissioners were not abolished but they could not levy taxes or make other major decisions unless a majority of the justices concurred. And this was only the general law—in some counties, the commissioners were also made subject to legislative appointment.

This hobbling arrangement lasted for twenty years. In 1895 the right of the people to elect commissioners was restored in most counties, and the requirement that the boards' decisions be approved by the justices of the peace was repealed. The right of the people to elect the commissioners was finally restored in all counties in 1905.

The County as a Body Politic and Corporate

Counties, as defined geographic subdivisions of the state, serve many purposes. Churches, civic clubs, and other societal institutions use them as convenient subdivisions for their own purposes. The business world may assign sales territories and franchises to areas composed of one or more counties. The county may play a role in the psychology of people born and raised "in the country": it serves to establish where they are from and who they are, thus becoming a part of their personal identity. But the county was created in the first instance by the state as a political unit, and this remains its primary purpose.

Many years ago the North Carolina Supreme Court was called on to define a county from a legal point of view. (The case before the court was one in which Wake County was a litigant; thus the court spoke in terms of that county, but what it had to say is equally true of the other ninety-nine.) Here is that description:

> Wake County is a body politic and corporate, created by the General Assembly of North Carolina for certain public and political purposes. Its powers as such, both express and implied, are conferred by statutes, enacted from time to time by the General Assembly, and are exercised by its Board of Commissioners. . . . Speaking of the counties of this State, this Court has said, in *Jones v. Comrs.*, 137 N.C. 579, 50 S.E. 291: . . . "In the exercise of ordinary governmental functions, [counties] are simply agencies of the State, constituted for the convenience of local administration in certain portions of the State's territory, and in the exercise of such functions they are subject to almost unlimited legislative control, except when the power is restricted by constitutional provisions." In *O'Berry, State Treasurer v. Mecklenburg County*, 198 N.C. 357, 151 S.E. 880 (1930), it is said: "The weight of authority is to the effect that all the powers and functions of a county bear reference to the general policy of the State, and are in fact an integral portion of the general administration of State policy." [2]

It is instructive to examine some of the phrases used in this quotation. A county is a "body politic and corporate," according to the court. A body politic is a civil division of the state for purposes of governmental administration. A body corporate is a legal entity. In private law, a corporation is a legal person. A county is a legal entity or corporation of a special sort and with a public function. As such, it can buy and hold property, sue and be sued, and enter into contracts—all functions necessary to make its work as a body politic effective.

Historically, the primary reason for establishing a county was to serve state purposes and to perform state functions in a given area rather than to satisfy the needs of a particular geographic community. By way of contrast, a city was formed primarily at the request of the people within its jurisdiction to serve the needs of the inhabitants.

For the supreme court to say that "all the powers and functions of a county bear reference to the general policy of the State and are in fact an integral portion of the general administration of State policy" is not as restrictive as it might appear at first reading. "State policy" is a very broad frame of reference; it can touch any aspect of local government. Thus the significant nugget in the supreme court's definition of the role of counties is its statement that in exercising their functions they "are subject to almost unlimited legislative control, except when the power is restricted by constitutional provisions." In effect, if the General Assembly can be persuaded to assign counties any given power or responsibility, that assignment becomes state policy for county administration unless prohibited by the North Carolina Constitution.

The court's phrases should not be drained of meaning, but they must be read in light of the General Assembly's freedom to withhold, assign, withdraw, and supervise the specific powers of any agency of government—state, county, municipality, or special district. The development of state policy with regard to the allocation of functions among government units and agencies is necessarily determined by successive legislatures' changing ideas of what is best calculated to achieve desired results.

Experience plays a major role in the determination of state policy. The experience of financial emergency and stress, for example, has sometimes produced a climate favorable to reexamining the allocation of government responsibilities. Until Governor Angus W. McLean's administration (1925–29), the state allowed counties, cities, and other local units unlimited freedom in borrowing money and issuing bonds. With no one to advise or warn them in marketing their securities, many counties overextended their obligations and saw their credit ratings drop so low that they had to pay crippling rates of interest; eventually some faced bankruptcy. On the basis of this experience and recognizing a statewide concern, in 1927 the legislature established the County Government Advisory Commission and gave it the supervisory powers necessary to correct the situation. This commission effected a reversal in local government financing; its successor, the Local Government Commission, remains a bulwark of North Carolina government today.

Experience with various local arrangements for road building and maintenance has had a comparable effect on state policy. It is not accidental that the counties are no longer responsible for this work. The legislature, reflecting the concerns of the people of the state, recognized a community of interest in roads that was wider than the single county and defined state policy on them accordingly. Comparable redefinitions of the appropriate areas of concern have affected governmental responsibility for operating schools, conducting elections, housing the state's system of lower courts and their records, maintaining property ownership and mortgage records, enforcing much of the state's criminal law, administering public health and social services programs, and carrying on state programs designed to foster agriculture. Some of these functions are the responsibility of the boards of county commissioners, and some are assigned to other boards with varying relationships to the boards of commissioners. Thus, apart from the direct role played by the commissioners in any of these fields, it is the policy of the state to make extensive use of its counties in carrying out a large number of essential government operations.

For example, from the beginning the county has been used as the basic local unit in the judicial system and for law enforcement—there one finds the court, courthouse, sheriff, jail, clerk of court, and court records. But the court is not a *county* court; it is a unit of the *state's* judicial system. The judge, district attorney, clerk, and magistrates are state officials who administer state law, not county law.

Legislative elections provide a good example of how the county's role in carrying out state policy can change. For many years the county was the basic unit for popular representation in the General Assembly because both House and Senate districts were composed of single or multiple counties. Vestiges of that system remain, but today census tracts rather than counties have become the building blocks of legislative representation. This has come about as a result of federal requirements that legislative districts be drawn in ways that respect the right of each citizen to cast an equally weighted vote and not dilute the voting strength of racial minorities.

The General Assembly expresses and codifies its state policy decisions by enacting statutes. In assigning duties and powers to counties, the legislature sometimes speaks in terms of mandate or command and sometimes in terms of permission and discretion. Thus, for example, counties are *required* to help finance the public schools, but have discretionary authority to exercise planning and zoning powers.

Forms of Legislation Affecting Counties

The General Assembly makes two kinds of laws. It enacts general statutes that apply statewide and local or special laws that pertain exclusively to named counties or cities. The North Carolina Constitution contains limitations on legislative authority to enact local laws dealing with a substantial list of topics, but in the absence of constitutional restriction, the legislature is free to permit local variety and experiment, a freedom once denounced by students of government but now seen as a useful device for exploring new ideas and approaches to government problems. Given this legislative freedom, any discussion of county powers and responsibilities must always be prefaced with a caution that what is being said about counties in general may not hold true for any particular county.

The Board of County Commissioners

As has been noted, the county, as a body politic and corporate, is a legal person capable of holding and managing property and possessed of many powers conferred on it by law. It exercises its powers and discharges its responsibilities through its board of commissioners. In the words of G.S. 153A-12, "Except as otherwise directed by law, each power, right, duty, function, privilege and immunity of the corporation [i.e., the county] shall be exercised by the board of commissioners." This statute goes on to say that the county's legal powers are to be carried into execution as provided by the laws of the state, but if a power is "conferred or imposed by law without direction or restriction as to how it is to be exercised or performed," the power or responsibility "shall be carried into execution as provided by ordinance or resolution of the board of commissioners."

Each county in the state has a board of commissioners. In many states, general laws prescribe a form of government for all counties, or for all counties in classes defined by population. In such states, one would expect to find essentially the same form of government in counties of comparable size. Not so in North Carolina. Its boards of county commissioners vary in size, term of office, method of election, procedure for selecting the chair, and administrative structure. And these variations bear no correlation to the population of the county or any other objective criterion. Boards of commissioners are authorized to initiate various changes in their makeup and manner of election, subject to voter approval (G.S. 153A-58 through -64).

The composition of county boards varies widely across the state. The number of members ranges from three to eleven, terms of office may be either two years or four years, and there is wide variety in the use of districting systems. The typical North Carolina county operates under the county-manager form of government with a five-member board of commissioners nominated and elected at large for four-year staggered terms. Table 1-1 shows the variety of forms in use as of 1997. There has been a long-term trend toward adoption of four-year staggered terms. Efforts to increase minority representation on county boards have led to more use of districting systems and larger boards. The board sets its own compensation and allowances.

Selection

All county commissioners are elected by the people in partisan elections held in November of even-numbered years—the same time as the elections for members of the General Assembly. But not every county elects all members of its board every two years. Because of the interplay of staggered four-year terms, two-year terms, and straight four-year terms, about half of the state's county commissioners are elected at each general election. Nomination by a political party is not required in order to run for this office, but candidates are almost invariably partisan nominees. As of the 1996 elections, 324 of the 564 county commissioners were affiliated with the Democratic party and 240 belonged to the Republican party.

Vacancies in the board of commissioners are filled by appointment of the remaining members. A person appointed to fill a vacancy must be a member of the same political party as the one replaced (if that person was elected as the nominee of a political party), and the executive committee of that party has the right to be consulted before the appointment is made. As of 1997 the board must appoint the executive committee's nominee in forty-two counties, if the recommendation is made within thirty days after the seat becomes vacant.[3] In the other fifty-eight counties, the board need not follow any advice given by the committee. If the vacancy occurs in a two-year term or in the last two years of a four-year term, the appointment is for the remainder of the unexpired term. If the vacancy takes place in the first two years of a four-year term, the appointment runs only until the next general election, when an election is held to fill the office for the remainder of the unexpired term.

Occasionally a board of commissioners finds itself deadlocked and unable to fill a vacancy. Since nearly all of these boards have an odd

Table 1-1
Form of Government of North Carolina Counties, 1997

Number of Boards with a Chief Administrative Officer

99	Appointed manager
1	Elected chair of the board is the county administrator

Number of Boards with This Number of Members

59 boards	5 members
27 boards	7 members
6 boards	3 members
3 boards	6 members
5 boards	More than 7 members

Number of Boards with These Terms of Office

77 boards	Four-year staggered terms
13 boards	Four-year terms
7 boards	Combination of two-year and four-year terms
3 boards	Two-year terms

Number of Boards with This Method of Election

41 boards	Elected at large
23 boards	Elected with various combinations of at large, at large with district residency requirements, and nominations by districts with election at large
22 boards	Elected at large; district residency required
10 boards	Nominated and elected entirely by districts
4 boards	Elected under limited voting plans

number of members, one vacancy means that the remaining members could become equally divided over two candidates, so that neither candidate could receive a majority vote. Recognizing this problem the law provides that when a board of commissioners fails to fill a vacancy in its membership for sixty days, the clerk to the board must report it to the clerk of superior court, who must fill the vacancy within ten days after the day the report is received.

The law also provides for another contingency that has not occurred to date. If the number of vacancies on the board is such that a quorum cannot be obtained, the chair must appoint enough members to make one up, and the board then fills the vacancies. If this situation exists and the office of chair is also vacant, the clerk of superior court may act in the chair's stead on petition of any remaining member of the board or any five registered voters of the county.

Whoever makes appointments to the board is bound by the rules that each appointee must be a member of the same political party as the person being replaced, that the party's executive committee must be consulted, and that in certain counties the committee's nominee must be appointed.

Taking Office

Under G.S. 153A-26 a county commissioner assumes the powers and duties of office by taking an oath of office and subscribing to (signing) a copy of it. The law gives several public officials the authority to administer oaths, but in most counties it is customary to have this done by the resident superior court judge, chief district judge, or clerk of the superior court for members of the board of commissioners, the sheriff, and the register of deeds. The clerk to the board of commissioners can also perform this function.

A person elected to public office may take the oath of office at any time on or after the date fixed by law for this to occur. For newly elected county commissioners, that date is the first Monday in December following their election. This is also the regular meeting date for the board in most counties. If newly elected commissioners are unable to take the oath at that time, they may take it later. The North Carolina Constitution provides, however, that public officers continue to hold office until their successors are chosen and qualified; thus, a member of the board of commissioners who was defeated in the election or did not seek reelection retains office until the successor takes the oath.

The Chair

In most counties, the chair of the board of commissioners is selected by the board itself. In a few counties, this is a separate office, and the chair is elected as such by the people. In all counties, the board itself must choose a vice-chair to act in the absence or disability of the chair (G.S. 153A-39).

When the board selects the chair, it does so at its first regular meeting in December of odd-numbered years or the first Monday in December in even-numbered years; the chair serves a term of one year and presides at all board meetings. By law, this official has not only the right, but also the duty, to vote on all questions before the board unless excused by a standing rule of the body or by consent of the remaining members. (Permission not to vote can be granted only in limited cases, as discussed in the "Procedure" section, later in this chapter.) However, the chair may not vote to break a tie vote in which he or she participated. The chair is generally recognized by law as the county's chief executive officer and may acquire considerable prestige and influence by virtue of the position. Although as a general rule, chairs have no more legal power than other members of the board, they do have special authority to declare states of emergency under the state laws governing riots and civil disorders, and they have authority to call special meetings of the board on their own initiative.

Meetings

Boards of commissioners are required by law to hold at least one meeting each month, although they may meet as often as necessary (G.S. 153A-40). Many boards hold two regular meetings each month. They may select any day of the month and any public place within the county for their regular meetings, but unless they select some other time or place by formal resolution, the law requires them to meet on the first Monday of the month at the courthouse. It does not specify the time of day. Some boards hold some of their regular meetings in the evening to allow greater public attendance.

Special meetings may be called by the chair or by a majority of the other board members. The law lays down specific rules for calling special meetings. They must be called by written notice stating the time, place, and subjects to be considered. This notice must be posted on the courthouse bulletin board and delivered to each board member at least forty-eight hours before the meeting. Unless all members attend or sign a written waiver, only business related to the subjects stated in the notice may be transacted at a special meeting.

Other notice requirements for special meetings are imposed by the North Carolina open meetings law (G.S. 143-318.9 through -143-318.16A). In addition to a written notice posted forty-eight hours in advance, notices of the meeting must be mailed or delivered to news media and other persons who have filed a written request for notice with the clerk to the board or other designated person forty-eight hours before the time of the meeting.

These rules do not apply to special meetings called to deal with an "emergency," which is not defined by the general law governing county commissioners' meetings. (The open meetings law defines an emergency meeting as one called because of generally unexpected circumstances requiring immediate board consideration.) Even then, the persons who call the meeting must take "reasonable action to inform the other members and the public of the meeting." The open meetings law requires local news media to be informed of emergency meetings as defined in that statute. Only business connected with the emergency may be discussed at such a meeting.

While county commissioners' meetings are generally held within the county, out-of-county meetings are permitted in four specific instances:

1. In connection with a joint meeting of two or more public bodies, as long as the meeting is within the boundaries of the political subdivision represented by the members of one of the participating bodies.

2. In connection with a retreat, forum, or similar gathering held solely to provide the county commissioners with information relating to the performance of their public duties (no vote may be taken during this type of meeting).

3. In connection with a meeting between the board and its local legislative delegation while the General Assembly is in session, as long as no votes are taken except concerning matters directly relating to proposed or pending legislation.

4. While the commissioners are attending a convention, association meeting, or similar gathering, if the meeting is held solely to discuss or deliberate on the board's position concerning convention resolutions, association officer elections, and similar issues that are not legally binding.

All such meetings held outside the county are considered "official meetings," as that term is used in the open meetings law, and are subject to that law.

The notice and other requirements of the open meetings law extend to all "public bodies." In county government they include the following:

1. The board of county commissioners itself
2. All committees of the board, whether standing or ad hoc
3. All groups established through the action of the board of commissioners, such as a planning board, board of adjustment, human relations commission, and the like, along with all committees composed of members of such groups

All "official meetings" of public bodies, including the board of county commissioners and any of its committees, are subject to the open meetings law. Official meetings must be open to the public at all times except when the public body is considering a topic for which the law specifically permits closed sessions. An official meeting occurs when a majority of the members of a public body gather to take action, hold a hearing, deliberate, or vote.

Before deciding to meet in closed session lawfully, a board of county commissioners should always consult its attorney for advice as to the precise provisions of the open meetings law that must be observed. Briefly, the procedure for holding a closed session requires that the public body first meet in an open session for which public notice has been given in accordance with the open meetings law. A member must then move to go into closed session. The motion must state a lawful reason for closing the session. If the reason is to prevent disclosure of privileged or confidential information, the motion must state the specific state or federal law that makes the information privileged or confidential. If the motion to close the session is approved, the board may then exclude from the meeting room any nonmembers it may choose. Most boards admit the county manager, clerk to the board, county attorney, and perhaps other staff members to closed meetings, and it is lawful to do so.

In most cases a public body may only deliberate in closed session; any formal action required of the board must usually take place in open session. There is one exception to this rule. The board may approve an offer of settlement of a lawsuit in closed session, but the terms of any settlement accepted by the other side in the lawsuit (other than a malpractice suit against a hospital) must be reported in an open session and recorded in the minutes.

At the end of the closed session, the public body must return to open session even though the only action remaining may be to adjourn the meeting. Minutes of the closed session must be kept, but they may be sealed "so long as public inspection would frustrate the purpose of a closed session." Whether sealed or not, the minutes of a closed session must give a *general account* of the session "so that a person not in attendance would have a reasonable understanding of what transpired." Although *minutes* and a *general account* will often be the same, there will be times when the board might choose to issue a general account of a closed meeting that does not contain as much detail as the minutes.

The purposes for which boards of county commissioners or other public bodies may meet in closed session are as follows:

- To prevent disclosure of information privileged or confidential pursuant to state or federal law
- To prevent premature disclosure of a special award such as a prize or honorary distinction
- To consult with an attorney in order to preserve the attorney-client privilege and to consider and give instructions to the attorney concerning the handling or settlement of litigation
- To reach agreement on a tentative list of economic development incentives that may be offered by the public body in negotiations
- To instruct the county's staff or negotiating agents with respect to the position to be taken in negotiations for the acquisition of real property or the amount of compensation or other terms of an employment contract
- To consider personnel matters with respect to a specific individual
- To discuss allegations of criminal misconduct

There are two basic sanctions for violations of the open meetings law. The most often used is an injunction against future violations. Such an injunction is a court order directing named public officials to stop violating the law. A public official who flouts such an injunction can be found in contempt of court, a serious offense that can lead to imprisonment. A less often used remedy is a court order declaring specific actions taken in violation of the open meetings law to be void.

The open meetings law provides that the court may award reasonable attorneys' fees to the prevailing party in any lawsuit that has been brought to enforce the act, to be paid by the losing party as a part of the costs of court. The court may also order that all or any part of attorneys' fees assessed against the county be paid personally by any individual board member who the court finds to have knowingly or intentionally violated the act. This cannot be done if the board or the individual member sought and followed the advice of an attorney before participating in the unlawful closed session.

Procedure

G.S. 153A-41 through -44 leave most procedural matters to the board's discretion, but they do establish a few rules that must be followed. The board may take no action unless a quorum is present. A quorum is defined as a majority of the full membership of the board without regard to vacancies. For example, a quorum of a five-member board is always three members, even though there may be two vacancies. Once a quorum is present at a meeting, a member may not destroy it by leaving the room without the remaining members' consent. The law provides that if a member withdraws from the meeting room without being excused by a majority of those remaining, he or she is counted as present for quorum purposes. The board also has the legal power to command the sheriff to take absent members into custody and bring them to the meeting place, but such action may be taken only when a quorum is already present.

The law places a duty on all members to vote on each question before the board unless they are excused by their colleagues. Abstention is not allowed except when the matter before the board concerns that member's financial interest or official conduct. Most boards enforce this duty by recording members as voting in the affirmative unless the member audibly votes in the negative. A few boards reverse this and record an abstention as a negative vote. At least one board records an abstention as a vote on the prevailing side.

The board must see that the clerk to the board keeps full and accurate minutes of its proceedings. The minute book must be open to public inspection, and the results of each vote taken by the board must be recorded in it. Each member has the right to demand a roll-call vote on any question put to the board; when such a demand is made, the names of those voting on each side of the question must be recorded.

The keeping of "full and accurate minutes" requires recording the board's actions in ways that demonstrate that any required conditions for taking action have been met (for example, the fact that a quorum was present or, in the case of a contract award after formal bidding, a list of the proposals received). Whether other information is included is up to the board. Generally, it is not helpful to record summaries of board discussions, although occasionally commissioners want this done.

The board has the power to adopt its own written rules of procedure. The only legal restraints on them are that they must be "in the spirit of generally accepted principles of parliamentary procedure" and must conform to the various general laws governing board actions.

Formal Actions

Except for the few special powers held by the chair, the legal powers and duties of county commissioners are vested in the board acting as a body. Individual commissioners have no powers of their own, but when they meet with their fellow commissioners in a validly called and validly held meeting, a majority may exercise control of those functions of county government confided to the care of the board of commissioners.

Formal action by the board may be taken in any of three forms: orders (or motions), resolutions, and ordinances. Although these terms are often used interchangeably, their definitions may be useful in illustrating how the board acts. An *order* is usually a directive to a county administrative officer to take or refrain from taking a specified action. For example, a board of commissioners may enter an order directing the county manager to advertise for bids for a new office building. An order may also formally declare the existence of a given state of fact—for example, an order declaring the results of a bond election. Finally, an order may sometimes be used to decide a question before the board, such as an order awarding a construction contract to the lowest responsible bidder. A *resolution* usually expresses the sense of the board on a question before it. For example, it may adopt a resolution requesting the county's legislative delegation to introduce a local bill, or it may resolve to petition the state's department of transportation to pave a rural road. An *ordinance* is an action of the board taken in its capacity as the county's legislative body. As such, an ordinance is analogous to an act of the General Assembly. The commissioners may adopt ordinances relating to such varied matters as zoning, subdivision control, dogs running at large, use of county parking lots, street numbers and rural roads, and use of the county landfill.

Ordinance Procedure

The law does not regulate the manner in which orders and resolutions are adopted by a board of commissioners beyond the minimum requirement of a valid meeting at which a quorum is present, but several laws govern the adoption of ordinances (G.S. 153A-45 through -50). An ordinance may be adopted at the meeting at which it is introduced only if it receives a unanimous affirmative vote, with all members of the board present and voting. If it passes at this meeting but with less than a unanimous vote, it may finally be passed by a majority vote at any time within

100 days of its introduction. This rule does not apply to the following ordinances:

- The budget ordinance (which may be passed at any meeting at which a quorum is present)
- The bond ordinance (which always requires a public hearing before passage and in most cases requires approval by the voters as well)
- Any ordinance on which the law requires a public hearing before adoption (such as a zoning ordinance)
- A franchise ordinance (which must be passed at two separate regular meetings of the board)

Once an ordinance is adopted, it must be filed in an ordinance book, separate from the minute book. The ordinance book must be indexed and made available for public inspection. The budget ordinance, bond ordinances, and ordinances of "limited interest or transitory nature" may be omitted from the book, but the book must contain a section showing the caption of each omitted ordinance and the page in the minute book at which it appears. An ordinance that is required to be included in the ordinance book cannot be enforced until it is properly filed and indexed.

The board of commissioners has authority to adopt and issue a code of ordinances.

Public Hearings

In the course of a normal year, a board of commissioners will hold several public hearings. Some of them will be required by law, such as those on the budget ordinance, a bond ordinance, or a zoning ordinance or amendment thereto. Some hearings may be held on the board's own initiative to give interested citizens an opportunity to make their views known to the board on a controversial issue, such as a dog-control ordinance. The laws that require public hearings do not specify the manner in which they must be conducted; the laws only require that they be held. Nevertheless, G.S. 153A-52 allows the board to adopt reasonable rules governing the conduct of public hearings. These rules may regulate such matters as allotting time to each speaker, designating who will speak for groups, selecting delegates from groups when the hearing room is too small to hold everyone who wants to attend, and maintaining order as well as decorum.

Organizing the Administration

The law dictates many features of county government organization. The sheriff and the register of deeds are elected by the people. Each county has a board of education, a board of social services, and a board of elections. Each county is served by a board of health and a mental health, mental retardation, and substance-abuse board. Many counties have a community college board and a board of alcoholic beverage control. The board of commissioners participates in choosing at least some of the members of all of these boards except the board of education (elected by citizens) and the board of elections (appointed by the State Board of Elections). Because these boards are established pursuant to the requirements of state law, the board of commissioners has little or no power to alter their structure or authority, although it may exercise control over the budgets of some of them. (The roles of most of these other boards are discussed elsewhere in this text.) The board of commissioners has authority to organize other local boards, agencies, departments, and offices not mandated by state law in any way it sees fit.

Principal Administrative Appointments

The board of commissioners is served as a board by three principal officials whom the board itself appoints directly: the county manager, the county attorney, and the clerk to the board. The manager's powers and duties are discussed in Chapter 2. The county attorney and the clerk to the board are discussed in Chapter 5. Each of these officials serves at the pleasure of the board.

Additional Resources

Corbitt, David L. *Formation of North Carolina Counties 1663–1943.* Raleigh, N.C.: North Carolina Department of Archives and History, 1950.

Ferrell, Joseph S., comp. *Forms of Government of North Carolina Counties.* Chapel Hill, N.C.: Institute of Government, The University of North Carolina at Chapel Hill, 1992.

————. *Rules of Procedure for the Board of County Commissioners.* 2d ed. rev. Chapel Hill, N.C.: Institute of Government, The University of North Carolina at Chapel Hill, 1995.

Liner, Charles D., ed. *State and Local Government Relations in North Carolina: Their Evolution and Current Status.* 2d ed. Chapel Hill, N.C.: Institute of Government, The University of North Carolina at Chapel Hill, 1995.

Lawrence, David M. *Open Meetings and Local Governments in North Carolina: Some Questions and Answers.* 5th ed. Chapel Hill, N.C.: Institute of Government, The University of North Carolina at Chapel Hill, 1998.

————. *Public Records Law for North Carolina Local Governments.* Chapel Hill, N.C.: Institute of Government, The University of North Carolina at Chapel Hill, 1997.

Whitaker, Gordon P. *Local Government in North Carolina.* Raleigh, N.C.: North Carolina City and County Management Association, 1993.

Notes

1. The gender-neutral term "chair" will be used throughout this chapter instead of "chairman" or "chairperson," although the statute uses the term "chairman."

2. Martin v. Commissioners of Wake County, 208 N.C. 354, 180 S.E. 777 (1935).

3. N.C. Gen. Stat. § 153A-27.1. Alamance, Alexander, Alleghany, Avery, Beaufort, Brunswick, Buncombe, Burke, Cabarrus, Caldwell, Carteret, Cherokee, Clay, Cleveland, Cumberland, Dare, Davidson, Davie, Forsyth, Graham, Guilford, Haywood, Henderson, Hyde, Jackson, Lincoln, Macon, Madison, McDowell, Mecklenburg, Moore, Pender, Polk, Randolph, Rockingham, Rutherford, Sampson, Stanly, Stokes, Transylvania, Wake, and Yancey counties.

2   County Management

Kurt Jenne

Contents

Kurt Jenne is an Institute of Government faculty member whose work includes teaching in
the Institute's schools for newly elected officials, assisting governing boards in hiring city
and county managers, and facilitating board retreats.
   The author expresses his thanks to Don Hayman, Institute of Government faculty
member, 1948–1985, the previous author of this chapter. He has been advisor, mentor,
and friend to countless city and county managers, the boards they served, and the
Institute faculty who have followed in his footsteps.

North Carolina has a long tradition of using professional managers to promote efficient and effective local government. In 1917 Catawba and Caldwell counties secured authorization by special acts of the General Assembly to appoint a county manager, although neither did so at the time.[1] In that same year, Buncombe County designated the chair of the board of commissioners as a full-time manager.[2] In 1927, following the success of the general law allowing cities to determine their form of government by local action, the General Assembly passed similar legislation to allow counties to choose their form of government without special legislation.[3] In 1929 Robeson County became the first county in the United States to adopt the county-manager form,[4] and in 1930 Durham County became the second in the country to do so.[5] Although they were ahead of their counterparts in other states, North Carolina counties were more cautious than cities in adopting this new form of government: while twenty-four towns and cities had adopted the council-manager form by 1933, up until 1960 only nine counties had used the general law to appoint county managers, and three other counties elected commissioners to serve in the capacity of county manager.[6] By 1970 thirty-five counties were using the county-manager form, and by 1980 eighty-two had adopted it. Today only one county does not employ a full-time professional county manager: in Jackson County the chair is elected to perform not only the duties of the chair on a full-time basis, but also the duties of the county manager, for which he or she is paid accordingly.

Reasons for the Growth in the Use of County-Manager Government

Where did this growth in professional management originate? The form of government employing a professional manager who is accountable to those elected to office appeared in the United States almost a century ago. It was created as part of an effort to reform the corruption in American local government that existed at the turn of the century. Nineteenth-century Jacksonian democracy—with its aversion to concentrated power in government—had created a system (the so-called long ballot) by which popularly elected officials filled most critical administrative positions. Few of these officials had the requisite skills or even incentives to cooperate with other officials to run an efficient or effective government. This inefficiency created a leadership void that was quickly filled by party machines, whose political bosses controlled and manipulated voting. In return for delivering the vote, political bosses told elected officials how to run operations, invariably in a way that enriched them and their friends. Public affairs were organized and conducted on the basis of personal favors, political deals, and private profit. Party machine politics resulted in such inefficiency and laid such waste to local government treasuries that it became a blatant affront to middle- and upper-class notions of a broader public good as the guiding principle of government. To change this, progressive reformers promoted widespread citizen access to accountable, elected officials through such devices as the short ballot, the strong executive, nonpartisan at-large elections, the initiative, the referendum, and the recall.

At the same time, reformers sought to introduce into local government the application of business and scientific management principles that were hugely popular at the time. One vehicle for doing this was the council-manager plan for cities, originated by reformer Richard Childs in 1910[7] and officially incorporated into the Model City Charter of the National Civic League in 1915. The plan sought to bring a balance of democratic political accountability and honest, competent administration to governance. In a move away from the reformers' previous support of the strong, elected executive, the plan called for a small, accountable, elected body with a presiding officer to employ a politically neutral, expert manager to serve at its pleasure. The manager would give objective, rational advice to the elected body and then faithfully execute whatever decisions the elected body made for the welfare of the citizens, using sound business practices to administer efficiently the day-to-day affairs of government.

While these government reforms were initially employed in cities, the impetus to use measures aimed at increasing the efficiency of local government affected counties as well, as they grew in population and became more urbanized in some parts of the country. In almost eighty years, the main elements of the plan have changed very little. Today the criteria of the International City/County Management Association (ICMA) for officially recognizing a jurisdiction as a *council-manager juris-diction* (the term applies to counties as well) include that the manager

- serve at the pleasure of the entire board of commissioners (not the chair alone);
- have direct responsibility for the operation of government services and functions;
- have joint responsibility, in partnership with the commissioners, for policy formulation;
- have direct responsibility for budget preparation and implementation; and
- have appointment, removal, and administrative authority over principal department heads.[8]

Adoption of the County-Manager Form of Government

The county-manager form of government is one of two forms under which counties in North Carolina may operate. If the board of commissioners takes no action in this respect, it operates without a county manager under the authority of G.S. 153A-76, which permits the board to organize county government however it wishes, consistent with the law. Among other things this would permit the commissioners to hire an "administrator" whose duties might not include all of those granted by statute to the county manager but might be prescribed by the commissioners themselves. Unlike city councils in North Carolina, boards of county commissioners have seldom used this more circumscribed position.[9] Under the municipal statute, adoption of the council-manager form requires that the manager be given hiring and firing authority over all employees not otherwise hired by the board. As a result, some councils that want to retain this authority but also want the help of a chief administrative officer retain the mayor-council form but hire an administrator. Conversely, county commissioners have a choice in whether or not to grant hiring and firing authority to the manager under the county-manager plan.

If the commissioners wish to employ the county-manager plan, they may do so by passing a resolution adopting the plan by authority of G.S. 153A-81. The plan can be carried out in any one of three ways:

1. The commissioners may employ a county manager who holds no other office simultaneously and who serves at the pleasure of the commissioners. In this alternative the county manager must be appointed solely on the basis of his or her administrative qualifications [G.S. 153A-81(a)].
2. The commissioners may confer the duties of county manager upon the chair or some other commissioner.[10]
3. The commissioners may confer the duties of county manager upon any other county employee, as did the Brunswick County Commissioners at one time when they appointed the county attorney to also serve as county manager.[11]

Unlike cities, counties have no requirement to continue to operate with or without the county-manager plan for any minimum period of time after passing a resolution to change from one arrangement to the other.[12]

Roles of the County Commissioners, the Chair, and the County Manager

Several assumptions implicit in the county-manager plan have influenced North Carolina's and other states' general laws regarding this form of government and have affected the way in which elected officials and managers perceive their roles in relation to each other. For the most part, the plan assumes that the board of county commissioners fairly represents the electorate, that a clear public interest can be found to guide most decisions, and therefore that the commissioners can, with some degree of consensus, give the manager clear direction for carrying out the board's policies. The plan has always promoted separation of the commissioners' responsibility for political judgments and policy direction from the manager's responsibility for administration in accordance with the commissioners' guidance and his or her own politically neutral expertise. By these assumptions the plan seeks to create an effective balance between objective, honest, expert government operation and democratic access and control through the authority and the accountability of the elected body.

Many of these underlying assumptions have always been difficult to achieve in reality and are becoming even more problematic in the political and social landscape of the late 1990s. In 1993 a task force of county and city managers from all over the country convened by ICMA to examine board-manager relations, began its work by talking about the forces of change that were affecting the county-manager and council-manager forms of government. Managers suggested that citizens seemed to be losing respect for both politics and government itself and that the public that managers served was increasingly fragmented into interest groups with competing narrow agendas, an unwillingness to cooperate, and a tendency to vie for absolute control. This last problem seemed to afflict counties where urban expansion into rural areas had brought newer citizens with expectations of government and its services into conflict with lifelong rural residents, who suddenly found themselves having to share space and increasing tax burdens with the newly arrived urbanites. As a result, managers said, they faced mixed signals and sometimes unresolvable conflicts of expectations from both elected officials and citizens. They felt that directly elected chairs and mayors often viewed managers as competitors in the arena of local leadership and that the old business traditions of the profession had themselves evolved into such a state of "thriving on chaos" that managers who played by the old rules might find themselves characterized as impediments to progress.[13]

These changes and managers' attempts to adjust to them have led to confusion over what the absolute elements of the county-manager plan are—which of the ideals are essential to its integrity and which can be changed or adapted to the needs of politics in local government. Today many managers and elected officials seem to be seeking ways to forge a true partnership in governance, one that recognizes that commissioners, chairs, and managers are mutually dependent on one another, share responsibility for most aspects of governance, yet must divide some responsibility for fulfilling certain expectations in order to make the whole system work for the benefit of the community. Such partnerships must often be formed and sustained in an arena in which personal interests, district interests, and confrontational politics make it difficult or impossible to obtain the kind of political consensus that used to exist on many boards. The responsibilities of the commissioners, the chair, and the manager that come from the law, from the managers' professional code, from realistic notions of roles in policy and administration, and from commonly understood expectations of behavior can be helpful in understanding how this partnership might work and how it is often challenged in the context of the county-manager form of government.

Statutory Responsibilities

The County Commissioners

Regardless of the form of government, G.S. 153A-76 gives the board of commissioners broad authority to organize county government:

> The board of commissioners may create, change, abolish, and consolidate offices, positions, departments, boards, commissions, and agencies of the county government, may impose ex officio the duties of more than one office in a single officer, may change the composition and manner of selection of boards, commissions, and agencies, and may generally organize and reorganize county government in order to promote orderly and efficient administration of county affairs, subject to the following limitations:
>
> (1) The board may not abolish an office, position, department, board, commission, or agency established or required by law.
> (2) The board may not combine offices or confer certain duties on the same officer when this action is specifically forbidden by law.
> (3) The board may not discontinue or assign elsewhere a function or duty assigned by law to a particular office, position, department, board, commission, or agency.
> (4) The board may not change the composition or manner of selection of a local board of education, the board of health, the board of social services, the board of elections, or the board of alcoholic beverage control.

This seemingly broad grant of responsibility nonetheless leaves many county functions outside the commissioners' direct control:

- The sheriff[14] and the register of deeds[15] are elected officers.
- Board of education members are elected and appoint the superintendent.[16]
- The state board of elections appoints the local board, which in turn appoints the director of elections.
- The directors of health and social services are appointed by their respective boards except in the state's two largest counties.[17]

These exceptions notwithstanding, the commissioners still have fairly broad authority to organize the administrative apparatus to carry out the board's policies, including the options for appointing a county manager to oversee the administration of county services.

The Chair

G.S. 153A-39 requires that the board of commissioners select a chair from among its members at its first regular meeting in December, unless the chair is elected by the people or otherwise designated by law. The board also elects a vice-chair to serve in the absence of the chair, and, when both are absent, the commissioners present may choose another member to act temporarily as chair. The statutory powers and duties conferred on the chair are few: G.S. 153A-39 designates the chair as the presiding officer and requires him or her to vote on measures before the board. The only other clearly stipulated duty of the chair is to use his or her authority under G.S. 143-318.17 to direct persons who disrupt a meeting to leave (the refusal to do so being a misdemeanor). Without any further enumeration of powers and no provision for the board of commissioners to confer additional powers and duties, the chair's ability to lead or guide the board is largely dependent on his or her personal and political skills and willingness to do so.

Unlike mayors of cities who are expressly prohibited from assuming the duties of the manager on any basis (G.S. 160A-151), chairs of county boards of commissioners are certainly able to do so by action of the board in accordance with G.S. 153A-81, as mentioned earlier.

The County Manager

North Carolina's laws authorizing the council-manager form of government, like those of most of the states, drew on the provisions contained in the National Municipal League's Model City Charter. Consequently, the specifications of the powers and duties of the county manager found in North Carolina's General Statutes (G.S. 153A-82) are fairly typical of those found nationwide and, with one exception, are consistent with the general elements of the council-manager plan:

> Section 82. Powers and duties of manager. The manager is the chief administrator of county government. He is responsible to the board of commissioners for the administration of all departments of county government under the board's general control and has the following powers and duties:
>
> (1) He shall appoint with the approval of the board of commissioners and suspend or remove all county officers, employees, and agents except those who are elected by the people or whose appointment is otherwise provided for by law. The board may by resolution permit the manager to appoint officers, employees, and agents without first securing

the board's approval. The manager shall make his appointments, suspensions, and removals in accordance with any general personnel rules, regulations, policies, or ordinances that the board may adopt.

Unlike the city manager in North Carolina, the county manager does not have automatic statutory authority to hire, fire, and discipline all employees not otherwise appointed by the council. The county manager performs these duties only with the approval of the board, unless the commissioners take positive action to grant the county manager the power to do so without their approval. Of course, the manager's hiring and firing authority does not extend to the administrative officers noted earlier who are elected by the people or to those who are appointed by authorities other than the commissioners. In addition, the board appoints the county clerk, the county attorney, and, except in the few cases where a local act provides otherwise, the tax collector.[18] Thus county managers preside over an administrative apparatus in which they have much less authority of appointment and removal than city managers do. Of course, county managers must exercise whatever authority of appointment and removal they have in accordance with personnel rules and regulations adopted by the board of commissioners.

(2) He shall direct and supervise the administration of all county offices, departments, boards, commissions and agencies under the general control of the board of commissioners, subject to the general direction and control of the board.

This provision makes the county manager responsible for the supervision of county operations in accordance with whatever laws, regulations, policies, direction, and guidance the board of commissioners might give. The commissioners' control is intended to be general in nature, leaving the manager to exercise professional judgment on how to carry out the board's intent. Obviously this can be a difficult line to draw clearly, and its actual practice varies from county to county, depending on a variety of factors such as tradition, confidence in the person who serves as manager, individual personalities and styles, and the issues involved. Because others elect or appoint several key department heads, as described earlier, and because the commissioners usually appoint the county clerk, county attorney, county assessor, and county tax collector, county managers' authority over the administrative apparatus for which they are responsible might seem less than clear. To be successful, North Carolina county managers probably have to be more tolerant of ambiguity in their authority and more facilitative than directive in their management styles than their counterparts in North Carolina cities.

    (3) He shall attend all meetings of the board of commissioners and rec-
          ommend any measures that he considers expedient.

The manager does not actually have to attend all meetings of the board of commissioners in person. However, this provision acknowledges that one of the manager's fundamental responsibilities is to give professional advice and counsel to the commissioners in their deliberations or, at the very least, to ensure that the board has access to and understands the information it needs to make informed choices in the matters coming before it. Thus the expectation is that the board of commissioners will have access to the advice of the manager or the manager's designee any time it gathers. Most managers will not miss a meeting if they can help it and will be careful to secure the concurrence of the chair or the entire board if they must be absent. They will also make sure that an assistant or other designee chosen to act in their place is fully able and prepared to give the board the support it needs.

    (4) He shall see that the orders, ordinances, resolutions, and regulations
          of the board of commissioners are faithfully executed within the
          county.

This general supervisory role of the manager is self-explanatory.

    (5) He shall prepare and submit the annual budget and capital program
          to the board of commissioners.

In a county that adopts the county-manager form of government, the manager is also the budget officer (G.S. 159-9) and is required by G.S. 159-11 to prepare a budget for consideration by the commissioners in whatever form and detail the board might specify. This is, of course, a *recommended* budget and capital program, which the commissioners may modify as they wish before adopting the budget ordinance (see Chapters 10 and 11).

    (6) He shall annually submit to the board of commissioners and make
          available to the public a complete report on the finances and admin-
          istrative activities of the county as of the end of the fiscal year.

In practice this is frequently done more often than once a year. The manager commonly makes periodic financial and administrative reports to the commissioners throughout the fiscal year.

    (7) He shall make any other reports that the board of commissioners may
          require concerning the operations of county offices, departments,
          boards, commissions, and agencies.

(8) He shall perform any other duties that may be required or authorized by the board of commissioners.

These responsibilities are also self-explanatory.

The ICMA Code of Ethics

The professional county manager has another set of expectations governing his or her behavior: a code of ethics originally developed in 1924 by the International City Managers' Association, (the original name of ICMA, now the International City/County Management Association)[19] and modified periodically since then. The ICMA Code of Ethics is a point of pride among professional managers. Any manager admitted to the association is bound by its ethical tenets and subject to censure by or even expulsion from the association for violations of this professional code. The code seeks to enforce and balance what ICMA believes to be the prerogatives that professional managers must have to do their jobs properly and the obligations that managers must meet in order to honor the authority of the board of commissioners and promote the overall welfare of the citizens.

The twelve tenets of the Code of Ethics might be paraphrased as follows:[20]

1. Be dedicated to effective, responsive local government by responsible elected officials and professional general management.
2. Be a constructive, creative, and trusted public servant.
3. Be dedicated to the highest ideals of honor and integrity.
4. Recognize the chief function of local government as serving the best interests of all citizens.
5. Propose policies, give the board of commissioners all the information it needs to make decisions, and carry out the board's decisions and policies.
6. Give credit to the commissioners for establishing policies; accept responsibility for carrying them out.
7. Refrain from involvement in local electoral politics.
8. Continually improve one's own and others' professional competence.
9. Keep citizens informed and promote effective communications and public service.
10. Resist any encroachment on one's professional responsibilities.
11. Handle all personnel matters on the basis of merit.
12. Seek no personal favor.

Recent censures of managers for violations of the tenets illustrate how they are applied by the profession. A local government manager in Texas was publicly censured for falsifying an expense report (violating tenets 2, 3, and 9). He was found accountable, even though he had been directed by an elected official to submit the misinformation. Private censures have involved the following:

- Job-hopping (violating tenet 4)
- Publicly engaging in the election process (violating tenet 7)
- Failing to disclose complete and accurate information about background and qualifications on the résumé (violating tenet 3)
- Joining in real estate investments within the jurisdiction in a manner that could appear to be a conflict of interest (even though there was no indication of actual conflict of interest in this case) (violating tenet 12)

Roles and Relationships in Policy and Administration

Although both the law and the ICMA Code of Ethics prescribe responsibilities for the manager and the governing board, they are very general and do not go far in describing exactly how these officials should actually interact with one another in order to be effective in the division of labor set out in these tenets. Popular wisdom used to promote the notion of a strict dichotomy between policy making and administration: the elected body should make policy, and the administration should carry it out, each without interference from the other as it performed its functions. The dichotomy probably arose originally from a misinterpretation of a highly respected paper by Woodrow Wilson in which he advocated the use of appointed officials to relieve legislators of the burden of administrative functions.[21] The fact that the popular interpretation of this dichotomy theory reduced board-manager relations to a simple, easy-to-follow formula probably accounts for its perpetuation. However, as anyone who works in local government for very long soon realizes, matters are just not that simple. The county manager often has training, analytical skills, experience in a wide range of jurisdictions, and an in-depth knowledge of the county and its government operations that would be extremely helpful to the commissioners in establishing policy. On the other hand, when constituents complain about the quality of service or the treatment they receive from county employees, commissioners are unlikely to feel that it is an administrative matter that does not concern them. John Nalbandian, a respected scholar of local government has observed,

> The practical world of city [and county] management often suggests a more complicated view [than the dichotomy theory]. The manager is deeply involved in policy-making as well as implementation, responds to a multitude of community forces as well as to the governing body, and incorporates a variety of competing values into the decision-making process.[22]

A more realistic relationship between elected officials and managers in policy and administration has been depicted by James H. Svara, as shown in Figure 2-1.[23] This depiction recognizes that there is no strict dichotomy; rather, there is involvement of both elected and administrative officials at all levels of policy and administration. The involvement and responsibility of each are proportionately different depending on the level at which they occur. At the highest level the county commissioners are responsible for setting the overall direction, or *mission*, of county government, including its purpose, scope, and philosophy, in carrying out both its functions as agent of the state and its local functions. Figure 2-1 suggests that although the board of commissioners has a clearly dominant role in this function, the manager can bring knowledge and experience to the table that enhances the board's ability to make informed choices and decisions.

The commissioners must enact *policy* to achieve the mission that is mandated or that they set for county government. They do this through functions such as budgeting, capital improvement programming, comprehensive planning, and making laws and policies regarding government operations. Although the commissioners have the final responsibility for adopting budgets, plans, and ordinances, the manager and his or her staff play a major role in developing technical studies and estimates and analyzing the impact of alternative choices. Thus in reality these kinds of policy making are a shared responsibility.

In government *how* something is done is often as important to citizens' satisfaction with the outcome as *what* is done. Consequently, although the manager and the staff are responsible for implementing the policies adopted by the commissioners, elected officials still have a stake in how those policies are carried out—that is, in *administration* and *management*. After making a decision to build a new animal shelter and budgeting funds for it, the commissioners will almost always have a continued interest in how the facilities actually look and work. They will be

Figure 2-1
Dichotomy-Duality Model
Mission-Management Separation with Shared Responsibility for
Policy and Administration

Dimensions of Governmental Process

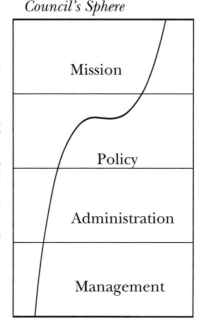

Illustrative tasks for Council	*Council's Sphere*	Illustrative tasks for administrators
Determine "purpose," scope of services, tax level, constitutional issues.	Mission	Advise (what city "can" do may influence what it "should" do), analyze conditions and trends.
Pass ordinances, approve new projects and programs, ratify budget. Make implementing decisions (e.g., site selection), handle complaints, oversee administration.	Policy	Make recommendations on all decisions, formulate budget, determine service distribution formulae. Establish practices and procedures and make decisions for implementing policy.
Suggest management changes to Manager: review organizational performance in Manager's appraisal.	Administration Management	Control the human, material, and informational resources of organization to support policy and administrative functions.

Manager's Sphere

The curved line suggests the division between the Council's and the Manager's spheres of activity, with the Council to the left and the Manager to the right of the line.

The division presented is intended to approximate a "proper" degree of separation and sharing. Shifts to either the left or right would indicate improper incursions.

Source: "Dichotomy and Duality: Reconceptualizing the Relationship Between Policy and Administration in Council-Manager Cities," *Public Administration Review* 45 (January/February 1985), 228.

concerned with how well the scheduling and execution of work on new water or sewer lines minimizes disruption of travel on roads and the effects of noise and dust on adjoining residential properties. The board will always have an interest in how overall employee morale is affected by internal operating policies developed by the administration.

Thus Figure 2-1 describes a partnership at every level of endeavor, with the elected body shouldering most of the responsibility, authority, and initiative at the mission level, the administration shouldering most of it in internal management, and the two sharing it significantly in policy and administration. In practice the line that is depicted in Figure 2-1 is symbolic; it would be expected to vary among jurisdictions and within a particular jurisdiction over time for the reasons described earlier. Some boards want the manager to push aggressively for policies that he or she thinks necessary; other boards want the manager to stay in the background and respond to the commissioners' initiatives. Some boards feel the need to be intimately familiar with day-to-day occurrences in county business; others want to concern themselves with administrative matters only when those matters might create public controversy. Agreement between elected officials and the appointed manager on where the line is drawn is essential to a good relationship and must be reviewed frequently to make sure everyone understands what the commissioners and the manager expect of each other.

Elected officials have to consider more than their own personal preferences and operating styles in this matter, taking into account how citizens perceive the relationship between elected and appointed officials. Citizens' most important expectation is that the commissioners will either represent or at least be attentive to their interests. If administrators do not satisfy this expectation on behalf of the commissioners by their service and behavior, citizens will usually expect the board to take a more dominant role, whereas if citizens' needs are being met routinely, they may be satisfied with elected officials taking a more passive role in day-to-day business.

Today it may be harder for either the board of commissioners or the administration to please everyone, harder for the board to achieve consensus on many issues that might have been routine in the past, and therefore harder for the commissioners to give the manager clear direction at all times. This, in turn, makes it harder for the manager to administer county operations in a way that satisfies the entire board. Some observers of local government bemoan the increase in confrontational politics on the part of constituents and the trend back toward district representation on elected bodies as undermining the principles of broad representation of the public good and efficient administration. Others, however, point out that these developments are just a manifestation of the reality of constituent politics and make for more open, fairer representation of all the diverse interests in the community, instead of just those of a powerful privileged few or an exclusive majority. Nevertheless, many managers feel it is now more difficult than it used to be to obtain and maintain the kind of clear consensus and direction from the elected body that is one of the fundamental assumptions of the county-manager form of government.

Common Expectations among the County Commissioners, the County Manager, and the Chair

Specific expectations and practices among the commissioners, the manager, and the chair vary greatly from county to county, depending on social and political norms and traditions. They can also vary over time with changes in the personalities involved as elected officials turn over and managers come and go. However, experience and research have shown that in some critical aspects of the partnership, there are fairly consistent expectations across jurisdictions and over time. For the most part these expectations may be regarded as basic and necessary to defining roles and maintaining a healthy relationship between the elected commissioners and the manager.

Expectation 1: The Manager Is a Valued Adviser to the Board of Commissioners

Both the General Statutes and the ICMA Code of Ethics require the manager to give policy advice to the commissioners and to carry out their policy decisions; however, neither tenet deals specifically with some subtle but important aspects of this process. The General Statutes require the manager to "recommend any measures that he considers expedient," and the Code of Ethics requires him or her to "submit policy proposals" and give "facts and advice" to help the commissioners make decisions and set goals. Commissioners expect the manager to offer balanced and unbiased advice:

- To provide all relevant information that is reasonably available on the different options

- To present the pros and the cons of each option
- To explain the professional reasoning that leads him or her to a recommendation
- To base that reasoning on established professional, technical, or legal principles, and not on personal beliefs, no matter how strongly held, unless the commissioners specifically solicit them

Even the appearance or suspicion that the manager is being selective in the information he or she gives, personally biased in the judgment he or she renders, or manipulative of the board's decision in the way he or she presents material, can severely damage the manager's credibility and thereby his or her effectiveness.

Most managers feel responsible for arguing for a professionally compelling course of action no matter how unpopular it might be with the public or with the board of commissioners. This often requires the manager to have the courage to make an unpopular recommendation that might not have very good prospects of being accepted. Commissioners or citizens who are upset over the facts that are presented or who disagree with the recommendations might, at best, attack the validity of the advice, or at worst, attack the competence, motives, or character of the manager who gives the advice. One of the most difficult tests of professional managers as policy advisers is to remain cool and undefensive during heated debate over the information and recommendations that they have brought to the commissioners.

Once the board has made a decision, the manager must support it fully and make sure that the administration does the same. The General Statutes require the manager to see that all actions of the commissioners are "faithfully executed," and the Code of Ethics requires him or her to implement all the board's policies. This sometimes requires managers to carry out something that they think is a bad idea. If the manager believes that the direction the commissioners have given is illegal or if it is professionally or personally repugnant, and if the manager cannot dissuade the board from its action, he or she can, of course, resign. If the manager chooses to stay, however, he or she is obliged to assist the commissioners in carrying out the will of the board. Sometimes the manager will be put in the awkward position of arguing strenuously for a course of action that the board subsequently rejects, and then having the press ask what he or she thinks of the commissioners' decision. Unless reasoned debate has changed the manager's mind, to agree completely with the commissioners will make the manager look like a toady. On the other hand, to criticize or denigrate the board for its decision will violate the Code of Ethics and court legitimate censure. Most professional managers who find themselves in this situation acknowledge the differences in judgment that were exhibited in the deliberations and try to explain the reasoning that brought the commissioners to the decision they made. In other words, they will help the commissioners explain the decision to the public and help the public understand the board's point of view. Obviously, carrying out this important responsibility often takes great emotional maturity.

Expectation 2: The Commissioners and the Manager Jointly Strive for Good Service to Citizens

Service to citizens is the ultimate test of the effectiveness of local government operations. Regardless of what the commissioners accomplish, if the government does not satisfactorily deliver basic services to citizens, citizens will be dissatisfied with the elected board, and the commissioners in turn will be dissatisfied with the manager and the administration. Everyone's fate ultimately rests on citizens' satisfaction with services. Therefore one of the most important responsibilities of managers is to be aggressive in ensuring that their administration provides the very best service possible to the citizens in the county. Careful planning, budgeting, and management help, but managers cannot be everywhere at all times to supervise day-to-day execution, so they have to create a culture of responsiveness in the organization, both in providing routine service to citizens and in handling special requests and complaints. This usually involves pushing down to the lowest levels of the organization the responsibility and the authority to make decisions and to act, supporting people who take initiative, and helping people learn from mistakes made in good faith. The manager must take personal risks on behalf of employees and fully accept responsibility with the commissioners when things go wrong.

On the other hand, if managers are going to accept such responsibility, they should be able to expect that commissioners will give the system a chance to work and will channel complaints through the manager. The gratitude that an elected official might enjoy as a result of personally wading into a problem and resolving it is ordinarily short-lived and transitory. More lasting credit usually comes from citizens' recognition that the commissioners have created a responsive workforce as an essential ingredient of efficient and effective governance, and are maintaining it. Even when an administration is very good at responding to citizens' needs, people will sometimes ask their elected officials directly for help, usually in good faith but sometimes for manipulative reasons. Managers expect commissioners to determine whether the citizen has tried the usual administrative remedies and to steer the citizen into the system if he or she has not. If the administration has in fact been unresponsive, then the manager expects to be informed and to have the opportunity to fix the problem, and the manager can be expected to give the commissioner the necessary information to follow up with the citizen if the commissioner wishes.

Expectation 3: Commissioners' Relationships with Employees Are Carefully Managed

From the standpoint of managing resources effectively, it is desirable to observe a chain of command in answering service needs. The problems that can arise when commissioners intervene directly in service operations include confusing employees with conflicting directives or priorities from supervisors and elected officials, weakening or destroying clear accountability for work results, or short-circuiting coordinated plans developed by the supervisors responsible for day-to-day operations. This does *not* mean that commissioners should not have periodic or even regular contact with county employees. To prohibit such contact would be to ask employees and commissioners to give up some of their basic rights as members of the community and would make it harder to build harmony among the critical roles in county government. It would also be inefficient. To funnel all communication through the manager would waste his or her time with unnecessary traffic and would be terribly awkward and inconvenient for commissioners.

A common arrangement to protect planned work flow and still reap the benefits of regular interaction is to encourage direct contact between commissioners and employees for routine inquiries or requests that do not affect administrative workloads, and to route more significant requests through the manager. This permits commissioners to obtain routine information that they need quickly and accurately from the persons who are closest to the action and most informed about details, just as citizens can (or should be able to do). It also provides an opportunity for regular informal communication between elected officials and employees, helping each become more familiar, more comfortable, and more trusting of the other over time. Anything a commissioner wants from employees that will involve significant and unplanned expenditures of time or money or might disrupt agreed-on work schedules, is taken up with the manager so as not to put employees on the spot. Then the manager and the commissioner can make informed choices about whether the request should take outright precedence over existing commitments, whether something can be done that would meet the commissioner's needs but not be disruptive, or whether it should not be done at all, given other commitments. The manager and the commissioner who made the request might also agree to submit the question to the whole board to decide as a body whether a change in resource allocation would make sense or not.

Sometimes managers have attempted to cut off direct contact between elected officials and employees to minimize problems with commissioners who meddle with or harass employees or with employees who are manipulative and disloyal. Like most treatments of a symptom alone, such an approach usually does little or nothing to solve the problems that underlie these dysfunctional behaviors. Often it makes matters worse by creating a siege mentality among administrators, anxiety among employees, and distrust and frustration among elected officials.

Expectation 4: The Board of Commissioners Acts as a Body and Is Dealt with as a Body

One of the tricky aspects of dealing with a board of commissioners is that by law it takes official action as a body, yet it is made up of three to eleven individual politicians with various constituencies, personal interests, and personalities. Without the benefit of consensus or at least formal support of a majority of the council, elected officials often find it hard to refrain from imposing their own personal agendas on the administration. Most managers will welcome, discuss, and frequently respond directly to suggestions at any time from individual commissioners, as long as they do not conflict with the pleasure of the board as a whole. However, if a request sets new directions or requires allocation of funds or staff time not anticipated by the board, the manager will usually ask the member making the proposal to put it before the entire board for consideration. It is important for the manager to treat all commissioners alike in this respect. There will always be some commissioners whom the manager likes better, gets along with better, or agrees with more than others. Unless he or she is scrupulous in avoiding even the appearance of favoritism, however, the manager can seriously undermine his or her effectiveness by permanently alienating the commissioners who feel slighted or barred from some inner circle, real or imagined. Even in the case of routine requests for information, most managers will keep all commissioners informed of transactions with individuals by sending copies of written responses or summaries of opinions rendered or actions agreed to in conversation, to all board members for their information.

One area in which the manager must take initiative in this matter is in keeping commissioners up-to-date on day-to-day events. Elected officials do not like surprises. It is embarrassing for an elected official to be asked about some newsworthy item of county business and have to admit that he or she does not know much about it, and it is unforgivable for someone to be the *only* commissioner who is ignorant about it. Boards of commissioners expect their managers to be sensitive, alert, and responsive to their needs for current information, which includes making occasional extraordinary efforts when necessary to ensure that every commissioner has the same level of information and understanding.

Expectation 5: The Manager and the Commissioners Give Each Other a Chance to Prove Themselves

One of the implicit foundations of county-manager government is that a professional manager, who is dedicated to serving whatever elected body is seated by the people, will provide smooth transitions, some institutional stability and memory, and some change, as different individuals or groups join and leave the board. Nevertheless, it is sometimes hard for commissioners who have sought election because they too want to bring about changes to trust the loyalty of the manager toward the new members or to have confidence in the ability of the manager to help bring about the changes they want. In short, the manager is sometimes viewed as inextricably tied to the old way of doing things and assumed to be an impediment to progress. Most managers strive to change the direction of the administration in whatever way the board decides (they can resign if they feel they cannot serve the new board's agenda in good conscience). Therefore managers expect newly elected officials to give them a chance to prove that they can serve the new board just as well as they served the old one.

On the other hand, sometimes after an election the manager finds himself or herself working for one or more new commissioners who as candidates roundly criticized the way in which the county was governed and managed. During their campaigns some of those commissioners may have called for the manager's dismissal. Many elected officials agree that even if they entered government with previous county experience on volunteer boards or commissions, the view of government from the inside is very different than the view from the outside. Candidates, on taking office, usually learn that the simplicity and the surety of campaign rhetoric seldom stand up to the complexity of governance or management. Recognizing the bluff and bluster of campaign rhetoric for what it is, experienced and mature managers will withhold judgment on new board members whose campaigning seemed threatening and will set about proving that they can serve the new board as well as they served the old. They hope that given a chance, they will eventually earn the trust and confidence of the new board members as those members learn the realities of governing, gain skill as legislators, and observe the manager's performance at close hand.

Expectation 6: The Manager and the Commissioners Freely Give and Seek Feedback

One of the key ingredients for building and maintaining a relationship of trust and confidence is open communication. County managers and county commissioners invariably find themselves caught up in a whirlwind of daily activity. There never seems to be quite enough time to do everything—especially to do it all just right. So elected officials and managers both make mistakes; they might overlook side effects of actions taken in the heat of urgency, or say or do things that convey unintended messages. All these occurrences can generate dissatisfaction, disappointment, offense, anger, or distrust if they are not recognized and resolved appropriately. The key to dealing effectively with such matters is to work hard at maintaining open communication between commissioners and their manager. The jobs of both elected officials and managers can make the persons in them feel very isolated. The manager, accountable to a board elected by citizens and responsible for a county workforce, might feel apart from both, a part of neither. The elected official, held accountable by fellow citizens for the county's administration, might feel that he or she has very little direct role to play in making sure things go well. Open communication is one effective cure for these feelings of isolation. Managers must provide all commissioners with accurate, relevant, and timely information, and commissioners should take the initiative to ask questions and make their interests, positions, and feelings known to their manager.

Most managers appreciate clear signals about how well they are satisfying the commissioners whom they serve, even when those signals are negative. Being criticized is not pleasant, but it is in fact more comforting than inferring all kinds of unexpressed dissatisfaction from elected officials' behavior. Many people find it easier to give faint compliments or remain silent than to confront others with criticism; however, dissatisfaction withheld is usually hard to conceal for very long without being revealed indirectly by behavior or rumor. This kind of indirect revelation almost always produces some inaccuracy and misinterpretation regarding facts, feelings, and underlying motivations; distracts the manager, who becomes unduly preoccupied with figuring out where he or she stands; and often has the effect of shutting down communication and producing an increasing spiral of tension between the manager and the elected official involved. On the other hand, when a commissioner openly directs constructive criticism at the manager, putting the issue on the table, the manager then can ask questions, provide information that the commissioner might not have, and respond to his or her concerns. Such dialogue gives commissioners the opportunity to clarify their expectations of the manager by means of concrete examples as they occur, and it gives the manager more certainty about what he or she has to do to satisfy the board and how well he or she is succeeding. Each board and its manager have to work out for themselves how publicly they are willing to give and receive this individual feedback. They should come to an agreement early in the manager's tenure and confirm or modify it when there is turnover among commissioners.

Many elected officials appreciate the same candor from the manager when they are behaving in a way that frustrates effective management. This attitude is by no means universal, however, and most managers are very careful to determine the comfort zone of a particular board and its individual members in offering them constructive criticism. Nevertheless, the benefits of freely giving and accepting feedback are potentially as great for elected officials as for the manager.

The Special Role of the Chair

As noted earlier, the role of the chair of the board of county commissioners in North Carolina is largely limited to serving as ceremonial head of the government and presiding over its affairs. The chair has no veto over the board's actions and no executive authority; yet many chairs continue to be very influential in exerting political leadership and in facilitating the work of both the commissioners and the administration by assuming roles for themselves that are not specifically prescribed by statute.

Political Leadership

Chairing the board of county commissioners still enjoys at least some of the popular image of the political chief executive. Those who are elected to the job are in a position to exert political leadership in the affairs of the board of commissioners if they have the skill and the disposition to do so. This might include proposing policy, organizing public support of or opposition to issues, mediating solutions to political struggles, and encouraging the manager to accomplish certain tasks. The actual performance of chairs in this situation seems to be highly personalized, depending on both the style of the chair and the degree to which the other commissioners are willing to cooperate with the chair's exercising such informal authority.

Facilitative Leadership

If the chair wins the trust and the confidence of the commissioners and the manager, then he or she is in a good position to enhance the performance of both elected and appointed officials by helping them channel their individual and collective energies into productive actions. By staying abreast of commissioners' interests, positions, and feelings, the chair can help stimulate thought and discussion among them, and facilitate understanding and possible consensus on issues. The chair is also in a position to communicate a developing board consensus on issues to the manager and to provide an effective sounding board by which the manager can sense the climate among commissioners for ideas, options, or issues that he or she and the staff are considering. The bigger the board, the more time and energy this can save for the manager, but the harder it can be to develop consensus or even to discern or predict any meaningful or dependable pattern among members' opinions. By the same token, if the manager can demonstrate the merit of an idea to the chair, then the chair can be effective in promoting understanding of the issue, possibly helping move commissioners toward its acceptance. This facilitative role becomes less tenable if the board suffers from fractiousness born of political conviction, representation of a divided constituency, or personal animosity. In addition, county managers who are lucky enough to have a chair who takes on this kind of facilitative role are usually very careful not to let it replace regular and direct contact with individual commissioners, recognizing how important that contact is to their relationship with the whole board.

Executive Leadership

Both of the foregoing roles cast the chair as a central figure in the affairs of the county—the "first among equals" on the governing board. Most commissioners are willing to accept the notion that the chair will spend more time with the manager than any one commissioner over time and that the chair is in a position to play a preeminent role among them in representing the county to the public and other governments. However, there is an important boundary that most chairs observe in order to maintain their relationship of trust with the commissioners and the manager. Although the chair might encourage administrative actions or suggest policy interpretations on the basis of his or her position on the board, he or she must be careful not to violate the prerogatives of the other commissioners. Indeed, the manager is accountable to the entire board and is ethically bound to ensure that at least a majority of the commissioners concurs before taking actions that would deviate significantly from the established county policies, expectations, or norms. On balance, it is usually a judicious combination of political leadership and facilitation of the process of governance that enables an effective chair to complement a competent manager and an active board of commissioners in a working relationship of harmony and trust.

The Search for an Effective County Manager

Hiring a county manager is one of the most important actions that a board of commissioners may be called on to take. From the preceding description of how the manager and the board might work together, it should be evident that their working relationship can have a significant influence on the effectiveness of the local government that they serve. Whether the commissioners are hiring their first manager or replacing one who has resigned or been fired, they can take several basic steps to ensure that they make a good choice:[24]

1. *Determine the future needs of the county and county government.* It is well worth the commissioners' time to spend a few hours discussing what they think will be the future demands on the manager's position. What will be happening in the county? What will the prominent or controversial issues be? What will the major challenges or projects be? What will the workforce be like, and how will it change? The answers to these questions are likely to be different for every county. By thinking about and planning for them the commissioners increase the probability that they will find somebody who has the right talents to deal with the issues facing their county.

2. *List the critical skills required to deal with those needs.* Almost 4,000 men and women have met ICMA's stringent criteria for professional membership, and there are many other capable public administrators working in the public and private sectors who are not members. Many of the applicants for a county-manager position will have educational credentials and experience that are at least adequate and often impressive, but no two of them will be exactly the same. Each applicant will have slightly different strengths and weaknesses. The challenge facing the commissioners is to choose from many capable applicants the person who comes closest to having the unique set of skills and abilities that is needed to deal with their own county's issues and personality.

3. *Recruit and screen applicants.* This step typically includes setting a salary range within which the commissioners are willing to negotiate, advertising to attract persons with the attributes sought, screening applications, and deciding on and arranging to interview a set of top candidates. Normally the board of commissioners needs a staff person to assist it in this process, and it is important that this be somebody who has the confidence of the entire board. Care must be taken to preserve the confidentiality of the applications[25] unless and until the applicants release the county from that obligation. The commissioners typically seek a

release in the interview stage when it becomes very difficult to ensure confidentiality to any applicant. Some boards have arranged for five to ten semifinalists to have screening interviews with a committee of commissioners or to have videotape interviews conducted by a contractor, after which they invite three to five finalists for an interview with the whole board of commissioners. Most others have found it effective to narrow the field down to three to five finalists simply by reviewing and discussing the applications.

4. *Interview applicants.* The structure of the interview process varies quite a bit in practice, from simply interviewing each candidate to bringing all the candidates and their spouses in together to see the county, meet key people in and outside county government, and participate in an assessment center or highly structured interview. At the very least the interviews should be structured to allow commissioners to make reliable judgments about the important attributes that they have agreed they need in a manager, and to make valid and consistent comparisons among the candidates. G.S. 143-318-11(6) in the open meetings law allows these interviews to be conducted in a closed session.[26]

5. *Hire the manager.* After the interviews the commissioners will usually try to reach consensus on one candidate, sometimes with a backup candidate in case the chosen candidate does not accept the offer. Many managers insist on consensus before they will accept a board's offer, feeling that anything less would make their position too tenuous to survive the stress and strain that the demands of governance and management put on the relationship between the board and the manager. Some managers, however, are willing to start with no more than the tentative security of support from a simple majority. Sometimes the commissioners choose to send one or more members to the leading candidate's community for confirmation of their impressions, but usually the board simply arranges for a final background investigation while it negotiates the terms and conditions of employment with the prospective manager. When these negotiations are complete, the other candidates are notified, and the commissioners take formal action in open session to hire the successful candidate. The entire recruitment, screening, selection, and hiring process can normally be completed in about six months.

6. *Conclude an employment agreement.* An increasing number of local governments in North Carolina have formal employment agreements with managers. Sometimes called contracts, they may set out a variety of conditions specific to the manager's employment, such as leave, use of a car for official business, expense accounts, participation in professional activities, and virtually anything else that establishes a clear understanding between the commissioners and the manager about the responsibilities, benefits, and privileges of the office. Many boards now include severance provisions in these agreements, which specify the manager's responsibility for notifying the commissioners in advance of his or her intention to resign and which provide a lump-sum severance payment in the event that the manager's employment is involuntarily terminated for reasons other than illegal or improper behavior. These agreements do not and cannot guarantee any tenure to the manager, inasmuch as G.S. 153A-81(1) provides that the board shall appoint the county manager to serve at its pleasure.

Establishment and Maintenance of a Good Relationship

The relationship between a board of commissioners and its manager can enhance or impede the process of governance significantly, so it is important that they devote some time to establishing and maintaining a good one. As soon as possible, they should establish what they expect of each other beyond the very general tenets of statutory and professional responsibilities. No two boards are exactly alike, nor are any two managers. No matter how much previous experience a new manager has had or how many managers the board has had, the relationship between a particular board and a particular manager is certain to be different in some ways than any previously experienced by either party.

Soon after a new manager is hired, if a significant turnover in commissioners occurs or a new chair is elected, the commissioners, the chair, and the manager may find it useful to discuss their specific expectations of one another. Such a discussion allows them to understand what each thinks he or she needs from the others to be effective in carrying out major responsibilities. The chair's and the other commissioners' expectations of the manager provide a sound basis for them to be effective in both formally evaluating the manager and giving the manager informal feedback about his or her specific behavior and general performance. Most boards find it effective and convenient to conduct a formal evaluation of the manager once a year, usually associated with their consideration of adjustments in the manager's compensation. Typically the evaluation is held in closed session, with the manager present when his or her performance is discussed and rated with respect to general behavior and the achievement of specific tasks or objectives previously set out by the commissioners.[27]

More and more boards use retreats to set out these initial expectations among themselves and the manager and to achieve other purposes that contribute to effective governance. The idea behind a retreat is for the commissioners and whomever else they invite to convene at a time and place outside of the board's regular meetings[28] to deliberate about matters that are difficult to fit into the crush of routine formal business that fills the board's regular agendas. Commissioners commonly use retreats to identify agreements and differences among themselves with respect to their beliefs and goals for the county, to plan how they will achieve common goals and accommodate differences, and to understand one another's expectations about working together.[29] Most boards and managers that have tried retreats have found them to be an effective way to build a unity of effort that is otherwise difficult to develop in the course of regular meetings.

The county-manager form of government has a long and successful history in the United States and especially in North Carolina. Like any government arrangement, it has potential advantages that are not automatically realized in practice; however, it provides many advantages to the process of governance if the elected officials and the manager work together in a good faith effort to observe the tenets on which the system is based. The General Statutes constitute a clear foundation for the county-manager form of government, but they are only a starting point in a very complex working relationship. Using the county-manager form successfully depends on the commissioners and the manager establishing clear expectations, maintaining good communication, and developing a sense of shared vision and teamwork on behalf of the community.

Additional Resources

Publications

International City/County Management Association. *Employment Agreements for Managers: Guidelines for Elected Officials.* Washington, D.C.: ICMA, 1984.

——. *Employment Agreements for Managers: Guidelines for Managers.* Washington, D.C.: ICMA, 1992.

——. *Partnerships in Local Governance: Effective Council-Manager Relations.* Washington, D.C.: ICMA, 1989.

——. *Recruitment Guidelines for Selecting a Local Government Administrator.* Washington, D.C.: ICMA, 1987.

Nalbandian, John. *Professionalism in Local Government.* San Francisco: Jossey-Bass, 1991.

Organizations

International City/County Management Association, 777 North Capitol Street, NE, Washington, D.C. 20002.

National Association of Counties, 440 First Street, NW, Washington, D.C. 20001.

National Association of County Administrators, 500 South Grand Central Parkway, Las Vegas, Nev. 89155.

North Carolina Association of County Commissioners, Albert Coates Local Government Center, 215 North Dawson Street, Raleigh, N.C. 27602.

North Carolina City and County Management Association, P.O. Box 3069, Raleigh, N.C. 27602.

Notes

1. 1917 N.C. Pub.-Local Laws ch. 433 (Catawba); 1917 N.C. Pub.-Local Laws ch. 690 (Caldwell). Neither special legislation was used. At its organizational meeting in 1936, the Catawba Board of County Commissioners, having decided the county needed an executive to manage the county's affairs when the board was not in session, voted to hire Nolan J. Sigmon as county accountant with the intention of making him county manager. In March 1937 the commissioners passed a resolution adopting the county-manager form, which had by then been authorized by Chapter 91 of the Public Laws of 1929 (now G.S. 153A-81), and appointed Sigmon to the post of county manager.

2. This arrangement continued until December 1984 when the offices of county manager and chairman were separated pursuant to special legislation passed by the 1983 session of the General Assembly (1983 N.C. Sess. Laws ch. 129). This arrangement continues in effect.

3. 1927 Pub. Laws ch. 91, §§ 5–8, modified and recodified in 1973; now G.S. 153A-81 (*adoption of county manager plan; appointment or designation of manager*) and G.S. 153A-82 (*powers and duties of manager*).

4. Robeson County is the only county in the United States to have had the appointed-manager form of government continuously since that time.

5. ICMA lists Durham County as having adopted the form in 1930.

6. In Catawba, Davidson, Durham, Forsyth, Gaston, Hertford, Rockingham, Guilford, and Robeson counties, commissioners appointed a separate county manager. In Buncombe, Haywood, and Mecklenburg counties, the chair served as county manager.

7. Richard Childs first articulated the plan in a proposal to combine the commission form of government with a professional city manager. (The commission form of government became popular after its successful use in resurrecting Galveston, Texas, from almost complete destruction from a hurricane in 1900.) Childs drafted a bill incorporating the plan and persuaded the Lockport (N.Y.) Board of Trade to sponsor its introduction in the New York State Legislature with the public support of reform organizations. Thus the earliest version is known as the Lockport Plan.

8. See "Criteria and Guidelines for Recognition," in *Who's Who in Local Government Management, 1997–1998* (Washington, D.C.: ICMA, 1997), 390.

9. At the end of 1997, Tyrrell County employed a county administrator without adopting the county-manager form of government. Columbus and Swain counties use the title "county administrator" but have adopted the county-manager form of government by passage of a resolution.

10. G.S. 153A-81(2), which is consistent with the provisions of G.S. 128-1.1(b), allowing any person holding an elective office in state or local government to hold concurrently one other appointive office in either state or local government. At the end of 1997, this arrangement existed only in Jackson County, where the chair is elected with the incumbency of serving as county manager.

11. G.S. 153A-81(3). This arrangement was used from 1990 until 1993, when the county manager/county attorney left the position and the commissioners chose not to continue to combine the offices.

12. G.S. 160A-107 requires that a city that changes its charter to create or eliminate the council-manager plan keep the change in effect for at least two years after adoption.

13. These were the main conclusions drawn by participants in the initial meeting of the ICMA Task Force on Council-Manager Relations, in San Francisco in February 1993. They formed the basis of the task force's inquiry into how ICMA could help foster citizen support for the council-manager form of government and strengthen the partnership between elected officials and appointed administrators. The task force's conclusions were summarized in three parts in *ICMA Newsletter* 74, no. 10 (May 17, 1993), no. 11 (May 31, 1993), and no. 13 (June 28, 1993).

14. Elected by provision of Article VII, Section 2, of the constitution.

15. Elected by provision of G.S. 161-1.

16. Appointed by provision of G.S. 115C-271.

17. By exception, if and when a county reaches a population of 425,000, then G.S. 153A-77 allows the commissioners to combine or assume direct control of social services, health, mental health, developmental disabilities, and substance-abuse area boards as well as any other commission, board, or agency appointed by the commissioners. This option was legislated in 1973 specifically to allow the Mecklenburg

County Commissioners to assume direct responsibility for several health and social services agencies. Since the state constitution does not allow special acts affecting health, it was enacted as a general law, which, by virtue of the population threshold, could only apply to Mecklenburg County at that time. Wake County has since passed the threshold and took similar action under the current law, which now provides for the creation of a consolidated human services board.

18. At the end of 1997, four counties, Haywood, Henderson, Madison, and Transylvania, elected the tax collector.

19. Originally called the International City Managers Association, ICMA has modified its name twice since 1924. In 1969 it changed Managers to Management to recognize the inclusion of members who were deputies, assistants, directors of councils of governments, and local government chief administrative officers who did not have the title or the traditional authority of a manager. In 1991 it included a reference to county managers, who had become a significant proportion of the membership—thus the International City/County Management Association. Because of tradition and widespread recognition of the original acronym ICMA, the association decided to continue it in that form.

20. Paraphrased from "ICMA Code of Ethics with Guidelines," in *Who's Who in Local Government Management, 1997–1998* (Washington, D.C.: ICMA, 1996), 4–5.

21. Woodrow Wilson, "The Study of Administration," *Political Science Quarterly* 2 (June 1887): 197–222. When Wilson wrote that "administration lies outside the proper sphere of politics. Administrative questions are not political questions. Although politics sets the tasks for administration, it should not be suffered to manipulate its offices" (p. 210), he was arguing for the provision of administrative support to legislative bodies, not prescribing a strict separation of duties between the two.

22. John Nalbandian, *Professionalism in Local Government* (San Francisco: Jossey-Bass, 1991), xiii.

23. A more thorough discussion of the relationships among the elected body, the manager, and the chief elected official over a continuum from mission to management as depicted in Figure 2-1, can be found in a series of articles written for *Popular Government* by James H. Svara: "Understanding the Mayor's Office in Council-Manager Cities," 51 (Fall 1985): 6–11; "Contributions of the City Council to Effective Governance," 51 (Spring 1986): 1–8; and "The Responsible Administrator: Contributions of the City Manager to Effective Governance," 52 (Fall 1986): 18–27. Although these articles deal with the relationships among the council, the mayor, and the manager in a municipal setting, the research results and the principles discussed are largely relevant to the county setting, with some exceptions.

24. For more detailed guidelines on recruiting and hiring a county manager, see Kurt Jenne, "Hiring a City or County Manager," *Popular Government* 62 (Spring 1997): 26–33, available in reprint.

25. *See* Elkin Tribune v. Yadkin County Bd. of Commissioners, 331 N.C. 735, 417 S.E. 2d 465 (1992). The court held that applications for employment were personnel records under G.S. 153A-98 and therefore their disclosure was prohibited.

26. The commissioners must nevertheless follow all the other procedural requirements contained in the open meetings law, G.S. Ch. 143, Art. 33-C. These interviews are typically conducted in closed session; however, that is not required. In 1997 the Buncombe County Commissioners chose to conduct a round of semifinal inter-

views in closed session and then to interview the three finalists in open session so that interested citizens could observe this final stage.

27. For a detailed treatment of the evaluation process, see Margaret S. Carlson, "'How Are We Doing?' Evaluating the Performance of the Chief Administrator," *Popular Government* 59 (Winter 1994): 24–29, available in reprint.

28. A retreat must still meet all the requirements set out in the open meetings law.

29. For a more thorough discussion of retreats, see Kurt Jenne, "Governing Board Retreats," *Popular Government* 53 (Winter 1988): 20–26.

3 Performance Measurement: Its Use in Productivity Improvement

David N. Ammons

Contents

David N. Ammons is an Institute of Government faculty member whose work includes performance measurement, benchmarking, and productivity improvement in local government.

As the service responsibility of county government continues to grow, so does public insistence that services be provided efficiently and effectively. Citizens depend on county services and are increasingly adamant that they be produced in sufficient quantity and with adequate timeliness to satisfy public needs, and that they meet reasonable standards of quality. Resource constraints demand that they be provided efficiently.

Those county governments that have been most aggressive in their pursuit of service quality and efficiency tend also to be the counties that have been most interested in measuring their performance. For them, performance measurement is a useful tool that confirms their successes and alerts them to programs in need of greater scrutiny.

Uses of Performance Measures

A typical set of performance measures reveals how many units of service were delivered. More sophisticated sets of measures provide this basic information and much more. A good set also reveals how efficiently a given service was rendered, at what level of quality it was delivered, and, ideally, what effect it is having on recipients or the community as a whole.

Good sets of performance measures have multiple uses. A partial list of these uses includes the following:

- Accountability
- Program planning
- Budgeting/resource reallocation
- Identification of operational strengths and weaknesses
- Analysis of the effectiveness of performance improvement initiatives
- Program evaluation/performance appraisal
- Direction of operations
- Contract monitoring

Local governments that are among the leaders in performance measurement rarely limit the application of their measures to a single use. Almost invariably, their measures support two, three, or even more of the functions noted in the list. Almost always, one of these uses is accountability.

Citizens like to be reassured that someone in their local government is minding the store. Even if they have little interest in most of the detailed facts and figures of service delivery, citizens rightfully expect that elected and appointed officials will collect and monitor those facts and figures, and will ensure that quality service is provided at a fair price.

A good set of performance measures is a vital tool for building accountability throughout an organization. By compiling key indicators of performance, supervisors can ensure that work crews are meeting expectations and delivering quality products—in short, they can ensure the accountability of front-line employees. Periodic reporting of selected measures allows supervisors to be accountable for their work to department management, department management to be accountable to central administration, and central administration to be accountable to the board of commissioners. In turn, the periodic publication of key performance indicators allows elected officials to be accountable to the citizenry for county operations as a whole.

True accountability means more than just assuring the public that revenues are properly collected and reported and that expenditures are made in accordance with prescribed procedures. Accountability includes these important assurances but also entails assurances to the public that their resources are being spent wisely as well as legally and that services of good quality are being produced efficiently. Performance measurement offers a tool for providing such assurances.

Jurisdictions that are leaders in performance measurement conscientiously report their accomplishments. Rarely, however, are performance measures in these jurisdictions used solely for public information reporting. Other uses are common. The county manager, for instance, may recite parks, recreation, and library performance statistics as background for a planning retreat on leisure services needs. As the county prepares for a major change in a given program, it might use performance measures to establish a baseline prior to program change and to continue monitoring these measures after implementation to see if the performance improvement initiative is working. The county undoubtedly applies performance measures to various contractual services to be sure that contractors are living up to their promises.

The Importance of Performance Measurement for Management

Good performance measures support a variety of management functions. From the targeting of service improvements to the defense of good performance, measures of program efficiency and effectiveness provide a solid foundation for objective decisions and prudent management.

By general observation and careful attention to the comments of service recipients, department heads and other management officials often develop a perception of operating strengths and weaknesses—a general notion about which units are performance leaders and which units lag behind. Often, such impressions are correct and are borne out by systematic assessments. More frequently than many managers care to admit, however, systematic assessments reveal a picture that differs from that suggested by occasional observation and anecdotes. Occasionally, strong performers do not look quite so strong when examined in the light of objective evidence, and weak performers are revealed to be more proficient than previously imagined. With appropriate measurement systems, managers and supervisors can more objectively detect operating deficiencies and target additional attention where it is needed most.

It is difficult to imagine any measurement system that could completely replace the value of on-site supervision. No measurement system can match a skillful supervisor's ability to develop the skills of workers, to instruct them in their tasks, to plan and schedule their work, to draw upon the pride and commitment of a work unit, or to motivate greater performance. But a good measurement system can enhance that supervisor's ability to do all these things. Instruction can be more focused, planning more precise, and feedback more objective. In this way, a systematic gauge of program efficiency and effectiveness can augment the value of on-site supervision, with greater value provided not only to upper management but also to the supervisor and the workforce in general.

Service complaints, often revolving around isolated incidents, sometimes produce a broader unfavorable image in the mind of the complainant. An unfortunate incident, perhaps misinterpreted, becomes symbolic of the service as a whole. Without a systematic means of judging departmental performance, the best hope for program officials confronted by uncomplimentary tales is that they have a few positive stories on hand to balance the negative ones told by their critics.

With systematic performance measurement and reporting, county programs and the budgets that support them are less vulnerable to isolated anecdotes that misrepresent the normal state of affairs in service delivery. With good performance measures, a service complaint can be viewed in the context of the norms for that service rather than in the absence of such context. Service units with strong performance can more adequately be defended, and weaker units can be identified with greater confidence and targeted for corrective action.

The Value of Performance Measurement to Governing Bodies

Even when a county's board of commissioners hires a county manager to handle matters of day-to-day administration, the board retains responsibility for general oversight of county government and for establishment of program priorities. It also retains responsibility for assessing the performance of the county manager in directing county operations. Good performance measures can be helpful in performing these duties.

Are county services being provided efficiently and equitably? Do they meet expectations in terms of quality? Could better services be provided at a more reasonable cost by contracting out some functions? Have deficiencies been identified, and are improvements being made where needed? Do service results indicate that proper management is being provided? Each of these questions can be answered adequately only if reliable data are available.

In recent years, many management experts have advocated more decentralized decision making, allowing field unit supervisors and even front-line employees to make decisions as long as they are consistent with a vision or culture established and nurtured by central authorities. Much can be said in favor of a strategy that places greater discretion in the hands of those who know the program best and are closest to the problems. However, without a dependable system for guaranteeing accountability, few governing bodies will be willing to increase managerial discretion or to encourage managers to permit greater discretion at lower levels of the organization. In the absence of a system for compiling and reporting evidence that county programs are being run efficiently and effectively, top officials are more likely to believe that their oversight responsibilities require involvement in or approval of a large portion of the individual decisions made on behalf of the government. If, on the other hand, reductions in administrative red tape are accompanied by clear evidence of favorable program results, upper management and governing bodies are more likely to be receptive.

The expense of administering a good performance measurement system is not trivial, but neither are the benefits of a good system. Because of its value to elected officials, appointed administrators, and the general citizenry, performance measurement has been endorsed by a host of professional associations, including the International City/ County Management Association, the Government Finance Officers

Association, the Governmental Accounting Standards Board, and the National Academy of Public Administration.

Types of Performance Measures

Over the years several efforts have been made to identify the various types of performance measures. In some cases, these efforts have produced lengthy lists with dubious categories. A shorter list with simple labels presents a clearer picture of the array of practical performance measures for local government. Virtually every relevant performance measure falls into one of these four categories:

- Workload measures
- Efficiency measures
- Effectiveness measures
- Productivity measures

Workload Measures

When a county department reports the number of applications processed, inspections made, or cases handled, it is reporting on its workload. These statistics say nothing about the quality or efficiency of the service. They only report how many units of a service were produced or how much of an activity was undertaken.

Although counting and tabulating workload numbers is the most common form of performance reporting in local government, the value of raw workload measures for policy and management purposes is extremely limited. This is not to suggest that keeping track of workload is unimportant. Comparing workload numbers from year to year provides an indication of growing or declining demand for a given service. More important, workload numbers are often critical ingredients in the calculation of higher-order measures that hold greater value for managerial and policy decisions. Unfortunately, however, too many county governments depend almost entirely on raw workload measures to report their performance. With workload measures alone, the message conveyed by a department or program cannot be, "We are efficient" or "We provide quality services." With raw workload measures, the only message is "We are busy!"

Efficiency Measures

Measures of efficiency report the relationship between resources used and services produced. Often, this relationship is expressed in terms of unit cost—for example, cost per application processed or cost per inspection. Efficiency measures may also be expressed as a variation of unit cost, either reversing the ratio or substituting another form of resource input—for example, applications processed per $1,000 or inspections per eight-hour inspector-day.

Effectiveness Measures

Measures of effectiveness gauge the quality of services and the extent to which a program's objectives are being achieved. Among the wide variety of possibilities, these may include measures of responsiveness (for example, average response time to emergencies) and citizen satisfaction (for example, percentage of citizens who are "satisfied" or "very satisfied" with the county recreation program).

Productivity Measures

A good productivity measure depicts important aspects of program efficiency and effectiveness *simultaneously* in a single indicator. For instance, mechanics' efficiency can be calculated based on a comparison of the actual time required for a job and the standard time for that type of repair. If the time required for reworking because of any improper repairs is added to the ratio as a penalty, the resulting measure accounts for both the efficiency of mechanics and the effectiveness of their repairs; hence, it becomes a productivity measure.

Although well-designed productivity measures can be very informative, they are also quite rare in local government performance reporting. Unfortunately, a few ill-fated efforts by county governments to develop sophisticated productivity measures have produced indicators that are illogical or difficult to interpret. Unless productivity measures are both logical and easily understood, local governments are better served by a good set of basic performance measures that includes several solid efficiency measures and effectiveness measures to accompany its workload measures, simply forgoing the sometimes complex productivity measures.

Use of Performance Measures in Budgeting

The budget process offers the opportunity to influence program design and priorities among county services. The budget itself is a financial document—but really it is much more than that. It is a financial document that reflects program planning and service priorities in financial terms and also, ideally, in terms of performance expectations.

Although some public-sector budgets continue to retain a strictly line-item format, listing appropriations for each detailed expenditure category, many governments have adopted formats more conducive to management or policy deliberations. Program budgets, for example, omit most of the object-of-expenditure details that characterize line-item budgets. Instead, they are organized around particular programs or types of service and report only broader categories of anticipated expenditures. Program budgets often include several measures of performance that reveal past performance and reflect performance expectations of the future.

Another prominent budget format is the performance budget. Once again, many line-item details are omitted from the document itself, and broader categories of expenditure are organized around departments, activities, or programs. In the case of performance budgeting, measures of performance become the central focus of budget deliberations as managers and governing bodies discuss performance successes and disappointments, hammer out plans for performance improvement and resource reallocation, and focus on budgetary decisions that will enable operating units to achieve desired performance levels.

A county government's decision to choose a program or performance budget format over a line-item format does not guarantee a change in the focus or nature of budgetary debate. However, it does set the stage for budgetary deliberations that focus a little less on supplies and other categories of expenditure, and a lot more on services and program results. Budget formats that incorporate good performance measures—especially efficiency and effectiveness measures—recognize and advance the planning and managerial opportunities in the budgetary process. They are designed to equip decision makers with performance facts and figures for a given program—as well as resource facts and figures—that will help them plan wisely and manage prudently.

Although the Government Finance Officers Association (GFOA) refrains from endorsing one particular budget format over all others, it nevertheless strongly advocates the use of performance measures. Included among the criteria for GFOA's Distinguished Budget Presentation Award is this guideline: "The document should provide objective methods (quantitative and/or qualitative) of measurement of results by unit or program."[1]

Echoing GFOA's assertion that performance measurement is an ingredient of a good budget, the National Advisory Council on State and Local Budgeting considers performance assessment to be one of the four fundamental principles of budgeting.

> Performance measures, including efficiency and effectiveness measures, should be presented in basic budget materials, including the operating budget document, and should be available to stakeholders. . . . At least some of these measures should document progress toward achievement of previously developed goals and objectives. More formal reviews and documentation of those reviews should be carried out as part of the overall planning, decision-making, and budget process.[2]

Despite all the advantages that performance measurement offers and the numerous endorsements it boasts, the act of incorporating performance measures into the budget process will not make the often arduous task of budget decisions suddenly simple. Performance measures will help identify operational strengths and weaknesses and will gauge changes in efficiency and progress toward meeting objectives, but they can neither formulate the perfect budget nor prescribe remedies for operational deficiencies. Governing bodies will still struggle to set priorities—and struggle to stretch resources to fund those priorities. Operating officials must still design program improvement strategies, but performance measures can provide a baseline and a gauge for the success or failure of those strategies.

Rarely will budget decisions be made solely on the strength of performance measures. Well-intentioned strategies of rewarding good performance with budgetary increases and penalizing poor performance with budget reductions inevitably deteriorate when crucial programs, struggling and seemingly losing ground to intractable problems, might be helped by a budgetary boost. When crime statistics are climbing, should the governing body penalize the sheriff's office with a blanket reduction, or should it reinforce law enforcement efforts with a budgetary increase?

Even if performance measures rarely yield clear budgetary direction, they almost always contribute positively to the process. Difficult decisions are best made with clear evidence of program performance and realistic expectations of future impact. Perhaps more important, awareness of downward performance trends often will prompt managers to design remedies to performance deficiencies prior to budget deliberations. These suggested remedies may then be presented in the budget process. Furthermore, meaningful performance measures can enhance communication between managers and governing bodies regarding performance expectations and service priorities.

Performance Measurement as a Tool for Productivity Improvement

Local government productivity may be defined as "the efficiency with which resources are consumed in the effective delivery of public services."[3] Not only should the quantity of outputs be considered in assessing productivity but also the quality of outputs. Productivity improvement occurs when the ratio of outputs to inputs is increased, with output considered in both a quantitative and a qualitative sense.

In other words, a county department may appropriately claim a gain in productivity when, for a given amount of dollars, it is able to provide services to more citizens without reducing quality or it is able to improve the quality of the service without reducing the number of service recipients. If increased quantity comes at the expense of quality, or if improved quality comes at the expense of quantity, overall productivity may not be increasing at all. Similarly, if expanding quantity or enhanced quality is matched by an even greater increase in required resources, there is no productivity gain; rather, there is a productivity loss.

Although productivity improvement strategies do not spring magically from performance measures, it is difficult to imagine effective strategies in the absence of performance measures. A good set of performance measures will identify areas of performance deficiency in which improvement strategies are likely to yield the greatest return, and if a formal approach is taken to the design of corrective action, measures are likely to support that approach. Improvement strategies, for example, may be guided by a formal benchmarking project or may develop as elements of a reinvention initiative—both of which rely on performance measurement. On the other hand, a strategy for productivity improvement in a given operation may be completely ad hoc, the product of careful observation, knowledge of techniques that have worked elsewhere, and a well-reasoned hunch that a particular adaptation will work in this organization.

Whether the source of a given productivity improvement strategy is systematic or informal, the effects of the strategy should be monitored carefully using appropriate performance measures. Such measures will yield feedback that may prompt mid-course corrections in strategies and improve the odds of success. And performance measures will help policy makers decide whether a given strategy is working and should be funded for continuation.

Identifying Strengths and Weaknesses

Often, county government officials have a notion about where the operating strengths and weaknesses lie in their organization, based upon personal observation and a history of complaints and compliments. In many cases their hunches are correct and can be substantiated by more objective performance measures. In other cases, however, their guesses are incorrect. They may be surprised to discover evidence that a favorite program is not as effective as previously thought or that a department once presumed to be wasteful is instead rather efficient.

Serious productivity efforts are neither simple nor inexpensive. Done properly, they require considerable time, analysis, and careful implementation. It makes sense, then, to direct these substantial efforts toward opportunities most likely to yield ample return. In most cases, services with the greatest performance deficiencies offer the greatest opportunity for improvement.

Benchmarking

Benchmarking projects in the public sector have taken one of three forms:

- Corporate-style benchmarking
- Targets as benchmarks
- Comparison of performance statistics as benchmarks[4]

Several government units have applied the private sector's formal benchmarking model, popularized when corporate giants such as Xerox analyzed the procedures of benchmarking partners from other industries to improve their own practices. Local governments that follow this model focus on a single process in their operation (for example, the procurement process, the issuance of permits, or emergency dispatching), identify other organizations that achieve superior results from that process, carefully analyze the process in their own organization and in their benchmarking partners, identify factors that contribute to superior results, and figure out how to modify their own process to improve their results. Because this approach focuses on processes and identifies performance leaders, it is often linked to the search for "best practices" and frequently carries that label.

A second form of benchmarking sets targets—sometimes administrative or operational targets but more often societal targets—and tracks progress toward achieving them. While corporate-style benchmarking focuses narrowly on key processes, this form of benchmarking focuses broadly on results and community conditions—for example, illiteracy, teen pregnancy rates, pollution, and unemployment. And while corporate-style benchmarking uses actual performance results from "best practices" as its benchmarks, the benchmarks in the second form often are set arbitrarily.

The third form is perhaps the most common type of benchmarking in the public sector. Apart from a few celebrated projects of significant scale, however, it rarely receives much fanfare. In this form of benchmarking, government units compare their own performance statistics with performance standards or with the performance targets and actual results of other units. For example, a property appraisal unit might compare its appraisal accuracy, based upon the market price from actual sales, with the appraisal accuracy of other units, or it might compare the daily workload of its appraisers with the typical production rates reported by the International Association of Assessing Officers.[5] Occasionally, major projects of considerable scope are developed around this form of benchmarking. Recent examples include the multijurisdictional performance measurement projects involving local governments across the nation, sponsored by the International City/County Management Association and The Innovation Groups; and a project involving local governments in North Carolina, coordinated by the Institute of Government.[6]

Comparison of performance statistics differs from the second form of benchmarking in that the performance statistics typically focus on government services rather than social indicators or broad quality-of-life measures, and benchmarks are more often tied to externally established standards or to the records of leading performers rather than being set arbitrarily. It differs from corporate-style benchmarking in two major ways. First, it typically focuses broadly on multiple services or operations, rather than narrowly on a single key process. Second, it focuses primarily on results and only secondarily, if at all, on the details of the processes that produce these results.

Local government officials who choose to compare performance statistics rather than to apply corporate-style benchmarking accept a trade-off. They trade the depth of analysis associated with corporate-style benchmarking for the breadth of coverage that comes with the comparison of performance statistics across several government operations. Those who make this trade do not necessarily rule out more detailed analysis at a later point. In fact, the broad comparison of performance statistics across several departments may help them identify functions that would benefit most from corporate-style benchmarking or from reinventing.

Reinventing

By the mid-1990s many governments across the nation—local, state, and federal—were engaged in cost-cutting or performance-enhancing initiatives that claimed the label *reinventing government,* after the popular 1992 book by that title.[7] The fundamental notion propelling the push for reinvention was the idea that merely tinkering with the system, making small procedural changes here and there, would not yield a government that was efficient and effective. Basic changes that would challenge the status quo in service delivery, that would force government units to be competitive, and that would even question the role of government, were needed.

Among the county governments in North Carolina that were inspired by the reinvention movement was Catawba County. The hallmarks of reinvention in Catawba County include the following:

- Increased discretion and flexibility for department managers, including more liberal purchasing authority, greater salary- setting discretion, and, among selected departments, the authority to move funds where they were needed and to create or abolish positions within the constraints of department appropriation
- The opportunity for prudent managers of selected departments to carry over budget savings for future use
- Department accountability for performance and results in exchange for greater discretion and authority

These operating characteristics deviate sharply from the status quo in most local governments, where departments are bound up in red tape, restricted by line items and rigid constraints on personnel practices, and perversely encouraged to "spend it or lose it" by year's end. They also mark expanded territory in managerial responsibility for quality services and program results.

In Catawba County, performance expectations are negotiated in advance, and performance is tracked and reported as part of the greater-accountability-for-greater-authority arrangement. The results of that arrangement are encouraging. By 1996, for instance, the Personnel Department was "providing departments with a pool of qualified applicants within five working days of receiving a recruitment request and recommending the most qualified applicants for interviews within three working days after the closing date." Similarly, the Social Services Department reported "96.4 percent of child protective services cases in treatment for six months had no repeat child abuse/neglect; 98.7 percent of TEEN-UP program participants did not become pregnant"; and "98 percent of TEEN-UP participants had no incidence of violence."[8] Other departments reported positive results as well.

Gauging the Success of Operational Improvements

Benchmarking, reinvention, and various other techniques for productivity improvement are promising but hardly fail-safe. Often, operational changes achieve the desired results, but sometimes they do not. Sometimes adjustments are needed. And occasionally new techniques fail and should be abandoned. The monitoring of performance *before, during,* and *after* operational change, therefore, is very important.

Keys to the Successful Use of Performance Measures

Many county governments have undertaken performance measurement with the best of intentions, but some have been disappointed by meager results. More often than not, their disappointment can be attributed to falling short on one or more of the following keys to success:

- *Measure efficiency and effectiveness—not just workload.* Systems that do nothing more than "count beans" have very limited managerial and policy value. Systems that report a department's efficiency, the quality of its services, and the effectiveness of its programs receive a lot more attention from managers—and they deserve to receive it because they are much more valuable.
- *Link the performance measurement system to important policy processes and to other management systems.* Although even a stand-alone performance measurement system can enhance accountability, the

systems that are most valued do that and more, because they are linked to important processes and contribute meaningfully to important policy or managerial decisions. The presentation of key performance measures as background for policy retreats held by the governing body, the review of performance measures during managerial or department head appraisals, and the use of performance measures to diagnose employee training needs are but a few examples of possible applications.

- *Present performance measures in context.* A performance measure reported out of context is "just a number" to all but the best-informed consumers of that information. Is a five-minute average response time to law enforcement emergencies good? What about a library circulation rate of five items per capita? Or a citizen satisfaction rate of 87 percent? When the information is presented out of context, it is difficult to know. Last year's numbers are the easiest context to provide for this year's numbers, but a more informative context might be applicable standards or the performance of other respected units. Presented in context, performance statistics become more valuable—and even interesting!

Additional Resources

Ammons, David N., ed. *Accountability for Performance: Measurement and Monitoring in Local Government.* Washington, D.C.: International City/County Management Association, 1995.

———. *Municipal Benchmarks: Assessing Local Performance and Establishing Community Standards.* Thousand Oaks, Calif.: Sage Publications, 1996.

Hatry, Harry P., L. H. Blair, D. M. Fisk, J. M. Greiner, J. R. Hall, Jr., and P. S. Schaenman. *How Effective Are Your Community Services? Procedures for Measuring Their Quality.* 2d ed. Washington, D.C.: Urban Institute and International City/County Management Association, 1992.

Tigue, Patricia, and Dennis Strachota. *The Use of Performance Measures in City and County Budgets.* Chicago: Government Finance Officers Association, 1994.

Notes

1. Government Finance Officers Association, "Detailed Criteria Location Guide: Distinguished Budget Presentation Awards Program" (Chicago: GFOA, 1997).

2. National Advisory Council on State and Local Budgeting, *Recommended Budget Practices: A Framework for Improved State and Local Government Budgeting* (Chicago: GFOA, 1998), 62. Quoted material is drawn from Practice 11.1.

3. Nancy S. Hayward, "The Productivity Challenge," *Public Administration Review* 36 (Sept.–Oct. 1976): 544.

4. David Ammons, "Raising the Performance Bar . . . Locally," *Public Management* 79 (Sept. 1997): 10–16.

5. Richard R. Almy, Robert J. Gloudemans, and Garth E. Thimgan, *Assessment Practices: Self-Evaluation Guide* (Chicago: International Association of Assessing Officers, 1991).

6. Paula K. Few and A. John Vogt, "Measuring the Performance of Local Governments," *Popular Government* 62 (Winter 1997): 41–54.

7. David Osborne and Ted Gaebler, *Reinventing Government: How the Entrepreneurial Spirit Is Transforming the Public Sector* (Reading, Mass.: Addison-Wesley, 1992).

8. Judy Ikerd, "End-of-Year Report on Reinventing Department Outcomes," Catawba County Budget Office memorandum dated Sept. 31, 1996.

4 Civil Liability of the County and County Officials

Anita R. Brown-Graham

Contents

Anita R. Brown-Graham is an Institute of Government faculty member who works in the area of public liability.

The author wishes to express her appreciation to Michael R. Smith, Director of the Institute of Government, and to Jeffrey S. Koeze, a former Institute of Government faculty member, whose authorship of this chapter in previous editions of this book is reflected in this edition's chapter.

The performance of governmental services sometimes results in injury to people or property and related lawsuits brought against counties and their officers and employees. The expense and inconvenience of these lawsuits are an unavoidable cost of carrying out the public's business. But the cost can sometimes appear higher than it actually is because of the significant number of frivolous lawsuits filed against public servants and local governments. Anyone with a pencil, a piece of paper, and the filing fee can bring a lawsuit. On the other hand, to hold a public servant or county liable, the individual, group, or entity (the "plaintiff") bringing the lawsuit must prove that the public servant or county violated the plaintiff's legal rights and the court must find that there are no laws that protect the defendant from liability.

Therefore, in assessing legal risks, public servants must distinguish between "being sued" and "being held liable" to pay damages. Very little can be done to control the former, but a number of basic legal principles seek to protect local governments and public servants from the latter. This chapter sets forth those principles under two basic areas of liability: tort liability under North Carolina law, and liability under federal law for violations of someone's protected civil rights. The latter liability is created by Section 1983 of the Civil Rights Act of 1871 (often referred to as Section 1983). Except perhaps for employment-related claims, these two kinds of claims are the most common ones brought against county public servants and governments. However, they are obviously not the only types of public liability claims. This chapter does not attempt to cover the remainder of the universe of both state and federal claims, which include environmental claims, tax claims, and contract claims, to mention only a few.

The term public servant is used throughout this chapter to refer to all the people who do the county's work, from elected officials to employees. At times, however, employees will be distinguished by position and duty and elected officials will be distinguished from employees.

Liability under state law and federal law are discussed separately. It is important to note, nonetheless, that although a person bringing a lawsuit can be compensated only once for his injuries, overlap between state and federal law may mean that the same action violates both state and federal law, rendering the unit of local government and its public servants liable under both.

The chapter uses the following framework to discuss state tort law and Section 1983 liability:

Tort liability under North Carolina law
- liability of the county
- liability of public servants

Section 1983 liability
- liability of the county
- liability of public servants

Liability under State Law

Civil liability in state court may arise for either intentional acts or negligence (conduct not considered reasonable under the circumstances) that cause personal injury or property damage. The North Carolina courts have classified these harmful acts as torts—that is, civil wrongs—as opposed to criminal conduct, and a person may recover damages for injuries or other harm caused by them.

The most significant function of tort law is to make persons who injure others pay for the harm they inflict. Individuals who are harmed through no fault of their own are not required to bear the loss; instead, the person whose wrongful act caused the harm must pay the injured party damages sufficient to compensate for the loss. Another purpose of tort law is to deter people from engaging in conduct likely to cause personal injury or property damage. Tort law makes an underlying assumption that people will be more careful in conducting their day-to-day activities if they are held accountable for any resultant harmful consequences.

In considering how the law of torts affects the liability of counties and their officers and employees, it is important to understand the types of civil wrongs that may be remedied by an award of damages in a tort lawsuit.

Intentional Torts

Intentionally committed wrongful acts that cause personal injury or property damage generally give rise to liability. The concept of intent relates to the desire to commit an act, not the desire to cause a specific harm or even any harm at all. A court need only find that the public servant intended the offensive *act* to hold him or her liable for an intentional tort; the court does not need to find that the public servant intended the resultant *injury*. A public servant could be held liable, therefore, for an intentional tort even though he honestly believed that his act would not cause injury.

Following are some examples of common intentional torts.

Battery

The intentional touching or striking of another person without either that person's consent or a legally recognized authorization is the intentional tort of battery. The case of *Munick v. City of Durham*[1] provides a useful illustration. An elderly man named Munick sought to pay his water bill with cash that included a wrapped roll of fifty pennies. The water department manager became outraged, threw the pennies to the floor, and commanded Munick to pick them up. When he did not respond, the manager locked the office door, struck him in the face, pulled him into a back room, and beat him. The state supreme court found that Munick could recover damages for a battery because the attack was unprovoked and without legal excuse.

Striking another person without consent is not a battery if the contact is legally authorized. For example, a sheriff's deputy may use reasonable force to effect a legal arrest [N.C. Gen. Stat. § 15A-1401(d)(1)]. The use of reasonable force, even if it includes striking a suspect to prevent an escape, does not constitute a civil battery. But if more force is employed than is reasonably necessary to make the arrest, the deputy may be sued in state court for the intentional tort of battery and be required to pay damages.[2]

False Imprisonment

The intentional tort of false imprisonment is committed when someone restrains the movement of another without that person's permission or without a legally recognized authorization. Keeping an inmate in the county jail beyond the court-ordered release date is an example of false imprisonment.[3] The tort of false imprisonment can arise in other contexts as well. In one case, the manager of a county hospital told a female patient that she could not leave until her bill was paid. If the patient stayed because of a reasonable belief that force would be used to prevent her departure, false imprisonment would be established and an award of damages might be allowed.[4]

Defamation

Defamation is false, written, or oral communication that tends to injure a third party's reputation. If the communication is written, it is called *libel*; if oral, it is called *slander*. It includes accusations that a person is a criminal, statements that injure someone in his or her occupation, and charges that an individual has an offensive disease. It would be defamation, for example, for a health department doctor to spread a false rumor that a particular patient had a venereal disease. Defamation would also be established if the county manager falsely told a local newspaper that a county employee was dismissed for stealing.[5]

A county officer or employee who is sued for making a public statement that harms someone's reputation has two possible defenses. First, the truth of a statement is always an absolute defense to liability for damages in a defamation lawsuit. Second, a public officer may avoid liability for a false statement by showing that it was made under circumstances in which a qualified privilege exists.[6] A qualified privilege exists when (1) the statement is made in good faith, (2) the person who makes it has a valid interest or a legal duty with respect to its subject, and (3) it is made to someone with a corresponding interest or duty. For example, in *Davis v. Durham City Schools*,[7] the court held that a school principal has a qualified privilege to report to the department of social services a student's concern that a teacher had physically abused another student. The privilege applies because the principal has a duty to report the allegations of abuse under G.S. 115C-400 and the department has a corresponding interest in the information. Of course, the privilege may be destroyed if the report is not made in a proper manner.

Negligence

The law imposes a duty on all people to exercise *reasonable care* in conducting their daily affairs. Negligence is the failure to act reasonably under a given set of circumstances. The court can find a local government defendant liable for negligence either for something that he or she has unreasonably done or something that he or she failed to do. Negligence may occur in an infinite variety of situations. Moreover, whether particular conduct is negligent cannot be determined in the abstract; a jury must decide in each specific case whether the defendant acted as a reasonably prudent person would have under the same circumstances. If the jury finds that the defendant did not act reasonably and that this caused the plaintiff's injury, the defendant may be required to pay for the harm caused by the negligence.

In order to prove that a public servant was negligent, a plaintiff must first demonstrate that the law imposed a duty on the public servant to conform his or her actions to a certain standard of conduct to protect the interests of the plaintiff. This first requirement is typically not difficult to meet in cases where the defendant's action, rather than omission, is the basis of the claim for negligence. Second, the plaintiff must demonstrate that the defendant failed to meet that duty. Third, an injury or damage to the plaintiff must have resulted from the defendant's action or inaction. Fourth, there must be sufficient factual and legal connection between the defendant's conduct and the plaintiff's harm or injury. The fourth requirement obligates the plaintiff to establish that the failure to exercise reasonable care under the circumstances *directly* caused the harm and that the defendant should have foreseen that his or her conduct would result in some harm. In addition, a person who is sued for negligence may under North Carolina law invoke the defense of contributory negligence—a legal rule that bars recovery by any individuals whose own negligence contributes to their injury.

Some examples will help to illustrate the operation of these rules. The failure to put up warning signs in this example is the failure to act. In *Clark v. Scheld*,[8] two local government employees drove a truck equipped with a machine that discharged a thick insecticide fog along a public highway. The fog covered the highway and totally obscured the view of approaching traffic. No warning signs were displayed to give oncoming vehicles notice of the hazard. A man rounded a curve into the fog and slowed his truck, but he was blinded by the fog and sideswiped a car that had pulled off the road to wait for it to clear. The court held that the two employees were negligent because of the following:

1. They had a duty to take reasonable precautions to protect other highway drivers from the hazardous condition they created.
2. They failed to take those reasonable precautions.
3. The man was injured by the employees' unreasonable actions.
4. It was highly probable that the employees' actions would result in injury to highway travelers.

In *Dunn v. Swanson*,[9] a county jailer took custody of a sick and helpless man who had been arrested and placed him in a cell with another man who was known to be violently insane. During the night, the latter used a leg torn from a table in the cell to beat the helpless inmate from head to foot, and the victim died the next morning. The state supreme court ruled that the plaintiff (the legal representative of the deceased inmate) could prove all of the requirements of a negligence case, and therefore, that a jury could find that the jailer had failed to act reasonably—in other words, that he was negligent—in placing a helpless individual in the same cell with a violent one.

Liability of the County

Governmental Immunity

The general legal rule governing the liability of employers for the torts of their employees is that they may be required to pay damages for any harm caused by employees who are acting within the scope of their employment at the time they cause the harm (see the "Acts within the Scope of Employment" subsection, later in the chapter). An additional rule may determine the result, however, when a county is the employer. From the legal point of view, county functions are of two kinds: governmental and proprietary.

Counties in North Carolina are protected from liability for injuries caused when their officers and employees are engaged in *governmental* activities, unless they waive their immunity by the purchase of insurance pursuant to G.S. 153A-435.[10] No such immunity protects counties from liability for injuries caused while the county's officers or employees are engaged in *proprietary* activities. The county's immunity from liability is limited, therefore, by the nature of the activity causing the plaintiff's injury. If the activity involved is characterized as governmental, the immunity will apply. If the activity is characterized as proprietary, the immunity will not.

The state supreme court has distinguished between governmental and proprietary activities as follows:

> Any activity . . . which is discretionary, political, legislative or public in nature and performed for the public good on behalf of the State, rather than to itself, comes within the class of governmental functions. When, however, the activity is commercial or chiefly for the private advantage of the compact community, it is private or proprietary.[11]

The distinction between governmental and proprietary activities, albeit often difficult to make, is one of the most important concepts in municipal liability under North Carolina state law. Unfortunately, the absence of a precise standard makes it difficult to predict whether a county will be liable for the torts of an employee who is engaged in a particular activity.

Factors Courts Consider in Determining Whether an Activity Is Governmental or Proprietary

Courts have looked to several factors in determining whether an activity is governmental or proprietary. The following are most common:

1. **Who traditionally performs the function?** It appears that all of the activities courts have held to be governmental functions are those historically performed by the government, and not ordinarily engaged in by private corporations. Examples include operation of county jails,[12] operation of traffic lights,[13] driving a police car,[14] use of a police or fire alarm,[15] administration of social services programs,[16] zoning enforcement,[17] storm drain maintenance,[18] furnishing water to firefighters,[19] condemnation of property,[20] franchise granting,[21] administration of sanitation programs,[22] and operation of libraries.[23]

2. **Is a fee charged for the service?** Every activity that has been found to be proprietary in nature has involved a monetary charge of some sort.[24] Examples of proprietary activities include operating a landfill where fees are charged for its use,[25] distributing water for profit,[26] distributing electricity for profit,[27] and operating an airport[28] or municipal golf course.[29]

    The fact that a fee is charged does not necessarily mean, however, that the activity is proprietary. Services that are truly governmental in nature are not made proprietary merely because a cost of the service is charged to a recipient.[30] For example, mass transit systems typically charge a user fee. However, these systems are so heavily subsidized that it is unlikely that a court would find the activity to be proprietary. If the local government is charging fees to the extent that a profit is made, however, the court will consider the existence of a profit strong evidence that the activity is proprietary.[31]

3. **Does public policy support a finding that the activity is governmental?** A specific municipal activity may be of such benefit to the state that public policy requires it be classified as governmental even though citizens of the municipality benefit more than the general citizens of the state. An example is sewerage, which is considered a governmental function in recognition of statewide public health concerns.[32]

Waiver by the Purchase of Insurance

As noted earlier, governmental immunity protects counties from liability for injuries arising from governmental activities. The immunity is granted by the state of North Carolina, so the state is entitled to determine the extent of the immunity, including the circumstances under which it may be waived. Currently, the General Assembly has provided only one way for a county to waive its governmental immunity—through the purchase of liability insurance.

G.S. 153A-435, which provides for waiver through the purchase of insurance, makes clear that the board of county commissioners has full discretion to determine the specific torts and officials or employees to be covered under the insurance policy. The governing body may even decide not to purchase insurance at all. If a county purchases insurance, a plaintiff may not recover damages for his or her injuries in excess of the insurance policy amount for injuries arising from a governmental activity. This is true irrespective of the extent of plaintiff's actual damages, because governmental immunity is only waived to the extent of insurance coverage. Similarly, a local government retains governmental immunity for damages that exceed the insurance amount.[33]

A county's participation in a local government risk pool is considered purchase of insurance and results in a waiver of governmental immunity up to the dollar amount agreed to by the participants. Local government risk pools are defined in G.S. 58-23-15. Generally, these risk pools are agreements between two or more local governments to either jointly purchase insurance or to pool resources to pay claims for property losses or liability. On the other hand, self insurance by a county does not waive governmental immunity. There must be some shifting of risk to another entity in order to meet the policy mandate behind the immunity; that is, the protection of public funds. The courts have taken this mandate seriously. In an illustrative case, the court found that there had not been a waiver of immunity under the statute where a city created an independent corporation to handle claims below the $1 million its insurance policy covered.[34]

County commissioners may often question the wisdom of purchasing insurance, when the consequence is a waiver of an immunity that completely protects the unit of local government from liability for injuries arising out of governmental activities. Yet there are several reasons to purchase insurance. First, the immunity does not cover proprietary acts, and insurance coverage may be desirable for those acts. As discussed earlier, the distinction between governmental and proprietary acts is often difficult to make without court direction. Those failing to seek insurance coverage do so at the risk of significant liability exposure for activities that the court may find to be proprietary. Second, the immunity does not extend to claims for violations of the North Carolina constitution,[35] for breach of contract,[36] or for an action for diminished property value due to a nuisance created by the unit of local government.[37] A county may wish to be insured with respect to such claims. Third, governmental immunity does not protect local governments from liability under federal laws, even if they are engaged in a governmental activity. Fourth, the purchase of insurance allows the local government to protect officials and employees who may be sued personally for job-related activities. Although other immunities may protect some of these individuals, those immunities are significantly more limited than governmental immunity. Fifth, the public is demanding increased accountability from governments. Since the only way to waive governmental immunity is through the purchase of insurance, an uninsured county may well find that, despite public expectations, it is unable to settle a claim for injuries caused while engaged in a governmental activity.[38] A county simply has no authority to make payment on a liability claim and compensate an injured citizen without a legal obligation to do so.[39] Finally, it is important to note that courts have willingly articulated a strong trend toward limiting governmental immunity,[40] meaning that the number of instances where a county is found liable for damages may be increasing.

The Nuisance Exception

The tort of nuisance is committed when a person engages in an activity that substantially and unreasonably interferes with the use and enjoyment of someone else's land. A county may be required to pay for damage to another's land caused by a county-created nuisance, *even if* this comes about through the performance of a governmental function. In one case, for example, a town's sewage treatment plant (the operation of which is a governmental function) released odorous gases that permanently reduced the value of the plaintiff's nearby home.[41] The state supreme court held that the plaintiff was entitled to recover damages from the municipality to compensate for the reduced value of his residential land.

Discretionary Immunity

Discretionary immunity is another doctrine that protects the county against liability under state law for certain actions. It provides that North Carolina courts will not review decisions that have been left to the sound discretion of a local legislative body. Although this type of immunity is sometimes characterized as one of the governmental functions covered within the broader doctrine of governmental immunity,[42] it is more appropriately discussed separately as a special category of immunity.

The treatment by courts of local ordinance-making power provides a good example of how the discretionary immunity doctrine is applied. They will not usurp the discretionary power granted local governing bodies to enact ordinances. That is, they will not substitute their judgment for that of a local governing body by imposing liability for the exercise or non-exercise of that body's ordinance-making power.

For example, Charlotte's city council once temporarily suspended an ordinance against the use of fireworks inside the city limits. A man's building was destroyed when fireworks landed on the roof and caught fire. He sued the city to recover damages, alleging that the board's negligence in suspending the ordinance caused his loss. The state supreme court denied recovery against the city on the grounds that a local government is not liable for the exercise or non-exercise of a discretionary power, such as the power to enact ordinances.[43]

Acts within the Scope of Employment

Absent an applicable immunity, a county will be held responsible for the acts of its officers and employees if their conduct falls within the "scope of the employment." The scope of employment includes not only those duties that are part of the formal job description but also all actual and customary duties.

Generally, the county will only be held liable for acts that are authorized, either expressly or implied. However, even acts that are contrary to the explicit instructions of an employer may be within the scope of employment if the act furthers the business of the county.

On the other hand, if the act is done wholly for the personal pleasure of the employee and it does not further the employer's business, the employer will not be held liable. A driver's use of a town's truck for personal reasons, for example, is not within the scope of employment and the town will not be held liable for injuries caused by the negligent use of the truck.[44]

Liability of County Officers and Employees

A county can conduct its daily affairs only through the actions of its officers and employees. An injured person may usually choose whether to sue the offending public servant in an official or individual capacity, or both. If the lawsuit is brought against the public servant in an "official capacity," it is in all respects other than name an action against the entity for which he or she works[45] and the same defenses and immunities available to the entity if it were sued in its own name are available. On the other hand, an action against a public servant in an "individual capacity" represents an allegation by the plaintiff that the public servant has personal liability to the plaintiff. Immunities separate and distinct from those available to the entity often insulate the public servant from liability for acts within the scope of his or her duties. These immunities are discussed in this section.

The immunities that may protect a public servant sued in an individual capacity reflect a balancing of the need to protect persons involved in certain functions of government from suit and the need to compensate injured plaintiffs and hold individuals accountable for their wrongdoing. Thus the extent of the immunity depends on the particular function of government involved.

Legislative Immunity

Legislative immunity provides absolute protection from personal liability for local legislators (county commissioners) and those executives acting in a quasi-legislative function (boards of health or zoning members, for example) for injuries caused by their legislative acts. Legislative immunity under state law was not recognized by the North Carolina Court of Appeals until 1996 in *Vereen v. Holden*.[46] Prior to *Vereen*, trial courts routinely applied the doctrine but looked to federal decisions for guidance. The Court of Appeals confirmed in *Vereen* that the parameters of legislative immunity are the same under both North Carolina and federal law. Legislative immunity applies if (1) the defendant was acting in a legislative capacity at the time of the alleged incident, and (2) the defendant's acts were not illegal. A more extensive discussion of legislative immunity is included under the Section 1983 segment of this chapter.

Public Official Immunity

In North Carolina, differing standards of liability apply to public servants deemed to be "public officials" than those that apply to "public employees." A public official is shielded from liability for injuries that arise from the exercise of a discretionary act, unless he or she acted with malice, for corrupt reasons, or outside the scope of his or her official duties. "Discretionary acts are those requiring personal deliberation, decision and judgment; [in contrast,] duties are ministerial [and not discretionary] when they are 'absolute, certain, and imperative, involving merely the execution of a specific duty arising from fixed and designated facts.'"[47] Put simply, and in keeping with the public policy goal of protecting the decision making of public officials, a public official will not be held personally liable for a properly motivated judgment made in using or failing to use a governmental power within the scope of his or her authority. A public employee, on the other hand, is not shielded from liability by public official immunity, and therefore may be held personally liable for injuries proximately caused by his or her negligence in the performance of his or her duties.[48]

Defining "Public Official"

The insulation from personal liability afforded to public officials means whenever a public servant is sued in his individual capacity, the court must determine whether the servant is an official or employee. In *Pigott v. City of Wilmington*,[49] the court of appeals considered four factors in determining whether a city building inspector was a public official or employee: (1) whether the inspector held a position created by legislation; (2) whether his position normally required an oath of office; (3) whether he performed legally imposed public duties; and (4) whether he exercised a certain amount of discretion in doing his job. A public servant does not have to meet all four criteria to be deemed a public officer for purposes of public official immunity. Since the *Pigott* ruling gave no indication of the weight that should be accorded each criterion, subsequent courts have focused on different sets of the criteria depending on the facts of the case.[50]

Based on the four factors listed in the *Pigott* ruling, North Carolina courts have held the following public servants to be public officials: notaries,[51] school trustees,[52] park commissioners,[53] a school district superintendent,[54] a principal,[55] coroners,[56] the state banking commissioner,[57] the Commissioner of Motor Vehicles,[58] the County Director of Social Services,[59] the director of a county health department,[60] building inspectors,[61] a chief of police,[62] police officers,[63] and elected officials.[64]

Defining "Public Employees"

Public servants who do not meet the test for public officials are usually deemed public employees. Public employees typically act at the direction of others, and their duties are more administrative or ministerial in nature than discretionary. The North Carolina Supreme Court has defined a ministerial duty as one which a person performs in obedience to legal authority, without exercising his or her own judgment.[65] A ministerial duty is one in which nothing is left to discretion.[66] It is a simple, definite duty arising under the law.[67] North Carolina courts have found public employees to include social workers,[68] police department personnel who test and repair radios,[69] and public works employees who sweep and clean the streets.[70]

Limitations of Public Official Immunity

The court's determination that the defendant is a public officer does not necessarily guarantee the defendant will be cloaked by public official immunity for his negligent acts. In its analysis the court need only answer one of the following questions in the affirmative for the immunity to fail:

1. Did the activity complained of entail ministerial duties, rather than the exercise of discretion or judgment?
2. Was the defendant motivated by malice?
3. Was the defendant motivated by corruption?
4. Did the defendant act outside of the scope of his authority?
5. Is there a statute that specifically imposes liability, thus overriding the general rules of public official immunity?

If the answer is "no" to all the questions, then the public official in question will be protected by public official immunity from liability for the complained-of action.

Liability of Sheriffs

Sheriffs are independent constitutional officers and historically have had the right to appoint deputies, who are their personal representatives and act exclusively in their name.[71] As a result, North Carolina courts have traditionally treated the two officials as one person and have held sheriffs accountable for all actions taken by deputies within the scope of their employment.[72] This harsh rule of liability applies even if the sheriff acted reasonably under the circumstances and was totally unaware of a deputy's particular misconduct.

Liability under Section 1983 of the Civil Rights Act of 1871

Local governments and their officials or employees may be held liable under a host of federal statutes. No source of liability, however, is more common than liability created under 42 U.S.C. Section 1983. Section 1983 authorizes a person to sue and recover damages against a county or its board members, officers, and employees for violating one of the person's federal constitutional or statutory rights when the violation is caused by official conduct. Section 1983 creates a framework of liability that is separate from that of state tort law discussed above. It provides a remedy under federal law for the violation of rights that are protected by a federal statute or the United States Constitution. Section 1983 may allow for a finding of liability in some cases where there is none under state law. In other cases, an official action may violate both sets of liability rules and expose the public officer and the county to potential liability under both state and federal law.

Notwithstanding their differences, the federal liability rules under Section 1983 serve many of the same functions as those of the state under tort law. Compensation of victims is an example: a person who violates someone's federal rights can be required to compensate the injured party, just as an individual who commits a civil wrong under state law must. In addition, the federal rules, like those of the state, are designed to deter county officers and employees from engaging in conduct that is likely to violate someone's rights under law. In analyzing how the federal liability rules affect the civil liability of counties and their officers and employees, we must first examine the type of official conduct that can give rise to federal civil liability under Section 1983.

Violation of Constitutional Rights

Section 1983 permits a person to sue and recover damages if the county or any of its board members, officers, or employees violate that person's federal constitutional rights. Several common constitutional violations are illustrated in the following sections.

First Amendment: Free Speech and Political Affiliation

The Constitution's First Amendment guarantees everyone's freedom of expression, which includes religion, assembly, petition, the press, and association. Thus, for example, the First Amendment is violated if a county official prevents a person from holding a non-obscene protest sign at a political rally.[73] The First Amendment also guarantees a citizen's right to affiliate with any political party. Generally, dismissing an employee solely because of such affiliation violates this guarantee.[74] Suppose, for example, that an incoming Republican board of county commissioners acknowledges that the planning director, a Democrat, has done a good job, but nevertheless dismisses the individual solely because of party affiliation and appoints a Republican. The dismissed director could bring a Section 1983 lawsuit and recover damages for the violation of the right of political-party affiliation caused by the board's official conduct. Similarly, the First Amendment would prohibit the commissioners from dismissing the planning director simply because of his or her religion.

Fourth Amendment: Wrongful Search and Seizure

The Fourth Amendment to the United States Constitution guarantees everyone's right to be free from unreasonable searches and seizures. When law enforcement officers attempt to control suspects during an arrest, for example, the Fourth Amendment requires that they only exercise that amount of force reasonably necessary under the circumstances.[75] The Fourth Amendment is also violated if one is arrested (seized) by a county sheriff who lacks probable cause (that is, good reason) to believe that the person arrested committed a crime or searches someone's person or property without a search warrant. In one case, for example, the plaintiff alleged that his constitutional rights were violated when a law enforcement officer broke into his home unannounced, searched the entire house without a warrant, shot and killed the family dog, arrested the home owner, and pushed him out into public with a gun pointed at his head.[76] The federal district court held that the plaintiff could recover damages under Section 1983 because his Fourth Amendment constitutional rights had been violated by the official action of the officer.

Fourteenth Amendment: Due Process

The Fourteenth Amendment to the federal Constitution provides that no person may be deprived of life, liberty, or property without due process of law—that is, the person must receive prior notice of the reasons for the deprivation and an opportunity for a hearing to consider those reasons. "Property" and "liberty" are defined broadly for purposes of this guarantee. For example, some county employees have a continued right to public employment because the personnel ordinance requires that there be a legitimate cause for firing them. They are said to have a "property" interest in their jobs and must be granted a due-process hearing before they may be discharged.[77] Similarly, county employees whose reputations are seriously injured by official accusations of illegal or immoral conduct at the time they are discharged have been deprived of a "liberty" interest in their professional reputation. They are therefore entitled to a due-process hearing to clear their names.[78] If no name-clearing opportunity is given, Section 1983 authorizes discharged county employees to sue and recover damages for the deprivation of their liberty interest (their protected professional reputation) without due process of law.

Violation of Statutory Rights

Section 1983 also authorizes a person whose rights under a federal statute have been violated to sue for and recover damages. The variety of federal statutes that might be violated by a county officer or employee, resulting in a Section 1983 lawsuit, is very large. In one case, for example, a man alleged that social services officials improperly reduced his Aid to Families with Dependent Children benefits because they misinterpreted the Social Security Act. The United States Supreme Court held that he could sue for damages in federal court under Section 1983.[79] In another case, the Supreme Court held that an error in billing low-income housing tenants for their utilities might violate the Housing Act of 1937 and result in a recovery of damages under Section 1983.[80]

There are two exceptions that limit the use of a Section 1983 lawsuit to remedy alleged violations of federal statutes by county officers and employees. First, a lawsuit under Section 1983 is not possible if the federal statute allegedly violated provides an exclusive remedy for its own enforcement.[81] Title VII of the Civil Rights Act of 1965, which prohibits employment discrimination, cannot be the basis of a Section 1983 lawsuit because Title VII provides a comprehensive remedial scheme for violations of its substantive provisions. Second, no Section 1983 lawsuit is permitted if a federal statute such as the Model Cities Act does not create an enforceable right.[82]

Liability of the County

The rules that govern a county's liability *under federal law* for violating federal constitutional or statutory rights differ from those that govern tort liability *under state law*. It will be recalled that state tort law holds a county liable for any actions of its employees within the scope of their employment whenever they are carrying out a proprietary function. In contrast, a county may be required to pay money damages in a lawsuit brought under Section 1983 only if the violation of federal rights is caused by the county's *official policy*.[83] The mere fact that an officer or employee violates someone's federal rights does not automatically make the county liable in federal court under Section 1983. If an official policy *is* involved, however, it is irrelevant under federal law whether the violation occurred in the pursuit of a governmental or a proprietary function.

As just mentioned, a county may be required to pay damages in a lawsuit brought under Section 1983 only if the violation of a plaintiff's federal rights (illustrated earlier) is caused by the county's "official policy or custom." Some examples may help to illustrate the meaning of this phrase.

A county may be held liable if someone's federal rights are violated by the implementation of an *ordinance, regulation,* or *decision officially adopted by the board of county commissioners.* For example, a county could be held liable if the commissioners enacted an unconstitutional zoning ordinance that arbitrarily violated someone's federal constitutional rights (for example, one that prohibited unmarried couples from living together). A county also may be required to pay damages under Section 1983 if someone's federal rights are violated by a *county board* or *county official with final decision-making authority in the area involved.* For example, the county could be held liable in a Section 1983 lawsuit if the county manager dismissed an employee solely for political reasons in violation of the employee's First Amendment right to affiliate with any political party. In each case, the violation of federal rights was caused by someone (the board of commissioners or the manager) with final authority to make official policy.

Significantly, official county policy also may be established by the *failure* of board members and officers to make policy, and it may be established by boards largely independent of the board of commissioners. Consider, for example, the case of *Avery v. Burke County*,[84] which involved a woman who was sterilized on the advice of a health department doctor after a health department nurse incorrectly interpreted her blood test as showing the presence of sickle-cell trait. The Fourth Circuit federal court of appeals ruled that Burke County could be required to pay damages if the board of health's failure to establish adequate sterilization procedures caused the violation of the woman's constitutional right to privacy and procreation. The court found that the board of health had final authority to make health policy for the county, and that its policy (or lack of one) was therefore automatically official policy.

The most common local government liability cases under Section 1983 are those alleging unconstitutional customs. A custom may be inferred from continued inaction in the face of a known history of widespread constitutional deprivation on the part of county employees.[85] For example, a sheriff's department may not ignore repeated complaints of excessive force by its officers, and therefore if local government officials know of a need to develop a policy on a particular matter and fail to do so, liability may arise. A plaintiff cannot prove the existence of a custom, however, based solely on the failure to prevent a single incident of unconstitutional action by a non–policy-making employee.[86]

As noted earlier, a county may be held liable under state law for torts committed by its employees in the course of their employment solely because it is the employer, without regard to whether or not the employees were carrying out official county policy. The county will not, however, be required to pay damages in a Section 1983 lawsuit if the violation of federal rights was caused by the independent, isolated act of an officer or employee who had no authority to make final policy for the county. For example, unlike under state law, a county is *not* liable automatically under Section 1983 if a sheriff's deputy makes an illegal arrest and conducts a warrantless search in violation of someone's Fourth Amendment rights. The reason: the constitutional violation was the deputy's independent wrongful act and did not result from official county policy.

Liability of County Officers and Employees

County board members, officers, and employees also may be sued individually in a Section 1983 lawsuit if they violate someone's federal rights. In some cases, however, they may be entitled to the protection of either absolute or qualified immunity from personal liability for damages. (In contrast, the county is never entitled to immunity from liability for damages in a Section 1983 lawsuit if its official policy caused the violation of someone's federal rights.)[87]

Legislative Immunity

Members of local legislative bodies such as boards of county commissioners are *absolutely immune* from personal liability for damages if the board's legislative acts violate someone's federal rights.[88] This absolute immunity means that county commissioners may never be required to pay damages for acts taken within the scope of their *legislative* duties. In contrast, they could be held personally liable for acts taken within the scope of their *administrative* duties, although *qualified immunity* (see the next section) may sometimes protect them.

An example will illustrate the difference between legislative and administrative duties. Board members are absolutely immune from per sonal liability if the board enacts a personnel ordinance that lists Republican political-party affiliation by any county employee as cause for dismissal, even though it violates employees' First Amendment right to affiliate freely with any political party, since enacting an ordinance is a legislative action.[89] But they are *not* absolutely immune from damage liability if they enforce such an ordinance by wrongfully dismissing an employee solely because he or she is a Republican when party affiliation is not necessary on the job. Enforcement of the ordinance involves an administrative action. Employment decisions are approved by boards of county commissioners as part of their administrative rather than their legislative duties.[90]

Absolute immunity is considered necessary to ensure that local legislators will discharge their legislative duties for the public good without fear of personal liability. The grant of absolute immunity guarantees that Section 1983 claims against individual county commissioners for legislative acts will be dismissed without subjecting them to the cost and inconvenience of a trial.

Qualified Immunity

Other county officers and employees who violate someone's federal rights while performing their official duties (and county commissioners who are performing administrative tasks) are entitled to *qualified*—not absolute—*immunity* from personal liability.[91] Such immunity is necessary to ensure that county officials will make decisions without fear of personal liability for honest mistakes in judgment. The qualified immunity defense provides that a public servant may not be held personally liable in a Section 1983 lawsuit unless his or her conduct violated clearly established statutory or constitutional rights that a reasonable person in similar circumstances would have known about.[92] In other words, public officials are shielded from Section 1983 liability if they reasonably could have thought that their conduct was lawful.[93] The qualified immunity defense protects county officials if the law governing their conduct is unclear at the time they act, even if a court later declares their conduct unconstitutional. But the reverse is also true: qualified immunity will not protect county officers if the law is clear and they ignore it.[94]

For example, suppose that a county manager has dismissed an employee. The personnel ordinance provides that employees may be dismissed only for cause (that is, for a good reason). The manager gave the dismissed employee neither a reason for the action nor a hearing to challenge it. A year before the dismissal occurred, the United States Supreme Court held that public employees who may be dismissed only for cause have a property interest in their job and must be granted a due-process hearing before they may be dismissed. When the employee brings a Section 1983 lawsuit against the manager on the basis of not receiving due process, the manager claims entitlement to qualified immunity from liability for damages on the basis of never hearing about the Supreme Court decision. The manager, who will lose the argument, is not entitled to qualified immunity from liability because of ignorance of settled law that a reasonable person under the circumstances would have known about. While qualified immunity offers complete protection to county officers and employees who unintentionally violate someone's constitutional rights, it only protects them if they could not reasonably have predicted that their conduct was unlawful.

Defense of Employees and Payment of Judgments

Each county is authorized, but not required, to provide for the defense of any civil or criminal action brought against current or former officers and employees in state or federal court on account of alleged acts or omissions committed in the scope and course of their employment [G.S. 153A-97, 160A-167(a)]. A county may provide a defense through the county attorney or by hiring a private attorney. Also, as discussed above, the county may purchase liability insurance that requires the insurer to defend lawsuits brought against certain officers or employees. Whether to provide a defense at all is of course the county commissioners' decision.

Each county also is authorized, but not required, to pay all or part of any settlements or judgments in lawsuits against officers or employees for acts committed in the scope and course of their employment (G.S. 160A-167(b) and (c)]. No statutory limit is placed on the amount of money a county may appropriate to pay a settlement or judgment. But funds may not be appropriated to pay an employee's or officer's settlement or judgment if the county commissioners find that the individual acted or failed to act because of fraud, corruption, or malice.

Certain procedural requirements must be satisfied before a county may pay an employee's settlement or judgment. (No such requirements need be met before providing for the defense of an employee.) First, notice of a claim or litigation against an employee must be given to the county *before* a settlement is reached or a judgment is entered, if the county is to pay the settlement or judgment. Also, the county must have adopted, prior to the reaching of the settlement or entry of the judgment, a set of uniform standards under which claims against officers and employees will be paid. These standards must be made available for public inspection. Adopting uniform standards for paying claims does *not* obligate the county to pay all settlements and judgments against officers and employees that satisfy the adopted criteria. The commissioners are still entitled to decide whether to pay on a case-by-case basis.

Notes

1. Munick v. City of Durham, 181 N.C. 188, 106 S.E. 665 (1921).

2. In Houston v. De Herrodora, 192 N.C. 749, 136 S.E. 6 (1926), for example, three police officers who chased the plaintiff in their car and fired twenty shots at him before identifying themselves as police officers were held liable for battery and required to pay a total of $2,000 in damages.

3. *See* Williams v. State, 168 N.Y.S. 2d 163 (Ct. Cl. 1957) (a prison inmate who was detained for one and one-half years after his maximum sentence expired was awarded damages for false imprisonment).

4. *See* Hoffman v. Clinic Hosp., Inc., 213 N.C. 669, 197 S.E. 161 (1938). *See generally* Blackwood v. Cates, 297 N.C. 163, 254 S.E.2d 7 (1979) (mayor individually liable for false imprisonment when, acting in his official capacity, he ordered the plaintiff illegally arrested, handcuffed, and confined in a room for 40 minutes).

5. *See* Jones v. Brinkley, 174 N.C. 25, 93 S.E. 372 (1917).

6. *But see* Presnell v. Pell, 298 N.C. 715, 260 S.E.2d 611 (1979); Towne v. Cope, 32 N.C. App. 660, 233 S.E.2d 624 (1977). In some instances, there are state statutes that expressly extend this qualified privilege to designated public officers and employees. For example, the 1987 General Assembly created a privilege for written communications made by members of nursing and domiciliary home advisory committees. See N.C. Gen. Stat. §§ 131O-31(i) and 131E-128(i).

7. Davis v. Durham City Sch., 91 N.C. App. 520, 372 S.E.2d 318 (1988).

8. Clark v. Scheld, 253 N.C. 732, 117 S.E.2d 838 (1961).

9. Dunn v. Swanson, 217 N.C. 279, 7 S.E.2d 503 (1940).

10. Not all local governments are authorized to waive immunity through the purchase of insurance. For example, water and sewer districts are not municipal corporations for the purpose of Chapter 160A, which contains such an insurance purchase/waiver provision for municipalities. They are special-purpose municipal corporations and may not waive immunity by the purchase of insurance. Thrash v. City of Asheville, 95 N.C. App. 457, 470 383 S.E.2d 657, 665 (1989); *rev'd on other grounds*, 327 N.C. 251, 393 S.E.2d 842 (1990).

11. Millar v. Town of Wilson, 222 N.C. 340, 341, 23 S.E.2d 42 (1942).

12. North Carolina *ex rel* Hayes v. Billings, 240 N.C. 78, 81 S.E.2d 150 (1954).

13. Hamilton v. Hamlet, 238 N.C. 741, 78 S.E.2d 770 (1953).

14. Lewis v. Hunter, 212 N.C. 504, 193 S.E. 814 (1937).

15. Cathey v. City of Charlotte, 197 N.C. 309, 148 S.E. 426 (1929).

16. Whitaker v. Clark, 109 N.C. App. 379, 427 S.E.2d 142, *disc. review* and *cert. denied*, 333 N.C. 795, 431 S.E.2d 31 (1993).

17. Orange County v. Heath, 14 N.C. App. 44, 187 S.E.2d 345, *aff'd*, 282 N.C. 292, 192 S.E.2d 308 (1972).

18. Stone v. City of Fayetteville, 3 N.C. App. 261, 164 S.E.2d 542 (1968).

19. Howland v. Asheville, 174 N.C. 749, 94 S.E. 524 (1917) (furnishing water to firefighters).

20. Dale v. City of Morganton, 270 N.C. 567, 155 S.E.2d 136 (1967).

21. Denning v. Goldsboro Gas Co., 246 N.C. 541, 98 S.E.2d 910 (1957).

22. See James v. City of Charlotte, 183 N.C. 630, 112 S.E. 423 (1922); Koontz v. City of Winston-Salem, 280 N.C. 513, 186 S.E.2d 897 (1972) (operating a landfill for disposal of garbage collected within territorial limits is also a governmental function).

23. Siebold v. Kinston-Lenoir County Pub. Library, 264 N.C. 360, 141 S.E.2d 519 (1965).

24. *See, e.g.*, Sides v. Cabarrus Mem'l Hosp., 287 N.C. 14, 21, 213 S.E.2d 297, 302 (1975).

25. Koontz v. City of Winston-Salem, 280 N.C. 513, 186 S.E.2d 897 (1972).

26. Foust v. Durham, 239 N.C. 306, 79 S.E.2d 519 (1954).

27. Rice v. Lumberton, 235 N.C. 227, 69 S.E.2d 543 (1952).

28. Rhodes v. City of Asheville, 230 N.C. 134, 52 S.E.2d 371 (1949).

29. Lowe v. Gastonia, 211 N.C. 564, 191 S.E. 7 (1937).

30. Casey v. Wake County, 45 N.C. App. 522, 263 S.E.2d 360 (1980) (fee charged for public health measure which is a governmental activity).

31. See Hare v. Butler, 99 N.C. App. 693, 394 S.E.2d 231 (1990), *disc. review denied*, 327 N.C. 634, 399 S.E.2d 121 (1991).

32. McCombs v. City of Asheboro, 6 N.C. App. 234, 170 S.E.2d 169 (1969).

33. Jones v. Kearns, 120 N.C. App. 301, 462 S.E.2d 245 (1995). Plaintiffs may be required to submit a statement of damages indicating that their damages exceed the amount of an insurance deductible.

34. Blackwelder v. City of Winston-Salem, 332 N.C. 319, 420 S.E.2d 432 (1992); *See also* Hickman v. Fuqua, 108 N.C. App. 80, 422 S.E.2d 449 (1992); Lyles v. City of Charlotte, 344 N.C. 676, 477 S.E.2d 150 (1996) (local government risk pool agreement must contain a provision that the pool pay all claims for which a member incurs liability; pool has not paid a claim if it is reimbursed for it).

35. Corum v. University of N. C., 330 N.C. 761, 786, 413 S.E.2d 276, 291 (1992). It would indeed be a fanciful gesture to say on one hand that citizens have constitutional individual civil rights that are protected from encroachment actions by the state, while on the other hand saying that individuals whose constitutional rights have been violated by the state cannot sue because of the doctrine of sovereign immunity.

36. Smith v. State, 289 N.C. 303, 222 S.E.2d 412 (1976).

37. Moser v. City of Burlington, 162 N.C. 141, 78 S.E. 74 (1913).

38. Galligan v. Town of Chapel Hill, 276 N.C. 172, 171 S.E.2d 427 (1970); Town of Hillsborough v. Smith, 10 N.C. App. 70, 178 S.E.2d 18 (1970), *cert. denied*, 277 N.C. 727, 178 S.E.2d 831 (1971).

39. Leete v. County of Warren, 341 N.C. 116, 462 S.E.2d 476 (1995); Brown v. Board of Comm'rs of Richmond County, 223 N.C. 744, 746, 28 S.E.2d 104, 105–06 (1943) ("[A] municipality cannot lawfully make an appropriation of public moneys except to meet a legal and enforceable claim").

40. *See* Smith v. Phillips, 117 N.C. App. 378, 451 S.E.2d 309 (1994).

41. Glace v. Town of Pilot Mountain, 265 N.C. 181, 143 S.E.2d 78 (1965).

42. Blackwelder v. Concord, 205 N.C. 792, 795, 172 S.E. 392 (1934) (declaring that "[t]he exercise of discretionary or legislative power is a governmental function, and for injury resulting from the negligent exercise of such power a municipality is exempt from liability").

43. Hill v. City of Charlotte, 72 N.C. 55 (1875), 21 Am. Rep. 451. *See* Moye v. McLawhorn, 208 N.C. 812, 182 S.E. 493 (1935).

44. Rogers v. Town of Black Mountain, 224 N.C. 119, 122, 29 S.E.2d 203, 205 (1944).

45. *See* Dickens v. Thorne, 110 N.C. App. 39, 45, 429 S.E.2d 176, 180 (1993), *citing* Whitaker v. Clark, 109 N.C. App. 379, 427 S.E.2d 142, *review denied*, 333 N.C. 795, 431 S.E.2d 31 (1993).

46. Vereen v. Holden, 121 N.C. App. 779, 468 S.E.2d 471 (1996), *citing* Scott v. Greenville County, 716 F.2d 1409, 1422 (4th Cir. 1983).

47. *Id.* at 309, 404, *citing* Wiggins v. City of Monroe, 73 N.C. App. 44, 49, 326 S.E.2d 39, 43 (1985).

48. Harwood v. Johnson, 92 N.C. App. 306, 374 S.E.2d 401 (1988), *aff'd in part, rev'd in part on other grounds*, 326 N.C. 231, 388 S.E.2d 439 (1990).

49. Pigott v. City of Wilmington, 50 N.C. App. 401, 403–04, 273 S.E.2d 752, 754, *disc. review denied*, 303 N.C. 181, 280 S.E.2d 453 (1981); *see also* State v. Hord, 264 N.C. 149, 155, 141 S.E.2d 241, 245 (1965).

50. *See, e.g.,* EEE-ZZZ Lay Drain Co. v. North Carolina Dep't of Human Resources, 108 N.C. App. 24, 422 S.E.2d 338 (1992) (focusing on the first, second, and third *Pigott* factors).

51. McGee v. Eubanks, 77 N.C. App. 369, 335 S.E.2d 178 (1985).

52. Smith v. Hefner, 235 N.C. App. 1, 68 S.E.2d 783 (1952).

53. *Id.*

54. Gunter v. Anders, 114 N.C. App. 61, 441 S.E.2d 167 (1994).

55. *Id.*

56. Gilikin v. United States Fid. & Guar. Co., 254 N.C. 247, 118 S.E.2d 606 (1961).

57. Sansom v. Johnson, 39 N.C. App. 682, 251 S.E.2d 629 (1979).

58. Thompson Cadillac-Olds v. Silk Hope Automobile, Inc., 87 N.C. App. 467, 361 S.E.2d 418 (1987).

59. Hare v. Butler, 99 N.C. App. 693, 394 S.E.2d 231 (1990).

60. *EEE-ZZZ Lay Drain Co.,* 108 N.C. App. 24, 422 S.E.2d 338 (1992).

61. *Pigott,* 50 N.C. App. at 405, 273 S.E.2d at 755.

62. State v. Hord, 264 N.C. 149, 141 S.E.2d 241 (1965).

63. *Id.*

64. Town of Old Fort v Harmon, 219 N.C. 241, 12 S.E.2d 423 (1941).

65. Hare v. Butler, 99 N.C. App. 693, 699, 394 S.E.2d 231, 236 (1990).

66. *Id.*

67. *Id.*

68. *Id.*

69. *Id.*

70. Miller v. Jones, 224 N.C. 783, 32 S.E.2d 594 (1994).

71. Styers v. Forsyth County, 212 N.C. 558, 2 S.E.2d 366 (1937).

72. Davis v. Moore, 215 N.C. 449, 2 S.E.2d 366 (1939).

73. Glasson v. City of Louisville, 518 F.2d 899 (6th Cir. 1975).

74. *See* Branti v. Finkel, 445 U.S. 507 (1980); Elrod v. Burns, 427 U.S. 347 (1976); Jones v. Dodson, 727 F.2d 1329 (4th Cir. 1984). *See generally* Stephen Allred, *Employment Law: A Guide for North Carolina Public Employers,* 2d ed. (Chapel Hill, N.C.: Institute of Government, The University of North Carolina at Chapel Hill, 1995), 190–203.

75. Graham v. Connor, 490 U.S. 386 (1989).

76. Ellis v. City of Chicago, 478 F. Supp. 333 (N.D. Ill. 1979).

77. Board of Regents of State Colleges v. Roth, 408 U.S. 564 (1972).

78. Bishop v. Wood, 426 U.S. 341 (1976); *Roth,* 408 U.S. 564.

79. Maine v. Thiboutot, 448 U.S. 1 (1980).

80. Wright v. City of Roanoke Redevelopment and Hous. Auth., 479 U.S. 418 (1987).

81. Middlesex County Sewerage Authority v. National Sea Clammers Ass'n, 453 U.S. 1 (1981).

82. Pennhurst State Sch. v. Haldermann, 451 U.S. 1 (1981).

83. Monell v. Department of Soc. Servs., 436 U.S. 658 (1978).

84. Avery v. Burke County, 660 F.2d 111 (4th Cir. 1981).

85. *See* Milligan v. City of Newport News, 743 F.2d 227 (4th Cir. 1984), *citing* Wellington v. Daniels, 717 F.2d 932 (4th Cir. 1983).

86. Slaken v. Porter, 737 F.2d 368 (4th Cir. 1984), *cert. denied,* 470 U.S. 1035 (1985).

87. Owen v. City of Independence, 445 U.S. 622 (1980).

88. Bruce v. Riddle, 631 F.2d 272 (4th Cir. 1980); Bogan v. Scott-Haris, ___ U.S. ___, 118 S. Ct. 988 (1998).

89. *See generally id.*

90. Visser v. Magnarelli, 542 F. Supp. 1331 (N.D.N.Y. 1982); Detz v. Hoover, 539 F. Supp. 532 (E.D. Pa. 1982).

91. *See* Wood v. Strickland, 420 U.S. 308 (1975).

92. Harlow v. Fitzgerald, 457 U.S. 800 (1982). *See* Michael R. Smith, "Qualified Immunity from Liability for Violations of Federal Rights: A Modification," *Local Government Law Bulletin,* no. 23 (Institute of Government, 1983).

93. Anderson v. Creighton, 483 U.S. 635, 107 S. Ct. 3034 (1987). In *Anderson,* the United States Supreme Court stated that qualified immunity protects public officials from damage liability "so long as their actions could reasonably have been thought consistent with the rights they are alleged to have violated." 107 S. Ct. at 3038.

94. One purpose of qualified immunity is to protect county officials from the cost and disruption of a trial by expediting the resolution of insubstantial lawsuits. For this reason, judges usually decide *before trial* whether to grant qualified immunity to county officers.

5 The County Attorney and the County Clerk

A. Fleming Bell, II

Contents

A. Fleming Bell, II, is an Institute of Government faculty member who specializes in local government law. He coordinates the Institute's programs for county attorneys and clerks to the boards of county commisssioners.
The portion of this chapter on the county attorney has been adapted, with updated data, from Grainger R. Barrett, "County Legal Representation: Retained or Full-Time County Attorney?" *Local Government Law Bulletin,* no. 20 (Oct. 1980), published by the Institute of Government.

The county attorney and the clerk to the board of county commissioners are mainstays of the board of county commissioners as it attempts to govern wisely and well. Together they help to ensure that county government activities are carried out in a legally correct manner. The documents created and maintained by the attorney and the clerk provide the written record needed to ensure that the board is accountable to the county's citizens and to other public and private officials. Ideally the attorney and the clerk work as partners with the manager and the board, the attorney advising on the legal consequences of commissioners' actions, the clerk keeping a record of those actions, and both officials ensuring that proper procedures are followed to enable the corporate entity, the county, to "speak" and "act" clearly and effectively.

The County Attorney

Every board of county commissioners in North Carolina must appoint an attorney to be its legal adviser (G.S. 153A-114). All counties in fact have a county attorney, but the diversity of arrangements they have made for legal representation is notable; it reflects the varied legal needs of the state's 100 counties. The typical county attorney in North Carolina is an independent practitioner or a member of a law firm who works for the county on a contractual basis. About twenty-four counties, however, have at least one full-time attorney—the county attorney or an assistant or staff attorney—who is an employee of the unit, is paid a salary, and works only on county legal matters. The number of full-time attorneys has increased steadily though slowly in recent decades. This section reviews some of the issues that a board of county commissioners might consider in deciding what sort of legal representation it needs.[1]

Typical Arrangements

The typical county attorney is an independent contractor. In over half of North Carolina's counties, the county attorney is paid a yearly retainer to provide agreed-on basic services. In some other counties, a retainer is apparently not used, so all legal work is "fee for service." This retainer fee can run to over $47,000 annually, but retainers of $15,000 or less are more common. The retainer usually covers such services as the following:

- Attending all meetings of the board of commissioners
- Being available for routine consultation with commissioners and department heads
- Drafting ordinances and resolutions
- Preparing routine legal documents like deeds and simple contracts
- Preparing legal advertisements

In some counties, all of a retained attorney's work is charged against the retainer on a per-hour basis; the retainer then is a minimum annual fee for legal representation. Services beyond established retainer services are reimbursed on a per-hour or other fee basis. As independent contractors, attorneys are responsible for providing their own health and hospitalization insurance, disability insurance, life insurance, and pension plan. Their retainer and hourly charges also pay for office and secretarial expenses.

As noted earlier, roughly twenty-four counties have at least one full-time salaried attorney with the larger ones having legal staffs of varying sizes. An experienced full-time county attorney in an urban county can receive a salary in the $65,000 to $100,000 range. In addition, the county provides fringe benefits, office space and supplies, and secretarial and other assistance.

The range of legal costs is illustrated by the following examples. Chatham County, with an estimated 1996 population of 41,049, uses a retained attorney. In the 1996–97 fiscal year, it had a total legal budget of $33,650, $30,000 of which was the retainer, for a per capita cost of $ .82. Guilford County's estimated population in 1996 was about 354,000, and it has a full-time legal staff. The county had a total legal budget of $535,274 in the 1996–97 fiscal year, $445,278 of which was for personnel services. The per capita cost was $1.52. (These figures may not include all legal expenses.)

A number of counties have "hybrid" arrangements for legal representation. Several, for instance, retain as county attorney a law firm or attorney who is an independent contractor, even though the attorney spends upward of 80 percent of his or her time exclusively on county legal matters. The advantage of this arrangement for attorneys quite often is that they can remain partners in their law firms and thus share in the firms' overall economic success. The advantage to the county is the knowledge that one person brings to his or her legal service who has represented the county's affairs over a period of time and knows its personalities, issues, and operations. Still other counties classify their attorney as an employee even though the attorney may devote less than half of his or her time to county matters. This arrangement may be advantageous to the attorney in the area of fringe benefits such as insurance and pension provisions. Some counties retain a member of a law firm but also employ a full-time staff attorney as an assistant. This arrangement gives the county the benefit of a valued legal counselor while maintaining a full-time lawyer on hand for day-to-day legal matters.

Considerations in Providing Legal Services

The best way to provide legal services for a particular county depends on that county's legal needs. Most counties' legal matters have become steadily more complex and costly to handle over the last few decades. The proliferation of state and federal laws and programs and their consequent demands on local governments suggest that the trend will not reverse itself in the foreseeable future. Commissioners should regularly assess what sorts of legal representation will be best for a county as it changes over the years. They should not be afraid to ask hard questions and to expect clear answers as they conduct this evaluation.

Take the issue of "better service," for example. The quality of service a county attorney provides depends primarily on his or her professional capability and personality. Whether the county attorney is an independent contractor or an employee, the county is best served by a capable lawyer who is well versed in a variety of general legal subjects and also is familiar with the specific legal principles and statutes that apply to local governments. Thus ideally a county attorney should be both a generalist and a specialist. He or she should be knowledgeable in such general legal areas as contracts, civil procedure and litigation, torts, and constitutional law and should also feel at home with such local government legal matters as governing board procedures, open meetings, public records, purchasing, property tax assessment and collection, budget and financial procedures, and federal civil rights, equal opportunity, and environmental regulations and laws.

A county attorney should be able to work and communicate effectively with public officials, county employees, the press, and the public. Commissioners want to rely on the attorney's judgment and his or her ability to articulate ideas clearly when asked an unanticipated question during a public meeting. Also, the attorney must represent the board of commissioners effectively even when those commissioners do not agree among themselves. The attorney must be able to understand the job requirements of administrators such as the county manager and department heads and give them accurate and practical legal advice. He or she must develop a relationship with separately elected county officials such as the sheriff and the register of deeds. The attorney may also represent the county social services board or the county board of health, and must be able to deal with it effectively even when it and the commissioners do not see eye-to-eye. The attorney must be both forthright and discreet in dealing with representatives of the news media, who often assume a watchdog role over the affairs of the county. The attorney must maintain credibility while not disclosing his or her client's confidences. Finally, he or she should be able to represent the county to the public on occasion, even though it is not usually the attorney's role to be a spokesperson for the county. All these criteria suggest that an ideal county attorney should be talented and well rounded.

The question of political affiliation and relationships may also arise when the commissioners choose the county attorney. While a board or a dominant faction on the board may feel comfortable with a political ally as county attorney, appointing a county attorney mainly on the basis of political qualifications may be unwise. Commissioners can come and go with each election, but the board and the county are best served by impartial advice that is not unduly influenced by close party affiliation or by fear of partisan retribution.

In addition to its regular attorney, a county may sometimes employ expert counsel for specialized matters such as a title search for a major acquisition of real estate. A county may also retain outside counsel for unusually complex litigation. Certain civil rights, tax, or environmental cases might fall into this category. Litigation like this requires either professional specialization in the field or the full-time attention of the attorney, or both. The county attorney, whether retained or full-time, will likely need assistance with complex or unusual litigation if he or she is to continue providing routine and day-to-day legal assistance to the county in an effective manner.

Retained or Full-Time Attorney

General Factors

Whether hiring a full-time county attorney is appropriate for a particular county depends on the county's specific legal needs, its county commissioners, and other relatively subtle issues such as what *type* of litigation a county anticipates and whether a contract or full-time attorney will be more effective with county officials and personnel. Perhaps the salient advantages of hiring a full-time attorney are his or her intimate knowledge of the county's day-to-day affairs and ability to practice preventive law. Because of the economics of legal fees and the social environment within which local government law is practiced, one can expect a steady increase in the number of counties employing full-time attorneys. But not all counties will need such an attorney—particularly those without continuous, recurring legal needs.

In practice, most county attorneys who are retained as independent contractors place an emphasis on advising the commissioners and the county manager and on attending their meetings. To minimize their retainer fee, some county attorneys provide routine legal service to only those parties. A full-time county attorney, on the other hand, handles the full range of the county's legal needs. This might be "better" service in the sense that a full-time attorney is available to consult with and provide advice to all county departments and offices (such as a purchasing or recreation department), to other county boards and commissions (such as a social services board or a board of adjustment), and to other elected county officials (such as the sheriff and the register of deeds).

Officials and employees in a county with a full-time attorney may also feel that legal consultation is more convenient when the attorney is available full-time. Full-time attorneys may be more accessible simply because they have offices close to other county offices. Or they may not feel the constraint they might experience consulting with an independent-contractor attorney, which may involve escalating legal fees as the consultation becomes more complex or extensive. In a county with a full-time attorney, county personnel know that his or her client is the county and that they will not be interrupting the attorney while he or she is handling matters for other clients. Similarly, on occasion, retained county attorneys may not be readily available because they are entirely occupied with a major matter—perhaps a trial—for another client. A full-time attorney should be in closer touch with developments affecting the county's business than retained counsel because of his or her day-to-day presence and exposure. Full-time attorneys will not need to be briefed as extensively on certain matters because they are already somewhat familiar with the background. Of course, because they are full-time salaried employees, no additional charges are associated with legal consultations either.

Cost Concerns

Whether having a full-time county attorney will save the county money depends on whether it has "full-time" legal needs—which in turn may depend significantly on the amount and the type of litigation in which the county is engaged. If the county is frequently in court, a full-time attorney may be justified. Court cases tend to raise the cost of a county's legal services sharply. A full-time attorney ordinarily can handle much of the county's recurring litigation such as tax foreclosures, social services child support suits, and zoning disputes. If the commissioners are contemplating a full-time county attorney, they should also keep in mind the nature of the county's litigation as they decide what experience and capabilities that attorney should have.

On the other hand, the county may incur significant additional costs if it hires a full-time attorney, costs that are ordinarily covered by the fees charged by a retained attorney. Paralegal and secretarial support, law books, subscriptions to legal research services, and computer equipment are among the overhead expense items that a county must plan to absorb if it has full-time legal representation.

Other matters should also be considered. Will county departments and commissions need legal consultation frequently enough to keep an attorney busy throughout the year? A great advantage of "in-house" attorneys is that they can practice "preventive law" by counseling county personnel regarding appropriate policies and practices, exploring legal considerations before disputes erupt into law suits, advising employees regarding courses of action when problems suddenly arise, and so on. The daily presence of an attorney can have an intangible value in avoiding legal expenses that might otherwise be incurred without timely legal advice.

Does the cost of the county's litigation fluctuate sharply from year to year? If so, having a salaried attorney can give the county a more predictable measure of its annual legal expense, assuming that a full-time attorney is justifiable in other respects. A retainer, on the other hand, is more likely to represent a minimum cost of legal representation. Even if complex or time-consuming litigation is routed to specialized counsel, a full-time attorney may be better able to absorb much of the county's unforeseen legal requirements without a large corresponding increase in legal fees. The county can better anticipate and estimate its budget requirements for legal representation if a full-time county attorney can handle most of its routine legal affairs. The attorney and legal support staff's salaries and benefits, other overhead expenses, and a contingency reserve for outside counsel's representation in extraordinary litigation will be a fair measure of the county's annual budget requirement for legal services.

Options for Full-Time Representation

If the county decides that it needs full-time representation, it has at least three options with varying costs. It can hire either a less experienced and less expensive attorney or a more experienced but more costly attorney, or it can adopt a hybrid arrangement involving a younger staff attorney and a more experienced attorney on retainer. Several questions need to be asked concerning each arrangement.

Are the personalities in county government and its legal needs such that the county can hire an unseasoned or inexperienced attorney? Inexperienced attorneys command lower salaries, but to some degree they will be training and acquiring experience on the job. Will the county commissioners give due weight to an unseasoned attorney's legal advice? Will they respect his or her judgment and counsel? Will an unseasoned attorney become rattled in a public meeting when suddenly confronted with an unanticipated query? There are mature young attorneys in North Carolina who are very capable county attorneys, but character and potential should be more carefully evaluated for young candidates than when evaluating a seasoned attorney with years of experience summarized on a résumé.

Other considerations emerge if a county decides to hire a more experienced lawyer as its full-time county attorney. Since such a person's salary requirements will be substantially more than a less experienced attorney's, yearly cost-of-living adjustments will have more impact because they are made from a substantially larger base. A policy should be agreed on for merit increases. Pension arrangements may have to be examined closely. The shorter funding period for an older attorney in the Local

Government Employees' Retirement System may result in less than optimum retirement payments if an inflationary environment follows retirement. If a more experienced attorney is taking a significant cut in remuneration to become county attorney, the board of commissioners should satisfy itself that he or she will devote an appropriate amount of energy and initiative to continuing employment on a public salary.

Hiring a younger full-time staff (or assistant) attorney when the county needs more legal services than a retained attorney can provide may be an appropriate arrangement for some counties. The county that follows this plan continues to retain an outside attorney, at a reduced retainer. The county's costs rise at first as it picks up the salary for a full-time younger attorney. The retained county attorney can devote most of his or her time to private law practice, which is typically more remunerative than representing local government, while still being available to the commissioners as counsel on policy questions. The retained attorney will also be available to the staff attorney when the staff attorney feels that guidance or supervision would be appropriate for certain issues. As the staff attorney gains experience, the commissioners, manager, and department heads should come to rely on his or her advice in his or her areas of expertise.

Conclusion

The position of county attorney is a very important and sensitive one. A wide range of factors should be considered as county commissioners seek to determine what amount of legal representation, at what costs, will best serve the needs of the county government and the county's citizens. The best balance of cost, experience, and service level will vary from county to county and from year to year. Commissioners should review their legal representation on a regular basis, asking questions and making adjustments as needed to ensure that they are getting what they need and pay for from the county's lawyers.

The Clerk to the Board of Commissioners

The position of clerk is one of the oldest in local government, dating back to biblical times at least. For example, the book of Acts in the Christian New Testament records that when a conflict arose between the people of Ephesus and the missionary Paul and his companions, the town clerk quieted the crowd and prevented a riot.[2]

The term "clerk" has long been associated with the written word. Indeed, an archaic definition of a clerk is a person who can read or read *and* write, or a learned person, scholar, or person of letters. "Clerk" can also mean cleric or clergyman; during the Middle Ages, the clergy were among the few literate people in many European communities.

Those who can read and write can keep records for their fellow citizens; so it is that modern-day clerks are official record keepers for their counties. Each county in North Carolina must have a clerk for its board of commissioners (G.S. 153A-111), and the most important county records maintained by the clerk, such as minutes of commissioners' meetings, must be kept permanently for the use of future generations.[3] Under G.S. 153A-111 the board of county commissioners appoints or designates the clerk to the board who serves as such at the board's pleasure. The clerk performs any duties required by the board or by law. Although any county officer or employee may be designated as clerk, most counties have created a separate position with these responsibilities.

Some counties also have deputy or assistant clerks. Boards of county commissioners may rely on their general authority under G.S. 153A-76 to create offices and positions of county government to create this position.

County clerks and their deputies have a variety of duties in addition to creating and maintaining records. This chapter discusses the diverse responsibilities of clerks.[4] The specific legal requirements that clerks must follow as custodians of county records are discussed in Chapter 6.

Record Keeping

Minutes

One of the clerk's most important statutory duties is to prepare the minutes of county commissioners' meetings and maintain them in a set of minute books.[5] Many of the legal powers of a county are exercised by the board of commissioners, and the minutes of a board's meetings are the official record of what it does.

G.S. 153A-42 and 143-318.10(e) state that the minutes prepared by the clerk must be "full and accurate," because they are the legal evidence of what the governing board has said and done. The board "speaks" only through its minutes, and their contents may not be altered nor their meaning explained by other evidence.[6]

"Full and accurate" does not generally mean, however, that the clerk must make a verbatim transcript of a meeting's proceedings. Rather, according to G.S. 153A-42, the minutes must record the results of each vote taken by the commissioners, and they should also show the existence of any condition required before a particular action may validly be taken.[7] The clerk should record the full text of each motion, including the full text of all ordinances and resolutions passed by the board. This permanent, unchanging record of board actions can be extremely important in later years to supplement and back-up information sources that are frequently revised, such as ordinance books and codes of ordinances.

The clerk must attend to other important details in preparing the minutes. The minutes should state that the meeting was legally convened and show that a quorum was present at all times during the meeting. They should note the late arrival and early departure of members (including whether someone leaving was excused by the remaining members). They must also include a list of the members who voted each way on a particular question (the "ayes and noes") if any member so requests (G.S. 153A-42).

The minutes should show as well that any other legally required conditions for taking action were met—for example, that a properly advertised public hearing on a proposed rezoning was held or that an ordinance received a sufficient number of votes to be adopted finally on first reading. As another example, if the board awards a formally bid contract, G.S. 143-129(b) requires the minutes to include a list of the bids received.

Minutes and General Accounts of Closed Sessions

G.S. 143-318.11(a) permits public bodies to hold closed sessions for certain specified purposes. Like other minutes, the minutes of these sessions must be "full and accurate" [G.S. 143-318.10(e)], recording any actions taken and the existence of the conditions needed to take particular actions. In addition to the minutes, G.S. 143-318.10(e) requires the board also to keep a "general account of the closed session so that a person not in attendance would have a reasonable understanding of what transpired." The general account may be either a written narrative or audio or video recordings. If the clerk does not attend the closed session, he or she should designate someone who does attend to record the minutes and general account.

While the minutes of a closed session need only record actions, if any,[8] and conditions needed to take action, it is less clear what must be included in the general account. In many cases it may need to be somewhat more detailed than the minutes,[9] but the county attorney should be consulted for advice on this point. The clerk should record in the board of commissioners' public minutes the motion to go into the closed session, including the information required by the open meetings law [G.S. 143-318.11(c)], and the fact that the board came out of the session. If desired, the board and the clerk may combine the minutes and general account into a single document serving both purposes.

A public body may seal the minutes and the general account of a closed session for as long as necessary to avoid frustrating the purpose of the session [G.S. 143-318.10(e)]. A recorded vote to seal the minutes is advisable. Many clerks maintain sealed closed-session minutes in a separate minutes book.

A Circumstance Requiring a Verbatim Transcript

As noted earlier, the clerk generally does not need to include a verbatim transcript or even a summary of the discussion that took place at a board of commissioners meeting in the minutes. Indeed, including a detailed record of comments may well be counterproductive; the board may find itself spending an excessive amount of time at its next meeting discussing the details of this record.

A verbatim transcript of board proceedings may be required in one limited circumstance, however. When the board of commissioners is sitting as a quasi-judicial body—for example, when it is considering issuance of a special-use permit under a zoning ordinance—it must act somewhat like a court, and the clerk must prepare a full transcript of the proceedings if one of the parties appearing before the board so requests.

Audio or Video Recordings

The law does not require the clerk to make an audio or video recording of county commissioners' meetings. (Persons attending the meeting may make their own recordings if they desire.) If the clerk or another county official does record a meeting, he or she may dispose of the recording after the minutes of that meeting are approved if the board of commissioners and the county attorney are comfortable with so doing. Should the attorney or the board wish the clerk to retain meeting tapes for a longer period, the board should establish a clear, uniform policy for the clerk's guidance. The county's tape of a meeting is a public record available for public inspection and copying, just as the minutes are a public record.

Approval of the Minutes

The clerk generally sends draft copies of board of commissioners' minutes—except minutes and general accounts of closed sessions—to the board members several days before the meeting at which the board will consider the minutes for approval. The circulated draft minutes are a public record that must also be made available for public inspection.

Commissioners should carefully review the minutes and bring their suggested changes and corrections to the meeting for consideration by the full board. Although the clerk prepares the draft minutes for the board of commissioners, the board itself, acting as a body, must finally determine what the minutes will include. The minutes do not become the official record of the board's actions until they are approved by the board.

The board may handle approval of closed-session minutes and general accounts in one of several ways, depending on the situation and the preferences of the clerk and the board:

1. If the minutes and the general account are fairly short, an easy way to handle their approval is to prepare them on the spot and have the board vote to approve them before the closed session ends.
2. The board might also approve the minutes and the general account in a later closed session. In this case the motion to go into the closed session should state that one of the session's purposes is "to prevent the disclosure of information that is made privileged or confidential by G.S. 143-318.10(e)." [10]
3. Finally, the board might approve the minutes and the general account of a closed session in an open session. This option is probably most desirable if the board does not plan to seal these documents. However, approval in open session may pose the risk of disclosure of the documents' contents, especially if a board member wants to amend them.

The board of commissioners may correct minutes that it has already approved if it later finds that they are incorrect. [11] In such a case, the clerk should note the correction in the minutes of the meeting at which the correction is made, with an appropriate notation and cross-reference at the place in the minutes book where the provision being corrected appears.

Meetings of Other Public Bodies

The open meetings law requires that "full and accurate" minutes also be kept of the meetings of other "public bodies" that are part of county government. Included are all boards, committees, and other bodies of the county that perform legislative, policy-making, quasi-judicial, administrative, or advisory functions. These public bodies must also keep minutes and general accounts of their closed sessions. The board of commissioners, generally with the clerk's help, should establish procedures to ensure that the minutes of all public bodies under its direction are properly recorded and maintained. The minutes of these various public bodies may be kept either in written form or, at the option of the public body, in the form of sound or video-and-sound recordings [G.S. 143-318.10(e)].

Ordinance Book

Among the other records of board of commissioners' actions maintained by the clerk is the ordinance book (G.S. 153A-48). The clerk must file each county ordinance in an appropriately indexed ordinance book, with the exception of certain kinds of ordinances discussed in the next paragraph. This book, kept separately from the minutes book, is maintained for public inspection in the clerk's office. If the county has adopted and issued a code of ordinances, it must index its ordinances and keep them in an ordinance book only until it codifies them.

The law provides that the ordinance book need not include transitory ordinances and certain technical regulations adopted in ordinances by reference, although the law does require a cross-reference to the minutes book (at least for transitory ordinances). If the board of commissioners adopts technical regulations in an ordinance by reference, the clerk must maintain an official copy of the adopted items in his or her office for public inspection (G.S. 153A-47).

Code of Ordinances

A county may adopt and issue a bound or loose-leaf code of its ordinances (G.S. 153A-49, 153A-50). It should update any such code annually unless there have been no changes. Counties may reproduce their codes by any method that gives legible and permanent copies. A county is also free to select a code-preparation method that meets its needs. For example, a private code-publishing company or the county attorney may prepare the code in consultation with the clerk.

A county may include separate sections in a code for general ordinances and for technical ordinances or they may issue the latter as separate books or pamphlets. Examples of technical ordinances are those pertaining to the following:

- Building construction
- Installation of plumbing
- Electric wiring, or cooling and heating equipment
- Zoning
- Subdivision control
- Privilege license taxes
- The use of public utilities, buildings, or facilities operated by the county

Also included are similar ordinances designated as technical by the board of commissioners.

The board may omit from the code classes of ordinances designated by it as having limited interest or transitory value (for example, the annual budget ordinance), but the code should clearly describe the classes of ordinances that have been left out. The board may also provide that certain ordinances pertaining to zoning area or district boundaries be maintained on official map books in the clerk's office or in some other county office generally accessible to the public.

One reason that clerks maintain ordinance books and codes is to make the county's laws readily accessible to its citizens. Accordingly, ordinances may not be enforced or admitted into evidence in court unless they are properly filed and indexed or codified. The law presumes, however, that a county has followed the proper procedure unless someone proves otherwise.

Other Records

The clerk to the board of county commissioners and the board itself are generally the custodians of many county records besides minutes and ordinances.[12] Board resolutions, contracts, governing board correspondence, signed oaths of office, copies of legal and other notices, and a variety of miscellaneous documents (for example, commissioners' travel records and applications from citizens to be appointed to various county boards) are all to be maintained in the county clerk's office or under the clerk's guidance.

The clerk and other county records custodians have primary responsibility for ensuring that local government records are kept safely, are accessible for use by the public and county officials (except as restricted by law), and are disposed of in accordance with the appropriate schedule for records retention and disposition promulgated by the North Carolina Department of Cultural Resources, Division of Archives and History.[13] For the general rules on this subject, see Chapter 6.

Notice-Giving

The clerk is usually responsible for giving notice of board of commissioners meetings and for a variety of other public notices. Clerks give notice of the regular meetings of all public bodies that are part of county government through regular meeting schedules, which the clerk's office must keep on file by law [G.S. 143-318.12(a)]. The clerk often handles the posting and distribution of special meeting notices as well, and frequently oversees the legal advertisements required for public hearings, bid solicitations, bond orders, and other matters.

Oaths of Office

The clerk is one of the few county officials who may administer the oaths of office [G.S. 11-7.1(a)] that are required of elected and appointed county officers (G.S. 153A-26). The clerk should also take such an oath. Deputy clerks, when discharging the clerk's duties, are also permitted to administer oaths as long as they are themselves sworn officers (G.S. 11-8). The text of the main required oath of office is found in Article VI, Section 7, of the state constitution. The oaths in G.S. 11-7 and 11-11 are sometimes administered in addition to the constitutional oath.[14] A signed copy of all oaths administered to county officials must be filed with the clerk (G.S. 153A-26).

General Assistance to the Governing Board

Research and General Assistance

In addition to the responsibilities previously outlined, clerks must perform other duties "that may be required by law or the board of commissioners" (G.S. 153A-111). Individual board members or the board as a whole frequently call on the clerk to find answers to questions. They may ask the clerk to learn how others have solved a particular problem, to find sample ordinances for the county attorney, or to search the minutes for information about the actions of a previous board. Individual members also look to the clerk for help in arranging official appointments and making official travel plans.

Acting as a researcher and an information provider is both a rewarding and challenging part of the clerk's responsibilities. Commissioners can help the clerk serve them more effectively by remembering the limits of the clerk's role. For example, a professional clerk generally performs research and provides information for the benefit of the entire board. A board member's seeking research assistance from the clerk to win a squabble with another board member is inappropriate. Also, although clerks expect to make travel arrangements and perform other official tasks for individual board members, the members should expect to share the clerk's time and energy.

Agendas and Preparations for Meetings

One of the most important services that the clerk provides to the board of commissioners is assistance with preparations for meetings. The clerk is often involved in preparing the tentative agenda for board meetings and in compiling background information for the board's agenda packet. He or she may also arrange for the recording of meetings and may set up other audiovisual equipment and the meeting room.

Clear procedures for handling these matters can serve both the board members and the clerk. The board of commissioners should establish and enforce a realistic schedule for placing items on the agenda that allows adequate time to compile and duplicate background materials and it should clearly state any preferences concerning the order of items on the agenda. The board should also support the clerk in complying with public and press requests for information about upcoming meetings and for access to tapes and other records of prior meetings. (For more information, see the discussion of the laws governing access to public records in Chapter 6.)

Information Source

The clerk is sometimes described as "the hub of the wheel" in county government because of the central role that he or she plays in the government's communication network.[15] Clerks provide information to commissioners, county employees, other government officials, citizens, and the press daily. A clerk in a larger North Carolina county expressed the following thoughts about her position:

> Your description of a clerk as the hub of the wheel is much the way I think of my position here. The clerk is the hub and serves as one of the major sources of information on board actions. I communicate daily with the commissioners, the county manager, and the county attorney. I interact frequently with the planning director, other department heads, other government employees, and the press. The clerk also serves as a link between citizens and government. One of my primary functions is to provide information.[16]

Dealing with such a wide variety of information requests requires tact, judgment, empathy, organizational skills, energy, and a good sense of humor. Although clerks work *for the board of commissioners*, they truly provide *public* service, from helping the press understand the meaning of a complicated motion, to assisting a citizen in finding the correct person to help with a complaint, to keeping department heads advised of board actions and keeping board members informed of administration proposals. As local government becomes larger and more complicated, the clerk's role as a professional, dispassionate provider of information to citizens, government officials, and the media becomes more and more important.

Combination of the Clerk's Position with Other Jobs

Many county clerks perform still other tasks. Roughly thirteen are assistant managers or assistants to the manager. Some counties may combine the duties of the clerk with those of the manager (fourteen counties) or another county official (five counties).[17]

Wearing many hats can be both stressful and invigorating for a clerk. Giving clerks appropriate authority can help them perform the varied duties of their office well or blend their position effectively with other roles. Adequate financial rewards are also important. Historically and currently the salary for the clerk's position is often not commensurate with the broad responsibilities involved.

Professionalism and Continuing Education

County clerks have one of the most active professional associations of public officials in North Carolina. The North Carolina Association of County Clerks to the Boards of County Commissioners is dedicated to improving the professional competency of clerks through regular regional and statewide educational opportunities and through a nationally recognized certification program. It is also developing a general job description for the clerk's position. To quote from a brochure published by the association, such professional groups provide clerks with "opportunities to exchange ideas and techniques relating to their jobs," making them "better able to create and improve efficiency in their individual offices."[18] The association also operates an informal mentor program to provide guidance for new clerks and clerks serve on various committees of the North Carolina Association of County Commissioners. The clerks' organization publishes a reference guide to assist clerks in their day-to-day work and it has a home page and a listserv on the World Wide Web where clerks can exchange ideas and information.[19]

Additional Resources

Lloyd, Carolyn. "The Hub of the Wheel," *Popular Government* 55 (Spring 1990): 36–43. Additional information about the role of county and city clerks may be found in this article, which is based on interviews with several clerks.

MAPS Group for the Institute of Government. *County Salaries in North Carolina 1998.* Chapel Hill: N.C.: Institute of Government, The University of North Carolina at Chapel Hill, 1998. This is an excellent source for information about retainer arrangements and the salaries of county attorneys and county clerks.

Notes

1. Financial and other numerical information is derived from MAPS Group for the Institute of Government, *County Salaries in North Carolina 1998* (Chapel Hill, N.C.: Institute of Government, The University of North Carolina at Chapel Hill, 1998), 61–63.

2. Acts 19: 23–41.

3. North Carolina Department of Cultural Resources, Division of Archives and History, *Records Disposition Schedule* (Raleigh, N.C.: Division of Archives and History, May 1991) (applicable to county administrative, financial, legal, and personnel offices). Other disposition schedules are published by the Division for other county departments.

4. The materials on the county clerk are based on "City and County Clerks: What They Do and How They Do It," *Popular Government* 61 (Summer 1996): 21–30, and "The City Clerk and City Records," in *Municipal Government in North Carolina*, 2d

ed., David M. Lawrence and Warren Jake Wicker, eds. (Chapel Hill, N.C.: Institute of Government, The University of North Carolina at Chapel Hill, 1996), 105–18, both by A. Fleming Bell, II.

5. *See* G.S. 153A-42 (requiring the clerk to a board of commissioners "to keep full and accurate minutes of the proceedings of the board of commissioners"); and G.S. 143-318.10(e) (part of the open meetings law, requiring public bodies to keep full and accurate minutes of their official meetings but allowing the sealing of minutes and general accounts of closed sessions in certain instances).

6. *See* Norfolk S. R.R. v. Reid, 187 N.C. 320, 326, 121 S.E. 534, 537 (1924).

7. For a discussion of the meaning of "full and accurate minutes," see Maready v. City of Winston-Salem, 342 N.C. 708, 732–34, 467 S.E.2d 615, 630–31 (1996).

8. The law allows boards to take only a few types of action in a closed session. One must examine the specific statutory provision authorizing the particular closed session to determine whether an action is allowed. *See* G.S. 143-318.11(a). Closed sessions and permitted actions are discussed in detail in David M. Lawrence, *Open Meetings and Local Governments in North Carolina: Some Questions and Answers*, 5th ed. (Chapel Hill, N.C.: Institute of Government, The University of North Carolina at Chapel Hill, 1998), 16–31.

9. The legal requirements for general accounts of closed sessions are discussed in detail in David M. Lawrence, "1997 Changes to the Open Meetings and Public Records Laws," *Local Government Law Bulletin*, no. 80 (Institute of Government, Aug. 1997).

10. Under G.S. 143-318.11(a)(1), a closed session may be held to prevent the disclosure of information that is privileged or confidential pursuant to North Carolina law. However, G.S. 143-318.11(c) requires that a motion to close a meeting based on this provision state the name or cite the location of the law that renders the information to be discussed privileged or confidential. In the case of closed-session minutes, this statute is G.S. 143-318.10(e), which allows them to be withheld from public inspection as long as public inspection would frustrate the purpose of the closed session.

11. Norfolk S. R.R. v. Reid, 187 N.C. 320, 326–27, 121 S.E. 534, 537–38 (1924).

12. See G.S. 132-2, which provides that the person in charge of an office having public records is the custodian of those records.

13. See the publications cited in note 3.

14. For a discussion of the oaths to be taken by North Carolina public officials, see Joseph S. Ferrell, "Questions I Am Frequently Asked: What Form of Oath Should a Public Officer Take?" *Popular Government* 62 (Fall 1996): 43.

15. Carolyn Lloyd, "The Hub of the Wheel," *Popular Government* 55 (Spring 1990): 36–43.

16. Lloyd, "The Hub," 38.

17. Derived from MAPS Group, *County Salaries*, 31–32.

18. North Carolina Association of County Clerks to the Boards of County Commissioners, Brochure for 1994 Clerks' Conference, Winston-Salem, N.C., March 24–26, 1994.

19. The county clerks' home page and the clerk's listserv can be reached through Clerk-Net at http://ncinfo.iog.unc.edu/clerks/.

6 Records Management and Access, including Register of Deeds

A. Fleming Bell, II, and William A. Campbell

Contents

A. Fleming Bell, II, is an Institute of Government faculty member who specializes in local government law. He regularly answers questions about public records access and retention. William A. Campbell is an Institute of Government faculty member whose work includes state and local taxation, land records, and environmental law.

Taken together, the public offices of the 100 North Carolina counties constitute the largest depository of public records in the state. Much that is essential to public and government affairs as well as to commercial and private matters is affected by the records and documents maintained by county officials. While many of the factors relating to the creation of, maintenance of, disposition of, and access to records are regulated directly by law, the attitude, interest, and cooperation of the board of county commissioners can considerably influence the quality and general usefulness of county records. This chapter summarizes briefly some of the commissioners' statutory duties and responsibilities in records management and describes some of the services available to counties in this regard. It also discusses the rules governing access to public records. As used in this chapter, "public records" means any documents, tape recordings, photographs, films, or computer tapes or discs that are created, filed, or recorded in county offices pursuant to a statutory duty or in the conduct of government business (see G.S. 132-1).

County Records Defined

Generally speaking, most county records are kept in the offices of the register of deeds, the clerk of the superior court, the local school superintendent, the county finance officer, the county assessor, the tax collector, the director of social services, the clerk to the board of county commissioners, and the sheriff, in roughly that order, on the basis of volume of records. The two major custodians are the register of deeds and the clerk of superior court. Most of the register's records are instruments and documents that either affect the title to real or personal property (deeds, deeds of trust, maps, and financing statements) or relate to vital statistics (births, deaths, and marriages); the clerk of court's records, although extremely varied, primarily concern operation of the courts and matters affecting the administration of estates of deceased persons.[1]

In recent years the volume of public records, particularly those of permanent or long-term value, has increased greatly in most counties, and this trend seems likely to continue, particularly in the register of deeds' and clerk of court's offices. Therefore the costs of creating and maintaining these records will continue to present problems for boards of commissioners.

Office of the Register of Deeds

The major custodian of records in county government is the register of deeds. All Uniform Commercial Code filings, deeds and deeds of trust affecting real property in the county, and records of births, deaths, and marriages are recorded in the register of deeds' office. By statute the office is elective, and each register serves a four-year term (G.S. 161-1, -2). After a person is elected register, but before he or she may take the oath of office and begin exercising the duties of the office, the board of county commissioners must approve the register's bond [G.S. 161-4(a)]. The bond must be for at least $10,000 but not more than $50,000 [G.S. 161-4(a)]. In addition to the bond, it is important that the register of deeds be provided with liability insurance to protect him or her against personal liability from errors and omissions in the recording and indexing of documents. If the county provides liability insurance to other county officials, the register must be included in the policy; if the county provides no liability insurance, the register must be informed in writing of that fact (G.S. 161-4.2).

The county must provide the register with at least one deputy (G.S. 153A-103), and in counties of most sizes, numerous deputies and assistants are required to perform the work of the office. In most counties the register's recording fees are a substantial budget item and more than cover the costs of operating the office. These fees are, of course, remitted to the county's general fund and are not retained by the register. The register's salary, the salaries of all office personnel, and the register's operating budget are all set by the commissioners in the annual budget ordinance.

The office hours of the register of deeds are set by the board of commissioners (G.S. 161-8), and with one exception, these hours are always the same as those of other county offices. In some counties, the commissioners, by resolution, have provided that the register must stop recording instruments at some time before the office closes for the day, usually fifteen to twenty minutes before the close of business. This arrangement enables the office to complete the recording process for the day so that persons presenting documents for recording do not have to stand in line after hours, thus requiring the members of the office staff to work a minimum of overtime.

When a register of deeds resigns, retires, or dies during his or her term, the executive committee of the political party from which the register was elected has thirty days in which to submit the name of a successor to the board of commissioners. If the committee meets this deadline, the commissioners must appoint the person recommended (G.S. 161-5). This procedure does not apply in Camden, Chowan, Pasquotank, and Perquimans counties; in those counties the board of commissioners selects the person to be appointed.

Commissioners' Authority over Records

The statutes that relate to the commissioners' authority with respect to public records are scattered through the General Statutes, with some overlap among the various sections. This authority generally involves administering and managing the county's public records and not methods of operation for a particular office or officer. No attempt is made here to discuss the various laws that regulate the creation, filing, or recording of particular types of records as applied to a specific county official or office. The records procedures in the office of the register of deeds are discussed in the *North Carolina Guidebook for Registers of Deeds*,[2] published by the Institute of Government. The procedures in the office of the clerk to the board of county commissioners are covered in the county clerks' *Reference Guide*, available from the North Carolina Association of County Commissioners.

The county commissioners' responsibility for records in the various county offices is one of general supervision and oversight. The custodians are the officials—such as the register of deeds, the tax collector, and the sheriff—in whose offices the records are created or filed (see G.S. 132-2) and who have day-to-day responsibility for maintaining and protecting them. In their supervisory role, the commissioners have a duty to ensure that the records are being managed in accordance with the statutory directions for safety and security[3] and are not being disposed of improperly.

Disposal of Records

Perhaps the county commissioners' most important general authority regarding records concerns the destruction or permanent removal from offices of records that no longer have any local official use or value. Such records are generally of two types: those that have no official use or value at the county level but have historical value, and those that have neither official nor historical value. As the volume of records in many offices increases, the statutory procedures for disposing of unneeded ones take on great importance. Eliminating those that have no official value has a direct bearing not only on the efficient use and management of valuable public records but also on the cost to the county of maintaining and operating the record custodians' offices. The statutes provide a two-tiered procedure by which unneeded records may be removed from county offices [G.S. 121-5(b)]. Under this procedure both the Division of Archives and History (of the Department of Cultural Resources) and the board of county commissioners play important roles.

In accordance with the statutory requirement that the Division of Archives and History administer a statewide program of local records management (G.S. 132-8.1), the division has published a series of Records Retention and Disposition Schedules. The primary purpose of these publications is to provide a recommended retention and disposition schedule for most types of records to be found in the office of each major custodian of county records. Each schedule deals with the office or official with custody of records, with a recommendation as to how long each type of record should be kept and of how it should ultimately be disposed of. Records of continuing legal or historical value are required to be preserved in the county or sent to the state archives, in Raleigh, for permanent safekeeping; others may be disposed of after the time listed in the schedules has elapsed. The purpose of the schedules is not to compel public officials to destroy records when the time periods indicated expire; rather, they provide the division's permission, pursuant to G.S. 121-5(b), to dispose of certain types of records after the required time periods have elapsed so that custodians may free storage space for records that have permanent or current temporary value.

As county officials dispose of records under the disposition schedules, they should be aware not only of which records must be kept permanently but also of the forms that permanent records may take. At present, only paper copies and microfilm copies that meet certain technical standards specified by the Division of Archives and History may be used as permanent records. Counties may *not* use records on computer, optical disk, or other electronic media as their permanent file copy. Many counties that maintain their records on computer are generating computer output microfilm (COM) as a means of making a permanent record on microfilm. As long as the microfilm meets the state's technical standards, this is an inexpensive means of creating a permanent record.

However, approval by the Division of Archives and History is only half the authority required for the destruction of county records. Records should never be destroyed except as authorized by resolution of the board of commissioners. Once custodians have determined that destruction is necessary, they must submit a description of the records to the board of commissioners with a request for permission to dispose of them. If this permission is granted, it must be done by a resolution entered in the minutes [G.S. 121-5(b)]. Records may be transferred legally to the Division of Archives and History without the commissioners' consent, although some officials may prefer to obtain consent first. When records are destroyed or disposed of in accordance with this procedure, the custodian is protected from any later liability that might otherwise be imposed as a result of the destruction or disposition of public records [G.S. 121-5(b)].

When the destruction of records is authorized, they should in fact be destroyed and not permitted to fall into unauthorized hands. State law does not permit records to be removed permanently from the custodian's office except for destruction or transfer to the Division of Archives and History. Individuals, local historical societies, and similar groups often ask county officials to release records intended for destruction to them. Since records with any significant historical value may not be destroyed (but may be transferred to Archives and History), it is not likely that those that may be destroyed legally would be of much value to such unofficial groups, and—as noted—the law does not provide for such disposition. Nonconfidential records probably may be sold to commercial concerns as waste paper if there is reasonable assurance that they will be handled and processed carefully to destroy their identity. Otherwise, destruction should be accomplished by burning, shredding, pulping, burying, or other effective means.

A permanent account should be kept of all records disposed of or destroyed. This may be done by means of a separate log maintained by each custodian or by inclusion of the complete list in the county commissioners' minutes. These accounts should include a description of the type and quantity of records destroyed in each group, the inclusive dates covered by the various types, and the date as well as method of destruction. It is also prudent to maintain a similar log of records transferred to the Division of Archives and History.

Copies and Replacement of Records

The statutory provisions regarding photographic reproduction of county records for the purpose of making permanent copies of them are contained in G.S. 153A-436. Counties are authorized to establish systems for reproducing records photographically. The copies, which must be legible and permanent because they are to serve as the permanent record copies, must be stored in a fire-resistant file, vault, or similar container. When a county establishes a system for photographing or microphotographing records, the originals may be removed from their regular repositories for up to twenty-four hours for filming, outside of the county if necessary. If more time is required, records may be removed from their regular repositories for more than twenty-four hours but only with the county commissioners' permission. When a photographic copy of a recorded instrument is made pursuant to G.S. 153A-436, the reproduction is a sufficient recording for all purposes.

Role of the Division of Archives and History

Although the Division of Archives and History has been assigned some statutory responsibility concerning county records since 1935, only in recent years has its legal authority been broadened and have funds been made available to enable the division to undertake a substantial program of assistance to the counties. Its primary interest is in preserving records and documents of historical value, but its services can also be helpful in managing all local records. These services can generally be divided into three categories of programs: the Records Retention and Disposition Schedules (discussed previously in connection with the destruction of records); inventory, repair, and microfilming; and records-management assistance and advice.

Inventory, Repair, and Microfilming of Records

In 1959 the Division of Archives and History began a program of inventory, repair, and microfilming that is perhaps the nation's largest undertaking concerned with permanently preserving valuable local records. Under this program the division visited the various offices in each county (starting with the oldest county), made complete inventories of the records in each office, repaired all those of permanent value when necessary, and microfilmed all records of this type for security storage. The cost of the program, including the repair service, was borne by the state. Copies made from the security microfilm are available to the counties at cost and may be used to replace permanent records destroyed by disaster. The division no longer visits each county, but it will microfilm records sent to it and maintain a security copy of the film. Some counties are microfilming their permanent records themselves and providing the division with the microfilm negatives of them.

Records-Management Advice and Assistance

The third aspect of the Division of Archives and History's records-management program involves aid and advice to individual counties or officials in connection with creating, using, maintaining, retaining, preserving, and disposing of official records. The division may be particularly helpful in such matters as the selection of equipment to be used in a records-management program, specifications for microfilming records, and the use of various filing systems. Many kinds of equipment are available for various purposes, and it is important to ascertain that a particular machine will render the service needed before a considerable investment of funds is made. The division is also available to assist counties in protecting and reconstructing records that have been damaged by water, fire, and other natural disasters.

Land Records Management Program

The Land Records Management Program (G.S. 147-54.3), a part of the Department of the Secretary of State, advises registers of deeds, local tax officials, and local planning officials about sound management practices and seeks to bring about greater uniformity in local land records systems. As part of the program, the secretary of state is directed to establish standards and specifications for reproducing these records by photography, microphotography, and other means as well as for keeping recorded documents secure.

The secretary of state, in cooperation with the secretary of cultural resources, is directed to undertake research and to provide advice and technical assistance to local governments on the following matters: uniform indexing of land records; uniform recording and indexing procedures for maps, plats, and condominiums; and computerized land records systems. On the joint request of the board of commissioners and the register of deeds, the secretary may make a management study of the register's office and offer appropriate recommendations.

The secretary has promulgated uniform indexing rules for indexing documents in the registers of deeds' offices. The rules became effective January 1, 1997, in every county except Brunswick.

Recent Developments in Records Management

Two related developments in county records management offer the promise of more efficient storage of records and increased accessibility to the users of records. An increasing number of registers of deeds and tax offices are storing their records on optical disks or CD-ROMs. Because hundreds of pages of documents can be stored on a single optical disk, much less storage space is used than would be required for paper records. These records, and the indexes to them, are in an electronic format and are accessible by computer. As a result, several counties, including Caldwell, Guilford, Harnett, Orange, and Wake, have arrangements for remote access to the records. A user of the records with a personal computer can obtain—for a fee—access to the records from any location at any time of the day. Several counties are currently considering the next step of making their indexes and records accessible on the Internet.

Access to Records

Inspection and Copying of Public Records

Most of the records of counties, regardless of where they are maintained, must be made available for public inspection. Unless a record is exempted from disclosure by a specific statute (see next section and Table 6-1, page 130), it must be made available for inspection and examination "at reasonable times and under reasonable supervision by any person" [G.S. 132-6(a)], not just by local residents or those with a special interest in the record. The use that a person plans to make of county records is irrelevant to his or her right of inspection [G.S. 132-6(b)], with two exceptions: (1) a person obtaining geographic information system records may be required to agree in writing not to resell or otherwise use them for trade or commercial purposes (G.S. 132-10), and (2) specified lists of recipients of public assistance may not be used for commercial or political purposes [G.S. 108A-80(b), (c)].

Making public records available for inspection is an important legal duty of custodians of records. Generally no fee should be charged for the right of inspection. Adequate space for inspection should be provided, and inspection should generally be allowed during most hours for which the office is open. The originals of the public records must usually be made available.[4]

The right of access is a right to make reasonable requests to inspect the particular records maintained by the records custodian. The person requesting the records may not require creation or compilation of a record that does not exist [G.S. 132-6.2(e)]. Thus the custodian is not required to sort or tabulate individual paper or computer files to place them in an order more usable by the person requesting them. Nor is he or she required to make a transcript of a tape recording just because the person requesting the tape would like to have its information in written form. If the custodian voluntarily elects to create or compile a record as a service to a person requesting it, he or she may negotiate a reasonable charge on behalf of the county for doing so, if authorized [G.S. 132-6.2(e)]. Records custodians are required to make copies of records when requested, as well as to make the records available for inspection. Copies must generally be furnished "as promptly as possible" [G.S. 132-6(a)].[5]

If the records requested contain confidential as well as public information, the custodian must separate the two [G.S. 132-6(c)]. The person requesting copies may elect to obtain them in any medium (for example, computer disk or paper copy) in which the local government is capable of providing them [G.S. 132-6.2(a)].

Records Exempt from Inspection

While most of the records of counties must be made available for public inspection, some records are exempt from inspection because of a specific statute. Examples of statutory exemptions include the following:

- Most county personnel records (G.S. 153A-98)
- Certain attorney-client records (G.S. 132-1.1)
- Basic social services records (G.S. 108A-11, -73, -80)
- Various medical and patient records (G.S. 8-53; 122C-52; 131E-97; 130A-12, -102, -131.17, -143, -212, -289)
- Certain law enforcement records (G.S. 132-1.4)
- Specified records concerning industrial development (G.S. 132-6 and -9)

Table 6-1 lists statutes that exempt particular local government records from public access and regulate when access may occur. Some of these, as noted, are discussed in other chapters of this book.

Fees for Copies of Public Records

Fees for copies of public records usually may not exceed the actual cost to the county of making the copy, unless a statute specifically authorizes a different fee. In general, personnel and other costs that the unit would have incurred had the copying request not been made may not be recovered [G.S. 132-6.2(b)], although there are exceptions for certain requests that involve extra work.[6] Fee schedules should be uniform and established in advance.

Regulation of Access to Records

As noted earlier, reasonable regulations to protect the records and to minimize disruption of public offices are permissible as long as the rights of access, inspection, and copying are not unduly limited. For example, county departments need not respond to requests for copies of records outside their usual business hours [G.S. 132-6.2(d)]. Like fee schedules, such regulations should be established in advance by the board of county commissioners or in appropriate cases by the records custodian, perhaps pursuant to policies established by the board. Persons desiring access to the county's records should be informed of the rules. Ad hoc rule making should be avoided to prevent arbitrary and unreasonable limitations on the rights of access, inspection, and copying.

The law establishes special rules for electronic data-processing records. These include requirements for indexing computer databases [G.S. 132-6.1(b)], and for purchasing data-processing systems that do not impair or impede the accessibility of public records [G.S. 132-6.1(a)], and provisions governing the way in which copies of computer databases are to be supplied [G.S. 132-6.2(c)].

Legal Remedies if Access Is Denied

Any person who is denied access to public records for purposes of inspection and examination, or who is denied copies of public records, may seek a court order compelling disclosure or copying [G.S. 132-9(a)]. If the records have been withheld without substantial justification, the county may in some cases be required to pay the person's attorneys' fees [G.S. 132-9(c)]. On the other hand, an attorney's fee may be

Continued on p. 134

Table 6-1
Statutes Regulating or Restricting Public Access to Certain Records

Type of Record and Applicable General Statute	Description
Personnel Records (Chapter 13 of *County Government*)	
G.S. 115C-319 to -321	Public school employees
G.S. 115D-27 to -30	Community college employees
G.S. 122C-158	Area authority employees
G.S. 130A-42	Health department employees
G.S. 131E-97.1	Public hospital employees
G.S. 153A-98	County government employees
G.S. 160A-168	City government employees
G.S. 162A-6.1	Water and sewer authority employees
Criminal Investigation Records (Chapter 31 of *County Government*)	
G.S. 132-1.4	Criminal investigation and criminal intelligence records
Trade Secrets (Chapter 14 of *County Government*)	
G.S. 132-1.2	Trade secrets
Local Tax Records (Chapter 9 of *County Government*)	
G.S. 153A-148.1	County tax records
G.S. 160A-208.1	City tax records
Medical and Patient Records (Chapter 22 of *County Government*)	
G.S. 8-53	Privileged physician-patient records
G.S. 122C-52(a)	Area authority client records
G.S. 130A-12	Privileged medical records of health department
G.S. 131E-97	Medical and financial records of health-care facility patients
Minutes of Closed Sessions (Chapter 1 of *County Government*)	
G.S. 143 318.10(e)	Minutes of closed sessions

Continued on next page

Table 6-1 *(continued)*

Type of Record and Applicable General Statute	Description
Settlements	
G.S. 132-1.3	Settlements of suits brought against governments
G.S. 143-318.11(a)(4)	Settlements discussed in closed session
Confidential Legal Materials	
G.S. 132-1.1	Communications from attorney to client regarding litigation
G.S. lA-1, Rules of Civil Procedure (RCP) 26(b)(3)	Attorney work product
Geographic Information System Records	
G.S. 132-10	Geographic information system databases
Contract Bid Documents and Construction Diaries (Chapter 14 of *County Government*)	
G.S. 133-33	Contract cost estimates and bidders' lists
Records Concerning Public Employees Chapter 13 discusses the various personnel privacy acts. There are also a number of more specific statutes dealing with criminal record checks of prospective employees.	
G.S. 114-19.2	School employee criminal records checks
G.S. 114-19.3	Medical facility employee criminal records checks
G.S. 115C-332	School employment applicant criminal history checks
Records Containing Private Business Information Chapter 14 discusses the exemption from the public records law of business trade secrets. Three more specific statutes also exempt business information from public access.	
G.S. 66-169	Records of precious metals transactions
G.S. 95-194 and 95-197	Hazardous chemical information

Continued on next page

Table 6-1 *(continued)*

Type of Record
and Applicable
General Statute   Description

Economic Development Information
G.S. 132-6(d)   Information about economic development
                                projects

Taxpayer Information
G.S. 105-289(e)   Taxpayer information from the state Depart-
                                ment of Revenue
G.S. 105-296(h)   Information about business property
G.S. 105-164.14(f)   Information on sales tax refunds

Medical Information (partial listing)
G.S. 130A-102   Medical information on birth certificates
G.S. 130A-131.17   Information on birth defects
G.S. 130A-143   Information on communicable diseases
G.S. 130A-212   Information about cancer patients
G.S. 130A-389   Information about certain autopsies

Peer Review and Other Information about Medical Professionals
G.S. 131E-95   Records of hospital medical review committees
G.S. 131E-97.2   Information about persons with practice
                                privileges at public hospitals
G.S. 131E-97.1(c)   Information about health-care independent
                                contractors
G.S. 122C-30   Records of mental health hospital medical
                                review committees
G.S. 122C-191   Records of area authority facility medical
                                review committees

Government Operations in Competition with Others
G.S. 131E-97.3   Competitive health-care information
G.S. 131E-99   Information about health-care contracts
G.S. 159B-38   Records of joint-agency contract discussions

Student Records
G.S. 115C-402   Public school student records
G.S. 115C-114   Records about children with special needs
G.S. 115C-174.13   Student test scores
G.S. 130A-441   Kindergarten-student health assessments

Continued on next page

Table 6-1 *(continued)*

Type of Record and Applicable General Statute	Description
Records about Children	
G.S. 7A-675	Juvenile justice system records
G.S. 7A-544	Information about investigations of child abuse, neglect, or dependency
G.S. 48-9-102	Adoption records
G.S. 143-578	Child abuse and neglect records
Social Services Records	
G.S. 108A-80 and -73	Basic social services records
G.S. 108A-11	Access to certain social services records by members of boards of social services
G.S. 110-90.2	Criminal records checks of child day-care providers
G.S. 131D-10.3A	Criminal records checks of foster parents
G.S. 110-139	Child-support enforcement records
G.S. 131D-2	Certain information about adult care homes
G.S. 131D-27	Information about violations of rights of residents of adult care homes
G.S. 131E-124	Information about violations of rights of nursing home residents
Election Records	
G.S. 163-82.4	Certain voter registration information
Miscellaneous Private Information	
G.S. 125-19	Library records
G.S. 62A-9	Telephone numbers held by 911 systems
G.S. 159E-11	Municipal-bond registration records

Source: Adapted from David M. Lawrence, *Public Records Law for North Carolina Local Governments* (Chapel Hill, N.C.: Institute of Government, The University of North Carolina at Chapel Hill, 1997), 69–75.

Continued from p. 129

assessed against the person bringing the action if the court determines that the legal action was frivolous or was brought in bad faith [G.S. 132-9(d)].

Additional Resources

Lawrence, David M. *Public Records Law for North Carolina Local Governments.* Chapel Hill, N.C.: Institute of Government, The University of North Carolina at Chapel Hill, 1997.

North Carolina Department of Cultural Resources, Division of Archives and History. *Records Retention and Disposition Schedule.* Raleigh, N.C.: Division of Archives and History, various dates. This series of schedules, which deals with records retention and disposition, applies to various county departments.

Notes

1. The records of the clerks of superior court occupy an unusual position. Although they are housed at the county level, they are state records, and their management falls under the jurisdiction of the Administrative Office of the Courts (see G.S. 7A-101 and -343). The county commissioners' authority over the clerk's records extends only to the designation of office and repository space.

2. William A. Campbell, *North Carolina Guidebook for Registers of Deeds,* 7th ed. (Chapel Hill, N.C.: Institute of Government, The University of North Carolina at Chapel Hill, 1994).

3. G.S. 132-7: "Insofar as possible, custodians of records shall keep them in fireproof safes, vaults, or rooms fitted with noncombustible materials and in such arrangements as to be easily accessible for convenient use. All public records should be kept in the buildings in which they are ordinarily used. Record books should be copied or repaired, renovated or rebound if worn, mutilated, damaged or difficult to read."

4. Records that could be damaged during inspection or copying because of age or condition may be subjected to reasonable restrictions intended to preserve the records [G.S. 132-6(f)].

5. In the case of computer databases, the law provides that (1) persons may be required to make or submit requests for copies in writing and (2) the records custodian is to respond to all such requests "as promptly as possible." If the request is granted, the copies are to be provided "as soon as reasonably possible" [G.S. 132-6.2(c)]. It is unclear whether the latter phrase means something different from "as promptly as possible."

6. *See* G.S. 132-6.2(b), -6(c). The latter statute establishes a timetable for counties and cities to assume the cost of separating confidential from nonconfidential information.

7 Interlocal Cooperation, Regional Organizations, and City-County Consolidation

David M. Lawrence and Warren Jake Wicker

Contents

David M. Lawrence is an Institute of Government faculty member who works in the area of local government law. Warren Jake Wicker is an Institute of Government emeritus faculty member whose work included special attention to municipal incorporation and annexation and city-county consolidation.

135

Government officials frequently discover that some facilities and services can be operated more efficiently or provided through collaboration among two or more local governments. North Carolina counties have entered into a wide variety of agreements establishing such collaborations. The number and success of joint efforts have led to continuing interest in the consolidation of governments themselves, especially cities with counties, but no city-county consolidations have yet occurred in North Carolina.

Interlocal Cooperation

Cooperation among local governments has become common in recent years. As urbanization has spilled beyond city limits, counties have had to begin providing urban services to residents. They often have found that an efficient way of doing so is by cooperating with one or more of their cities. In this way a county may benefit from a city's experience as it begins a new activity. Also, counties have continued to cooperate among themselves in providing services more traditional to county government.

Cooperation offers several advantages.

1. It may be the most efficient and least expensive way of providing a new service. As a county begins to provide fire inspection services, for example, a contract with an ongoing city inspection department can make the services of experienced inspectors available immediately, with no administrative overhead. Similarly, a county may not need or be able to afford full-time specialized services such as the more sophisticated types of police activities. However, if such services are jointly sponsored by a county and one or more cities or by two adjacent counties, such services may be financially feasible and fully used by all parties.

2. Cooperation also allows governments to achieve economies of scale, lowering the per-unit cost of a service and perhaps providing it at a higher level. A good example is a district (multi-county) health department.

3. Cooperation permits a more effective response to problems that refuse to respect government boundaries. For example, air pollution may drift from one county to another and require a regional problem-solving approach.

4. By cooperating, two units of government may coordinate functions that each has been carrying on independently. Such coordination may be needed, for instance, to provide water and sewer services in areas just beyond city limits. There, counties must often work with cities to establish policies on extensions, supplies, costs, and the like.

5. Cooperation permits local governments to adjust inequitable situations concerning payment for and use of services. For example, cities often provide recreation programs used by people from throughout the county, so many counties contribute funds to these city-sponsored programs.

6. Cooperation is flexible. It can usually begin by simple action of the governing boards involved. A county may engage in several cooperative ventures, each differing from the others in scope, administrative structure, and financial support. While a cooperative relationship established for one service may provide a model for another, it in no way establishes a mold that must be followed.

Types of Cooperation

Cooperation between local governments may assume a variety of forms. The most frequently used categories are contributions, mutual aid contracts, transfer of functions, service contracts, joint agreements, and new units of government.

Contributions

Occasionally one local government will provide a program that benefits the property or citizens of another government but without direct financial support from these beneficiaries. In this case the government that benefits might contribute funds to the government that provides the program. County financial support for a city recreation program is such a contribution.

Mutual Aid Contracts

In a mutual-aid agreement, two or more governments agree to come to each other's aid (if possible) in emergencies or other special situations. Assistance with law enforcement, fire fighting, or natural disasters may be involved.

Transfer of Functions

Sometimes a county and a city, each authorized to perform a particular function, will agree that the county should assume total responsibility for the activity. Such transfers of responsibility have frequently occurred for libraries, hospitals, and, most recently, solid-waste disposal.

Service Contracts

Under this type of agreement, one government contracts with another to provide a service. The contract may involve either administrative assistance to the receiving government or a service provided directly to its citizens. A county might contract to collect the taxes of or provide data-processing for a city; or a city might contract to treat the sewage of a county-owned collection system.

Joint Agreements

The line between joint agreements and service contracts is often a thin one. In theory, a joint agreement involves two or more government units exercising jointly a power that each could exercise individually. Thus a city and a county might employ a joint manager, or two counties might hire a joint social services director. City-county planning boards fit this category, as do councils of governments and other regional councils.

New Units of Government

On occasion, two or more local governments may cooperatively create a new political subdivision to provide service to the citizens of each cooperating government. This form of cooperation is not often found in North Carolina, but examples include some airport authorities, water and sewer authorities, metropolitan water or sewerage districts, and regional solid waste management authorities.

Authority for Cooperation

The General Assembly, through a series of statutes, has provided ample authority for intergovernmental cooperation among counties and other local governments. Table 7-1 sets out the principal statutes authorizing counties to cooperate with other local governments.

Provisions of Interlocal Agreements

Some types of cooperative arrangements are quite simple. When one government contributes to an ongoing program of another, the contributing government typically does not concern itself with the administration of the program; it simply includes an appropriation in its budget ordinance. The amount of the appropriation may have been negotiated, but the negotiations probably will not extend to other subjects. The same disinterest in program administration will probably exist when functions are transferred. Once the transfer is made, the function becomes the sole responsibility of the recipient government.

Other arrangements, however, become more complex, and negotiations may be difficult. Questions may arise concerning financing, operations, administration, property, and many other matters. This chapter cannot suggest correct solutions, because the needs, administrative structures, traditions, and services involved all differ. Nor can it even suggest all the questions that need to be asked. But it can point out the most common decisions that negotiating governments might face (see Table 7-2, page 142). Perhaps this partial list will suggest other questions more particular to a specific situation.

Regional Organizations

The conditions that have given rise to cooperative relationships between local governments have also prompted the creation of substate regional organizations. The development of highway systems, the operation of water and sewer facilities, the protection of air quality, and the regulation of land use are examples of activities that when undertaken by one unit will affect people and property in neighboring units. Sometimes, as noted in the preceding section, these common interests may be recognized and managed by cooperative relationships. At other times, however, the administration of some joint interests may be accomplished most effectively by creating a joint, regional agency.

Impetus for Regional Organization

By 1960 an increasing number of federal agencies required some form of regional planning and the creation of multicounty organizations to administer categorical programs under their jurisdictions. State agencies, of course, have a long history of dividing the state into administrative

Table 7-1
Statutes Authorizing Counties to Cooperate with Other Local Governments

Function	General Statute
General Powers of Cooperation	
Administrative and governmental powers	160A-460 through -464
Property transactions	160A-274
Buildings	153A-164
Councils of governments	160A-470 through -478
Consolidation study commissions	153A-401 through -405
Education	
Merger of school administrative units	115C-67, -68
Community colleges	115D-59; 153A-450
Elections	
Registration of voters	163-288
Conduct	163-285
Officials	163-281(a)
Voting machines	163-161
Health Services	
Public health	130A-36
Mental health	122C-115
Hospitals	131E-7
Planning and Regulation of Development	
Transfer of territorial jurisdiction	160A-360
Planning contracts	153A-322
Historic preservation commissions	160A-400.7
Appearance commissions	160A-451
Open space	160A-404
Inspection services	153A-353
Housing	157-35, -39.5
Community development	153A-376
Regional planning commissions	153A-391 through -398
Regional economic development commissions	158-8 through -15
City-county redevelopment commissions	160A-507.1
Environmental Matters	
Air pollution control	143-215.112
Sedimentation control	113A-60

Continued on next page

Table 7-1 *(continued)*

Function	General Statute
Public Safety	
Law enforcement	
Training	153A-211
Auxiliary police	160A-283
Personnel and equipment	160A-288
Local confinement facilities	153A-219
Fire protection	160A-293
Civil disorders	14-288.12, -288.14
Civil preparedness	166A-7
Ambulance services	153A-250
Hospitals	131E-7
Social Services	
Social services directors	108A-12
Human relations programs	160A-492
Manpower	160A-492
Community action programs	160A-492
Senior citizens	160A-497
Library services	153A-270
Recreation, generally	160A-355
Regional sports authorities	160A-479 through -479.17
Public enterprises	
Airports	63-56; 153A-278
Off-street parking	153A-278
Water services	153A-278
Sewer services	153A-278
Solid waste services	153A-278; 160A-192(b)
Utility emergencies	160A-318
Public transportation systems	153A-278
Regional public transportation authorities	160A-600 through -625
Regional solid waste management authorities	153A-421 through -432

regions. In 1961 the General Assembly authorized the creation of regional planning commissions (G.S. 153A-391, -400) and economic development commissions (G.S. 158-8, -15) by general law. These actions built on the successful experience with regional planning and economic development organizations that had been established in previous years by local legislation. Today's most frequently used form of regional organization, the regional council of governments, was authorized by legislation in 1971 (G.S. 160A-470, -484).

Table 7-2
Common Decisions Facing Negotiating Governments

Administrative Structure	Should the units jointly supervise the function, or should one simply contract with the other to supervise it for both?
Finances	Are user charges to be levied? Should the agreement establish the schedule of charges? Should the agreement establish the basis of charges? How should charges be modified? Should charges be the province of the operating government alone? On what basis are costs to be divided? What should be included as costs attributable to the activity? What will be the timing and the manner of payment between governments? What budgeting procedures should be established? Are special assessments to be used? On what basis? In capital projects, who will make expenditure decisions?
Operations	What will be the territorial scope of activity? What performance levels will be expected? Can they be modified? How? In capital projects, will the parties mandate specific features? On facilities, what limitations or priorities on use will be necessary?
Personnel	How are personnel to be selected? Whose employees will they be? Should there be special provisions in regard to position classification, pay plan, fringe benefits, etc.?
Property	How will decisions to buy real or major personal property be made? How are sites to be selected? How are specifications to be established? How will acquisitions be made? Who will own the property? How will the property be disposed of?

Continued on next page

Table 7-2 *(continued)*

Miscellaneous	What reports will be required? What records must be retained? What rights of inspection should be allowed? How will potential tort liabilities be paid?
Joint Agencies	How will joint agencies be structured? What will the size of the coordinating body be? What will the terms of members be? Who will appoint them? How often will the body meet? What powers and duties will be conferred on/ delegated to the body? What provisions should be made for budgeting? What reports and records will be required?
Duration	How long will the cooperative activity continue?
Termination and Renewal	What should be the provisions for renewal and termination?

The big push for multicounty regional organizations, however, came from the federal government after Congress enacted the Intergovernmental Cooperation Act of 1968. This act encouraged the states to establish a uniform system of areawide planning and development districts. Regional review of local grant and program proposals, as required by Circular A-95 of the Office of Management and Budget, became a standard procedure. In 1969 the General Assembly directed the Department of Administration to cooperate with "the counties, the cities and towns, the federal government, multistate commissions and private agencies and organizations to develop a system of multicounty, regional planning districts to cover the entire State" [G.S. 143-341(6)(i)]. This charge was part of the department's broader role in undertaking and supporting state and regional planning and development.

Lead Regional Organizations

In May 1970, Governor Robert Scott designated seventeen multicounty regions by executive order. One of these, Region G, was further divided in 1979 to create Region I. There have been eighteen regions since that time. Following the designation of the multicounty regions, many state agencies took action to align their regional administrative organization with the new regional designations. Cities and counties in the regions also moved to create a new regional organization or to reshape an existing one to fit the new pattern. In 1971 the state announced a policy of designating a single organization in each region as the *lead regional organization* (LRO). This organization is open to all cities and counties in the region and is the organization through which many state and federal programs are channeled. In 1998 four of these LROs were planning and economic development commissions, and fourteen were councils of governments.

The governing bodies of the LROs comprise representatives from the member governments. Most counties and municipalities are members.[1] A 1994 study found 615 local governments that were eligible to be members. Of these, 515 were members and 100 were not. In six regions, all the eligible local governments were members. Populations of the regions varied from 135,000 to 1,220,000. Staff size varied between twelve and fifty-five. An executive director is the administrative head of each LRO.

Because the LROs may not levy taxes, they must depend on membership dues, earnings from technical assistance, and grants from other governments for their financial support. In 1994 that support was principally from federal (82 percent) and state (8 percent) grants. Membership dues and revenues from local projects and miscellaneous revenues accounted for the remainder of their financial support in that year.

Programs and activities of the LROs vary. All engage in economic planning and development, provide intergovernmental review, serve as a data center for the region, administer programs for the aging in cooperation with state and federal agencies, and advise and assist counties in providing emergency medical services. Most participate in administering community development block grants and the Job Training Partnership Act, and provide technical assistance in local solid waste and land-use planning, housing, and programs to enhance water quality. For a number of LROs, transportation services, regional transportation planning, management consulting, and land and water conservation are significant activities. In short, although the LROs focus principally on planning and coordinating activities and technical assistance in the areas within which they work, they are also available to carry out almost any function or activity that their members may wish.

City-County Consolidation

City-county consolidation is the merger of a county government with one or more city governments. As a general rule, the city government is abolished, and the county government is legally transformed into one that has all the powers and functions previously held by both governments. Authority for counties and cities to create special commissions to study consolidation and other forms of cooperative action, including the drafting of a charter for a consolidated government, is found in Article 20 of G.S. Chapter 153A.

The History of City-County Consolidation

City-county consolidation has a long history in the United States. New Orleans City and Parish were consolidated in 1813; Boston and Suffolk County in 1821; and Philadelphia City and County in 1854.

In North Carolina, interest in city-county consolidation also has a long history, beginning with a 1927 plan (never submitted to the voters) to consolidate the City of Charlotte and Mecklenburg County. Since that time, consolidation plans have been placed before the electorate four times in Wilmington and New Hanover County, twice in Durham and Durham County, and once each in Charlotte and Mecklenburg County and Asheville and Buncombe County. All the plans were rejected, but the margins of defeat have decreased in the places that have had more than one consolidation attempt. The results of the eight referenda on consolidation are shown in Table 7-3.

In every case, voters inside the city proposed for consolidation were more favorable toward the merger than those outside the city but inside the county. However, only in the three most recent votes—Wilmington and New Hanover County in 1987 and 1995, and Asheville and Buncombe County in 1982—have a majority of the voters inside the city involved favored merger.

Other moves toward city-county consolidation in the four counties mentioned earlier have been made in the past sixty years, but they all stopped short of producing a charter that was the subject of a referendum. Interest in consolidation, as evidenced by the creation of study groups, has also been present in recent years in a number of other cities and counties, including Brevard and Transylvania County, Fayetteville and Cumberland County, Roxboro and Person County, and Sanford and Lee County.

Table 7-3
Results of City-County Consolidation Referenda in North Carolina

Governmental Units Involved	Date of Referendum	Results			
		Number		Percentage	
		For	Against	For	Against
Wilmington and	March 28, 1933	1,189	4,128	22	78
New Hanover County	February 27, 1973	4,040	11,722	26	74
	October 6, 1987	7,051	10,337	41	59
	October 10, 1995	11,377	15,923	42	58
Durham and	January 28, 1961	4,115	14,355	22	78
Durham County	September 10, 1974	6,198	13,124	32	68
Charlotte and Mecklenburg County	March 22, 1971	17,313	39,464	31	69
Asheville and Buncombe County	November 2, 1982	12,642	20,883	38	62

Source: Official election returns

Advantages and Disadvantages of City-County Consolidation

The people who have supported consolidation have done so on the grounds of efficiency. They note that the county is a single social and economic community, and argue that it could be better served by one local government than by two. They see better coordination of all government services and improved management of growth flowing from consolidation. Merger would also result in greater equity in taxation, in their view, because it typically involves the use of service districts in which taxation is tied to service levels. Proponents also argue that a single governing board, serving all citizens for all local government purposes, would be more responsive and responsible. Furthermore, they assert, consolidation would eliminate city-county conflicts and the objections to municipal annexation decisions being made by a governing board not responsive to those being annexed.

The opponents of consolidation, for their part, have put forth a host of objections. Citizens outside the central city have feared that merger would, in effect, result in their being "swallowed up" by the "big city." They note that a merged government would be a larger one and have argued that this would mean a less responsive and less efficient government. The fear of higher taxes, especially among residents outside the city, has usually been a major objection to consolidation.

Most of the plans for consolidation proposed in North Carolina have called for changes in the manner in which the governing board was elected and for the merger of administrative departments and offices. These proposed changes have caused some citizens to fear a loss of political influence or jobs or both. Members of rural fire departments and employees of sheriffs' offices, for example, have usually opposed consolidation.

Residents of small towns in counties proposed for merger with a central city have usually opposed consolidation, even though their towns would continue to exist after the merger. They have seen the initial consolidation as a first step that might lead eventually to the merger of their towns and a loss of their identity.

The efforts at city-county consolidation have not yet culminated in a merger of any city and county governments in North Carolina. Almost all of them, however, have been a factor in promoting city-county cooperation by the merger of functions or by an increase in the joint use of facilities.

Additional Resources

Glendening, Parris N., and Patricia S. Atkins. "City-County Consolidations: New Views for the Eighties" in *The Municipal Year Book, 1980,* 68–72. Washington, D.C.: International City/County Management Association, 1980.

Temple, David G. *Merger Politics: Local Government Consolidation in Tidewater Virginia.* Charlottesville, Va.: The University Press, 1972.

Notes

1. Information in this and the following paragraph is from "Regionalism in North Carolina," a report prepared in 1995 for Governor James B. Hunt, Jr., by his Working Group on Regions and Regionalism.

II
County Revenues and Finance

8 Revenues

David M. Lawrence

Contents

David M. Lawrence is an Institute of Government faculty member whose interests include the legal aspects of local government finance.

Counties must raise revenues to support the services they provide. Revenues increase a county's net worth or financial resources. Revenues are usually cash receipts, but not all cash receipts are revenues. For example, when a county redeems an investment, one asset—the investment—is exchanged for another—cash. Except for interest earnings from the investment, the county's net worth does not increase, and no revenues accrue. Likewise, when a county issues bonds, its cash receipts increase by the amount of the bond proceeds, but the county also incurs a debt or a liability equal to the proceeds. The addition to cash receipts in this case is balanced by the liability, and neither the county's net worth nor its revenues are increased.

The major types of revenues available to North Carolina counties are local taxes, state-shared taxes, user charges, other local fees and charges, and federal and state grants and aid. *Taxes* are compulsory charges that governments levy on persons or property. They need not bear any relation to the benefit from public services received by the taxpaying persons or property. The most important taxes for North Carolina counties are the property tax and the local-option sales tax. On a statewide average, property taxes constitute about 37 percent of total county revenues, and local-option sales taxes about 14 percent.

User charges are levied on those who avail themselves of certain county services, in proportion to the benefit they receive from the services. Water supply and distribution and sewage collection and treatment are the most important county activities supported by user charges. Other user charges levied by the state's counties are for solid waste collection and disposal, health and mental health services, ambulance services, recreation and cultural activities, airports, and several other functions.

Besides taxes and user charges, counties have other local revenue sources available to them. The more important of these are fees levied to cover the cost of regulation, special assessments, profits from alcoholic beverage control (ABC) stores, and investment earnings.

Finally, North Carolina counties receive intergovernmental grants and aid, including state reimbursements for property removed from the property tax base. One major change in public finance since the early 1980s has been the reduction in federal aid to local governments. In 1979, direct federal aid to local governments as a percentage of general revenues from local sources was more than 17 percent nationally; twelve years later, such aid had dropped to less than 6 percent.[1]

Local Taxes

As creations of the legislature, counties may impose only the local taxes specifically authorized by the General Assembly. The following local taxes are available to them under the general law: the property tax, the local-option sales and use tax, the privilege license tax, the cable television franchise tax, the animal tax, and the charge for 911 services. A number of counties levy other local taxes as authorized by local acts of the legislature.

The Property Tax

The property tax is levied against real and personal property and generally is an obligation of the property, not its owner. That is, if the tax is not paid, the usual enforcement procedure is to sell the property and pay the tax from the proceeds of the sale. For total county property tax levies in North Carolina in recent years, see Table 8-1. Part of the annual increase in property tax levies evident in that table is due to increases in the tax rate and in part to growth in the tax base, that is, the value of property.

Tax Base

The property tax base consists of real property (land, buildings, and other improvements to land); personal property (business equipment, automobiles, and so forth); and the property of public service companies (electric power companies, telephone companies, railroads, airlines, and certain other companies). Not all property is subject to taxation. Government-owned property is exempt under Article V, Sections 2(2) and (3) of the state constitution. In addition, the General Assembly may exempt property from taxation or classify property to exclude it from the tax base, give it a reduced valuation, or subject it to a reduced tax rate. It must do so, however, only on a statewide basis (G.S. 105-275 through -278.9). A local government itself may not exempt or classify or otherwise give a tax preference to property within its jurisdiction. For the assessed value of property subject to taxation in North Carolina's counties, see Table 8-1.

Tax Rate Limitations and Voter Approval

Property taxes levied for certain purposes are subject to rate limitations and, in certain cases must be approved by the voters. These restrictions are pursuant to Article V, Section 2(5) of the state constitution, which reads as follows:

> The General Assembly shall not authorize any county, city or town, special district, or other unit of local government to levy taxes on property except for purposes authorized by general law uniformly applicable throughout the State, unless the tax is approved by a majority of the qualified voters of the unit who vote thereon.

This provision means that unless the General Assembly specifically authorizes the levy of property taxes for a particular purpose, and does so on a statewide basis, property taxes may be levied for that purpose only with voter approval.

To implement Article V, Section 2(5), the General Assembly has enacted G.S. 153A-149. This statute places functions that counties are authorized to undertake in three groups. Counties may levy property taxes for

Table 8-1
Property Taxation in North Carolina, 1987–88 through 1996–97

	Countywide Property Tax Levies		Assessed Value of Taxable Property	
Year	Amount ($ in millions)	Percent Increase from Prior Year	Amount ($ in billions)	Percent Increase from Prior Year
1987–88	1,263.0	10	208.3	9
1988–89	1,349.1	7	214.9	3
1989–90	1,495.7	11	231.6	8
1990–91	1,660.1	11	248.2	7
1991–92	1,812.3	9	269.7	9
1992–93	1,927.9	6	288.7	7
1993–94	2,130.3	10	302.8	5
1994–95	2,305.6	8	328.7	9
1995–96	2,392.1	4	349.1	6
1996–97	2,498.9	4	372.7	7

Source: North Carolina Department of Revenue, Tax Research Division.

Table 8-2
Group I Functions, for Which There Is No Limit on County Tax Rates

Courts	Jails
Debt service	Schools
Deficits	Social services (mandated programs)
Elections	Joint undertakings of any of the preceding

Group I functions without restriction on tax rate or amount. This group includes the most important state-mandated functions for counties: schools and social services. For a list of Group I functions, see Table 8-2. Counties may levy property taxes for Group II functions without a vote, to a maximum rate of $1.50 per $100.00 valuation of taxable property. For a list of Group II functions, see Table 8-3. They include most of the remaining functions of county government. A county may hold a referendum on the levy of property taxes for any Group II function. If such a referendum passes, the tax levied under it does not count against the $1.50 limitation. A county may also hold a referendum to raise the $1.50 limitation. Group III functions include all authorized activities that the General Assembly has not specified as either Group I or Group II functions. The statute

Table 8-3
Group II Functions, for Which Property Taxes May Be Levied
by a County without a Vote, within a $1.50 Rate

Administration	Law enforcement or sheriffs' department
Agricultural extension	Libraries
Air pollution	Mapping
Airports	Medical examiner or coroner
Ambulance service	Mental health
Animal protection and control	Off-street parking
Armories	Open space
Arts programs and museums	Parks and recreation
Auditoriums, coliseums, and	Planning
convention centers	Ports and harbors and cooperative
Beach erosion and natural disasters	programs with North Carolina Ports
Cemeteries	Authority
Civil defense	Register of deeds
Debts and judgments	Sewage collection and disposal
Defense of employees and officers	Social services (nonmandated programs)
Drainage	Solid waste collection and treatment
Economic development	Surveyors
Fire protection	Veterans' service officers
Forest protection	Water resources development in federal
Health	water resources development projects
Historic preservation	Water supply and distribution services
Hospitals	Watershed improvement projects
Human relations	Joint undertakings with other local
	governments for any Group II function

Table 8-4
Group III Functions, for Which a City May Levy Property Taxes
Only after an Approving Vote of the People

Bus lines and mass transit	Public housing
Community action	Redevelopment
Community development	Sedimentation control
Employment service offices	Streets
Game commissions functions	Joint undertakings of any of the
Manpower programs	preceding functions

does not identify Group III functions. For a list of the most important ones for counties, see Table 8-4. If the voters approve the levy of property taxes for a Group III function, any tax levied for that function does not count against the $1.50 rate limitation.

Tax-Levy Formula

The formula for setting the property tax rate and enacting property taxes is relatively simple. One determines the amount of property tax revenue that must be *collected* to balance the budget, considering estimated expenditures and the amount of money that other revenue sources are likely to yield. (The full property tax levy—the total dollar value of the tax enacted—is never collected. Most North Carolina counties collect 95 to 99 percent of the levy; the statewide average is almost 97 percent.) In calculating the amount of tax expected to be collected, the county may not use an estimated collection percentage that exceeds the current year's collection percentage [G.S. 159-13(b)(6)].

To illustrate the procedure for determining the tax levy and rate, let us say that a county must collect $10,000,000 in property tax revenue to balance its budget and that its finance officer expects 96 percent of the property tax levy to be collected. Being a little conservative, the finance officer assumes that the collection percentage for the coming budget year will be 95 percent. She divides the $10,000,000 of required property tax revenue by 0.95, which yields a property tax levy of $10,526,000. She then divides that levy by taxable valuation—say, $1.6 billion—which yields $ .007017. This figure is multiplied by 100 to produce a tax rate of $ .7017 per $100.00. (Fractional cents may be but are not usually levied in the tax rate. Therefore the actual rate might be set at $ .70 or $ .71.) To check her arithmetic, the finance officer multiplies the $1.5 billion by 0.007017, which yields $10,526,000, the levy. Ninety-five percent of the levy is $10,000,000 in collected property taxes.

Collection of Property Taxes and Cash Flow

Property taxes are due on September 1, but taxpayers may delay payment until January 5 without incurring a penalty. In one county in a recent year, 5 percent of the tax levy was paid in August; 4 percent in September and October; 15 percent in November; 36 percent in December; 28 percent in January; and 6 percent in all other months of the year.[2] Such a concentration of property tax collections in the middle of the fiscal year is typical of most North Carolina cities and counties. It means that cities and counties must rely on fund balances and other revenue sources to finance expenditures during the first part of the fiscal year.

Uniformity of Taxation and Service Districts

With one exception the state constitution requires that the county property tax rate be uniform throughout the county. The uniformity rule applies only to the levy of the tax, not to the use of its proceeds, which may be spent wherever needed. The exception arises from Article V, Section 2(4), of the state constitution, which authorizes the General Assembly to permit counties and cities to define special service districts within their borders and to levy additional taxes in those areas to provide services or facilities that are not offered throughout the unit or that are offered at a lower level in the rest of the unit.

Pursuant to this constitutional provision, the General Assembly has enacted the County Service District Act of 1973, G.S. Chapter 153A, Article 16, Part 1. It authorizes counties to define a part of the county as a service district, to levy a property tax in the district additional to the countywide property tax, and to use the proceeds to provide services to the district. A service district is in no way a separate unit of government. It is simply a geographic designation, a defined part of the county in which the county government levies extra taxes and provides extra services. Counties may define a service district for any of the following functions:

1. Beach erosion control and flood and hurricane protection works
2. Fire protection
3. Recreation
4. Solid waste collection and disposal
5. Sewage collection and disposal
6. Water supply and distribution
7. Watershed improvement
8. Ambulance and rescue services
9. Cemeteries

A service district does not have its own governing body separate from the board of county commissioners that established it. Occasionally, though, the board of commissioners will create an advisory board within the district, especially for districts established for fire protection.

G.S. 153A-302 establishes the standards for creating a service district. A district is defined by simple action of the board of commissioners. No petition from district residents is required, although the commissioners could establish a policy of defining districts only when they receive such a petition. A vote need not be held within the district in order to create it. In fact, there is no authority to hold a vote even if the board of commissioners thinks one is desirable. The commissioners have only to find that the district needs the proposed service or services "to a demonstrably greater extent" than the rest of the county. Usually a county sets the effective date for a new service district at the beginning of the first new fiscal year after its commissioners adopt the resolution approving the district, though the board may postpone that date. Once the district becomes effective, the unit must "provide, maintain, or let contracts for" the service or services involved within a reasonable time, not to exceed one year.

All of the services or facilities that a county may provide in a service district are Group II functions (see Table 8-3) for purposes of the application of tax rate limitations. Because of this the property tax rate for taxes levied exclusively in such a district, when taken together with the general county tax rate attributable to Group II functions, may not exceed the rate limitation of $1.50 per $100 of valuation.

Reimbursements

As noted earlier the General Assembly establishes the kinds of property that will be included in the property tax base, through its power to exempt and to classify and exclude property from taxes. Traditionally, when the General Assembly has sought to subsidize an activity or a group by excluding property from the tax base, it has placed the fiscal burden of the subsidy on local governments through reductions in their tax bases. In recent years, however, the legislature has sometimes coupled tax-base exclusions with state reimbursement to local governments of some or all of the lost tax revenues.

The earliest of these reimbursements partially compensates local governments for taxes lost to the so-called homestead exemption, under which the principal residence of certain older or disabled taxpayers is partially excluded from the tax base. There has since been a series of reimbursements triggered by the exclusion from the tax base of retailers', wholesalers', and manufacturers' inventories and of intangible personal property. By 1996–97 the annual statewide total of such reimbursements to counties was $232.3 million.[3]

Table 8-5
North Carolina Local-Option Sales and Use Tax Revenue,
1987–88 through 1996–97

Fiscal Year	County Government Share Amount ($ in millions)	County Government Share Percent Increase	City Government Share Amount ($ in millions)	City Government Share Percent Increase
1987–88	515.4	26	219.5	26
1988–89	580.7	13	250.9	14
1989–90	611.3	5	264.7	6
1990–91	624.8	2	271.7	3
1991–92	640.8	3	269.2	0
1992–93	677.6	6	282.3	5
1993–94	740.7	9	300.3	6
1994–95	815.5	10	325.8	8
1995–96	875.9	7	356.1	9
1996–97	933.0	7	382.0	7

Source: Data for years before 1994–95, from Patricia A. Seawell, North Carolina Department of Revenue, Tax Research Division, telephone conversation with A. John Vogt, July 3, 1995; all other data from Richard Jones, North Carolina Department of Revenue, Tax Research Division, telephone conversation with Alex Hess, Dec. 19, 1997.

The Local-Option Sales and Use Tax

The local-option sales and use tax is in fact two taxes. The *sales tax* is basically a tax on the retail sale or lease of tangible personal property and on the rental of motel and hotel rooms. The *use tax* is an excise tax on the right to use or consume property in North Carolina or elsewhere. The use tax produces about 10 percent of the total sales and use tax yield. For the total amounts of sales and use tax proceeds received by counties and cities in recent years, see Table 8-5. The large increases in the mid-1980s were due in part to a half-percent increase in the tax rate.

The local sales and use taxes are levied by counties (not cities), and all 100 counties now levy the full amount—2 percent—authorized statewide. (In addition, Mecklenburg County has been authorized to levy a 0.5 percent tax, to be used for mass transit only.) North Carolina has three separate local sales and use taxes; as noted, together they total 2 percent. (The state levies a 4 percent sales and use tax for its own purposes; thus the total sales tax in North Carolina is 6 percent, except in Mecklenburg County, where it is authorized to be 6.5 percent.) The three separate local sales and use taxes are distributed differently and carry different expenditure requirements, and for that reason they must be discussed separately. The three taxes, characterized by the articles in G.S. Chapter 105 under which they are levied, are the *Article 39 one-cent tax*, the *Article 40 half-cent tax*, and the *Article 42 half-cent tax*.

Each of the local sales and use taxes is collected by the state, along with the state's comparable tax. After collection costs (slightly less than 1 percent of collections) are subtracted, the net proceeds are allocated among the 100 counties. Net proceeds of the Article 39 tax are returned to the county of collection. Net proceeds of the Article 40 and Article 42 taxes, however, are placed in a statewide pool and allocated among the counties on a per capita basis.

The allocation of the proceeds among government units in the county is based on either of two distribution formulas: per capita or *ad valorem* (property) tax. The county commissioners select the distribution formula and may change it in April of each year, to take effect in the ensuing fiscal year. The per capita formula uses the annual population estimates of the State Department of Administration. The county's total population is added to the population of all cities in the county. This adjusted population figure is divided into the sales and use tax revenue available to the county to determine the county's per capita sales and use tax amount. The resultant figure is then multiplied by the population of the county and each city within it to determine each unit's share of the county's allocation. Under the *ad valorem* tax formula, the dollar amounts of *ad valorem* taxes levied by the county and each city in the county are added. The proportion that the levy of each of these units bears to the total levy of all the units in the county is the proportion of the county sales and use tax revenue that each unit receives. *Ad valorem* tax figures used in the formula are those of the fiscal year immediately preceding the year in which the distribution is made. For the 1996–97 fiscal year distributions, sixty-two counties used the per capita formula, and thirty-eight used the *ad valorem* tax formula for the allocation of local sales and use tax proceeds.[4]

Counties may spend the proceeds of the Article 39 one-cent tax for any public purpose that they are authorized to undertake. The proceeds of the two half-cent taxes, however, are partially earmarked: for the Article 40 half-cent tax (authorized in 1983), 30 percent is earmarked until the tax has been in effect for fifteen years; for the Article 42 half-cent tax (authorized in 1986), 60 percent is earmarked until the tax has been in effect for sixteen years. The earmarked portion must be used for school capital outlay or for debt service on county borrowing for school projects. The counties did not initially levy these half-cent taxes at the same time, so the earmarking periods begin at slightly different times in different counties.

Other Local Taxes

Other county taxes permitted by general law are the privilege license tax, the local franchise tax, the animal tax, and the charge for 911 services. In addition, some counties may levy occupancy taxes, prepared-food taxes, deed transfer taxes, and motor vehicle taxes pursuant to local act of the legislature. Although none of these local taxes are significant in the overall revenue picture for North Carolina's counties, they produce hundreds of thousands of dollars for many counties and up to several million dollars for some of the state's largest counties. Except for the 911 service charge, revenue from the taxes authorized by general law may be spent for any public purpose. Revenue from the taxes permitted by local act is usually earmarked for specific purposes.

The Privilege License Tax

The privilege license tax is imposed on the privilege of carrying on a business or engaging in certain occupations, trades, employment, or activities. Under G.S. 153A-152 a county may levy privilege license taxes only as specifically authorized by law. The authorizations appear primarily in Article 2, Schedule B, of G.S. Chapter 105. The state formerly levied a privilege license tax on a few categories of businesses under that article and frequently permitted some county taxation of the same businesses. Although the state has repealed its own privilege license tax, the Schedule B authorizations remain valid for counties. An Institute of Government publication entitled *North Carolina City and County Privilege License Taxes* is a useful guide to this subject.[5]

The Cable Television Franchise Tax

Under federal and state law, a county may levy a tax on franchised cable television companies up to 5 percent of gross receipts.

The Animal Tax

Counties may levy taxes on the privilege of keeping dogs and other pets (G.S. 153A-153). These taxes evolved from local dog taxes, and most counties still tax only dogs. A county is free to decide which pets to tax and to set the rate of the tax. Rates usually do not exceed $5 per animal. It is no longer legally required (or lawfully authorized, for that matter) to use the proceeds of dog taxes to compensate people for damage done to their livestock by dogs running at large.

The Charge for 911 Services

Counties (and cities) may impose a charge on telephone subscribers for certain costs associated with 911 services. (These charges are typically levied throughout a telephone exchange and, because an exchange rarely follows city boundaries, are more likely to be levied by counties than cities.) The telephone company collects these charges.

Taxes Permitted by Local Act

Local governments in more than seventy counties are permitted by local act to levy occupancy taxes, which are taxes on the occupancy of hotel and motel rooms. Although most of these taxes are levied by county governments, a few are levied by cities, and cities frequently receive a share of the tax even if the county levies it. In most cases the local act authorizing the tax limits the use that the levying government may make of the proceeds, often to travel- or tourism-related programs. In some instances, though, the levying government may use the money for any public purpose.

A much smaller number of counties are authorized to levy taxes on prepared food (or restaurant meals), on the transfer of real estate, and on motor vehicles garaged in the county. The prepared-food taxes and deed transfer taxes are levied at the rate of 1 percent. The motor vehicle taxes are normally levied at $5 per vehicle.

State-Shared Taxes

State taxes that are shared with counties are the beer and wine taxes and the real estate transfer tax. In 1996–97 the county share of beer and wine taxes statewide was about $9 million; the county share of the proceeds from the excise stamp tax on conveyances of interest in real estate was about $22.9 million.[6]

Beer and Wine Taxes

The state levies a number of taxes on alcoholic beverages. These include license taxes, excise taxes on liquor, and excise taxes on beer and wine.[7] The state shares 23.75 percent of its excise tax on beer, 62 percent of its excise tax on unfortified wine, and 22 percent of its excise tax on fortified wine with cities and counties. A city or a county is eligible to share in beer or wine excise tax revenues if beer or wine may legally be sold within its boundaries. If only one beverage may be sold, the city or county shares only in the tax for that beverage. General law permits beer and wine to be sold statewide but allows any county to hold a referendum on prohibiting the sale of either beverage (or both) within the county. The statutes also allow a city in a dry county to vote to permit the sale of beer or wine within its boundaries.

Distribution of state beer and wine tax revenue that is shared with local governments is based on the population of eligible cities and counties. Counties are given credit only for their *nonmunicipal* population. Since 1983–84 such revenue has grown slowly but steadily to its present level. The money is distributed annually, around Thanksgiving. Counties may spend state-shared beer and wine tax revenue for any authorized public purpose.

Real-Estate Transfer Taxes

The state imposes an excise stamp tax on the conveyance of any interest in real estate. The tax is levied on each recorded deed and is measured by the price paid for the property. The tax rate is $1 for each $500 of the sale price. (The local deed transfer taxes in effect in a few counties are in addition to this statewide tax.) The tax is collected by the county, which must remit one-half of the proceeds to the state; the county's portion may be used for any authorized public purpose.

User Charges

Revenues from user charges finance in whole or in part numerous local government functions. *User charges* means charges to those who voluntarily receive or use certain government services or facilities. In this context the phrase does not include fees that are incidental to a regulatory program or fees established by law for the performance of official acts, such as the recording of deeds or the serving of legal papers.

Many revenues from user charges are placed in the general fund and are available to support any general fund activity or program. Charges for recreation and cultural activities, ambulance services, and even solid waste collection and disposal are budgeted in the general fund in most counties. User charges for these and most general fund services typically cover only a portion of the cost of providing the service.

Some activities supported by user charges are set up and operated as public enterprises. A *public enterprise* is an activity of a commercial nature that could be provided by the private sector. Most public enterprises are self-supporting or predominantly so. North Carolina counties may operate public enterprises for water supply and distribution, sewage collection and treatment, solid waste collection and disposal, airports, public transportation, off-street parking, and stormwater systems (G.S. 153A-274). A county must set up a separate accounting fund for each enterprise that it owns or operates,[8] and user-charge revenue generated by the enterprise must be deposited in that fund and applied first to pay operating expenses, debt service, and capital outlay for the enterprise [G.S. 159-136(b)(4)]. If any user-charge revenue from the enterprise remains, it may be transferred from that enterprise fund and made available to support general government activities or another enterprise. The authorizing statutes for county public enterprises are contained in G.S. Chapter 153A, Article 15.

Reasons for Charging Fees to Users

User charges are feasible for any service that directly benefits individual users, is divisible into service units, and can be collected at a reasonable cost. For example, a county landfill provides a direct benefit to each user (his or her garbage is disposed of), the service is divisible into units (each ton of waste disposed of), and the fee for landfill use can be collected at a reasonable cost (by weighing solid waste and charging and collecting so much per ton before it may be disposed of in the landfill). User charges also allocate limited services and resources efficiently. For example, free water, financed by general taxes, tends to be wasted. But when people are charged for water, they use it more economically.

Counties may choose to impose user charges for services that are used by nonresidents—for example, airports, parking facilities, cultural facilities, coliseums, and convention centers. The county cannot tax these people unless they own property in the county, but it can levy charges on them to recoup its cost for providing a service that directly and individually benefits them. Similarly, user charges can be imposed on owners of property that is exempt from property taxes, such as churches and other nonprofit organizations. Some county officials favor making such owners bear a larger share of the cost of providing services.

On the other hand, other considerations sometimes argue against adoption or expansion of user charges. Compared with the property tax, user charges can be regressive in nature. Furthermore, user charges might cause poor persons and families to decide not to use certain public services. For example, imposing a high fee for use of county recreation facilities might reduce use of the facilities by poor children, and such children are often a primary target for public recreation services. These concerns often lead county officials to retain some tax support for activities that could, in a technical sense, be fully supported by user charges.

Types of User Charges

Water and Sewer Services

Basic charges may be made for receiving county water and using a county sewer system. While the rates of private utilities are regulated by the state Utilities Commission, the charges for county water and sewer services are not. Almost all counties with water systems meter water consumption and charge for water use on this basis. Sewer charges are usually set at some percentage—often at or close to 100 percent—of the water cost. Sewer services to large industries are increasingly metered, and the charge for service to them is based on how much sewage is treated and how difficult it is to treat.

Increasingly, county water and sewer systems in North Carolina are operated as public enterprises. A water and sewer system is self-supporting when its charges for service plus other recurring revenues—for example, interest earned on water and sewer investments—equal or exceed operating expenses, interest on outstanding water and sewer debt, and depreciation. In recent years many counties have received grants from the state Clean Water Bond program and from the United States Environmental Protection Agency to construct water and sewer systems; to receive the grants, the counties have to agree to keep their water and sewer systems self-supporting.

Solid Waste Collection and Disposal

Counties are authorized to collect and dispose of solid wastes. In practice a few counties collect solid waste (although more provide collection sites throughout the county) while many more provide disposal facilities. (The private sector also provides both collection services and disposal facilities.) Revenues from collection services include the basic service fee, charges for additional or special services, and proceeds from the sale of bags or the rental or sale of commercial or industrial solid waste containers. Revenue generated by disposal facilities comes from fees per weight of load and from sales of recyclable materials. In addition, a county may levy an "availability fee" for the "availability of a disposal facility provided by the county."

Airports

A variety of fees, charges, and rents raise revenue for an airport operation: landing fees; rentals of hangar space, terminal space, and land; franchise fees for ground transportation services; sale of gasoline, aircraft materials, and the like; and parking receipts.

Hospitals

A county-operated hospital typically charges in the same manner as a privately operated hospital does for patient care.

Ambulance and Rescue Services

A county that provides or contracts for the provision of ambulance services may charge fees for them. These fees may include a flat amount per trip within the county; a mileage charge for trips to distant locations; and scheduled charges for medically related services such as providing oxygen.

Recreation and Cultural Activities

Counties may operate recreation programs, art galleries, museums, auditoriums, coliseums, convention centers, libraries, and the like. A variety of support sources are available in this category of service: admission charges, concessions, facility rentals, and parking receipts. For most recreation and cultural programs, user charges are not the principal means of support; rather, the programs are largely financed by tax proceeds. Auditoriums and coliseums can more readily be supported by user charges. G.S. 153A-264 entitles any resident of a county or city that operates or contributes to a public library to free use of the library; user charges are therefore generally inappropriate for libraries.

Public Transportation

A small but growing number of counties operate bus or van transit systems to serve unincorporated areas. Start-up and capital costs for these systems have been financed largely with federal grants, but a significant portion of the annual operating costs are financed by user charges. A county may not subsidize a bus or mass transit service by means of property taxes without voter approval.

Other Local Revenues

Other local revenues for counties include statutory fees charged by public officers; facilities fees assessed as part of the cost of court operation; fees that are incidental to regulation; special assessments; profits from ABC stores; investment earnings; and revenues from many miscellaneous sources.

Statutory Fees of Public Officers

At one time the entire cost of operating the offices of the county sheriff and the register of deeds was financed by the statutory fees charged by these officers for the performance of official duties. They collected the fees, hired their own help, paid their own expenses, and kept the remainder as their compensation. Although this financing system has been abolished throughout the state, the statutory fees remain. They are collected by the sheriff or register of deeds and deposited in the county's general fund.

Sheriff

The sheriff collects a $5 fee for executing a criminal warrant and for serving any civil process paper. A sheriff who is also the jailer collects a $5 per day jail fee from persons held awaiting trial, if the person being held is convicted. When conducting sales of real estate or personal property, the sheriff receives a commission of 5 percent of the first $500 and 2.5 percent of the remainder of the property's value, in addition to associated expenses [G.S. 7A-304(a)(1), -311, -313].

Register of Deeds

The register of deeds collects fees for virtually every official act performed, ranging from $40 for issuing marriage licenses to $1 for certifying probate instruments. The largest revenue-producing fee is for recording deeds and other instruments that affect land titles: $5 for the first page and $2 for each additional page. Fees for recording security interests under the Uniform Commercial Code and for issuing marriage licenses are also major sources of revenue. In many counties, the fees received by the register of deeds exceed the cost of operating the office (G.S. 161-10).

Each county must deposit an amount equal to 4.5 percent of register of deeds fees collected under G.S. 161-10 with the state treasurer. This money is earmarked for a supplemental pension payment for eligible retired registers of deeds. Other than this provision, there is no legal restriction on the use of register of deeds' fees paid into the county's general fund.

Court Facilities and Related Fees

The state assesses fees against criminal defendants and civil litigants to offset in part the costs of operating the court system. As part of these charges, a facilities fee for each court case is paid to the local government unit (usually the county) that provides the courtroom in which judgment in the case is rendered [G.S. 7A-304(a)(2), -305(a)(1), -306(a)(1), and -307(a)(1)]. The facilities fee in criminal actions is $6 in district court and $24 in superior court. For civil actions, the fee is $4 for special proceedings and administration of estates, $6 for cases heard before a magistrate, and $10 for those heard in district or superior court. Each county is also paid a facilities fee of 4 percent of the principal amount of money held in a trust or agency capacity by the clerk of superior court in an interest-bearing checking account, up to a maximum of $750 in interest per principal amount deposited (G.S. 7A-308.1).

The proceeds of the facilities fee may be used only for providing courtrooms and related judicial facilities, including jails and law libraries. In most counties, the fees barely cover the cost of utilities, insurance, and maintenance of the building(s) occupied by the court system. (Financing of the court system is discussed further in Chapter 30 of this volume.)

Fees Incidental to Regulation

Local governmental regulatory programs frequently have associated fees and charges. The person being regulated is required to meet some or all of the costs occasioned by the regulated action. Programs that often have such fees and charges are building inspection, land use regulation, health and sanitation regulation, and the like.

The authority to impose reasonable charges for regulatory activities is subsumed in the power to regulate.[9] There is no general statutory limit to such charges, although occasionally the amount of a regulatory fee is set by statute. A rough limit to reasonableness for these fees is the amount necessary to meet the full cost of a regulatory program. Fees and charges for regulatory programs may be used for any public purpose that counties are authorized to undertake, except that fees imposed for public health and sanitation regulation [*see* G.S. 130A-39(g)] must be expended for public health purposes.

Impact Fees

In rapidly growing areas of the state, officials are seeking new ways to finance the many new public facilities needed to accommodate development. Impact fees are one device serving that need. These fees require a developer to pay a substantial capital fee upon the issuance of a building permit, and the local government then uses the proceeds of the fees to construct new public infrastructure, such as streets, utilities, parks and open spaces, and other facilities. A county may impose impact fees for water and sewer infrastructure under existing general law. For other sorts of facilities, however, local legislation is necessary from the General Assembly. Several counties and cities have received such legislation, and others are watching those governments' experiences to decide whether they should seek comparable legislation.

Special Assessments

Special assessments are levied against property to pay for public improvements that benefit that property. Like user charges and unlike property taxes, special assessments are levied in some proportion to the benefit received by the assessed property. Unlike user charges, special assessments are levied against property rather than persons and are typically for public improvements rather than for services. Although special assessments are a relatively minor revenue source in the overall revenue picture of North Carolina's counties, they are significant in reimbursing the units that use them for such projects as extensions of water distribution or sewage collection lines.

Under G.S. 153A-185, counties may levy special assessments to finance the following public improvements: water systems; sewage collection and disposal systems (including septic tank systems); beach erosion control and flood and hurricane protection works; watershed improvement, drainage, and water resources development projects; and the local cost of improvements made by the Department of Transportation to subdivision and residential streets outside municipalities. Although most special assessments are levied for capital projects, counties may also levy them on benefiting property for annual maintenance and operating costs for beach erosion control or flood or hurricane protection works (G.S. 153A-204.1).

The amount of each assessment must bear some relationship to the amount of benefit that accrues to the assessed property. The most common basis of assessment is front footage: each property is assessed on a uniform rate per foot of property that abuts on the project. Other bases include the size of the area benefited and the value added to the property because of the improvement.

The board of commissioners may levy special assessments without a petition except for street improvements. For such improvements the council must first receive a petition requesting the assessments from 75 percent of the property owners to be assessed, and those who petition must own at least 75 percent of the frontage on the street.

Special assessments may be paid (and often are) in annual installments along with interest on the amount outstanding in any year. Special assessment revenue, including the interest portion, generally is not earmarked and may be used for any public purpose. Local improvements are often financed from special-assessment revolving funds; assessment revenues generated from finished projects are used to finance new improvements.

Special assessments may not be levied until the improvement being financed has been completed. Therefore the county must advance its own funds to construct the improvement.

Profits from ABC Stores

Both counties and cities may establish and operate ABC stores. By the end of 1997, 48 counties had their own ABC systems, while there were 110 city systems. Together, these local systems generated about $25.5 million in annual profits.[10] Net profits equal gross sales minus state taxes; the per-bottle add-on tax; the cost of goods; the contributions for ABC law enforcement, education, and rehabilitation programs for alcoholics; and operating expenses. About 80 percent of the net profits is distributed to the units that are authorized to share in the profits. The rest of the profits is kept by the ABC systems as working capital.

ABC profits are constitutionally subject to no limitations except public purpose. However, local acts of the General Assembly frequently earmark all or some portion of a system's profits.

Investment Earnings

G.S. 159-30 authorizes counties to invest their idle cash. Funds for investment come from bond proceeds, capital and operating revenues, and fund balances. Local governments' most common investments are certificates of deposit in banks and savings and loan associations, obligations of the United States Government (called *Treasuries*), obligations that mature no later than eighteen months from the date of purchase of certain agencies set up under federal law (called *Agencies*), and the North Carolina Cash Management Trust, a mutual fund for local government investment. The interest earned on investments must be credited proportionately to the funds from which the moneys that were invested came.

Investment income has become a much more important revenue source in recent years because of high interest rates and more sophisticated case management practices by North Carolina local governments. North Carolina's counties often earn investment income that is the equivalent of 5 or more cents on the property tax rate, exclusive of income on invested bond proceeds. For total cash and investments, and investment earnings of North Carolina counties for recent years, see Table 8-6. The ups and downs in earnings reflect shifts in interest rates from one year to another.

Table 8-6
Cash and Investments by County Governments, 1987–88 through 1995–96

Year	Cash and Investments, June 30	Investment Earnings
1987–88	$ 909,953,192	$ 70,094,308
1988–89	1,059,479,561	96,430,877
1989–90	1,151,798,224	106,025,533
1990–91	1,213,110,073	98,391,573
1991–92	1,292,711,239	72,439,882
1992–93	1,353,253,342	55,719,203
1993–94	1,542,152,442	54,450,280
1994–95	1,973,034,682	107,602,161
1995–96	2,272,163,449	129,516,885

Source: North Carolina Department of State Treasurer, Local Government Commission.

Minor Sources

Counties have numerous minor sources of local revenue. For example, many units receive payments from other local governments for joint or contractual programs. Some units receive funds from the management of their property, such as from leasing of county-owned building space or land, or sale of surplus equipment. Further, counties receive refunds on the state gasoline and sales taxes that they pay. Occasionally a county receives a bond forfeiture from a prospective vendor or a contractor.

Additional Resources

Campbell, William A. *North Carolina City and County Privilege License Taxes.* 4th ed. Chapel Hill, N.C.: Institute of Government, The University of North Carolina at Chapel Hill, 1996.

Lawrence, David M. *Local Government Finance in North Carolina.* 2d ed. Chapel Hill, N.C.: Institute of Government, The University of North Carolina at Chapel Hill, 1990.

Notes

1. Bureau of the Census, *Government Finances, 1978–79* (Washington, D.C.: Government Printing Office, 1979), 64; and *Government Finances, 1991–92* (Washington, D.C.: Government Printing Office, 1993), 1.

2. These data were supplied by the county finance director.

3. North Carolina Department of Revenue, Tax Research Division.

4. Richard Jones, North Carolina Department of Revenue, Tax Research Division, telephone conversation with Alex Hess, acting librarian at Institute of Government, Dec. 19, 1997.

5. William A. Campbell, *North Carolina City and County Privilege License Taxes*, 4th ed. (Chapel Hill, N.C.: Institute of Government, The University of North Carolina at Chapel Hill, 1996).

6. North Carolina Department of Revenue, Tax Research Division.

7. North Carolina Department of Revenue, Tax Research Division, *Statistics of Taxation 1980* (Raleigh, N.C.: North Carolina Department of Revenue, 1981), 172.

8. Water and sewer systems operated as a consolidated enterprise may be accounted for in the same fund. G.S. 159-26(b)(4).

9. Homebuilders Ass'n of Charlotte v. City of Charlotte, 336 N.C. 37, 442 S.E.2d 45 (1994).

10. North Carolina Alcoholic Beverage Control Commission.

9   The Property Tax

William A. Campbell and Joseph S. Ferrell

Contents

William A. Campbell is an Institute of Government faculty member whose work includes state and local taxation, land records, and environmental law.

Joseph S. Ferrell is an Institute of Government faculty member whose fields of interest include general county government and the legal aspects of property tax listing and assessing.

Part 1: Characteristics of the Property Tax

From colonial times to the present, North Carolina has used taxes on land and other forms of property to finance the operations of government.[1] At one time property taxes were the major revenue source for both the state and its local governments. Today, the property tax is levied only by local governments. Counties, cities, and special tax districts use property tax proceeds to support public schools and community colleges, social services, public health and mental health services, police and fire protection, city streets, solid waste collection and disposal, and many other government services provided at the local level.

Kinds of Property That Can Be Taxed

Two major paragraphs of the state constitution determine the General Assembly's authority to decide what kinds of property are to be subject to the property tax. The older of these exemptions removes property belonging to the state, counties, and municipalities from the property tax; authorizes the General Assembly to exempt property used for certain specific purposes; and prohibits the General Assembly from delegating its power to exempt property [N.C. CONST. Art. V, Sec. 2(2)]. The other authorizes the General Assembly to classify any property for taxation, prohibits the General Assembly from delegating this power, and commands that each class of taxable property be taxed by uniform rule [N.C. CONST. Art. V, Sec. 2(2)]. Why should the property tax be the subject of such extensive and detailed constitutional regulation? The answer to this question lies in the history of the long struggle to devise a state and local tax system that was both equitable in theory and capable of being equitable in practice.

Taxation by Uniform Rule

North Carolina has always used some form of the property tax,[2] but in the earliest days it took second place behind the capitation tax (often called the *poll tax*).[3] In colonial times the property tax took the rudimentary form of land tax known as "quit rents" that was derived from English feudal land tenures.[4] Quit rents were levied at a fixed rate per acre and had nothing to do with the value of the land or how it was improved. During the Revolutionary War, North Carolina experimented with a uniform property tax that was levied according to value and reached almost every form of property. Poll taxes were relegated to a minor role. This farsighted plan did not survive the war. By 1784 it had been replaced by a system that was not too different from the colonial system. There was little or no effort to tax tangible or intangible personal property. Taxes were imposed on land holdings at a fixed rate per acre rather than in proportion to the value of the property. There was no effort to tax buildings and other improvements to land. Town lots, on the other hand, were taxed according to value. The difference in treatment was probably due to the greater ease of estimating the value of town lots, which were bought and sold more often than farm and forest land.

Taxation of land according to value first appeared in North Carolina in 1814. Efforts to tax personal property began in 1836 with a special property tax on gold and silver plate, watches, pleasure carriages, harps, pianos, bowling alleys, and playing cards. These items were considered luxuries that identified their owners as able to pay more taxes than ordinary citizens. Although land was to be taxed according to value, the estimation of value was left largely up to the taxpayer. Property owners were expected to declare the extent of their taxable property and to give an honest estimate of its value under oath. In an era when most people sincerely feared that God would punish them for swearing a false oath, self-assessment was probably not as bad a system as it seems today, but it is also likely that many people, believing that the meek and humble of heart would indeed inherit the earth, felt that they could avoid the sin of pride by modestly estimating their property's value.

Two features of the pre–Civil War property tax system stand out: only selected classes of property were taxable, and valuation was determined primarily by the property owner. When a taxpayer declared his annual tax liability, he was said to *give in his list*. The official to whom the list was given was the *list taker*, and the process of determining what property was taxable was termed *listing* property for taxes. These familiar terms are still in use today. Self-assessment of real property has been obsolete for many years, but it survives to a degree in the modern practice of listing some forms of business property by dollar value rather than by item.

The modern concept of the property tax originated as a reform movement in the early nineteenth century but was not implemented in North Carolina until after the Civil War. The reform movement advocated a general property tax on all species of property *by uniform rule*, that is, according to the same valuation standard and at the same tax rate. During the nineteenth century the American economy changed from one based predominantly on agriculture to an industrialized economy in which land was no longer the only major form of wealth. Instead of rents and profits from land, the wealthiest people now derived their income from ownership of corporate stock, interest on money loaned, profits from commercial enterprises, salaries, and wages. One way to access these new forms of wealth was through a tax on incomes. This was begun in North Carolina as early as 1849. Another way to tap them was to tax the capital assets that formed the basis of the economy. This idea forms the kernel of the general property tax. Instead of trying to reach agreement on what kinds of property to tax, thereby having to weigh the interests of those who will pay much against those who will pay little, the reformers advocated taxing all forms of property under the same valuation standard, at the same rate, and according to the same procedures.

The movement toward the general property tax began in North Carolina by legislative action in 1860, but unsettled conditions during the Civil War limited its implementation. Nevertheless, widespread support for the general property tax throughout the nation and among reform-minded North Carolinians formed a broad base of popular support for a new tax system. This movement found expression in the North Carolina Constitution of 1868, which contained a clause requiring a general property tax but provided that "no income shall be taxed when the property from which the income is derived is taxed" [N.C. CONST. (1868) Art. V, Sec. 3]. The General Assembly had a choice about whether to levy property taxes, no choice as to what kinds of property would be "on the list," and no choice as to what valuation standard to use. The provision also limited severely the use of the income tax as a major source of revenue by prohibiting taxation of income derived from taxable real or personal property. As a practical matter, this left only salaries and wages subject to the income tax.

Kinds of Property Exempt from Taxes

Proponents of the general property tax agreed that some kinds of property should not be taxed. The states cannot tax property owned by the federal government without violating the United States Constitution, and it does not make much sense for a taxing unit to tax its own property. It would be futile to attempt to tax cemeteries, and no one wanted to tax churches, educational institutions, or charitable organizations. Furthermore, many people believed that every citizen was entitled to a minimum amount of property that would be protected from taxation. These considerations led the framers of the 1868 constitution to add a clause allowing exemption of those kinds of property [N.C. CONST. (1868) Art. V, Sec. 5]. The General Assembly promptly exercised its discretion to exempt cemeteries and property used for religious, charitable, and educational purposes, and has continued that policy to the present day.

Authority to Classify Property for Taxation

The general property tax fell short of the high ideals held by its supporters because owners of real property would not accept market value assessments and owners of intangible personal property would not disclose a complete list of their holdings. It is relatively easy to list land but difficult to assign a precise value to it. The same is true of tangible personal property. Since list takers relied primarily on the owner's estimate of value to determine the tax value of real property and tangible personal property, it should not be surprising that these species of property were, on the whole, assessed for taxes at only a small fraction of true value. The problem with taxing intangible personal property was just the opposite. It is easy to value but difficult to find unless the owner cooperates. A taxpayer listing money on deposit or shares of stock had little room to argue about their value. Instead, owners of intangible personal property conveniently forgot the extent of their holdings when listing their taxes. The constitution required that all property be taxed "by uniform rule," meaning that the same rate of tax had to be levied on all listed property. Thus the underassessment of real and tangible personal property required high tax rates, which tended to drive even more intangible personal property into hiding.

There were two other major problems with the state's system of taxation as mandated by the 1868 constitution. The section requiring a general property tax prohibited taxing income derived from taxable property, and the constitution placed an absolute limit on the combined state and county property tax rate. A detailed discussion of the former constitutional rate limitation is beyond the scope of this chapter. It is enough to point out that the combined state and county property tax rate could not exceed $ .6667 per $100 of assessed value. The revenue raised by a rate this low would have been insufficient even if assessments had been close to market value. With real property assessments generally at a small fraction of value and most intangible personal property unlisted, the property tax was incapable of producing enough revenue to satisfy the demands of the people for more and better services from their government.

The income tax offered an attractive alternative to the property tax as a source of revenue for statewide services, such as public schools. It had been in use in North Carolina since the 1840s, but because the constitution commanded that income derived from taxable property not be taxed, the income tax could not reach such sources of income as dividends, interest, rents, farm profits, and capital gains. These were the primary sources of income for wealthy individuals. If the property producing the income had been taxed at close to market value, the exclusion of these income sources from taxation would have been more equitable than it was, but in practice, income taxes levied on salaries and wages took a proportionately much larger share of the taxpayer's disposable income than did property taxes levied on income-producing real and personal property. That made it politically difficult to increase reliance on the income tax.

Any solution for the state's problems with its system of taxation would require constitutional amendments that addressed these and other problems. The General Assembly needed the authority to expand the base of the income tax to include more than salaries and wages. In return, some more equitable means of taxing intangible personal property were needed. The complex constitutional rate limitation needed to be abandoned, and the state government itself needed to look to sources of revenue other than the property tax to finance statewide programs.

Between 1913 and 1935 the General Assembly went to the voters seven times with constitutional amendments that would allow reform of the tax system.[5] Amendments authorizing special tax treatment for intangible personal property were defeated in 1913, 1927, and 1929, but the voters approved a 1919 amendment authorizing a state income tax without the restriction on taxing income from taxable property. This amendment made it possible for the state to abandon the property tax as a source of state revenue after 1921.

One measure attempted in the course of the reform movement has had a lasting effect on property tax administration. Governor Thomas W. Bickett (1917–21) made one last attempt to make the old tax system work by persuading the 1919 General Assembly to commission a state-wide revaluation of real property in 1920.[6] If land could be put on the tax books at close to its true value, tax rates could be lowered and intangible personal property could be coaxed out of hiding. The statewide revaluation was conducted under the auspices of the State Tax Commission. Up to this time, property had been assessed at the township level by township list takers working independently of each other. Valuation was largely a matter of accepting the taxpayer's estimate of value. The list taker's completed work was reviewed at the county level by the county board of equalization and review, but there was no coordination of the work at the beginning of the process and no uniform guides for estimating property values. The State Tax Commission addressed both of these problems by appointing a tax supervisor in each county to co-ordinate and oversee the work of the list takers in preparing for the 1920 revaluation. The new position proved so useful that it was soon made a permanent feature of the property tax system. As time passed, the role and powers of the tax supervisor grew constantly, and the list taker system declined. Today the office carries the title of county assessor, and independent list takers have become extinct.

The reform process culminated in 1936 when the voters approved a constitutional amendment permitting the General Assembly to classify property for taxation. This swept away the last vestiges of a constitutionally mandated general property tax. The 1936 amendment made it possible for the General Assembly to establish a new revenue system for the state and its local governments. The state would finance statewide services primarily from income and sales tax revenues, while local governments would provide local services primarily from property tax revenues. That basic division, somewhat modified, remains in place today [N.C. CONST. (1937) Art. V, Sec. 3].

For property tax purposes, the heart of the 1936 amendment was a provision that "taxes on property shall be uniform as to each class of property taxed." This substituted for the former requirement that all property be taxed, and permitted the General Assembly to be selective in deciding whether and under what conditions certain classes of property would be taxed, subject only to the basic requirement that all items in each class be treated uniformly.

The General Assembly promptly exercised its newfound authority to classify property by enacting the intangibles tax on the most common forms of intangible personal property and removing them from the general mass of property subject to the locally administered property tax. The intangibles tax remained on the books until 1995 when it was repealed. A few types of intangible personal property remained subject to local taxation for many years. In 1997 virtually all intangible personal property was exempted from *ad valorem* taxation [G.S. 105-275(31)].

Uniformity of the Statewide Tax Base

The final two elements that make up the constitutional underpinnings of the modern property tax were added in 1961 and 1971. A 1961 constitutional amendment prohibited the General Assembly from passing legislation that excused certain types of property from property taxes on less than a statewide basis.[7] This amendment nipped in the bud the practice of granting exemptions or other kinds of preferential tax treatment by local acts of the General Assembly that applied in only one taxing unit. The 1971 amendments eliminated a constitutional limitation on the tax rate and gave the General Assembly the authority to decide when voter approval would be required for property tax levies. Previously, the state constitution had required voter approval for purposes that were not "necessary expenses" of the taxing unit, and the state courts decided what kinds of government functions qualified as "necessary expenses."

Contemporary Significance of Taxation by Uniform Rule

One consequence of the constitutional requirement that property taxes be levied "by uniform rule" is that each parcel of real property or item of personal property can have only one assessed value for tax purposes. Several levels of government may levy property taxes on a given parcel. When the state levied property taxes, city lots were subject to property taxes levied by the state, the county, and the city. Today city residents are subject to both county and city property taxes, and many rural residents pay special district taxes as well as county taxes. Taxation by uniform rule prevents these overlapping taxing jurisdictions from adopting different tax values for the same item of property. This is why the job of appraising and assessing property for taxes is exclusively a county function in North Carolina. Municipalities and special tax districts must accept the county's tax value for all property within their boundaries.

A second consequence of the uniform rule requirement is that a taxing jurisdiction must levy the same rate of tax on all taxable property; it cannot choose to tax some classes of property at a higher rate per dollar of value than others, and it cannot levy taxes in different geographic areas at different rates. This explains why it is necessary to set up a special tax district if a city or county wants to provide certain services to a part of its territory that it does not provide throughout its jurisdiction.

Characteristics of the Property Tax

Two characteristics of the property tax distinguish it from other forms of taxation and underlie the methods of determining tax liability and enforcing collection. These characteristics are that a tax is levied *in rem* and that tax liability is determined *ad valorem.*

Property Tax as an *In Rem* Tax

The first of these characteristics is that the property tax is levied on property itself, not on the owner. It is said to be an *in rem* tax, from the Latin phrase meaning "on the thing," as opposed to other forms of taxes that are said to be *in personam*, from the Latin phrase meaning "on the person." The concept of the property tax as *in rem*, levied on the property itself, underlies the legal principle of the property tax lien. The obligation to pay the tax attaches directly to land and other forms of real property without any intervention on the part of the tax collector. The obligation to pay can be attached directly to personal property by seizure. Because the property tax is an *in rem* tax, the obligation to pay an unsatisfied property tax lien passes along with the land when the title is transferred to another, and personal property that has been seized by the tax collector can be sold to satisfy tax liens. The *in rem* nature of the tax finds its strongest expression in the lien on land and other forms of real property.[8] Here, taxing authorities look to the land itself for payment of the tax. If taxes remain unpaid when title is transferred, the new owner will have to come up with the money to pay the tax or risk losing the land, even though the tax liability was incurred when someone else owned the land.

Property Tax as an *Ad Valorem* Tax

The second distinctive characteristic of the property tax is that it is measured by the value of the thing being taxed. It is said to be an *ad valorem* tax from the Latin phrase meaning "according to value." The *ad valorem* character of the tax has two main consequences. First, a property owner's ability to pay property taxes from his or her current income is irrelevant. Only the current market value of the property is taken into account. The second consequence is that tax liability is determined by assessment officials with little or no direct involvement by the taxpayer. As noted earlier, self-assessment does not work. This means that almost all of the cost of property tax administration is located in the public sector. By contrast, much of the cost of administering taxes in which tax liability is initially computed and declared by the taxpayers themselves is located in the private sector. This distinction accounts for the apparently high cost of property tax administration in comparison to income and sales taxes.

Steps in the Process of Taxing Property

There are six basic steps in property tax administration:

1. The property to be taxed must be identified as to ownership, location, and whether it is taxable or not. This step is called *listing.*
2. The tax office must estimate the market value of the listed property. This step is *appraisal.*
3. The portion of the market value to be taxed must be calculated, and the property must be formally placed on the roll of taxable property. This step is *assessment.*
4. Once property has been formally assessed for taxation, the taxing authorities must allow a time for *review and appeal* of assessments. The owner may want to challenge the valuation placed on the property or whether the taxing jurisdiction has authority to tax it all, and the board itself may want to correct assessment inequities.
5. Once the review process has concluded, the governing body of the taxing unit sets the *tax rate* for the current tax year, and the tax office begins the *billing* process that notifies each taxpayer how much he or she owes and where to pay the tax.
6. The last step is *collection* of the tax levy.

The Property Tax Calendar

North Carolina local governments levy property taxes to support government operations for a *fiscal year* that opens on July 1 and closes on the following June 30. County commissioners and city council members adopt their budgets and set the property tax rate around July 1 of each year. The county and city then mail notices to taxpayers, usually in late July or early August. The due date of the current year's tax is September 1, but taxpayers are allowed to pay their property taxes without penalty at any time until the delinquency date, which is the following January 6. The great majority of taxpayers pay voluntarily on or before December 31 to take advantage of the income tax deduction for property taxes in the current calendar year. After the delinquency date (January 6), local tax collectors begin to use enforced collection remedies against those who have not paid on time.

The local governing board cannot make its tax levy until the assessment list has been compiled and reviewed. Only then can the board make a reliable estimate of the probable yield of the property tax at any given tax rate. Therefore the steps of listing, appraisal, assessment, and review must begin well in advance of the July 1 opening of the fiscal year.

To tax property according to value in the correct taxing jurisdiction and bill the taxes to the proper owner, the taxing authorities must know three things about all taxable property: where it is, what it is worth, and who owns it. All of these characteristics change constantly, which means there must be a fixed assessment date as of which time ownership, value, and location (tax status) will be determined. That date in North Carolina is January 1. All taxable property is assessed for taxes at its value as of January 1, the taxing jurisdictions that have authority to tax it are ascertained by the property's location as of January 1, and ownership is determined by ownership records as of January 1. The information needed to make these determinations is compiled each year during the listing period, which begins in January and normally runs for about thirty days. During this time taxpayers must submit to the county assessor a list of all their taxable property. In most counties taxpayers are not required to list their real property each year; they need only list any taxable personal property that they own (other than motor vehicles) and disclose information about any improvements they have made to their real property in the previous year. Also, property owners who want to claim the benefit of exemption or other special tax treatment must submit their applications at this time. The form on which taxable property is declared is called the *abstract*.

After the listing period closes, the county assessor determines the appraised and assessed value of each taxable item and compiles the *scroll*, which is a tentative list of taxable property showing the owner's name and address and the aggregate assessed value of his or her taxable property. The scroll is then submitted to the board of equalization and review for approval. Most counties begin this process on the first Monday in May. Normally the board of equalization and review remains in session for four weeks, during which time it may make any changes in the scroll needed to bring the listing and assessments into conformity with legal requirements. Most changes are made as a result of reviews requested by property owners.

After the board of equalization and review has completed its work and the tax rate has been set, the tax office computes the precise amount of taxes due from each person entered on the scroll, which is now more properly called the *tax list and assessment roll* because it has been finalized for the current year. The list of taxpayers with the amount of taxes due from each is called the *tax book*. In most counties it is combined with the tax list and assessment roll in one document. It may take the form of a computerized database, a paper document, or both.

The tax book is the basic documentation for preparing tax receipts for each entry on the tax list and assessment roll. The tax receipt doubles as a billing notice to the taxpayer and, once the tax has been paid, as legal evidence that the tax has been paid and the tax lien discharged.

Table 9-1 shows a simplified calendar of important dates in the 1998–99 property tax cycle for a county that begins the review and appeal process in May and is not conducting a general revaluation of real property. When certain deadlines fall on a holiday or a weekend, the taxpayer is given extra time. The example takes this into account.

The Tax Year

The property tax calendar examined in Table 9-1 makes it clear that property taxes are levied on the basis of the fiscal year, not the calendar year. The tax levy occurs at the beginning of the new fiscal year. Tax collections go to support the operations of the taxing unit for the ensuing fiscal year. To be precise, taxes billed in July or August of 1998 should be referred to as "1998–99 taxes" because they are levied to pay for government services to be provided in the 1998–99 fiscal year. It is customary, however, to refer to taxes by the year in which they are levied. So taxes levied and billed in July 1998 will be referred to as "1998 taxes." This and other features of the tax cycle, such as listing in January and paying in December, lead most taxpayers to assume that property taxes are levied on the calendar basis and cover government services provided during that calendar year. This incorrect assumption often leads to misunderstandings that can be difficult to explain.

Table 9-1
Simplified Calendar of Dates in the 1998–99 Property Tax Cycle

Date	Process
Thursday, January 1, 1998	Assessment date.
Friday, January 2	Listing period begins (first business day after January 1).
Tuesday, January 6	Delinquency date for 1997 taxes.
Monday, February 2	Listing period ends (deadline for 1998 is moved forward to first business day after Saturday, January 31).
Monday, March 2	Tax collector advertises unpaid 1997 taxes that are liens on real property.
Wednesday, April 15	Listing deadline for taxpayers who have been granted extensions of time in which to list.
Friday, April 24	Assessor publishes legal notice of beginning of review and appeal process.
Monday, May 4	Review and appeal process begins when board of equalization and review holds its first meeting.
Monday, May 23	Deadline for taxpayers to file requests for review of listings and assessments by board of equalization and review.
Tuesday, June 30	Close of 1997–98 fiscal year.
Wednesday, July 1	Beginning of 1998–99 fiscal year. (Counties and cities should adopt their 1998–99 budgets and set their tax rates before start of new fiscal year. Statutory deadline for budget adoption is July 1.)
Mid-July to mid-August	Tax notices should be mailed as soon as possible after tax rate is set.
Tuesday, September 1	Due date for 1998–99 taxes.

The laws governing property tax administration make no provision for prorating property tax liability when real property is sold. The land remains subject to the full amount of taxes levied for the current fiscal year no matter who owns it at what point in the tax cycle. This basic fact is obscured, however, by the universal custom of prorating property taxes between the buyer and the seller when land is sold. Usually, the seller's share will be deducted from the price to be paid by the buyer. For purposes of property tax administration, it is important to emphasize that these proration agreements are nothing more than private bargains between buyers and sellers.

The other circumstance that leads to much misunderstanding of the property tax cycle arises when a city or town takes in new areas by annexation. The municipal annexation law provides that newly annexed areas are subject to property taxes in proportion to the period of time that the area will have been within the city during the current tax year. Usually, taxpayers in the annexed area are surprised when they are billed for prorated municipal taxes because they think of the property tax in terms of the calendar year, not the fiscal year. On the other hand, there is no statute requiring proration of property taxes for territory added to fire districts, sanitary districts, and other special taxing districts. In the case of special taxing districts, the critical date is July 1. If property is within the tax district on July 1, it is subject to the full tax levy for the current year; if not within the district on July 1, it cannot be taxed by the district for the current year. There are special statutes that require cities annexing portions of fire tax districts to make partial refunds of fire district taxes to property owners in the annexed area.[9] Otherwise, the statute requiring proration of municipal taxes upon annexation would result in property owners paying twice for fire protection in the same fiscal year.

The Machinery Act

The North Carolina statute that governs property tax administration is called the Machinery Act. This quaint title dates from the nineteenth century and uses the word "machinery" in the sense of the means or procedures by which a desired result is obtained. When the state levied a property tax and all state taxes were levied anew with each biennial session of the General Assembly, each legislative session adopted a Revenue Act to finance the operations of state government for the upcoming biennium and a Machinery Act to specify how taxes levied in the Revenue Act would be assessed and collected. Local governments used the same procedures, or "machinery," to levy their own property taxes. The Machinery Act was made permanent in 1937, as was the Revenue Act. The Revenue Act now forms Subchapter I of Chapter 105 of the General Statutes of North Carolina. The Machinery Act forms Subchapter II of Chapter 105. When the state ceased levying property taxes after 1921, the Machinery Act became exclusively concerned with local tax administration. Nevertheless, it remains in the chapter of the General Statutes that includes the statutes levying state taxes and providing for their administration.

Real and Personal Property

A full understanding of the property tax requires a basic understanding of the legal concepts that underlie ownership of land and other things. The concept of property embodies the idea that one person or a group of persons can claim exclusive ownership of a specific area of land or some other thing, and is a very ancient concept. In the United States, ideas about the nature of property are derived from English common law.

The common law divided all property into two great categories, real and personal. Real property was by far the most important of the two, and for that reason the laws defining the nature of real property ownership soon became very complex. In the earliest days the types of personal property with which the law concerned itself were few. Horses and other livestock were important forms of wealth, as were armor, weapons, furniture, jewels, fine clothing, and gold and silver plate. The laws were structured so that land was seldom sold and often could not be disposed of by will. Ownership of land was established by written documents and passed from one generation to the next in accordance with the terms of the original land grant or the laws of intestate succession. Only the king was considered capable of owning land absolutely; every other landowner held his land subject to feudal obligations to an overlord. Disputes about land ownership were resolved in the common law courts.

The laws governing personal property were much simpler. There usually were no written documents establishing one's ownership of such things as horses and furniture. Possession of such things was considered sufficient proof of ownership in the absence of controversy. Personal property could, on the whole, be freely sold and disposed of by will.

At first, personal property consisted of things that could be picked up and carried around and had intrinsic value. Even money shared these characteristics. The value of coins came from the gold or silver of which they were made; the king's imprint on the coin was nothing more than assurance that the precious metal content of the coin met certain minimum specifications. In modern times a new species of personal property has come into being. These are types of property that have no intrinsic value in and of themselves, but might represent great value. Paper money is perhaps the best example. The paper itself is essentially worthless, but the value it represents may be great or small depending on the solvency of the government that issues it and the denomination of the bill. Shares of stock in corporations are similar. Some stock certificates can be very valuable; others are worthless.

Real Property Defined

The Machinery Act defines *real property* as the land itself; all buildings, structures, improvements, and permanent fixtures on the land; and all rights and privileges attached to the land [G.S. 105-273(13)]. This definition draws no distinction between the concept of the property itself and the nature of the ownership of the property. Real property includes all rights in the land, no matter how ownership may be divided among several owners, and all buildings, structures, and other improvements on the land. Minerals under the surface of the land are real property, and so is the air above it. Old writers used to say that ownership of the surface extended down to the center of the earth and up infinitely into the heavens. The invention of aircraft has made obsolete the idea of owning an infinite quantity of air space, but landowners still retain air rights that adjoining landowners cannot invade. Other forms of real property include standing timber and water rights.

Taxability of All Rights in Land

This concept of real property has important consequences for the property tax. In North Carolina it is not the value of the listing owner's interest in the land that is subject to taxation but the entire value of all property interests in the land. It is possible that the ownership of land may be split into several rights that are held by different people. The traditional metaphor for thinking of rights in land is a bundle of sticks. Sometimes one person owns all of the sticks. Sometimes one or more sticks have been removed from the bundle and belong to someone else. For property tax purposes all of the bundle is potentially taxable. Two illustrations will make this clear: land held in a life estate, and rental property subject to long-term leases.

The classic example of property interests divided among several people is the life estate. Here, one owner, the *life tenant*, has the right of current possession and the right to all of the rents and profits from the land for his or her lifetime but does not have the right to sell the land or dispose of it by will. Some of the sticks have been removed from the bundle and belong to other owners, who are known as *remaindermen*. Upon the death of the life tenant all of the sticks in the bundle will belong to the remaindermen, who only then become full owners of the property. North Carolina taxes the entire value of all interests in this form of ownership. The property is appraised as if both the life tenant and all the remaindermen were willing to sell their respective interests at the same time to the same buyer.

Rental property subject to long-term leases provides a similar example. Here, the right of possession of the property has been leased to another for a specific term of years, often at a fixed monthly or annual rent that cannot be adjusted for inflation or other changes in market conditions. The landlord can sell his or her underlying ownership of the property but cannot evict the tenants until the lease expires. A purchaser will take the building subject to the outstanding leases. If the rent being paid under the leases is less than the current market demands for similar space, the value of the landlord's ownership interest can be adversely affected. The difference will depend on the gap between market rent and rent under the leases, and how long the leases have to run. Conversely, the value of the leasehold interests held by the tenants will be enhanced. This kind of property is also taxed as if all of the sticks in the ownership bundle belonged to one owner.[10]

Personal Property Defined

The Machinery Act adds little to the definition of personal property beyond what has already been related. Essentially, the statute says that personal property includes everything that is not real property [G.S. 105-275(14)]. There are two kinds of personal property, tangible and intangible. Tangible personal property consists of things like machinery, furniture, and vehicles. The principal types of tangible personal property that are subject to *ad valorem* taxes are motor vehicles, aircraft, boats, manufactured homes, and business machinery, furnishings, and equipment. Intangible personal property consists of things like money, shares of stock, copyrights, and patents. Except for some types of computer software and leasehold interests in exempt real property, no intangible personal property is now subject to *ad valorem* taxes.

Leasehold Interests in Exempt Real Property

The one item of taxable personal property that seems odd at first glance is leasehold interests in exempted real property. For historical reasons that are beyond the scope of this chapter, leasehold interests in real property did not fit comfortably into the theories underlying the English common law of land ownership. Lessees were never recognized as landowners, although they did enjoy some of the perquisites that went along with ownership. The best the common law could do was to invent the idea of the *chattel real* to describe possessory interests that did not qualify as ownership. This term simply combined the common law term for personal property—chattel—with the word used to describe ownership of land. Ordinarily, whether leasehold interests in real property are real or personal property is of no concern to property tax administrators because the entire bundle of rights is taxed to the landlord. It only becomes a concern when all of the ownership rights except the leasehold interest are exempt from taxes. In that case, the Machinery Act categorizes the possessory rights of the lessee as a species of taxable intangible personal property.

The Listing Owner

For the convenience of taxpayers and property tax administrators alike, the Machinery Act specifies who is to be considered the owner of property for purposes of property taxes. This owner is said to be the *listing owner*. Noted earlier are two major instances when the listing owner does not own the entire bundle of rights: property subject to a life estate and property subject to long-term leases. A third example is owners of time-share interests in resort property. In each of these instances and others, the Machinery Act specifies who is to be considered the listing owner and places on that person the duty to list the property. Taxes will then be billed in the name of the listing owner, and the tax collector looks to that person for payment.

The Administrative Structure

The Machinery Act prescribes the basic administrative structure for listing, assessing, and collecting property taxes. Two county officers stand at the heart of this structure: the county assessor and the county tax collector. Supervising them are the county commissioners, who name them, pay them, and provide them with assistance. Working for them are employees whom they select and who work under their direction. At the state level these officers come under the jurisdiction of the Department of Revenue and the Property Tax Commission.

The Machinery Act assumes but does not require that the county assessor and the tax collector head separate departments and that they report to the board of commissioners and relate to the county manager independently of each other. That is the pattern in some counties, but increasingly, counties have found advantages in locating all property tax functions in a single tax department under one department head. Some counties accomplish this by appointing the same person as both assessor and tax collector. Others appoint a tax administrator who heads a combined tax department. The tax administrator may also be appointed as county assessor or tax collector or both, but often another person is appointed to hold one of those offices. The Machinery Act is flexible enough to permit almost any form of administrative organization for the tax department that the county commissioners and county manager prefer, as long as the statutory duties of assessor and collector are formally conferred on someone and are carried out according to law.

The work of the county assessor is subject to review by the county board of equalization and review. The principal function of this board is to hear and decide taxpayer appeals. In many counties the board of equalization and review is composed of the county commissioners, who sit for that purpose for a limited time each year. In other counties there are special boards of equalization and review appointed by the county commissioners. Some of these special boards have been created by local act of the General Assembly. Others have been created by resolution of the board of county commissioners pursuant to general enabling legislation.

At the state level, over and above the county officials, are the Department of Revenue and the Property Tax Commission. As an administrative agency, the Department of Revenue is charged with supervising the valuation and taxation of property by local units of government and, in limited cases, with appraising property for local taxation. The Property Tax Commission is an administrative appeals board that has the power to review and change listing and valuation decisions made by local officials or the Department of Revenue.

Terms and Qualifications of the County Assessor

The county assessor is appointed directly by the board of county commissioners rather than by the county manager. The term of office is two years, beginning on July 1 of odd-numbered years. An assessor who has completed a two-year term and has been certified by the Department of Revenue may be reappointed for a four-year term, at the discretion of the board. The commissioners may remove the assessor at any time for good cause after giving him or her notice in writing and an opportunity to appear and be heard at a public session of the board.

Persons appointed as assessor must be certified by the Department of Revenue. A prospective assessor must complete satisfactorily four basic training courses and a comprehensive examination. New appointees have two years to complete these requirements and are not eligible for reappointment if they fail to do so within the time allowed. Assessors are also required to complete at least thirty hours of continuing education instruction every two years in order to remain eligible for reappointment upon expiration of their terms.

The Listing Process

Under G.S. 105-301 through -312, all taxable property, both real and personal, must be listed for taxation each year. In all counties, persons and business entities that own taxable personal property have the legal responsibility to list that property with the appropriate taxing units. In counties that have adopted a permanent listing system for real property, responsibility for listing taxable real property rests on the county assessor. The owner of real property in those counties has only a duty to report to the assessor any change that has occurred in the previous year. In counties that have not adopted permanent listing, taxpayers must list all their taxable real property each year. Failure to comply with these listing and reporting requirements results in an automatic penalty: 10 percent of the amount of tax that will become due for the following fiscal year.

Roles of the County and the City in the Listing Process

Real and personal property must always be listed with county officials. The *abstract*, that is, the listing form, must indicate the city and the special districts, if any, in which the property is also situated. The county commissioners are almost always the tax-levying authority for special districts; therefore they perform the listing function for those districts as well as for the county.

Cities have a choice in listing property. They may copy their listings from the county records, or if they prefer, they may set up their own machinery for securing lists of property subject to municipal taxation. Cities that copy their listings from county records remain responsible for deciding for themselves whether specific property should be listed for taxation or be granted immunity. This responsibility is independent of county decisions about the same property. If a county and a city differ on whether certain property is entitled to exemption or other preferential treatment, the owner may appeal to the Property Tax Commission for resolution of the dispute.

Although a city may elect to do its own listing, it must accept the property valuations fixed by the county authorities unless it lies in more than one county. (In that case G.S. 105-328 grants special appraisal authority to the city.) The requirement that cities accept county valuations of property has led most of them to copy county listings rather than make their own.

Location of Property for Listing Purposes: A Matter of Jurisdiction

G.S. 105-301, -304, and -305 determine where property is taxable. By its nature, real property is fixed in one location; thus the law logically provides that taxable real property must be listed in the county in which it is situated. If real property is located within the boundaries of a city or a special tax district, that fact must be indicated on the abstract when the property is listed.

On the other hand, the very essence of personal property is its mobility. Determining the place where it is taxable demands more complicated rules. In general, if personal property is within the jurisdiction of the state, the Machinery Act makes the owner's North Carolina residence (or lack of residence) the key fact in determining where his or her personal property is to be listed. Thus the local unit in which the owner resides ordinarily has the right to tax his or her personal property. If the property is held or used at the owner's business premises, however, it must be taxed there. This requirement makes it essential to determine the "residence" of business firms as well as of individuals.

The Listing Period

Taxable property must be listed in the name of the person who owned it on January 1 of a given year. In counties using a permanent listing system, the assessor lists taxable real property each year. Property owners submit reports of new construction and other changes to their property, and persons owning taxable personal property submit the appropriate listing forms. In counties not using a permanent listing system, each taxpayer must submit a listing form disclosing all of his or her taxable real and personal property situated in the county. Listing forms must be returned to the county tax office during the regular listing period, which runs through the month of January. Extensions of time in which to list may be obtained on written application filed during the regular listing period. Extensions may not run later than April 15.

Property Not Subject to Taxation: Requests for Tax Relief

Under G.S. 105-282.1, exempt and excluded property is not required to be listed, but owners of such property have the burden of demonstrating to tax authorities that it qualifies for this preferential treatment by filing a request for tax relief. This is normally done during the regular listing period. (No request need be made for government-owned and certain other types of property.)

For most of the property currently granted tax immunity or other preferential treatment by the Machinery Act, requests for relief must be made only once, then revised thereafter when improvements or additions are made or a change in use occurs. However, for some types of business-related exempt and classified property, annual requests for relief must be made.

As the requests are made or revised, tax officials are expected to review them to ensure that the property in question qualifies for the relief requested. If a request for relief is required but has not been made, the property involved is treated the same as property for which a required listing was not made.

The board of county commissioners has authority to allow a property owner to file a late application for exemption or exclusion "for good cause" but not after the close of the calendar year for the current year's taxes. Thus a property owner who fails to apply for exemption for 1998 taxes during the 1998 listing period may ask the board of commissioners to accept a late application at any time up until December 31, 1998.

The Homestead Exclusion

One of the most widely applicable exclusions from the tax base is the *homestead* exclusion, which provides partial property tax relief for elderly or disabled low-income people who own their own homes. An individual who is sixty-five or older or who is permanently and totally disabled and who had a disposable income of not more than $15,000 in the preceding calendar year may have excluded from property taxes the first $20,000 in tax value of his or her permanent residence. Social Security, retirement benefits, public assistance payments, and any other form of income except gifts or inheritances are counted against the income limit. Homeowners must apply for the benefit of this exclusion, but once an application is approved, it remains valid for succeeding tax years, assuming there has been no change in circumstances that affects eligibility. Local governments are reimbursed for the revenue loss occasioned by this exclusion by annual appropriations in the state budget.

The Valuation Process

Statutory Elements of Value

The North Carolina Constitution contains no instructions on how property is to be valued for tax purposes. It simply states that if property is taxed, the General Assembly may divide it into classes, and as long as the taxes are uniform in their application within a class, they will be upheld.

Market-Value Standard

Although the state constitution is silent on the valuation process, the Machinery Act specifies in detail the valuation standard, the factors to be considered in arriving at an estimate of value, and the procedures that assessors must follow in appraising property for taxes. All property not singled out for preferential treatment is subject to a single valuation standard. G.S. 105-283 defines the *market-value standard* as follows:

> All property, real and personal, shall as far as practicable be appraised or valued at its true value in money. . . . that is, the price estimated in terms of money at which the property would change hands between a willing and financially able buyer and a willing seller, neither being under any compulsion to buy or to sell and both having reasonable knowledge of all the uses to which the property is adapted and for which it is capable of being used.

The standard draws no distinction between real and personal property and allows no room for arbitrary methods of appraisal that are not directly based on the operation of the free market.

Use-Value Appraisal of Farmlands

In 1973 the General Assembly enacted the only instance in the Machinery Act of a departure from the market-value standard of tax appraisal (G.S. 105-277.2 through -277.6). Land used for agricultural, horticultural, or forestry purposes, if it meets certain other qualifications, may be taxed on the basis of its value in its present use, even though it may have a greater market value for other uses. G.S. 105-277.2 defines *present-use value* as "the value of land in its current use as agricultural land, horticultural land, or forestland, based solely on its ability to produce income, using a rate of nine percent (9%) to capitalize the expected net income of the property and assuming an average level of management."

Market value still plays an important part in the taxation of farmland and forestland, however. If the land ceases to be used for agricultural, horticultural, or forestry purposes, or if title passes to someone outside the immediate family of the owner, a *deferred tax* must be paid. The amount of this tax is the difference between the taxes paid based on the use value and the taxes that would have been paid based on the market value for the preceding three years. The county has responsibility for performing use-value appraisals when requested, just as it must make market-value appraisals.

Time for Appraisal

G.S. 105-285 through -287 establishes the time for appraisal.

Personal Property

Personal property must be appraised each year when it is listed for taxation. The law assumes that the true value of personal property fluctuates rapidly; therefore the law insists that the value of personal property be examined annually. This annual appraisal may be a simple process, as in determining the value of an automobile, or it may be highly complex, as in selecting an appropriate depreciation rate for unusual industrial machinery. The day as of which the value of property is to be determined is January 1.

Real Property

The North Carolina law adopts a different attitude toward real property. It assumes that real property values do not fluctuate rapidly and, accepting some of the practical arguments against too frequent appraisal, requires that all real property be reappraised only every eight years.

G.S. 105-286 divides the counties of the state into eight groups and establishes an *octennial revaluation schedule*, that is, a base revaluation year for each group. Each county must conduct a general revaluation of real property in the base year for its group and every eighth year thereafter. This establishes the minimum level of effort required of the county.

A county may find it desirable to revalue real property before the end of its current eight-year cycle. The law places no obstacles in the path of a county wanting to do so. Several counties are moving toward cycles of four or five years rather than eight. The legal effect of conducting a revaluation earlier than the law specifies is simply to require that the next revaluation take place within eight years thereafter; the county is not thereafter bound to adhere to the shorter cycle.

Appraisal Techniques

Having established market value as the appraisal goal, the North Carolina tax statutes go on to indicate what factors should be considered in determining the value of property (G.S. 105-317, -317.1). With regard to personal property, the appraiser must consider the following for each item (or each lot of similar items): replacement cost; sale price of similar property; age; physical condition; productivity; remaining life; obsolescence; economic utility (that is, usability and adaptability for industrial, commercial, or other purposes); and any other factor that may affect its value. Although this statement is not entirely satisfactory, it is valuable as a guide for the appraiser. In effect, it requires him or her to employ every reasonable factor available in deciding on the true value of personal property.

County appraisers have developed many techniques for estimating the market value of various types of personal property. Industry pricing guides are available for such major categories as motor vehicles, mobile homes, boats, and aircraft. For machinery and equipment the current value may be estimated by depreciating the original cost to acquire the item according to a standard depreciation schedule. This technique is further refined in many counties by factoring or "trending" the original cost to current market levels before applying the standard depreciation factor.

Mass Appraisal of Real Property

A general revaluation of real property is a big undertaking. The typical county has more than 40,000 parcels of land that must be individually appraised. The process must begin early enough to have the results ready in time for tax billing in the revaluation year but not so early that the value estimates will be out of date by the time they take effect. Also, the cost of the revaluation must be reasonable. A person who is borrowing money from a lending institution to buy a new house can expect to pay about $275 for an appraisal of the house and the lot. A tax appraisal must cost much less than that. Most counties want it done for $16 to $18 per parcel (these figures assume that the revaluation does not entail extra features, such as installing a new computer-based office system). Obviously, to accomplish a job of such magnitude at reasonable cost requires specialized appraisal techniques that rapidly, efficiently, and economically yield a high degree of accuracy.

Development of an Appraisal Manual for Establishing Market Value

G.S. 105-317 lays out the essential elements of a modern mass appraisal system that accomplishes the objective just summarized. The foundation of the system is the assessor's *appraisal manual* or, as the statute describes it, a "uniform schedule of values, standards, and rules to be used in appraising real property in the county." The manual is formulated from two basic sources: the local real estate market and nationally developed data on the cost of building construction, adjusted to reflect local building costs. The manual identifies a large number of characteristics exhibited by real property in the county and indicates the dollar amount that each characteristic can normally be expected to contribute to the value of a given parcel of land or a given building according to a unit of measure appropriate to the characteristic. For example, the appraisal manual contains a land schedule. For agricultural land or forestland the appropriate unit of measure is usually the acre, whereas urban land is typically measured by square footage, front footage (the number of feet of a lot that fronts on a street), or standard-size lot (such as the 100- by 200-foot lot often found in newer subdivisions). Buildings are usually measured by square footage.

The value increments attributed to the various units of measurement vary considerably. Some land may be worth $5,000 per acre, other land only $400 per acre. Buildings of top-quality construction may be priced at $80 or more per square foot, lower-quality buildings at $50. Other characteristics may increase or reduce the value indicated by the basic unit of measurement. Agricultural land may be decreased in value by poor soil or topography. The value of an urban residential lot may be adversely affected by other development in the neighborhood. The value of buildings is always adjusted to reflect accrued depreciation.

The characteristics just mentioned are but the tip of the iceberg; a well-conceived appraisal manual will identify many more. The manual is a comprehensive, complex document designed to enable the assessor to estimate the value of thousands of parcels and buildings accurately, efficiently, and rapidly by means of a manageable number of characteristics that influence value.

Developing the appraisal manual is the single most important step in a revaluation. The manual's designation of the property characteristics to be examined and the value increment to be attributed to each determines the accuracy with which the assessor can estimate the fair market value of real property in the county. If the manual sets values too high, most properties will be appraised higher than market value. If the values are too low, most properties will be underappraised. If too few characteristics are used, the accuracy of appraisals will vary widely from parcel to parcel. If too many are used, the assessor may not be able to complete the job on time. Because the appraisal manual is so important, the Machinery Act requires that it be formally approved by the board of county commissioners. The act also permits any property owner of the county to test the validity of the appraisal manual before the Property Tax Commission.

Development of a Special Schedule for Establishing Present-Use Value

Similarly, the assessor establishes a special schedule for appraising eligible agricultural land, horticultural land, and forestland at its present-use value. For this purpose he or she has available a statewide valuation manual prepared by the Department of Revenue with the assistance of the Use-Value Advisory Board, which is composed of representatives of the Agricultural Extension Service, the state Department of Agriculture, and the state Division of Forest Resources. This manual is based on the net income per acre that can be anticipated from growing corn and soybeans in each soil type found in the state. Use of the Department of Revenue's manual is not mandatory, but it carries great authority.

Approval of the Manuals

After the manuals on market value and present-use value have been prepared and a public hearing has been held, the board of county commissioners adopts them and places a newspaper notice stating that it has done so. Property owners then have thirty days to challenge the manuals by appeal to the state Property Tax Commission on grounds that the manuals do not adhere to the appropriate statutory valuation standard (that is, that they will produce values that are too high, too low, or inconsistent). The commission has the power to order the board of county commissioners to revise the manuals if they do not adhere to the statutory valuation standard, and it has done so on occasion. The commission's decision may be appealed to the North Carolina Court of Appeals.

Preparation of Record Cards

After the manuals are adopted, the assessor prepares a record card for each parcel of land in the county. On this card he or she notes all the characteristics of the parcel that will be considered in making the appraisal. Although land and the buildings on it are appraised separately, data for both appear on the same property record card. The Machinery Act specifically directs the assessor to show on the card all characteristics considered in appraising the parcel, points out that they must be consistent with the appraisal manual, and requires that the data be accurate.

Collecting data about property characteristics is called *listing* the property. For buildings this process consists of measuring their outside perimeter, showing special features such as air conditioning and the number of bathrooms, and recording such crucial factors as depreciation and quality or grade of construction. For agricultural land and forestland, the process is similar but simpler. Characteristics of such land usually include the number of acres in the tract, its road frontage if the manual identifies this as a relevant characteristic, its fertility or productivity grade, and any crop allotments. Much of this information can be gathered by persons who are not trained appraisers; for example, no advanced training is needed to measure a house or compute the number of acres in a tract of land from the tax map. Other computations, such as estimating depreciation, require trained and experienced personnel.

Appraisal of Property

After the basic data have been gathered and recorded on the property record card, the parcel is appraised. G.S. 105-317 requires that a competent appraiser do this for each parcel individually. The first step is usually carried out mechanically. The property characteristics gathered by the listers are used to compute a preliminary value estimate according to the value increments set out in the manual for those characteristics. This value is tentatively recorded on the property record card. The appraiser then takes the cards into the field and revisits each property. This procedure, known as the *review*, is the critical fine-tuning step in which the training, experience, and judgment of the appraiser play a large part. Recognizing the crucial importance of appraising property on the basis of accurate data, G.S. 105-317 gives each property owner the right to have the assessor (or one of the assessor's agents or employees) actually visit and observe the property to verify the accuracy of characteristics on record for it.

Notice to Property Owners

The Machinery Act requires that when the final review has been completed, the assessor send each property owner a written notice of the appraised value on each parcel owned by that person. At this point nearly all assessors allow for a period of informal appeals that is not required by law. Typically the value notice sent to taxpayers states that they may contact the assessor for an appointment to review the appraisal if they believe it to be in error. Most counties engage the services of a professional appraisal company to assist in the revaluation, although the legal responsibility remains entirely in the hands of the assessor appointed by the county commissioners. If professional appraisers have helped in the revaluation, taxpayers may obtain an appointment with the company appraiser, at which they may be able to persuade him or her that a mistake was made in measurement, calculation, or judgment. The time allowed for these informal appeals is within the discretion of the assessor.

Formal Appraisal and Assessment

When the informal appeal process is over, the assessor formally appraises and assesses each parcel. Ideally the appraisals are adopted before January 1 of the revaluation year. This may not always be possible because the appraisal may take more time than was planned or there may be more informal appeals than were expected. In any event, after the assessor has adopted the appraisals, the taxpayer may appeal directly to the assessor at any time before the county board of equalization and review convenes.

Valuation Appeals

G.S. 105-322 governs listing and valuation appeals. The county board of equalization and review is the local body charged with hearing property tax appeals. It also has the power to correct the tax lists or to increase or reduce values on its own motion if it finds such action to be warranted. As explained earlier, in most counties the board of equalization and review is the board of county commissioners sitting in another capacity. In some counties, however, the board of commissioners has created a special board to hear appeals. In others a special board has been created by local act of the General Assembly. In all counties the primary work of the board of equalization and review is essentially the same: to hear and decide valuation appeals. The board convenes no earlier than the first Monday in April and no later than the first Monday in May. It sits for at least four weeks and may meet longer if needed. It may not sit later than July 1 except to decide appeals filed before that date. Before the board convenes, it must publish its hours of operation in a newspaper. It must also publish any change in that schedule.

A taxpayer appealing a listing or an appraisal may simply appear at a scheduled meeting of the board of equalization and review, but writing or calling for an appointment is always preferable. Proceedings before a county board of equalization and review are informal. However, the appealing taxpayer should expect that the board will want specific testimony on why the taxpayer is entitled to the relief he or she is seeking. The most persuasive evidence in a valuation appeal is the testimony (oral or written) of a qualified appraiser who disagrees with the assessor's appraisal.

The Property Tax Commission hears appeals from the county boards of equalization and review across the state. The commission's hearings are more formal than those of the county board's but are still relatively informal compared with court proceedings. Testimony is recorded and may be transcribed, documentary evidence is formally introduced, and both sides must be represented by attorneys except for a property owner who chooses to present his or her own case. An appellant taxpayer who believes that the Property Tax Commission made an error of law in reaching its decision on his or her property may appeal further to the North Carolina Court of Appeals. Normally this is the court of last resort. The North Carolina Supreme Court will hear a property tax appeal only if the court of appeals was not unanimous in its decision or if the supreme court believes that a major issue of law in the case warrants its attention.

Adjustment of Real Property Values in Nonrevaluation Years

The North Carolina plan for taxing property envisions annual appraisal of personal property and octennial appraisal of real property. Yet for the sake of equity and uniformity, some parcels of real property may need reappraisal in a year in which general revaluation of real property is not undertaken. G.S. 105-287 directs the assessor in a nonrevaluation year to reappraise specific parcels in order to correct clerical or mathematical errors in the former appraisal; correct appraisal errors resulting from misapplication of the county's appraisal manual; or recognize an increase or a decrease in value resulting from some factor other than normal depreciation, economic changes affecting property in general, or certain improvements such as repainting and landscaping. Reappraisals made under the authority of G.S. 105-287 must conform to the appraisal manual adopted in the last revaluation year so that they will represent market or present-use value as of January 1 of the revaluation year, rather than current value. Also, these appraisals take effect as of January 1 of the year in which they are made and do not affect previous tax years.

Discovered Property

To *discover* property, as the expression is used in the tax statutes, means to find that an item of taxable property has not been listed for taxation during the annual listing period established by law or has been listed at a substantial understatement of value, quantity, or other measurement. Under G.S. 105-312 it is the duty of the assessor to see that all property not properly listed during the regular listing period is accurately listed, assessed, and taxed. The assessor is also required to file reports of such discoveries with the governing boards of all taxing units affected by the discovery at such times and in such form as those boards may require.

When unlisted real or personal property has been identified, the county assessor must first sign an abstract listing it and then make a tentative appraisal of it, in accordance with the best information available. The assessor must then mail a notice to the person in whose name it has been listed. This notice must give the name and the address of that person, a brief description and tentative appraisal of the property, and a statement to the effect that the taxpayer has thirty days in which to object to the listing and the appraisal.

If the taxpayer objects in writing within the thirty-day period, the assessor must arrange a conference to give the taxpayer an opportunity to present any evidence or argument regarding the discovery. The assessor must make a final decision within fifteen days, and the taxpayer has fifteen days (measured from the time at which he or she is officially notified of the decision) to appeal that decision. Both the listing and the appraisal are subject to the right of appeal to the board of county commissioners and from there to the Property Tax Commission.

When property is found not to be listed for a given year, it has often not been listed for a number of years or perhaps has never been listed. Accordingly there is a statutory presumption that it should have been listed by the same taxpayer for the preceding five years. The taxpayer can overcome this presumption by showing that the property was not in existence, that it was actually listed for taxation, or that it was not his or her duty to list the property during all or some of the years in question.

The penalty for failing to list property for taxes is an amount equal to 10 percent of the tax for each listing period that has elapsed since the failure to list occurred. For example, if a taxpayer failed to list his or her property for 1992 taxes and was subjected to discovery procedures in September 1997, the penalty for the 1992 failure to list would be 60 percent of the tax. If the taxpayer had failed to list the same item of property for each of the intervening years, the penalty rates would be 50 percent for 1993, 40 percent for 1994, and so on down to 10 percent for 1997.

Special cases may arise in which the county commissioners feel that the statutory provisions place an undue burden on the property owner.

In such situations the board is empowered to reduce the penalty (or even the principal amount of the tax) to what it finds to be equitable. This authority does not arise until the discovery procedures have been completed, and it may be exercised only on written petition of the tax-payer. The assessor has no authority to waive any part of the penalty or the tax, and the board may not delegate such authority to him or her. Because each request for relief is unique, the board should act on it individually.

Part 2: Collection of the Property Tax

Office of Tax Collector

Counties with special legislation that provides a method (either elective or appointive) for selecting tax collectors must adhere to the provisions of that legislation relating to the tax collector's selection and term of office [G.S. 105-395(c)]. In the absence of special legislation, the governing body of each county must appoint a tax collector, for a term to be determined by the appointing body, to collect the taxes levied by the county [G.S. 105-349(a)]. Ordinarily, collectors are named early enough in the fiscal year to prepare themselves to take over the new taxes when the time comes for collection.

Often persons charged with tax collection also have other duties. For example, as noted earlier, it is increasingly common for the same person to serve as both assessor and tax collector. The Machinery Act declares the office of tax collector to be "an office that may be held concurrently with any appointive or elective office other than those hereinafter designated, and the governing body may appoint as tax collector any appointive or elective officer who meets the personal and bonding requirements" (discussed under the next section, "Qualification as Tax Collector") [G.S. 105-349(e)]. Only two restrictions are placed on double-office-holding by collectors, but they are important:

> A member of the governing body of a taxing unit may not be appointed tax collector, nor may the duties of the office be conferred upon him. A person appointed or elected as treasurer or chief accounting officer of a taxing unit may not be appointed tax collector, nor may the duties of the office of tax collector be conferred upon him except with the written permission of the secretary of the Local Government Commission who,

before giving his permission, shall satisfy himself that the unit's internal control procedures are sufficient to prevent improper handling of public funds [G.S. 105-349(e)].

Virtually all counties pay their collectors salaries, often a travel allowance as well. A few delinquent collectors are paid wholly or in part from commissions on collections. The Machinery Act provides simply that "[t]he compensation and expense allowances of the tax collector shall be fixed by the governing body" of the taxing unit [G.S. 105-349(d)].

Qualification as Tax Collector

Boards of county commissioners are not free to assign collection responsibility for any tax year to an individual unless the person selected can meet the prescribed legal standards [G.S. 105-352(b)]:

> Before the tax receipts for the current year are delivered to the tax collector, he shall have:
> (1) Delivered to the chief accounting officer of the taxing unit the duplicate receipts issued for prepayments received by the tax collector.
> (2) Demonstrated to the satisfaction of the chief accounting officer that all moneys received by the tax collector as prepayments have been deposited to the credit of the taxing unit.
> (3) Made his annual settlement . . . for all taxes in his hands for collection.
> (4) Provided bond or bonds as required by [law] for taxes for the current year and all prior years in his hands for collection. . . .

This could hardly be plainer. Proper settlement for prepayments, proper settlement for prior years' taxes, and a proper bond to cover the new and old taxes that the tax collector is to collect are prerequisites to delivery of the tax books to the collector. The word *settlement* as used in this connection has a technical meaning (see the discussion under the section "Settlements," later in this chapter).

The courts have not defined *satisfactory bond* for a local tax collector. A useful test might be a reasonable approximation of the maximum amount of money that the collector will have in his or her hands at any one time, plus a reasonable allowance for cumulative losses.

By law, any member of a governing body who votes to deliver the tax receipts to the tax collector before the collector has met the requirements just listed is individually liable for the amount of taxes charged against the tax collector for which he or she has not made satisfactory settlement. Any member who so votes is also guilty of a misdemeanor punishable by fine or imprisonment, or both, at the discretion of the court [G.S. 105-352(d)(1)].

Removal of the Tax Collector

Collectors who cannot meet the bonding and settlement requirements outlined in the preceding section are not entitled to serve and may be removed or simply not permitted to enter on collection work. However, cases may arise in which it is questionable whether a collector should be permitted to remain in office, even though he or she has met the statutory prerequisites and conditions. The manner in which a tax collector may be removed depends on the source of law under which he or she holds office. Because the Machinery Act preserves local legislation relating to the selection of tax collectors [G.S. 105-395(c)], pertinent provisions of the special act creating the tax collector's office in a given unit may control the circumstances and procedures under which he or she may be dismissed. Governing bodies of units subject to such local legislation should seek the advice of their attorneys before attempting to remove a tax collector from office, especially if the collector is an elected official. The Machinery Act gives the county commissioners express authority to remove the tax collector from office during the tax collector's term for good cause after giving notice in writing and an opportunity to appear and be heard at a public session of the council [G.S. 105-349(a)]. *Cause* in this sense refers to reasons recognized by the law and sound public policy as sufficient warrant for removal—that is, *legal cause*, not merely cause that the appointing power in exercising its discretion may deem sufficient. Moreover, the cause must relate to and affect the administration of the office and must be restricted to something of a substantial nature directly affecting the rights and the interests of the public.[11] For example, misappropriation of funds would be cause for discharge.

Deputy Tax Collectors

Boards of county commissioners are free to decide whether to name deputy tax collectors. They also have the authority to set the term and the pay of each deputy collector as well as the amount of his or her bond. Most importantly, unless the board specifically limits the scope of the deputy's authority, he or she has the authority to perform, under the direction of the tax collector, any act that the tax collector may perform [G.S. 105-349(f)].

Necessary Collection Records

The words *tax records* as used in the Machinery Act have a precise and technical meaning. Two records are included: the *scroll*, which the law defines as the record of property valuations; and the *tax book*, which the law defines as the record of taxes due. The two may be combined [G.S. 105-319(a)], and they customarily are. This combined record is usually called the scroll but not always. The originals of both county records must be kept in the office of the county assessor unless the board requires them to be filed in some other public office of the county. The law permits the governing body to give the collector a copy of the scroll when he or she is charged with collection [G.S. 105-319(a)].

Apart from the tax records, the most important document in the collection process is the *tax receipt*. The primary purpose of the tax receipt is twofold: to furnish the taxpayer with evidence of payment and to furnish the tax collector with the payment information necessary to support a credit in the settlement. Receipts may be prepared in sufficient copies to provide a tax notice, possibly a second notice, an official receipt for delivery to the taxpayer on payment, an auditor's copy, and an office or permanent copy, depending largely on the complexity of the accounting procedures of a particular county. The law specifies the minimum information to be shown on the receipt given the taxpayer [G.S. 105-320(a)]. One of the required entries is "[t]he rate of tax levied for each unit-wide purpose, the total rate levied for all unit-wide purposes, and the rate levied by or for any special district or subdivision of the unit" [G.S. 105-320(a)]. This breakdown may not be finally determined until shortly before the deadline for setting the tax rate (July 1 for all units; see Chapter 10); thus to avoid delay in having receipt forms printed, the statute allows this information to be furnished on a separate sheet of paper, properly identified, when the official receipt is delivered on payment [G.S. 105-320(a)(6)].

North Carolina law does not require that property owners be sent or receive bills or notices of taxes due. On the contrary, "[a]ll persons who have or may acquire any interest in any real or personal property" are charged with notice that their property is or should be listed for taxation, that taxes are or may become a lien thereon, and that if taxes are not paid, the proceedings allowed by law may be taken against the property. This notice is conclusively presumed, whether or not such persons have actual notice (G.S. 105-348). In only one place does the

Machinery Act mention tax notices: G.S. 105-350(8) empowers the governing body in its discretion at any time to require the collector to send out tax bills or notices. This practice is a means for improving collections and one that should always be used; nevertheless, no property owner has an enforceable right to a bill or a notice, and his or her failure to receive one cannot be considered a valid reason for not enforcing the full tax claim (principal and interest).

Reports of Progress in Collection

The tax collector must keep adequate records of all collections [G.S. 105-350(4)] and must submit a report showing the amount collected on each year's taxes with which the tax collector is charged, the amount remaining uncollected, and the steps being taken to encourage or enforce payment, at least as often as each regular meeting of the governing body [G.S. 105-350(7)]. Collectors usually comply with this reporting requirement, but governing board members often disregard the reports. Having to make a periodic statement with respect to their efforts may spur collectors to action, and no responsible board would ignore a periodic record placed before it of what is being done and what has and has not been collected. The board can draw comparisons between the current year's position and positions on the same date in prior years, with useful results.

Tax Due Dates: Periods Covered

As pointed out earlier, county property taxes are due and payable on the first day of September of the fiscal year for which they are levied [G.S. 105-360(a)]. They are legally collectible until their collection is barred by the statute of limitations. The statute of limitations requires all taxing units to initiate an action to enforce any legal remedy provided for the collection of tax claims within ten years of the date on which taxes are due (G.S. 105-378).

Order of Collection

The tax books and receipts are to be turned over to the collector between July 1 and September 1 if he or she has been able to meet the requirements pertaining to settlement and bond already discussed [G.S. 105-352(a)]. An important feature of this *turning over* or *charge* is the order of collection. The board of commissioners is to issue the order, deliver a copy to the collector, and insert a copy in its minutes [G.S. 105-321(b)]. The wording of the order is prescribed by statute [G.S. 105-321(b)]:

STATE OF NORTH CAROLINA

COUNTY OF _____

To the Tax Collector of the County of _____:

You are hereby authorized, empowered, and commanded to collect the taxes set forth in the tax records filed in the office of _____ and in the tax receipts herewith delivered to you, in the amounts and from the taxpayers likewise therein set forth. Such taxes are hereby declared to be a first lien upon all real property of the respective taxpayers in the County of _____, and this order shall be a full and sufficient authority to direct, require, and enable you to levy on and sell any real or personal property of such taxpayers, for and on account thereof, in accordance with law.

Witness my hand and official seal, this ____ day of _____, 19____.

(SEAL)
Chairman, Board of Commissioners of _____

Attest:

_____
Clerk of Board of Commissioners of _____ County

Examination of the order indicates that it commands the collector to collect, declares the already existing fact that taxes are a first lien on real property, and requires the collector to "levy on and sell" any real and personal property owned by the taxpayers if necessary to enforce collection. The order enumerates the lawful means for collecting taxes that the collector is, by virtue of his or her position, required to employ. Even if the governing body fails to issue the order of collection, the collector has full power and responsibility to levy, garnish, and prepare the necessary information on which the governing body may order sale of liens against real property and, eventually, initiate foreclosure (G.S. 105-350, -366, -369, -373 through -375).

Property Tax Lien

The North Carolina Supreme Court has defined *lien* as "the right to have a demand satisfied out of the property of another."[12] This right runs against the property rather than against the owner. As used in the property tax laws of this state, the lien for taxes runs in favor of the local government unit and may be enforced against the property of the taxpayer.

Each year the county acquires a lien against all real property that each taxpayer owns within the county on January 1; this lien attaches automatically, by operation of law, without any effort on the collector's part [G.S. 105-355(a)]. On the other hand, the taxing unit does not obtain a lien against personal property until the collector takes action to levy or garnish [G.S. 105-355(b)].

Because the lien attaches to real property as of January 1, obviously it attaches not only before the tax becomes due but also before the exact amount of the tax can be known. Thus until the amount of the tax is computed, the lien is indeterminate, but this in no way impairs either its validity or its priority. The lien against real property, it will be seen, includes not only the taxes levied on the real property itself but also the taxes levied on all the taxpayer's personal property by the taxing unit. Of the taxpayer's total tax bill, as it will be determined between July and September of the ensuing fiscal year, the only amount that does not attach to a given parcel of realty on January 1 is the amount levied on other parcels of real property. In addition, "[a]ll penalties, interest, and costs allowed by law shall be added to the amount of the lien for the principal amount of the taxes" [G.S. 105-355(b)].

The lien for taxes attaches to personal property of the taxpayer only when the property is seized by the tax collector, either under levy or under attachment and garnishment. Once attached, however, the lien against personal property includes all taxes due the county, not merely those levied on the particular item seized, nor merely those levied on the personal property of the taxpayer [G.S. 105-355(b)].

Once the lien attaches to either real or personal property, affirmative action is required to obtain its release. Ordinarily the tax lien on real property continues "until the principal amount of the taxes plus penalties, interest, and costs allowed by law [has] been fully paid" [G.S. 105-362(a)]. This is true with regard to personal property seized under levy or attachment as well as real property subjected to the automatic lien. Nevertheless, it is possible for a careless or untrained collector to release the taxing unit's lien by failing to require taxpayers and other interested persons in each instance to pay the full amount secured by the lien before he or she issues a full-payment receipt. Because the lien is the county's security, great care should be exercised to ensure that collectors adhere to the law, and a diligent collector should be given full support by the board of commissioners.

The lien of the property tax against real property is superior to all other liens and rights (except certain liens for other taxes), regardless of the claimant and regardless of whether the other liens or rights were acquired before or after the lien for taxes [G.S. 105-356(a)(1),(2)]. Furthermore, once the lien has attached to real property, its priority is not affected by transfer of title, by death, or by receivership of the property owner [G.S. 105-356(a)(3)].

As already pointed out, taxes, interest, penalties, and costs become a lien on personal property from and after levy or attachment and garnishment. What is the priority of such a lien when it attaches? The Machinery Act makes a distinction between (1) the status of a lien for taxes on the specific property seized and (2) the status of a lien for taxes on other property: the portion of the lien that is for taxes levied on the specific personal property is superior to all other liens and rights, both prior and subsequent [G.S. 105-356(b)(1)]; the portion that is for taxes levied on property other than the specific personal property is inferior to prior valid liens and perfected security interests but superior to all subsequent liens and security interests [G.S. 105-356(b)(2)].

Payment of Taxes

As a general rule, tax collectors are authorized to accept nothing in payment of taxes except existing national currency [G.S. 105-357(a)]. They may take a check (and all collectors do), but they do so at their own risk. Thus a collector who accepts a check in payment of taxes is permitted to issue the receipt immediately or withhold it until the check is collected [G.S. 105-357(b)]. Sometimes collectors require a certified or cashier's check as an alternative to withholding the receipt until an ordinary check has cleared.

When a collector has taken a check in payment of taxes, has issued a receipt, and has had the check returned unpaid, the taxes are treated as being unpaid. In such a case the collector has the same remedies for collection that he or she would have had if the receipt had not been issued (plus the right to bring a civil suit on the check), provided that the collector has not been negligent in presenting the check for payment [G.S. 105-357(b)].

In the course of their work, tax collectors are often asked for information on whether some individual owes taxes or whether any taxes are outstanding against a given parcel of real property. There is only one statutory provision on this subject in North Carolina, and it applies only to taxes that constitute a lien on real property. The statute requires the tax collector to give written statements of the taxes that constitute a lien on specified real property when requested to do so by the following people:

1. An owner of the property
2. An occupant of the property
3. A person having a lien on the property
4. A person having a legal interest or estate in the property
5. A person or a firm having a contract to purchase or lease the property
6. A person or a firm having a contract to make a loan secured by the property
7. The authorized agent or attorney of anyone in one of the first six categories

Before furnishing the statement, the collector should require the requester to identify the person in whose name the property was listed for each year for which tax information is desired. Of course, the collector need not furnish such a statement unless the taxes have become due and are "in his hands for collection" [G.S. 105-361(a)].[13]

When a qualified person requests and obtains a written statement and actually relies on it by (1) paying the amount of taxes certified as a lien on the property, (2) purchasing or leasing the property, or (3) lending money secured by the property, then a lien will exist against the property in relation to that person only to the extent that taxes and special assessments are stated to be due in the certificate. An understatement of the tax liability in the certificate causes the lien to be released to the extent of the amount of the understatement. Thus although the county's claim for the full amount of taxes due is in no way released or compromised by the taxpayer's reliance on an erroneous certificate, the tax collector should exercise care in preparing a certificate to avoid surrendering the county's security for payment.

Once a lien is lost, collectors are liable on their bond for any loss that the county suffers [G.S. 105-361(b)]. It must be emphasized that the statutory provisions are exclusive with respect to both the kind of information that may be compelled and the persons who are entitled to it: no one other than members of the enumerated categories is entitled to a binding certificate, and no one at all can force the collector to state the amount of personal property taxes owed by any taxpayer (other than those constituting a lien on the specified real property in which a qualified person is legally interested). Finally, an oral statement made by the tax collector about the amount of taxes, penalties, interest, and costs due binds neither the tax collector nor the county [G.S. 105-361(d)].

Partial Payments

Unless the board of county commissioners directs otherwise, the tax collector is required to accept partial payments on taxes and to issue partial-payment receipts for the amounts accepted (G.S. 105-358). The board may prohibit acceptance of partial payments altogether by resolution, and in no event is the county required to accept partial payment on taxes for any year before the annual budget estimate for that year has been filed [G.S. 105-358, -359(b)]. In addition to its power to refuse acceptance of partial payments, the board of commissioners has explicit authority to prescribe by regulation an amount or a percentage of the entire tax as the required minimum for a partial payment, as long as the amount or the figure adopted applies uniformly to all tax bills (G.S. 105-358). If partial payments are accepted, the statute requires that they be applied first against accrued interest, penalties, and costs, if any, and then against the principal amount of the tax (G.S. 105-358).

Prepayments

Taxpayers are permitted to pay taxes before they are legally due. That is, taxpayers may prepay. Unlike the situation with regard to partial payments, the county has no discretion to refuse a tender of full payment of a tax after the annual budget estimate has been filed [G.S. 105-359(a), (b)]. However, the obligation to accept prepayments carries with it no requirement that the taxpayer be given a discount for early payment. If the board of commissioners chooses to provide discounts for prepayment, that is, for payment before September 1, it may do so by adopting a resolution or an ordinance not later than the first day of May preceding the due date of the taxes to which the resolution or the ordinance first applies, specifying the amounts of the discounts and the

Table 9-2
Interest for Late Payment of Taxes

If taxes are paid . . .	The interest charged is . . .
September 1 through January 5	0
During remainder of January	2%
During February	2.75%
During March	3.5%
Thereafter	3.5% plus 0.75% per month, the additional 0.75% being added on the first day of each month

periods during which they are to be applicable [G.S. 105-360(c)(1)]. The resolution or the ordinance must be approved by the Department of Revenue, and the discount schedule must be published at least once in some newspaper that has a general circulation in the taxing unit [G.S. 105-360(c)(3)]. The Department of Revenue will not approve a discount schedule if in its opinion the rates are excessive or the discount period is unreasonable [G.S. 105-360(c)].

Interest for Late Payment of Taxes

The substance of the statewide statute establishing interest for late payment of taxes [G.S. 105-360(a)] can be reduced to the schedule shown in Table 9-2.

Enforcement of Collection of Property Taxes

Counties have a general power to bring suits to collect debts in their own names as government units. However, the tax statute itself supplies the collector, in administering the duties of tax collection, with specific legal means for enforcing collection against the taxpayer's property: in the case of real property, advertisement of the lien followed by foreclosure; and in the case of personal property, levy or attachment and garnishment. Having these remedies, neither the collector nor the county itself may bring a civil action to enforce collection of property taxes, except in certain limited instances.[14]

Enforcement against Real Property: Lien Advertisement and Foreclosure

The lien of taxes attaches to all of a taxpayer's real property in the taxing unit as of January 1 of the year in which the property is listed and assessed; the lien encompasses the owner's personal property taxes as well as the taxes on the real property itself [G.S. 105-355(a)]. Thus when any or all of the taxes are not paid, the lien against the real property may be enforced.

Report of Delinquent Taxes Constituting Liens on Realty

In February of each year the tax collector is required to report to the governing body of the taxing unit "the total amount of unpaid taxes for the current fiscal year that are liens on real property" [G.S. 105-369(a)]. When it receives this report, the governing body must order that the liens be advertised and must set a date on which advertisement is to occur [G.S. 105-369(a)].

Time and Place of Lien Advertisement

The board of county commissioners may choose any date from March 1 through June 30 on which to advertise the liens. It must advertise them at least once and may advertise them additional times [G.S. 105-369(c)]. The board must advertise them by posting a notice at the courthouse and by publishing a notice in a newspaper of general circulation [G.S. 105-369(c)].

Foreclosure

Foreclosure of the lien on real property and sale of the property should be viewed as the collection remedy of last resort. It is a complex and expensive remedy and should be used only after the collector has attempted to collect the delinquent taxes through attachment or levy.

The board of commissioners must decide which of the available foreclosure methods it will employ. For this it will need the county attorney's advice. Two methods of foreclosure are available under North Carolina law: one is characterized as being "in the nature of an action to foreclose a mortgage" [G.S. 105-374(a)], and the other is described as an action *in rem* [G.S. 105-375(a)]. The first method is a civil lawsuit that requires the services of an attorney. The second is a summary procedure that in most instances can be handled by the tax collector, or a paralegal, with occasional advice from an attorney. Both methods require a title examination to determine the persons who are entitled to receive notice of the foreclosure action. The *in rem* procedure can usually be concluded more expeditiously and less expensively than the mortgage-style foreclosure. Some counties use one method exclusively; other counties sometimes use the mortgage-style foreclosure and sometimes use the *in rem* method, depending on the nature of the property being foreclosed.

Enforcement against Personal Property: Levy and Attachment and Garnishment

The remedies for use in subjecting personal property to the satisfaction of tax claims are based on actual seizure of the property. What happens after the seizure differs according to the remedy being used, but the fundamental element in the remedies remains seizure. If the personal property to be seized is tangible, the appropriate remedy is levy, followed by public sale of the property seized. If the personal property to be seized is intangible, that is, incapable of manual seizure or delivery, the remedy is attachment and garnishment.

Kinds of Taxes Appropriate for Use of Levy and Attachment and Garnishment

Levy may be used against tangible personal property as a means of enforcing collection of taxes imposed on both real and personal property (the personal property levied on and any other personal property owned by the taxpayer). Similarly, attachment and garnishment of intangible personal property is available for enforcing collection of taxes imposed on both real and personal property of the taxpayer [G.S. 105-366(a)]. Tax collectors need no special authority from the board of county commissioners to use levy and attachment and garnishment; they have that authority by virtue of their office [G.S. 105-366(a)]. There are two cases, however, in which collectors have a legal duty to use one or both of these remedies before proceeding against the taxpayer's realty:

1. They must do so when "directed to do so" by the governing body [G.S. 105-366(a)(1)].

2. They must do so "[w]hen requested to do so by the taxpayer or
    by a mortgagee or other person holding a lien upon the real
    property subject to the lien for taxes if the person making the
    request furnishes the tax collector with a written statement de-
    scribing the personal property to be proceeded against and giv-
    ing its location" [G.S. 105-366(a)(2)].

Time Limitations on Use of Levy and Attachment and Garnishment

As a general rule, levy and attachment and garnishment may not be
used until the tax has become delinquent [G.S. 105-366(b)], that is, not
until after January 5 following the September 1 due date. The right to
use these remedies continues, in the case of taxes that are a lien against
real property, until foreclosure is initiated [G.S. 105-366(b)], and in the
case of taxes that are not a lien against real property, until foreclosure
is barred by the ten-year statute of limitations (G.S. 105-378).

There are four situations in which levy and attachment and garnishment may be used before the date on which the tax becomes legally due:

1. If before January 6 "the tax collector has reasonable grounds
    for believing that the taxpayer is about to remove his property
    from the taxing unit" [G.S. 105-366(c)].
2. If before January 6 "the tax collector has reasonable grounds
    for believing that the taxpayer is about to . . . transfer [his or her
    property] to another person" [G.S. 105-366(c)].
3. If before January 6 "the tax collector has reasonable grounds
    for believing that the taxpayer . . . is in imminent danger of be-
    coming insolvent" [G.S. 105-366(c)].
4. "Whenever any wholesale or retail merchant . . . sells or trans-
    fers the major part of his stock of goods, materials, supplies, or
    fixtures, other than in the ordinary course of business, or
    goes out of business" and the taxes on the transferred prop-
    erty that will fall due on the following September 1 are not
    paid within thirty days after the described action [G.S. 105-
    366(d)(3)].

Procedure in Making of Levy

As already indicated, levy is a procedure under which tangible personal property of the taxpayer is seized, advertised, and sold to the highest bidder for cash to pay a tax claim held by the taxing unit. The present law anticipates that the levy will be made by the tax collector or by a properly authorized deputy tax collector [G.S. 105-367(b)]. Ordinarily it is not the responsibility of a law enforcement officer to make levies for taxes. Nevertheless, the board of commissioners has authority to permit the tax collector to call on the sheriff to assist in this work [G.S. 105-367(b)]. As a matter of practice, it is much simpler not to adopt this procedure. If the collector needs protection in making the levy, a law enforcement officer can be called on to accompany him or her. Tax levies, however, should be made by tax collectors.

Procedure in Attachment and Garnishment

The key characteristic of attachment and garnishment is that it invariably draws a third person into the collection process, that is, a person other than the taxpayer and the tax collector. The third person is brought in because the item of intangible personal property to be attached is something that the third person owes the taxpayer or holds for the taxpayer. For example, an employer owes wages to the taxpayer; a bank holds money for its depositor-taxpayer. Debts owed to a taxpayer, though intangible, are nonetheless the property of the taxpayer, and it is this kind of property that the attachment and garnishment procedure enables the tax collector to reach to satisfy the unit's claim for taxes. Like levy, attachment and garnishment is designed to operate outside the courts, and the statute provides that any payment made to the tax collector by the garnishee "shall completely satisfy any liability therefor on his part to the taxpayer" [G.S. 105-368(c)].

The collector initiates the procedure by preparing a notice to be served on both the taxpayer and the person or the institution that holds the intangible item to be seized, informing them of

1. the taxpayer's name and address;
2. the amount of the tax (stating the years for which the taxes were levied);
3. the name of the taxing unit;
4. the property to be attached; and
5. the law under which the collector is proceeding by giving them a copy of G.S. 105-366 and G.S. 105-368 [G.S. 105-368(b)].

Usually the collector need take no further action; the garnishee will remit to the collector the amount demanded.

If the garnishee has a *defense* or *set-off* to assert against the taxpayer (which he or she must state in writing under oath, sending two copies of the statement to the collector by registered mail within ten days), or if the taxpayer asserts a defense in the same manner, then the collector must decide whether to admit the defense or the set-off or to deny it, in whole or in part [G.S. 105-368(d), (f)]. If the collector denies the defense, the collector must notify the garnishee or the taxpayer, as the case may be, in writing within ten days

> or within such further time as may be agreed on by the garnishee [or taxpayer] and at the same time the tax collector shall file a copy of the notice of garnishment, a copy of the garnishee's [or taxpayer's] statement, and a copy of the tax collector's objections thereto in the appropriate division of the General Court of Justice . . . where the issues made shall be tried as in civil actions. [G.S. 105-368(d), (f)]

In most cases the person or the institution garnished pays when it receives the collector's first notice of the taxing unit's claim against the taxpayer. (If wages are attached, no more than 10 percent per pay period may be reached by this procedure [G.S. 105-368(a)].) Only if the collector has not received the garnishee's response within fifteen days after the notice was served or if the garnishee [G.S. 105-368(e)] or the taxpayer asserts a defense to the garnishment that the collector refuses to allow [G.S. 105-368(d), (f)], is court action necessary.

Special Remedies for Motor Vehicle Taxes

Taxes on registered motor vehicles are not a lien on real property [G.S. 105-330.4(c)], but the collector still has the remedies of levy and attachment and garnishment to collect motor vehicle taxes, as well as an additional remedy. If a motor vehicle tax is unpaid four months after its due date, the collector must include that tax on a block list that is sent to the Division of Motor Vehicles. When the division receives this list, it will not permit the owner of the vehicle to renew the vehicle's registration until the taxes are paid. Aggressive tax collectors do not wait the four months until they can place the tax on the block list; rather, they begin levy or attachment and garnishment procedures to collect the tax just as soon as feasible after the tax becomes delinquent.

Reduction, Release, and Refund of Property Taxes

Reductions, refunds, and releases of tax claims are matters to be decided by the board of county commissioners; they are not left to the discretion of the tax collector. Furthermore, each claim should be dealt with on its own facts. Once a tax bill has been computed and turned over to the collector, it can be reduced, released, or refunded only on the specific authorization of the governing body [G.S. 105-380, -381(b), -373(a)(3)]. *Tax bill,* as used in this sentence, covers not only the principal amount of the tax but also all interest, penalties, and costs that may have accrued on the unpaid tax [G.S. 105-273(15)].

A strong public policy supports the stability of sources of government revenue, and property taxes constitute the major source of county and city tax revenue in this state. For this reason the statutes dealing with forgiveness of property tax claims are strict. G.S. 105-380 opens with the following statement of general policy:

> The governing body of a taxing unit is prohibited from releasing, refunding, or compromising all or any portion of the taxes levied against any property within its jurisdiction except as expressly provided in [the Machinery Act].

This is a rigid prohibition, and failure to abide by it carries personal liability for each member of the governing body:

> Any tax that has been released, refunded, or compromised in violation of this section may be recovered from any member or members of the governing body who voted for the release, refund, or compromise by civil action instituted by any resident of the taxing unit, and when collected, the recovered tax shall be paid to the treasurer of the taxing unit. The costs of bringing the action, including reasonable attorneys' fees, shall be allowed the plaintiff in the event the tax is recovered. (G.S. 105-380)

The express provisions referred to in G.S. 105-380's statement of general policy are that releases, refunds, or reductions of tax claims must be allowed if the tax was illegal, levied for an illegal purpose, or imposed through a clerical error [G.S. 105-381(a), (b)]. Specific instances in which refunds or releases should be granted are listed in G.S. 105-381 and include the following:

1. If the assessed valuation of the property taxed has been reduced under proper exercise of legal authority, a reduction in the tax bill follows as a matter of course.

2. If the property concerned is not taxable by the unit, that is, if the property is legally entitled to exemption or if it does not fall within the unit's jurisdiction, a release of the claim is justified.

3. If the property has been listed and taxed twice, that is, *double-listed*, one of the duplicate claims should be released.

4. If the rate of tax or any part of it has been illegally levied (as in the following examples), a release is warranted. That is, a release is warranted if the tax

    a. is levied for something other than a "public purpose,"

    b. is levied without a vote of the people in a situation in which such a vote is required by law, or

    c. is levied for an amount greater than that authorized by the state constitution, statutes, or a vote of the people.

5. If the amount of the tax has been erroneously computed, through clerical or mathematical error, at a figure higher than is proper, a release or a reduction is appropriate.

County commissioners should familiarize themselves with all of these grounds.

The procedures that must be followed before a release may be granted are relatively simple. The taxpayer must submit a written statement of his or her demand to the governing body of the taxing unit. The only time limit governing acceptance of the taxpayer's statement is that implicit in the relief requested: releases are granted only before the tax has been paid. As long as the tax has not been paid, a release may be requested regardless of when the tax first came due. Once the taxpayer's demand has been made, the governing board must decide whether legal grounds for the release exist. If it finds that grounds do exist, then it instructs the official who prepared the tax receipt to make the proper reductions and adjustments in the taxpayer's bill. When the taxpayer pays, he or she pays at the reduced amount (G.S. 105-381).

When a refund is requested after the taxpayer has already paid some or all of the bill but before the right to reduction or release has been determined, the problem is not so simple. In fact, under some circumstances a refund is not allowed, despite the existence of a right to reduction or release. The reason is that the statutes impose a limit on the time in which a dissatisfied taxpayer must act to establish an enforceable right to a refund. To obtain a valid refund, the taxpayer must comply with the following requirements:

1. He or she must have paid the tax or a part of it equal to the amount of the refund.
2. He or she must make the demand in writing.
3. His or her demand must be delivered to the governing body "within five years after said tax first became due or within six months from the date of payment of such tax, whichever is the later date" [G.S. 105-381(a)(3)].

If the taxpayer has satisfied these procedural requirements and if the governing body finds legal grounds for a refund, then the refund must be granted: the governing body has no discretion to refuse the refund on a valid claim. On the other hand, if the procedures are not followed, then the refund should not be allowed. In fact, as previously mentioned, members of the governing body who vote to make refunds when the procedures have not been followed strictly lay themselves open to possible suit and personal liability for the money refunded (G.S. 105-380).

The board of commissioners may delegate authority to make refunds and releases of less than $100 to the county attorney, finance officer, or manager. The officer to whom this authority is delegated must make a monthly report to the board of all releases and refunds granted.

Special refund procedures apply when the property owner has appealed the value to the Property Tax Commission and paid the tax, and after payment the commission orders a reduction in the value. In this case, the county may be required to pay interest on the amount refunded [G.S. 105-290(b)(4)]. The rate of interest to be paid is the rate set by the secretary of revenue under G.S. 105-241.1(i), which is the interest to be paid on delinquent state taxes. This rate may not be higher than 16 percent a year or lower than 5 percent a year. The secretary has authority to set the rate twice a year: on June 1, to take effect July 1; and on December 1, to take effect January 1. If no new rate is set, the current rate continues in effect. This interest is calculated on a daily basis. The rate on January 1, 1998, was 9 percent. The interest begins to accrue either from the date the tax was paid or from the date the tax would have become delinquent under G.S. 105-360, whichever is the later date. What this apparently means is that if the tax is paid before January 6 (the delinquency date), interest begins to accrue from January 6, but if the tax is paid after January 6, interest begins to accrue from the date of payment. The interest continues to accrue until a refund is paid. The date a refund is paid is the date determined by the governing body of the taxing unit, but it can be no sooner than five days after a refund check is mailed. Thus a governing board could adopt a uniform rule that interest is to cease in all cases five days from the date a refund check is mailed.

Settlements

Settlement refers to the tax collector's report to the board of commissioners concerning his or her tax collection efforts as well as an accounting of the funds collected. An audit disclosing that funds collected have been properly allocated and deposited is not equivalent to a settlement. In a settlement the governing body, in addition to determining whether the collector has been honest and careful, reviews his or her efforts to collect.

The governing body may call on the collector to make a full settlement at any time [G.S. 105-350(6)]. More commonly it relies on an annual settlement or a settlement when a vacancy occurs in the office. No matter when the settlement occurs, the legal effect for the collector remains the same:

> Approval of any settlement by the governing body does not relieve the tax collector or his bondsmen of liability for any shortage actually existing at the time of the settlement and thereafter discovered; nor does it relieve the collector of any criminal liability. [G.S. 105-373(e)]

Time for Annual Settlement

The tax collector is supposed to settle for the previous fiscal year's taxes after July 1 and before he or she is charged with taxes for the current fiscal year [G.S. 105-373(a)(3)]. This requirement fixes the time for annual settlement to a date shortly after the close of the fiscal year for which the taxes were levied. Although the governing body, as noted earlier, may require the collector to make settlement "at any other time," such other settlements as the governing body may require must be in addition to the mandatory settlement to be made annually in July; they may not take its place. Commissioners who permit settlements to be delayed until after taxes for the current year are charged to the collector should consult the following provision in G.S. 105-373(f):

> In addition to any other civil or criminal penalties provided by law, any member of a governing body . . . who fails to perform any duty imposed upon him by [the settlement statute, G.S. 105-373] shall be guilty of a misdemeanor punishable by fine or imprisonment, or both, in the discretion of the court.

An administrative matter must also be kept in mind. Settlement must be made before the new tax books are turned over to the collector [G.S. 105-373(a)(3)]. Any member of the governing body who votes to deliver the tax receipts to the tax collector before the collector has met the requirements prescribed (including making settlement) is individually liable for the amount of taxes charged against the tax collector for which he or she has not made satisfactory settlement. Any member who so votes or willfully fails to perform any duty imposed by the settlement law is guilty of a misdemeanor punishable by fine or imprisonment, or both, in the discretion of the court [G.S. 105-352(d)(1)]. This could become serious if the collector has not been diligent in cases in which diligence might have produced results.

Settlement Procedure

Tax collectors are supposed to carry out the law as it is written; they are not policy makers. They are personally responsible for collecting the taxes in their hands, and the law gives them ample authority to seize any property that the taxpayer may own in order to collect the unit's claim. The law presumes that, with this responsibility and with these remedies, collectors will do their utmost to collect and that they will, if necessary, seize whatever property of the delinquent taxpayer may be available to them. Thus the governing body rather than the collector has the responsibility for determining whether the collection work has been performed satisfactorily. Ultimately the governing body must decide in each case whether the collector has done everything that he or she could have done to reach whatever property may have been available. If the unit has no lien for taxes against real property, the collector's effort to enforce collection must be the subject of the special scrutiny described in the next section.

Insolvents

After July 1 and before he or she makes the annual settlement, the collector is supposed to present the governing board with "[a] list of the persons not owning real property whose personal property taxes for the preceding fiscal year remain unpaid," along with a statement under oath [G.S. 105-373(a)(1)b]

1. that he or she has made a diligent effort to collect these taxes out of the personal property of the taxpayers concerned.

2. that he or she has made use of the "other means available to him for collection."
3. that where applicable, he or she has tried to make collection outside the taxing unit.
4. that he or she has included any information concerning these taxpayers that may be of interest to or required by the governing body.

This is not to be a perfunctory report. Collectors are supposed to demonstrate that they have actually done everything possible under the law to collect the taxes for which the unit has no lien against real estate. The first affirmation that collectors must make means that they have been diligent in using levy and attachment and garnishment. The second means that they have done what they could to collect by working out partial-payment schedules for taxpayers and that they have used all the procedures available to them in collecting from estates, receivers, and bankrupts. The third affirmation means that in appropriate instances they have exercised their authority to call on collectors of other units to help them make collections.

The fourth item listed is not itself an affirmation, but a reminder of two things: (1) that collectors should include facts in their report to justify their failure to collect the accounts reported; and (2) that when the governing body desires to do so, it may require collectors to furnish whatever factual information is considered useful in connection with their report.

The mere fact that a collector, in making this report, swears that he or she has used diligence in attempting to collect from the persons listed as still owing personal property taxes is not determinative of the matter. The governing body has the power to reject the name of any taxpayer if, in its opinion or knowledge, the taxpayer is not insolvent. In the event of a rejection, the governing body is entitled to hold the collector liable on his or her bond for the uncollected tax [G.S. 105-373(a)(2), (3)]. Having reviewed the list submitted by the collector and having come to a conclusion about the collector's justification in asking that he or she be allowed credit in the settlement for the uncollected items on the ground of the taxpayers' "insolvency," the governing body must enter in its minutes the names of the taxpayers found to be insolvent and designate them as the insolvent list "to be credited to the tax collector in his settlement" [G.S. 105-373(a)(2)].

Table 9-3
Items Required to Be Charged against and Credited to the Tax Collector

Charges	Credits
1. The total amount of all taxes placed in the collector's hands for collection, including taxes on discoveries, increased assessments, and values certified by the Property Tax Commission	1. All sums deposited by the collector to the credit of the taxing unit or for which the proper official has given receipts
2. All late-listing penalties collected by the tax collector	2. Releases allowed by the governing body, including rebates, reductions, refunds, and so on
3. All interest on taxes collected by the tax collector	3. Discounts allowed for prepayments, if the principal amounts of such accounts were collected after the books were placed in the collector's hands
4. Any other sums collected or received by the tax collector, including, for example, fees allowed in levy and attachment and garnishment	4. The principal amount of unpaid taxes constituting liens against real property
5. Any fees that the tax collector may have taken for making collections for other taxing units	5. The principal amount of taxes found by the county commissioners to be uncollectible in the current year because the taxpayers who owe them are insolvent
	6. Any commissions to which the collector is entitled

Form of Settlement

A review of the North Carolina statutes will disclose that boards of county commissioners are given every opportunity throughout the year to keep abreast of the tax collector's work. The cornerstone of this scheme, mentioned earlier, is the requirement that the collector submit to the governing body at each of its regular meetings a report of the amount that he or she has collected on each year's taxes with which he or she is charged, the amount remaining uncollected, and the steps that he or she is taking to encourage or enforce payment of uncollected taxes [G.S. 105-350(7)]. If the collector is careful to comply with this requirement and if the governing body pays attention to these periodic reports, calling for additional information as desired, the annual settlement will follow in orderly culmination.

The law specifies the items that must be charged against the collector and the items that must be allowed as credits for him or her [G.S. 105-373(a)(3), (b)]. They are summarized in Table 9-3.

The charges and the credits should balance. The collector is liable on his or her bond for any deficiency disclosed. In addition to this civil liability, he or she is subject to the criminal penalties imposed by G.S. 105-373(f): "[A]ny . . . tax collector . . . who fails to perform any duty imposed upon him by [the settlement statute] shall be guilty of a misdemeanor punishable by fine or imprisonment, or both, in the discretion of the court."

Additional Resources

Campbell, William A. *Property Tax Collection in North Carolina.* 4th ed. Chapel Hill, N.C.: Institute of Government, The University of North Carolina at Chapel Hill, 1998.

———. *Property Tax Lien Foreclosure Forms and Procedures.* 4th ed. Chapel Hill, N.C.: Institute of Government, The University of North Carolina at Chapel Hill, 1992 (5th ed. forthcoming).

Notes

1. This section draws heavily on Charles D. Liner's article "The Origins and Development of the North Carolina System of Taxation," *Popular Government* 45 (Summer 1979): 41.

2. See generally Liner, "The Origins and Development," note 1.

3. A capitation or poll tax is one levied on individual persons at a fixed rate per person. It is one of the most ancient forms of taxation. In England its roots can be traced to Anglo-Saxon kingdoms predating the Norman Conquest. The capitation tax has no necessary connection with the right to vote, although it has been used in that regard. The North Carolina Constitution of 1776 limited the right to vote for members of the lower house of the General Assembly to persons who had "paid public taxes." If a person owned no land, this meant the poll tax. Therefore, if a person did not own land and did not pay the poll tax, the person could not vote.

4. Under the feudal system persons held title to land in return for services due to the overlord, usually the obligation to follow the king into battle or supply a number of armed men and horses or other military supplies. In later years the military tenures were often converted into a form of ownership in which the landowner rendered a fixed annual sum of money to the overlord in substitution for military service. This came to be known as the *quit rent* system.

5. See John L. Sanders and John F. Lomax, Jr., comps., *Amendments to the Constitution of North Carolina 1776–1989* (Chapel Hill, N.C.: Institute of Government, The University of North Carolina at Chapel Hill, 1990).

6. Message of Governor T. W. Bickett to the General Assembly of 1919, *North Carolina Public Documents, Session 1919,* Document No. 1, pp. 19–20.

7. The amendment revised the portion of the constitution now numbered as N.C. CONST. Art. V, § 2(2). The 1971 constitutional revision renumbered the section but made no other substantive or editorial changes in it.

8. See William A. Campbell, *Property Tax Collection in North Carolina*, 4th ed. (Chapel Hill, N.C.: Institute of Government, The University of North Carolina at Chapel Hill, 1998), 65–83.

9. N.C. GEN. STAT. §§ 69-25.15 (voted fire tax districts), 153A-304.1 (county fire service districts).

10. *In re* Greensboro Office Partnership, 72 N.C. App. 635, 325 S.E.2d 24, *cert. denied*, 313 N.C. 602, 330 S.E.2d 610 (1985).

11. *American Jurisprudence*, 3d ed., vol. 63, *Public Officers and Employees*, sec. 202 (Rochester, N.Y.: Lawyers Cooperative, 1972).

12. Thigpen v. Leigh, 93 N.C. 47, 49 (1885).

13. Taxes that are due but whose payment has been deferred under G.S. 105-277.4(c) must be included in the statement.

14. See William A. Campbell, *Property Tax Collection in North Carolina*, 4th ed. (Chapel Hill, N.C.: Institute of Government, The University of North Carolina at Chapel Hill, 1998), 146–47.

10 Budget Preparation and Enactment

A. John Vogt

Contents

A. John Vogt is an Institute of Government faculty member who specializes in budgeting, capital planning and finance, and financial management.

North Carolina counties budget and spend moneys under the Local Government Budget and Fiscal Control Act (LGBFCA) (G.S. Chapter 159, Article 3). This law requires that the budget be balanced and that county moneys be budgeted before being spent. Ongoing operating expenditures and the recurring revenues that support them must be included in the annual budget. Expenditures and revenues for capital assets and for projects financed wholly or partly with federal or state grants must be budgeted either in the annual budget or in project ordinances. Revenues and expenditures of a separate fund for a county's internal services may be included in a separate financial plan for that fund or in the annual budget.

The fiscal control portions of the LGBFCA require counties to maintain accounting systems in accordance with generally accepted accounting principles as well as the rules and regulations of the Local Government Commission. The commission is an agency in the Department of State Treasurer that approves and sells local government bonds and other debt and helps local governments with financial management. The LGBFCA also requires that expenditures be made in accordance with the approved budget, that cash and other assets be safeguarded, and that a county's financial accounts be audited annually by an independent public auditor.

The LGBFCA is neither too broad to leave doubt about what are proper financial procedures nor too narrow to impede improvements in financial practices or local government services. This chapter examines the budgeting portions of the LGBFCA, including budget practices. Chapter 11 deals with capital improvement programs, capital budgets, and debt, and Chapter 12 analyzes the fiscal control and cash management portions of the LGBFCA.

Definitions, and Purposes of the Budget

The LGBFCA defines the *annual budget* as "a proposed *plan* for raising and spending money for specified programs, functions, activities, or objectives during a fiscal year" (emphasis added) [G.S. 159-7(b)(1)]. The board of county commissioners reviews the budget and enacts it into law by adopting the *annual budget ordinance*, which the LGBFCA characterizes as "the ordinance that levies taxes and appropriates revenues for specified purposes, functions, activities, or objectives during a fiscal year" [G.S. 159-7(b)(2)]. The *fiscal year* runs from July 1 through June 30.

The LGBFCA's definition of the annual budget as a plan suggests that one purpose of the budget is to *allocate resources rationally*. In this process the objectives for a county's services are established and ranked in priority, and then the expenditures to be incurred to reach those objectives are estimated and balanced with available resources. Officials strive to make budgetary decisions that are *cost-effective*, that is, that yield the greatest benefit with the available resources.

The budget process in actual settings often does not measure up to this ideal. Where there are major disagreements among budget makers, the budget process is likely to seem more like a political than a planning exercise. In this case, budgeting *involves much bargaining among participants who represent different points of view*, and the result may be not the most effective or rational allocation of resources, but a compromise that decision makers and different community groups resign themselves to live with for another year.

Thus the annual budget process can be an opportunity to plan programs and activities for the coming year or a vehicle to deal with differences and reach a political compromise among groups in a county about what its government should do in the next year. Usually the budget is both. In some counties and at particular times, however, one of these concepts or purposes of budgeting predominates.

Whether the annual budget serves primarily as a planning vehicle or as a means of reaching political agreement about budgetary policies, it can and should serve several specific purposes. Most basically it *sets three legal limits* on what a county government may do:

1. The most important legal limit concerns the *property tax levy*. Under the LGBFCA, once the board of commissioners sets the tax levy in the budget ordinance, neither the levy (by explicit reference) nor the rate (by implication) may be amended or changed during the fiscal year (G.S. 159-15). This is the only part of the annual budget ordinance that may not be amended.
2. The LGBFCA requires the annual budget ordinance to be balanced.
3. Appropriations made in the budget ordinance set legal limits on what a county may spend. The sum of expenditures and encumbrances chargeable to an appropriation may not exceed the appropriation. The board of commissioners may also incorporate provisions in the budget ordinance that specify the manner in which appropriations must be spent.

The annual budget also provides the opportunity for officials to *review and evaluate county programs and activities*. During most of the year, officials are often hard-pressed to keep up with day-to-day duties and may not have the time to examine the full range of county programs to determine whether they are heading in the proper directions or need adjustments. Even if local officials make no changes after they review programs and activities, and the budget remains the same from year to year, such a review is valuable. It gives officials an overview of programs and a broader perspective for the decisions that they must make, issue by issue, during the following year.

The annual budget hardly ever remains the same from one year to the next. Besides having to accommodate changes in costs for continuing programs, the budget is also usually used to expand, improve, reduce, revise, or eliminate existing programs or to authorize or undertake altogether new programs.

The disadvantage of using the budget for this purpose is that preparing and approving cost estimates for just the existing programs is difficult and time-consuming enough; incorporating and executing many program or policy changes in the annual budget makes budget preparation and enactment even busier and more challenging. As a result, some proposed changes may slide through and be approved in the budget process without adequate review. This problem can be avoided if major program changes to be effected in the annual budget are considered during the year before the budget process begins. Then the budget is used mainly to implement the changes, rather than to review and study as well as implement them.

Finally, the budget can *serve management purposes.* By making appropriations to departments or divisions within departments, the budget assigns or renews the assignment of responsibility for providing services or programs for which the appropriations are made. A board of commissioners may also review and approve goals and objectives to be achieved by departments as well as dollar authorizations for them in the budget. Such board-approved goals and objectives can be translated into very specific targets for managers and supervisors to achieve during the year. All these goals, objectives, and targets taken together can constitute a plan of work that guides management efforts and for which managers can be held accountable.

The Public-Purpose Limitation

A fundamental restriction that underlies the LGBFCA is that public moneys, regardless of their source, may be budgeted and spent only for public purposes. This limitation springs from Article V, Section 2(1), of the North Carolina Constitution, enacted in 1936, which reads, "the power of taxation shall be exercised . . . for public purposes only." Rulings of the state's supreme court in the half century leading up to this constitutional provision and since have applied the provision to all public moneys, not just taxes, and have forbidden both raising and spending public moneys for private purposes.[1]

The twentieth century has been an era of expanding government responsibilities, spurred by citizens' needs and desires, and questions have been raised about whether some newly proposed programs or expenditures serve public purposes. The courts, and ultimately the state supreme court, determine what is a public purpose. Until a court does decide, a county may rely on a legislative declaration that a particular activity serves a public purpose.

In deciding whether an expenditure serves a public purpose, the courts have not tried to define what public purpose means in the abstract. They have decided public-purpose cases considering what have generally been accepted as legitimate and proper local government functions, yet recognizing that conditions change and functions that are not now considered public purposes may one day become such.

A basic principle at work in the public-purpose limitation is that some activities are reserved for the private sector. The courts have accepted as public purposes, traditional government functions, or activities that are perceived as extensions of traditional functions, and have maintained a cautious attitude toward government expansion into traditionally private-sector functions.

Some expenditures fail the public-purpose test because the benefits that they bring to particular persons or businesses significantly outweigh any benefit to the public at large. For example, in cases in which government sought to issue bonds to build facilities for private entities, the North Carolina Supreme Court found the benefit to the private organizations to be paramount, significantly outweighing any public benefit and causing the proposed bonding programs to fail the public-purpose test.[2] These specific cases have since been reversed by narrowly drawn constitutional amendments,[3] but they still reflect the basic point that the public benefits of a particular expenditure or activity may be so slight that the courts will hold that the expenditure or the activity serves no essentially public purpose. In a 1996 decision, the state supreme court upheld local government provision of economic development incentives to private firms as authorized in G.S. 158-7.1, as long as the incentives benefit the public interests of the units giving them rather than just the private interests of the firms or their employees.[4]

The public-purpose limitation does not prevent a county from appropriating money to a private agency for the performance of a public activity. Article V, Section 2(7), of the state constitution permits the General Assembly to authorize local governments to "contract with and appropriate money to any person, association, or corporation for accomplishment of public purposes only." Pursuant to this constitutional provision, G.S. 153A-449 expressly authorizes counties to appropriate money to any person, association, or corporation to carry out any public purpose that the county is authorized by law to undertake. (G.S. 160A-20.1 provides comparable statutory authority for cities.)

Although counties may contract with private agencies to provide public services, there are certain limitations or procedural requirements that they should respect or follow in doing so:

1. The activity must be one that the county itself is legally authorized to undertake.

2. In giving financial support to privately controlled agencies, a county should specify the purposes or the uses of the money.
3. The county should require the private agency to account for its expenditures of the money at the end of the fiscal period or year for which the money is given.[5]

A county may contract or cooperate with other local governments for the provision of authorized public services without raising a public-purpose issue as long as the county's citizens benefit from the arrangement (G.S. Ch. 160A, Art. 20, "Interlocal Cooperation").

Budgeting and Accounting

Budgeting estimates future revenues and makes appropriations for expenditures to support an organization, a program, or a project, whereas *accounting* records revenues raised and expenditures actually made and reports on the resulting financial condition of the organization, the program, or the project. Budget estimation and decision making depend on accounting records that are accurate and consistent from one period to the next. The importance of accounting records for budgeting may become apparent only when such records are absent or deficient. Three facets of governmental accounting have important implications for budgeting by counties and other governmental entities: fund accounting, budgetary accounting, and basis of accounting and budgeting.

Fund Accounting

An accounting *fund* is a separate fiscal and accounting entity, with its own set of accounts and its own cash and other assets, liabilities, equities or fund balance, revenues, and expenditures or expenses.[6] Governmental financial transactions are grouped into funds essentially to isolate information for legal and management purposes.

G.S. 159-8(a) requires the annual budget ordinance to be balanced by fund, as well as for the county as a whole. Individual funds may be balanced in part through interfund transfers.

G.S. 159-26(b) lists the types of funds that governments generally maintain: general, debt service, special revenue, enterprise, internal service, capital project, and trust and agency funds. Which ones and how many a particular county maintains will depend on what functions it performs and how it finances those functions, although to simplify accounting and reporting, a county should maintain as few funds as possible.

General Fund

The *general fund* is a catchall fund for all transactions not properly accounted for in another fund. The general fund typically budgets and accounts for all or most property tax revenue, most sales and use tax revenue, state-shared tax revenue, and other revenues that are not statutorily earmarked for particular purposes. Typically it also includes all county appropriations and contributions to the schools and community college; expenditures for social services, health, and mental health programs; the sheriff's department, jail, and other public safety activities; parks and recreation programs; and general county government and administration. The general fund may include expenditures for solid waste disposal (landfill) if it is not operated as a public enterprise. For purposes of budgeting, accounting, and financial reporting, there can be only one general fund.

Debt Service Funds

Debt service funds may be established for the payment of principal and interest on general obligation bonds and notes and other debt-financing instruments. Alternatively, generally accepted accounting principles permit debt service payments on such bonds, notes, or debt to be made directly from the general fund or from the applicable operating fund. Although the use of debt service funds was common in the past, a debt service fund should be used only if a county is legally or otherwise required to set aside money for debt service payments. For general obligation bonds and notes, debt service payments should generally be made from the general fund, or if such bonds or notes were issued for enterprise purposes, from the appropriate enterprise fund.

Special Revenue Funds

Special revenue funds account for the proceeds of revenue sources that are legally restricted to expenditures for specific purposes. The LGBFCA requires that a special revenue fund be established for activities supported in part or in whole with voted property taxes (property taxes levied pursuant to a voter referendum), for service districts, and for activities for which money is appropriated under grant project ordinances (see the discussion under the section "Project Ordinances," later in this chapter).

Enterprise Funds

A separate *enterprise fund* must be established for each public enterprise operated by a county. An *enterprise* is understood to mean a public service that is financed partly or wholly through charges to users or customers and that is operated in a proprietary or businesslike manner. Even when user charges cover only a portion of the cost of such a service, using an enterprise fund to account for it enables county officials to determine the extent to which the service is self-supporting. A county may establish enterprise funds for the following services: water supply and distribution, sewage collection and disposal, solid waste collection and disposal, airports, off-street parking, public transportation systems, and stormwater and drainage systems (G.S. 153A-274).

Internal Service Funds

Internal service funds account for activities that serve other departments or parts of the same government or other governments, rather than the public. County-owned and -operated central stores or warehouses, print shops, data-processing units, and motor pools are examples of internal services. Counties may account for internal services either in the general fund or in one or more separate internal service funds. If a county wants to operate an internal service like a business and charge county departments that use the service, it will set up an internal service fund for it.

Capital Project Funds

Bond and debt proceeds may be used only for the purposes for which the bonds were issued or the debt incurred. To ensure this, *capital project funds* must be established for bond- or debt-financed projects. Such funds should also be used to budget and account for the construction of most major capital improvements, whether or not bond or debt financing is involved. A single capital project fund may be used to account for multiple capital projects as long as a county's accounting system can segregate the revenues and the expenditures for each of the projects.

Trust and Agency Funds

Trust and agency funds are used to account for assets that are held by a county as a trustee or as an agent for another governmental unit, a private organization, or one or more individuals. Others besides the county have ownership rights in the assets of these funds, although the county holds and manages the assets. Counties establish trust or agency funds for pension system assets that they manage, deferred compensation programs for county employees, and other purposes. Most trust and agency funds do *not* have to be budgeted (see the discussion under the section "Moneys Not Having to Be Budgeted," later in this chapter).

Budgetary Accounting

Commercial accounting principles do not require a firm's budget to be recorded in its accounting system. The accounts record only actual revenues and expenses. In government, however, generally accepted accounting principles call for the approved budget to be entered into a government entity's accounting records.[7] The LGBFCA reflects this principle of governmental accounting by directing that a local government's accounting system show "appropriations and estimated revenues as established in the budget ordinance and in each project ordinance [G.S. 159-25(a)]. With appropriations and estimated revenues recorded in the accounting system at the beginning of the fiscal year, actual expenditures and revenues are then charged against the appropriations or the estimated revenues during the year. This whole process is called *budgetary accounting.*

Why do governments use budgetary accounting, and private firms not? In the private sector the principal yardstick of success is earnings or profit. The budget is useful as a guide to achieving that end, but meeting or staying within the budget is secondary to a private firm as long as revenues exceed expenses and a profit is earned. Thus in the private sector, revenues and profit rather than the budget generally serve to control or limit spending, and the budget is a plan but not, strictly speaking, a ceiling or a limit on spending. Therefore the budget is not recorded in a firm's accounting system. In the public sector, on the other hand, the budget is both a plan and a ceiling or a legal limit on spending, and the budget is entered into a government entity's accounting system.

Because the budget in government serves this important legal role, generally accepted accounting principles and the LGBFCA require that appropriations and estimated revenues from the approved budget be recorded in a local government's accounting system, and that actual expenditures and revenues be charged against the budgeted amounts. Of course, some county services, like certain county-owned and operated water system or combined water-sewer systems, generate sufficient revenues to cover their expenditures. Even so, the LGBFCA requires budgetary accounting for such self-supporting enterprise services as well as for non-self-supporting enterprises and general government functions.

Under the LGBFCA, budgetary accounting is not required for financial plans for internal service funds [G.S. 159-13.1, -28(a)]. If a county accounts for an internal service in an internal service fund, it may "budget" revenues and expenditures for the fund either in the annual budget ordinance or in a separate *financial plan*. Although the board of commissioners must approve any such financial plan, the approved amounts for revenues and expenditures in the plan are estimates and not legal limits. Consequently the LGBFCA does not require that these revenue and expenditure estimates be recorded in the unit's accounting system, although a county may choose to do so.

Basis of Accounting and Budgeting

Basis of accounting has to do with when revenues and expenditures or expenses are recorded in the accounting records and reported in the financial statements. It is of particular significance for revenue and expenditure or expense transactions that occur near the end of one fiscal year or at the beginning of the next one.[8] Basis of accounting provides criteria for determining the fiscal year in which such transactions should be recorded. There are three general bases of accounting:

1. *Cash basis,* by which revenues and expenditures are recorded when cash is received or disbursed.
2. *Accrual basis,* by which revenues are recorded when they are earned, regardless of when they are received in cash, and expenses are recorded when goods or services are received and

liabilities are created for them, regardless of when cash disbursements are made to pay for the goods and services.

3. *Modified accrual basis,* by which revenues are recorded when they are measurable and available, and, as with the accrual basis, expenditures, with a few exceptions, are recorded when goods and services are received and the liabilities for them are created.

Practically speaking, the modified accrual basis, as applied to North Carolina local governments, records many revenues when they are received in cash. However, some revenues to be received within a month or two after the start of a new fiscal year may be assigned to the prior fiscal year if their amounts can be determined (measured) at the end of the prior year and if they will be available soon enough after the close of that year to pay liabilities (bills) for expenditures incurred that year. Liabilities for many items and services received near the end of one fiscal year are often not paid until after the beginning of the next fiscal year. The quarterly distribution of sales tax revenues that the state makes to counties and municipalities in August each year may be budgeted and accounted for in the year ending on June 30, even though it is not received in cash until August of the next fiscal year. A county can estimate the amount of the August sales tax distribution with reasonable accuracy at the end of June, and that distribution is available early enough in the next fiscal year to cover expenditures incurred before June 30 of the prior year. Therefore the August sales tax payment may be recorded as a revenue for the year ending June 30.

The LGBFCA directs that counties and other local governments use the modified accrual basis of accounting except as otherwise provided by regulation of the Local Government Commission. Generally the commission requires local governments to record revenues and expenditures using the modified accrual basis of accounting.

Basis of accounting, as applied to budgeting, has to do with the year to which revenues and expenditures are assigned or for which they are estimated. Generally, estimates of revenues and expenditures in the budget should use the same "basis" as the recording of revenues and expenditures in the accounting system. Thus most or nearly all counties should use the modified accrual basis for budgeting revenues and expenditures. This means that counties should assign most revenues, including the property tax, to the year when they are received in cash, or if they are received shortly after the start of one fiscal year but are measurable and available at the end of the prior fiscal year, to the prior year's budget; and they should assign expenditures to the year in which the liabilities arising from those expenditures are expected to occur.

The Inclusiveness Requirement

The *inclusiveness requirement* means that a county or another local government may spend or disburse only moneys that have been budgeted [G.S. 159-8(a)]. Although the LGBFCA authorizes an exception for certain trust and agency fund moneys (see the discussion under the section "Moneys Not Having to Be Budgeted," later in this chapter), the inclusiveness requirement applies to all moneys, regardless of source, including property taxes, other local taxes, state shared revenues, user charges for specific services, federal and state grants, bond proceeds, fund balances, and any other money available to a county to fund its programs, activities, or projects. A county has several options for budgeting moneys: the annual budget ordinance, project ordinances, and financial plans. Board of commissioners' adoption is necessary for all these budgeting options.

The Annual Budget Ordinance

Any moneys that a county spends may be budgeted in the annual budget ordinance. If a county does not use project ordinances or financial plans for internal service funds, all county moneys that a county spends must be included in the annual budget ordinance. All revenues that support recurring operating expenditures are generally included in the annual budget ordinance, which is enacted for a July 1–June 30 fiscal year. More is written about the annual budget ordinance in subsequent sections of this chapter.

Project Ordinances

Expenditures and revenues for the construction or the acquisition of capital assets or for projects that are financed in whole or in part with federal or state grants or assistance, may be budgeted either in the annual budget ordinance or in one or more project ordinances. A *project ordinance* appropriates revenues and expenditures for however long it takes to complete the project rather than for a particular fiscal year or period (G.S. 159-13.2).

G.S. 159-13.2(a) specifies that a *capital project ordinance* may be used to appropriate revenues and expenditures for a project "financed in whole or in part by the proceeds of bonds or notes or debt instruments or a project involving the construction or acquisition of a capital asset." Practically speaking, counties are authorized to use bond or debt financing only for capital projects or acquisitions. Therefore the focus of attention here is the second part of this statutory language. What is a capital asset? According to generally accepted accounting principles, a *capital asset* is tangible property of significant value that has a useful life of more than one year. Such assets include land, buildings, improvements other than buildings, and equipment. The amount that establishes *significant value* for the purpose of identifying capital assets is determined locally and varies by size of jurisdiction. It usually falls somewhere between $100 and several thousand dollars. Although capital project ordinances may be used to appropriate revenues and expenditures for any capital asset, such ordinances are especially suitable and primarily used for capital improvements or acquisitions that are large relative to the annual resources of a county, that take more than one year to build or acquire, or that recur irregularly, that is, once every few years or less often. Expenditures for capital assets that are not expensive relative to a county's annual budget or that recur annually or with frequent regularity can usually be handled effectively in the annual budget.

A *grant project ordinance* may be used to appropriate revenues and authorize expenditures for operating or capital purposes in a project financed wholly or partly by a grant or other financial assistance from the federal or state government. A *grant* is a gift of cash or other assets from one government or entity to another that must be used or spent for a specific purpose. A *project* is a temporary activity. Thus a grant project ordinance should be used only to appropriate moneys for federally aided or state-aided activities that serve specific purposes and are temporary in nature. Grant project ordinances are often used for multiyear grants that counties receive, such as Community Development Block Grant moneys. Grant project ordinances should not be used to appropriate state-shared taxes or other federal or state revenue that is provided on a continuing basis to a county. Such revenue or aid, even if it is earmarked for a specific purpose, should be budgeted in the annual budget ordinance.

A project ordinance must identify and authorize the project, identify the revenue sources for financing it, make all appropriations necessary to complete the project, and must be adopted by the board of commissioners. A project ordinance may be adopted at any time during the year. A public hearing is not required in relation to the adoption of a project ordinance. Once a project ordinance has been adopted, it need not be readopted in subsequent fiscal years; it has a project life rather than an annual life. Correspondingly a project ordinance need not be balanced by year; it is balanced for the life of the project. A project ordinance may be amended at any time as long as it stays balanced. More is written about amending project ordinances later in this chapter.

A project ordinance must encompass all forecasted expenditures and revenues for the project. Revenues may include grant moneys, bond proceeds, transfers from capital reserve funds, annual revenues, fund balances, and other sources of revenue. Annual revenues may be appropriated directly into a project ordinance, or they may be appropriated initially in the annual budget ordinance and transferred from there into the project ordinance. If property taxes are used to finance a project authorized in a project ordinance, such taxes must be levied in the annual budget ordinance and then transferred into the project ordinance. A project may not be financed partly from appropriations in a project ordinance and partly from appropriations in the annual budget ordinance. If money is appropriated initially in the annual budget to finance a project for which a project ordinance exists, it must be transferred from the annual budget into the project ordinance and reappropriated there before it can be spent for the project. Appropriations for expenditures in a project ordinance may be a lump sum, that is, a single sum for the entire project, or they may be and usually are broken down into line-item or functional categories—for example, land, construction, and equipment.

The annual budget must include information about capital or grant project ordinances to be approved during the year and about previously adopted capital and grant project ordinances for which appropriations are available for expenditure in the budget year. Moneys appropriated and spent under grant project ordinances must be accounted for in a special revenue fund [G.S. 159-26(b)(2)]. Moneys appropriated and spent under a capital project ordinance in which bond or other debt financing is involved must be accounted for in a capital project fund [G.S. 159-26(b)(6)]. Generally accepted accounting principles encourage the use of a capital project fund for any major capital project authorized under a project ordinance, even if bond or debt financing is not involved.

Financial Plans for Internal Service Funds

As already mentioned, an internal service fund may be established to account for a service provided by one department or part of a local government to other departments or divisions in the same local unit, and in some cases to other local governments. In small counties, internal services, if they exist within the structure of county government, are typically budgeted and accounted for in the general fund and financed with general fund revenues. However, in many large counties and in a growing number of medium-size ones, many internal services are financed by charges to other departments for the use of the services, and they are budgeted and accounted for in internal service funds rather than in the general fund.

If a county uses an internal service fund, the fund's revenues and expenditures may be included either in the annual budget ordinance or in a separate financial plan adopted specifically for the fund [G.S. 159-8(a), -13.1]. The county board of commissioners must approve any financial plan adopted for an internal service fund, with such approval occurring at the same time that the board enacts the annual budget and running for the same July 1–June 30 fiscal year as the budget ordinance. In practice, a board of commissioners' approval of a financial plan often occurs simultaneously with its adoption of the annual budget ordinance; the ordinance may include a special provision indicating the board's approval of each financial plan. An approved financial plan must be balanced, and it may be amended only with the approval of the board of commissioners.

Moneys Not Having to Be Budgeted

The LGBFCA permits the revenues of certain local government trust and agency funds to be spent or disbursed without being budgeted [G.S. 159-13(a)(3)]. As already mentioned, a trust or agency fund accounts for moneys or other assets that are held and managed by a county but for which the county serves only as an agent or a trustee. For example, many counties collect property taxes as an agent for municipalities and other governmental units in the county. Although these collections are held temporarily by the county, they belong to the other units. They are therefore not revenues of the county collecting them, and it should not include them in its budget, even though it must account for them in a nonbudgeted agency fund. Many counties now set aside and manage moneys that finance special separation allowances and other retirement or special benefits for sheriff's department deputies and certain other county employees. Moneys set aside for such allowances or benefits do not belong to the county or to the county alone. The employees and the retirees for whom the county is managing these moneys have ownership rights in them. Although a county must budget its initial contributions on behalf of employees or retirees into the trust fund for such a benefit or pension system, usually calculated as some percentage of payroll, once the moneys are in the fund, earnings on the assets, payments to retirees or employees, and other receipts and disbursements of the fund should not be included in the county's budget.

Some counties have trust funds that generate income or provide other revenue that finances county services or projects. For example, a county may receive a donation that the donor requires be placed in a trust fund and be spent only for a specific function, for example, the county's parks and recreation programs. Because the money is to be spent for a county function, income or principal withdrawn from the fund to be spent for this function should be budgeted before being spent. Such trust funds are similar to special revenue funds; therefore income or withdrawals from them for financing county services should be budgeted.

The Balanced-Budget Requirement

A fundamental requirement of the LGBFCA is that the annual budget ordinance and any project ordinance or any financial plan for an internal service fund be balanced. The next section discusses the balancing requirement for the annual budget ordinance in some depth. The balancing requirements for project ordinances and financial plans differ somewhat from the requirement for the annual budget ordinance. Later sections discuss them.

The Annual Budget Ordinance

G.S. 159-8(a) states that the annual budget ordinance is balanced when "the sum of estimated net revenues and appropriated fund balances is equal to appropriations" (for expenditures). This law requires an exact balance; it permits neither a deficit nor a surplus. Further, each of the accounting funds that together make up the annual budget—the general fund, a water and sewer fund, and so forth—must also be balanced [G.S. 159-13(b)(16)].

During budget preparation, each of the variables in the balanced budget equation (estimated net revenues, appropriated fund balances, and appropriations for expenditures) is an estimate. The law makes this explicit with regard to revenues by referring to them as "estimated" net revenues. Both revenues and appropriations for expenditures remain estimates during budget preparation and through much of the budget year. Officials will not know whether their estimates for these variables are accurate until near the end of the budget year. Indeed, except for changing the property tax levy, the board of commissioners can amend the budget ordinance to increase (assuming unbudgeted money is available) or decrease appropriations during the year in order to accommodate changing conditions that cause estimates in the original annual budget to become outdated. Appropriated fund balance is taken from unrestricted money that is left over at the end of the current year that is legally available to budget in the coming year. During budget preparation for the coming year, which takes place before the current year ends, legally available fund balance at the end of the current year is also an estimate. It does not become an actual figure until the end of the current year, after all revenues for the year have been collected and all expenditures have been made.

Each variable in the budget equation for the annual budget ordinance is now examined.

Estimated Net Revenues

Revenues

Generally a *revenue* is an increase in cash or other financial resources, or in a few cases a decrease in liabilities, that increases an entity's net worth or fund balance and that can be made available in the budget to support spending.[9] An increase in cash or another financial resource that is balanced by an increase in one or more liabilities or by a decrease in other resources or assets does not increase an entity's net worth or fund balance and is therefore not a revenue.

For purposes of the LGBFCA, revenues or increases in financial resources (the equivalent of revenues under the LGBFCA) for a specific fund—for example, a capital project fund—may include proceeds from bonds or other debt that may be budgeted and spent from the fund, and transfers into the fund from other funds. However, what may be a revenue or an increase in financial resources for one fund of a county may not be a revenue or an increase in financial resources for the county as a whole. For instance, if a county issues bonds and deposits the bond proceeds into a governmental capital project fund, this increases that fund's cash and fund balance or equity, and when budgeted, would be considered a fund revenue or the equivalent under the LGBFCA. However, there is no increase in equity, net worth, or fund balance (assets minus liabilities) for the county as a whole because the county's general long-term debt, recorded in the general long-term debt group of accounts, increases by the amount of the bond proceeds. Under generally accepted accounting principles, the term *revenue* does not include debt proceeds or transfers into a fund from another fund of a county. Generally accepted accounting principles refer to debt proceeds and such transfers as *other financing sources* rather than revenues.

Some increases in cash or financial resources may appear to be revenues, but are actually collections of receivables under generally accepted accounting principles and also the LGBFCA. For instance, when a county buys materials or equipment, it pays state sales taxes on such purchases and then files for reimbursement from the state for the state sales taxes. Such sales taxes should be recorded as receivables rather than expenditures when the purchases for which they are paid are made. When the county receives reimbursement from the state for such sales taxes, the county should classify the reimbursement as the collection of a receivable rather than as a revenue under both generally accepted accounting principles and the LGBFCA. Such reimbursements should be budgeted neither as revenues nor as expenditures.

Net Revenues

The LGBFCA refers to "estimated net revenues" in the balanced-budget equation. The word *net* refers to revenues levied or billed, less discounts or amounts that a county does not expect to collect of the totals levied or billed. For example, some counties give property tax payers discounts for paying taxes before September 1 [G.S. 105-360(c)], which generally range from 1 to 3 percent of the tax levy. Moreover, counties and other units of local government seldom collect the full amounts of the property taxes that they levy or the water and sewer or other charges that they bill. The LGBFCA's explicit reference to net revenues in the balanced-budget equation directs local governments to budget only revenues that a county actually expects to collect or have available to fund expenditures during the budget year. Although not required by the LGBFCA, the annual budget ordinance may show or refer to gross, levied, or billed revenues as well as net revenues. However, the estimates of revenues used for the balanced budget equation should be net revenues only.

Budgeting of Revenues by Major Source

G.S. 159-13(a) requires that the annual budget ordinance "show revenues by major source." Generally accepted accounting principles as interpreted by the Local Government Commission define *major source* in this statute to include at least the following revenue categories: taxes, licenses and permits, intergovernmental revenues, charges for services, interest earnings, and miscellaneous revenues. The annual budget ordinances of most counties actually show or appropriate revenues in more specific categories-current year's property taxes, prior years' property taxes, sales taxes, and so forth, for general fund revenues.

Conservatism in Estimating Revenues

For any revenue source that is listed separately in the budget ordinance, one estimate must be selected from a range of possible figures. County officials should be conservative in estimating revenues. This means selecting an estimate for a revenue source that is somewhat below the midpoint of the range for that source. Some budget officials estimate revenues conservatively for all or most revenue sources. Others choose revenue estimates at the midpoint of the range for most sources, but are conservative on one or a few of the major sources, such as the property tax or the sales tax.

Property tax revenue is often estimated conservatively by underestimating the percentage of the levy that will be collected. Thus if a 98 percent collection percentage is anticipated for the coming year, the property tax revenue estimate in the budget might be calculated in terms of only a 97 percent collection rate. As a result, property tax revenue estimated in the budget is somewhat less than what will probably be collected.

County officials estimate revenues conservatively because the penalties for underestimating are usually less severe than those for overestimating.

Probably the most significant penalty that sometimes results from underestimating is the accumulation of a fund balance that is excessive, angering taxpayers. A range of unfortunate possibilities awaits the county that overestimates revenues. One possible consequence is having to cut appropriations and planned services that citizens were led to believe they would receive. If expenditures could not be cut and additional non-property-tax revenues could not be raised (the property tax levy may not be legally changed after the budget ordinance is adopted) to cover a shortfall caused by an overestimate of revenues, the year would end with a deficit to be funded from the next year's budget or from borrowing (strongly discouraged by the Local Government Commission). Either eventuality would likely hurt a county's standing with creditors or potential creditors. Awareness of these dangers tends to cause counties and other local governments to be conservative in estimating revenues for the budget.

Of course, a county or any local government can be too conservative in estimating revenues. There is a reasonable range of high to low forecasts for any revenue source, and budget makers cannot place their estimates below (or above) this range without being dishonest. However, because selecting this range depends as much on judgment as on calculation, there is no simple or definitive norm for determining what is an appropriately conservative estimate for major revenue sources. The extent of conservatism in estimating revenues should depend on one or more of various factors, including the following:

1. *The economic outlook.* If economists paint a bright picture for the coming year and the county is likely to benefit, the revenue estimates can be more optimistic. If the economy looks weak, however, and the weakness is likely to affect county revenues, revenue estimates should generally be more conservative.

2. *The tightness of the county's budgeting for expenditures.* If departments are expected to underspend their appropriations in the budget year, the need to be conservative in revenue estimates is reduced. On the other hand, if expenditures are tightly budgeted and departments are likely to spend all or nearly all their appropriations, revenue estimates should be more conservative.

3. *The size of fund balance and/or contingency appropriations.* If a county will close the current year with a significant general fund balance and/or significant working capital in enterprise funds that the county will carry as unappropriated operating

reserves into the next budget year, revenue estimates can be less conservative than they would otherwise be. However, if a county will have little or no unappropriated general fund balance or enterprise fund working-capital reserves to back up its budget for the next year, county officials should be more conservative in estimating revenue. A contingency appropriation can serve in place of an unappropriated fund balance as an operating reserve to support the budget, and although G.S. 159-13(b)(3) limits contingency appropriations to 5 percent of all other appropriations in a fund, a county that includes contingency appropriations in its budget can be somewhat less conservative in estimating revenues.

4. *The county's size.* A large county with considerable diversity in its revenue sources and specialized financial staff can operate closer to the margin in estimating revenue than a small county with fewer revenue sources and a small financial staff can. On this basis alone, a large unit could therefore estimate its revenues somewhat less conservatively than a small one, other things being equal.

Appropriated Fund Balance

The second variable in the balanced-budget equation for the annual budget is appropriated fund balance.

Available Fund Balance

Legally available fund balance is money that is left at the end of one fiscal year that may be appropriated to finance expenditures in the next year's budget. G.S. 159-8(a) defines such fund balance as "the sum of cash and investments minus the sum of liabilities, encumbrances, and deferred revenues arising from cash receipts, as those figures stand at the close of the fiscal year next preceding the budget year."

Legally available fund balance is calculated using this statutory formula. The calculation starts with an estimate of cash and investments at the end of the current year, and subtracts from them estimated liabilities, encumbrances, and deferred revenues from cash receipts at the end of the current year. All these figures are estimates because the calculation is being made for budget purposes before the end of the current year. If the estimate of available fund balance is for the general fund, typical liabilities are payroll owed for a payroll period that carries forward from the current year into the budget year, and accounts payable representing unpaid trade accounts for goods and services provided to the county toward the end of the current year. Such liabilities should be paid from the current year's moneys rather than the next year's; they will thus reduce cash and investments that would otherwise be part of available fund balance. Encumbrances arise from purchase orders and other unfulfilled contractual obligations for goods and services that are outstanding at the end of a fiscal year. They reduce legally available fund balance because cash and investments will be needed to pay for the goods and the services on order. A *deferred revenue* from a cash receipt is revenue that is received in cash in the current year, even though it is not owed to the county until the coming budget year. Such prepaid revenues are primarily property taxes. They should be included among revenues for the coming year's budget rather than carried forward as available fund balance from the current to the coming year.

Legally available fund balance is different from fund balance, equity, or net worth for financial reporting purposes as presented in the balance sheet of a county's annual financial report. Legally available fund balance includes only cash and investments. It may not include any receivables or other current assets. By contrast, fund balance, equity, or net worth for financial reporting purposes is calculated considering all assets of the fund, and includes receivables as well as cash and investments. In calculating or estimating fund balance available for appropriation into next year's budget, county officials should use the legal formula provided in G.S. 159-8(a) rather than the accounting or balance sheet amount for fund balance.

Some legally available fund balance, as defined by G.S. 159-8(a), may be restricted or reserved for particular purposes by other statutes. For example, a portion could represent restricted moneys that may be spent only for a specific function. Available fund balance attributable to such moneys will generally be reserved to show that it is not available for general purposes. It is a part of legally available fund balance under G.S. 159-8(a), but it is available only for the restricted purpose and not for general spending in the next year's budget. Other portions of legally available fund balance may be designated by local officials for particular purposes—for example, future capital improvements—and therefore may also not be available for general purposes in the next year's budget unless local officials remove the designations.

Sources of Fund Balance

Legally available fund balance at the end of the current fiscal year can originate from unbudgeted fund balance carried forward from the prior year or from conservative revenue estimates or underspent appropriations in the current year's budget.

Appropriated and Unappropriated Fund Balance

Fund balance that is legally available at the end of the current year does not have to be appropriated into the next year's budget except under one condition. If part or all of it is needed to balance the next year's budget, considering estimated revenues and appropriated expenditures for the year, at least that much of the available fund balance must be appropriated. Otherwise, none of the legally available fund balance need be budgeted, legally speaking. A county may choose to appropriate some or all of available and unrestricted fund balance for any purpose for which the county is authorized to spend money. The county might also budget available fund balance in a contingency appropriation; as already noted, the amount of this appropriation may not exceed 5 percent of all other appropriations in a fund. If a larger operating reserve is needed, as is often the case, it must remain outside the budget as unappropriated fund balance. Alternatively, if a county does not need any fund balance to balance its budget, it may choose not to appropriate any available fund balance. Any portion of legally available fund balance that a county budgets is generally called *appropriated fund balance*. Any portion that remains outside the budget is called *unappropriated fund balance*.

Reasons for Counties to Carry Fund Balances

Counties and other local governments carry significant fund balances to provide working capital to pay vendors and others in a timely way, to meet emergency or unforeseen needs, and to be able to take advantage of unexpected opportunities requiring the expenditure of money. If a county with low fund balance attempts to issue bonds, its bond rating may be hurt because of inadequate fund balance, causing the county to have to pay more in interest than it otherwise would. Without fund balances, some counties would face a cash-flow deficit during the first half of the fiscal year because most property tax revenue, the most important general revenue source, is not received until December, whereas expenditures are evenly distributed throughout the year. With Local Government Commission approval, such a deficit may be funded by borrowing against anticipated tax or other revenues, but the interest cost of such borrowing adds to expenditures, and such borrowing is discouraged by the Local Government Commission. Counties in North Carolina have traditionally used end-of-year fund balances rather than borrowing against anticipated tax or other revenues to meet cash-flow shortfalls in the first part of the budget year. Finally, even in periods of low interest rates, a county with significant fund balance can earn investment income that helps to hold down its property tax.

Recommended Amount of Available Fund Balance

Staff of the Local Government Commission recommend that counties end a fiscal year with legally available general fund balance equal to at least 8 percent of general fund expenditures for that year. Commission staff consider the 8-percent level to be a floor, representing only about one month's expenditures and needed just to meet operating or working-capital requirements. Therefore they encourage most counties to maintain fund balances larger than this. If a county's end-of-year general fund balance falls below 8 percent of general fund expenditures, commission staff will send county officials a letter noting this fact and advising them to rebuild available general fund balance at least to the 8-percent level. If county officials fail to do so, the county may be unable to secure the commission's approval in selling bonds or other debt instruments.

In deciding how much available general fund balance a county should carry, officials should consider the experiences of other counties of similar size. Generally, smaller and medium-size counties have larger available fund balance relative to expenditures than large counties do. It is not uncommon for counties with fewer than 100,000 people to have available general fund balance in a range between 20 to 30 percent of general fund expenditures. Such a fund balance may seem excessive. However, it usually is not, considering the actual dollar amounts that these percentages represent in relation to the large unforeseen expenditures that small and medium-size counties must occasionally make to meet emergency needs. Also, some counties rely heavily on pay-as-you-go financing of capital improvements and build general fund balance for such financing of future capital needs. Statistics on available fund balance for counties of different sizes are compiled and published each year by the Local Government Commission.

The amount of available general fund balance that a particular county carries should depend on a variety of factors, including how conservatively it estimates revenues, how tightly it budgets expenditures, whether it faces a cash-flow deficit during the first half of the fiscal year, and what economic prospects are. Generally officials should increase general fund balance to the extent that revenues are estimated less conservatively, actual spending takes most of appropriations, a cash-flow deficit exists, available reserves do not exist in other funds, or economic conditions affecting local revenues and expenditures worsen. Available fund balance carried by a particular county should also depend in part on how well the county manages its fiscal affairs. The better a county manages these affairs, the more likely it can get by with a somewhat lower available fund balance.

Presentation of Fund Balance Information in the Budget

The LGBFCA explicitly requires that any appropriation of fund balance be shown in the annual budget ordinance [G.S. 159-8(a), -13(a)]. By implication the recommended budget, which must be balanced unless the board of commissioners authorizes the budget officer to submit an unbalanced budget, must also show any appropriation of fund balance that the budget officer proposes to use to balance the budget. There are, however, no additional requirements for the budget or the budget ordinance to present fund balance information. As a matter of local policy, the recommended budget for a county should include the budget officer's estimate of legally available fund balance at the close of the current year as well as any amount of this fund balance that the budget officer is proposing for appropriation into the coming year's budget. The recommended budget should also include a brief discussion of the budget's fund balance policies. Because available fund balance on June 30 can only be estimated at the time of budget preparation, the presentation of much of this fund balance information in the budget must be tentative. Nonetheless, such information is important and should be part of the budget presentation. A county's annual financial report will eventually reveal actual fund balances on June 30 for the fiscal year preceding the budget year, changes in the county's fund balance during that year, and the amount of available fund balance appropriated into the budget, but that report will not be available for at least three months after the budget year begins.

Appropriations for Expenditures

The third variable in the balanced-budget equation is appropriations for expenditures. An *appropriation* is an estimate of future expenditures, a legal authorization to spend, and a ceiling on expenditures. Only the board of county commissioners may establish appropriations; neither the budget officer nor any other administrative official may do so. The expenditure figures that appear in the budget officer's recommended budget are only proposed appropriations and breakdowns of those appropriations.

An appropriation is a specified dollar amount set forth in the annual budget ordinance or in a capital or grant project ordinance. Financial plans for internal service funds estimate and authorize expenditures. However, the estimates and the authorizations are not ceilings for expenditures and therefore are not appropriations under the LGBFCA (G.S. 159-13.1).

Lump-Sum or Detailed Appropriations

G.S. 159-13(a) provides that appropriations in the annual budget ordinance shall be by department, function, or project. This raises the question of how general or specific appropriations should be. A very detailed budget ordinance makes appropriations by line item or by individual object of expenditure. The line items or the objects of expenditure are taken from the expenditure accounts in a county's accounting system. Some small counties may have annual budget ordinances with detailed line-item appropriations. Although such appropriations facilitate close control by the board of commissioners over departmental expenditures, they can cause the board to become enmeshed in the details of budget administration and correspondingly neglect the broader issues of budget development and execution.

Most counties make appropriations by department or by function or division within departments. This level of appropriation seems to be favored by G.S. 159-13(a), specifying that the annual budget ordinance "shall make appropriations by department, function, or project and show revenues by major source." With departmental, functional, or project appropriations, the board of commissioners delegates control over expenditures by line item to the budget officer (the manager in counties with the manager form of government), who is responsible for reviewing and approving expenditures from line-item accounts and transfers of money from one such account to another within the same departmental or functional appropriation. Usually this system works well because control over expenditures by line item is typically a management responsibility.

In some counties the board of commissioners permits the budget officer or the manager to delegate to department heads the authority to approve most transfers among line-item accounts within each departmental or functional appropriation, reporting such transfers to the budget or finance officer as or after they are made. In return for this flexibility, department heads are held accountable for achieving specific performance targets or objectives within appropriated funds. In units where such budget flexibility is practiced, certain transfers on or off salaries and wages lines or accounts may still have to be approved by the budget officer or staff before being made.

A lump-sum appropriation for the general fund or any fund from which more than one department or function is financed is too broad and is not in keeping with the intent of G.S. 159-13(a). Appropriation by fund is legally permissible only for a fund that finances the activities of just one department or function.

Nondepartmental Appropriations

Some appropriations authorize expenditures for what are called nondepartmental purposes or items—for example, premium payments for property and general liability insurance, and contributions to private nonprofit organizations that carry out functions that the county itself is authorized to undertake. The use of nondepartmental appropriations should be limited. The LGBFCA favors the allocation of expenditures among departmental, functional, program, or project appropriations in the annual budget ordinance. Moreover, generally accepted accounting principles require that nondepartmental appropriations be held to a minimum.[10]

Allocation of Appropriations for Shared Services

General fund departments often provide certain services to other funds. For example, if a county operates a water system from an enterprise fund, the county finance department, which is typically budgeted and accounted for in the general fund, often prepares and mails utility bills and processes utility payments for the water fund. Both the general fund and the water fund share the services of the finance department. Water and other enterprise or other funds should reimburse the general fund for billing, mailing, and collection services provided by the county finance department to these other funds. Such reimbursements should be budgeted and accounted for as expenditures (expenses) for the enterprise or other funds. On the general fund side of the transaction, some counties mistakenly budget and account for such reimbursements as revenues or "other financing sources." Generally accepted accounting principles call for these reimbursements to be accounted for as reimbursements of general fund expenditures. To avoid having to make the reimbursements, a county, in preparing the budget, may allocate or split the appropriation for the finance department between the general and enterprise or other funds based on the estimated use of finance department services by each fund. Such split or allocated appropriations are in accord with generally accepted accounting principles and may be the simplest way for counties to budget and account for expenditures for shared services.

Required Appropriations

Although counties generally enjoy discretion over what programs and expenditures they choose to provide, and at what levels, the LGBFCA places certain limits on this discretion. First, the full amount estimated by the county's finance officer to be required for debt service during the budget year must be appropriated [G.S. 159-13(b)(1)]. During the spring the Local Government Commission notifies each finance officer of that county's debt service obligations on existing debt for the coming year. If the county does not appropriate enough money for the payment of principal and interest on its debt, the commission may order the county to make the necessary appropriation; if the county ignores this order, the commission may itself levy the local tax for debt service purposes (G.S. 159-36).

Second, sufficient appropriations must be made for continuing contracts [G.S. 159-13(b)(15)]. *Continuing contracts* are those that extend over more than one fiscal year. G.S. 153A-13 requires that in each year of such a contract, the board of commissioners appropriate sufficient funds to meet payments that come due that year under the contract. G.S. 159-13 (b)(15) of the LGBFCA simply repeats that requirement.

Third, the full amount of any deficit in each fund must be appropriated [G.S. 159-13(b)(2)]. Three types of deficits may occur to which this requirement applies:

1. Despite the LGBFCA's provisions to the contrary, expenditures occasionally occur without an appropriation or exceed appropriations, creating a deficit for that appropriation and perhaps for the entire fund. If the fiscal year ends with such a circumstance and the expenditures are otherwise authorized by law, the resulting deficit must be funded by an appropriation in the budget ordinance for the coming fiscal year.

2. Revenue estimates may turn out to be higher than actual revenue collections for a year. Although expenditures may not exceed the revenue estimates, they may exceed revenue collections. If this occurs and if the legally available fund balance in the affected fund falls below zero, a deficit exists in that fund, and sufficient moneys must be appropriated in the next fiscal year's budget to make up the deficit.

3. A deficit is created when a county appropriates more fund balance in the budget than the amount that is legally available on June 30 of the year preceding the budget year (see the discussion under the section "Available Fund Balance," earlier in this chapter). If such an overappropriation of fund balance occurs, the budget ordinance must be amended to correct this situation.

Limits on Appropriations

Several LGBFCA provisions place upper or lower limits on certain appropriations. First, as already mentioned, contingency appropriations for each fund are limited to 5 percent of the total of all other appropriations in that fund.

Second, G.S. 159-13(b)(4) requires that tax limits and earmarked revenues be respected. For example, portions of the two half-percent local-option sales and use taxes are earmarked for school capital outlay or debt service. Appropriations or provisions in the budget ordinance for proposed expenditures of these two half-percent sales tax revenues must evidence compliance by the county with these statutory earmarking requirements for education.

Third, G.S. 159-13(b)(5) states that the total of all appropriations for purposes that require voter approval for expenditure of property tax moneys under Article V, Section 2(5), of the North Carolina Constitution must not exceed the total of all estimated nonproperty-tax revenues (not including nontax revenues required by law to be spent for specific purposes) and property taxes levied for such purposes pursuant to a vote of the people.

Restrictions on Appropriations for Interfund Transfers

The annual budget ordinance often makes appropriations to transfer money from one fund to another. A contribution, or *transfer-out*, from one fund becomes a financial resource, or *transfer-in*, to the receiving fund. The LGBFCA generally permits appropriations for interfund transfers, but it sets some restrictions on them, each designed to maintain the basic integrity of a fund in light of the purposes for which the fund was established. In addition, the LGBFCA prohibits certain interfund transfers of moneys that are earmarked for a specific service. The LGBFCA's restrictions on interfund transfers for counties affect voted property tax funds, agency funds for special districts, capital project funds involving bond or debt proceeds, enterprise funds, service district funds, a property tax reappraisal, and overhead and revenue-generation and -collection costs.

1. *Voted property tax funds.* Proceeds from a voted property tax may be used only for the purpose approved by the voters. Such proceeds must be budgeted and accounted for in a special revenue fund and may not be transferred from such a fund [G.S. 159-13(b)(10)].

2. *Agency funds for special districts.* Moneys collected by a county for a special district belong to that district, not to the county, and such moneys may not be appropriated from the agency fund for the district to any other fund of the county [G.S. 159-14(b)].

3. *Capital projects funds involving bond or debt proceeds.* Bond or debt proceeds may be spent only for the purposes for which the bonds or the debt was issued. Therefore the statutes permit the appropriation or the transfer of bond proceeds only (1) for the purposes stated in the bond order, (2) to a debt service fund to pay debt service on the bonds, or (3) to a capital reserve fund for eventual expenditure for the purpose stated in the bond order [G.S. 159-13(b)(13)]. Expenditure of the proceeds of debt instruments other than bonds is more circumscribed; such proceeds may be spent only for the project or the purpose for which the debt was approved and issued [G.S. 159-13(b)(19)].

4. *Enterprise funds.* Appropriations to transfer moneys from an enterprise fund to another fund may be made only if other appropriations in the enterprise fund are sufficient to meet operating

expenses, capital outlays, and debt service for the enterprise [G.S. 159-13(b)(14)]. This limitation reflects the policy that enterprise revenues must first meet the expenditures and the obligations related to the enterprise. Enterprise revenues are not absolutely earmarked, however; once all enterprise expenditures have been funded by appropriations, the law permits any remaining moneys to be transferred to another fund.

5. *Service district funds.* Although a service district is not a separate government, specific taxes and other revenues raised within it for the district belong to the district. Therefore no appropriation may be made to transfer moneys from a service district fund except for the purposes for which the district was established [G.S. 159-13(b)(18)].

6. *Reappraisal reserve fund.* The reappraisal reserve is established to accumulate money with which to finance the county's next real property revaluation, which must occur at least once every eight years. Appropriations may not be made from a reappraisal reserve fund for any other purpose [G.S. 159-13(b)(17)]. Although contracting with a private appraisal company is a commonly used means of conducting a revaluation, counties have the authority to do the work with their own staff. If an in-house revaluation capacity exists, personnel and other costs associated with it will be a part of the regular annual budget. Start-up costs, such as computer acquisitions for the reappraisal, may be paid from transfers of money from a reappraisal reserve fund.

7. *Overhead and revenue-generation and -collection costs.* Each prohibition or limitation on interfund transfers discussed in this section except the one relating to capital project funds, is subject to the modification that any fund may be charged for general administrative and overhead costs properly allocable to its activities, and for the costs of levying and collecting its revenues [G.S. 159-13(b)].

Project Ordinances

The LGBFCA requires a capital or grant project ordinance to be balanced for the life of the project, specifies that such an ordinance is balanced when "revenues estimated to be available for the project equal appropriations for the project," and requires the ordinance to identify the revenues for financing the project and to make the appropriations necessary to complete the project. A project ordinance may be amended at any time as long as the ordinance remains balanced (G.S. 159-13.2).

The key characteristic of a project ordinance is that it has a project life, which means that the balancing requirement for such an ordinance is not bound by or related to any fiscal year or period. Estimated revenues and appropriations in a project ordinance must be balanced for the life of the project, but do not have to be balanced for any fiscal year or period that the ordinance should happen to span.

A project ordinance does not have to be readopted after it is initially enacted, and spending authority created by a project ordinance continues in force for however long it takes to complete the project authorized by the ordinance. A project ordinance may be amended to change the scope of the project, to keep revenues and expenditures for the project in balance, or to accomplish other purposes.

Estimated revenues for a project ordinance may include bond or debt proceeds, federal or state grants, revenues from special assessments or impact fees, other special revenues, and annually recurring revenues. As already mentioned, annually recurring revenues may be budgeted initially in the annual budget ordinances and then transferred to a project ordinance, or appropriated directly into the project ordinance. If property tax revenue is used to help finance a project ordinance, it must be levied initially in the annual budget ordinance before being transferred to the project ordinance.

Appropriations for expenditures in a project ordinance may be general or detailed. A single lump-sum appropriation for a project fulfills the requirements of the LGBFCA. However, project ordinances for major capital improvements or large grant-financed projects generally break down appropriations into expenditure categories. For improvement projects the common categories are planning and design, land, construction, equipment and furnishings, and administrative and legal expenses. Appropriations for grant programs for operating purposes are often made by function or purpose authorized under the grant, by general line-item category, or some combination.

Fund balance is not part of the balanced-budget equation for project ordinances. Because project ordinances do not have fiscal year or period lives, they do not generate fund balances. Of course, projects are frequently completed with appropriated revenues remaining unspent. Practically speaking, such excess revenues are equivalent to a project fund balance. However, because a project ordinance's authority ends with the completion of the project, the LGBFCA's silence about such remaining project revenues suggests that a project's completion should occasion the transfer of any remaining project revenues to another appropriate project, fund, or purpose. Annual revenues budgeted in a project ordinance that remain after a project is finished may be transferred back to the annual budget ordinance. Bond proceeds remaining after a project is finished should be transferred to the appropriate fund for other projects authorized by the bond order or to pay debt service on the bonds.

Financial Plans for Internal Service Funds

The LGBFCA requires any approved financial plan for an internal service fund to be balanced. It specifies that such a plan is balanced when "estimated expenditures do not exceed estimated revenues."

Internal service fund revenues are principally charges to county departments that use the services of an internal service fund. These charges are financed by appropriated expenditures of the using departments in the annual budget ordinance. Internal service fund revenues or resources may also include an appropriated subsidy or transfer unrelated to specific internal service fund services, from the general fund to the internal service fund. Such a subsidy is often made during the start-up years of an internal service fund. It should be shown as a transfer-in rather than a revenue per se for the internal service fund. Internal service fund revenues may also include investment income and income from other sources.

Expenditures for an internal service fund are typically for items necessary to provide fund services, including salaries and wages; other operating outlays; lease, rental, or debt service payments and/or depreciation charges on equipment or facilities used by the fund; and other internal service expenditures. Estimates of fund expenditures might be by purpose or function within the fund rather than by line item.

The LGBFCA makes no mention of internal service fund balance and reserves or the equivalent (fund equity), even though the approved financial plan for any such fund is for the same fiscal year as the annual budget, and even though an internal service fund's revenues may exceed its expenditures in a year, creating fund balance or reserves for that year and possibly over time. In adopting the annual financial plan for an internal service fund, the board of commissioners must decide what to do with any available balance or reserves remaining from any previous year's financial plan. The law permits such balance or reserves to be used to help finance fund operations in the next year, or if the balance is substantial, to fund long-term capital needs of the fund. Alternatively such balance may be allowed to continue accumulating for the purpose of financing major capital needs of the fund in the future, or it may be transferred to the general or another fund and be used there. Generally accepted accounting principles discourage the buildup of internal service fund balance unrelated to specific present or future needs of the fund.[11] Accumulation of large balance or reserves may also create problems if internal service fund expenditures are charged to federal grant programs. Federal regulations prohibit excessive charges to federal programs, and unexplained internal service fund balance or reserves may be interpreted by auditors as resulting from excessive charges.

The Budget Officer

Authorities on budgeting distinguish between a budget developed or prepared by a legislative body or a governing board and one prepared by or under the direction of the jurisdiction's chief executive officer. When a local governing board formulates the budget, departmental budget requests flow directly to the board; it estimates revenues, balances the requests against available revenues, and then enacts the budget. This can be called a *legislatively prepared budget*. On the other hand, an *executive budget* is one prepared by a jurisdiction's chief executive officer, who receives departmental budget requests, reviews and balances the requests against available revenues, and submits a recommended and balanced budget to the legislative body for its review and approval.

The LGBFCA provides for an executive budget. It calls for each county to appoint a budget officer to be responsible for budget preparation (G.S. 159-9 and -11). By law a county's manager is *ex officio* its budget officer. The law gives the manager this responsibility because the budget is the basis for managing and providing public services. A few counties without the manager form of government nonetheless have a professional county administrator who also serves as county budget officer. In the one or two counties without a county manager or administrator, the board of commissioners must appoint a budget officer to serve at its pleasure. Any officer or employee, including a commissioner or the county finance officer, may serve as the budget officer—except for the sheriff and, in counties with more than 7,500 people, the register of deeds.

Having one official who is responsible for budget preparation focuses responsibility for timely preparation of the budget, permits a technical review of departmental estimates to ensure completeness and accuracy, and allows for administrative analysis of departmental priorities in the context of a county's overall priorities. This centered responsibility for budget preparation means that the council receives a budget already reviewed by someone who shares its overall perspective and who has the first-hand knowledge to evaluate and recommend services and priorities.

In many of the state's counties, the county manager delegates many of the duties associated with budget preparation to another official or employee, for example, the finance officer or a separate budget director or administrator. This is strictly an administrative arrangement, usually with the official or the employee performing these duties serving only as staff to the manager. Under the law and often in actual practice, the manager retains full responsibility for budget preparation and decision making, subject to board of commissioner review and approval.[12]

The Annual Budget Preparation Process

The LGBFCA provides for three general stages of annual budget preparation and enactment: formulation of expenditure requests by county departments, preparation of a recommended budget by the budget officer, and governing board review and enactment of the annual budget ordinance. Preceding these stages is a preliminary organizational stage.

Initiation of the Budget Process

Before the budget process begins, the budget officer, alone or often with the board of commissioners' direction and advice, generally establishes an administrative calendar for budget preparation and prescribes forms and procedures for departments to use in formulating requests. Budget officers in many counties also issue fiscal or program policies to guide department officials in formulating their budget requests.

Calendar for Budget Preparation

The LGBFCA specifies the dates by which each stage in the annual budget process is to be completed (G.S. 159-10 through -13). Departmental requests must be submitted to the budget officer before April 30. The recommended budget must be given to the board of county commissioners no later than June 1, and the board must enact the budget ordinance by July 1, when the fiscal year begins. The most important of these dates is the last one.

Even if the budget ordinance is not enacted by July 1, its legal validity is not impaired once it is enacted. Similarly, even if the departments and the budget officer miss their target dates, neither the budget process nor the budget is invalid in any way. The failure of a county to enact its annual budget by July 1, however, may suggest that it is experiencing problems in managing its fiscal affairs. The Local Government Commission and the national bond rating agencies are likely to look unfavorably on such a failure if it happens year after year.

If a county fails to enact its annual budget ordinance by July 1, it must enact an interim budget to provide legal authority for expenditures made between July 1 and whenever the budget ordinance is finally approved. In certain years over the last decade, some counties have delayed enactment of their budget ordinances several weeks to a month or more after July 1 because they were waiting for the General Assembly to pass the state budget. Officials in these units felt that they could not enact their budgets without knowing with certainty how much revenue the state budget was going to provide to them.

The statutory dates of April 30, June 1, and July 1 for budget preparation serve as targets for establishing an administrative calendar for annual budgeting. This calendar can be established by working back from the statutory dates. It should specify who is responsible for doing what in annual budget preparation and enactment.

Several key issues arise in setting the administrative calendar. The most obvious one is how much time the calendar should provide overall for budget preparation. The larger and more complex the budget, the more controversial the issues addressed in it, and the more departmental and citizen participation in the process, the longer the calendar needs to be. Most medium- and large-size counties allow four to six months or so for budget preparation and enactment.

A second issue concerning the administrative calendar for budget preparation is whether the board of commissioners and the budget officer should, at the very start of the process, set guidelines for departments to follow in making budget requests. Although the LGBFCA does not expressly address this early role for the board and the budget officer, it does not prohibit such a practice, and more and more boards of commissioners and budget officers are using it. Such a procedure enables elected and top administrative officials to take more initiative in setting policy in the budget. It also saves department heads' time: guidelines tell them early what the board's priorities and intentions are; therefore they need not waste time generating requests that have no chance of being funded.[13]

Budget Forms and Procedures

Forms are unavoidable in budgeting: they are necessary to calculate expenditures and revenues and summarize the budget; they are important because by structuring information, they can influence the outcome of budget decisions. The budget officer has the authority to prescribe the forms and the procedures for departments to use in preparing their requests. In the words of G.S. 159-10, requests "shall be made in such form and detail, with such supporting information and justifications, as the budget officer may prescribe." In large counties the budget officer usually prepares a budget manual—including forms, instructions, and sample requests—and provides other information such as historical data for department officials to use in making their requests.

Several types of forms are basic and are found in almost any budget preparation system, regardless of a jurisdiction's size and approach to budgeting. One type lists positions and corresponding salaries and wages. A second type lists expenditures by account, object, or line item. One of the line items is a total for salaries and wages that is taken from the salaries-and-wages form; other lines list expenditures for different expenditure accounts. G.S. 159-10 requires that a budget request show actual expenditures for the prior year, estimated expenditures for the current year, and requested expenditures for the coming year. This second budget form should show expenditures by line item for each of these three years. Many counties use additional request forms that are tailored to their needs in budget preparation. The information from the various forms used for preparing budget requests is usually consolidated as the process progresses from the request stage through the recommended budget to enactment of the budget ordinance.

Departmental Requests

A departmental budget request often includes estimated receipts from fees imposed for departmental services; expenditures for salaries, fringe benefits, supplies, other operating items, and capital or permanent property items; requests for new positions or improved or new services; and in a growing number of counties, a service plan focusing on program goals and objectives and including performance measures. In some counties, departmental budget requests distinguish between expenditures to continue services at current levels and those to expand or improve services. If budget reductions are to be made, departmental budget requests often identify where departmental services and the departmental budget might be cut.

Departmental Receipts

G.S. 159-10 requires that the budget request for a department include revenues or fees that it will collect in the budget year. The request must show such receipts whether they are earmarked by law or local policy exclusively to finance departmental expenditures or are available for financing any county programs or services. In many counties the county finance officer actually makes the estimates of revenues to be collected by a department. If department officials make these estimates, they should be reviewed by the county finance officer before they become part of the budget.

Line-Item Expenditures

Salaries and wages make up the largest share of expenditures in most departmental budget requests. To estimate these requirements, department officials typically start with a list of existing authorized positions. A budget request should include an estimate of how much of the amount to be authorized for salaries and wages will not be spent because of vacancies, and it should not overlook special salary payments such as overtime, premium pay for work on holidays or on second or third shifts, and longevity pay. Decisions on salary and wage increases or adjustments are usually made on a countywide basis; therefore the money to fund them is usually not included in departmental budget requests. That money is budgeted initially in a nondepartmental account or maintained in unappropriated fund balance. After the board of commissioners approves the increases or the adjustments, or at the start of the new budget year, the money is transferred to departmental salaries-and-wages accounts.

Fringe benefits are an increasingly expensive component of most departmental budgets. Such benefits include time away from work (for example, vacations and sick leave). Although time away from work may not require specific cash outlays by a county and therefore does not of itself have to be budgeted, it may create the need for expenditures for temporary employees or other permanent positions, which, of course, do have to be budgeted. Fringe benefits also include county contributions for Social Security, health and other insurance, retirement benefits, and other employee benefits, which all must be budgeted. Because of increasing fringe benefit costs for permanent employees, some counties are relying more on temporary or part-time employees (for whom they must usually pay only Social Security contributions) or on private contractors to perform certain county functions or work.

Supplies and operating expenditures are another component of departmental budget requests. In this category, inflation may have to be taken into account. On the items that a county buys, like gasoline or uniforms, inflation may run higher or lower than increases in the general consumer or wholesale price indexes. In budgeting for inflation, counties should refer to one or more of the special price indexes available to measure cost increases for supplies or services that local governments use. For instance, *American City and County* magazine publishes such indexes.[14] Some counties may require departments to use a single percentage-increase allowance to budget for inflation for all items; others may permit departments to use percentage-increase allowances that vary from item to item. The percentage-increase allowance(s) can be based on knowledge of what inflation has been over the most recent fiscal year or twelve-month period, or on a forecast of what it is projected to be in the budget year.

Acquisitions of capital assets such as equipment, vehicles, and furnishings are also a significant part of most departmental budget requests. A capital or permanent property item is one that is held or used for more than one year and is of significant value, for example, worth $500 or more. In budgeting for capital or permanent property, counties find it useful to distinguish between items that replace existing equipment, vehicles, or furnishings, and items that are in addition to existing items. Replacement capital items are usually more likely to be approved and funded in the budget than additional ones. The difficulties of budgeting for expensive capital or permanent property in the annual budget have been eased somewhat with the wide availability of lease and installment purchase arrangements for financing capital items. In the past a county had to pay cash in one lump sum up front to acquire most capital or permanent property items. Now a county has the choice of paying for capital items in cash up front or in installments over several years under leases or installment purchase contracts.

Service Plans

Many medium-size and large counties and some small ones require departments to include annual service plans with their budget requests. These plans identify objectives for departmental services and activities and include performance measures related to the objectives. The objectives are often derived from board of commissioner-approved goals for departmental services. A service plan can be the starting point— or one of them—in preparing a budget request. Too often the only formal starting point for a departmental budget request is its current year's budget. Boards of commissioners are increasingly asking about the levels and the quality of services that their counties are receiving for money budgeted, and departmental service plans help answer these questions.[15]

Continuation and Expansion Expenditures

Departmental budget requests may distinguish between continuation and expansion expenditures. *Continuation expenditures* are generally those that are made just to provide the same level and quality of service in the coming budget year that the department is providing in the current year. Such expenditures typically include outlays in the current year that will repeat in the budget year with adjustments for salary and wage increments, inflation or deflation on items to be purchased, rate changes on contractual obligations, necessary replacement of capital equipment, and certain nonrecurring items. *Expansion expenditures* typically include requests for new positions, for additional capital equipment or assets, and for program growth or new programs or services. Expansion expenditures are highlighted in almost any budget request and must usually be well justified to be approved and funded. The justification should refer to any law or contract that will be violated if the request is not funded; use statistics, if available, to show the need for what is being requested; indicate whether other similarly situated counties are funding the service or the item being requested; and include a forecast of probable expenditures for the request for several years beyond the coming budget year.

Identification of Budget Reductions

Resistance to tax increases and the need to provide county services more efficiently are causing more counties to require department officials to identify possible savings in operations, low-priority programs, and possible reductions in departmental budgets. This chapter addresses that important topic later in the section "Incremental and Zero-Base Budgeting and Budget Reductions."

The Recommended Budget

The LGBFCA requires that the budget officer's recommended budget be balanced unless the board of county commissioners insists that an unbalanced budget be submitted [G.S. 159-11(c)]. In the latter instance the budget officer might simply give to the board the departmental requests and revenue estimates at current rates, noting the property tax rate that would have to be levied to balance the budget. Even in this circumstance, however, the budget officer should conduct at least a technical review, checking the accuracy and the completeness of departmental requests.

This minimal role for the budget officer in compiling departmental budget requests and estimating revenues does not fulfill the intent of the LGBFCA. The budget officer should be much more than a clerk who compiles budget figures and passes them on to the board. The LGBFCA calls on the budget officer to prepare a balanced budget for the county. Until this happens, the various components of the budget may exist, but the budget for the county as a whole has yet to be created. Developing that budget requires the budget officer to exercise both judgment and skill with regard to fiscal requirements, program needs, and the political environment of the county. In short, the budget officer's role in preparing a county's budget is a crucial one. A board of commissioners should expect the budget officer to review departmental requests substantively, examine revenue estimates, recommend changes in services and revenue rates or sources, and present a budget that balances the needs and the resources of the county.

The Budget Officer's Review of Requests

In setting the administrative calendar for budget preparation, the budget officer can require that requests be submitted all at once or on staggered dates. Having the requests come in on a staggered basis over several weeks spreads the work of budget review.

What, specifically, should be the focus of the budget officer's review of departmental requests? First, the budget officer or staff should make sure that all expenditure items included in the base on which departments have built their budget requests are indeed needed. The base for building a budget request is most often an updated estimate of expenditures for the current year. This base is generally calculated by starting with the current year's budget as enacted, adjusted for amendments and actual expenditure experience from July 1 to date, and further adjusted by a revised forecast of expenditures for the remainder of the current year. In counties facing fiscal retrenchments, the budget base may be reduced to an amount equal to 95 percent or less of the revised estimate of the current year's expenditures. In a few counties the base may include all expenditures necessary to continue services at current levels into the coming budget year. In most situations this would provide a base somewhat above the revised estimate of the current year's expenditures.

Second, the budget officer should make sure that every additional dollar included in a budget request over the base is accounted for. Thus if the base—that is, the revised current year's estimated expenditures— for a particular department or program amounts to $4,200,000, and the budget request for next year for the department or the program is $4,600,000, the request should make clear how the additional $400,000 will be spent, and the budget officer should make sure that the additional money is needed.

Third, any new permanent position or capital improvement or equipment requests should be scrutinized. Although the cost of a new permanent position may be modest relative to the entire budget, approving a new permanent position represents a long-term commitment that will be expensive over time. The substantial acquisition or financing costs for most capital improvements and major equipment items require them to be examined, especially if they are associated with program expansion or the start-up of a new program, or if they will result in significant increases in operating expenditures in annual budgets in subsequent years.

Fourth, the budget officer must look carefully at the revenue side of the budget, making certain that revenues estimated for each source are realistic. G.S. 159-13(b)(7) states that the annual budget ordinance "shall include only those revenues reasonably expected to be realized in the budget year." The budget officer should also make sure that revenues that will not recur in future years are used only for nonrecurring types of expenditures and also that any alternative revenue sources that are locally available are not overlooked.

Fifth, the budget officer should formulate or review recommendations and options for salary and wage increases or adjustments. Such increases or adjustments can take various forms. The traditional alternatives are cost-of-living and performance or merit pay adjustments. Some local governments have begun giving employees bonuses. Both cost-of-living and performance pay increases are typically added to the salary-and-wage base and continue in that base each year thereafter. Bonuses, on the other hand, are usually not built into the salary-and-wage base and therefore are not continuing commitments in subsequent years. Cost-of-living or performance pay increases can be made effective on July 1 or later during the fiscal year.

Finally, and most important, the budget officer must decide what property tax rate to recommend to the board of commissioners. The tax rate is almost always the focal point of any budget. In selecting a tax rate to recommend, the budget officer must resolve the following questions:

1. Should the property tax rate remain the same? If so, what effect will the unchanged rate have on fund balance and county services?
2. Should the tax rate be lowered? If so, by how much, and what effect will the lower rate have on fund balance and county services?
3. Should the tax rate be raised? If so, by how much, and how will the additional tax revenue be spent? Will it finance new or expanded services or be used just to keep existing services going? Can the property tax rate be raised, given the views of the county commissioners and the citizens?

Submission of the Recommended Budget

The budget officer must submit a recommended budget to the board of commissioners "not later than June 1." Because this should be an occasion for summarizing and explaining the budget to both the board and the public, the law urges that the budget be submitted at a formal meeting of the board, when the explanation is most likely to reach the public. The board's first meeting in June is often the occasion for budget submission, even though the meeting date will only rarely fall on June 1. This is acceptable because like April 30, June 1 is primarily a guideline, a checkpoint on the way to adopting the budget by July 1. Of course, in some counties the budget is submitted well before June 1.

When submitting the budget, the budget officer must include a budget message. This message should introduce the budget to the board and members of the public who wish to study it, and summarize it for those who have no time to study it themselves or are perhaps intimidated by its detail. Thus the message should emphasize the major features of the proposed budget, especially significant changes or additions from the current year's budget. G.S. 159-11(b) states that the message should include the following:

- A concise explanation of the governmental goals fixed by the budget for the budget year
- Important features of the activities anticipated in the budget
- Reasons for stated changes from the previous year in program goals, programs, and appropriation levels
- Any major changes in fiscal policy

Although a written format for the budget message is not explicitly required, it is preferable to a simple oral statement. An oral statement will summarize the budget only for those who are present when it is made. The larger public will not benefit from the statement except to the extent that they learn of it in the press. Normally the budget message takes the form of a letter from the budget officer to the board of commissioners and is bound with or attached to the document presenting the full budget.

In most counties the budget is presented in a budget book that includes tables showing revenues by fund and source and expenditures by fund, department, function or program, and line item or line-item class. A growing number of county budget books also contain organization charts; statements of policies that guide budget preparation and financial operations for the county; goals, objectives, and performance indicators and data for departments and programs; and lists of positions authorized in the budget. The book should present full explanations of changes or increases in the recommended budget from expenditures for the current year. It may also contain special sections that highlight specific challenges facing the county, such as a slow-growing property tax base and the need to rely more on user fees.

The budget book may present only the budget officer's recommended budget or both the requested amount and the recommended budget for each department and program. The budget book provides the detailed backup to the annual budget ordinance. Once the board of county commissioners approves the ordinance, the book should be revised to reflect the changes made by the board. The book, along with the ordinance, then serves as the budget officer's guide in executing the budget.

When the budget is submitted, some boards of commissioners may adopt it as the tentative budget. Although such a step does no harm, the LGBFCA neither requires nor provides for it. Such an adopted tentative budget is not the equivalent of the annual budget ordinance and provides no appropriation authority for spending.

On the day that the budget officer submits the budget to the board of commissioners, he or she must file a copy with the clerk to the board. The clerk must then make the copy available to all news media in the county (G.S. 159-12).

The board must schedule a public hearing on the budget after it is submitted but before the budget ordinance is adopted [G.S. 159-12(b)]. After the budget is filed and the date for the hearing is set, the clerk to the board must publish, in a newspaper with general circulation, a legal notice stating that the budget has been submitted to the board and that a copy is available for public inspection in the clerk's office. The notice should also give the time, the date, and the place of the budget hearing. The notice need not but may include a summary of the proposed budget. The statute requires no specific minimum number of days between the date on which the notice appears and the date on which the hearing is held; however, the notice should be timely enough to allow for full public participation at the hearing.

Commissioner Review and Enactment of the Annual Budget

Commissioner Review

Once the proposed budget is before the board of county commissioners, several general legal provisions apply to board review and adoption of the budget ordinance. First, at least ten days must elapse between submission of the budget and adoption of the budget ordinance [G.S. 159-13(a)]. Second, during the interval between submission and adoption, the board may conduct its review at both regular special meetings, and the particular notice requirements of G.S. Chapter 153A and of any local acts applying to the county may be ignored. However, the notice requirements of the open meetings law (see G.S. 143-318.12) must be met, each board member must be notified of any budget review meeting to be held, and only budget matters may be discussed at such meetings (G.S. 159-17). Third, as just noted, the open meetings law (Article 33C of G.S. 143) applies to the budget preparation and adoption process. There is no provision allowing executive sessions for the local budget process (G.S. 143-318.11).

Board of commissioner practices in reviewing the budget vary from county to county and over time in the same county. In some counties or in some years, the board may hold the one statutorily required public hearing and stop there, accepting with little question the budget officer's recommendations. The review may be completed in a week or two. Most boards, however, take a month or so to review the budget. Board review of the proposed budget usually takes place in a series of briefings or meetings on the budget. Ordinarily, each meeting dwells on one part of the budget, and the budget officer, often with help from budget staff, the finance director, and other department heads, briefs the board on that part. Citizens and representatives of organizations or groups in the county also often comment on particular parts of the budget at these meetings. The board may make decisions on particular requests as the meetings progress, or it may hold its decisions until the review is finished.

Whether the board's review is short or long depends very much on what the recommended budget includes—that is, whether it requests new positions and programs, makes cuts in existing programs or activities, calls for a tax rate increase, and so on. The length of the review process may also depend on personal or political considerations. For example, if members of the board essentially agree on major issues and have confidence in the budget officer, their review may well be short. If the opposite is true, however, review by the board may be long and difficult.

Public Hearing(s) on the Budget

Although the board of commissioners may hold a series of budget review meetings or briefings that are called hearings, they do not satisfy the requirement for a budget hearing under G.S. 159-12(b). This law expects at least one hearing on the entire budget, primarily to allow citizens to speak to the board. As with most of the budget process, the law permits variety and flexibility in conducting the required budget hearing. The hearing may be the culminating step in the board's review of the budget. Even when this is not the case, the hearing is usually held nearer to adoption than to submission of the recommended budget.[16]

Enactment of the Annual Budget Ordinance

As noted earlier, G.S. 159-13(a) directs that the budget be adopted by July 1. If this does not occur and expenditures must be made before the annual budget ordinance is adopted, G.S. 159-16 requires that the board of commissioners adopt an interim budget, making "interim appropriations for the purpose of paying salaries, debt service payments, and the usual ordinary expenses" of the county until the budget ordinance is adopted. An interim budget should not include appropriations for salary and wage increases, capital items, and program or service expansion. An interim budget may not levy property taxes, nor should it change or increase other tax, user fee, or other revenue rates. The purpose of an interim budget is to keep operations going at current levels without funding new or expanded programs or changing fiscal policy. Although there must be cash available to fund interim appropriations, the interim budget need not include revenues to balance the appropriations. Any expenditures made under an interim budget must be charged against the comparable appropriations in the annual budget ordinance once it is adopted. In other words, the interim expenditures will be funded eventually with revenues included in the annual budget ordinance. If the annual budget ordinance will be adopted a few days late but before any payroll is due or other expenditures must be made, an interim budget may be unnecessary.

The LGBFCA specifically provides that the budget ordinance may be adopted at any regular or special meeting at which a quorum is present, by a majority of those present and voting (G.S. 159-17). Adoption of the budget ordinance is not subject to the normal ordinance adoption requirements of G.S. 153A-45.

The budget ordinance must contain appropriations for expenditures, estimates or appropriations of revenues, and the property tax levy. The ordinance must show revenues and expenditures by fund and demonstrate a balance in each fund. The property tax levy is stated in terms of a rate of so many cents per $100 of taxable value. The stated rate may be accompanied by the dollar amount of the levy, the taxable value to which the rate will be applied to produce the dollar amount of the levy, and the percentage of the levy that is estimated to be collected. The estimated collection percentage used for the property tax in the budget may not exceed the percentage of the property tax levy collected in the year preceding the budget year. Typically the annual budget ordinance devotes a section to appropriations and revenues for each fund and one to the levy of property taxes.

Although these sections are sufficient, the annual budget ordinance may contain other sections or provisions as well. For example, it might include instructions on its administration. If the ordinance makes appropriations very broadly, it might direct that expenditures comply not only with the ordinance but also with the more detailed budget book on which the ordinance is based. If a fund mixes legally earmarked revenues with general revenues, the ordinance might specify the use of the earmarked funds. The ordinance may also authorize and limit certain transfers among departmental or functional appropriations within the same fund pursuant to G.S. 159-15, put certain restrictions on interfund loans within the year (the board of commissioners should approve interfund loans that remain outstanding from one fiscal year to the next), set rates or fees for public enterprises or other municipal services, and so forth.

Finally, G.S. 159-13(d) directs that the budget ordinance be entered in the board of commissioners' minutes and that within five days after it is adopted, copies be filed with the budget officer, the finance officer, and the clerk to the board. Because the LGBFCA itself requires that this filing take place, the ordinance need not restate the filing requirements.

Budget Modification and Amendment

Once adopted, the annual budget ordinance is not merely a financial plan for the year but also the legal gauge against which expenditures must be measured. An expenditure must be authorized by an appropriation in the ordinance, and sufficient moneys must remain in the appropriation to cover the expenditure. Obviously, events during a fiscal year may occasion greater or less spending than anticipated for some activities, or needs may arise for which there is no appropriation or for which the existing one is exhausted.

To meet these situations, three types of changes to the annual budget may be made: first, certain budget modifications may be made without changing the ordinance; second, expenditures may be made from contingency appropriations; third, the annual budget ordinance itself may be amended. The next three sections discuss these types of changes.

Modifications in the Annual Budget

As pointed out earlier, the budget normally exhibits greater detail than the budget ordinance. Thus an ordinance may make appropriations by department within the general fund, while the budget on which the ordinance is based may break down departmental totals into line-item categories or accounts. For example, the budget might show the following breakdown for a county's recreation department for the fiscal year:

Recreation Department	**$2,500,400**
Personnel services	$1,358,700
Contractual services	660,000
Operating expenses	305,800
Capital outlay	175,900

If only the total departmental figure ($2,500,400) appears in the annual budget ordinance, it is only that figure against which expenditures are compared by law. In other words, as long as the recreation department's expenditures do not exceed $2,500,400, there is no violation of the annual budget ordinance nor of the LGBFCA.

To continue the example, events during the year result in these actual recreation department expenditures:

Recreation Department	**$2,464,900**
Personnel services	$1,370,600
Contractual services	635,000
Operating expenses	274,200
Capital outlay	185,100

Even though two of the accounts (personnel services and capital outlay) have been overspent, neither the annual budget ordinance nor the LGBFCA has been violated because the budget ordinance's appropriation for the department ($2,500,400) has not been exceeded.

Contingency Appropriations in the Annual Budget

Contingency appropriations are intended for funding unanticipated expenditures. Moneys may be transferred from contingency appropriations and spent by direct authorization of the board of commissioners, by order of the budget officer, or on the basis of express delegation from the board [G.S. 159-13(b)(3)]. If the budget officer is given the authority to approve transfers from and expenditures of contingency appropriations, he or she must report any such expenditure to the board at its next regular meeting, and the report must be recorded in the board's minutes. Money transferred from a contingency appropriation and spent should be charged to the departmental, functional, or project appropriation for which it is spent and not to the contingency appropriation.

Amendments to the Annual Budget Ordinance

A board of county commissioners has broad flexibility to amend the budget ordinance except that no amendment may increase a property tax levy (or the rate per $100 of taxable value) or alter a property tax payer's liability. The legal bar to amending the property tax levy and rate does not apply to other tax or revenue sources controlled by the board of commissioners, although practical difficulties may be involved. Thus the privilege license tax schedule may be revised during a year, but a change would not be effective until the next license year begins in July. On the other hand, user fees and charges—such as admission fees to public recreation facilities or landfill tipping fees—may be changed via an amendment to the budget ordinance and become effective at any time. Another change possible on the revenue side of the ordinance is the appropriation of additional fund balance if it is legally available.

If revenue estimates are increased or decreased, appropriations for expenditures or appropriated fund balance must be correspondingly adjusted so that all funds and the total annual budget ordinance remain in balance. When changes in appropriations are made, the directions and the limitations discussed earlier in this chapter must still be observed.

In amending the budget ordinance, the board of commissioners enjoys the same freedom from the procedural requirements set forth in G.S. 153A-45. Any amendment to the annual budget ordinance must be by ordinance. There are neither notice nor public hearing requirements for amendments, and they may be adopted by a simple majority of board members as long as a quorum is present.

As with contingency expenditures, the board may delegate to the budget officer the authority to make certain amendments to the budget ordinance. Subject to restrictions set by the board, the budget officer may be permitted to transfer moneys from one appropriation to another within the same fund (G.S. 159-15). Two elements of this statute authorization should be emphasized. First, the transfers must be within the same fund; transfers between funds by the budget officer are not permitted. Second, the transfers must be between appropriations; the budget officer may not make changes on the revenue side of the budget, such as increasing the amount of appropriated fund balance. By extension, this means that total fund appropriations may not be increased or changed by the budget officer or any other administrative official. If the power to amend pursuant to G.S. 159-15 is delegated to the budget officer, each amendment must be reported to the board at its next regular meeting, and it must record the report in its minutes.

Amendments to Project Ordinances

As mentioned earlier in the chapter, a project ordinance may make a single, lump-sum appropriation for the project authorized by the ordinance, or it may make appropriations in detail by line-item, functional, or other appropriate categories within the project. If the ordinance makes a single project appropriation, actual expenditures may exceed estimated expenditures in any budget or account category by which expenditures for the project may be classified without violating the project ordinance, as long as total expenditures do not exceed the total project appropriation. On the other hand, if the project ordinance makes appropriations by expenditure category, actual expenditures for a category may not exceed the appropriation for it without violating the project ordinance. If expenditures for a project will exceed the ordinance's appropriation, in total or for any expenditure category for which an appropriation was made, an amendment to the ordinance will be necessary to increase the appropriation and identify additional revenues to keep the project ordinance balanced. Only the board of commissioners may amend a project ordinance.

Modifications to Financial Plans for Internal Service Funds

As explained earlier, a financial plan for an internal service fund only estimates annual revenues and expenditures for the fund. The estimates are not legal limits on spending and therefore are not required to be recorded in a county's accounting system. Such spending flexibility is one of the reasons for including revenues and expenditures for an internal service fund in a financial plan rather than in the annual budget ordinance.

Nevertheless, G.S. 159-13.1(d) directs that any change in a financial plan be approved by the board of commissioners. Because a financial plan does not control expenditures, one interpretation of this provision is that it requires the budget officer or staff to report to the board differences between actual revenues and expenditures and the board-approved financial plan for the internal service fund. A narrower interpretation is that it requires board approval of major changes in internal service fund financing, especially those affecting departmental usage of and expenditures for fund services, and, correspondingly, internal service fund revenues.

Line-Item and Performance Budgeting

Line-item budgeting and *performance budgeting* refer to general systems or approaches for budget preparation, presentation, and review. Although not mutually exclusive, they are often viewed as alternative budget systems. A *line-item budget* organizes information principally by expenditure account or object of expenditure, that is, by the items or the resources that a government must acquire to provide public services. A *performance budget* organizes information principally in terms of the services to be provided or the objectives to be achieved. Depending on the stage of development and the particular emphasis given to it when used, performance budgeting has been called by various names: *program budgeting, objectives budgeting, planning-programming-budgeting system, results-oriented budgeting, service budgeting,* and, most recently, *outcome-oriented budgeting.*

The LGBFCA permits counties to select the particular system or approach for budgeting that they wish to use. Most of the state's small counties rely essentially on line-item budgeting systems, although some are incorporating aspects of performance budgeting into these systems. Many medium-size and most large counties use what can be characterized as mixed line-item and performance budgeting systems.

Line-Item Budgeting

A line-item or object-of-expenditure budget emphasizes the relationship between money budgeted and the item or the object that the county will acquire or purchase with that money. The items or the objects are expenditure accounts that are taken from an entity's accounting system, and they are typically organized into the conventional categories of salaries and wages, benefits on salaries and wages, operating supplies, contractual services, and capital or permanent property. Office supplies, for example, would be a line item or object within the operating supplies category. A line-item budget can present information by object or line-item *category*, providing a consolidated line-item budget, or by individual line-item or object *accounts*, creating a very detailed line-item budget. A few line-item budgets are so detailed as to show expenditures for individual positions in the proposed and even in the enacted budgets.

A line-item budget is principally a control tool. It provides information that elected and top administrative officials can use to make sure that revenues are spent only for personnel or items that they approve in the budget. By reviewing requested and recommended expenditures by line, they seek to prevent the misapplication of public moneys and generally to encourage frugality in the use of public funds. As suggested earlier, the line-item budget's main tool is the departmental accounting system, with its detailed listing of expenditure accounts within each department. These line-item accounts become the categories for budgeting as well as accounting, and in a bare-bones line-item budget format, they are *not* complemented by information about departmental goals, objectives, or activities.

Performance Budgeting

Performance budgeting emphasizes the relationship between money budgeted and the objectives that a county will achieve or the services that a county will provide by spending that money. This type of budgeting attempts to be specific about the demand for public services, the level (quantity) and the quality at which services are provided, and the results obtained from providing the services. In performance budgeting, mission statements and general goals are established by the governing board to guide budget preparation. Objectives and performance targets based on the mission statements and general goals are formulated by program managers in making their budget requests and are approved by top administrators and the board when reviewing and approving the budget. Performance measures or indicators relating to the objectives and the performance targets are also identified and approved in the budget. Then, while the budget is being executed, data on these measures are collected to determine the extent to which the program objectives and the performance targets have been achieved. In a full-fledged performance budgeting system, expenditure or cost data are related to performance measures to produce cost-performance ratios that officials can use for budget and management control.

Whereas line-item budgeting is oriented more toward administration and management, performance budgeting is oriented more toward policy or decision making. Because line-item budgeting shows expenditures by line or object, this brings to the fore the trade-offs between spending money for one item (such as salaries and wages for permanent positions) and spending that money for another item (such as contractual services). Such trade-offs have more to do with administration and budget execution than with policy making. A performance budget, on the other hand, highlights the trade-offs between spending money for one function or program (like parks and recreation) and spending it for another program (like public health). The directions that a county takes in providing public services are often at stake in these program trade-offs. Thus the performance budget tends to be more of a policy-making tool than the line-item budget is.

Renewed interest in performance budgeting has developed in recent years. This is arising from at least three sources:

1. The book *Reinventing Government* recommends that governments become mission driven and that governmental budgeting systems identify measurable objectives to be achieved with the funds that are budgeted.[17] As stated in the book, the premise that underlies these recommendations is, "What gets measured is what gets done."

2. The Governmental Accounting Standards Board (GASB), which establishes principles for governmental accounting and financial reporting, has issued a concepts statement recommending that government entities develop and include service effort and accomplishment measures in their external financial reports.[18] Such measures are generally comparable to what public officials have more commonly known as performance measures or indicators. If this GASB statement is approved in its present or a comparable form and comes to represent generally accepted accounting principles for government, it is likely to cause many local governments across the nation, including those in North Carolina, to adopt one form or another of performance budgeting. Even if GASB does not adopt the concept statement as generally accepted accounting principles, the statement itself and the research and work leading up to it have

had a great influence in furthering interest in performance measurement and budgeting in the public sector.

3. The Government Finance Officers Association of the United States and Canada (GFOA) has passed two resolutions calling on public entities to develop and use performance measurements in their budgeting systems.[19] The GFOA also sponsors a Distinguished Budget Presentation Awards Program for state and local government budgets. In this program, budget documents are evaluated as policy documents, financial plans, operational guides, and communication devices. Some of the specific criteria in several of these general areas are related to performance budgeting and have the effect of encouraging governments seeking the award to incorporate aspects of performance budgeting into their budgeting systems.

In performance budgeting, the county's budget officer and staff and department officials are primarily responsible for controlling expenditures by line item. They use line-item data on amounts budgeted and spent to enforce account ceilings and to prevent the misapplication or the extravagant expenditure of public funds. The board of county commissioners may call for and use the line-item data at any time, but they usually do so to spot-check line-item control by administrative officials or to resolve thorny budget problems involving particular line-item expenditures. Besides the line-item budget data, the budget officer and other administrative officials use the accounting system, purchasing procedures, and other fiscal tools for enforcing line-item budget control.

All this does not mean that in performance budgeting, the board of commissioners delegates all authority for executing and controlling the budget to the budget officer and other administrative officials. The board can and should hold that officer and the department heads accountable for achieving the objectives and the performance targets specified in the budget—and within the funds appropriated. These objectives and performance targets can be detailed and extend down to the operating levels in each department. Moreover, the board can and usually should continue to maintain general types of line-item control, such as ceilings on the number of positions in each department, function, or division, and should review specific expenditure items that are sensitive or potentially controversial. Also, as noted, the board can call for and review line-item data at any time.

A performance budgeting system is more complicated than a typical line-item one. This is why performance budgeting is more commonly used by larger counties than by smaller ones. A performance budget requires not only line-item data for costing out objectives and programs and for maintaining administrative control of expenditures by line but also program objectives and performance measures and data. Moreover, often several types of performance measures and data are collected and used in performance budgeting—for example, measures pertaining to the need or the demand for services; measures relating to the outcomes sought through the provision of public services; and measures dealing with the quantity and the quality of the services being provided.

In undertaking performance budgeting, some governmental units create programs apart from the regular organizational structure and formulate performance objectives for them. Creating such a separate program structure for budgeting requires "cross-walking" department and line-item expenditures into the programs in the separate program structure. Such cross-walking complicates the budget process and means that budgets are prepared and approved one way, on the basis of programs, and then executed another way, on the basis of the departmental and line-item accounting system. For most counties, objectives and performance data should generally be formulated for departments, divisions, and units in the existing organizational structure, rather than for a program structure that exists apart from the organizational structure. If the existing organizational structure meets management needs, it probably can serve budget purposes as well. If a county does use a separate program structure, the LGBFCA requires that the programs, as approved in the budget ordinance, be organized within accounting funds.

Counties that adopt performance budgeting and begin to use performance objectives and measures in the budget will not see results overnight. Almost any county or other local government will need several years to refine objectives and performance measures to the point that they are reliable enough for budget- and management-control purposes. Once good performance objectives and data are available, a county should begin to build a program- or activity-based cost-accounting system that relates expenditures or costs to individual objectives or performance targets approved in the budget. This process will give the county the cost- or expenditure-performance ratios mentioned earlier. These ratios are a major payoff of performance budgeting. They may be used not only for planning and decision making but also for control and evaluation.

Incremental and Zero-Base Budgeting and Budget Reductions

Budgeting in government over the past half-century has focused on the changes in the budget from year to year, especially on the ways in which additional funds are to be spent. Additional revenue resulting from growth in the property tax base, occasional increases in tax rate, and growth in other revenue sources have provided the increments to allow expenditures generally to grow from year to year. Some of the additional revenue available in any year is typically applied to finance expenditure increases for existing programs. The rest may be used to finance improvement or expansion in existing services or the start-up of new services, or it may be returned to the taxpayers by lowering taxes. *Incremental budgeting* focuses on these issues. Expenditures for existing services in the current year that repeat in the budget year, and the revenues that finance them, are the base in incremental budgeting, and they are usually approved and funded after limited review. Precedent enters into play in this situation: if expenditures were made in the past and are being incurred in the current year, budget makers are generally willing to approve them again for the next budget year.

A growing number of citizens and taxpayers question whether the base—roughly the current year's budget—should be accepted so readily in preparing the next year's budget. They point out that the need for an existing program may have diminished, and if so, budget makers should challenge its continuation and perhaps cut it back or eliminate it altogether. Such a course would permit revenues that would have been spent for the program to be reallocated to higher priority existing programs or to new programs, or to be returned to the taxpayers in tax reductions.

Zero-base budgeting has been advocated for reducing expenditures in existing programs and applying the money so freed to other, more pressing needs, or lowering taxes. In this kind of budgeting, the base is zero rather than the current year's expenditure and revenue level, and the current year's expenditures are not accepted as a given in preparing the next year's budget. In zero-base budgeting theory, all continuing or current-year expenditures must be justified anew each time the budget is prepared and approved.

Zero-base budgeting can be understood more fully by making two comparisons of what it calls for in theory and what it has actually achieved in practice. First, in zero-base budgeting, according to the theory, the starting point is zero, and review efforts are spread over the entire budget rather than concentrated on any one part of it. In practice, where zero-base budgeting has been tried, the starting point has not been zero but some level below the current year's budget or expenditure level—from 5 to perhaps 30 percent below the current expenditure level. This base may represent what officials consider to be a minimum level of effort for a service or a program if it is to be provided at all.

Second, in zero-base budgeting, in theory, no priorities exist when the budget process begins, and all requests, whether for ongoing programs or continuing expenditures or for new ones, are ranked during the budget process. In practice, the minimum level of service in zero-base budgeting—70 to 95 percent of the current year's expenditure level—has top priority, even at the beginning of the budget process. The process is then used to establish priorities among the requests for program expansion or new programs and also among the programs or the items in the 5 to 30 percent of the current year's budget that are not a part of the minimum level of service and expenditure. Even in zero-base budgeting, however, the ongoing expenditures that are not a part of the minimum level are usually more likely to be funded than are requests for service expansion or new programs or services.

Putting zero-base budgeting into practice entails some practical problems. First, it requires more time and work than conventional or incremental budgeting. The justification and the review of requests in zero-base budgeting focus not only on the changes from the current year's budget but also on at least some current year's expenditures. Second, zero-base budgeting involves some political risks that are not as present in conventional or incremental budgeting. Because existing services stand to be reduced or eliminated in zero-base budgeting, the clients who benefit from these services and the employees who provide them are likely to object to proposed reductions identified in the budgeting process. If such reductions must or should be made, this ought not to dissuade the budget officer and the board from using zero-base budgeting to select and make them. However, these officials should be prepared to cope with the political repercussions.

A county can use parts of zero-base budgeting rather than the full package. Zero-base budgeting includes many elements, and some are more useful than others. One of the most useful elements is the division of a budget request into alternative levels (increments and decrements) of service and expenditure. For example, at the top of Table 10-1, the current year's service level is 10,000 units, and the budget to provide it is $100,000. The request for the coming budget year presumes a mini-

Table 10-1
Alternative Service and Expenditure Levels

	Service Level (in units)		Expenditure	
	Increment	Total	Increment	Total
Current Year	NA	10,000	NA	$100,000
Budget Year				
Base Level	NA	7,500	NA	79,000
Increment 1	1,500	9,000	$17,000	96,000
Increment 2	1,000	10,000	11,000	107,000
Increment 3	1,000	11,000	11,000	118,000
Increment 4	Quality improve-ment	11,000+	9,000	127,000

mum level of service of 7,500 units, requiring total expenditures of $79,000. The $79,000 includes $75,000 of recurring expenditures plus a $4,000 increase to cover salary and wage increases and other increased costs. Additions or increments above the minimum level are also identified. Increment 1, at 9,000 units and a cost of $96,000, is below the current year's service level. Increment 2, at 10,000 units and a cost of $107,000, is at the current year's service level. Increments 3 and 4, both at 11,000 units but one at a cost of $118,000, and the other, of improved quality, at a cost of $127,000, are above the current year's service level. They are called *betterment* increments. By presenting budget requests for public services in this way, department officials show the effects on services of reductions in or additions to their current year's budget. The type of general budget format shown in Table 10-1 has been used by several North Carolina local governments at one time or another.

A few governments have applied the thorough budgetary review characteristic of zero-base budgeting to one or two programs or departments each year. After five or six years, all departments have been examined in such a thorough review. This practice is a rotating approach to zero-base budgeting. The reasons for undertaking it may have as much to do with the need periodically to assess and update departmental policies, organization, and methods as with any need to reduce or change budgets.

A county can of course cut existing services or shift funding among them without resorting to zero-base budgeting or a modified version of it. For example, officials can simply ask departments to rank existing services, activities, or items according to priority, thereby identifying expenditures that they would probably cut first if they had to make budget reductions. Alternatively officials can review programs and budgets and identify areas where they can make improvements in productivity, thereby saving money without intending to cut services. However, a caution is in order: significant and true improvements in productivity often cannot be achieved without at least some initial investments of money, for example, to purchase labor-saving equipment, reorganization expenses, and other purposes.

Multiyear Financial Forecasting

A multiyear financial forecast projects revenues and expenditures over a future planning period, usually for a term of somewhere from three to six years. If a county has a multiyear capital improvement program (see Chapter 11), the forecast usually covers the same future period as that program. Most local governments' multiyear financial forecasts embrace all funds included in the budget and one-time or nonrecurring as well as annually recurring revenues and expenditures.

Multiyear financial forecasting helps county officials plan more effectively for the future. A forecast can be useful to officials in anticipating long-term program needs and thinking through the most cost-effective ways to meet those needs, and it can provide a context for long-range management planning. A multiyear forecast is especially important for county-operated utilities and enterprises, which are often capital intensive and for which long lead times are needed to plan and put infrastructure, facilities, and equipment into place. Multiyear forecasting is useful for any county that is undertaking major capital improvements. Regardless of how capital projects are financed initially, through debt or from current revenue and reserves, they must ultimately be paid for from operating revenues. Future operating revenues must cover not only future operating expenditures but also annual principal and interest payments on bonds and other debt issued to finance capital projects, as well as capital projects and outlays financed on a pay-as-you-go basis directly from future operating revenues. A multiyear forecast can reveal a county's ability or inability in the future to cover these future debt service, capital, and operating requirements.

The LGBFCA does not require a county or any other local government to prepare a multiyear financial forecast. Preparing one is a matter of local policy.[20] In counties where multiyear revenue and expenditure forecasts are prepared, the forecasts are generally presented to the board of commissioners. The forecast may be included in a special section of the annual budget document or in an altogether separate document. The board may pass a resolution approving the forecast. Such approval has no legally binding effect. It does not commit the board to raise revenues or make expenditures at the levels shown in the forecast or at any other levels. Board approval is tantamount to acceptance of the forecast and indicates board recognition of the financial situation forecasted for the county.

The methodology for a multiyear financial forecast typically carries forward revenue and expenditure trends from prior years and adjusts them for events that officials know or expect will affect the trends during the forecast period. The forecast of revenues is typically by fund and by major source within each fund. For the general fund, separate forecasts would ordinarily be made of revenues from the property tax, the sales and use taxes, major intergovernmental revenues, and other sources. For utility or enterprise funds, separate forecasts would be made of revenues from each major operating or user charge and from other sources. The forecast of some revenues should involve a projection of the tax base—for example, taxable value for the property tax—with the forecast resulting from application of the current or an adjusted tax rate to the projected base. Most forecasts assume the continuation of current tax or revenue rates through the forecast period. The advantage of this is that it avoids assumptions about board actions during the forecast period to increase rates or charges. The disadvantage is that the forecast could show imbalances between revenues and expenditures for particular years that could be difficult to explain to interested members of the public. Because of this and for certain other reasons some multiyear forecasts assume and provide for changes in the property tax rate or other charges that the forecast shows will be necessary to balance revenues and expenditures in years during the forecast period.

The forecast of expenditures is typically by fund and by line-item category or by department and function within each fund. A forecast of expenditures by line item across departments within a fund rather than by department within a fund is less likely to influence department officials' judgments about what growth or changes in expenditures will be expected or accepted for their respective departments during the forecast period. However, such a forecast may be less accurate than one by department and line item within each department. Forecasts of expenditures can be based on carrying current per capita expenditures into the forecast period, on analyzing probable changes in expenditures in each expenditure category, or some combination of these approaches. An expenditure forecast based partly or wholly on an analysis of probable changes or increases in expenditures would have to make some assumptions about salary and wage adjustments, inflation or deflation, replacement of capital equipment and property, creation of new positions, expansion of existing programs and creation of new ones, and acquisition or construction of new capital infrastructure during the forecast period.

Appropriations for Education

County appropriations for public schools and community colleges account for a quarter to a third of most county budgets. In 1995–96, county expenditures for education were 29.7 percent of total county spending, on average, in all 100 counties; 32.6 percent of total county spending, on average, in counties above 100,000 in population; and around 25 percent of total county spending, on average, in counties below 100,000 in population.[21] The overwhelming portion of this spending goes toward public schools.

The North Carolina General Statutes divide the responsibility for county budgeting of local education among the board of commissioners (who have general control of the county's fiscal policy), the county board of education, one or more boards of education for city school administrative units in those counties where they exist, and the community college board of trustees. Ideally, these boards would agree among themselves each year on the best allocation of scarce resources for local public schools and community college programs. In practice, consensus is typically elusive. Boards of education are especially sensitive to citizen demands for better schools. Boards of county commissioners are especially sensitive to citizen demands concerning taxes. In the school area, perhaps more so than for any other function of local government, the budget process is very much a matter of bargaining and compromise.

The county board of commissioners is the local tax-levying authority for school administrative units and community colleges. The fiscal affairs of school administrative units are governed by the School Budget and Fiscal Control Act (G.S. Ch. 115C, Art. 31). Similar provisions for community colleges appear in G.S. Chapter 115D, Article 4A. The budget portions of these statutes roughly parallel the LGBFCA. Both school administrative units and community colleges adopt and administer their own annual budgets independently of the county government, but both depend on county appropriations for a significant portion of their annual revenues.

A full treatment of the statutes and issues that are most central to county budgeting for public schools and community colleges occurs in Chapters 27 and 28. The more important of these issues are listed and briefly commented on here.

1. *Request deadline for school and community college requests* [G.S. 115C-429(a) and G.S. 115D-55(a)]. The school and community college budgets must be submitted to the board of commissioners no later than May 15, unless the board of commissioners agrees to a later date. The May 15 deadline is late in the county budget preparation calendar. This schedule gives the county budget officer and staff little time to review budget requests and formulate a recommended county budget for submission to the board of commissioners, which must occur no later than June 1. Of course, the statutes requires submission of the school and community college budget request directly to the board of commissioners rather than to the county budget officer. In most counties, however, the county commissioners expect the budget officer to analyze these requests and recommend what action the board of commissioners should take.

2. *Allocation of public school appropriations* [G.S. 115C-426 and -429(b)]. County appropriations to a school administrative unit are made to the unit's school current expense fund and school capital outlay fund. The current expense fund includes instructional, support, and other operating expenditures of the school system. The capital outlay fund includes appropriations for site acquisition, new buildings and renovations of existing ones, vehicles, and other capital assets. The board of commissioners may make lump-sum appropriations to these two funds, or it may allocate all or part of its appropriations to particular purposes or functions in the current expense fund or to specific projects in the capital outlay fund. This allocation issue is a key one in county budgeting for the schools; see Chapter 27 for a more thorough discussion of this topic.

3. *Continuing contracts for school capital outlays* [G.S. 115C-441(c1) and G.S. 115C-528]. When a school administrative unit enters into a contract for multiyear capital improvement projects or outlays, the county commissioners must approve the contract. Approval of the contract by the board of commissioners obligates it to appropriate funds in future fiscal years to pay the amounts falling due under the contract in those years. However, a local school board does not have to obtain board of county commissioner approval of a multiyear lease- or installment-purchase contract under the continuing contracts statute if the contract is for automobiles, school buses, mobile classroom units, copiers, or computer hardware or software; and if the contract has a term of less than three years and the total amount financed under the contract is below the lesser of $250,000 or an amount equal to three times the local school system's annual allocation from the state for classroom materials and equipment.

4. *School supplemental taxes.* Under G.S. Chapter 115C, Article 36, the voters of a school administrative unit may approve the levy of supplemental taxes for "any item of expenditure in the school budget." If the voters have approved such a supplemental school tax, the board of county commissioners, as the tax-levying authority for the administrative unit, decides each year how much supplemental tax revenue the administrative unit needs and levies the supplemental tax accordingly. The board of education does not have the power to require the board of commissioners to levy any particular rate of supplemental tax. Even though school supplemental taxes are levied and collected by the county government, they are revenues of the school administrative unit and not county revenues appropriated to the school unit by the commissioners. Therefore, the power to allocate appropriations by purpose, function, and project does not extend to voted supplemental taxes.

5. *Apportionment of county current expense appropriations in counties with multiple school systems.* In counties with two or more school administrative units, G.S. 115C-430 requires that the board of commissioners appropriate exactly the same amount per pupil to each unit for current operating expenses. Capital outlay appropriations need not be so apportioned.

6. *Resolving disputes over county appropriations to schools* (G.S. 115C-431). The locally elected school board is responsible for setting local education policy and administering the schools, yet the board of county commissioners has the responsibility for levying the taxes and providing the local money needed to support the schools. As already mentioned, this creates an opportunity for a clash between citizens' demands for improved education and their demands for maintaining or lowering the tax rate. North Carolina law provides a curious if not unique process for a board of county commissioners and a school board to resolve this kind of conflict over the school budget. In this process, the courts can ultimately determine the amount of county funds needed to support the schools. The dispute resolution process is described in Chapter 27 of this volume.

7. *Appropriations to community colleges.* County appropriations to a community college are made to its county current fund and its plant fund. As with the schools, the board of commissioners has the power to allocate its appropriation to the community college by purpose, function, or project. The allocation process and its consequences are virtually identical to those that apply to school administrative units. With respect to the community college, however, the commissioners are essentially free to exercise their budgetary discretion without possible review by the courts.

Appropriations to Human Service Agencies

In 1995–96, total county expenditures for human service programs were 28.4 percent of total county spending, on average, in all 100 counties. In nearly all of the state's counties, county spending for these programs is between a quarter and third of the county budget.[22]

County appropriations for human services programs go predominantly to three agencies: the county social services department; the county health department (or for county participation in a district health department or health authority that serves the county); and to the area mental health authority serving the county. Each such agency is headed by an appointed board that exercises statutory responsibilities for the programs provided by the agency, appoints the agency's chief administrative officer, and establishes policies or advises the board of county commissioners about policies in the areas of work done by the agency. In the state's two largest counties—Mecklenburg and Wake, the board of county commissioners has assumed direct responsibility as authorized under G.S. 153A-77 for local policy-making and administration (including budgeting) of social services, public health, and mental health programs.

County appropriations to these human services agencies must address complicated funding streams, involving federal, state, as well as local sources; frequent federal and state changes in eligibility and program requirements; market-driven changes for health and mental health services; accountability and performance measurement challenges; and except in Mecklenburg and Wake counties, divided responsibility between the board of county commissioners and their staff, on the one hand, and the appointed boards that head the agencies and their staffs, on the other, that are directly involved in administering human services programs.

Important budget and fiscal relationships between the board of county commissioners and the social services, health, and mental health agencies are identified and briefly addressed here. The programs and financial affairs of these county agencies are discussed in more detail in Chapters 22, 24, and 26 of this volume.

Social Services Appropriations

Social services spending occurs in three major categories: public assistance for low-income recipients; service programs for dependent children, disabled adults, and others; and administration. The discussion here addresses five questions related to county budgeting for social services programs. Chapter 24 of this volume provides a fuller description of the programs themselves and of their organization and financing.

1. *Responsibility for preparing social services budget request* [G.S. 108A-9(3) and (4)]. The county director of social services is responsible for "planning budgets" and preparing the budget request for the department of social services. The county board of social services is suppose to "assist" the director in this duty and transmit or present the department's request to the board of commissioners. In some counties, the social services budget

request goes directly to the county commissioners, who then refer it to the county manager for analysis and recommendation before the commissioners themselves review the request. In other counties, the social services request goes initially to the county manager, who reviews it and then passes the request along with the manager's recommendations on to the commissioners.

2. *Information from the state* (G.S. 108A-88). Before February 15 of each year, the state Department of Health and Human Services informs county directors of social services of the amounts of federal and state aid that are likely to be available for public assistance and social services programs in the coming fiscal year, an estimate of related administrative expenditures, and the percentage of county participation that will be required in each program. These estimates are revised as necessary when the General Assembly or Congress changes eligibility requirements or the level of state or federal funding.

3. *Mandated county spending for public assistance and social services programs* (G.S. 108A-90 and -93). Within the direct public assistance and services categories are programs that are mandated and other non-mandated or discretionary programs. Medicaid is the most expensive mandated program for counties. The new Work First program for needy families with children is another mandated program requiring county outlays at least for administration and services. Other mandated programs include child and adult protective services, adoption services, foster care, guardianship of certain incompetent adults, and others. The county's budgetary discretion varies from virtually none with respect to some mandated programs to complete discretion with respect to "local" nonmandated programs. State notification of a county's percentage contributions to the costs for mandated programs requires the county to appropriate sufficient funds for these programs. If the county fails to pay its full share of public assistance costs, the governor, as director of the state budget, has authority to withhold distributions of revenues from certain taxes that the state shares with and/or collects for counties, for example, the 1 percent local-option sales tax, to any county that refuses to appropriate its full share of the cost of mandated public assistance and social services programs.

4. *Estimating the county's share of costs for public assistance, services, and administrative costs.* Counties face certain challenges in budgeting their contributions for public assistance, services, and related administrative costs. First, although federal and state moneys cover much of these costs, county contributions take a significant portion of the county budget. Second, county appropriations for public assistance, services, or administration can increase substantially and sometimes unpredictably when the federal government or the state increases benefit levels or opens the programs to new recipients. Third, funding for Medicaid and some other mandated public assistance programs is open-ended, with total expenditures by each level of government, including the county, dependent on the number of eligible recipients. That is, any person who meets eligibility criteria for one of these programs is entitled to assistance, which must be made even though the moneys appropriated for them are insufficient to cover the program's total costs. As a result, a county can face actual outlays for these programs that are in excess of the budgeted or state forecasted amounts. The LGBFCA recognizes this state of affairs by authorizing contingency appropriations for public assistance programs in an amount greater than the 5-percent limit that applies to other contingency appropriations [G.S. 159-13(b)(3)].

5. *Capped federal and/or state aid for service programs and for Work First.* Federal and/or state funding for some mandated programs, for example, protective services for children and adults, are capped at certain dollar levels, and because the programs are mandated, counties must have the staff and resources necessary to carry out these mandates, regardless of whether there is federal or state financial participation in covering the costs. There has been little growth in federal funds since the early 1980s for the social service block grant that funds many of the mandated services, causing the county share of the costs for these services to increase. Besides the mandated services, counties may provide and fund, with only county money, services that are not mandated. The new Work First program for needy families is both a public assistance and services program. Federal and state funds for it are capped, which means that counties would be responsible for all Work First costs in excess of the federal and state money available for this program.

Public Health Appropriations

The board of commissioners may provide public health services in the county through the county's own public health department, by participation in a district health department that serves the county as well as one or more other counties, through a public health authority, or by contract with the state or other entities.[23] Chapter 22 of this volume provides a full description of public health programs, organization, and financing. The brief discussion here highlights some issues that county commissioners and managers and their staffs must consider in budgeting for public health programs.

1. *Mandated public health services.* The statutes do not explicitly require boards of county commissioners to appropriate minimum levels of funding for public health, although county appropriations, when added to revenues from the state and other sources, must be sufficient to support mandated services. The mandated services include some functions that the local public health department must provide directly, for example, setting and enforcing standards for individual water supply sites and vital records; and services that the county must assure are available in the county, such as certain child health services.

2. *Consolidated contract.* State funding for county public health services is provided under a consolidated contract between the state and the county health department or the district or authority serving the county. If the health department, district, or authority fails to fulfill the terms of the contract, the state can reduce or eliminate state funding for the program that is not in compliance with the contract.

3. *Fees for public health services or programs.* Fees may be charged to help cover the costs of public health medical services and the costs of certain regulatory programs. Fees charged by county or district health boards must be based on a plan submitted by the local health director and approved by the county board of health and the board of county commissioners; or for a district, by the district health board and the boards of county commissioners in all counties served by the district [G.S. 130A-39(g)]. The board of a public health authority may establish a fee schedule for public health services [G.S. 130A-45.3(a)(5)]; under this statute, there is no authorization or requirement for

county commissioner approval of the schedule. Fees are prohibited for immunizations (G.S. 130A-153); sickle cell syndrome testing and counseling (G.S. 130A-130); examination and treatment of tuberculosis and sexually transmitted diseases [G.S. 130A-144(e)]; and for any programs for which local health department employees act as agents for the state [G.S. 130A-39(g)]. The last prohibition does not apply to sanitary sewer and swimming pool programs and to inspections of tattooing businesses. Like other fees for services, public health fees must not unreasonably exceed the cost of providing the services for which the fees are charged. Generally, the fees generated in a public health program must be spent for that program. Any fees not restricted to the specific programs generating them must nonetheless be spent for public health [G.S. 130A-39(g)].

4. *Public health fund balances.* Certain public health programs have generated so much fee revenue that the programs in some counties may have significant fund balances. These balances, like the fee income that produced them, are generally restricted to spending for the fee-supported services and are not available for other public health services or general county needs.

5. *Non-supplant requirements.* Finally, boards of county commissioners may consider reducing county appropriations for public health services when revenues from fees or from state or federal sources increase. Although there is no general statutory prohibition against this practice, "non-supplant" statutes exist (G.S. 130A-4.1 and -4.2) that seek to prevent boards of commissioners from doing this when the state increases its funding for health promotion and maternal and child health programs. Also, the consolidated contract prohibits cuts in county appropriations when revenues from fees and charges increase during the term of the contract. The contract's term is annual.

Mental Health and Related Appropriations

Local mental health services are administered and provided by area mental health, developmental disabilities, and substance abuse authorities.[24] There are forty separate authorities in the state, with twenty-four serving multicounty areas and sixteen each serving a single county. Each area authority has its own governing board, called the "area board." For most purposes, area authorities, including those serving single county areas, are separate local government entities rather than agencies of county government. However, area authorities that serve a single county area are departments of county government for budget and fiscal control purposes (G.S. 122C-116), meaning that the area authority's budget is subject to review by the county budget officer and approval by the board of county commissioners. Chapter 26 of this volume describes area authority organization, services, and financing in detail. The brief discussion here focuses on four issues that are important to county budgeting for area authorities.

1. *County influence over the area authority budget.* The ability of the board of county commissioners to approve the budget of single county area authorities gives the commissioners a substantial role in determining the budget, the magnitude of programs, and the number of positions that the area authority may have. Boards of commissioners in counties served by multicounty area authorities also can shape or influence the area authority's budget through appropriations that the county commissioners make to the area authority. However, the area authority board rather than the board of commissioners is the local governing body responsible for determining the mental health and related needs of area residents and deciding what services to provide to meet these needs (G.S. 122C-117).

2. *Memorandum of agreement.* State funds are provided under an annual memorandum of agreement between the area authority and the state Division of Mental Health, Developmental Disabilities, and Substance Abuse Services. One purpose of the agreement is to assure that area authorities spend state funds and provide services according to state priorities. The agreement establishes prospective reimbursement rates that the state uses to provide funds to area authorities for the services that they provide. Thus preparation of the agreement necessarily involves budgeting, with the need for county appropriated funds possibly affected by the reimbursement rates approved in the agreement.

3. *Fees for area authority services and salaries for area authority employees.* In the case of both single county and multiple county area authorities, the area authority rather than the board of com-

missioners approves fee schedules for mental health services (G.S. 122C-146) and establishes the salary plan that sets salaries for area authority employees (G.S. 122C-156).

4. *Non-supplant requirements.* Although boards of commissioners may but are not required to appropriate money for the support of area authority programs [G.S. 153A-248 and G.S. 122C-115(b)], counties "shall not reduce county appropriations and expenditures for area authorities because of the availability of State-allocated funds, fees, capitation amounts, or fund balance to the area authority" (G.S. 122C-115 and -146). This "non-supplant" requirement limits the ability of boards of commissioners to reduce appropriations to area authorities in response to the availability of funding from other sources. Of course, counties may allocate little or no new county money to area authority programs that receive substantial amounts of "new" revenue from other sources.

Appropriations to Community Agencies

Counties and other local governments seldom provide all the local public services that citizens in their communities want or need. A great variety of private community agencies serve people in ways that county governments might, but often choose not to do. Some of these agencies, like councils of churches, provide services such as homeless shelters or soup kitchens to disadvantaged persons or groups. Others, such as local arts councils or historical societies, sponsor cultural programs, events, or exhibits that are open to the public. Still others, like chambers of commerce or downtown business associations, promote economic development in the community or administer certain civic programs. Many of these typically nonprofit community agencies seek funding from the counties that they serve, as well as from private and other public sources.

As previously discussed under the section "The Public-Purpose Limitation," counties are authorized to contribute money to private community agencies to carry out any public purpose that counties themselves are authorized by law to undertake.[25] Despite statutory authorization, county commissioners may disagree philosophically on whether the county should provide funds for social or other programs administered by private community agencies. Some commissioners may argue that funding such agencies is the responsibility of the private sector. Other commissioners may believe that county government support of community agency programs is necessary to address specific problems or to take advantage of opportunities, and that community agency provision of these programs is likely to be more cost-effective than direct county involvement. Still other commissioners may not object on philosophical grounds to funding community agencies, but still be unwilling to do so because county funds are already stretched too far to fund county services.

Many North Carolina counties receive significant funding requests from private community agencies.[26] There seems to be growing interest in relying more on community agencies and the private sector to meet certain public needs and counties are likely to receive more funding requests for increasing amounts from private community agencies in the future.

How counties handle requests for funding from community agencies in the budget process is important. Are requests from community agencies treated differently than those from county departments, or do all budget requests, regardless of source, go through the same budget review process? Counties should require community agencies to submit requests on county-prescribed forms, and the county budget officer or staff should review community agency requests before they go to the board of county commissioners. Submitting budget requests from community agencies to the same procedural and review requirements as requests from county departments fosters a perception that all requests are treated on the same basis. It also enables county budget officials to review community agency requests for legality and consistency.

Even if a county does not submit budget requests from community agencies to the same procedural and review requirements as it does other requests, county contributions to any such agency should occur only under a written contract or agreement between the county and the agency. The contract should specify the purposes for which the county's contributions are to be spent and should require an end-of-year, or in some cases a more frequent, accounting of how the community agency spends county contributions.[27] If the county's contribution to an agency is more than $1,000 in a year, the county may require an audit of the agency's finances, although certain community agencies, such as volunteer fire departments and rescue squads, are exempt from this requirement (G.S. 159-40). Of course, a county is not legally required to make contributions to community agencies, and a county could require an annual audit of any agency to which it gives funds as a contractual condition of the contribution.

In sum, officials in a county must decide the following issues:

1. Whether and to what extent they will contribute to the support of private community agencies
2. What budget procedures they will require community agencies to follow in making requests for county funding
3. What contractual and expenditure-control requirements they will impose on community agencies to which they make contributions.

Budgeting for Federal and State Grants

Although the amount of federal and state grant revenue available to local governments has dropped over the last twenty years both in absolute terms and as a proportion of county revenues, such grants can be important sources for financing specific projects or programs. Counties have several devices to help them budget federal and state grants. The most important is probably the grant project ordinance, which was examined in earlier sections of this chapter.

Counties also follow certain administrative procedures to address the challenges involved in budgeting federal and state grants. One is to require department officials to secure the manager's or the board of commissioner's approval before applying for any such grant. The budget officer should also carefully analyze any federal or state grant that department or other officials apply for or say will be received in the budget year to ascertain in fact whether the grant will be forthcoming. Once the county receives notice of a grant award, the county can budget it by amending the annual budget ordinance or by adopting a grant project ordinance at that time. Another precaution in budgeting federal and state grants is for a county to maintain a locally funded contingency or reserve for programs or projects funded with federal or state grants, which can be a part of the unappropriated fund balance. Such a contingency or reserve can provide a ready source of matching funds if the county is unexpectedly awarded a federal or state grant. Alternatively, if federal or state moneys are unexpectedly cut for an existing grant-funded program, but the county wishes to continue the program, the contingency or reserve gives the county the wherewithal to do so for a time while it searches for or arranges permanent funding for the program.

Finally, although most federal grants and aid are now provided on a letter-of-credit basis, by which federal funds are wired to a county to pay expenditures as they are incurred, a few federal and some state grants continue to be provided to counties on a reimbursement basis, under which a county must incur and pay expenditures for a program or a project with its own money and then apply for reimbursement of its payments from the federal or state government. In these latter instances a county must have its own front-end money to undertake the program or the project.

Additional Resources

Few, Paula K., and A. John Vogt. "Measuring the Performance of Local Governments," *Popular Government* 62 (Winter 1997): 41–54.

Lawrence, David M. *Local Government Finance in North Carolina*, 2d ed., Chapel Hill, N.C.: Institute of Government, The University of North Carolina at Chapel Hill, 1990, especially chaps. 5–8, 14, and 15.

Rabin, Jack, W. Bartley Hildreth, and Gerald J. Miller, eds. *Budgeting: Formulation and Execution*. Athens, Ga.: Carl Vinson Institute of Government, 1996.

Vogt, A. John, and Charles K. Coe. "A Close Look at North Carolina City and County Budget Practices," *Popular Government* 59 (Summer 1993): 16–28.

Notes

1. See, for example, Greensboro v. Smith, 241 N.C. 363, 85 S.E.2d 292 (1955), and the discussion of this case in David M. Lawrence, *Local Government Finance in North Carolina*, 2d ed. (Chapel Hill, N.C.: Institute of Government, The University of North Carolina at Chapel Hill, 1990), 3.

2. Mitchell v. Financing Auth., 273 N.C. 137, 159 S.E.2d 745 (1968); Foster v. Medical Care Comm'n, 283 N.C. 110, 195 S.E.2d 517 (1973); Stanley v. Department of Conservation and Dev., 284 N.C. 15, 199 S.E.2d 641 (1973).

3. N.C. CONST. ART. V, §§ 8, 9.

4. Maready v. City of Winston-Salem, 342 N.C. 708, 467 S.E.2d 615 (1996).

5. Dennis v. Raleigh, 253 N.C. 400, 116 S.E.2d 923 (1960).

6. Government Finance Officers Association, *Governmental Accounting, Auditing, and Financial Reporting* (Chicago: GFOA, 1994), 332.

7. *Id.* at 15–17, 317.

8. For a discussion of basis of accounting, see *id.* at 23–24.

9. *Id.* at 351.

10. The Local Government Commission and independent public accountants auditing local government finances discourage the use of nondepartmental appropriations.

11. GFOA, *Governmental Accounting*, ch. 11. The Local Government Commission discourages the accumulation of fund balances in internal service funds.

12. A 1990 survey of local government budget practices in forty-seven North Carolina counties found that regardless of who served legally as the budget officer, the work associated with preparation of the 1990–91 budget was the responsibility of the manager or the administrator in nineteen of these counties, the finance director in another twelve counties, a separate budget director or administrator in another eleven counties, and other officials in five counties. A. John Vogt and Charles K. Coe, unpublished results of 1990–91 survey of North Carolina city and county budget practices, available from the Institute of Government, The University of North Carolina at Chapel Hill.

13. The 1990–91 survey of city and county budget practices for 1990–91 found that boards of county commissioners in thirty-four of the forty-seven counties surveyed held meetings at or near the start of budget preparation to discuss the upcoming budget. For twelve of these counties, such meetings took the form of retreats at which the board of commissioners could discuss budget issues in depth. In twenty of the forty-seven counties, the board approved policies or goals to guide budget preparation at these meetings or retreats. See A. John Vogt and Charles K. Coe, "A Close Look at North Carolina City and County Budget Practices," *Popular Government* 59 (Summer 1993): 17.

14. See, for example, *American City and County*, vol. 3, no. 1 (January 1996): 76.

15. The survey of budget practices for 1990–91 addressed the use of service plans, including objectives and performance or workload measures, in departmental budget requests. Of the forty-seven counties in the survey, twenty-six required the inclusion of goals and objectives in departmental budget requests, and twenty required the inclusion of performance or workload measures in departmental requests. See Vogt and Coe, "A Close Look," 21.

16. The survey of budget practices for 1990–91 revealed that forty-four of forty-seven counties held just the one legally required public hearing on the budget; the other three counties held two or more budget hearings. Of the units holding just one hearing, twenty-seven counties held it just before adoption of the annual budget ordinance, nine held it sometime during the period when the board was holding briefings on the budget, and eight held it immediately after the budget officer presented the proposed budget. Vogt and Coe, unpublished results, available from the Institute of Government.

17. David Osborne and Ted Gaebler, *Reinventing Government: How the Entrepreneurial Spirit Is Transforming the Public Sector* (Reading, Mass.: Addison-Wesley Publishing Company, 1992).

18. Governmental Accounting Standards Board, *Concept Statement No. 2 on Service Efforts and Accomplishment Reporting* (Norwalk, Conn.: GASB, April 1994). The *Concept Statement* is a draft recommendation of GASB; it does not constitute generally accepted accounting principles.

19. Government Finance Officers Association of the United States and Canada, *Recommended Practices for State and Local Governments* (Chicago: GFOA, 1995), 44–47.

20. In the 1990–91 survey of local government budget practices, ten of the forty-seven counties in the sample responded that they had such forecasts. Multiyear forecasting was more common among the larger counties; three of the five counties above 200,000 in population and four of the ten counties from 100,000–199,999 in population had such forecasts. Vogt and Coe, "A Close Look," 26.

21. North Carolina Association of County Commissioners and the North Carolina Department of State Treasurer, *Fiscal Summary of North Carolina Counties for the Fiscal Year Ending June 30, 1996,* A-12–A-16.

22. *Ibid.*

23. This discussion about county appropriations for public health draws heavily on Anne M. Dellinger, Jeffrey S. Koeze, and Vicki Winslow, "Public Health," in Charles D. Liner, ed., *State and Local Government Relations in North Carolina: Their Evolution and Current Status,* 2d ed., (Chapel Hill, N.C.: Institute of Government, The University of North Carolina at Chapel Hill, 1995), ch. 9, especially 129–135. In counties with more than 500,000 in population, G.S. 153A-77 authorizes the board of county commissioners to assume direct responsibility for providing public health services.

24. This discussion about county appropriations for mental health and related programs draws heavily on Mark F. Botts, *Area Mental Health, Developmental Disabilities, and Substance Abuse Boards in North Carolina* (Chapel Hill, N.C.: Institute of Government, The University of North Carolina at Chapel Hill, 1995), especially 3–8 and 24–31.

25. N.C. CONST. ART. V, §2(7); G.S. 153A-449.

26. The survey of local government budget practices for 1990–91 revealed that forty-three of forty-seven counties received budget requests from community agencies for that year. As one would expect, the number of community agencies making requests and the amount of the requests varied by size of unit. Charles K. Coe and A. John Vogt, "How North Carolina Cities and Counties Budget for Community Agencies," *Popular Government* 58 (Winter 1993), 26.

27. These requirements are mentioned in the earlier section "The Public-Purpose Limitation." They are based on Dennis v. Raleigh, 253 N.C. 400, 116 S.E.2d 923 (1960).

11 Capital Budgeting and Debt

David M. Lawrence and A. John Vogt

Contents

David M. Lawrence is an Institute of Government faculty member whose fields of interest
include the legal aspects of local government finance.
    A. John Vogt is an Institute of Government faculty member who specializes in
budgeting, capital planning and finance, and financial management.

Planning, financing, and providing the capital facilities and equipment needed for public services are among the most important responsibilities of county officials. The North Carolina General Statutes give local governments, including counties, specific powers that are important in capital budgeting. The Local Government Bond Act, G.S. Chapter 159, Article 4, prescribes procedures for the authorization and the issuance of general obligation bonds secured by taxing power for a broad range of capital purposes. G.S. Chapter 159, Article 5, authorizes revenue bonds secured by the net earnings of a self-supporting enterprise to finance capital projects for such enterprises. Under the security interests statute (G.S. 160A-20), installment purchase or certificate of participation debt, which is secured by the asset being financed with the debt, may be used to finance the acquisition or construction of capital assets. The Solid Waste Management Loan Program (G.S. Ch. 159I) authorizes special obligation debt, secured by revenues from any available source as long as city taxing power is not pledged, for certain solid waste projects. G.S. 159-18 through -22 permits the accumulation of moneys in capital reserve funds to meet future capital needs. G.S. 159-13.2 permits the appropriation of moneys for capital projects or expenditures in capital project ordinances. Finally, one statutory duty of managers in counties with the council-manager form of government is to prepare and submit a capital program [G.S. 153A-82(5)].

Although these statutes grant major powers, they do not define what a capital budget is. Nor do they specify a process for local governments to use in capital budgeting; this absence contrasts with annual budgeting, for which the Local Government Budget and Fiscal Control Act (G.S. Ch. 159, Art. 3) sets forth a process for local units to follow (see Chapter 10 of this volume).

What, then, is *capital budgeting and finance*? It may be defined as a process that has the following steps, which are the subjects of the next six sections.

1. *Identification and classification of capital requests and expenditures.* This consists of deciding whether particular requests are in fact capital (see next section) and whether they belong in the capital budget, as well as making sure that specific expenditure items properly chargeable to a capital project or outlay are so charged and others are not.

2. *Capital improvement programming.* This involves planning for and scheduling major capital needs for approval, funding, and implementation over a future period—usually five to six years.

3. *Assessment, maintenance, and improvement of a county's ability to finance capital needs.* This involves maintaining or improving a county's bond or credit ratings, determining present financial

condition, and projecting the resources that will be available to finance capital needs over the same forecast period covered by the capital improvement program.

4. *Selection of the financing source(s) for individual capital projects and expenditures.* Major capital projects are often financed by issuing bonds or other forms of debt. Other sources of capital financing include current revenues, capital reserves, and gifts or grants.

5. *Authorization of capital projects or expenditures and appropriation of funds for them.* Authorization and appropriation may occur together or in separate steps. Appropriation may be made in the annual budget ordinance or in one or more capital project ordinances.

6. *Implementation of the capital budget.* This step consists of managing the funds that have been accumulated for capital projects and expenditures; acquiring equipment; and designing, contracting for, supervising, and accounting for construction projects.

Identification and Classification of Capital Requests and Expenditures

Broadly conceived, a *capital expenditure* is an outlay of significant value that results in acquisition of or addition to a fixed asset.[1] The term *fixed asset* refers to property that is held or used for more than one year, usually for many years. *Fixed* does not mean "immobile"; an automobile is usually a fixed asset.

According to the Department of State Treasurer's *Policies Manual,*[2] which recommends fiscal policies and practices for local governments, fixed assets that are owned and used in city operations can be classified into the following categories:

1. All land or rights to land.
2. All buildings.
3. Additions to or renovations of buildings that cost $500 or more and that add value to the building or improve it.
4. Improvements to land other than buildings that cost $500 or more and that add value to land or improve its utility. These improvements can include drainage systems, parking lots, and similar construction on land.

5. Equipment and furnishings that cost $500 or more. According to the *Policies Manual,* additions to or refurbishing of capital equipment that cost $250 or more are capital expenditures and should be recorded as additions to fixed assets.

Expenditures for fixed assets owned by a county and used in its operations that are for general governmental purposes should be budgeted for in the general fund, a capital projects fund, or another governmental fund, and then recorded or carried as *general* fixed assets in a county's accounting system. Expenditures for fixed assets owned by a county that are used in enterprise or proprietary fund activities should be budgeted for and recorded or carried as fixed assets in the appropriate enterprise or proprietary funds. If a county acquires a fixed asset for the purpose of selling or donating the asset to another organization—for example, to the local area mental health agency—the county must of course budget for the expenditure but does not have to record or carry it as a fixed asset.

Counties also occasionally make capital expenditures for infrastructure that is used by the public, such as drainage facilities or open space. Such assets are typically immovable and have value only to the government entity that builds them and the public that uses or benefits from them. Expenditures for such infrastructure must be budgeted—usually in a capital projects fund—but the recording or the capitalizing of such public domain infrastructure in a county's accounting system is optional and is often not done, except that all enterprise or other proprietary fund infrastructure is capitalized.

The general definition of capital expenditure just given says that such an expenditure must be of *significant value*—$500 as a minimum for improvements to land and for equipment and $250 for additions to or refurbishing of equipment, according to the *Policies Manual.* The selection of this minimum is a local decision and should depend on the size of the county. Minimums for most counties in North Carolina currently range between $500 and several thousand dollars.

Generally, in governmental budgeting and accounting, only expenditures to acquire *tangible* assets or property are recorded as fixed assets.[3] Tangible assets are touchable or physical items; for example, land, buildings, and equipment. Expenditures to acquire *intangible* assets, such as a patent or a license for a specific technology, are seldom recorded as fixed assets for governmental funds in the general fixed asset account group[4] (intangible fixed assets should be capitalized in an enterprise fund).[5] Despite general practices, a growing number of

North Carolina counties are recording expenditures for computer software programs as fixed or capital assets. If the software is an operating system, comes with the hardware, and without it the hardware cannot run, the software should probably be capitalized as part of the computer's costs. If the software is an application program, it may have market value of its own. In this instance the software could be capitalized separately from the hardware.

Not all capital expenditures have to be included in the capital budget. *Inexpensive capital expenditures and those that recur every year* may be reviewed in the annual budget process, approved in the annual budget ordinance, and accounted for in the general fund or in another operating fund. The meaning of *inexpensive* will vary with the size of the county. A small county might establish a dollar cutoff for this determination of anywhere from $5,000 to $25,000 or so, and include all capital assets with an acquisition or construction cost below this amount in its annual budget and all more costly capital assets in a separate capital budget. A medium-size or large county would use a higher cutoff—for example, anywhere from $25,000 to $100,000 or even more—and put only capital assets that cost more than this amount in its capital budget.

Many *annually recurring capital expenditures* are made to replace vehicles or equipment. For example, many counties replace some of their sheriff's patrol vehicles annually. Because each patrol vehicle is generally used by the sheriff's department for more than one year and is of significant value—that is, it costs more than the minimum dollar amount used for capitalization—each is a fixed asset, and the expenditures to acquire one or more of them are capital. But annually recurring expenditures to replace patrol vehicles or other relatively inexpensive capital expenditures may be included in the annual budget. They can be reviewed and approved in the annual budget, which can accommodate them just as readily as expenditures for salaries, supplies, and operating items, which also recur yearly.

It is the very expensive, long-lived, and irregularly recurring capital projects and acquisitions that deserve the special treatment and planning called capital budgeting. Such projects and acquisitions must often be identified and planned ahead of actual need through a multiyear capital improvement program. They require large amounts of financing, for which debt is often issued, and they are frequently budgeted in capital project ordinances and accounted for in special capital project funds.

Problems occasionally arise in deciding whether to charge specific items of cost to a capital project or expenditure. A capital project or acquisition should include all expenditures or items that are incurred to put the capital asset being built or acquired into operating condition. For construction projects these items would include all costs for labor and construction materials; planning as well as architectural and engineering design; legal services; the acquisition of land or other property for the project, including brokerage fees, and the preparation of land for construction; easements; equipment and furnishings that are affixed to the project; interest and other financing charges during construction; and project administration charges. For equipment acquisitions the capital cost or expenditure includes not only the purchase price of the equipment per se, but also any transportation charges to move the equipment to its place of intended use and costs for installation and testing, if any.

Expenditures for certain items associated with a capital asset or facility may not be charged as a capital cost of the asset. Instead, they are operating expenditures. For example, although expenditures to buy land for a landfill and ready it for use are properly charged as capital costs for the landfill, expenditures for certain closure and post-closure purposes at a landfill are considered to be operating expenditures, according to interpretations of the bond statutes and generally accepted accounting principles, and may not be included among capital costs. Furthermore, although some expenditures for maintenance and repair—for example, a major repainting project on a large building—are very expensive and may preserve the useful lives of capital assets and seem like capital expenditures, they should be budgeted and accounted for as operating expenditures.

Capital Improvement Programming

One useful approach for planning capital acquisitions and improvements is a *capital improvement program* (CIP). A CIP forecasts future capital project and expenditure needs of a county, identifies sources of financing for those projects and expenditures, and points to the effect that the projects and the expenditures, if approved and implemented, will have on future annual budgets. More and more cities have instituted CIP processes in recent years to plan major infrastructure programs needed to meet growth and in response to recommendations of the Local Government Commission and the debt rating agencies.[6]

CIP Forecast Period and Allocation of Costs by Year

Most CIPs forecast five or six years into the future. A shorter period generally does not allow enough time to plan and obtain clearances and funding for major projects, although some, mostly small municipalities have successfully used three- or four-year CIPs. A few of the state's largest local units have used ten-year forecast periods, but such long forecasts involve considerable guesswork with the projection of needs for the latter part of the forecast period necessarily remaining general.

The essential feature of a CIP is the apportionment of capital expenditures among the years of the forecast period. On the CIP summary form (Figure 11-1), the columns designated Prior Years and Current Year are used for capital projects that are in process. Expenditures have been incurred for them, are being incurred for them, or both; but the projects are not finished, and expenditures will be incurred for them in the coming Budget Year and possibly in one or more of the Planning Years. The column designated Budget Year lists capital expenditures that will be incurred in the next year. These expenditures may be for projects in process or for projects or expenditures that are in the final stage of review in this year's CIP, for which money will be spent in the Budget Year if they are approved. The columns on the CIP form designated Planning Years can show expenditures to be incurred in the future for multiyear projects that are in process, for projects that are getting under way in the Budget Year but will not be completed until a later year, and for projects that are scheduled to start in one of the Planning Years. The column designated Subsequent Years is for expenditures on projects that get under way in the CIP forecast period, usually in one of the Planning Years, but will not be finished until sometime after the CIP forecast period.

The CIP's phasing of projects and expenditures by year is important not only in scheduling but also in setting priorities. A capital project or expenditure that is scheduled in the Budget Year or an early CIP Planning Year is often placed there because it has a higher priority than other projects and outlays scheduled for one or more of the later Planning Years.

As Figure 11-1 suggests, CIPs often distribute costs over the years covered by the CIP based on when expenditures will be made. Alternatively, costs can be allocated among a CIP's years based on when a city council is expected to make appropriations for projects or outlays or when contractual obligations will be incurred for projects or outlays. Of

Project Expenditures, Funding Sources, and Operating Budget Impact by Year

	Prior Years	Current Year	Budget Year	Planning Years					Subsequent Years	Total Project
				Year 1	Year 2	Year 3	Year 4	Year 5		
Project Expenditures by Function										
Schools										
Community college										
Human services										
Library system										
Public safety										
Parks and recreation										
Solid waste										
Water-sewer										
General government										
Other										
Total Expenditures for All Projects										
Funding Sources										
General fund revenues										
Enterprise fund revenues										
General capital reserves										
Enterprise capital reserves										
General obligation bonds authorized										
General obligation bonds to be authorized										
Revenue bonds										
Certificates of participation or leases										
Special obligation bonds										
Impact fees or assessments										
Grants and gifts										
Total All Funding Sources										
Effect of Projects on Annual Budget										
Salaries, wages, and benefits										
Other operating and maint. expenditures										
Capital expenditures										
Debt service and lease payments										
Revenues										
Net Impact on Annual Budget										

course, appropriation, contracting, and expenditures for a project or an acquisition can all occur in the same year, especially if the project or the item is relatively small or modest in size. However, they often occur in different years for relatively large projects or acquisitions. A hypothetical example illustrates the difference among these alternatives. A multiyear construction project for a county will cost $9 million. All $9 million will be appropriated for the project in the coming Budget Year, using a capital project ordinance (discussed further on in the chapter); $6 million in contracts will be left for it in that year and $3 million in Planning Year 1; and $3 million will be spent for the project in the Budget Year, $3 million in Planning Year 1, and $3 million in Planning Year 2. If the county's CIP allocates costs by year based on when appropriations for projects are made, the CIP will show the full $9 million in the Budget Year. However, if the CIP allocates project costs by year based on when contracts are let, it will show $6 million in the Budget Year and $3 million in Planning Year 1. If costs in the CIP are allocated by year based on spending, then the CIP will show $3 million in the Budget Year, $3 million in Planning Year 1, and $3 million in Planning Year 2.

A CIP that distributes costs by year based on when appropriations are made focuses attention principally on the decisions that officials must make to approve projects. The approval of projects or expenditures often occurs via appropriations. Even if effective approval of a project occurs before appropriations are made for it, the appropriation of funds is usually a key step in getting the project going. A CIP that distributes costs by year based on when contracts are let or on when expenditures occur addresses both decision-making and implementation concerns: decision-making concerns because appropriations are generally associated with contracts let or expenditures made for a project in its first year, and implementation concerns because contracting and spending are integral parts of project execution. A county should use one basis for distributing costs by year in its CIP and not switch among bases for different projects.

The CIP is conceived as an annual process, and most counties that use one revise it each year. Annual review provides for a recurring assessment of capital needs and updates the CIP to accommodate new projects and expenditures. New capital requests should be anticipated before the time of need and first placed in the CIP in one of the later Planning Years (Planning Years 3, 4, or 5). Then, as the CIP process is repeated annually, the standing requests are reviewed, those that pass muster move up a year or more toward approval and funding, and marginal requests are weeded out. When the requests that survive reach the Budget Year, they are approved and funding arrangements are made. Of course, not all capital needs can be foreseen years in advance. Some capital requests must be approved and funded almost immediately after the need for them becomes apparent. If this happens with many projects, however, the CIP loses much of its value as a planning tool.

The CIP Preparation Process

The total time needed for CIP preparation, review, and approval may span up to six months or so in the state's largest counties. It may span only a month to several months in small- and medium-size counties.

An important issue is whether the CIP process should occur before, along with, or after the annual budget process. Both processes involve much time and work, and running them simultaneously can be difficult. Some counties prepare and present CIPs before the annual budget process begins. In this way, decisions about major improvements that are made in the CIP process establish a framework for follow-up decisions on operating issues that are made in the annual budget. As a result, the annual budget process can be less complex and difficult. Other counties run the CIP process and present the CIP concurrently with the annual budget process. Indeed, CIP preparation is treated as just one part, albeit an important one, of the annual budget process in some of these counties. Linking the CIP to annual budget preparation in this way helps ensure that program operation and capital project decisions, which arise from the same general needs, are adequately coordinated. Few jurisdictions prepare their CIPs after the annual budget has been prepared and presented.[7]

Coordination

One official in a county is typically assigned the responsibility of coordinating preparation of the CIP. In smaller counties this official may be the county manager or administrator. In medium-size and large counties, the manager is likely to delegate the responsibility to another official, for example, the county finance or budget director, the planning director, or an assistant manager.[8] In some counties an administrative committee composed of the manager and top staff officials oversees CIP preparation. However, even with this arrangement, one of the officials on the committee typically has day-to-day responsibility for coordinating the CIP.

A county's CIP should be coordinated with other multiyear plans that relate to the county's growth in future years. For instance, a county may have a strategic plan that addresses long-term growth over the next decade, a utility system expansion plan, a comprehensive land use development plan, or a capital or needs assessment that forecasts county capital projects five to ten years beyond the CIP planning period. A CIP often is a vehicle for implementing these and any other plans that directly address or have implications for a county's capital needs.

Requests

The CIP preparation process typically begins with the issuance of request forms and instructions to departments and other agencies that participate in the CIP process. In many counties, only county departments may submit CIP project requests. In some counties, special-purpose government entities in the county such as a public housing authority, or community service agencies that provide services to county residents such as a homeless shelter, may be allowed to submit project requests in the county's CIP process.

Instructions for CIP requests usually specify what types of capital projects and expenditures may be included in the CIP. Counties vary, principally according to size, in the types of capital items that their CIPs include. For example, in one county with a population of about 50,000, CIP projects or items include any project requiring debt financing or borrowing; any acquisition or lease of land; purchases of equipment and vehicles that cost more than $10,000 and have a useful life of more than five years; construction of new buildings or facilities; major, nonroutine improvements to buildings or facilities that enhance their value; and equipment or furnishings required to furnish new buildings or other projects. One of the state's largest counties limits CIP requests to construction or renovation projects that cost $100,000 or more, have a useful life of five years or more; and take a year or more to complete. Items or projects not meeting these criteria are planned, budgeted, and financed entirely in the city's annual budget process. Most counties in the state include expensive equipment and vehicles in their CIPs.

The description of and the justification for any CIP project or acquisition should do the following:

- Summarize the project or the acquisition and explain how it fits with the objectives and the future plans of the requesting department or agency.

- Indicate the clients whom the project or the acquisition will serve and explain the effect of the project or the acquisition on them.
- Identify any alternatives to the requested project or acquisition.
- Provide expenditure estimates for completing the project or the acquisition, and address the probability that the expenditure estimates will escalate over time.
- Identify funding sources that may be available to fund the project or the acquisition. Program officials in most county departments are not likely to be knowledgeable about suitability and availability of general financing sources for most CIP requests. Nevertheless, program officials are often in a position to identify grants or other special funding sources for CIP projects that they propose. The city's finance director and other administrative officials are generally in the best position to identify and make recommendations about the applicability and the selection of funding sources for specific CIP requests. Figure 11-1 shows the typical funding sources that are available for financing capital projects in North Carolina. The most important ones are discussed in detail under the heading "Capital Financing Methods," later in this chapter. However, a comment is appropriate here about whether a CIP should include projects that are to be financed with general obligation bonds yet to be authorized by the voters. The inclusion of these projects presumes that the voters will approve a referendum. Nevertheless, the CIPs of many of the state's counties include this source of financing and identify projects to be funded from it. In these jurisdictions the CIP serves as a springboard for seeking voter approval of general obligation bonds for the projects or purposes to be funded from them.
- Provide a schedule for completing the project or making the acquisition, and indicate the relationship of this project to other projects in general, to other projects or acquisitions that must be completed before this one is undertaken, and to other projects that should await completion of this one.
- Comment on the status of any feasibility studies, architectural or engineering plans, land or right-of-way acquisitions, or construction already done for the project or the acquisition.
- Show the effect of the project or the acquisition on the annual operating budget, considering additional operating and maintenance expenditures and debt service or lease payments that

are likely to result, and any one-time or recurring savings or revenues that the project is likely to generate.

- Indicate the project's or acquisition's priority among other CIP requests that the department is making.

Review and Approval

After CIP project and acquisition requests have been submitted, county administrative staff need to review the requests from several standpoints. Requests should be checked for appropriateness for inclusion in the CIP and for technical feasibility. Project justifications, expenditure estimates, and the impact of projects on the operating budget must be verified. The availability of proposed financing sources for particular projects needs to be confirmed, and the ability of the county to incur new debt to finance CIP projects or acquisitions should be determined. Finally, relationships among CIP requests, of CIP requests to other multiyear development plans that the county may have, and of CIP requests to capital improvement plans of other governments that serve county residents—for example, a city within the county—need to be taken into account.

Once the review of CIP requests is finished, a recommended CIP for the county is usually prepared. This is likely to involve hard choices because the total of CIP requests almost always exceeds the availability of capital financing over the CIP forecast period. Even if the county were to issue debt to finance all or most CIP requests, the amount of debt that it could issue would be limited by its ability to service the debt during the forecast period and beyond. Many counties incorporate ranking criteria or systems into their CIP process to help put CIP project and acquisition requests in priority order. For example, officials in one North Carolina local government use the following ranking criteria, the first criterion having the highest priority:

1. Is mandated: Is clearly and specifically required by federal or state laws or court rulings.
2. Removes hazard: Removes an existing or potential hazard that threatens public health or safety.
3. Maintains service: Permits an existing standard of service to be maintained. If the request is not funded, a decrease in service will occur.
4. Improves efficiency: Reduces operating expenditures in the annual budget.

5. Increases revenues: Yields a net gain in revenues, considering increases in gross revenues and expenditures over the useful life of the project.

6. Expands or improves existing service: Increases the population served, the quantity of the service or the product provided, or the quality of the service or the product.

7. Creates new service: Makes possible the provision of an altogether new service or program.

8. Increases convenience, and Other: Increases the ease with which a service is provided, or does not fit into another category.

Many capital project and acquisition requests are likely to be excluded from the CIP that is recommended for a county. Some requests are likely to be excluded because they are not justified or because they are not technically feasible. Others that are justified and technically feasible are likely to be excluded because they are of lower priority given the financing capabilities of the county. In some future year the latter requests may take on a higher priority and be included in the CIP. Because of this, some CIPs contain a special section that lists currently low-priority but otherwise justified CIP requests that are not included in the current CIP but may be included in it in later years.

The county manager or administrator usually presents the recommended CIP to the board of commissioners. If this presentation occurs as part of the annual budget process, the recommended CIP is typically included in the document presenting the annual budget. In many counties the recommended CIP is presented to the board of commissioners in a separate CIP document.

Whether the CIP is presented to the commissioners in the annual budget document or as a separate document, the board may hold one or more review sessions focused exclusively on the CIP and capital projects or acquisitions included in it. Although there is no statutory requirement for a board of commissioners to hold a public hearing on the recommended CIP, a board can choose to do so to give citizens the opportunity to comment on the entire program or specific projects.[9]

After considering and making changes in the recommended CIP, boards of commissioners in some counties pass a resolution approving it.[10] The resolution approves the CIP as a plan for the forecast period. Generally it does not represent commissioner approval of or commitment to any one project or expenditure, nor does it appropriate money for any project or expenditure. However, as already mentioned, projects and expenditures in the first year of the CIP typically become the proposed capital budget for that year, and unless such projects and expenditures are in process with appropriations made for them in prior years, they are up for board of commissioner approval and appropriation.

Board appropriation of moneys for projects and expenditures in the Budget Year of the CIP can be accomplished either in the annual budget ordinance, in amendments to that ordinance, or in one or more capital project ordinances (see the section "Use of Capital Project Ordinances," later in the chapter).

In some counties, board approval of the CIP as a plan may occur almost simultaneously with board appropriation of funds for projects and expenditures in the Budget Year of the CIP. Because of this, approval of the CIP itself and appropriation of money for projects or expenditures may be difficult to distinguish. Moreover, in counties where the board of commissioners does not pass a resolution approving a CIP, appropriation of funds for projects and expenditures in the CIPs first year can be seen as approval of the CIP itself. Nevertheless, approval of the CIP, on the one hand, and approval of CIP projects and appropriation of money for them, on the other hand, are typically and should be separate steps.

Reasons for Preparing a CIP

Why should a county undertake a CIP? There are numerous reasons:

1. Having such a program helps a county meet capital replacement and new capital needs in an orderly fashion.

2. By forecasting, officials allow enough time for project planning and design. Without a CIP these functions are often rushed, and errors in design are much more likely to result.

3. A CIP can be a helpful fiscal planning tool because forecasting capital demands on local revenues and borrowing power helps a county avoid overextending itself financially during the forecast period and even beyond.

4. A CIP enables a county to schedule the implementation of projects, helping it phase related projects in the most efficient sequence and avoid having to cope with an unmanageable number of major projects at any one time.

5. By identifying major capital requirements before they are needed, a CIP can put county officials in a better position to secure grants and generally to arrange funding for projects.

6. A CIP can be an effective springboard for an effort to secure voter approval for general obligation bonds for certain purposes or projects.

7. Having a workable CIP can improve a county's debt rating.

Debt Ratings, Evaluation of Financial Condition, and Forecasting of Resources for Capital Financing

Counties must be able to raise the moneys that they need to undertake capital projects and acquire capital assets. Such moneys may come from annual revenues remaining after current operating needs are met, accumulated capital reserves, bond or other debt proceeds, special assessments or facility fees, federal or state grants, and other sources. Any capital budgeting process should address the county's bond or debt ratings, its current financial condition, and specifically the ways in which its ability to finance capital needs is likely to change over the planning period covered by the CIP.

Debt Ratings

A debt or bond rating generally evaluates the capacity and the willingness of the issuer to repay debt and to make timely interest payments on debt.[11] North Carolina's counties are rated by several national bond rating agencies—Standard & Poor's Corporation (S & P), Moody's Investors Service (Moody's), and Fitch Investor's Service (Fitch's)—and by the North Carolina Municipal Council, which is an association of banks, investment banking firms, securities dealers, bond attorney firms, and regulatory agencies that are involved in the municipal debt market in North Carolina. Municipal debt commonly refers to all bonds and other debt sold by state and local government entities, including counties. In rating such debt and debt issuers, the rating agencies rely on annual financial reports, annual budgets, CIPs, and other reports and information as well as official offering statements for bond or debt issues themselves.

All three of the national bond rating agencies have headquarters in New York, although each has regional offices in different parts of the country.[12] S & P and Moody's rate nearly all North Carolina local government debt that is sold nationally. Fitch's became active (again) in rating municipal debt in the late 1980s, and rates some but not all North Carolina local government debt that is marketed nationally. The national agencies evaluate the creditworthiness of a county or any issuer with regard to a specific bond or debt offering. In other words, the rating applies to a specific bond or debt issue rather than to the entity issuing the debt, although the rating on the debt, especially if it is general obligation debt, depends heavily on the strength and the prospects of the issuer. A national debt or bond rating addresses not only the ability and the willingness of the issuer to make debt service payments but also the legal protection afforded by the bond or the debt contract to investors. Such protection is a function of the contract and of the statutory and constitutional provisions that authorize and regulate this type of debt. A national rating may also take into account credit support, if any is provided, from bond insurance or other sources of guaranty for a debt or bond issue. Bond insurance guarantees to investors the payment of interest and the repayment of principal on an insured bond or debt issue. Insurance from a highly rated national bond insurance company gives the insured debt the rating of the insurance company. The national agencies rate all types of municipal debt: general obligation bonds or notes, revenue bonds, certificates of participation and other debt secured by the asset being financed with the debt (and sometimes other property), special obligation bonds, and different types of short-term debt.

The national rating agencies use letter-rating systems for bonds and other long-term debt. For instance, S & P uses ten general rating categories: AAA, AA, A, BBB, BB, B, CCC, CC, C, and D. The ratings from AA to CCC may be modified by the addition of a plus or minus sign (+ or −) to indicate relative quality within the general categories. The four highest categories, AAA through BBB, are referred to as *investment grade* or *bank eligible* ratings. Banks and certain other financial institutions are not supposed to invest in state and local government or other debt that is otherwise a permissible investment for them unless the debt has a bank eligible rating. Bonds or other long-term debt rated BB or below are regarded as speculative (popularly called *junk bonds*). Debt rated D is in default.

Moody's uses a similar rating system for bonds and long-term debt, although it consists of nine rather than ten general categories: Aaa, Aa, A, Baa, Ba, B, Caa, Ca, and C. Debt in each of the Aa through B groups carries an additional rating symbol of 1, 2, or 3 to indicate relative quality within the general categories. Debt in the first four general rating groups is bank eligible. Debt in the lower-rated groups is considered to be speculative.

To secure a rating from a national rating agency for new bonds or debt, a city or any other issuer generally must request it. The Local Government Commission recommends that a North Carolina local government obtain at least one national rating when it sells $1 million to $2 million in debt, and two national ratings when it sells over $2 million. The national rating agencies charge from around $4,000 to about $25,000, depending on the size of an issue, for a rating on general obligation bonds. Ratings of very large general obligation bond issues— more than $100 million—can cost up to $60,000 or so. To maintain a national rating, a county must send the agency annual financial reports, budgets, CIPs, and other positive or negative information that bears on its financial condition and prospects and therefore on the rating. If the rating agencies do not receive such information regularly, they will most likely suspend or withdraw their rating for the city's debt. If there is any material change in a county's financial condition, its rating may change. S & P provides *rating outlooks* for all debt that it rates. These forecast the potential direction of an entity's debt rating. A rating outlook may be *negative*—the rating may be lowered; *stable*—the rating is unlikely to change; *positive*—the rating may be raised; or *developing*—the rating may be raised or lowered.

General obligation bond ratings from the national rating agencies are based on similar criteria, which fall into four areas: economic base, financial performance and flexibility, debt burden and management, and administration and governance. Economic base tends to be the most important element in general obligation ratings from the national agencies. Many of the criteria that enter into debt ratings from the national agencies are discussed under the next heading, Evaluation of Financial Condition.

The North Carolina Municipal Council is located in Raleigh.[13] It rates counties, cities, and special-purpose local governments in the state that have outstanding general obligation bonds or other debt, such as certificates of participation, issued to finance general-purpose public improvements.[14] The Council does not rate local governments that have issued only revenue bonds or debt. Currently the Council maintains ratings on all 100 North Carolina counties, 255 cities and towns, and about 25 special purpose districts in the state. Council ratings apply to the county or the unit issuing debt rather than to a specific bond or debt issue. Because of this, Council ratings do not reflect bond insurance or other guarantees for specific debt issues. Council ratings focus preponderantly on the ability and the willingness of the issuer to repay debt and make timely payments of interest. The Council uses a numeric rating system that ranges from 0 to 100, with 100 being the highest or best rating. Bonds or debt of a county with a Council rating of 75 or more is considered to be eligible for investment by banks. The Council does not charge a local government for its rating service. Members of the Council pay for ratings through membership fees and assessments. The Council reviews and updates its rating for any unit with outstanding, rated debt at least once every three years or sooner if a unit is marketing new general obligation or publicly offered general purpose debt. Council staff typically visit a county whenever the Council is reviewing the county's rating.

A Council rating is based on three general factors: general obligation and other general-purpose debt burden relative to wealth; administrative and financial record, which encompasses budgetary operations, accounting, level of taxes compared with similar units, tax collection, and other areas of financial operations; and payments program and resources, which considers debt structure and ability to make debt payments. Debt burden and structure are very important factors in the Council's rating system.

North Carolina's local governments are generally among the best rated in the country. As of the spring of 1998, about fifty cities and counties in the country had AAA general obligation bond ratings from S & P. Ten of these are North Carolina units.[15] Among these AAA-rated entities are Durham, Forsyth, Mecklenburg, and Wake Counties. Because of the importance that economic size and diversity have in determining a general obligation bond rating from one of the national agencies, it is most difficult for medium- and smaller-size counties to secure AAA or Aaa ratings. All counties in the state that have general obligation bond ratings from one or more of the national rating agencies have ratings of BBB or Baa and above, that is, bank eligible or investment grade ratings.

The North Carolina Municipal Council's rating system results in few ratings in the 90s. As of December 31, 1997, the Council rated only five of the state's counties in the 90s. Five counties, all small, rural counties, had ratings below 75. Most of the state's counties have ratings in the 80s and the upper 70s.

Because of their generally excellent debt ratings, the state's counties and other local governments are able to sell their bonds and debt at lower interest rates than local governments in virtually any other state. Indeed, North Carolina local governments are often able to sell bonds at lower interest rates than comparably rated local governments in other states. The generally excellent credit of the state's counties and other local governments enables them to save millions of dollars in interest costs.

What accounts for the good debt ratings of North Carolina's counties and other local governments? The state's economy has grown and become more diverse. Local government financial management in North Carolina is professional and recognized throughout the country. Good local government leadership, the prevalence of the county-manager form of government, and conservative yet forward-looking budgeting and financial planning also underlie the good bond ratings of the state's local governments. Last but certainly not least, Local Government Commission oversight of debt policies and management, accounting and financial reporting, and budgeting and financial management has contributed greatly to the high local government ratings.[16]

Evaluation of Financial Condition

A county's debt rating and general financial position depend on the size and the strength of the local economy and the financial condition and practices of the city.

Size and Strength of the Local Economy

The local economy is a critical factor in determining the creditworthiness of any local government. The ability to provide services, to raise money, and to pay the cost of capital financing ultimately depends on the health of the local economy. A county's economic base is a function of income and wealth; economic activity, diversity, and stability; and the presence of infrastructure that is vital to strong economic performance.

Per capita income is one measure of wealth. Growth in per capita income for a county should be compared with that of the state as a whole and with that of other North Carolina counties of similar size in order to evaluate relative position. Data on per capita income are available from the Bureau of Economic Analysis of the United States Department of Commerce. Retail sales figures, which are another significant measure of wealth and economic activity, are available from the Sales and Use Tax Division of the North Carolina Department of Revenue.

The measure of wealth or economic activity that is most directly related to a county's ability to finance general public improvements is the value of property subject to taxation. Growth in property tax valuation can be compared with that of other counties of similar size. If a county's taxable value is growing relatively slowly, officials should be concerned and determine why: Is the cause underassessment or failure to discover taxable property for the tax rolls? The removal of property from the tax base due to state exemption of certain property or some other reason? A falloff or problems in an industry or an economic sector important to the county's tax base? Some other factor? New construction and industrial growth increase the property tax base of a county. Therefore economic development programs focused on these sectors can be vital in contributing to a county's long-term economic and fiscal well-being.

Economic diversity, which is important for a strong local economy, depends on having several major industries or economic sectors rather than just one. One measure of economic diversity is the level of employment by industry or sector; employment statistics are available from the North Carolina Employment Security Commission. A second measure is the portion of property tax revenue that comes from a county's largest taxpayer or from a single industrial or economic sector. If more than 10 percent of property tax proceeds are attributed to any single taxpayer or if a significant portion—20 percent or more—of tax revenues comes from one industrial sector (for example, textiles), county officials should monitor the prospects of that industry or sector closely and promote the growth of different types of local economic activity, thereby diversifying the county's tax base.

The economic stability of a county is related to how the local economy holds up in a recession or in the face of general economic problems. One measure of economic stability is the rate of unemployment in the local labor force. This figure can be compared with unemployment rates in other counties, in the state, and in the nation as a whole. The analysis of comparative and historical data on employment can reveal how stable a local economy has been over a long period.

A county's ability to maintain a strong local economy depends on whether it has the infrastructure needed to support economic growth: transportation facilities, utilities, schools, housing, and health care facilities. Important questions with regard to infrastructure include the following: Is the county served by an airport and a railroad? Is it served by an interstate highway? What other roads are available for truck transportation? Are the facilities for water supply and sewage treatment, through city, county, or other systems, large enough to meet economic and residential growth? Are community college or other technical training facilities adequate, and are their programs responsive to the need of the county and its surrounding region for skilled labor? Will schools and health care facilities be available to serve a growing population, and are the schools giving young people the education they need to function effectively in the workforce and in the community at large? What is the age and the composition of the local housing stock? How fast is new housing being built, if at all?

A county can attempt to strengthen its economic base by fostering economic development and providing the infrastructure needed to support growth. G.S. 158-7.1 gives counties the statutory authority to offer important incentives to industries and other businesses. If successful, economic development programs typically lead to improved financial conditions for the county government itself and also strengthen the county's capacity to finance capital projects. However, the results of economic development efforts are seldom immediate and cannot be guaranteed. (For further discussion of economic development activities, see Chapter 17). A county's financial position and practices are more directly under the control of its officials, and they also affect its ability to acquire and pay the cost of capital financing.

Financial Condition and Practices

A county's financial condition depends on its revenues, expenditures, fund balances or other reserves, outstanding debt, and debt service schedule. Revenues directly or indirectly support all county capital financing. They are necessary to provide current funding for capital outlays financed on a pay-as-you-go basis, to build capital reserves or fund balances to meet capital needs, and to pay debt service on debt obligations incurred to finance capital projects.

One measure of whether revenues are keeping pace with the need for services and capital facilities is growth of important general fund revenues (for example, property and sales taxes and user fee revenues) in relation to growth in the city's population and in general fund expenditures. The property tax is the most important general revenue source for counties. Officials should closely monitor the annual increases in property tax revenue and the property tax base. They should know how much property tax revenue growth results from tax-rate increases and how much from growth in the tax base. Separate sources of growth in this base—that is, new construction versus revaluation—should be distinguished.

Expenditures for operating purposes—for example, salaries and wages, fringe benefits, contractual services, and supplies—absorb revenues so they are otherwise not available for capital projects and expenditures. Expenditures for salaries, wages, and fringe benefits account for the largest share of operating expenditures for many county services. Officials can keep track of the number of authorized county positions per 1,000 population, counting part-time positions on a full-time-equivalent basis. This will permit a comparison with similar counties to determine relative staffing levels. Likewise, expenditures per capita for salaries, fringe benefits, and contractual services can be compared with those of similar counties. Officials for a county can compare the county's expenditures per capita for general line-item and functional categories with the averages for all of the state's counties of similar size by referring to the *Fiscal Summary of North Carolina Counties*.[17]

The available fund balance for a county at any one point in time consists of its cash plus investments less liabilities, encumbrances, and deferred revenues arising from cash receipts. Chapter 10 discusses fund balance in relation to annual budgeting. All that need be said here is that a county should maintain some fund balance and reserves for emergency capital replacement purposes. The general fund should have such fund balance or reserves, and enterprise funds should also have them. Such fund balance or reserves are in addition to the minimum general fund balance that the Local Government Commission recommends local governments carry to support their general fund annual operating budgets, equal to 8 percent of general fund expenditures. Maintaining adequate fund balance is one factor underlying the good debt ratings that North Carolina's local governments enjoy.

Outstanding debt and the annual debt service that a county must pay affect its financial condition and are crucial factors in determining its ability to finance future capital projects. If a county is already heavily in debt and making large annual debt service payments, it is unlikely to be able to borrow major new amounts of money to finance new capital projects. One measure of whether more debt can safely be issued is annual debt service on *net* (non-self-supporting) general obligation debt and on other general purpose or tax-supported debt, as a percentage of general operating expenditures and debt service. Some authorities say that this should ordinarily not exceed 15 to 20 percent.[18] Most North Carolina local governments hold it to less than 10 percent.

A second measure of safety in borrowing is outstanding general obligation debt as a percentage of the appraised value of taxable property. The statutes in fact set a legal limit on this percentage; according to G.S. 159-55, the net debt for any county may not exceed 8 percent of its taxable property valuation. *Net debt* is total authorized and outstanding general obligation debt plus other forms of general debt (for example, certificates of participation and lease purchase agreements issued for general government purposes), less debt issued for utility facilities and certain other deductions. (More is written about the calculation of net debt later in this chapter.) Although the legal net debt limit is 8 percent, all counties restrict outstanding net general obligation debt to a percentage far below 8 percent of taxable valuation. For instance, net debt (including authorized and unissued as well as outstanding general obligation bonds and outstanding certificate of participation debt for general public improvements but excluding enterprise debt) as a percentage of appraised property valuation for all North Carolina's counties was only 1.17 percent as of June 30, 1997.[19] For counties above 250,000 in population, on average, this percentage was 1.46; for counties with 10,000–24,999 people, 1.28 percent; and for counties with fewer than 10,000 people, 0.60 percent.

Of course, one problem with any debt measure stated as a percentage of taxable value is that the latter can change significantly with the revaluation of real property. Before the revaluation a county could have net debt equal to 1.25 percent of taxable valuation. After the revaluation, however, this figure might drop to 1 percent or less. This occurs simply because real property in the unit has been reappraised and has a higher value for tax purposes; it has nothing to do with any change in the existing outstanding or authorized debt.

Per capita debt is another measure widely used to compare the debt levels of counties and other local governments. As of June 30, 1997, net debt, as defined above, for all North Carolina's counties was $583 per capita. Such debt was $901 per capita for cities above 250,000 in population, $584 for counties from 10,000 to 24,999 in population, and $341 for counties with fewer than 10,000 people.[20]

Care must be exercised in interpreting these and other measures of debt burden. For instance, a fast-growing county with significant resort development may have issued general obligation debt and some certificates of participation to build public improvements to meet growth and resort needs. The county's permanent resident population may be small relative to this debt, making debt per capita relatively high. On the other hand, the value of the county's taxable property, including expensive vacation homes, may be quite large, causing net general obligation and certificate of participation debt as a percentage of tax valuation to be modest or low.

Moreover, these general debt measures are useful for comparing counties only with regard to general obligation and other debt serviced or paid from taxes and other general revenues. Judgments about a county's ability to carry revenue bonds or other special types of debt must be based on feasibility studies of the projects or enterprise systems financed with the bonds or the debt, and of the specific revenue streams earmarked for debt service on the bonds or the debt.

A county's financial practices also affect its financial position, creditworthiness, and ability to raise financing for capital projects at affordable rates. The most important of these practices are the budget, tax and revenue administration, and accounting and the annual audit. Key questions to ask about the annual budget are: Is the budget enacted by July 1—the start of the budget year—every year? Do actual revenue collections during the year meet or exceed estimates included in the budget? Do expenditures made during the year remain within the appropriations approved in the budget? Does the budget carry any operating reserve in the form of a contingency appropriation, or is there an unappropriated fund balance to meet cash-flow needs and provide for unforeseen expenditures?

A significant measure of effective revenue administration is the percentage of the current property tax levy collected by the end of the fiscal year. The average property tax collection percentage for all North Carolina cities in 1995–96 was 96.8.[21] For counties above 100,000 in population, the average collection percentage was 97.5, and for counties with fewer than 25,000 people, it was 93.9. A collection percentage below 92 indicates significant problems in revenue administration, and the Local Government Commission may not approve a county's bond or debt issue if its collection percentage is less than 90. (Property tax collection is discussed further in Chapter 9.)

The General Statutes require all cities to maintain accounting systems in accordance with generally accepted accounting principles and rules and regulations of the Local Government Commission [G.S. 159-25(a)(1)]. Counties in North Carolina, including the smaller ones, maintain accounting systems that are up to standard. Counties must also undergo an end-of-year independent audit (G.S. 159-34; see Chapter 12). Auditors examine accounting systems, financial statements, internal control procedures, and compliance with grant requirements, after which they draft and publish an opinion. An *unqualified* opinion suggests that a county's accounting system and procedures meet the applicable standards. If the auditor renders a *qualified* opinion, the Local Government Commission will normally not approve the issuance of debt by the county.

Forecasting of Resources for Capital Financing

Capital planning must go beyond the evaluation of a county's present fiscal position. It is important to forecast a county's future status and, more specifically, the financial resources that will be available to meet future capital needs. The forecast should cover the same period that the CIP covers. A forecast should first consider how a county's economic base is likely to grow or change in the forecast period, and then trace the effect of the change on annual revenues and operating expenditures. Annual revenues that remain after necessary operating needs are met and an operating reserve is provided, will be available to finance future capital needs.[22]

Counties can prepare multiyear financial forecasts using a form like that presented in Figure 11-2. The form is for a county's general fund and general public improvements. A similar and even simpler form might be used to forecast enterprise revenues, expenditures, and capital financing capacity.

Forecasting Annual Revenues

Forecasts of annual revenues are usually based on past trends. Because revenues from different sources grow at different rates, a forecast should be made for each major revenue source. In the general fund the key sources for most counties are the property tax, the local sales and use taxes, and intergovernmental revenue. Each of these sources should be forecast separately, with specific forecasts done for major sub-categories within intergovernmental revenues. Most other revenue sources can be combined and forecast together. In an enterprise fund, such as a water and sewer fund or a solid waste fund, user charges are the major revenue source. They should be projected separately from the handful of other significant sources in the fund—for example, assessments and connection fees.

In looking at past revenue trends, growth that resulted from economic expansion must be distinguished from growth that resulted from legal redefinition of the tax base, revaluation, or from changes in the tax rate or rates for user fees. If changes in revenue classifications have been made during the trend period being studied, past classifications must be adjusted to make them consistent with existing ones. In

Figure 11-2
Multiyear Financial Forecast, General Fund

	Two Years Ago Actual	Immediate Past Year Actual	Current Year Estimate	Budget Year Estimate	Planning Years					Totals
					Year 1	Year 2	Year 3	Year 4	Year 5	
Annual Revenues										
Property taxes										
Sales & use taxes										
Licenses & permits										
Intergovernmental revenue										
Social services										
Other										
Charges for services										
Health/mental health										
Solid waste										
Other										
Reimbursements										
Inventory tax										
Intangibles tax										
Other										
Other revenues										
Total General Fund Revenues										
Annual Expenditures										
General government										
Public safety										
Human services										
Schools										
Community college										
Library system										
Parks & recreation										
Environmental services										
Solid waste										
Other										
Debt service										
Other										

making the revenue forecast, present tax or utility rates will generally be assumed to continue through the forecast period unless a policy is in place that provides for changes in the rates during the forecast period.

Forecasting Annual Operating Expenditures

Once annual revenues have been projected, the amount that will be used to finance operating expenditures during the forecast period needs to be estimated. This can be done by line-item category for each fund—salaries, fringe benefits, operating expenditures, contractual services, and so on—or by department and program within a fund. If the forecast is done by line-item category for each fund, forecasted amounts are less likely to become a floor or a base for the annual budget requests that department and program managers submit each year. On the other hand, forecasts of expenditures by department and program within a fund are likely to reflect future program and service requirements more accurately than a line-item forecast by fund. Expenditure forecasts should be based on past trends. In some cases the trends can simply be carried forward; in others they will have to be adjusted for changes or new conditions that are likely to prevail in the forecast period.

Forecasting Annual Debt and Debt Service Requirements

Forecasting outstanding debt and debt service requirements is also essential in determining what capital financing will be available to a county in the future. The goal is to learn how much new debt a county can issue and how much total debt it can carry or have outstanding during the forecast period. Two limits or measures of safety in borrowing have already been discussed. One is annual debt service on net general obligation and other tax-supported or general purpose debt as a percentage of annual operating expenditures, including debt service, for general government purposes. The Local Government Commission normally arranges debt service schedule on general obligation bonds and other general purpose debt so that annual debt service declines from year to year until the bonds are fully repaid. A declining debt service schedule, compared with a level or ascending schedule, frees up debt issuance capacity more quickly in the future. Thus debt service on *existing* net outstanding general obligation and other general purpose debt as a percentage of annual operating expenditures for general purposes should also decline from year to year through the forecast period. This happens not only because annual debt service on such debt is declining but also because annual expenditures (and revenues) for general purposes typically grow from year to year.

A second measure of safety in borrowing is net general obligation and other general purpose debt as a percentage of taxable property valuation. Existing outstanding debt is a given figure. It will decline each year during the forecast period as principal payments, which make up part of annual debt service, are made. Taxable property valuation typically will grow during the forecast period. Thus if no new net general obligation or other general purpose debt is issued, such debt as a percentage of taxable valuation will decline during the forecast period.

Capital Financing Methods

Counties, like individuals, have essentially four methods for raising the money necessary to finance capital projects:

1. *Payment from current income.* Revenues earned during the current fiscal year are used to finance projects undertaken during that fiscal year.
2. *Payment from savings.* Revenues earned in earlier fiscal years have been set aside, or reserved, and after a sufficient amount has been accumulated, these savings are used to finance capital projects undertaken during the current fiscal year.
3. *Payment from gifts.* Moneys given to the county (including state and federal grants) are used to finance capital projects.
4. *Payment from borrowed moneys.* Moneys borrowed by the county, to be repaid in future fiscal years, are used to finance capital projects undertaken during this fiscal year.

The most important of these methods is the last, borrowing. If the capital project is at all large, it will almost always be financed, in whole or in part, by borrowing. Neither current revenues nor reserved moneys are likely to be sufficiently large to finance such a project without borrowed funds; and with the large-scale cutback in the number of federal grant programs, it is unlikely that large amounts of money will be acquired by gift. Therefore this section focuses on borrowing, briefly addressing current revenues and capital reserve funds at the end.

Forms of Security

A county that borrows money has a contract with its lenders, whether they are banks or brokerage houses that lent the money and retained the loan, or holders of bonds or certificates of participation. Under that contract the county agrees to pay the principal and the interest on the loan as they come due and to honor any other promises that it has made as part of the loan transaction. One of the most important provisions of the loan contract is the pledge or the designation of one or more forms of *security*, that to which the lender may look to compel repayment.

North Carolina counties currently may choose among four forms of security when they borrow money. It is appropriate to begin this section with a description of these forms of security because many of the other features of a borrowing flow from the choice that is made with respect to security. The form of security affects what form the loan transaction takes, whether voter approval is required, whether the Local Government Commission or the borrowing unit sells the debt securities, certainly what the credit rating on the loan is and thus what interest rate the borrower will have to pay, and even whether bond counsel is necessary for the loan.

The General Obligation

The strongest form of security that a county can pledge for debt is its full faith and credit, making the debt a *general obligation* of the borrowing government. All the resources of that government stand behind such a pledge, but specifically, a full-faith-and-credit pledge of a North Carolina county is a promise to levy whatever amount of property tax is necessary to repay the debt. (The property tax is singled out because it is the major revenue source over which counties have control; the state's general obligations are in effect secured largely by the state's income and sales taxes.) Because by law there is no statutory limit on the rate of property tax that may be levied for this purpose, such a promise is a pledge of unlimited taxing power.

Three statutes permit counties to incur general obligation debt. G.S. 159-43 through -79, the Local Government Bond Act, authorizes the issuance of general obligation *bonds*; G.S. Chapter 159, Article 9, Part 1 (G.S. 159-160 through -165), general obligation *bond anticipation notes*; and G.S. 159G-18, general obligation *debt instruments*. (Neither general obligation bond anticipation notes nor general obligation debt instruments may be issued without a government's having followed the procedures and met the requirements of the Local Government Bond Act.) These three authorizations are exclusive: G.S. 159-45 provides that "no unit of local government in this State shall have authority to enter into any contract or agreement, whether oral or written, whereby it borrows money and makes an express or implied pledge of its power to levy taxes as security for repayment of the loan," except pursuant to one of the three statutes.

The Revenue-Backed Obligation

A traditional form of security, although much more common nationally than in North Carolina, is a pledge of revenues generated by the debt-financed asset or by the system of which that asset is a part. For example, revenue bonds might be issued for a parking garage and secured by the revenues from charges for parking in the garage; or they might be issued for an expansion of a water system and secured by revenues of the entire system. By law (G.S. 159-91) such a pledge creates a lien on the pledged revenues in favor of the bondholders, and normally the bondholders have the contractual right to demand an increase in the user charges generating the revenues if those revenues prove inadequate to service the debt. The bondholders do not, however, have any right to demand payment from any other source, or to require an increase in taxes, if facility or system revenues continue to be inadequate even after charges are increased.

The nature of the security in a revenue-secured transaction leads to some uses of loan proceeds that are not found in general obligation loans. Two of these are using loan proceeds to pay any interest due to the lenders during the period of construction and to establish a reserve for future debt service payments. One effect of these uses of loan proceeds is that a county borrowing money secured by revenues will normally have to borrow more than it would have had to do had it financed the same project with general obligation debt.

Because the security for the debt is the revenues from the debt-financed asset (or the system of which it is a part), the lenders are naturally concerned about the construction, the operation, and the continued health of that asset or system. This concern is expressed through a series of *covenants*, or promises, that the borrowing government makes to the lenders as part of the loan transaction. The most fundamental of these is the *rate covenant*, under which the borrowing government promises to set and maintain the rates, the fees, and the charges of the revenue-producing facility or system so that net revenues will exceed annual debt service requirements by some fixed amount. For example, a common requirement is that the rate structure generate annual net revenues at some specified level—usually between 120 and 150 percent—of either the current year's debt service requirements or the maximum annual debt service requirements during the life of the loan. This margin of safety required by the rate covenant is referred to as *times-coverage* of the loan. Generally, as long as net revenues continue to maintain the required coverage, the borrowing government may modify the rate structure as it pleases. If net revenues fall below the required coverage, however (even if they are still adequate to service the debt), the covenant frequently requires the government to engage an independent consultant to study the operation of the revenue-producing facility or system and recommend changes in the rate structure and in operations necessary to return net revenues to a level above times-coverage. Typically the covenant further requires the government to revise its rate structure in conformity with the consultant's recommendations and permits the trustee (who represents the bondholders) or some percentage of lenders to sue the government to force such a rate revision.

A variety of statutes permit counties to borrow money and secure the loan by a pledge of asset- or system-generated revenues. The principal statute is the State and Local Government Revenue Bond Act, found at G.S. Chapter 159, Article 5 (G.S. 159-80 through -97), which authorizes the issuance of revenue bonds. G.S. 159-161 permits any government authorized to issue revenue bonds under the aforementioned statute also to issue revenue bond anticipation notes. A second important statute is G.S. 159I-30, which permits counties to issue *special obligation bonds* for solid waste projects. This statute permits the issuance of bonds and bond anticipation notes secured by any revenue source that "does not constitute a pledge of the unit's taxing power," and that language includes revenues generated by the financed asset or system. G.S. 159I-30(b) permits a borrowing government, when the revenue source securing a special obligation bond or note is within its control, "to enter into covenants to take action in order to generate the revenues." Finally, G.S. 159G-18 permits counties to borrow moneys from the Clean Water Revolving Loan Fund for the capital needs of water or sewer systems and to give debt instruments, payable to the state, in evidence of the loan. Among the kinds of security that the borrowing

Table 11-1
Authorized Purposes of Revenue Bonds

Water facilities	Electric facilities
Gas facilities	Public transportation
Solid waste facilities	Airports
Parking	Hospitals
Marine facilities	Stadiums
Auditoriums	Recreation facilities
Convention centers	Storm water drainage
Economic development	Facilities for the federal government
Sewer facilities	

government may give for the loan is a "pledge [of] user fee revenues derived from operation of the benefited facilities or systems." Table 11-1 sets out the purposes for which revenue bonds may be issued.

The Special Obligation

The defining characteristic of the special obligation lies in what it is not: a general obligation. A special obligation is secured by a pledge of any sort of revenue source or asset available to the county, as long as that pledge does not amount to a pledge of the county's taxing power. Neither the General Assembly nor the courts have definitively established what sorts of pledges, other than a pledge of property taxes, constitute a general obligation, but there is a working understanding in the state's finance community. This understanding focuses on the general obligation as a pledge of the government's taxing power and holds that as long as a county does not pledge *any local tax under its control*, it has not created a general obligation.

Thus in this broad sense a revenue bond is a special obligation because it pledges project revenues and does not pledge taxes of any sort. It is only one kind of special obligation, however; indeed, the term *special obligation*, as used in North Carolina, generally refers to debts secured by something other than project revenues. That something else has usually been the proceeds from one or more nontax revenues or from one or more kinds of taxes that are levied by some government other than the government making the pledge. Thus, for example, a county might pledge proceeds from fees charged for building permits or from state payments made to reimburse counties for the repeal property taxes; or it might pledge taxes levied by the state and shared with local governments. The principal sources of revenue available to counties for a special obligation pledge are state beer and wine tax revenues, property tax reimbursements, solid waste revenues, other enterprise revenues, regulatory fees and charges, and local ABC revenues.

What are the lender's rights under a special obligation pledge if the borrowing government does not meet its debt service obligations? Because the borrower does not control the levy of any tax that is part of a special obligation pledge, the lender cannot force an increase in the amount or the rate of the tax. Rather, the sole recourse of the lender is to exercise its lien and in essence to attach the pledged moneys on their coming into the possession of the borrower. Thus if the pledge was of a county's share of the state's intangibles tax reimbursements, the lender would take possession of those moneys and direct their first, and if necessary exclusive, use to pay debt service. If the moneys were inadequate, the lender would have no other recourse.

Because the debt market perceives the security for special obligation debt as weaker than the security for general obligation debt, the market normally demands of special obligation debt some of the same safeguards demanded of revenue bonds. Therefore if the loan is offered publicly—that is, if it is sold to investors—the borrowing government will almost always be required to establish a debt service reserve fund. As with the fund for revenue bonds, this fund will be initially supplied with money from the loan proceeds. Proceeds of special obligation debt may also have to be used to pay interest during project construction. Whether this is necessary depends on the particular revenues pledged to repayment.

Currently only two statutes specifically authorize a county to borrow money and create a special obligation pledge as security. Both are found in G.S. Chapter 159I. G.S. 159I-13 permits a county that borrows money from the state's Solid Waste Management Loan Fund to secure the loan, among other ways, from "any available source or sources of revenue" as long as the pledge "does not constitute a pledge of the [borrowing] unit's taxing power." G.S. 159I-30 uses similar language to permit a county to issue bonds, for solid waste projects only, with the same sort of security.

The Pledge of the Financed Asset

The final form of security available to North Carolina counties is a pledge of the asset being financed with the proceeds of the loan. Thus a county might secure a loan to construct a new jail or build an office building by pledging the jail or the office building. Unlike the sources of security discussed earlier, this source is not a stream of revenues. It is not the proceeds from the property tax, the county's share of a state-levied tax, or the revenues from a financed asset. Although the lender will receive the asset if the borrower defaults, that occurs only if there is in fact a default. Both the lender and the borrower will have to look elsewhere for the actual payment of the loan. As a practical matter, both will look to the general revenues of the local government. Therefore the market treats loans secured by the financed asset as if they were general obligations, although weaker than the real general obligations of the borrowing government.

No lender wants to rely on the asset as the real security for such a loan. The market does not judge the attractiveness of asset-secured loans on the basis of the suitability of the pledged asset for private use. Rather, the market rates such loans on its perception of the willingness or the unwillingness of the borrower to lose the asset. If the asset is perceived as essential to the continued operation of the county, the loan will be a stronger credit than if the asset is perceived as one the county could lose without much harm to basic operations.

The debt market perceives the security for asset-secured debt as weaker than the security for general obligation debt, so it normally demands of such debt some of the same safeguards demanded of revenue bonds. Therefore if the loan is offered publicly—that is, if it is sold to investors—the borrowing government is almost always required to establish a debt service reserve fund. As with the fund for revenue bonds, this fund will be initially supplied with money from the loan proceeds. Proceeds of asset-secured debt may also have to be used to pay interest during project construction. Whether this is necessary depends on the market's response to that particular financing.

Only two current statutes authorize loans secured by a pledge of the financed asset. The more important is G.S. 160A-20, which expressly permits counties to borrow money for purchases and for construction and to give as the sole security a lien in the financed asset. The second is G.S. 159I-30, which permits a government that issues special obligation bonds for a solid waste project, additionally or in lieu of a revenue pledge, to secure the bonds with a pledge of the financed asset. In either case, if the borrowing government defaults on the loan, the lender's sole recourse is to repossess or foreclose on the asset; it may not bring an action to sue the borrowing government for any difference between the amount due and the value of the asset.

School Projects

One of the most common uses of debt secured by the financed asset is to finance school construction projects, but not all counties may borrow money secured in this way for school projects. School facilities are normally owned by the local board of education, not the county, and when that is the case a county has no asset to give a security interest in. Therefore, counties began seeking and receiving local-act authority from the General Assembly to own school facilities; when that authority is exercised, the county does have an asset to pledge to lenders. By the end of 1997, fifty-eight of North Carolina's counties had received such authority from the General Assembly (G.S. 153A-158.1).

Use of a Nonappropriation Clause

Normally if a county borrows money and then during the life of the loan fails to make a scheduled payment of debt service, the county is considered in default on the loan. With asset-secured loans, however, the loan documents will usually give the county the annual choice of appropriating money to meet debt service requirements that year or not appropriating money. If the county chooses not to appropriate money, it will obviously be unable to make its debt service payments that year. Because the loan contract permitted it to make the choice, however, failure to pay debt service in these circumstances is not a default on the loan, but the exercise of a contractual right. The contract provision that gives this right to the borrowing government is known as a *nonappropriation clause.*

Nationally, nonappropriation clauses have become a standard part of asset-secured financing. The market does not exact much of a price for including them in such financing because it does not expect any local government borrower to make use of the clause. If local governments began to exercise this right with any frequency at all, it would quickly become an expensive addition to any financing.

The Structures of the Borrowing Transaction

If a private person wants to borrow money to buy a car or a house, he or she simply goes to the bank and does so, signing a note as evidence of his or her debt. If a county wants to borrow money, however, it can never proceed as simply as that. This section describes the common forms that loan transactions take.

A generation ago, if a North Carolina county borrowed money, it did so through the issuance of bonds. No other structures for borrowing money were available or used. That is no longer true. Although bonds remain the predominant loan form, North Carolina local governments currently borrow money through a variety of transactional structures.

General Obligation Bonds

The traditional mechanism by which counties borrow money is the issuance of *bonds*. A bond itself is simply an evidence of a debt, a fancy IOU, in the same way that the note a person gives his or her bank is the evidence of the bank's mortgage loan to him or her. Historically the bond differed from other evidences of debt in that it bore the seal of the borrower. In current local government finance the essential difference between a bond and a *note* is the length of time for which the underlying debt is outstanding. A note evidences a debt that will fall due in a short time—a few months to a year or, rarely, somewhat longer. A bond evidences a longer debt—from a few years to thirty-five or forty years.

The general obligation bond is the simplest form of borrowing generally available to local governments. The promise of the borrowing government is straightforward—it will levy whatever amount of tax is necessary to pay principal and interest—and can be enforced by the legal action of any bondholder. Furthermore, the promise is relatively unaccompanied by the additional promises characteristic of other forms of security. Therefore the documents generated by a general obligation bond issue are considerably fewer and shorter in length than those generated by other forms of borrowing.

The central document of the proceeding to secure local authorization of a general obligation bond issue is the *bond order*, which is adopted by the board of county commissioners. The order serves a double purpose. First, it authorizes issuance of the bonds, stating the purpose for which the proceeds will be spent and the maximum amount of bonds that may be issued. If a county is proposing bonds for more than one purpose, it will need a separate bond order for each purpose. Second, the order publicizes the bond issue, not only setting out purpose and amount but also indicating the security for the bonds. As the North Carolina Supreme Court has said, the bond order is "the crucial foundation document which supports and explains" the issue.[23]

The statutory procedure that leads to adoption of a bond order is intended to serve two primary purposes: (1) it concludes with the commissioners' formal authorization of the bond issue; and (2) it provides an opportunity for the public to learn of and comment on the proposed issue and the project or projects it will finance. In fact, however, the procedure is usually a *pro forma* exercise. It does not begin until the county has met informally with the Local Government Commission's staff and received informal approval of the proposed borrowing. The necessary documents are prepared by bond counsel, who also suggest a schedule for the statutory procedure. That schedule is normally established by setting a tentative date for the bond referendum, if one will be necessary, and then counting back from that date. Generally, then, by the time it begins the formal procedure, the board of commissioners has already decided to adopt the bond order. Occasionally testimony at the public hearing will cause a board to modify, delay, or drop its plans, but the real opportunity for citizens to comment on the bond issue is the referendum.

Revenue and Special Obligation Bonds

North Carolina law permits bonds to be issued with each of the other forms of security besides the general obligation: (1) revenue bonds, which pledge revenues from the bond-financed project; and (2) special obligation bonds, which pledge any revenues available to the issuing government that will not create a general obligation pledge or pledge the financed asset (or both). Because of the nature of their security, neither revenue bonds nor special obligation bonds require voter approval. For that reason the careful statutory procedure that must be followed to issue general obligation bonds (and which is intended to provide public notice of the issue) has no counterpart with these other kinds of bonds. The statutes contain no required procedures at all for commissioner authorization of these bonds, and as a result, the authorization process is legally simple. The documents that underlie such a bond issue, however, are anything but simple, and again the reason is the nature of the security behind the bonds. Furthermore, also because of the nature of the security, revenue and special obligation bond issues require the participation of new entities not necessary to a general obligation issue.

The most important new entity is the *bond trustee*, normally a bank, which represents the interests of the bondholders. When the bonds are issued, the proceeds are paid to the trustee, which controls disbursement of the moneys. Furthermore, the county is normally required regularly to pay debt service through the trustee rather than directly to bondholders. Finally, the borrowing county is often required to secure the trustee's approval of various operational matters, such as changes in consulting engineers or amount of insurance coverage.

As noted earlier in the discussion of security, borrowings secured by revenues, special obligation moneys, or the financed asset typically require that the borrowing government agree to a variety of special covenants that protect the lenders. The major part of the issuance process for revenue or special obligation bonds is negotiating these covenants with the *underwriters*, who will sell the bonds, and sometimes with the rating agencies. Once the documents are prepared, the county commissioners simply approve them, and the loan is thereby authorized.

Bond Anticipation Notes

Sometimes a county will authorize a bond issue, but will not wish to borrow the full sum at one time. Alternatively, if the county plans to sell the bonds to the Rural Development Administration, the bond sale will not take place until the project is fully constructed. In either case the county might decide to borrow, pursuant to the bond authorization, on a short-term basis. If it does so, it will issue *bond anticipation notes*. These are short-term notes, usually maturing in a year's time, that are primarily secured by the proceeds of the eventual bond issue itself. Because such notes are issued in anticipation of the eventual issuance of bonds, there is no separate authorization process for the notes. The county must, however, receive the approval of the Local Government Commission before the notes are issued, and the commission will sell the notes on the county's behalf.

Installment Financing Agreements

If the loan is to be secured by the financed asset and issued under G.S. 160A-20, it will be structured not as a bond issue but as an *installment financing agreement* (sometimes called a *lease purchase agreement* or, somewhat less often, a *capital lease*). Even though the government has in fact borrowed money and agreed to pay it back, the documents will describe a transaction in which the government has purchased an asset, agreeing to pay for it over time. The installment payments, however, will be divided into principal and interest components, and they are the equivalent of debt service payments on bond issues. The original reasons for this transactional disguise are no longer necessary, but the form continues from habit.

The statutory procedures incident to entering into an installment financing agreement are only slightly more elaborate than the total lack of procedure associated with revenue and special obligation bonds. G.S. 160A-20 requires that if the installment financing agreement involves real property (either acquisition or construction of it), the county must hold a public hearing on the financing. Otherwise there are no local steps required of the county, and once the documents are prepared, the board of commissioners may simply approve them and authorize the transaction.

The documentation for an installment financing agreement varies depending on whether the county borrows from one lender or a few, or from the broad investing public. If the former, which is likely if the loan is to acquire equipment of some sort, the basic document will be the installment financing agreement itself, often executed on forms developed by the vendor of the equipment or the financing bank.[24] If the loan is larger, however, which is likely if it is to finance a construction project, the transaction becomes considerably more complex.

Certificates of Participation

Once an installment financing agreement reaches a certain size—currently around $8 or $9 million—it almost certainly has to be publicly sold. That is, rather than the government borrowing the money from a single bank or vendor, the government has to turn to the bond market itself and the millions of individuals, companies, and mutual funds that invest in the market. To reach the market, however, the loan must be divided into much smaller units, affordable by the various participants in the bond market. With a standard bond issue those smaller units are the bonds themselves, normally issued in denominations of $5,000. As noted earlier, however, a bond is direct evidence of a debt of the unit; because of the transactional form of the installment financing agreement, bonds cannot be issued. Therefore some other investment instrument is necessary, and that instrument is the *certificate of participation.*

The *certificate of participation* (COP) entitles its holder to a share in the periodic payments made by the government under the installment financing agreement; the investor participates in receiving those payments, and the certificate is the evidence of his or her right to do so. Although the legal nature of the COP differs from that of the bond, it has been fully accepted by investors, and the bond market treats COPs as more or less interchangeable with true bonds.

If a local government borrows through COPs, the documentation for the transaction is probably the most complicated of any of the forms of borrowing. Typically a nonprofit corporation is established to enter into the financing agreement with the borrowing government. This agreement is considerably more complicated than an installment financing agreement made directly with a vendor or a single lender. In addition, there is a thick trust indenture, under which the corporation (not the government) issues COPs and assigns its rights to payments, under the installment financing agreement, to a trustee; the trustee is then in charge of making payments to the certificate holders.

Debt Instruments and Loan Agreements

Two final forms of borrowing are the *debt instrument* and the *loan agreement.* These are the labels the statutes give to the documents that evidence the debts when a county borrows money from a state agency. Debt instruments are used when counties borrow under the Clean Water program, loan agreements when counties borrow from the Solid Waste Management Loan Fund. Neither program is used very much.

Voter Approval of Borrowing

Article V, Section 4, of the state constitution requires voter approval before a local government may borrow money and secure the loan by a pledge of its faith and credit—that is, before it may borrow money secured by a pledge of its taxing power. The constitution does not require voter approval if any other form of security is used, and therefore voter approval is never necessary for loans secured by revenues, by special obligations, or by the financed asset. In fact, voter approval is not even always necessary for general obligation loans. The following section describes the rules for determining when the voters must, or need not, approve general obligation debt.

Rules for Determining Need for Voter Approval

Refunding Bonds

Refunding bonds are issued to refinance existing debt, usually because interest rates have fallen and the county wishes to reduce its debt service payments. No new debt is being created; rather, one evidence of a single debt is being replaced by another. Therefore the constitution excuses refunding bonds from the requirement of voter approval.

New General Obligation Debt for Certain Purposes

By statute the General Assembly has required that new general obligation debt incurred for a few purposes always be approved by the voters. (That is, debt for these purposes may not be incurred under the two-thirds rule, discussed next.) The purposes in this category are auditoriums, coliseums, stadiums, convention centers, and like facilities; art galleries, museums, and historic properties; urban redevelopment; and public transportation.

Two-Thirds Rule

All other general obligation debt is subject to the *two-thirds rule,* under which counties may incur relatively small amounts of such debt without voter approval. This rule allows a county to issue bonds in an amount up to two-thirds of the amount by which the county's outstanding general obligation indebtedness was reduced in the preceding fiscal year. For example, if a county reduces its net general obligation indebtedness by $900,000 in Year 1, then it may incur general obligation debt up to $600,000—two-thirds of $900,000—in Year 2 without voter approval. The simple thrust of the limitation is to prevent an increase in a government's total indebtedness unless the voters have approved the increase.

Several points should be made about the two-thirds rule. First, in determining the amount of debt reduction during a fiscal year, a county counts only principal payments; interest paid is irrelevant. In addition, it is not the amount of principal retired that is counted; rather, it is the net reduction in principal owed. If a county borrows during a fiscal year, it may actually have a net increase in outstanding debt and therefore no two-thirds capacity at all. Second, the county must use its two-thirds capacity in the fiscal year immediately following the year in which the debt was reduced. If it is not used in that immediately following year, the chance to use it is lost; two-thirds capacity cannot be accumulated from year to year. Finally, in using its two-thirds capacity, the county is not restricted in any way by the purposes for which the retired debt was issued. That is, if all a county's outstanding bonds were issued for public school purposes, so that all reductions are in school debt, a county may still issue two-thirds bonds for any authorized purpose (except those listed earlier as always requiring voter approval). To continue the example, the two-thirds bonds could be issued for water lines, park acquisition, a new fire station, and so on.

Public Funds in a Referendum Campaign

A frequent question is, To what extent may a county use county moneys in the campaign for voter approval of a proposed general obligation bond issue? No North Carolina statute or decided case deals with this question, but the law nationally is well settled and is commonly observed in this state. The basic rule is quite simple: public funds may be used to provide information about a bond issue and the proposed project for which the bonds will be issued; public funds may not be used to urge voters to vote yes in the referendum. Obviously differences of opinion may arise about whether a particular expenditure is informational or promotional; counties should be careful to err on the side of caution. There have been a number of cases in other states in which the officials responsible for improper expenditures have been required to repay the money personally. (There do not, however, appear to be any cases in which improper expenditures threatened the validity of a successful vote.)[25]

State Approval of Borrowing

North Carolina is quite unusual among the states in requiring state approval before most local government borrowing transactions. The approval is the responsibility of the Local Government Commission, an agency in the Department of State Treasurer. The commission was created during the Great Depression, when North Carolina had more local governments in default on debt than any other state in the United States. The commission's initial task was to help those defaulting governments out of their fiscal troubles; its task since then has been to ensure, as much as possible, that such a situation does not arise again. Thus the commission's responsibility is to review the borrowing plans of local governments, to judge whether the governments are borrowing only an amount that they will be able to afford to repay, and to approve the borrowing only after it is assured that repayment is indeed within the local government's means.[26]

For most forms of borrowing transactions, commission approval is always necessary; the only forms of borrowing for which it may not be necessary are some instances of loans secured only by the asset being financed. Two complementary rules determine when the Local Government Commission must approve loans, whether installment financing agreements or special obligation bonds, secured by an asset. First, if the proceeds of the loan will be used to finance improvements to real property, commission approval is always necessary. That is, any *construction* project so financed requires state approval. Loans that finance *acquisition* of property, whether real or personal, are subject to the second rule. Under this rule, such financings must have state approval if they meet both of two conditions:

1. The agreement must extend for at least five years, or sixty months.
2. The total amount paid by the county under the agreement (which includes both principal and interest) must be larger than a threshold amount: the lesser of $500,000 or 0.1 percent of the total appraised value of property subject to taxation in the county.

Again, both conditions must be met. If an agreement is for only fifty-nine months, it does not require state approval, regardless of the amount of money to be paid by the county. If the amount to be paid is less than the threshold, state approval is unnecessary, regardless of the length of the loan.

There is one final exception: the statute provides that state approval is never necessary for agreements or bonds that finance the acquisition of either motor vehicles or voting machines.

Other Methods of Capital Financing

The introduction notes other forms of capital financing. Any county will finance some capital assets from current revenues. In a small county, such assets may be no more expensive than motor vehicles, whereas in a large county, more expensive personal property may be paid for from current revenues. These kinds of expenditures are treated no differently than any other expenditures included in the annual budget ordinance.

A county might also receive capital financing from a grant or a gift, although this is much less likely now than during the 1970s or earlier. When that occurs, the grantor or the donor normally will specify what uses may be made of the money, and the county will be bound to those specifications. Once received, such moneys are fully public moneys and must be appropriated and accounted for in the same manner as any other public funds.

Finally, G.S. 159-18 permits counties to establish capital reserve funds for any capital purpose. A board of county commissioners does this by adopting an ordinance or a resolution that includes at least four points: the purpose or purposes for which moneys will be reserved; the length of time for which moneys will be accumulated; the approximate amounts to be accumulated for each purpose; and the source of the reserved moneys. The board may amend this ordinance or resolution at any time, including changing the purpose for which moneys have been reserved. Moneys may be removed from the fund only for a designated purpose; because only capital purposes can be designated, moneys may not be removed and used for operating expenses. Otherwise, a county has complete flexibility in the use of capital reserve funds.

Authorization of Capital Projects and Expenditures and Appropriation of Funds for Them

Authorization versus Appropriation

Authorization in this context refers to approving a capital project or acquisition; *appropriation,* to making revenues or financing available for expenditure on it. Authorization often occurs by an appropriation, as when annual revenues or fund balances are appropriated to finance an equipment acquisition or a construction project. In such a case the appropriation serves as authorization and provides the funding as well.

In contrast, when bonds are issued to finance a capital project, authorization of the project and appropriation of moneys for it usually take place in separate steps and at different times. For a project financed by general obligation bonds, authorization might be thought to occur when the voters approve the bonds. However, the board of county commissioners may still choose not to issue the bonds; final authorization occurs only with the decision to issue the bonds, which is typically associated with the letting of major contracts for the project. Once bonds are issued and contracts are let for a project, there is no turning back. Although issuance of bonds constitutes final project approval, it does not of itself appropriate or make the bond proceeds available for expenditure. This must occur in the annual budget ordinance or in a capital project ordinance.

Authorization of capital projects and acquisitions and appropriation of moneys for them also often occur separately when a county has a CIP. In such a case the board of county commissioners may pass a resolution approving capital projects and expenditures listed in the first year of the CIP as the capital budget for the year. This resolution may be part of a broader resolution approving the entire CIP. Although such a resolution may authorize the projects and the outlays, by itself it does not appropriate moneys for them; this may be done, again, only in the annual budget ordinance or in a capital project ordinance. Of course, if board approval of the projects and the expenditures in the first year of the CIP occurs by incorporation of the projects and the expenditures in the annual budget ordinance, by amendment(s) to the annual budget ordinance, or by enactment of one or more capital project ordinances, then project authorization and appropriation effectively take place in one step and at one time.

Counties occasionally undertake major capital construction projects that take several years to complete. If a multiyear project is financed with revenues that are appropriated in the annual budget ordinance each year during the construction period, project authorization and appropriation of at least part of the funds for the project occur separately. The board of commissioners authorizes the full project the first year, but it appropriates from the annual budget ordinance only enough money to meet project expenditures for that year. Then as construction proceeds, the board appropriates enough funds from each year's annual budget to cover project expenditures for that year. This practice is sometimes called *cash-flow budgeting* because appropriations for a project in any year are based on expenditures to be made for the project in that year. Cash-flow budgeting is a less-than-conservative approach to capital budgeting because contracts are let for the full or nearly the full project amount in the year of the project's inception, but appropriations enacted for the project that year cover only expenditures to be made in the year. Nevertheless, such budgeting is legal under the continuing contracts and preaudit statutes [G.S. 153A-17 and G.S. 159-28(a)].

In this last example, if annual revenues are appropriated in a capital project ordinance rather than as part of the annual budget ordinance, authorization and appropriation of the full amount of revenues needed for the project occur at the same time, that is, when the capital project ordinance is passed. Of course, even then, funds can be raised and appropriated initially in the annual budget ordinance and then transferred by board of commissioners action to the capital project ordinance on a year-to-year basis. Such transfers to the capital project ordinance fund the appropriations already there, not increase them.

Use of Capital Project Ordinances

Counties may use their annual budget ordinance or one or more capital project ordinances to appropriate moneys for capital projects or expenditures. If a county appropriates all revenues or financing for capital projects and expenditures in the annual budget ordinance or by amendment to it, this helps to ensure that capital expenditure decisions are coordinated with operating budget decisions. Moreover, because appropriation authority in the annual budget ordinance lasts for only a year, this practice helps to insure periodic review of capital projects under construction.

The disadvantages of appropriating money for capital projects and expenditures in the annual budget ordinance apply mainly to large multiyear projects. One drawback is the incongruity of appropriating funds for a project for only a year at a time, when in fact spending for it will take several years. A more difficult problem is that including major capital projects in the annual budget ordinance can cause the annual budget to fluctuate greatly in amount from year to year so that confusion arises about what amount is budgeted for ongoing operating programs annually.

These disadvantages are addressed by using a capital project ordinance. Such an ordinance continues in force until the project is complete—a capital asset is acquired or built. Also, by separating appropriations for capital projects from appropriations for operating expenditures, the distinction is clearer between current expenditures, with their immediate benefits, and capital projects and expenditures, with their long-term benefits.

In general, funds for small recurring capital expenditures should be appropriated in the annual budget ordinance, usually in the general fund or another operating fund, whereas those for major capital projects should usually be appropriated in project ordinances and accounted for in a capital project fund. The dividing line between these types of capital expenditures, however, is not always clear.

G.S. 159-13.2(c) specifies the content of a capital project ordinance. It must "identify and authorize the capital project to be undertaken, identify the revenues that will finance the project, and make the appropriations necessary for the project." The project ordinance should identify each revenue source and specify the amount from each one to be spent for the project. If a project will extend over more than one year and the county includes annual revenues from several years in estimating project revenues, the project ordinance should specify the amount of such revenues that will come from each year's receipts. The Local Government Budget and Fiscal Control Act (G.S. Ch. 159, Art. 3) says nothing about the level of detail for appropriations in a project ordinance. G.S. 159-13(a), however, permits appropriations in the annual budget ordinance to be by project. This would seem to permit a comparable appropriation in a project ordinance—that is, a single one for each project. A county could, of course, appropriate in greater detail. Indeed, most project ordinances for large construction projects make appropriations by general line-item categories—planning and design, land acquisition and preparation, construction, and contingency.

A separate capital project ordinance may be used for each individual project, or one comprehensive capital project ordinance may be enacted for all new projects authorized by the board of county commissioners in a particular year. Such a comprehensive capital project ordinance might be passed annually when the board approves new projects in the capital budget for the year. This budget may be taken from the CIP and consist of projects and expenditures in the Budget Year of the five- or six-year forecast made by that program (see Figure 11-1 under the heading "Capital Improvement Programming," earlier in the chapter).

Implementation: Construction or Acquisition of Capital Assets

The last step in capital budgeting is implementation. Key facets in this phase are managing the funds that are available for a capital project or expenditure; making equipment purchases; designing, contracting for, and constructing buildings or improvements; and accounting for capital construction or acquisition outlays.

The building or the acquisition of capital assets must be timed so that enough cash from the financing sources is on hand to make payments to vendors and contractors as the payments fall due. This can mean delaying major equipment acquisitions and the start-up of construction projects that are financed with annual revenues until the second half of the fiscal year, after most property tax revenue has been collected. If a large construction project is to be built and the financing will come entirely or largely from annual revenues, fund balances or capital reserves may have to be accumulated over several years before construction begins to provide enough money for the project.

If federal, state, or other outside grant money will finance part of a project but be provided on a reimbursement basis, a county must have its own money to start the project and finance construction until reimbursements start arriving. Such up-front money for grant-financed projects usually comes from county fund balances or capital reserves. Although counties have rarely used grant anticipation notes, they may issue them (G.S. 159-171) to pay for capital projects for which federal or state grant commitments have been obtained. The amount of the notes may not exceed 90 percent of the portion of the grant commitments yet to be received in cash by the county, and the notes must mature within twelve months of completion of the project financed with the notes. The Local Government Commission must approve and sell the notes.

Federal Arbitrage Regulations

If tax-exempt bond or debt proceeds are used to finance a capital project, federal arbitrage regulations must be followed to preserve the tax-exempt status of the interest paid on the bonds or the debt. Generally, *arbitrage* refers to profit made by selling securities and investing the resulting proceeds in other, higher-yielding securities. In the case of tax-exempt debt, arbitrage occurs when a governmental or other tax-exempt entity borrows money by selling its tax-exempt debt at a relatively low interest rate, and invests the proceeds in taxable securities that carry higher yields or interest rates.

Federal arbitrage restrictions, which became effective in 1969, and arbitrage rebate requirements, which are based on regulations developed pursuant to the Tax Reform Act of 1986, generally prohibit arbitrage profits on tax-exempt debt—profits made by investing the proceeds of tax-exempt debt in higher-yielding taxable securities.[27] However, under certain conditions, the earning of such arbitrage profits does not violate federal law. Even though arbitrage profits may be earned on the proceeds of certain tax-exempt debt, federal arbitrage rebate requirements provide that such profits be rebated to the United States Treasury unless the issuer of the debt qualifies for one of the following exemptions:

- *Tax-exempt exemption.* The issuer invests proceeds from the tax exempt debt in tax-exempt obligations.
- *Small issuer exemption.* The issuer has general taxing power and issues no more than $5 million of tax-exempt debt in a calendar year and spends the proceeds on government projects or activities. Federal tax changes enacted in 1997 increase this small issuer exemption by $5 million for bonds sold after December 31, 1997, to finance school capital expenditures.
- *Six-month exemption.* The issuer spends the gross proceeds from a tax exempt issue, except retainage that does not exceed the lesser of $100,000 or 5 percent of the issue, within six months after issuance. Any portion of the $100,000 or 5 percent that is not spent within six months must be spent within twelve months after issuance. Gross proceeds do not include money from the issue put into reasonably required reserves. Such reserves may not exceed the lesser of 10 percent of the gross proceeds, maximum annual debt service on the issue, or 125 percent of average annual debt service. Rebate calculations would have to be done for such reserves, possibly leading to the rebate of arbitrage profits earned by investing the reserves.
- *Eighteen-month exemption.* The issuer spends 15 percent of the gross proceeds of a tax-exempt issue within six months, 60 percent within twelve months, and all gross proceeds, less retainage not to exceed 5 percent of the issue, within eighteen months of issuance. As with the six-month exemption, gross proceeds do not include proceeds from the issue that go into reasonably required reserves, limited in the same way as for the six-month exemption. Rebate calculations would be necessary on such reserves, possibly leading to the rebate of arbitrage profits earned by investing the reserves. Any retainage must be spent within twenty-four months of issuance. This exemption is available only on debt issued after June 30, 1993.
- *Construction or two-year exemption.* This exception allows for the *bifurcation* of a debt issue into two components: a nonconstruction portion to be used for land or other acquisitions, which must be spent within six months to avoid rebate; and a

construction component which must be at least 75 percent of the total debt issue. The issuer must spend at least 10 percent of the available construction proceeds within six months of issuance, 45 percent within twelve months, 75 percent within eighteen months, and 100 percent, less retainage not to exceed 5 percent of the construction proceeds, within two years of issuance. Any retainage of construction proceeds must be spent within thirty-six months of issuance. If the issuer fails to spend the required proportion of available construction proceeds by any six-month interval, it will have either to rebate to the United States Treasury all arbitrage profits earned on the full debt proceeds or to pay to the Treasury a penalty equal to 1.5 percent of any portions of the proceeds that should have been spent but were not spent by each six-month interval. The issuer must choose between these options—rebating or paying the 1.5 percent penalty—at the time that it issues or sells the debt.

Besides the exemptions listed here, there are additional, less important exemptions to arbitrage rebate requirements. Clearly, federal arbitrage regulations are very complex. Moreover, they have been modified frequently over the years. Therefore counties should seek advice from bond counsel, the Local Government Commission, and other competent sources in trying to meet arbitrage restrictions and rebate requirements and in devising an investment plan for tax-exempt bond or debt proceeds. If a county does not comply with the United States Treasury's arbitrage regulations, it might have to pay penalties and interest to the federal government, and if the county fails to rebate arbitrage profits pursuant to regulations, the unit's bonds or debt could lose its tax-exempt status retroactively to the date of issuance.

Because of federal arbitrage regulations and its own longtime practice, the Local Government Commission urges that bonds or almost any form of debt not be sold or issued at least until a county has advertised for and opened the construction bids on the bond- or debt-financed project. The commission needs about ninety days to sell bonds or other debt and deliver the proceeds to a county. A county should contact the commission for the sale at least thirty days before it expects to receive bids on the project. The sale of the bonds will occur about sixty days after this initial contact, and the county will have the bond proceeds about thirty days after that, or not more than sixty days after the bid opening.

Other Considerations

Investment Plan

Adequate management of the financing or revenue proceeds for a major capital construction project typically requires an *investment plan*. The plan should

1. cover the period from the date when cash proceeds for the project begin to be received, to the date when the final disbursement is made;
2. show project receipts, disbursements, and cash balances available by month or quarter;
3. lay down a general strategy to guide the investment of balances that are not immediately needed for project payments at any point; and
4. estimate the approximate interest earnings on the investments, calculate arbitrage rebate requirements, if any, and provide for the use of the net earnings.

Bidding for Equipment Acquisitions and Construction Projects

Equipment purchases and construction and repair projects must comply with the applicable North Carolina bidding laws. For example, the purchase, or the lease with option to purchase, of any equipment that costs $30,000 or more and any construction or repair work costing $100,000 or more must be contracted for through formal bid procedures (G.S. 143-129). Further, informal bid procedures—for example, bids secured by telephone—must be used for equipment and projects costing less than the formal bidding minimums but $5,000 or more (G.S. 143-131). G.S. 143-29 addresses preparation of specifications, solicitation of bids, selection of multiple contractors for different types of work versus a single prime contractor, and use of minority- and women-owned business enterprises on construction projects for buildings. A full discussion of purchasing and contracting laws and procedures appears in Chapter 14.

Use of an Architect or an Engineer

Implementing a capital construction project is a complex undertaking. If the project is of any magnitude, a registered architectural or engineering firm is typically employed to prepare plans and specifications, oversee or inspect construction, and advise the county. An architect or the engineer also generally does a feasibility study as an initial step for any utility or enterprise projects. An architect or engineer must be used when the cost of a project exceeds $45,000 (G.S. 133-1.1). However, if the project is a repair project and involves no major structural change, an architect or an engineer is required to prepare plans and specifications only when the cost of the project is more than $100,000.

Architects and engineers are chosen through negotiation or requests for proposals that focus as much on considerations of design and qualifications as on considerations of cost. Indeed, G.S. Chapter 143, Article 3D, makes it the public policy of the state and its local governments to select architects and engineers based primarily on qualifications. Local governments may exempt themselves from this policy when architectural and engineering fees for a project will be less than $30,000 or when local government officials state the reasons for such an exemption.

Architectural and engineering fees are generally charged as a percentage of project costs, ranging from 7 or 8 percent to as much as 12 percent or so, depending on project size and type. Fixed-fee and other arrangements are also sometimes used. The architect or the engineer is responsible for assessing the feasibility of a project, designing it, drawing up blueprints and specifications, preparing and advising on construction contracts, and overseeing construction. For some projects one architectural or engineering firm does the feasibility study, and another plans, designs, and carries out the project. Occasionally a different firm is hired just to oversee and inspect construction. A county should provide guidelines about what and what not to include in the design for a project. Sometimes the architect or the engineer is asked to design *add-ons* or *drops* so that the county can more readily adjust the scope of a project to fit the amount of money available.

Capital Project Fund

A capital project fund should be used to account for the purchase or the construction of a major capital facility. G.S. 159-26(b)(6) requires all local governmental units to use such a fund when bond or other debt proceeds finance part or all of a project. Capital project funds are ordinarily not used to account for the acquisition of equipment and small construction or renovation projects. Such acquisitions or projects are normally budgeted and accounted for in the general fund or another operating fund. A separate capital project fund need not be established for each major project. Multiple projects can be accounted for in one capital project fund. Indeed, a single capital project fund can be used to account for all major general public improvements. However, one or more separate capital project funds should be used for major enterprise system projects.

Additional Resources

Lawrence, David M. *Financing Capital Projects in North Carolina*. Chapel Hill, N.C.: Institute of Government, The University of North Carolina at Chapel Hill, 1994.

Moody's Investors Service—Public Finance Group. *Guide to Moody's Ratings, Rating Process, and Rating Practices*. New York: Moody's, 1997.

Standard & Poor's Corporation. *Municipal Finance Criteria*. New York: S & P, 1997.

Vogt, A. John. "Budgeting Capital Outlays and Improvements," in Jack Rabin, W. Bartley Hildreth, and Gerald J. Miller, eds., *Budgeting: Formulation and Execution* (Athens, Ga.: Carl Vinson Institute of Government, 1996), 276–91.

Notes

1. Government Finance Officers Association, *Governmental Accounting, Auditing and Financial Reporting* (Chicago: GFOA, 1994), 318, 330.

2. North Carolina Department of State Treasurer, *Policies Manual* (Raleigh, N.C.: NCDST, Oct. 1990), sec. 20, "Fixed Assets Policy," especially pp. 5–8.

3. NCDST, *Policies Manual*, sec. 20, p. 1, refers to fixed assets as "tangible in nature."

4. GFOA, *Governmental Accounting*, recognizes the appropriateness of including certain intangible property among general fixed assets (p. 104), although its glossary defines a fixed asset as a "long-lived, tangible asset" (p. 330).

5. Accounting for public enterprises follows commercial accounting principles, which provide for the inclusion of intangible as well as tangible property among fixed assets.

6. A survey of North Carolina local government budget practices for 1990–91 revealed that eighteen of forty-seven counties included in the survey had CIPs in that year. Selected results of this survey are reported in A. John Vogt and Charles K. Coe, "A Close Look at North Carolina City and County Budget Practices," *Popular Government* 59 (Summer 1993): 16–28. The survey, conducted by the Institute of Government in November 1990, focused on preparation of the 1990–91 budget. One hundred twenty-one cities and counties of different sizes responded to the survey. Seventy-four of these units were cities, and forty-seven were counties. If a

county or city reported having a CIP, follow-up questions were asked about the CIP process. Results from some of these follow-up questions are reported further in the chapter.

7. The 1990–91 survey of local government budget practices revealed that among the eighteen counties with CIPs, the CIP was presented to the board of county commissioners before presentation of the annual budget in five counties, concurrent with presentation of the annual budget in nine cities, and after presentation of the annual budget in just one county. Three counties did not respond to this question. A. John Vogt and Charles K. Coe, unpublished results of 1990–91 survey of North Carolina city and county budget practices (Chapel Hill, N.C.: Institute of Government, The University of North Carolina at Chapel Hill, 1991).

8. The 1990–91 survey of local government budget practices found that the county manager or administrator coordinated the CIP process in five of the eighteen counties with CIPs, the budget director or a budget analyst in six counties, the finance officer in four counties, and an assistant manager in one county. Two counties did not respond to this question. Vogt and Coe, unpublished results, 1991.

9. The 1990–91 survey of local government budget practices found that among the eighteen counties surveyed with CIPs, the boards of commissioners in six of these counties held one or more public hearings on the recommended CIP. Boards of commissioners in the other twelve counties did not hold such public hearings. Vogt and Coe, unpublished results, 1991.

10. The 1990–91 survey of local government budget practices found that boards of commissioners in seven of the eighteen counties with CIPs enacted such resolutions. Vogt and Coe, unpublished results, 1991.

11. Standard & Poor's Corporation, *Municipal Finance Criteria* (New York: S & P, 1997), 4.

12. Information presented about the national debt rating agencies draws on S & P, *Municipal Finance Criteria*; Moody's Investors Service—Public Finance Group, "On Municipal Ratings," January 13, 1997; and conversations with staff of S & P and the Local Government Commission.

13. Information about the North Carolina Municipal Council is based on the council's brochure *North Carolina Municipal Council, Inc.* (Raleigh, N.C.: the Council, undated) and conversations with staff of the council.

14. If certificates of participation are issued to finance a general public improvement, e.g., to construct a new county office building, the money for debt service on the certificates is likely to come from tax or other general revenues, even though the certificates are secured by the county office building rather than taxing power. The Council rates counties and other local governments that issue certificates of participation or privately placed installment-purchase debt for general public improvements because debt service comes from taxes or general revenues, regardless of the security or pledge for the debt.

15. This information was provided by Diane P. Prosen and LaVerne M. Thomas, S & P officials. Also, see Standard & Poor's Corporation, *CreditWeek*, 4 January 1993, 50.

16. The rating agencies have specifically recognized the central contribution of the Local Government Commission. See S & P, *CreditWeek*, 4 January 1993, 50.

17. North Carolina Association of County Commissioners and the North Carolina Department of State Treasurer, *Fiscal Summary of North Carolina Counties* (Raleigh, N.C.: North Carolina Association of County Commissioners and the North Carolina Department of State Treasurer, 1996).

18. S & P, *Municipal Finance Criteria,* 21.

19. This and the debt percentages or ratios that follow it are taken from the Department of State Treasurer, division of State and Local Government Finance, "Analysis of Debt of North Carolina Counties at 6/30/97."

20. Department of State Treasurer, *Analysis of Debt of North Carolina Counties,* June 6, 1997.

21. Property tax collection percentages for individual North Carolina counties and average collection percentages for counties of different sizes are presented in *Fiscal Summary of North Carolina Counties.* See in particular p. A-6.

22. The 1990–91 survey of local government budget practices found that of the forty-seven counties included in the survey, ten had multiyear revenue and expenditure forecasts. Such forecasting was much more common among the larger counties. Vogt and Coe, "A Close Look," 26.

23. Rider v. Lenoir County, 236 N.C. 620, 631, 73 S.E.2d 913, 921 (1953).

24. If such forms are used, the borrowing government should review them carefully because they are likely to be particularly protective of the vendor's or lender's interests.

25. The rules on expenditure of public funds in bond referenda are discussed at length in David M. Lawrence, "Use of Public Funds in a Bond Referendum Campaign," *Popular Government* 53 (Spring 1988): 48–49.

26. Cities are subject to one other statutory mechanism that is intended to ensure they do not borrow more than they can repay: the *net debt limitation.* A city determines its net debt by adding together all general obligation debt and installment purchase debt, then subtracting debt incurred for water, electricity, and gas. The resulting sum of outstanding debt may not exceed 8 percent of the appraised value of property in the city subject to taxation. In fact, however, it is quite rare for a city's net debt to exceed 2 percent of its tax base; therefore, as a practical matter, the net debt limitation is unimportant.

27. I.R.C. § 148 (1986). A good summary of federal arbitrage restrictions and rebate requirements appears in Terence P. Burke, *Guide to Arbitrage Requirements for Governmental Bond Issues* and *1994 Supplement to the Guide to Arbitrage Requirements for Governmental Bond Issues* (Chicago: Government Finance Officers Association, 1992 and 1994). The discussion here of federal arbitrage requirements is based on this book and the supplement and on conversations with Meredith Fraley and Kim Anderson of Bingham–Arbitrage Rebate Services, Inc.

12 Fiscal Control and Cash Management

Gregory S. Allison, K. Lee Carter, Jr., and A. John Vogt

Contents

Gregory S. Allison is an Institute of Government faculty member who specializes in governmental accounting and financial reporting for state and local governmental entities.

K. Lee Carter, Jr., is a former Institute of Government faculty member who specialized in local government accounting and financial management.

A. John Vogt is an Institute of Government faculty member who specializes in budgeting, capital planning, and financial management.

Public confidence in government depends on proper stewardship of public money. The North Carolina Local Government Budget and Fiscal Control Act sets forth requirements for fiscal control that provide a framework for ensuring accountability in a county's budgetary and financial operations. This chapter discusses these requirements. They pertain to the appointment and the role of the county finance officer, the accounting system, control of expenditures, cash management and investments, the annual audit, and audits of federal and state financial assistance.

The Finance Officer

G.S. 159-24 requires that each county have a finance officer who is legally responsible for establishing the accounting system, controlling expenditures, managing cash and other assets, and preparing financial reports. The Local Government Budget and Fiscal Control Act (LGBFCA) does not specify who is to appoint this official, leaving the decision to each county. In many counties, the county manager appoints the finance officer (G.S. 153A-82). In other counties, the board of commissioners makes the appointment. According to G.S. 159-24, the finance officer serves at the pleasure of whoever makes the appointment.

In most counties the official exercising the statutory duties of finance officer carries that title, but in some this official may have another title, such as finance director. In a few, smaller counties, the county manager is also the legally designated finance officer. In some counties, the finance officer also serves as an assistant county manager. The LGBFCA permits the duties of the budget officer and finance officer to be conferred on one person. In contrast, G.S. 105-349(e) specifies that the duties of tax collector and those of the "treasurer or chief accounting officer," by which should be understood finance officer, may not be conferred on the same person, except with the written permission of the secretary of the North Carolina Local Government Commission. Currently no one person serves as both the finance officer and tax collector in any county in the state.

The finance officer's duties are summarized in G.S. 159-25(a): establish and maintain the accounting records, disburse moneys, make financial reports, manage the receipt and deposit of moneys, manage the county's debt service obligations, supervise investments, and perform any other assigned duties.

Official Bonds

The finance officer must give "a true-accounting and faithful-performance bond" of at least $10,000 and no more than $250,000; the amount is to be fixed by the board of commissioners (G.S. 159-29). The usual public official's bond covers faithful performance as well as true accounting. In determining the amount of the bond, the board should seek protection against both a large single loss and cumulative smaller ones. The bond insures the county for losses that it suffers as a result of the actions or negligence of the finance officer; it offers no insurance or protection to the officer. The county must pay the bond's premium.

G.S. 159-29 also requires that each "officer, employee, or agent . . . who handles or has in his custody more than one hundred dollars . . . at any time, or who handles or has access to the [county's] inventories" be bonded for faithful performance. If separate bonds for individuals are purchased, the $100 minimum should be understood to mean that the bonding requirement applies only to those persons who frequently or regularly handle that amount or more. The board of commissioners fixes the amount of each such bond, and the county may (and normally does) pay the premium.

In lieu of requiring a separate bond for each employee, counties may purchase a "blanket" faithful-performance bond, and nearly all counties do (primarily for cost reasons, as blanket bonds are more economical than the total cost of separate bonds).The blanket bond does not substitute for the separate bond required for the finance officer or other county officials (tax collector, sheriff, and register of deeds), who must still be bonded individually and separately.

The Accounting System

A county's accounting system exists to supply information. It provides the manager and other officials with the data needed to ascertain financial performance, as well as to plan and budget for future activities with projected resources. The accounting system is also an essential part of internal-fiscal control.

The board of commissioners depends on accounting information in making its budgetary and program decisions, as well as in determining whether or not they have been carried out. This kind of information is also valuable to outside organizations. The investment community and bond-rating agencies rely on it as they assess a county's financial condition. Also, in counties where bonds have recently been issued, the county is often required to provide various annual financial information to meet continuing disclosure requirements. State regulatory agencies such as the Local Government Commission review data generated by the accounting systems to determine whether counties have complied with the legal requirements regulating accounting and finance. Federal and state grantor agencies use the information to monitor compliance with the requirements of the financial assistance programs that they administer. The media and the public depend on the information to evaluate a county's activities.

County accounting practices are formed in response to the general statutory requirements set forth in G.S. 159-26, generally accepted accounting principles promulgated nationally by the Governmental Accounting Standards Board (GASB) and other organizations. In North Carolina the rules and regulations of the Local Government Commission, as well as the county's own needs and capabilities, directly impact the county's accounting practices.

Statutory Requirements

G.S. 159-26 requires that each county maintain an accounting system, which must do the following:

1. Show in detail its assets, liabilities, equities, revenues, and expenditures.
2. Record budgeted as well as actual expenditures and budgeted or estimated revenues as well as their collection.
3. Establish accounting funds as required by G.S. 159-26(b). A fund is a separate fiscal and accounting entity having its own assets, liabilities, equity or fund balance, revenues, and expenditures. Government activities are grouped into funds to isolate information for legal and management purposes. The types of funds that are set forth in G.S. 159-26(b) for use by counties are discussed in Chapter 10 of this volume.
4. Use the modified accrual basis of accounting. *Basis of accounting* refers to criteria for determining when revenues and expenditures should be recorded in the accounting system.[1] The *modified accrual basis* requires that expenditures be recorded when a liability is incurred (time of receipt) for a good or service provided to the county. The expenditure should be recorded then, usually before the funds are disbursed. This type of accounting also requires that revenues be recorded when the revenues are measurable and available. *Measurable* means that they can be reasonably estimated, and *available* means that they will be received within the current fiscal year or soon enough thereafter to be able to pay liabilities of the current fiscal year. In actual practice for various reasons, some revenues are recorded when they are received in cash. For example, in North Carolina, property tax revenues are generally recorded on the cash basis because taxes receivable are not considered to be collectible soon enough after the year's end to meet the availability criterion. Permits and fees are also recorded on the cash basis because they are not considered to be measurable at the year's end. However, certain revenues collected after the fiscal year end but soon enough thereafter to pay liabilities outstanding as of June 30 would be reflected as revenue for the year ending June 30 because they would be considered measurable and available. For example, the quarterly sales tax

payment received by counties in August is recorded by many counties as a revenue for the year ending June 30 because the payment can be measured at June 30 and it is received soon enough after June 30 to be able to pay liabilities at the fiscal year's end.

The modified accrual basis of accounting helps keep financial practices on a prudent footing: expenditures are recorded as soon as the liabilities for them are incurred, and some revenues are not recorded until they have actually been received in cash. In addition, the modified accrual basis enhances the comparability of financial reporting for counties and reduces the opportunity for manipulation of financial information.

5. Record encumbrances represented by outstanding purchase orders and contractual obligations that are chargeable against budgeted appropriations. An *encumbrance* is created when a contract that will require a county to pay money is entered into or when a purchase order is issued.

Although the LGBFCA does not explicitly mention any exceptions, in practice, expenditures for salaries and wages, fringe benefits, and utilities are usually not encumbered. Salaries, wages, and fringe benefits are not encumbered because they are generally budgeted at the full amounts expected for all positions, and this significantly reduces the risk of overexpenditure. Utilities expenditures are normally not encumbered because the amounts are generally not known in advance.

An encumbrance exists as long as the contractor or supplier has not delivered the goods or the services and the contract or purchase order is outstanding. While this is the case, the county is not yet liable to pay for the goods or the services and has not yet incurred an expenditure for it. G.S. 159-26(d) requires that a county's accounting system record encumbrances as well as expenditures. This recognizes that the encumbrance is a potential liability, and, once the purchase order is filled or the contract fulfilled, liability for payment is created and an expenditure is incurred. Although this requirement applies only to counties with more than 50,000 citizens, nearly all counties record encumbrances in their accounting systems.

Generally Accepted Accounting Principles for Governments

Governmental accounting, as a branch of general accounting practice, shares basic concepts and conventions with commercial accounting. However, because of major differences in the governmental environment, a distinct set of national accounting and financial-reporting principles has evolved in this field. They are promulgated by the Governmental Accounting Standards Board (GASB). Established in 1984 with the support of national organizations representing the public accounting profession and government finance officers, the GASB succeeded the National Council on Governmental Accounting (NCGA), which had formerly established generally accepted accounting principles (GAAP) for government entities. Although the GASB accepted the NCGA pronouncements, it has actively set forth standards in areas of accounting and finance that the NCGA did not formally consider.

The Local Government Commission plays a key role in defining and interpreting accounting standards and procedures for local governments in North Carolina. It issues rules and regulations that interpret state statutes as well as national professional standards, and it provides advice about requirements and improvements in accounting and financial-reporting practices. The commission's staff has focused much attention in recent years on annual financial reports, working closely with local officials and the state's public accounting profession to keep local government accounting systems up to date with the increasingly more rigorous reporting and disclosure standards being promulgated by the GASB.

Counties' Own Needs and Capabilities

Counties' own needs and capabilities also shape their accounting and financial-reporting systems. For example, a growing number of counties have improved their annual financial reports to the point that they have earned the Certificate of Achievement for Excellence in Financial Reporting, awarded by the Government Finance Officers Association of the United States and Canada to recognize outstanding achievement in governmental financial reporting. While all North Carolina counties issue professionally acceptable annual financial reports, those winning the Certificate of Achievement provide full disclosure and relate current financial conditions and performance to past financial trends. Approximately 3,000 local governments in the United States participate in the Certificate of Achievement program, which offers a tremendous resource for local governments to continually improve their financial reporting. Currently, close to fifty percent of North Carolina's counties actively participate in this program. Accordingly, their annual reports reflect a high standard of reporting excellence.

Fixed asset recording presents one of the more significant challenges in government accounting. In recent years, the Local Government Commission and the independent public accountants auditing local governments have placed increased emphasis on fixed-asset records. If they are inadequate, the annual auditor's opinion may be qualified, and this may adversely affect a county's bond rating. Also, a qualified audit opinion may affect a county's ability to obtain approval from the Local Government Commission for debt issuance. In addition, a fixed-asset accounting system can provide significant advantages. It helps fix responsibility for the safekeeping of such assets, thereby improving internal control. It also serves as a basis for establishing maintenance and replacement schedules for equipment and for determining the level of fire and hazard insurance that should be carried on buildings and other capital assets.

Control of Expenditures

Preauditing Obligations

Through the annual budget ordinance and any project ordinances (see Chapters 10 and 11 in this volume), the board of commissioners authorizes the county manager and other officials to undertake programs and projects and to spend moneys. Except for trust or agency funds and internal service funds, which may be excluded from the budget ordinance, G.S. 159-8 directs that no county "may expend any moneys . . . except in accordance with a budget ordinance or project ordinance."

The proper functioning of the budgeting process depends on adherence to the terms of these two types of ordinances. For example, budget and project ordinances are required by law to be balanced. If they are complied with, deficit spending should not occur. Just as important, these ordinances embody the county's policies and priorities, which are carried out if the ordinances are followed.

The preauditing of obligations, required by G.S. 159-28(a), is a principal legal mechanism for assuring compliance with the budget ordinance and each project ordinance. The preaudit rule provides that no obligation may be incurred in an activity accounted for in a fund included in the budget ordinance or for a project authorized by a project ordinance unless two requirements are met. First, the obligation must be authorized; that is, one of the ordinances must contain an appropriation to cover it. Second, the authorization must not be exhausted; sufficient unspent and unencumbered funds must remain in the appropriation to meet the obligation when it comes due. Only if both requirements are met is the obligation validly incurred.

The Meaning of "Appropriation"

The *appropriations* that may not be overspent without violating the law are the figures that *actually appear* in the annual budget ordinance or a project ordinance. For example, the annual budget ordinance may make appropriations by department. If $2,200,000 is appropriated to the recreation department and the ordinance contains no further breakdown of that amount, the $2,200,000 is the maximum that the recreation department may spend, and all its expenditures are charged against that figure. Various line items or *objects of expenditure* within the overall departmental appropriation could be overspent without violating the budget ordinance or the Local Government Budget and Fiscal Control Act as long as total departmental expenditures do not exceed $2,200,000.

In counties where the board of commissioners make appropriations by department in the annual budget ordinance, the budget officer, sometimes at the board's direction, typically imposes a further requirement that each operating department stay within the object of expenditure amounts set out in its budget. Typically, the budget officer's or finance officer's permission is needed to exceed these line-item limits. However, such a requirement is administrative rather than legal in nature because the legally binding appropriations in the budget ordinance are only made by department, not by line item.

Encumbrances

To find out whether a particular contract or purchase will cause an appropriation to be overspent, it is not enough to know the unexpended balance of the appropriation. The preauditor must also ascertain whether contracts or purchase orders are outstanding and chargeable against the appropriation. As already mentioned, an encumbrance is created when a county enters into a contract that will require it to pay money, or when it issues a purchase order. This encumbered portion of an appropriation is as unavailable for a proposed expenditure as if the funds had already been expended; once the contract is completed or the purchase order is filled, the encumbrance is replaced by an expenditure. To make the required preaudit, one must know the *unexpended and unencumbered balance* (which is often referred to simply as the *unencumbered balance*) of the proper appropriation.

The Preaudit Certificate

An obligation is invalid if incurred without meeting the preaudit requirements [G.S. 159-28(a)]. For this reason, those who deal with counties—vendors, contractors, consultants, and others—understandably want to be told whether the purchase order they have received or the contract they have been offered is a valid obligation. This information is provided by the *preaudit certificate.* G.S. 159-28(a) requires that any contract or agreement requiring the payment of money and any purchase order for supplies or materials include on its face "a certificate stating that the [contract, agreement, or purchase order] has been preaudited to assure compliance" with the preaudit requirements, namely that the budget includes an appropriation for the contract or the agreement and that unspent and unencumbered moneys remain in the appropriation to cover payments in the current year for the contract or the agreement. The certificate, which may be printed or stamped, should read substantially as follows: "This instrument has been preaudited in the manner required by the Local Government Budget and Fiscal Control Act." It must be signed by the finance officer or by a deputy finance officer approved for this purpose by the board of commissioners.

Besides providing some assurance to a vendor, the certificate emphasizes to the person who signs it the importance of the preaudit to the entire budget and fiscal control system. Any finance officer or deputy finance officer giving a false certificate is personally liable for any sums illegally committed or disbursed thereby [G.S. 159-28(e)].

Disbursements

Two Stages of Review

G.S. 159-28(b) outlines a two-stage procedure for approving payment of any "bill, invoice, or claim" (these include any item for which an expenditure may be made). First—and this stage applies to transactions involving moneys in any of the county's funds—the finance officer must determine that the amount claimed is owed to the claimant. Second—and this stage applies only to transactions authorized by the annual budget ordinance or a project ordinance—the finance officer must ascertain that the expenditure is authorized and that either an encumbrance exists for it or a sufficient unencumbered balance remains in the appropriation to pay the claim. Only if the finance officer has made both determinations may the disbursement be made.

The Finance Officer's Certificate

Completion of the two-stage review is evidenced by placing the *finance officer's certificate* on the face of the check or draft that makes payment. The certificate, which may be printed or stamped on the check, must follow substantially the following form: "This disbursement has been approved as required by the Local Government Budget and Fiscal Control Act." Normally the certificate is signed by the finance officer or by a deputy finance officer approved for this purpose by the board of commissioners [G.S. 159-28(d)]. Having a deputy finance officer authorized to sign checks is especially important. The sickness or other absence of the finance officer could delay their issuance if that officer were the only one authorized to sign the certificate. In some counties, the board of commissioners designates a deputy finance officer in the county finance department or another county department to regularly sign checks on a limited basis to make certain specific payments, for example, monthly benefit payments to public assistance recipients. Such delegation of the payment function should occur only with the approval of the county finance officer and only if adequate internal controls are built into the payment procedures that are used.

Board of Commissioners Approval of Bills, Invoices, or Claims

The LGBFCA authorizes the board of commissioners to approve by formal resolution a bill, an invoice, or another claim that has been disapproved by the finance officer. The board may do this only for a valid claim for which an encumbrance exists or an unencumbered appropriation remains in the budget ordinance or a project ordinance, and only by following certain specified procedures. Commission members approving invalid payments under this statute may be held personally liable for the payments. These procedures are rarely, if ever, used.

Form of Payment

Payment of obligations by cash are not allowed. G.S. 159-28(d) directs that all bills, invoices, salaries, or other claims be paid by check or draft on an official depository. This statute, by implication, also permits payment by wire transfer from or automated clearing house (ACH) charges to official depositories. Wire transfers are used, for example, to transmit the money periodically required for debt service on bonds or other debt to a paying agent, who in turn makes the payments to individual bondholders. ACH transactions are used by local governments to make retirement system contributions to the state, to make payroll payments, and to make certain other payments. The state has extended the use of the ACH system to most transfers of moneys between the state and local governments that are related to grant programs and state-shared revenues.

G.S. 159-25(b) requires each check or draft to "be signed by the finance officer or a properly designated deputy finance officer and countersigned by another official . . . designated for this purpose by the governing board." The finance officer's signature attests to completion of review and accompanies the certificate described above. The second signature may be by the chair of the board of commissioners or some other official. (If the board does not expressly designate the countersigner, G.S. 159-25(b) directs that it be the chair or the county's chief executive officer, that is, the county manager.)

The purpose of requiring two signatures is internal control. The law intends that the finance officer review the documentation of the claim before signing the certificate and check. The second person can independently review the documentation before signing and issuing the check. That two persons must separately be satisfied with the documentation should significantly reduce the opportunities for fraud.

In many counties, however, the second signer does not exercise this independent review, perhaps relying on other procedures for the desired internal control. Recognizing this, G.S. 159-25(b) permits the board of commissioners to waive the two-signature requirement (thus requiring only the finance officer's or a properly designated deputy finance officer's signature on the check) "if the board determines that the internal control procedures of the unit or authority will be satisfactory in the absence of dual signatures."

As an alternative to manual signatures, G.S. 159-28.1 permits the use of signature machines, signature stamps, or similar devices for signing checks or drafts. In practice, these are widely used in counties all across North Carolina. The board of commissioners must approve the use of such signature devices through a formal resolution or ordinance, which should designate who is to have custody of the devices. For internal control purposes it is essential that this equipment be properly secured. The finance officer or another official given custody of the facsimile signature device(s) by the board of commissioners is personally liable under the statute for illegal, improper, or unauthorized use of the device(s).

Cash Management

Daily Deposits

G.S. 159-32 generally requires that "all taxes and other moneys collected or received by an officer or employee of a local government" be deposited daily, either with the finance officer or in an official depository. (Deposits made under the second alternative must immediately be reported to the finance officer.) If an agency is part of a county for purposes of budget adoption and control, it and its officers and employees are also part of the county for purposes of the daily-deposit requirement.

In many counties, the daily deposit(s) to an official depository are made before the cutoff time (for example, 1:00 p.m.) set by the depository for crediting interest earnings on deposits made that day. A deposit should be made intact; all money collected up to the deposit time should be included. There need be only one deposit per day, although in some counties a second one is made toward the end of the day if substantial moneys are received after the first deposit.

There is a potential exception to the requirement for daily deposit. If the board of commissioners approves, an officer or employee need make deposits only when moneys on hand amount to $250 or more, although one must always be made on the last business day of each month. Note that only the board of commissioners may approve the use of this exception. Managers, finance officers, other officers or advisory boards or commissions may not authorize it.

Official Depository

All moneys belonging to a county (including those transmitted to a fiscal agent for payment of debt service) must be deposited in an official depository [G.S. 159-31(a)]. The board of commissioners designates which banks or financial institutions are to serve as the official depositories. It also decides how many of them there will be. It may so designate any bank, savings institution, or trust company in the state. With the permission of the secretary of the Local Government Commission, the board may also designate a nationally chartered bank located in another state to serve as an official depository. For a number of reasons the secretary to the Local Government Commission will approve the use of out-of-state depositories only in rare circumstances, such as when authorizing a board of county commissioners to designate a nationally or state-chartered out-of-state bank as a depository or fiscal agent for payment of debt service.

G.S. 14-234 generally forbids county commissioners and other officials involved in the contracting process to make contracts for the county in which they have an interest. An exception exists, however, for transacting business with "banks or banking institutions." Therefore, a county may designate as a depository a bank or a savings institution in which a commissioner, for example, is an officer, owner, or stockholder.

Depository accounts may be non-interest bearing accounts with unlimited check-writing privileges; interest-bearing accounts with unlimited check-writing privileges (NOW or superNOW accounts); interest-bearing money-market accounts for which check-writing privileges are restricted; or certificates of deposit which have no check-writing privileges. Generally, the use of interest-bearing accounts is recommended.

Counties follow a variety of methods in selecting or designating official depositories. Some name each bank and savings institution with an office in the county as a depository and place an account in each. Others maintain just one account, rotating it among the local financial institutions that are qualified to serve as official depositories, changing according to a predetermined schedule (commonly every one to three years). Although these methods demonstrate county support of local banks and financial institutions, they can complicate a county's cash-management procedures, hinder its investment program, and cause it to pay more than it would otherwise for banking services. For these reasons, a growing number of counties follow a third method, selecting the bank or financial institution to serve as the depository through a request-for-proposals process. This method is currently recommended by the Local Government Commission staff. It awards the business to that institution offering the most in services for the fees charged or for the lowest compensating balance that the county must maintain at the bank or financial institution.

Insurance and Collateralization of Deposits

G.S. 159-31(b) requires that funds on deposit in an official depository (except funds deposited with a fiscal agent for the purpose of making debt service payments to bondholders) be fully secured. This is accomplished through a combination of methods. First, government funds on deposit with a bank or savings institution or invested in a certificate of deposit (CD) issued by such an institution are insured by the Federal Deposit Insurance Corporation (FDIC). If the funds that a county has on deposit or invested in a CD do not exceed the maximum amount of FDIC insurance—currently $100,000 per official custodian for interest-bearing accounts and an additional $100,000 per official custodian for non-interest-bearing accounts—no further security is required. For purposes of FDIC regulation, the finance officer is always the official custodian.

Uninsured county funds in a bank or savings institution may be secured through a collateral security arrangement. Under one type of arrangement, the institution places securities with a market value equal to or greater than the county's uninsured moneys on deposit or invested in CDs into an escrow account with a separate, unrelated third-party institution (usually the trust department of another bank, the Federal Reserve, or the Federal Home Loan Bank). The escrow agreement provides that if the depository bank or savings institution defaults on its obligations to the county, then the county is entitled to the escrowed securities in the amount of the default less the amount of FDIC insurance coverage. Under this method the county must execute certain forms and take certain actions to ensure that deposits are adequately collateralized. Responsibility for assuring that the deposits are adequately secured under this method rests with the finance officer, who should closely supervise the collateral-security arrangement.

Alternatively, a bank or savings institution may choose to participate in a pool of bank- and savings-institution-owned securities sponsored and regulated by the state treasurer to collateralize state and local government moneys on deposit or invested in CDs with these institutions. A third-party institution, chosen by the various pooling-method banks, holds the securities in the pool. Participating depository banks and savings institutions are responsible for maintaining adequate collateral securities in the pool, although each financial institution's collateral balances are monitored by the state treasurer. In the unlikely event of defaults or similar financial troubles, the state treasurer would be considered the beneficiary of reclaimed deposits and collateral. Certain standards of financial soundness are required by the state treasurer before a financial institution is allowed to participate in this system.

Investments

Counties cannot afford to let significant amounts of cash lie idle in non-interest-bearing depository accounts. Investment income can amount to the equivalent of several cents or more on the property tax rate. G.S. 159-30 makes the finance officer responsible for managing investments, subject to policy directions and restrictions that the commissioners may impose. Because of the expanded opportunities and risks associated with the investments that North Carolina counties may legally make, both national investment authorities and the Local Government Commission recommend that boards of county commissioners establish general investment policies and restrictions for their finance officers to follow.

Such board-adopted policies could, for example, limit the maximum maturities for investments of general fund moneys; require the use of informal competitive bidding for the purchase of securities; authorize the finance officer to invest in the cash and/or term portfolios of the North Carolina Capital Management Trust (discussed later); and make clear that safety and liquidity should take precedence over yield in the county's investment program. In a growing number of counties, boards of commissioners are adopting such investment policies.

In conducting their investment programs, finance officers must forecast cash resources and needs, thus determining how much is available for investment and for how long. They must also investigate what types of investment securities are authorized by law as well as by their own internal investment policies, and decide which ones to purchase. If an investment security is to be sold before maturity, the finance officer must make that decision.

Custody of Investment Securities

G.S. 159-30(d) states: "Securities and deposit certificates shall be in the custody of the finance officer who shall be responsible for their safe-keeping." Investment securities come in two forms: *certificated* and *noncertificated*. Ownership of certificated investments is represented by an actual physical security. Some certificates of deposit and certain other securities are issued in certificated form. To obtain proper custody of certificated securities, the finance officer should hold the securities or the certificates in the county's vault or its safe deposit box at a local bank or trust company. Alternatively, certificated securities may be delivered to and held by the county's third-party safekeeping agent, which can be the trust department of a North Carolina bank.

Many investment securities—United States Treasury bills, notes, and bonds; federal agency instruments; some commercial paper; and other types of securities—are not certificated. Ownership of them is evidenced by electronic "book entry" records that are maintained by the Federal Reserve System for banks and certain other financial institutions, and by the financial institutions themselves. Additionally, for certain other securities the Depository Trust Company in New York maintains the electronic records of ownership. When a county buys noncertificated securities from a bank or a securities dealer, the record of ownership is transferred electronically from the seller or the seller's bank to the county's custodial agent. To obtain proper custody of book-entry securities, a county should have a signed custodial agreement in place with the financial institution that serves as its custodial agent and the securities should be recorded on the custodial agent's books "in the name of the county." The custodial agent should be a member of the Federal Reserve System and be authorized to conduct trust business in North Carolina. Counties may not use securities brokers and dealers and the *operating divisions* of banks and savings institutions as custodial agents for their investment securities. Generally, the trust department of a bank or financial institution that sells securities to a county may act as the custodial agent for the securities, as long as the trust department itself did not sell the securities to the county and provided that the institution is licensed to do trust business in North Carolina and is a member of the Federal Reserve. It is essential that a county or its custodial agent obtain custody of all county investments. Major losses from investments suffered by local governments in other states have been due to the failure of those governments to obtain proper custody of their investments.

Authorized Investments

Among the securities or the instruments in which counties invest are CDs or other forms of time deposit approved by the Local Government Commission that are offered by banks, savings institutions, and trust companies located in North Carolina [G.S. 159-30(b), (c)(5)]. CDs issued by banks in the state have traditionally been the most widely used investment instrument, especially by small- and medium-sized counties. Other investments authorized by G.S. 159-30(c) include the following:

1. United States Treasury obligations (bills, notes, and bonds)— called *Treasuries*—and U.S. *agency* obligations that are fully guaranteed by the United States government. Because these obligations are full-faith-and-credit obligations of the United States, they carry the least credit risk—that is, risk of default—of any investment available to counties. As a result, short-term Treasuries are usually lower yielding than alternative investment securities. Long-term Treasuries and Government National Mortgage Association (GNMA) securities (fully guaranteed by the United States Government) can experience significant price variations. This is characteristic of long-term securities in general; therefore such securities should be carefully evaluated and be considered only for investing certain, limited funds, for example, capital reserve moneys that will be needed for many years.

2. Direct obligations of certain agencies that are established and/or sponsored by the United States government but whose obligations are not guaranteed by it. Examples are the Federal Home Loan Bank Board, the Federal National Mortgage Association, and the Federal Farm Credit System. Direct debt issued by these agencies generally carries very low credit risk although economic conditions adverse to an economic sector the agency finances (for example, housing), can create some risk for counties or others who invest in its securities. Some

securities of these agencies are not their direct debt and are therefore not eligible investments for North Carolina counties. Moreover, longer-term direct debt of these agencies, although carrying low credit risk, can experience significant price fluctuations before maturity.

3. Obligations of the State of North Carolina or bonds and notes of any of its local governments or public authorities, with investments in such obligations subject to restrictions of the secretary of the Local Government Commission. Because the interest paid to investors on these obligations, bonds, and notes is typically exempt from federal and state income taxes, they generally carry lower yields than alternative investment instruments available to counties. However, should the state and local governments in North Carolina begin to issue significant amounts of securities on which the interest paid is subject to federal income taxes, those securities would carry higher interest rates than tax-exempt state and local government obligations. This could make the taxable obligations attractive as investment instruments to counties.

4. Top-rated U.S. commercial paper issued by domestic United States corporations. Commercial paper is issued by industrial and commercial corporations to finance inventories and other short-term needs. Such paper is an unsecured corporate promissory note that is available in maturities of up to 270 days, although maturities from 30 to 90 days are most common. For any local government to invest in commercial paper, the paper must be rated by at least one national rating organization and earn its top commercial paper rating. If the paper is rated by more than one such organization, it must have the highest rating given by each.

   Commercial paper is relatively high yielding, and many counties invest heavily in it. In economic recessions, some commercial paper issuers are downgraded. This means that their commercial paper is no longer eligible for investment by North Carolina local governments. However, as long as a commercial paper issuer is top-rated and the finance officer closely monitors its ratings, the risk for this type of investment is small. County officials should also understand that eligible commercial paper issued by banks is not a deposit and consequently is not covered by insurance and collateralization.

5. Bankers acceptances issued by North Carolina banks or by any top-rated United States bank. *Bankers acceptances* are bills of exchange or time drafts that are drawn on and guaranteed by banks. They are usually issued to finance international trade or a firm's short-term credit needs and are usually secured by the credit of the issuing firm, as well as by the general credit of the accepting bank. Most bankers acceptances have maturity terms of 30 to 180 days. Counties may invest in bankers acceptances issued by any North Carolina bank; only the largest banks in the state issue them. For a county to invest in bankers acceptances of non–North Carolina U.S. banks, the institution must have outstanding publicly held obligations that carry the highest long-term credit rating from at least one national rating organization. If the bank's credit obligations are rated by more than one national organization, it must have the highest rating given by each.

6. Participating shares in one of the portfolios of the North Carolina Capital Management Trust. This trust is a mutual fund established specifically for investments by North Carolina local governments and public authorities. It is certified and regulated by the Local Government Commission, and unlike other state-sponsored investment pools for public entity investments, it is registered with the United States Securities and Exchange Commission, which imposes reporting and other requirements that ensure the safety of money invested in the trust. The trust manages two separate investment portfolios. One is the money-market portfolio, which was started in 1982 and is intended for the investment of short-term or operating cash balances. The principal value of money invested in a share in this portfolio remains fixed at $1. The term portfolio, which was established in 1987, is intended for capital reserve funds and other moneys that are not subject to immediate need. The principal value of investments in this portfolio fluctuates with changes in market interest rates. Because of this, the term portfolio should primarily be used for the investment of funds that will not be needed immediately or in the short term.

Either portfolio permits the return of funds invested with it within one day of notice; however, the managers of the portfolios do request that local governments provide longer advance notice if large withdrawals will be made. The trust's portfolios may invest only in securities in which local governments may invest under G.S. 159-30(c).

7.　Repurchase agreements. A *repurchase agreement* is a purchase by an investor of a security, with the stipulation that the seller will buy it back at the original purchase price plus agreed-upon interest at the maturity date. These agreements were once popular for short-term or overnight investments by North Carolina local governments. Unfortunately, some local governments in other states suffered substantial losses by buying repurchase agreements from unscrupulous securities dealers. As a result, strict laws and requirements for the safe use of these agreements have been enacted, both in North Carolina and across the country. G.S. 159-30(c) authorizes local governments to invest in repurchase agreements, but only under very limiting conditions.[2] These conditions have greatly reduced the cost-effectiveness of local government investments in repurchase agreements, and such agreements are no longer used to any significant degree by counties. Occasionally, some counties will meet the extensive criteria and use such instruments on a limited basis. Most often the investments will be made on a short-term basis with debt proceeds.

8.　Evidences of ownership of, or fractional undivided interests in, future principal and interest payments of *stripped* or *zero-coupon instruments* that are issued directly or guaranteed by the United States government. These instruments were first authorized as a local government investment in 1987. They are sold at discount from face or par value and pay no interest until maturity. At maturity, the investor receives the face value, with the difference between that value and the discounted purchase price of the security representing the effective interest earned. Stripped or zero coupon securities may be a useful investment vehicle for certain limited moneys, such as those held in a capital reserve fund that will not be needed until after the instrument matures. However, because most strips or zero coupons have long maturities, they are subject to considerable price fluctuations before maturity and should not be used for the investment of general county funds. If investments were made in these securities and market interest rates later rose substantially (as they did in 1994), a county that had to cash in the investment before maturity could lose a significant portion of the principal invested in the securities.

9.　Certain mutual funds for moneys held by a county that are subject to the arbitrage and rebate provisions of the Internal

Revenue Code. The LGBFCA authorizes unspent proceeds from bonds or other financings subject to the Internal Revenue Code's arbitrage and rebate provisions to be invested in tax-exempt and taxable mutual funds under strict procedures. Operating moneys and proceeds from financings that are not subject to the arbitrage and rebate provisions may not be invested in these mutual funds. Because of the complexity of the federal tax code and the wide variety of available mutual funds, a county should consult with its bond counsel before placing moneys in this type of investment.

10. Derivatives issued directly by one of the federal agencies listed in G.S. 159-30(c)(2) or guaranteed by the United States Government. Derivatives are not specifically mentioned in the law, but may be eligible investments if they are otherwise authorized in G.S. 159-30(c). *Derivatives* refer to a broad range of investment securities that can vary in market price, yield, and/or cash flow depending on the value of the underlying securities or assets, or changes in one or more interest rate indices. Derivatives commonly include mortgage pass-through instruments issued by federal agencies, mortgage obligations "guaranteed" by federal agencies (but not by the United States Government), callable step-up notes, floaters, inverse floaters, and still other securities that go by even more interesting names. It is beyond the scope of this chapter to explain these different types of derivatives. It shall suffice to say that derivatives are generally complex instruments, and many of them are subject to rapid and major changes in value as market interest rates change. Some local governments in other states have lost vast amounts of money by investing in derivatives. The volume of derivatives available to investors has grown dramatically, and investment brokers and dealers often try to sell various types of derivatives to county and other local government finance officers. Many derivatives are not legal investment instruments for North Carolina's local governments. Those that are direct debt (i.e., a balance sheet liability) of the federal agencies listed in G.S. 159-30(c)(2) or guaranteed by the United States Government are usually legal investments. However, many if not most of these are inappropriate as investment vehicles for counties, except in very special circumstances. Even though legal, many of them are subject to extreme price and cash-flow

volatility. A finance officer considering investing the county's money in one or more derivatives should do so only pursuant to a board of commissioners' investment policy that explicitly authorizes such an investment, only if the finance officer understands the nature of the security and the risks associated with it, and only for a short maturity.

Guidelines for Investing Public Funds

Because of great changes and technological innovation in financial markets, challenges presented by international events to these markets, and the availability of many new types of investment instruments, the investment and general management of public moneys have become very complex. North Carolina counties can avoid many of these problems that have harmed local governments in other states by adhering to the following guidelines in conducting their investment programs:

1. *The investment program should put safety and liquidity before yield.* A county should not put funds that it is investing at risk of loss for the purpose of obtaining higher investment earnings. The substantial highly-publicized losses of several county governments as well as other local governmental entities across the nation in 1994 and 1995 underscore the potential problems faced with risky investments. The temptation to sacrifice safety for yield is particularly great when interest rates are falling and a county's officials are attempting to maintain investment earnings and revenues. A county should always have funds available to meet payment obligations when they become due. This requires maintaining adequate liquidity in an investment portfolio and limiting most investments to securities with short-term maturities.

2. *A county should invest only in securities that the finance officer understands.* Many investment vehicles, including most derivatives, are extremely complex. Before purchasing a security, a finance officer should thoroughly understand all its components, especially how its value is likely to change with changes in market interest rates. Whenever the finance officer is considering investing in a type of security that the county has not used before, the finance officer should obtain and study the prospectus or equivalent information for the security and talk to Local Gov-

ernment Commission staff and other informed, "disinterested" parties about the nature and risks of the security.

3. *The finance officer and other officials involved in investing county funds should know the financial institutions, the brokers, and the dealers from which the county buys investment securities.* Investment transactions are made by phone, and investment funds and securities are often electronically transferred in seconds. Funds and securities can be lost or "misplaced" quickly in such an environment. To protect the county, the officials conducting a county's investment program must be sure that they deal only with reputable and reliable institutions, brokers, and dealers. In fact, the authoritative literature that establishes GAAP also refers to the importance of knowing one's brokers or dealers. The finance officer should obtain a list of North Carolina local government clients of any firm or person attempting to sell the county investment securities and obtain references from officials in these other governments. The finance officer should also obtain and evaluate current financial statements from any institution, broker, or dealer that sells or wishes to sell securities to the county. Local governments in other states have lost invested funds because they placed moneys with firms that later went bankrupt and were unable to return the funds. A discussion of how to analyze the financial position of banks and similar financial institutions can be found in the North Carolina Department of State Treasurer's *Policies Manual.*[3] A county should also enter into an investment trading agreement with any firm or person from which it buys investments; model investment trading agreements are used by and are available from several of North Carolina's large counties.

4. *The finance officer should ensure that the county adequately insures or collateralizes all investments in CDs (as well as other deposits in banks), and that it has proper custody of all investment securities.*

5. *The county's investment program should be conducted pursuant to cash management and investment policy approved by the board of commissioners.* Such a policy should be based on G.S. 159-30 and related statutes, setting forth the board's directions and expectations about which investments will be made and generally how they will be made, and establishing general parameters for the receipt, the disbursement, and the management of moneys.

6. *The finance officer should report periodically to the board on the status of the county's investment program.* Such a report should be made at least semi-annually and preferably quarterly or monthly and show the securities in the county's investment portfolio, the terms or the maturities for investments, and their yields. If possible, average investment maturity and yield should be calculated and also shown in this report.

7. *The use of investment managers does not relieve the finance officer of the responsibility of the safety of public funds.* A few counties in North Carolina have considered the engagement of outside professional investment managers to administer their routine investment functions. Obviously, there are advantages and disadvantages to this arrangement. The most obvious disadvantage is the inability of the finance officer to have direct control of the investments even though the responsibility for them remains with that role. Also, because of the legal restrictions on the investments that local governments can make, the return that an investment manager can earn once management fees have been deducted may be lower than the return the unit can earn on its own. It should be noted that local legislation may be required for an entity to engage outside investment managers. If it is determined that an outside investment manager would be beneficial, a written agreement should be executed outlining permissible investments, safekeeping arrangements, diversification requirements, maturity limitations, the liability to be assumed by both parties, and the fees of the contract.

The Annual Audit

Contents of the Comprehensive Annual Financial Report

G.S. 159-34 requires local governments to have their accounts audited by independent auditors after the close of each fiscal year. The auditor's opinion is set out in an annual financial report, which must include "the [county's] financial statements prepared in accordance with generally accepted accounting principles, all disclosures in the public interest required by law, and the auditor's opinion and comments relating to [the] financial statements."

Preparation of the report's financial statements and their accompanying notes is the county's responsibility. They may be prepared by county finance officers and their staffs or the county may contract with an independent auditor for their preparation. Nearly all the larger counties and many medium-size and small ones are now preparing their own financial statements and notes. This requires much work by the county's finance staff, but it can result in significant savings in audit fees.

If a county prepares a comprehensive annual financial report (CAFR), it will contain three sections: introductory, financial, and statistical. A fourth section consisting of the compliance or single audit reports and schedules may be included. Table 12-1 summarizes the contents of the CAFR. If a county does not prepare a CAFR, only the financial section, including financial statements and notes, will be found in the annual financial report.

Introductory Section

The introductory section of a CAFR includes the transmittal letter, an organization chart, and a list of principal officials. The transmittal letter, which presents an overview of county operations and activities, should be of particular interest to county officials, who may not be aware of all the county does.

Financial Section

The financial section of a CAFR contains the financial statements, which present information in various formats and levels of detail. Generally the most summarized information is found at the beginning of the financial section, immediately followed by the notes to the financial statements. This portion of the financial section is commonly referred to as the general purpose financial statements (GPFS) and represents the minimum information required to be reported by a local government to be in accordance with generally accepted accounting principles (GAAP). The GPFS are combined statements which include all of the county's funds and highly summarized information, as well as the aforementioned note disclosures. In these combined statements, information for each fund type (for example, general, special revenue, capital projects, enterprise, internal service) is presented in a series of columns, one type to a column. The combining and individual fund statements follow the note disclosures (and, accordingly, are not considered part

Table 12-1
Contents of a Comprehensive Annual Financial Report

Section	Description
Introductory Section	
Letter of transmittal	Overview of the county's operations and financial statistics
Organizational chart	Diagram of the county's organizational structure
List of principal officials	List of elected and appointed officials
Financial Section	
Auditor's opinion	Independent auditor's opinion on financial statements
Combined financial statements	Summarized information, one column for each type of fund (general, special revenue, enterprise, etc.)
Notes to the financial statements	Explanations of accounting policies, statutory violations, explanations of financial statement items, etc.
Combining statements	Summarized information, one column for each fund of a particular type (e.g., each special revenue fund) and combined-total column
Individual fund statements	Detailed information about individual funds (prior year amounts, budgeted amounts, actual amounts, etc.)
Supplemental schedules	Additional information for such items as fixed assets
Statistical Section	
Statistical tables	Tables, usually on multiyear basis (i.e., ten years), showing information on property taxes, debt, revenues, expenditures, etc.
Compliance Section (optional)	
Single audit reports	Reports from independent auditor on compliance and internal control
Schedule of findings and questioned costs	Listing of grant findings and questioned costs
Schedule of expenditures of federal and state awards	Listing of federal and state financial assistance programs

of the GPFS) and provide more detailed information about the county's finances. A combining statement shows the individual funds of a particular fund type, as well as a combined total for all funds of that type. Statements for each individual fund, such as the general fund or a water and sewer fund, may also be presented in this portion of the financial section.

The "disclosures in the public interest" are primarily found in the notes to the financial statements, which are also located in the financial section. As mentioned earlier, the note disclosures are considered part of the GPFS along with the combined statement presentations. The content and form of the notes are prescribed by GAAP as established by the GASB. Through written advisory memoranda and illustrative financial statements interpreting GAAP, the Local Government Commission provides guidance to local officials and their independent auditors on the content of the note disclosures. These disclosures contain significant information for anyone attempting to interpret the financial statements and understand a county's finances. Disclosures of interest to county officials include such items as the following: the reporting entity; statutory violations, if any; budgetary overexpenditures, if any; significant accounting and budgetary policies; and detailed information concerning a county's deposits and investments, fixed assets, and long-term debt.

Statistical Section

The statistical section follows the financial section. It includes multiyear trend information on revenues, expenditures, debt, property taxes, and other items. Economic and demographic data are also reported. This section is useful in analyzing a county's financial trends and it is considered an invaluable tool for bond rating agencies as well as potential investors and creditors.

The Auditor's Opinion

The auditor's essential task is to render an independent opinion on the accuracy and reliability of the financial statements and the notes thereto, as well as on their conformity with GAAP. The auditor opines not that the financial statements and disclosures are perfect, but that they are reliable enough for a knowledgeable reader to use them to make informed judgments about a county's financial position and operations.

The auditor's opinion might take one of four forms. First, it may be *unqualified*: the auditor says that the statements present fairly the county's financial position at the close of the fiscal year, in conformity with GAAP.

A *qualified* opinion is a second possibility. If in some way a county's practices vary from GAAP, the opinion may state that the statements fairly present the county's financial position except for any such deviation. For example, the county may not have fully accounted for fixed assets. Also, an opinion qualification may be due to a *scope limitation*. This occurs when the independent auditor is unable to perform certain tests that are an essential part of the audit. For instance, when a county's accounting system fails to provide adequate documentation for some revenue and expenditure transactions, the auditor's ability to test such transactions is limited. This limitation may result in a qualified opinion.

Third, deviations from GAAP may be so material that the statements as a whole do not present fairly the county's financial position. If that occurs, an *adverse* opinion is rendered.

Fourth, and rarely, the auditor may *disclaim* any opinion at all as to the statements. In this case, the county's accounting system is in such disarray that an opinion cannot be rendered.

The auditor normally suggests improvements to the county's internal-control procedures in a *management letter* that accompanies the audit report. This letter is addressed to the board of commissioners. A public document, it typically makes various specific suggestions for improving internal control and financial procedures. These suggestions normally arise from the audit, and the letter is delivered at the same time as the audited financial statements. Often the suggestions have been informally made earlier, and some may already have been acted on. Significant weaknesses in internal controls will also be addressed by the independent auditor in the internal control reports that are required as part of the single audit on federal and state financial assistance programs. These are discussed in the next section.

Apart from the management letter, the independent auditor can often be an excellent source of advice on accounting system design, internal control procedures, and finance in general.

Selection of an Independent Auditor

G.S. 159-34 establishes certain requirements and procedures regarding contracting for the annual audit. First, the auditor must be selected by and report to the board of commissioners. The auditor should not report to the manager, the budget officer, or the finance officer.

Second, the board may choose any North Carolina certified public accountant (CPA) or any accountant certified by the Local Government Commission as qualified to audit local government accounts. In practice, no non-CPA accountants have requested certification or met the requirements for certification to perform local government audits in recent years. Board members should assure themselves that the person or firm selected is familiar with the particular features of government accounting and auditing. Auditors should be engaged early in the fiscal year so that they can become familiar with the county's procedures and can complete some of the necessary testing before the fiscal year's end. This also ensures that the auditor can plan the audit engagement and complete it in a timely manner.

Many counties select the auditor through a *request-for-proposals* (RFP) process. Although this is not required by state statute, using an RFP is recommended by the Local Government Commission staff to secure the best audit proposal. Also, selecting an independent auditor through a competitive procurement process is required by federal regulations if a county is allowed by a grant agreement and intends to charge some of the audit costs to the grant. Most counties that use RFPs engage an auditor for a term of three to five years. The RFP should cover both the technical qualifications of a potential audit firm and the firm's cost proposals. Local officials should give more weight to an auditor's technical skills than to its proposed audit fees. References from other local government clients should be requested from an auditor. These references should be contacted so that county officials may obtain information on other local governments' experiences with a potential auditor.

Contrary to popular belief, government entities are not required to rotate auditors periodically. As mentioned earlier, the Local Government Commission recommends governments issue an RFP at least every three to five years. This does not preclude, however, current auditors from retaining the engagement if they continue to meet the service and price requirements established in the RFP. Many government entities have retained the same audit firm for years. Some benefits of these established relationships are the auditor's familiarity with the government's environment, as well as the government body's avoidance of costs (particularly in staff time) incurred in changing auditors. On the other hand, some governing boards choose to contract with different auditors to provide a "fresh look" or allocate the work to other qualified auditors in the region. Either approach has merit, yet neither have been endorsed or encouraged by the Local Government Commission. It should again be noted that rotation is not statutorily required, but is a policy left to the discretion of each entity's governing board.

Third, a county's contract with an auditor must be approved by the Local Government Commission. Payment may not be made for audit services until the secretary of the commission has approved it.

Audits of Federal and State Grants

Federal and state grants and other financial assistance programs provide moneys to support certain county programs. In the past, individual federal and state agencies providing these moneys would audit county expenditure of them to verify that the moneys were spent for the purposes intended and in accordance with prescribed procedures. However, since the mid-1980s the federal government has required local governments to have a *combined financial and compliance audit,* or single audit, of all federal financial assistance programs that meet certain expenditure thresholds.

To build on the federal single audit, the 1987 General Assembly, with the support of local officials, passed a law requiring state financial assistance programs to be included with federal programs in a combined single audit. In North Carolina this combined single audit is performed in conjunction with the annual financial audit by the county's independent auditor. Federal and state agencies are allowed to build on the single audit and perform monitoring work on the programs they administer. However, they should not duplicate the work performed by the independent auditor.

The independent auditor issues a number of compliance and internal control reports to disclose findings from the single audit. These reports usually are included in the last section of the annual financial report. The most significant items for local officials in these reports are the internal control weaknesses, findings, and questioned costs identified by the auditor. Internal control weaknesses are usually significant deficiencies and should be corrected unless corrective actions would not be cost-effective. For example, an internal control weakness commonly cited is the lack of proper segregation of duties. However, especially for small counties, complete correction of the problem could involve additional hirings, the costs of which could outweigh the benefits. In these situations, mitigating controls can be put into place that lessen the risks and weaknesses involved. Otherwise, findings and questioned costs almost always require corrective action, which may necessitate the repayment of grant funds. County officials' formal responses to findings and questioned costs and material internal control weaknesses are included in the single audit reports.

The Local Government Commission monitors the single audit of grant funds as part of its review of the annual financial report. If the commission staff determines that the single audit reports and schedules are not prepared according to the applicable standards, then the independent auditor may be required to revise them before the annual financial report can be accepted. If the commission staff finds that the single audit is satisfactory, then all state grantor agencies must accept the audit. Subsequent to the acceptance of the annual financial report, if the commission determines that the single audit is not reliable, it may revoke its approval. This opens a county to individual federal and state agency audits.

Additional Resources

Allison, Gregory S. *Accounting Issues and Practices: A Guide for Smaller Governments.* Chicago: Government Finance Officers Association, 1996.

————. *A Preparer's Guide to Note Disclosures.* Chicago: Government Finance Officers Association, 1994.

Allison, Gregory S., K. Lee Carter, S. Grady Fullerton, and Fiscal Management Section, Department of State Treasurer. *Carolina County, North Carolina, Comprehensive Annual Financial Report,* 3d ed. rev. Chapel Hill, N.C.: Institute of Government, The University of North Carolina at Chapel Hill, 1998.

Governmental Accounting Standards Board. *Codification of Governmental Accounting and Financial Reporting Standards as of June 30, 1997.* Norwalk, Conn.: GASB, 1997.

Government Finance Officers Association. *Governmental Accounting, Auditing and Financial Reporting,* 1994 ed. Chicago: GFOA, 1994.

Larson, Corinne, ed. *A Public Investor's Guide to Money Market Instruments.* Chicago: GFOA, 1994.

Lawrence, David M. *Local Government Finance in North Carolina,* 2d ed. Chapel Hill, N.C.: Institute of Government, The University of North Carolina at Chapel Hill, 1990.

Notes

1. Although the LGBFCA requires the use of the modified accrual basis of accounting, it also requires that financial reporting be in conformity with generally accepted accounting principles (GAAP). Enterprise, internal service, and certain trust funds primarily follow commercial (accrual) accounting standards for

reporting in accordance with GAAP. A county's annual financial report must both demonstrate compliance with legal requirements (i.e., the LGBFCA) and report on operations in conformity with GAAP. Therefore, enterprise funds should be reported on both the modified accrual and accrual basis in a county's financial statements, and internal service and certain trust funds should also be reported on the accrual basis in the annual financial report.

2. The following restrictions apply to local government investments in repurchase agreements: (a) The underlying security acquired with a repurchase agreement must be a direct obligation of the United States or fully guaranteed by the United States. (b) The repurchase agreement must be sold by a broker or a dealer that is recognized as a primary dealer by a Federal Reserve Bank, or be sold by a commercial bank, a trust company, or a national bank whose deposits are insured by the FDIC. (c) The security underlying the agreement must be delivered in physical or in electronic book-entry form to the county or its third-party agent. (d) The value of the underlying security must be determined daily and be maintained, at least, at 100 percent of the repurchase price. (e) The county must have a valid and perfected first security interest in the underlying security. This can be achieved through delivery of the security to the county or its third-party safekeeping agent under a written agreement. (f) The underlying security acquired in the repurchase agreement must be free of a lien or third-party claim.

3. North Carolina Department of State Treasurer, *Policies Manual* (Raleigh, N.C.: NCDST, October 1990).

III
General County Government Functions

13 Personnel Law and Administration

Stephen Allred

Contents

Stephen Allred is an Institute of Government faculty member whose fields include public personnel law. The author expresses his appreciation to Donald Hayman, who retired from the Institute of Government faculty in 1985 after thirty-seven years of service. He specialized in personnel administration and was the author of this chapter in the previous editions of this book. His earlier work is reflected in this edition's chapter.

Recruiting, supervising, and disciplining employees poses challenges to any employer, public or private. At the county level there are additional challenges that come about as a result of the multiple hiring authorities established under the North Carolina General Statutes. Counties, like municipalities, have increasingly turned to the manager plan.[1] Unlike a city council and manager, however, a board of county commissioners and its manager do not have direct authority over all those who work for the county. This makes personnel administration at the county level more difficult than at the municipal level.

Public personnel administration in North Carolina counties is governed by the North Carolina General Statutes, federal statutes, the United States Constitution, the North Carolina Constitution, and court decisions. Additional sources of governance are the personnel policies adopted by the county commissioners and the regulations set forth in the North Carolina Administrative Code. This chapter summarizes these sources of personnel law and provides an overview of personnel administration at the county level.

The Employment "At Will" Rule

When a North Carolina employer hires someone, the legal presumption that governs the working relationship is that the employment is "at will." That is, employment is at the will of either party, and the employer is free to dismiss the employee at any time without explanation or legal penalty.[2] The employment-at-will presumption applies to both public- and private-sector employment.

For some county employees, their status as at-will employees is explicitly stated in the General Statutes. For example, G.S. 153A-103(2) provides that sheriff's deputies "serve at the pleasure of the appointing officer." Similarly G.S. 153A-81 provides that the county manager serves at the pleasure of the board of county commissioners. For other public employees the presumption of employment at will holds unless the employee proves otherwise.

The employment-at-will rule does not mean that a county may always discharge employees without worrying about possible legal challenges. Three broad categories of exceptions to the employment-at-will presumption have developed: statutory exceptions, common law exceptions, and property right exceptions.

Statutory exceptions represent legislative restrictions, by both Congress and the General Assembly, of an employer's right to discharge employees. Federal statutes that modify the employment-at-will rule include the Civil Rights Act of 1964, which prohibits discharge for discriminatory reasons; the Age Discrimination in Employment Act, which prohibits discharge solely on the basis of age; and the Americans with Disabilities Act of 1990, which bars dismissal of otherwise qualified employees if reasonable accommodation of their disabilities can be made. Similarly the North Carolina General Statutes modify the employment-at-will rule in several ways.[3]

In addition to statutory exceptions, judicially created exceptions to the employment-at-will rule restrict an employer's right to fire employees. These common law exceptions take the form of breach of contract or the tort of wrongful discharge. They arise when the court finds either that the parties themselves, through their actions, have created a contractual exception to the employment-at-will rule, or that the employer's motive in dismissing an employee violates some tenet of public policy.

For example, in *Coman v. Thomas Manufacturing Company*,[4] the North Carolina Supreme Court heard a claim in which an employee alleged that he had been fired for refusing to drive his truck longer than the time allowed under United States Department of Transportation regulations, and for refusing to falsify the logs required to be maintained by the department to ensure compliance with the law. The court held that the employee had stated a cause of action for wrongful discharge, stating "[W]hile there may be a right to terminate a contract at will for no reason, or for an arbitrary or irrational reason, there can be no right to terminate such a contract for an unlawful reason or purpose that contravenes public policy."[5]

A third source of exceptions to the employment-at-will rule is found only in public-sector employment: the vesting of a "property right" to employment. The Fourteenth Amendment's guarantee that no person may be deprived of property without due process has been construed to extend to a property interest in employment.[6] A property interest arises when a public employee can demonstrate a reasonable expectation of continued employment because the employer has established a binding policy that dismissal will occur only for stated reasons. For example, county employees subject to the State Personnel Act may be fired only for "just cause" (G.S. 126-35).

The effect of this language is to create a property right in employment that may be taken from the employee only after the constitutional requirements of substantive and procedural due process have been met.[7] Whether a county's personnel policies confer a property right in employment depends not only on the wording of the policies but also on the form in which those policies were adopted by the board of county commissioners. In *Pittman v. Wilson County*,[8] the court held that personnel policies adopted by resolution, not by ordinance, by the Board of County Commissioners of Wilson County were not sufficient to vest county employees with a property right. Instead the court held that because the restrictions were set forth only in a resolution, not in an ordinance or a statute, they were not binding. Stated the court:

> The resolution is a part of a manual that describes itself as merely a "Welcome to All Employees of Wilson County." The language simply is not typical of that used in an ordinance or statute having the effect of law. Moreover, the subject matter of the personnel resolution is administrative in nature. It supplies internal guidelines to County officials for the administration of the County's employment positions, including the disciplining and discharge of employees.

Having found no basis for the plaintiff's claim that she was other than an at-will employee, the court concluded that she was not entitled to due process in the termination of her employment.

The North Carolina Supreme Court most recently addressed the employment-at-will rule in November 1997 with its decision in *Kurtzman v. Applied Analytical Industries, Inc.*[9] In that case the plaintiff was recruited to move from Rhode Island to North Carolina to accept a new position with the defendant employer. During negotiations, the plaintiff inquired into the security of his proposed position with the employer and was told: "If you do your job, you'll have a job"; "This is a long-term growth opportunity for you"; "This is a secure position"; and "We're offering you a career position." He took the job, but was fired six months later.

The plaintiff argued that the combination of the additional consideration of moving his residence and the defendant's specific assurances of continued employment removed the employment relationship from the traditional at-will presumption and created an employment contract under which he could not be terminated absent cause. The question of first impression for the court was whether it should recognize a "moving residence" exception to the general rule of employment at will. But the North Carolina Supreme Court rejected the plaintiff's claim, stating:

> The employment-at-will doctrine has prevailed in this state for a century. The narrow exceptions to it have been grounded in considerations of public policy designed either to prohibit status-based discrimination or to insure the integrity of the judicial process or the enforcement of the law. The facts here do not present policy concerns of this nature. Rather, they are representative of negotiations and circumstances characteristically associated with traditional at-will employment situations.
>
> Further, as we recognized in *Coman*, "adoption of the [at-will] rule by the courts greatly facilitated the development of the American economy at the end of the nineteenth century." A century later, the rule remains an incentive to economic development, and any significant erosion of it could serve as a disincentive. Additional exceptions thus demand careful consideration and should be adopted only with substantial justification grounded in compelling considerations of public policy.
>
> We perceive no such justification here. The society to which the employment-at-will doctrine currently applies is a highly mobile one in which relocation to accept new employment is common. To remove an employment relationship from the at-will presumption upon an employee's change of residence, coupled with vague assurances of continued employment, would substantially erode the rule and bring considerable instability to an otherwise largely clear area of the law. We thus hold that plaintiff-employee's change of residence in the wake of defendant-employer's statements here does not constitute additional consideration making what is otherwise an at-will employment relationship one that can be terminated by the employer only for cause.

The employment-at-will rule in North Carolina continues to evolve as the courts hear claims from employees asserting that the rule does not apply to them. Continued monitoring of this developing area of the law is essential for those who advise counties on personnel matters.

County Commissioners' Personnel Powers

Although boards of county commissioners are limited by the North Carolina Constitution, state and local laws, and federal law, they have major responsibility for determining county personnel policies. County commissioners exercise their power over personnel because of the following responsibilities:

1. Appropriating or refusing to appropriate funds
2. Appointing, supervising, and dismissing some groups of employees
3. Approving or refusing to approve the appointments of the county manager or administrator
4. Fixing the qualifications for appointive office
5. Fixing the pay and expense allowances of officials and employees
6. Adopting rules and regulations governing hours and days of work, holidays, leave, pay, expense allowances, and working conditions, and any other measures that promote the hiring and retention of capable, diligent, and honest career employees
7. Prescribing the office hours, workdays, and holidays to be observed by the various offices, departments, and agencies of the county

Perhaps a board of commissioners' two greatest powers over personnel are the power of the purse—the power to appropriate or withhold funds—and the power of appointment. The board of commissioners in effect determines the number of county employees when it approves a budget for each department and establishes a pay plan that sets salary ranges for each class of positions. The board receives and appropriates the funds that pay all or a part of each county employee's salary. The power to withhold funds is limited by political and legal considerations, but unless the board of commissioners appropriates funds there will be no county employees and no county programs.

As noted at the beginning of this chapter, the structure for appointment and dismissal authority is more complex in county government than it is in municipal government in North Carolina. Many positions are under the control of the board of county commissioners or the county manager; others are under the control of elected officials; still others are under the control of various county boards subject to the State Personnel Act. The provisions are discussed in the following subsections.

General Appointment and Dismissal Authority

G.S. 153A-87 provides that in counties not having a county manager, the board of commissioners shall appoint, suspend, and remove all county officers, employees, and agents except those who are elected by the people or whose appointment is otherwise provided for by law. Counties may choose to adopt the manager plan, which allows them to hire a county manager to serve at the pleasure of the board of commissioners. If a manager plan is adopted (as it has been in 99 of 100 counties in North Carolina), the manager is vested with appointment authority. However, the manager's appointment power is subject to the approval of the board of commissioners unless the board passes a resolution permitting the manager to act without first securing the board's approval [G.S. 153A-82(1)].

Dismissal authority is also vested in the county manager but without the requirement that the dismissal action be ratified by the board. There are certain county officers whose appointment and dismissal are required by law to be made by the board of commissioners (even in counties in which the county manager plan has been adopted). The clerk of the board (G.S. 153A-111) and the county attorney (G.S. 153A-114) are appointed by the board and serve at its pleasure. The tax collector [G.S. 105-349(a)] and the deputy tax collector [G.S. 105-349(f)] are board appointees who serve for a term determined by the board. The tax collector may be removed only for good cause after written notice and an opportunity for a hearing at a public session except that no hearing is required if the tax collector is removed for failing to deliver tax receipts properly. Finally, the county assessor is a board appointee who serves a term of not less than two nor more than four years. G.S. 105-294(b) requires that within two years of appointment as assessor, the incumbent must achieve a passing score in courses of instruction approved by the Department of Revenue. The assessor may be removed only for good cause after written notice and an opportunity for a hearing at a public session [G.S. 105-294(a)]. The county assessor may in turn hire listers, appraisers, and clerical assistants [G.S. 105-296(b)].

Employees Whose Appointments Are Made through Boards or Are Subject to Requirements of Boards

Certain positions are filled either by designated boards or by the manager (where the manager plan exists) in accordance with the requirements established by the board of commissioners. A county manager may appoint one or more individuals as fire prevention inspectors. The board of commissioners, subject to the approval of the State Building Code Council, is to set the duties of any person appointed or designated as a fire prevention inspector (G.S. 153A-235). Similarly, an individual employed as a building inspector who enforces the State

Building Code as a member of a county or joint inspection department must be certified by the North Carolina Code Officials Qualification Board (G.S. 153A-351.1).

Public library employees are appointed through a library board of trustees. The board, not to exceed twelve members, is appointed by the board of commissioners for a term set by the county. Library trustees may be removed only for incapacity, unfitness, misconduct, or neglect of duty (G.S. 153A-265). The trustees, in turn, appoint a chief librarian or a director of library services. The trustees also appoint other library employees upon the advice of the chief librarian or the director of library services [G.S. 153A-266(4)]. G.S. 153A-267 states that the employees of a county library system are, for all purposes, employees of the county.

County boards of elections are composed of three members appointed by the State Board of Elections for two-year terms. The board's clerk, assistant clerks, and other employees, including precinct transfer assistants, are appointed and dismissed by the county board of elections [G.S. 163-33(10)]. The county director of elections is appointed and dismissed by the State Board of Elections, upon recommendation by the county board of elections (G.S. 163-35).

Officers Elected by the People

Article VII, Section 2, of the North Carolina Constitution provides that each county shall have a sheriff elected by the people for a four-year term, subject to removal for cause as provided by law. G.S. 153A-103(1) states that each sheriff has the exclusive right to hire, discharge, and supervise the employees in the sheriff's office[10] except that the board of commissioners must approve the appointment of a sheriff's relative or of a person convicted of a crime involving moral turpitude. Each sheriff is entitled to at least two deputies who serve at the pleasure of the sheriff.

The register of deeds is also an elected officer, with a four-year term [G.S. 153A-103(2)]. As is the case with the sheriff, each register of deeds has the exclusive right to hire, discharge, and supervise the employees in the register of deeds' office, except that the board of commissioners must approve the appointment of a relative of the register of deeds or of a person convicted of a crime involving moral turpitude [G.S. 153A-103(1)]. Each register of deeds is entitled to at least two deputies, provided that the register of deeds justifies to the board the necessity of the second deputy. Deputies serve at the pleasure of the register of deeds [G.S. 153A-103(2)].

Employees Appointed by Boards Subject to the State Personnel Act

The State Personnel Act (G.S. 126) governs recruitment, selection, and dismissal of four county departments: health, social services, mental health, and emergency management. These departments receive federal funds that require the use of "competitive" recruitment and selection procedures as a condition for their receipt.[11] Thus these employees are sometimes called competitive service employees. Health department employees are competitive service employees. A county board of health is composed of eleven members appointed by the board of commissioners to serve three-year terms (G.S. 130A-35). A district health department including more than one county may be formed instead of county health departments, upon agreement of the county boards of commissioners and local boards of health having jurisdiction over each of the counties involved (G.S. 130A-36). The board of health, in turn, appoints the local health director, after consultation with the board(s) of commissioners having jurisdiction over the area served by the health department (G.S. 130A-40). The local health director may be dismissed only in accordance with the due process requirements of the State Personnel Act.[12] Similarly, health department employees are appointed and dismissed in accordance with the act [G.S. 130A-41(b); G.S. 126-5(a)].

Social services department employees are also subject to the State Personnel Act. The county board of social services is composed of three or five members, appointed for three-year terms (G.S. 108A-1 through G.S. 108A-5). The county director of social services is appointed by the board according to the merit system rules of the State Personnel Commission, and is dismissed in accordance with the State Personnel Act (G.S. 108A-9). Social service employees are appointed and dismissed by the county director of social services, also in accordance with the act[13] [G.S.108A-14(2)].

Employees of the mental health, developmental disabilities, and substance abuse authority constitute the third category of competitive service employees at the county level. G.S. 122C-115 states that a county shall provide mental health, developmental disabilities, and substance abuse services through an area authority. An area authority is a local political subdivision of the state except that a single-county area authority is considered a department of the county in which it is located for purposes of Chapter 159 ("Local Government Finance," G.S. 122C-116). The governing unit of the area authority is the area board, composed of fifteen to twenty-five members appointed by the board(s) of county commissioners. Area board members may be removed with or without cause [G.S. 122C-318(b)]. The director of the area mental health, developmental disabilities, and substance abuse authority is appointed by the area authority [G.S. 122C-117(a)(7)]. The director is an employee of the area board who serves at its pleasure (G.S. 122C-121). Employees under the direct supervision of the area authority are employees of the area authority and are appointed and dismissed in accordance with the State Personnel Act [G.S. 122C-154; G.S. 126-5(a)].

Emergency management employees are the fourth category of county employees subject to the State Personnel Act. G.S. 166A-(7)(a) states that the governing body of each county is responsible for emergency management within the county, and is authorized to establish and maintain an emergency management agency. The governing body of each county that establishes an emergency management agency is to appoint a coordinator who will have a direct responsibility for the organization, administration, and operation of the county program, and will be subject to the direction and the guidance of such governing body [G.S. 166A-7(a)(2)]. Although there is no General Statutes provision on the dismissal of the coordinator, dismissal must presumably be made in accordance with the State Personnel Act. Employees of the emergency management agency are appointed and dismissed in accordance with the act [G.S. 126-5(a)].

"Substantially Equivalent" Personnel Systems

Revised federal personnel standards issued by the U.S. Office of Personnel Management after the passage of the Civil Service Reform Act of 1978 give greater flexibility to state and local governments in developing merit systems governing competitive service employees. One result of this increased flexibility has been the elimination of state competitive-selection requirements for certain county competitive-service employees. Local health and mental health positions, as well as clerical classes of social services employees, are no longer subject to the state's competitive system of selection. However, counties are expected to use merit standards—that is, recruiting and selecting employees on the basis of their relative ability, knowledge, and skills, and assuring fair treatment of applicants and employees—in filling vacancies, and to select only applicants who meet minimum qualification standards established for their class of position by the Office of State Personnel.

In addition, G.S. 126-11 permits the State Personnel Commission to exempt all county competitive service employees from portions of the State Personnel System when the commission finds that the county has a substantially equivalent personnel system for all county employees. The commission may approve as "substantially equivalent" such portions of a local personnel system as the position classification plan, the county's selection procedures, the salary administration plan, and the grievance and dismissal procedures.

Boards of county commissioners also have the option of extending the State Personnel System's coverage to other county employees besides health, mental health, social services, and emergency management personnel (G.S. 126-5). To date, however, no board of commissioners has done this.

Agricultural Extension Service Employees

Agricultural extension service employees are appointed and dismissed jointly by the board of commissioners and the Agricultural Extension Service of North Carolina State University or North Carolina Agricultural and Technical State University under a memorandum of understanding executed between the university and the county. The legal authority under which agricultural extension service agents are appointed is derived from the Smith-Lever Act; the basic memorandum of understanding; Schedule A, Section 213.3113(a)(1) of the regulations of the United States Office of Personnel Management; and an agreement between the university and the United States Department of Agriculture. The agents are entitled to certain federal benefits, including participation in the Civil Service Retirement Program, the Federal Employees' Group Life Insurance Program, and the Federal Employees' Health Benefits Program. Appointments are designated as excepted service because they are made separately from the federal competitive civil service system.

Position Classification and Salary Determination

G.S. 153A-25 provides that the board of county commissioners may fix qualifications for any appointive office. The board's most important use of this authority is to adopt a position classification plan.

A position classification plan is the basic tool of personnel administration. By adopting such a plan, the commissioners determine the duties and responsibilities of each position in advance and set the minimum qualifications as to education, training, and experience that will be required of each employee and each applicant for employment. The manager, the personnel director and staff, or an outside consultant prepares the classification plan for presentation to the board. Plan preparation involves identifying the duties and responsibilities of each position, and grouping jobs into classes similar enough in duties and responsibilities that the same job title, the same minimum qualifications, and the same pay range can apply to all positions in that class. An accurate description of duties and responsibilities and minimum qualifications can serve as a basis for or assist in all aspects of county administration, including planning, organizing, budgeting, selecting, training, paying, promoting, transferring, demoting, and discharging employees. In most counties, it is difficult if not impossible to give equal pay for equal work and unequal pay for unequal work without a classification plan.

In addition to position management, the board of commissioners has the responsibility to make compensation determinations for all county personnel.

The board of county commissioners may fix the compensation and allowances of the chairman and other board members by including their compensation and allowances in the annual budget ordinance when it is adopted. If the chair or a commissioner undertakes the duties of county manager full time, his or her salary and allowances may be adjusted during the fiscal year. Otherwise, the compensation of board members may not be changed until the next budget is adopted. The same is true of the expense allowances of board members.

The board of commissioners may fix the compensation and allowances of all other county officers and employees by adopting or amending the pay plan and approving departmental budgets. There are, however, certain restrictions on the board's authority under North Carolina law.

- Neither the register of deeds' nor the sheriff's compensation may be reduced during a term of office without the officeholder's approval or unless ordered by the Local Government Commission (G.S. 153A-92). Commissioners must give notice of intent to reduce the compensation for the next term of either office no later than fourteen days before the last day for filing as a candidate for that office. Further, the sheriff or register of deeds must approve any reduction in the salaries of employees assigned to his or her office, unless the board has made a general reduction of all county salaries subject to its control. If the board wants to reduce salaries of one or more employees of the sheriff or register of deeds and the elected officer will not agree, the board may refer the matter to the senior regular resident superior court judge for binding arbitration.

- The salaries paid to competitive service employees must conform to the pay plan approved for those departments by the State Personnel Commission (G.S. 126-9).
- All agricultural extension personnel salaries are set jointly by the North Carolina Agricultural Extension Service and the board of county commissioners, under a "Memorandum of Understanding"—a contract—entered into by the service and the board.

In addition to complying with the requirements of the North Carolina General Statutes, counties must be mindful of the requirements of the federal Fair Labor Standards Act (FLSA), 29 U.S.C. Sections 201 through 219. The FLSA is discussed in the section "Federal Statutes and County Personnel Administration," later in this chapter.

State Personnel Commission policies allow counties considerable discretion in developing local salary schedules applicable to health, mental health, social services, and emergency management employees, in order to conform to local ability to pay and fiscal policy. (As noted earlier, these persons are called "competitive service" employees because they are subject to federally mandated merit selection requirements.) With the State Personnel Commission's approval, counties may add to or reduce the number of salary steps in the state's salary schedule and may vary the percentage change between steps. The pay plan adopted by the county for these employees is subject to the State Personnel Commission's approval, and the commission may require the county to provide data and information to justify the deviation from the standard state salary ranges. A county's failure to adhere to the State Personnel Act's provisions for compensating county competitive service employees not only makes the county ineligible for certain state and federal funds but also results in an unauthorized expenditure of public money.

Despite these restrictions, the board of commissioners has an important role in determining the salaries of competitive service employees. For example, G.S. 108A-13, which authorizes the board of social services to set the social services director's salary, requires that board to obtain the approval of the board of commissioners for the salary paid. Similarly, a local health department has no authority to raise the salaries of health department employees without the board of commissioners' approval, since all county expenditures must be made in accordance with the provisions of the Local Government Budget and Fiscal Control Act (G.S. Ch. 159, Art. 3).

Merit- and longevity-based plans for giving salary increases are common in North Carolina. Longevity pay plans are popular among long-term employees, who stress several advantages of such plans:

1. They reward employees who have given the best years of their lives to the county.
2. They help to compensate for the low salaries at which many long-term employees were originally hired.
3. They provide some relief to long-term employees who are "frozen" at the top of their salary range.
4. They reduce turnover and training costs.
5. They do not cost much money.

Critics of longevity pay plans assert in response that the plans are not effective in recruiting desirable or better employees, retaining employees during the early years when turnover is higher, or retaining truly outstanding employees. They charge that the plans encourage marginal employees to stay when they should move on to other jobs.

Personnel Policies

The commissioners may adopt rules and regulations concerning matters such as annual leave, sick leave, special leave with full or partial pay supplementing workers' compensation payments, hours, workdays, holidays, service award and incentive award programs, and any other measures that promote the hiring and retention of capable, diligent, and honest career employees (G.S. 153A-94). If a board of commissioners adopts rules for county employees governing annual leave, sick leave, hours of work, holidays, and the administration of the pay plan, and files the rules with the state personnel director, these county rules supersede the State Personnel Commission rules as to leave, hours of work, and holidays that would otherwise apply to competitive service employees (G.S. 126-9). Such adopted and filed local rules as to leave, hours, and holidays also apply to county agricultural extension employees, superseding rules and regulations on these matters adopted by the Agricultural Extension Service that would otherwise govern these persons (G.S. 153A-439).

G.S. 153A-92(d) authorizes a county to provide benefits such as life or health insurance or both, for all or for any class of county officers and employees as part of their compensation. A county may also provide health insurance for all or any class of former officers and employees who are receiving benefits from the Local Governmental Employees' Retirement System. The premium for hospital, medical, or dental insurance provided by a county may be paid by the county, by the employees, or jointly. If the county pays the entire premium, all eligible employees, or all except those whose individual insurability is not satisfactory to the insurer, must be insured [G.S. 58-210(1)]. Similarly, the premium for a group life insurance policy for county employees may be paid either by the county or the employees, or the cost may be shared. The amount of life insurance under a group policy must be based on some plan that precludes individual selection by either the employees or the employer [G.S. 58-210(1),(6)]. The county may also offer its employees group accident and health insurance. Again, the premium may be paid by the county, by the employee, or jointly. If part or all of the premium is to be paid by the insured employees, the group must be structured on an actuarially sound basis [G.S. 58-254.4(b),(c)].

G.S. 153A-95 authorizes the board of commissioners to establish a personnel board with authority to administer tests; to conduct appeal hearings for employees who have been suspended, demoted, or discharged; to hear grievances; and to undertake any other duties relating to personnel administration that the commissioners may direct. The board's authority extends only to the employees under the board of commissioners' general control.

Federal Statutes and County Personnel Administration

A number of federal statutes limit a county's discretion in employment, promotion, and dismissal of employees. These are briefly summarized in the following sections.

Title VII of the Civil Rights Act of 1964

No single piece of legislation has had greater impact on the employment relationship than Title VII of the Civil Rights Act of 1964 (42 U.S.C. 2000e). Originally applicable only to private employers of fifteen or more employees, the act was amended in 1972 to apply to public employers, irrespective of the number of employees hired. The act was substantially modified by the Civil Rights Act of 1991 to provide greater rights and remedies to plaintiffs. Title VII is enforced by the United States Equal Employment Opportunity Commission (EEOC).

Title VII bars employers from hiring or dismissing or making other decisions with respect to terms and conditions of employment on the basis of race, color, religion, sex, or national origin [42 U.S.C. 2000e-2(a)(1)]. The courts have recognized two kinds of violations: disparate treatment and disparate impact. In the first, the employer is found to have intended to discriminate. In the second, what the employer intends does not matter; rather, the court considers only the question of whether the employer's personnel practices disproportionately exclude members of a protected class and, if so, if the practices be justified as job related. Most claims brought under Title VII are disparate treatment claims.

Disparate treatment claims allege intentional discrimination. An employer violates Title VII if it treats some employees or applicants less favorably than it treats others because of race, color, religion, sex, or national origin. Disparate treatment may be shown either by direct evidence or, as is usually the case, by indirect evidence.

The United States Supreme Court has created a straightforward way for an aggrieved employee or applicant to claim that he or she is the victim of unlawful discrimination. In *McDonnell Douglas Corporation v. Green*,[14] the court ruled that an applicant may create a prima facie case of discrimination in hiring (that is, enough of a case to require the employer to come forward to rebut) by showing the following:

1. The applicant belongs to a protected class.
2. The applicant applied and was qualified for a job for which the employer was seeking applicants.
3. The applicant was rejected, despite the fact that he or she met the qualifications for the job.
4. After the applicant was rejected, the employer continued to seek applicants from persons with the same qualifications as the applicant.

The employer then has the burden of presenting evidence that the applicant was rejected not because of race (or sex or another unlawful basis at issue), but because of a legitimate, nondiscriminatory reason. Such reasons might be, for example, another applicant's superior qualifications or the applicant's poor performance in the employment interview.[15] Finally, once the employer has advanced its legitimate reason for the applicant's rejection, the applicant has an opportunity to show that the employer's proffered reason is just a pretext and that the real reason is discrimination.

The Fair Labor Standards Act

The Fair Labor Standards Act (FLSA) (29 U.S.C. 201), first enacted during the Great Depression, is designed to ensure that employers meet federally mandated minimum-wage and overtime standards and maintain specified wage and hour records (29 C.F.R. Part 516). It also places certain restrictions on child labor (29 C.F.R. Part 570). The FLSA is administered and enforced by the United States Department of Labor (DOL).Under the FLSA, counties must pay the federal minimum wage and overtime to all non-exempt employees. Overtime is paid, either in wages or in comp time, at a rate of time-and-a-half for all work over forty hours in a seven-day work week for most employees, and to fire-protection employees working more than 212 hours and law enforcement officers working more than 171 hours in a twenty-eight-day work period.

The Fourth Circuit Court of Appeals recently handed down two decisions dealing with the status of emergency medical technicians (EMTs) under the FLSA, and in each case the news was not good for counties. In both cases, the counties relied on Section 7(k) of the FLSA in scheduling their EMTs, and in both cases the schedules were held to violate the Act.

Section 7(k) provides a partial exemption for public agencies employing persons "engaged in fire protection or law enforcement activities," by increasing the number of hours such employees must work above the regular forty-hour workweek before they are entitled to overtime compensation. Section 7(k) provides that a public employer need not compensate firefighters at the overtime rate until they have worked an aggregate of 212 hours for a period of twenty-eight consecutive days (fifty-three hours per week), or compensate law enforcement employees at the overtime rate until they have worked a total of 171 hours for a period of twenty-eight consecutive days (forty-three hours per week) (29 C.F.R. 553.230).

The Secretary of Labor has promulgated a regulation that permits employers to treat "ambulance and rescue service employees . . . as employees engaged in fire protection or law enforcement activities" for purposes of Section 7(k) if their services are "substantially related to fire fighting or law enforcement activities" [29 C.F.R. § 553.215(a)]. The Act, however, does not mention EMTs.

The first case, *West v. Anne Arundel County*,[16] invalidated the use of the Section 7(k) exemption as applied to EMTs on a 212-hour work schedule. The court held that because the EMTs were not performing work relating to fire fighting, the Maryland county employer could not use the 212-hour standard under the FLSA to calculate overtime entitlement.

The second case, *Roy v. County of Lexington*,[17] held that a South Carolina county could not classify its EMTs as firefighters or law enforcement officers for purposes of calculating their overtime pay, but could exclude their meal periods and sleep periods from hours worked for purposes of this calculation. As in *West*, the court held that the employees did not perform work related to fire fighting; but the court went one step further and held that the EMTs also did not perform work related to law enforcement, and thus were ineligible for participating in the lower 171-hour standard under the FLSA.

Indisputably, the court held that the EMTs in this case were employed neither "in fire protection activities" nor "in law enforcement activities"; rather, they were employed in emergency medical service activities. The court noted that sometimes employees of independent emergency service agencies assist public employees who do engage in fire and law enforcement activities. However, the court added, firefighters and police officers are assisted by a myriad of other public employees, including central communication workers, animal control and public health officers, and hospital and correctional employees. If Congress had intended to extend the scope of the Section 7(k) exemption to include employees of independent emergency service agencies, the court concluded, it certainly could have done so. Congress, however, provided no equivalent statutory exclusion for personnel of agencies engaged in "emergency medical response activities."

Although the court did not rule out the possibility that an EMT operation might be structured in a manner that would meet the Section 7(k) requirements (in that a county could demonstrate that EMTs were "regularly dispatched" to fires, crime scenes, riots, natural disasters and accidents, as provided in 29 C.F.R. 553.215), the court implied that this burden would be difficult to meet. The court held that the term "regularly dispatched" must be determined on a case by case basis, but required a showing that EMTs are dispatched with some frequency to the situations listed previously.

The bottom line in these cases is that it is increasingly unlikely that a county may successfully defend its use of the Section 7(k) exemption as applied to EMTs. A better alternative may be to place these employees under a fluctuating work week using a forty-hour standard.

The act provides that salaried executive, administrative, and professional employees are exempt from its minimum-wage and overtime provisions [29 U.S.C. 213(a)(1)]. Two tests, the "long test" and the "short test," have been adopted by the DOL to determine whether an employee meets one or more of these exemptions. An employee is exempt if he or she meets either one of the tests, found at 29 C.F.R. Part 541.

The long test for executives requires a showing that the individual meets the following criteria:

1. Has a primary duty (i.e., 50 percent or more of the time) of managing an enterprise or a department
2. Customarily and regularly directs the work of two or more employees
3. Has the authority to hire and fire employees or effectively to recommend such actions
4. Customarily and regularly exercises discretionary powers
5. Devotes no more than 20 percent of the time to nonmanagerial duties
6. Is paid on a salary basis at least $155 per week

The short test for executives requires a showing that the individual meets the following criteria:

1. Is paid on a salary basis at least $250 per week
2. Regularly directs the work of at least two employees
3. Has a primary duty of managing an enterprise or a department

The long test for administrative personnel requires a showing that the individual meets the following criteria:

1. Has a primary duty of office or nonmanual work directly related to management policies or general business operations of the employer, or responsible work directly related to academic instruction or training in an educational institution
2. Customarily and regularly exercises discretion and independent judgment
3. Regularly assists an executive or an administrator, or works under only generalized supervision along specialized or technical lines that require special training, experience, or knowledge, or executes special assignments under general supervision
4. Devotes no more than 20 percent of the time to other duties
5. Is paid on a salary basis at least $155 a week

The short test for administrative personnel requires a showing that the individual meets the following criteria:

1. Is paid on a salary basis at least $250 per week
2. Has a primary duty of office or nonmanual work directly related to management policies or general business operations of the employer, or responsible work directly related to academic instruction or training in an educational institution
3. Performs work requiring the exercise of discretion and independent judgment

The long test for professional employees requires a showing that the individual meets the following criteria:

1. Performs work requiring advanced knowledge in a field of science or learning customarily obtained by a prolonged course of specialized study
2. Consistently exercises discretion and judgment
3. Does work that is predominantly intellectual and varied in character
4. Devotes no more than 20 percent of the time to other duties; and except for physicians who qualify if they meet the preceding four conditions irrespective of salary
5. Is paid on a salary or fee basis at least $170 per week

The short test for professional personnel requires a showing that the individual meets the following criteria:

1. Is paid at least $250 a week
2. Performs work requiring advanced knowledge in a field of science or learning

The Civil Rights Acts of 1866 and 1871

After the Civil War, Congress passed two civil rights enforcement statutes to give effect to the Thirteenth, Fourteenth, and Fifteenth amendments to the United States Constitution. These acts, codified at Sections 1981 and 1983 of Title 42 of the United States Code, have been used by plaintiffs to bring claims of discrimination in employment separate and apart from Title VII.

The Civil Rights Act of 1866 is found at Section 1981. When enacted, its primary purpose was to provide an enforcement mechanism for the Thirteenth Amendment generally and to outlaw the "Black Codes" enacted by the Southern states after the Civil War. It provides that "all persons . . . shall have the same right . . . to make and enforce contracts . . . as is enjoyed by white citizens." This language allows a plaintiff to sue a government or private employer for discrimination in employment on the basis of race or national origin.

Until recently Section 1981 was limited to remedying claims of discrimination in hiring. A 1989 United States Supreme Court opinion made Section 1981 inapplicable to claims of racial harassment or other acts that occur on the job.[18] In 1991, however, Congress enacted and the President signed the Civil Rights Act of 1991, which broadens Section 1981 claims to include all aspects of employment. Under Section 1981 litigation, however, a government is not liable for discrimination by one of its employees unless that decision is traceable to an official policy or practice of the local government employer.[19]

The Civil Rights Act of 1871, found at Section 1983, provides as follows:

> Every person who, under color of any statute, ordinance, regulation, custom or usage, of any State or Territory, subjects, or causes to be subjected, any citizen of the United States or other person within the jurisdiction thereof to the deprivation of any rights, privileges or immunities secured by the Constitution and laws, shall be liable to the party injured in an action at law, suit in equity, or other proper proceeding for redress.

There is one key difference between this act (Section 1983) and the Civil Rights Act of 1866 (Section 1981): Section 1983 applies only to persons acting "under color of" state law. In other words, private employers may not be sued under this statute; only actions taken by local government entities, such as cities or counties, are covered. Also, states and state officials are not "persons" subject to liability under Section 1983 because of the Eleventh Amendment, among other reasons.[20]

The Age Discrimination in Employment Act of 1967

The Age Discrimination in Employment Act (ADEA) of 1967 (29 U.S.C. 621) prohibits discrimination on the basis of age for all persons aged forty and above. The ADEA makes it unlawful for an employer to fail or refuse to hire, to discharge any individual, or otherwise to discriminate against any individual with respect to compensation, terms, conditions, or privileges of employment because of such individual's age. The ADEA is enforced by the EEOC.

The Rehabilitation Act of 1973 and the Americans with Disabilities Act of 1990

The Rehabilitation Act of 1973 29 (U.S.C. 701) prohibits discrimination in employment against handicapped persons. The act defines the term handicapped person as any person who "(i) has a physical or mental impairment which substantially limits one or more of such person's major life activities, (ii) has a record of such an impairment, or (iii) is regarded as having such an impairment" (29 U.S.C. 706). The term "major life activities" is defined by the United States Department of Labor, Office of Federal Contract Compliance, as "communication, ambulation, selfcare, socialization, education, vocational training, employment, transportation, adapting to housing, etc." (41 C.F.R. 60-741). The act covers only recipients of federal contract funds[21] and bars discrimination against otherwise qualified handicapped persons in any program or activity receiving federal financial assistance [29 U.S.C. 794(a)]. The term "program or activity" includes a department, an agency, a special-purpose district, or another instrumentality of a state or local government [29 U.S.C. 794(b)(1)(A)].

Closely related to the Rehabilitation Act of 1973 is the Americans with Disabilities Act (ADA) of 1990 (42 U.S.C. 1201). The ADA prohibits discrimination against individuals with disabilities. Title I of the act prohibits discrimination in employment; the other titles prohibit discrimination in public services and transportation, public accommodations, and telecommunications. Title I of the ADA prohibits covered employers from discriminating against a qualified disabled individual in any aspect of employment, including hiring, promotion, dismissal, compensation, training, or any other term, condition, or privilege of employment. Specific prohibitions include limiting, segregating, or classifying a job applicant or an employee in a way that adversely affects the opportunities or the status of that individual because of a disability; using standards or criteria that have the effect of discriminating against the disabled; denying job benefits or opportunities to someone because of his or her association or relationship with a disabled individual; not making reasonable accommodations; using employment tests or selection criteria that screen out the disabled and are not job related; and failing to use tests that accurately measure job abilities.

The Family and Medical Leave Act of 1993

The Family and Medical Leave Act (FMLA) of 1993 (29 U.S.C. 2601) generally requires private sector employers of fifty or more employees, and all public agencies, to provide up to twelve workweeks of unpaid, job-protected leave to eligible employees for certain specified family and medical reasons. The act also ensures that while employees are on FMLA leave they are able to maintain health care coverage. Employees who take FMLA leave are entitled to return to the same position they left or an equivalent position at the conclusion of their leave.

State Employment Statutes

The North Carolina General Assembly has enacted various employment laws that govern both private and public employers, including counties. Selected North Carolina employment statutes are summarized in this section.

Unemployment Compensation

G.S. Chapter 96, Article 2, sets forth an employer-financed program to provide partial income-replacement benefits to employees who lose their jobs or have their work hours reduced to less than 60 percent of their last schedule. The program is authorized by the Federal Unemployment Tax Act, which levies a tax of 6.2 percent of payroll, with tax credits of up to 5.4 percent for state unemployment taxes paid. The program is administered by the North Carolina Employment Security Commission (ESC). County governments have been covered under the program since 1976 [G.S. 96-8(5)(p)]. Individuals are eligible for benefits if they register for work and continue to report at the ESC employment office, make a claim for benefits, and are able and available to work [G.S. 96-13(a)]. The procedure for filing unemployment insurance claims, including appeals from denials of benefits, is set forth in G.S. 96-15. There is a right of appeal from ESC decisions to superior court; however, the court's review is limited to two inquiries: (1) whether there was evidence before the commission to support its findings of fact; and (2) whether the facts found sustained the conclusions of law and the resultant decision of the commission.[22] An individual may be disqualified for benefits if he or she has left work voluntarily and without good cause attributable to the employer. Further, if the ESC determines that an individual was discharged for misconduct connected with the work, or was discharged for substantial fault, then benefits will be denied.

The term *misconduct connected with the work* is defined as

> conduct evincing such willful or wanton disregard of an employer's interest as is found in deliberate violations or disregard of standards of behavior which the employer has the right to expect of his employee, or in carelessness or negligence of such degree or recurrence as to manifest equal culpability, wrongful intent or evil design, or to show an intentional and substantial disregard of the employer's interests or of the employee's duties and obligations to his employer. . . . [The term also includes] reporting to work significantly impaired by alcohol or illegal drugs; consuming alcohol or illegal drugs on employer's premises; conviction by a court of competent jurisdiction for manufacturing, selling, or distribution of a controlled substance punishable under G.S. 90-95(a)(1) or G.S. 90-95(a)(2) while in the employ of said employer.[23]

A finding of a voluntary quit or discharge for misconduct by the ESC results in disqualification of the claimant for benefits. A finding of substantial fault results in disqualification for a period of four to thirteen weeks, after which the claimant is eligible for benefits. A claimant may also be disqualified for refusal of a suitable offer of work.

Collective Bargaining

G.S. 95, Article 12, is a comprehensive ban on collective bargaining by public employees. One provision, G.S. 95-97, which purports to prohibit public employees from becoming members of trade unions or labor unions, was held unconstitutional in *Atkins v. City of Charlotte*[24] and is of no effect. Thus municipal employees may exercise their First Amendment right of association and speech by belonging to labor unions, despite the statute. In contrast, G.S. 95-98, which makes contracts between any city, town, or municipality and any labor organization "illegal, unlawful, void, and of no effect," was upheld in *Atkins* as a valid and constitutional exercise of the legislature's authority. Nothing in the statute affects the right of employees and labor organizations to present their views to city councils and officials, however, to the same extent as other citizens.[25] Finally, G.S. 95-98.1 and G.S. 95-98.2 prohibit strikes by public employees, and G.S. 95-99 makes the violation of Article 12 a misdemeanor. The constitutionality of these latter provisions has never been tested.

Restrictions on Political Activity

North Carolina law makes it a crime to give or promise any political appointment or support for political office, in return for political support or influence [G.S. 163-274(9)]. Similarly, it is unlawful for any county officer or employee to intimidate or oppress any other officer or employee on account of the way that person or any member of his family exercises his right to vote (G.S. 163-271).

In 1991 the General Assembly enacted G.S. 153A-99 to prohibit county employers and employees from engaging in certain political activities. Employees are barred while on duty or in the workplace from using official authority or influence to interfere with or affect the result of an election or a nomination for political office, or to coerce, solicit or compel contributions from employees for political or partisan purposes. No employee may be required to contribute funds to a political campaign, and employees are barred from using county funds, supplies, or equipment for partisan political purposes.

Several boards of county commissioners have adopted additional restrictions on political activity by appointive county employees, including prohibitions on running for partisan office.

Workers' Compensation

All county employees are automatically covered by North Carolina's workers' compensation law (G.S. 97-2 and 97-7). A county may not reject coverage. Under the law, a county is liable only for accidents that arise out of and in the course of employment. It may cover its liability for compensation payments either by purchasing insurance or by self-insuring.

Volunteer members of rural fire departments are also covered by the workers' compensation law. Most counties that aid rural fire departments financially require them to carry workers' compensation insurance. Compensation payable to a volunteer firefighter disabled under compensable circumstances is calculated from the firefighter's earnings in his principal employment, and must be at least two-thirds of the maximum weekly benefit. The North Carolina Industrial Commission, which hears workers' compensation cases, considers members of volunteer rescue squads as county employees for purposes of workers' compensation coverage.

Defense of Employees

G.S. 153A-97 and G.S. 160A-167 authorize counties, on request, to provide for the defense of any civil or criminal action or proceeding brought against a present or former county employee, officer, or governing board member or a member of a volunteer fire department or rescue squad that receives public funds, on account of that person's conduct in the scope and course of his employment. Similarly, local health department sanitarians are entitled to legal defense by the state attorney general for their actions arising from the enforcement of state public health. In either case, assistance may be provided whether the person is sued or charged as an individual or in his official capacity (G.S. 143-300.8).

The county may defend either by employing legal counsel or by purchasing insurance. If certain conditions are met, the county may also pay claims or civil judgments for its officers, employees, or governing board members. The county is also authorized to insure itself and any officer or employee against liability for wrongful death or negligent or intentional damage to person or property caused by the officer or employee acting within the scope of his authority and in the course of his employment.[26]

Personnel Records

G.S. 153A-98 exempts the personnel files of county employees from the provisions of G.S. 132-6, the statute requiring that public records be made available for inspection and copying. Under G.S. 153A-98, certain information in personnel files is open to the public and other information is not to be disclosed except under special circumstances. Both present and former employees are covered by the statute.

The contents of the personnel file or personnel record are broadly defined. Under the statute, a "personnel record" consists of any information relating to an employee's application, selection or nonselection, performance, promotions, demotions, transfers, suspensions and other disciplinary actions, evaluation forms, leave, salary, and termination of employment. G.S. 153A-98 divides the contents of the personnel file into three types of information and then states special circumstances that pertain to each category.

The first type of information is open to the public. It includes each employee's name; age; date of original employment; current position title; current salary; date and amount of most recent salary change; date of most recent promotion, demotion, transfer, suspension, separation, or other change in position classification; and the office to which the employee is assigned. Anyone may inspect and copy these records during regular business hours, subject only to rules established by the board of commissioners for the records' safekeeping. Anyone who is denied access may seek a court order compelling disclosure.

The second type of information is closed to the public but is open to six groups of persons. The act does not list the items that fall into this category but they presumably include the application, previous salary, home address, telephone number, previous title, previous employment, amount of sick leave used, performance rating, and nature of personnel actions. This information is available to the following persons:

1. The employee or former employee
2. His or her authorized agent
3. The employee's supervisor
4. A public official whose inspection of the information is deemed essential to the performance of the official's duties by the custodian of the personnel records
5. The professional representative of a training, research, or academic institution (the board of commissioners must approve

this release and must require the researcher to make certifications concerning the use of the files and the maintenance of
anonymity)

6. A person authorized by a court

One of the special provisions concerning records in this category
allows an employee, by signing a written release, to permit all or a part
of the previously listed information to be released in person, by telephone, or by mail to prospective employers, educational institutions, or
others. A second special provision specifies that reference letters secured before an employee was hired are not to be made available to
either the employee or his or her representative. A third provision prevents an employee from seeing information in his or her file concerning a mental or physical medical disability that a prudent physician
would not divulge to his or her patient. However, a licensed physician
designated in writing by the employee may examine the employee's
medical record.

The third type of information may be made available to the employee or others listed previously, but need not be. This category includes testing or examination materials and information that identifies
an undercover agent. Investigative reports or memoranda concerning
possible criminal action need not be disclosed until the investigation is
completed or the criminal action concluded. At that time, the report
must be made available to the employee or his representative upon request. Similarly, notes, preliminary drafts, and internal communications
concerning an employee need not be disclosed until they have been
used for an official personnel decision.

No information in the personnel file is to be divulged for the purpose of assisting in either a criminal prosecution of the employee or an
investigation of the employee's tax liability. On the other hand, the
name, address, and telephone number from a personnel file may be
released for the purpose of otherwise aiding a criminal investigation.

G.S. 153A-98 also allows county officials in certain circumstances to
release information telling the "county's side" of a personnel action. If
the county manager, with the board of commissioners' concurrence, or
the board of commissioners if the county has no manager, determines
in writing that the release of information is essential to maintaining
public confidence in the administration of services or the level and
quality of public services, the manager or board may inform any person
of any personnel action and the reason for the action. A copy of this

written determination must be retained in the office of the manager or the clerk to the board for public inspection. The written determination must also be made a part of the employee's personnel file.

If an employee thinks that material in his or her personnel file is inaccurate or misleading, he or she may seek to have it removed through procedures established by the board of commissioners or may place a statement relating to the material in the file.

A public official who knowingly, willfully, and with malice gives anyone access to information contained in a personnel file, except as G.S. 153A-98 permits, is guilty of a misdemeanor. Any unauthorized person who knowingly and willfully examines, removes, or copies any portion of a confidential personnel file also commits a misdemeanor.

Additional Resources

Allred, Stephen. *Employment Law, A Guide for North Carolina Public Employers,* 2d ed. (Chapel Hill, N.C.: Institute of Government, The University of North Carolina at Chapel Hill, 1995).

Notes

1. As of 1997, 99 out of 100 counties had managers. The MAPS Group, *County Salaries in North Carolina 1998* (Chapel Hill, N.C.: Institute of Government, The University of North Carolina at Chapel Hill, 1998), 2–4.

2. The general statement of the employment-at-will rule in North Carolina is found in Soles v. City of Raleigh Civil Serv. Comm'n, 345 N.C. 443, 446, 480 S.E.2d 685, 687 (1997); Harris v. Duke Power Co., 319 N.C. 627, 629, 356 S.E.2d 357, 359 (1987); and Still v. Lance, 279 N.C. 254, 259, 182 S.E.2d 403, 406 (1971).

3. For example, Article 21 of Chapter 95 of the General Statutes prohibits dismissal of an employee because the employee files a complaint or otherwise participates in a proceeding under the Workers' Compensation Act, the Occupational Safety and Health Act, the Wage and Hour Act, or the Mine Safety and Health Act.

4. 325 N.C. 172, 381 S.E.2d 445 (1989).

5. *Id.* at 176, 381 S.E.2d at 447.

6. *See, e.g.,* Cleveland Bd. of Educ. v. Loudermill, 470 U.S. 532, 541–42 (1985) and cases cited therein.

7. Faulkner v. North Carolina Dep't of Correction, 428 F. Supp. 100 (W.D.N.C. 1977).

8. 839 F.2d 225 (4th Cir. 1988).

9. *Id.* at 229.

10. 347 N.C. 349, 492 S.E.2d 355 (1997).

11. *See* Peele v. Provident Mut. Life Ins. Co., 90 N.C. App. 447, 449, 368 S.E.2d 892, 894 (1988) (summary judgment granted for sheriff in wrongful discharge action by former dispatcher: "It is clear to this court that plaintiff was an employee of the sheriff and not Watauga County and its Board of Commissioners").

12. The federal standards for a merit system of personnel administration are found at 29 C.F.R. § 900.603 (1983). Section 900.605 authorizes federal agencies to require the establishment of a merit personnel system as a condition for receiving federal funds. Section 900.603(a) requires recruitment, selection, and advancement of employees on the basis of their relative ability, knowledge, and skills and requires open consideration of qualified applicants for initial appointment. The regulations of the State Personnel Commission incorporate the federal standards by reference at 25 NCAC 01 .0601.

13. *In re* Brunswick County, 81 N.C. App. 391, 344 S.E.2d 584 (1986) (director has exclusive power to hire and fire department personnel).

14. 411 U.S. 792, 802 (1973).

15. The Supreme Court has elaborated on the standard originally set forth in *McDonnell Douglas* no less than five times since its inception. See Teamsters v. United States, 431 U.S. 324, 335 n.15 (1977); Furnco Constr. Corp. v. Waters, 438 U.S. 567, 577 (1978); Board of Trustees of Keene State College v. Sweeney, 439 U.S. 24, 25 (1978); Texas Dep't of Community Affairs v. Burdine, 450 U.S. 248, 253–55 (1981); and United States Postal Serv. Bd. of Governors v. Aikens, 460 U.S. 711, 715 (1983).

16. 137 F.3d 792 (4th Cir. 1998).

17. 4 Wage & Hour Cas. 2d (BNA) 869 (4th Cir. 1998).

18. In St. Francis College v. Al-Khazraji, 481 U.S. 604 (1987), and Shaare Tefila Congregation v. Cobb, 481 U.S. 615 (1987), the United States Supreme Court held that Section 1981 claims were not limited to race discrimination but included claims by persons "who are subjected to intentional discrimination solely because of their ancestry or ethnic characteristics," such as Arabs. 481 U.S. at 613.

19. Patterson v. McClean Credit Union, 491 U.S. 164 (1989).

20. Jett v. Dallas Indep. Sch. Dist., 491 U.S. 701 (1989).

21. Will v. Michigan Dep't of State Police, 491 U.S. 58 (1989). It should be noted, however, that state officials who are sued in their individual capacities are "persons" subject to suits under Section 1983; the Eleventh Amendment does not bar such suits in federal court. Hafer v. Melo, 502 U.S. 21 (1991).

22. Consolidated Rail Corp. v. Darrone, 465 U.S. 624, 636 (1984).

23. Employment Sec. Comm'n v. Kermon, 232 N.C. 342, 60 S.E.2d 580 (1950).

24. *See* Lynch v. PPG Industries, 105 N.C. App. 223, 412 S.E.2d 163 (1992) (conviction of employee for possession of cocaine with intent to sell or deliver was misconduct); West v. Georgia-Pacific Corp., 107 N.C. App. 600, 421 S.E.2d 395 (1992) (employee who reported to work under the influence of alcohol and who refused offer to participate in employee assistance program was discharged for misconduct); Hester v. Hanes Knitwear, 61 N.C. App. 730, 301 S.E.2d 508, *cert. denied*, 308 N.C. 676, 304 S.E.2d 755 (1983) (use of marijuana on employer's property during working hours in violation of employer's rules constituted misconduct).

25. 296 F. Supp. 1068 (W.D.N.C. 1969).

26. Hickory Fire Fighters Ass'n, Local 2653 v. City of Hickory, 656 F.2d 917 (4th Cir. 1981).

14 Purchasing and Contracting and Conflicts of Interest

Frayda S. Bluestein

Contents

Frayda S. Bluestein is an Institute of Government faculty member who specializes in local government purchasing and contracting.

The author wishes to express her appreciation to Warren Jake Wicker whose work in public purchasing and authorship of this chapter in the previous editions of this book are reflected in this edition's chapter.

Obtaining the goods and services for the operation of county government is a major administrative responsibility. This chapter discusses the following:

- state laws that establish the governing board's authority to contract
- the legal requirement that each expenditure be supported by an appropriation
- the organization of the contracting function within county government
- competitive bidding procedures that must be followed for certain types of contracts
- the laws governing conflicts of interest in contracting (The laws governing board member conflicts of interest in voting are discussed in Chapter 1.)

Contracting Authority

The authority to contract is among the basic powers the General Assembly delegates to counties in G.S. 153-11, a statute that provides counties with the broad corporate powers necessary to govern and conduct the basic activities of the county. Other statutes authorize counties to perform particular functions and contain specific contracting powers.

The authority to contract generally rests with the governing board. The governing board may delegate contracting authority to other county officials unless a statute specifically requires board action. For example, competitive bidding laws require the governing board to award construction or repair contracts that are subject to the formal bidding requirements, but the board may delegate the authority to award smaller contracts and contracts not subject to bidding to other county officials.

Counties have specific authority to enter into contracts that extend beyond the current fiscal year. G.S. 153A-13 allows the governing board to approve continuing contracts and requires the board to appropriate the amount due in each subsequent year for the duration of the contract. Contracts generally continue to bind the county despite changes in board membership or philosophy. Courts have held that this rule does not apply to any contract that limits essential governmental discretion, such as an agreement not to annex property, or a contract in which the county promises not to raise taxes. Most county contracts, however, involve basic commercial transactions and, assuming compliance with all applicable procedures, will be enforceable against the county for the duration of the contract.

Expenditures Supported by Appropriations

State laws governing local government finance require counties to establish internal procedures designed to ensure that sufficient appropriated funds are available to pay contractual obligations. Contracts involving the expenditure of funds that are included in the budget ordinance must be "preaudited" to ensure that they are being spent in accordance with a budget appropriation and that they have not already been committed to another obligation. All written contracts must contain a certification of the finance officer or deputy finance officer, as specified in G.S. 159-28(a), stating that the instrument has been "preaudited in the manner required by the Local Government Budget and Fiscal Control Act." The statute provides that the finance officer is personally liable for any funds committed in violation of the preaudit requirement, and contracts that do not contain the preaudit certificate are void and cannot be enforced against the county.[1]

Most local governments use computerized financial systems that automatically conduct the preaudit procedure. These programs keep track of appropriated funds by category or account and *encumber* obligations as they are created by removing them from the pool of available funds. The system will notify the user if a requested expenditure exceeds the funds available, requiring either that the transaction be canceled or that funds be transferred from another account sufficient to cover the obligation.

Organization of the Contracting Function

Responsibility for contracting within the county should be allocated in a manner that best balances the need for efficiency and flexibility with the need to comply with legal contracting and fiscal internal control requirements. Under G.S. 153A-76 the county governing board has the authority to establish organizational arrangements for administration, including contracting. The main organizational consideration for contracting is the degree to which the function will be centralized.

Degree of Centralization

Most counties have some degree of centralization. In large counties it is common to appoint a full-time purchasing agent who has responsibility for complying with competitive bidding procedures and with locally established contracting procedures on behalf of the separate departments. Centralization can generate cost savings and efficiencies by accumulating needs, taking advantage of economies of scale, and eliminating duplication of effort. In addition, a purchasing staff has expertise in developing specifications and contract terms, identifying and evaluating sources of supply, and overseeing inspection and delivery. When these functions are handled by a purchasing staff, officials in other departments can better concentrate on their core missions and functions.

Centralization may not be an option in small counties with limited staff. In these situations, purchasing may be combined with other tasks within the finance office or within each separate department. In addition, centralization is sometimes criticized as creating delays and lacking flexibility in obtaining needed goods and services for departments. As a result of management philosophies that emphasize empowerment of front-line workers and departmental independence, some local governments have decentralized some or all contracting responsibility. It is also common for certain county departments, such as the health, mental health, social services, and sheriff's departments, to handle their own contracting. In the case of human services programs, this is largely due to their separate funding, reimbursement, and accounting requirements. In the case of the sheriff's department, this pattern reflects the sheriff's separate statutory responsibility for the administration of the jail and law enforcement activities within the county. Despite the decentralization of contracting in these cases, it is clear that all county departments are subject to the state laws governing contracting, as well as to the local procedures established by the county commissioners, regardless of how the responsibility for contracting is allocated.

Local Procedures for Small Purchases and Other Special Cases

Organization of the contracting function includes not only assigning staffing responsibility but also establishing policies for contracting procedures where they are not specified by state law. Mainly this involves establishing procedures for contracts that fall below the informal bidding threshold (discussed later), and for service contracts, which are not subject to competitive bidding requirements. It is common for some service contracts to be handled by the department needing the service because these contracts often involve specialized needs better understood by the department needing the service than by a centralized contracting authority.

For small purchases it is important to establish procedures that provide sufficient documentation of the expenditure but do not involve too much paperwork. It is also important to consider paperwork when setting the local threshold below which competitive bidding is not required. It may not be cost-effective to require competition for very small purchases because the administrative effort probably outweighs any cost saving. Examples of approaches to small purchases used by local governments in North Carolina include the following:

1. Procurement cards (cards issued to individuals or departments within the unit, with limited purchasing authority for small purchases paid on a master monthly bill)
2. Term contracts with fixed prices (for commonly used items, such as office supplies)
3. Blanket purchase orders (preaudited, open purchase orders to be used for unpredictable needs)

Cooperative Arrangements

North Carolina local governments also have the option of joining with other local governments in cooperative or joint purchasing arrangements. Under G.S. 160A, Article 20, local governments can enter into interlocal agreements to carry out jointly or cooperatively any function they have the authority to conduct. Under this authority, local governments can accumulate needs to realize economies of scale. Recent examples include the cooperative purchase of poles for electrical systems, chemicals for water and wastewater treatment plants, and recycled products. Typically in cooperative arrangements, the units agree to designate one unit to handle the contract on behalf of the rest. Local governments also have the option of participating in term contracts awarded by the state purchasing agency, commonly referred to as "buying off state contract," which is another form of cooperative purchasing that is discussed in more detail later.

Another opportunity for cooperation is the merger of city and county purchasing departments. At least two counties in North Carolina (Forsyth and Mecklenburg) have merged their purchasing departments with the major city located in the county (Winston-Salem and Charlotte, respectively), creating a joint purchasing arrangement.

Competitive Bidding Procedures

Contracts Covered by Bidding Laws

State law requires counties to obtain competitive bids before awarding certain types of contracts. The competitive bidding process is designed to prevent collusion and favoritism in the award of contracts and to generate favorable pricing to conserve public funds. As discussed later, the law does not always require contracts to be awarded to the lowest-dollar bid, and the bidding requirements are best viewed as requiring prudent investment of public dollars. This means that quality and value can be as important as initial price in evaluating products and contractors in competitively bid contracts.

The two key bidding statutes, G.S. 143-129 (formal bidding) and G.S. 143-131 (informal bidding), apply to two categories of contracts: (1) contracts for the purchase or lease-purchase of "apparatus, supplies, materials, or equipment" (hereinafter purchase contracts), and (2) contracts for construction or repair work. Contracts that do not fall within these two categories are not subject to the competitive bidding requirements. Informal bidding procedures apply to contracts costing from $5,000 to the formal limit. The formal procedures apply to contracts for construction or repair work estimated to cost $100,000 or more, and to purchase contracts estimated to cost $30,000 or more. Construction or repair contracts or purchase contracts costing less than $5,000 do not require competition of any kind, although it is common for counties to continue to use some form of informal bidding process for contracts costing $1,000 or more.

Contracts for services, such as janitorial, grounds maintenance, and solid waste collection, as well as contracts for professional services, such as attorneys and auditors, fall outside the scope of the competitive bidding statutes. (As discussed later, special rules apply to contracts for architectural, engineering, and surveying services.) Contracts for the purchase of real property and contracts for the lease (rental) of real or personal property also fall outside the scope of the laws that require competitive bidding. It is important to note that contracts for the lease-purchase of property, the installment purchase of property, or the lease with option to purchase property *are* subject to competitive bidding.

It is common for counties to seek competitive bids on contracts even when state law does not require it. This is a good practice whenever there is competition for a particular service or product. Counties often use the statutory procedures when seeking competition voluntarily, but this is not required. It is important for the county to specify what procedures and standards it will use for awarding contracts in solicitations that are not subject to state statutes, especially if the procedures will be different from those set forth in the statutes. The county is legally bound to adhere to the procedures it opts to use when bidding is not required by statute, or it may terminate the procedure and contract using some other procedure if it deems this to be in its best interest.

Exceptions to Bidding Requirements

State laws contain a number of exceptions to the competitive requirements. County officials should be cautious when contracting without bidding to make sure that the situation falls within an exception. Courts have recognized the importance of the public policy underlying the bidding requirements and have strictly scrutinized local government justifications for claiming an exemption from bidding.

The major exceptions to the competitive bidding requirements are as follows:

- **Emergencies—G.S. 143-129(a).** An exception applies "in cases of special emergency involving the health and safety of the people or their property." The only North Carolina case interpreting the emergency exception indicates that it is very limited, applying only when the emergency is immediate, unforeseeable, and cannot be resolved within the minimum time required to comply with the bidding procedures.[2]
- **Purchases from other governments—G.S. 143-129(e).** Counties may purchase directly from any other unit of government or government agency (federal, state, or local) and may purchase at government surplus sales.
- **Sole sources—G.S. 143-129(f).** This exception applies to purchase contracts only, when performance or price competition is not available, when a needed product is available from only one source of supply, or when standardization or compatibility is the overriding consideration. The governing board must approve each contract entered into under this exception, even if the board has delegated authority to award purchase contracts under G.S. 143-129(a).
- **Purchase from existing contractor ("piggybacking")—G.S. 143-129(g).** Counties may purchase from a contractor who has entered into a competitively bid contract with any other unit of government or government agency (federal, state, or local) within the past twelve months and who is willing to extend the same or more favorable prices and terms to the county. This exception applies to purchase contracts only. The governing board must approve each contract entered into under this exception at a regular board meeting on ten days' public notice, even if the board has delegated authority to award purchase contracts under G.S. 143-129(a).
- **State contract purchases—G.S. 143-49(6).** The Division of Purchase and Contract, the state agency charged with responsibility for purchasing on behalf of all state agencies, local schools, and community colleges, has legal authority to make its services available to cities, counties, and other nonstate agencies under G.S. 143-49(6). The division gives counties an opportunity to participate in state term contracts for a wide variety of goods, usually by requiring the county to indicate in writing its

commitment to participate in each contract before the division puts it out to bid. Counties are not *required* to participate, but once a county commits to do so, it is required to purchase all of its needs for that particular commodity from the state contract vendor. The differences between this procedure and the piggybacking exception described above are that (1) once a county signs on to participate in a state contract, the state contract vendor is obligated to extend the state contract terms and prices to the county; and (2) no further board approval or public notice is required to purchase under the contract. There is no explicit exception in the competitive bidding laws for purchases under state contracts in which the unit has agreed to participate, but it is considered a form of cooperative purchasing that is implicitly authorized by the authority in G.S. 143-49(6).

- **Gasoline, fuel, oil—G.S. 143-129(a).** Purchases of gasoline, diesel fuel, alcohol fuel, motor oil, or fuel oil are exempt from the formal bidding procedures but must be carried out using the informal procedures under G.S. 143-131.

- **Force account work—G.S. 143-135.** For construction or repair work, bidding is not required for projects to be completed using the county's own employees. This exception actually operates as a limitation on the amount of work that may be done by county forces. The exception limits such work to projects estimated to cost no more than $125,000 including the cost of labor and materials, or to projects on which the cost of labor does not exceed $50,000. The competitive bidding statutes still apply to materials to be used on force account projects. Some have argued that the exception to the bidding requirements does not limit the use of the county's own forces as long as the county itself submits a bid. There does not appear to be any authority in the statutes for a county to submit a bid to itself as a way of complying with bidding requirements and avoiding application of the force account limit.

Specifications

Competitive specifications are essential elements of a bidding process. On the other hand, there is no need for the county to invite bids on products that do not meet the county's minimum quality standards or functional requirements. There are no statutory procedures governing the preparation of specifications for purchases. County officials may develop specifications they deem most appropriate except that they cannot intentionally or unjustifiably eliminate competition by using overly restrictive specifications. If only one brand of product is suitable, the specification can be limited to that brand, although the county may be called upon by competitors to consider products alleged to be comparable, or to justify the elimination of other products from consideration. A brand-specific specification is not necessarily a sole-source purchase since there may be more than one supplier of a particular brand.

A separate statute imposes specific limitations on the development of specifications for construction or repair projects. G.S. 133-3 requires that specifications for materials included in construction projects be described in terms of performance characteristics, and it allows brands to be specified only when performance specification is not possible. In such cases, at least three brands must be specified unless it is impossible do so, in which case the specifications must include as many brands as possible.

Trade-ins

G.S. 143-129.7 authorizes local governments to include in specifications a trade-in of surplus property to be included in the bid, and to consider the price offered, including the trade-in allowance, when awarding a contract. This statute effects an exemption from otherwise applicable procedures for disposing of surplus property. See Chapter 15 for a full description of procedures for disposing of property.

Summary of Bidding Procedures

Informal Bidding

Contracts for construction or repair work, or for the purchase of apparatus, supplies, materials, or equipment costing between $5,000 and the formal bidding limit, are subject to the informal bidding statute, G.S. 143-131. The statute requires the county to obtain informal bids. No advertisement is required, and the statute does not specify a minimum number of bids that must be received. Informal bids can be obtained in the form of telephone quotes, faxed bids, or written bids. The statute requires that the county maintain a record of informal bids received and specifies that such records are subject to public inspection after the contract is awarded. This prevents bidders from having access to bids already submitted when preparing their bids, a situation not present in formal bidding because bids are sealed until the bid opening. The standard for awarding contracts in the informal range is the same as the standard for formal bids. It is discussed later in this chapter.

Formal Bidding

Advertisement

The formal bidding statute, G.S. 143-129, requires counties to advertise opportunities to bid on contracts for construction or repair, or purchase of apparatus, supplies, materials, and equipment, within the formal bid thresholds listed earlier. The advertisement must appear at least one time no less than one week before the date of the bid opening. It is common practice to place the advertisement more than once or for a long period of time prior to the bid opening, but the minimum requirement under the statute is one week. The advertisement must list the date and time of the bid opening, identify where specifications may be obtained, and contain a statement that the board reserves the right to reject any or all bids. For construction projects, the advertisement may also contain information about contractor licensing requirements that apply to the project.

Sealed Bids

Bids must be sealed and must be submitted prior to the time of the bid opening. Bids must be opened in public and must be recorded in the governing board's minutes. Staff generally conduct bid openings, and a summary of bids is reported to the board and incorporated into the minutes later. If the board has delegated the authority to award purchase contracts as authorized in G.S. 143-129(a), the summary of bids may be reported to the board after the contract is awarded.

Once bids are opened, they are public records and are subject to public inspection. The only exception to this rule is contained in G.S. 132-1.2, which allows a bidder to identify trade secrets that are contained in a bid and protects that information from public disclosure.

Number of Bids

According to G.S. 143-132, three bids are required for construction or repair contracts that are subject to the formal bidding procedures. If three bids are not received after the first advertisement, the project must be readvertised at least one week before the next bid opening. Following the second advertisement, a contract can be awarded even if fewer than three bids are received.

Note that the statute only applies to contracts for construction or repair work in the formal bidding range. This means that three bids are not required for purchase contracts in the formal range, or for any contracts in the informal range. Some counties may have local policies that require three bids for all contracts, but this is not required by state law.

Bid, Performance, and Payment Bonds

Bids submitted in the formal process must be accompanied by a bid deposit or bid bond of at least 5 percent of the bid amount. For purchase contracts, the statute authorizes the board or official to whom responsibility has been delegated, to waive the bid-deposit requirement. The bid bond or deposit guarantees that the bidder to whom a contract is awarded will execute a contract and provide performance and payment bonds when they are required. The statute specifies the forms in which the bid security may be submitted: a bid bond, a bid deposit in cash, a cashier's check, or a certified check.

For construction or repair contracts, specific procedures are set forth in G.S. 143-129.1 for the withdrawal of a bid. A bid may be withdrawn under those procedures without forfeiting the bid bond only if the bidder can demonstrate that he or she has made an unintentional error as opposed to an error in judgment. The law does not allow a bidder to correct a mistake, only to withdraw a bid if proof of an unintentional error is shown. There is no comparable statute for purchase contracts, but most local governments follow the withdrawal procedures in the statute governing construction contracts for mistakes in bids on purchase contracts.

The formal bidding statute also requires that the county obtain performance and payment bonds from the successful bidder. For construction or repair contracts, this requirement applies to any contract of $100,000 or more, as well as to any contract of $15,000 or more if it is part of a project costing $100,000 or more. The governing board or person to whom authority has been delegated may waive the performance and payment bond requirement for purchase contracts. The statute authorizes the county to accept a deposit of cash, a certified check, or government securities in lieu of bonds.

A performance bond guarantees performance of the contract and provides the county with security in the event that the contractor defaults and cannot complete the contract. The payment bond is obtained for the benefit of subcontractors who supply labor or materials to the project and provides a source of payment to those contractors in the event that they are not paid by the general contractor.

Evaluation of Bids; Responsiveness

Once received, bids must be evaluated to determine whether they meet the specifications and are eligible for award—that is, whether they are responsive bids. The bid evaluation process is important to maintaining the integrity of the bidding process. If the county accepts bids that contain significant deviations from the specifications, the other bidders may object. Indeed, courts have recognized that a government unit receiving bids does not have unlimited discretion in waiving deviations from specifications. In *Professional Food Services Management v. North Carolina Department of Administration,* the court held that the unit must reject a bid that contains a "material variance" from the specifications, defined as a variance that gives the bidder "an advantage or benefit not enjoyed by the other bidders."[3] Thus if a bid offers something outside the scope of the specifications that the unit finds desirable, the appropriate response is to reject all the bids, revise the specifications to incorporate the desired feature, and rebid the contract.

Standard for Awarding Contracts

Both the formal and informal bid statutes require that contracts be awarded to the "lowest responsible bidder, taking into consideration quality, performance, and the time specified in the proposals for the performance of the contract" [G.S. 143-129(b), 143-131]. Although this standard probably creates a presumption in favor of the bidder who submits the lowest dollar bid, it clearly does not require an award to the lowest bid in all cases. The North Carolina Court of Appeals has held that the statute authorizes the board to request information from the bidders about their experience and financial strength and to consider this information in determining whether the low bidder is responsible.[4] The court held that the term *responsibility* refers to the bidder's capacity to perform the contract and that the statute authorizes the board to evaluate the bidder's experience, training and quality of personnel, financial strength, and any other factors that bear on the bidder's ability to perform the work.

It is somewhat less clear whether this standard of award allows the county to award a contract for the purchase of apparatus, supplies, materials, or equipment to a bidder who proposes a more expensive, higher quality piece of equipment than the lowest bidder. Assuming all of the items proposed are within the scope of the specifications, it seems reasonable to interpret the statute as allowing the board to choose a higher quality item if this is the best investment of public funds.

The county must carefully document the factual basis for any award to a bidder who did not submit the lowest dollar bid and be diligent in investigating the facts to make sure that the information it relies upon is accurate and reliable. The county does not necessarily have to demonstrate that a contractor is not responsible generally, only that the contractor does not have the skills, experience, or financial capacity for the job in question.

Construction or repair contracts that are subject to the formal bidding requirements must be awarded by the governing body. For purchase contracts, G.S. 143-129(a) authorizes the board to delegate to the manager or chief purchasing official the authority to award contracts, reject bids and readvertise, and waive bonding requirements where otherwise allowed by statute. The informal bidding statute does not dictate who must award contracts. This responsibility is usually delegated to the purchasing agent or other employees responsible for handling informal contracts.

Special Rules for Building Contracts

Multiple-Prime Contracting

A separate statute, G.S. 143-128, establishes two significant requirements in addition to the bidding requirements in G.S. 143-129 for construction or repair contracts involving buildings. For building construction projects costing $500,000 or more, bids must be solicited separately in at least four categories of work:

1. General contracting
2. Heating, ventilating, and air conditioning
3. Plumbing
4. Electrical

This method of contracting is called *multiple-prime* or *separate-prime* contracting. The statute authorizes counties to receive bids on a single-prime basis (that is, one bid for the entire project), in addition to the multiple-prime basis. Local governments do not have the legal authority to solicit bids *solely* on a single-prime basis if the project exceeds $500,000.

The multiple-prime requirement, in most cases, eliminates the option of constructing buildings using a "design-build" system, in which a single contract is awarded for the design and construction of a project. The county can apply to the State Building Commission under G.S. 143-135.26 for approval of an alternative contracting method to be used on a particular project, but such approval is difficult to obtain and generally requires the applicant to demonstrate that the project cannot be completed using the multiple-prime method.

When bids are received on a multiple-prime basis only, contracts are awarded to the lowest responsible bidder in each category of work. When bids are received on both the single-prime and the multiple-prime basis, the lowest single-prime bid is compared with the total of the lowest set of multiple-prime bids, and the contract is awarded to the lowest responsible bid or set of bids for the entire project.

A second requirement in G.S. 143-128 relates to minority business enterprises. It is discussed later in the section "Local Preferences; Minority Business Enterprise Programs."

Requirements for Design; Architect and Engineer Selection

State law requires that plans and specifications for public building projects involving new construction or renovation that calls for foundation or structural work estimated to cost $45,000 or more, must be prepared by a registered or licensed architect or engineer. The same requirement applies to renovation that does not involve structural or foundation work and is estimated to cost $100,000 or more. This requirement applies even if the work is to be done by the county's own forces, subject to the force account limits discussed earlier.

Counties are not required to seek competitive bids on contracts for design services. Instead, G.S. 143-64.31 requires that design professionals be selected on the basis of their qualifications and that the contract price be negotiated with the best-qualified person or company. The governing board can exempt itself from the qualification-based selection process under G.S. 143-64.32 for all projects in which the design fee is less than $30,000, or for other projects, at the sole discretion of the board. The statute requires the board to exempt itself in writing, which can be accomplished by adopting a resolution. Once exempt, the board can either negotiate a contract or conduct a competitive bidding process to select an architect or engineer.

Local Preferences; Minority Business Enterprise Programs

Local governments in North Carolina do not have the legal authority to establish preferences in awarding contracts, such as preferences for local or minority contractors. Furthermore, although some may think it economically or politically desirable, it is not legal to assume that a local contractor is more responsible than others under the standard for awarding contracts.

G.S. 143-128(f) requires local governments to establish a percentage goal for participation by minority contractors in building construction contracts. Counties must require that contractors make a good faith effort to meet the goal, but the law does not establish or authorize a set-aside of particular contracts for minority contractors or a preference for minority contractors in awarding contracts. In fact, the statute specifically states that contracts must be awarded to the lowest responsible bidder and prohibits consideration of race, sex, religion, national origin, or handicapping condition in awarding contracts. Counties also have authority under G.S. 160A-17.1 to comply with minority business enterprise program requirements that may be imposed as a condition of receiving federal or state grants and loans.

Both the lack of statutory authority and the constitutional limitations on awarding contracts on the basis of race or sex[5] severely limit a county's authority to establish minority preference programs. Counties do have authority to establish race-neutral programs to encourage participation by small firms or local firms, and can establish procedures to identify local and minority contractors and notify them of contracting opportunities.

Protests and Legal Challenges

Unlike the laws governing state and federal contracting, North Carolina laws governing local government contracting do not establish protest procedures. North Carolina courts have held that if a contract is subject to the statutory competitive bidding procedures and those procedures are not followed, the contract is void.[6] If a bidder is dissatisfied with a decision of the county—for example, to award a contract to the second lowest bidder or to accept a bid that does not meet specifications—the bidder can register his or her complaint with the county official responsible for the contract or directly with the board. As a practical matter, it is best for the county to attempt to resolve the matter, but there is no legal requirement for a hearing or other formal disposition of the complaint. If the matter is not resolved administratively, the only legal option is for the aggrieved party to sue the county, typically for an injunction to prevent the county from going forward with an illegal contract. It is not unusual for protests to be lodged with county officials or with the governing boards, although legal challenges are rare.

Conflicts of Interest

Several state laws place limits on the ability of elected officials and public employees to derive personal benefit from their offices. These laws reflect the public's need to ensure that contracting and other decisions are made in a neutral, objective way, based on what is in the public interest and not in consideration of actual or potential benefit to the decision maker. However, these laws do not outlaw all activity that the public might consider improper. Instead, they identify particular activities that the legislature has identified as serious enough to constitute a criminal offense. Situations that are not illegal may nonetheless be inappropriate, so public officials should always consider the public perception of their actions as well as the legal consequences.

Contracts for Personal Benefit

A criminal statute, G.S. 14-234, makes it a misdemeanor for an elected or appointed official who is involved in contracting on behalf of a county to make contracts in which he or she has a personal, financial interest. This broad prohibition is modified by several exceptions, which are summarized in the following paragraphs. It is important to recognize that the prohibition applies to any kind of contract and that it applies with equal force whether the contract involves a public official selling to the county (for example, the owner of a business selling supplies or services to the county) or buying from the county (for example, a board member buying property sold at a county surplus-property auction).

At least one case suggests that a violation of this statute occurs when a contract between the county and a board member's business comes into being, even if the board member was not directly involved in the making of the contract and does not vote to approve it.[7] Another case interpreting a related statute, G.S. 14-236, which applies to public schools and other public educational entities, held that the statute does not apply to contracts with a business owned by the spouse of a board member or public official.[8] Despite this precedent, counties should avoid entering into contracts with the spouse of either a board member or a public employee who has contracting authority. Another case might be decided differently if it were shown that the board member or public employee benefited from the spouse's earnings.

The statute provides that persons are not considered interested in a contract with the county if their personal interest consists of an ownership interest of 10 percent or less, or if the person is an employee—as opposed to an owner—of the entity that is contracting with the county. For this exception to apply, the governing board must approve the contract by a specific resolution, on which the interested public official is not allowed to vote. The statute also exempts contracts with banks, savings and loan associations, and regulated public utilities, provided that the special approval process just described is completed.

Another exemption applies only in counties in which there is no incorporated municipality with a population of more than 7,500 (according to the most recent federal census). In these counties, under G.S. 14-234(d1), governing board members as well as certain members of the social services, local health or area mental health boards, and members of a board of directors of a public hospital, may benefit from contracts with the county as long as the contract does not exceed $10,000 for medically related services and $15,000 for other goods or services in any twelve-month period. The exemption does not apply to any contract that is subject to the competitive bidding laws, currently set at $5,000 or more for the purchase of apparatus, supplies, materials, or equipment, or for construction or repair work. The statute imposes additional public notice and reporting requirements for these contracts and prohibits the interested board member from participating in the development of or voting on the contract.

The statute also allows a board member to receive payment for services, facilities, or supplies provided to needy persons under state or federal assistance programs. Conditions on this exemption include the following:

1. The persons receiving the services or supplies are allowed to select the provider.
2. The payment is in the same amount as the county would pay to any other provider.
3. Participation is open to all providers, and the county does not limit who may provide the goods or services.
4. The board member takes no part in approving his or her own invoice.

Contracts entered into in violation of G.S. 14-234 violate public policy and are not enforceable. Prosecutions under the statute are not common, but situations in which board members or public officials stand to benefit from contracts involving public funds often make headlines.

Gifts and Favors

Another criminal statute, G.S. 133-32, is designed to prevent the use of gifts and favors to influence the award and administration of public contracts. The statute makes it a misdemeanor for a current contractor, a contractor who has performed under a contract with the county within the past year, or a person who anticipates bidding on a contract to give any gift or favor to public officials who have responsibility for preparing, awarding, or overseeing contracts. The statute also makes it a misdemeanor for those officials to receive the gift or favor.

The statute does not define gift or favor. A reasonable interpretation is that the statute prohibits gifts and the receipt of anything of value unless it is covered by a statutory exception. Items excepted from the statute include advertising items or souvenirs of nominal value, honoraria for participating in meetings, and meals at banquets. Inexpensive pens, mugs, and calendars bearing the name of the donor firm clearly fall within the exception for advertising items and souvenirs. A gift of a television set, use of a beach cottage, or tickets to a professional sports event is probably prohibited. Some local governments have adopted local policies establishing a dollar limit for gifts that may be accepted. Since meals at banquets are allowed, free meals offered by contractors under other circumstances, including lunch, should be refused.

The statute also allows county officials to accept customary gifts or favors from friends and relatives as long as the existing relationship, rather than the desire to do business with the county, is the motivation for the gift. The statute specifies that it does not prohibit contractors from making donations to professional organizations to defray meeting expenses, nor does it prohibit public officials who are members of those organizations from participating in meetings that are supported by such donations and are open to all members.

It is important to distinguish between gifts to individuals and gifts to the government entity itself. It is not illegal for a contractor to donate goods to the county for use by the county. For example, a local business can legally donate products to the county for county use or for the county to raffle to employees for an employee appreciation event. Gifts or favors delivered directly to individuals for their personal use should be returned, or in some cases, may be distributed among employees such that each person's benefit is nominal. The latter approach is common for gifts of food brought to a department by a vendor. Public officials should inform contractors and vendors about the existence of the gifts-and-favors statute, and about any local rules in effect within the county addressing this issue.

Misuse of Confidential Information

G.S. 14-234.1 makes it a misdemeanor for any state or local government officer or employee to use confidential information for personal gain, to acquire a pecuniary benefit in anticipation of his or her own official action, or to help another person gain from these actions.

Additional Resources

Bell, A. Fleming, II. *Construction Contracts with North Carolina Local Governments.* 3d ed. Chapel Hill, N.C.: Institute of Government, The University of North Carolina at Chapel Hill, 1996.

———. *Ethics, Conflicts, and Offices: A Guide for Local Officials.* Chapel Hill, N.C.: Institute of Government, The University of North Carolina at Chapel Hill, 1997.

Bluestein, Frayda S. *A Legal Guide to Purchasing and Contracting for North Carolina Local Governments.* Chapel Hill, N.C.: Institute of Government, The University of North Carolina at Chapel Hill, 1998.

Bluestein, Frayda S., and Warren Jake Wicker. *An Outline of Statutory Procedures Controlling Purchasing by North Carolina Local Governments.* Chapel Hill, N.C.: Institute of Government, The University of North Carolina at Chapel Hill, 1996.

Council of State Governments. *State and Local Government Purchasing.* 4th ed. Lexington, Ky.: The Council, 1994.

Haney, Donald. *Service Contracting: A Local Government Guide.* Washington, D.C.: International City/County Management Association, 1992.

Notes

1. G.S. 159-28(a); L & S Leasing v. Winston-Salem, 122 N.C. App. 619, 471 S.E.2d 118 (1996).

2. Raynor v. Commissioners of Louisburg, 220 N.C. 348, 17 S.E.2d 495 (1941).

3. 109 N.C. App. 165, 169, 426 S.E.2d 447, 450 (1993).

4. Kinsey Contracting Co. v. City of Fayetteville, 106 N.C. App. 383, 386, 416 S.E.2d 607, 609 (1992).

5. *See* Frayda S. Bluestein, "Local Government Minority- and Women-Owned Business Programs: Questions and Answers," *Popular Government* 59 (Spring 1994): 19–26.

6. *Raynor,* 220 N.C. at 353, 17 S.E.2d at 499.

7. State v. Williams, 153 N.C. 595, 68 S.E.2d 900 (1910).

8. State v. Debnam, 196 N.C. 740, 146 S.E.2d 857 (1929).

15 Property Acquisition, Sale, and Disposition

David M. Lawrence and Ben F. Loeb, Jr.

Contents

David M. Lawrence is an Institute of Government faculty member who works in the area of local government law.
    Ben F. Loeb, Jr., is an Institute of Government faculty member whose interests include eminent domain, alcoholic beverage control, fire protection, and animal control law.

As business entities, counties need to acquire and dispose of property. In acquiring property, counties generally are no different from private persons or corporations, although some acquisition procedures are available only to governments. In disposing of property, counties usually must follow detailed statutory procedures.

Acquisition of Real Property

Counties have broad statutory power to acquire the fee or any lesser interest (such as an easement) in real or personal property for their use or for the use of any of their departments, boards, commissions, or agencies. (Acquisition of personal property, which is generally subject to competitive-bidding requirements, is discussed in Chapter 14 of this volume.) Under the General Statutes and the common law, counties may acquire property by the following methods:

1. Gift: a voluntary transfer of property, without any cost to the county

2. Purchase: a voluntary transfer of property, for a price
3. Devise: a voluntary gift of property by a person's last will and testament, without any cost to the county
4. Dedication: a voluntary setting aside of an interest in land, usually an easement, for public use, which is accepted on behalf of the public by the county
5. Exchange: a voluntary transfer of property for something of equivalent value
6. Lease: a contract giving the county possession of a property for a determinate period
7. Adverse possession or prescription: an involuntary transfer of property, without payment, because of long occupation of the property by the county
8. Eminent domain: an involuntary transfer of property on payment of just compensation

A county may acquire property as a sole owner or as a joint owner with another government. When it does acquire property, it may not, as a part of the transaction, give a mortgage or another security interest in the property[1] unless a statute specifically permits it to do so.[2] G.S. 160A-20 (discussed in detail in Chapter 11) allows a county to give a security interest in limited circumstances:

1. To the seller of real or personal property to secure the purchase price when the county is paying for the property in installments
2. To the lender if the county finances such a purchase
3. To a construction lender if the loan is structured as an installment purchase contract

No other statute permits security interests, however; therefore they may not be given in other circumstances.

Eminent Domain

The 1981 General Assembly enacted a new eminent domain law for private condemnors and local public condemnors, including cities and counties. This act is essentially a General Statutes Commission bill that went through approximately twelve drafts over more than five years. As enacted, it does not affect state agencies. For example, the Department of Transportation continues to use the condemnation procedures set forth in G.S. Chapter 136.

The new law repealed all of G.S. Chapter 40, the eminent domain provisions of G.S. Chapter 160A, and most local condemnation acts (a few have since been added). These repealed provisions were replaced with a new G.S. Chapter 40A. Article 1 of the new act contains general provisions (such as definitions); Article 2 sets forth the condemnation procedures to be used by private condemnors (power companies, railroads, and so forth); Article 3 describes the condemnation procedures for public condemnors; and Article 4 concerns *just compensation.*

G.S. 40A-1 states in part:

> It is the intent of the General Assembly that the procedures provided by this Chapter shall be the exclusive condemnation procedures to be used in this State by private condemnors and all local public condemnors. All other provisions in laws, charters, or local acts authorizing the use of other procedures by municipal or county governments or agencies or political subdivisions thereof, or by corporations, associations or other persons are hereby repealed.

There are two express exceptions to this broad rule: (1) the new act did not repeal any provision of a local act enlarging or limiting the purpose for which property may be condemned; (2) nor did it repeal any local act creating any substantive or procedural requirement or limitation on the authority of a local public condemnor to exercise the power of eminent domain outside its boundaries. In addition, G.S. 136-66.3 (which authorizes counties to use the Chapter 136 procedure when condemning for a state-highway-system street) was not expressly repealed and apparently survived.

The definitions for Chapter 40A are contained in G.S. 40A-2. The word *property* is given the broadest possible meaning, being defined as any right, title, or interest in land, including leases and options to buy or sell. It also includes rights of access, rights-of-way, easements, water rights, air rights, and any other privilege in or appurtenance to the possession, the use, and the enjoyment of land. *Judge* is defined to include only judges of superior court; therefore district courts have no jurisdiction even when the amount of money in controversy falls within the range normally assigned to district court.

Allowable Purposes of Condemnation

The purposes for which counties may use the power of eminent domain are listed in G.S. 40A-3(b):

1. Public enterprises listed in G.S. 153A-274[3] (these include water, sewer, solid waste collection and disposal, airports, off-street parking, public transportation, and stormwater drainage)
2. Parks, playgrounds, and other recreational facilities
3. Storm sewer and drainage systems
4. Hospital facilities, cemeteries, and libraries
5. Fire stations, office buildings, jails, or other buildings for use by any department, board, commission, or agency
6. Drainage programs and programs to prevent obstruction to the natural flow of streams or to improve drainage facilities
7. Acquisition of designated historical properties
8. Public wharves

A county does not possess the power of eminent domain with respect to property owned by the state of North Carolina unless the state consents to the taking, nor may a county condemn property owned by the federal government. The state's consent is given by the Council of State or by the secretary of administration if the council delegates that authority to him or her. When state property is taken, the only issue is the compensation to be paid (G.S. 40A-5).

Except as otherwise provided by statute, a county may condemn the property of a private condemnor if such property is not in actual public use or is not necessary to the operation of the owner's business. It may also condemn the property of another local or public condemnor if the property proposed to be taken is not being used or held for future use for any government or proprietary purpose [G.S. 40A-5(b)].

Prior Offer and Right of Entry

G.S. 40A-4 provides that the power to acquire property by condemnation does not depend on any prior effort to acquire the same property by gift or purchase. Nor is the power to negotiate for the gift or the purchase of property impaired by initiation of a condemnation proceeding.

A condemnor may enter on any lands (but not structures) to make surveys, borings, examinations, or appraisals without filing a complaint, making a deposit, or taking any other action required by G.S. Chapter 40A. However, it must give the owner (at his or her last known address) thirty days' written notice of the intended entry. Also, it must reimburse the owner for any damages resulting from these activities (G.S. 40A-11).

Notice

G.S. 40A-40 requires that a public condemnor notify each owner of its intent to institute an action to condemn property not less than thirty days before it files a complaint. This notice must describe the property to be taken and state the amount estimated by the condemnor to constitute just compensation.

Complaint and Deposit

A public condemnor institutes action by filing a complaint (in the superior court of the county where the land is located) that contains a declaration of taking. When it files the complaint, the condemnor must deposit a sum of money that it estimates to be just compensation. A summons is then issued. The summons, together with a copy of the complaint and a notice of the deposit, is served on the person or persons named therein in the manner specified by G.S. 1A-1, rule 4. G.S. 40A-41 sets forth the contents for the complaint.

Quick Take

When a county condemns property for certain listed purposes, the title to the property and the right to immediate possession vest when the complaint is filed and the deposit is made (hence the name *quick take* for this procedure). Counties use the quick-take procedure for such public enterprises as water supply and distribution systems, wastewater collection and treatment systems, and solid waste collection and disposal systems. They may *not* use it for public transportation systems, off-street parking facilities, airports, and certain other purposes [G.S. 40A-42(a)].

Not-So-Quick Take

When quick take is not available to a county, the condemnation proceeds pursuant to G.S. 40A-42(b). Under that subsection, the title to the property specified in the complaint vests in the condemnor (1) when the answer filed by the owner requests only that there be a determination of just compensation, (2) if the owner fails to file an answer within the 120 days specified by G.S. 40A-46, or (3) when the deposit is disbursed in accordance with the provisions of G.S. 40A-44. The owner may seek an injunction to prevent title from vesting under either subsection (a) or (b) of G.S. 40A-42.

If the owner's answer raises questions other than the amount of just compensation, a judge—on motion and ten days' notice by either party—hears and determines the issues. These issues may include the condemnor's authority to take, questions of necessary and proper parties, the title to land, the interest taken, and the area taken (G.S. 40A-47).

Memorandum of Action and Disbursement

G.S. 40A-43 requires the condemnor, when it files the complaint and deposits the estimated compensation, to record a memorandum of action with the register of deeds in any county where the land to be condemned is located. This section also sets out the contents of the memorandum.

When there is no dispute as to title, the persons named in the complaint may apply to the court for disbursement of the deposited money (or any part thereof), "as full compensation or as a credit against just compensation without prejudice to further proceedings to determine just compensation" (G.S. 40A-44).

Answer

The contents of the owner's answer are set forth in G.S. 40A45. G.S. 40A-46 gives the owner or owners 120 days from the date of service to answer. Failure to answer within this period constitutes an admission that the amount deposited is just compensation and is a waiver of any further proceedings to determine just compensation. In such a case the judge enters final judgment and orders disbursement of the deposited money.

Appointment and Duties of Commissioners

Within sixty days of the answer being filed either the owner or the condemnor may request the clerk of superior court to appoint commissioners to determine just compensation. The clerk then appoints three competent, disinterested persons who reside in the county to serve as commissioners. G.S. 40A-48 requires that they be sworn and then visit the property to appraise its value. The commissioners have the power to inspect the property, hold hearings, swear witnesses, and take evidence as they deem necessary. When they have completed these tasks, they must file a report with the court as set out in G.S. 40A-48(c).

When the commissioners' report is filed, the clerk mails a copy to each of the parties or his or her counsel. Either party has thirty days after the report is mailed to file exceptions to it and demand a trial *de novo* by jury on the issue of compensation. If no exception is filed, the judge enters final judgment on a finding that the report awards just compensation to the property owners.

Costs and Interest

G.S. 40A-13 requires that the condemnor pay all court costs. In addition, the court in its discretion may award the owner a sum to reimburse him or her for charges paid for appraisers, engineers, and plats if the appraisers or engineers testify as witnesses and the plats are received in evidence by court order (G.S. 40A-8, -13). The judge also adds interest at the rate of 6 percent from the date of taking to the date of judgment (G.S. 40A-54).

Just Compensation

The determination of just compensation must reflect the value of the property immediately before the complaint is filed (G.S. 40A-63). The measure of compensation for the taking is the property's fair market value unless only part of the tract is taken, in which case the measure of compensation is either (1) the amount by which the fair market value of the entire tract immediately before the taking exceeds the fair market value of the remainder immediately after the taking, or (2) the fair market value of the property taken, whichever is greater (G.S. 40A-64). The value of the property taken does not include an increase or decrease in value before the date of valuation that is caused by the proposed improvement or project for which the property is taken (G.S. 40A-65).

Sale or Disposition of County Property

County governments generally dispose of property in accordance with the procedures set forth in G.S. Chapter 160A, Article 12 (G.S. 160A-265 through -279). Article 12 authorizes several methods for selling or disposing of property and sets forth the procedures for each one. Before examining these methods, it is useful to discuss one introductory matter: the need for consideration when disposing of county property.

Consideration

Under the North Carolina Constitution it is generally unconstitutional for a local government, including a county, to dispose of property for less than its fair market value.[4] A gift of property or a sale at well below market value constitutes the granting of an "exclusive privilege or emolument" to the person receiving the property, which is prohibited by Article 1, Section 32, of the constitution. Most of the procedures by which a county is permitted to sell or otherwise dispose of property are competitive, and the North Carolina Supreme Court has indicated that the price resulting from an open and competitive procedure will be accepted as the market value.[5] If a sale is privately negotiated, the price will normally be considered appropriate unless strong evidence indicates that it is so significantly below market value as to show an abuse of discretion.[6]

It is not always constitutionally necessary that a county receive *monetary* consideration when it conveys property. If the party receiving the property agrees to put it to some public use, that promise constitutes sufficient consideration for the conveyance.[7] (The receiver in this case is often, but not always, another government.) The General Statutes expressly permit such conveyances in the following circumstances:

- To governments (G.S. 160A-274)
- To volunteer fire departments and rescue squads (G.S. 160A-277)
- To nonprofit preservation or conservation organizations [G.S. 160A-266(b)]
- To nonprofit agencies to which the county is authorized to appropriate money (G.S. 160A-279)

Disposition Procedures

G.S. Chapter 160A, Article 12, sets out three competitive methods of sale, each of which is appropriate in any circumstance: sealed bid, negotiated offer and upset bid, and public auction. Article 12 also permits privately negotiated exchanges of property in any circumstance (as long as equal value changes hands) and privately negotiated sales or other dispositions of property in a number of limited circumstances. These various methods of disposition are summarized in the following sections. In undertaking any of them, county personnel must remember that the statutory procedure must be followed exactly or the transaction may be invalidated by a court.[8]

Sealed Bids

A county may sell any real or personal property by sealed bid (G.S. 160A-268).

Procedure

The procedure is based on that set forth in G.S. 143-129 for purchasing property, with one modification for real property. An advertisement for sealed bids must be published in a newspaper that has general circulation in the county. Publication must occur one week before the bids are opened if personal property is being sold and thirty days before the bids are opened if real property is being sold. The advertisement should generally describe the property; tell where it can be examined and when and where the bids will be opened; state that a 5 percent bid deposit is required and will be retained if the successful bidder fails to consummate the contract; and reserve the board of commissioners' right to reject any and all bids. Bids must be opened in public and recorded in the commissioners' minutes. The award is made to the highest bidder.

Comment

This procedure appears to be designed to obtain wide competition by providing public notice and good opportunity for bidders to examine the property. Invitations to bid may be mailed to prospective buyers, just as they are typically sent to prospective sellers in the formal purchasing procedures for personal property. Except for the bid-deposit requirement, this procedure is essentially the one used by the Division of Purchase and Contract in disposing of almost all surplus personal property owned by the state.

Negotiated Offer and Upset Bids

A county may sell any real or personal property by negotiated offer and upset bids (G.S. 160A-209).

Procedure

The procedure begins when the board of county commissioners receives and proposes to accept an offer to purchase specified county property. (The offer may be either solicited from the offeror or made directly by it on its own initiative.) The board of commissioners then requires the offeror to deposit a 5 percent bid deposit with the clerk to the board and causes a notice of the offer to be published. The notice must describe the property; specify the amount and the terms of the offer; and give notice that the bid may be raised by not less than 10 percent of the first $1,000 originally bid, plus 5 percent of any amount above $1,000 of the original bid. Upset bids must also be accompanied by a 5 percent bid deposit. Prospective bidders have ten days from the date on which the notice is published to offer an upset bid. This procedure is repeated until ten days have elapsed without the commissioners' receiving an upset bid. After that time the board may sell the property to the final offeror. At any time in the process, it may reject any and all offers and decide not to sell the property.

Public Auction

A county may sell any real or personal property by public auction (G.S. 160A-270).

Procedure

The statute sets out separate procedures for real and personal property sold at public auction. For real property the board of commissioners must adopt a resolution that authorizes the sale; describes the property; specifies the date, time, place, and terms of the sale; and states that the board must accept and confirm the successful bid. The board may require a bid deposit. A notice containing the information set out in the resolution must be published at least once and not less than thirty days before the auction. The highest bid is reported to the board of commissioners, which then has thirty days in which to accept or reject it.

For personal property the same procedure is followed except that (1) the board may in the resolution authorize an appropriate county official to complete the sale at the auction and (2) the notice must be published not less than ten days before the auction.

Comment

Public auction is a traditional method of selling both real and personal property. Open competitive bidding may under some circumstances encourage the offering of higher prices. The possibility of immediately acquiring possession of personal property makes this approach attractive to many buyers.

Exchange of Property

A county may exchange any real or personal property for other real or personal property if it receives full and fair consideration for the property (G.S. 160A-271).

Procedure

After the terms of the exchange agreement are developed by private negotiations, the board of commissioners authorizes the exchange at a *regular* meeting. A notice of intent to make the exchange must be published at least ten days before it occurs. The notice must describe the properties involved, give the value of each as well as the value of other consideration changing hands, and cite the date of the regular meeting at which the board proposes to confirm the exchange.

Comment

The exchange procedure is probably most useful in connection with a trade of real property when boundaries must be adjusted or when an individual owns land needed by the county and wants some other tract of county land. G.S. 143-129.7 permits local governments to convey surplus property as a "trade-in" when the government is purchasing apparatus or equipment; such an exchange need not comply with the procedures of G.S. 160A-271.

Private Negotiation and Sale: Personal Property

A county may use private negotiation and sale to dispose of personal property valued at less than $30,000 for any one item or any group of similar items (G.S. 160A-266, -267).

Procedure

At a *regular* meeting, the board of commissioners by resolution authorize an appropriate official to dispose of identified property at private sale. The board may set a minimum price but is not required to do so. The resolution must be published at least ten days before the sale.

The board of commissioners may also establish procedures under which county officials may dispose of personal property valued at less than $5,000 for any item or any group of similar items without further board action. The procedures may permit one or more officials to declare qualifying property to be surplus, to set its market value, and to sell it by public or private sale. The statute requires the selling official to make a semiannual report to the board on property sold under any such procedures.

Private Negotiation and Conveyance to Other Governments

G.S. 160A-274 authorizes any government unit in the state, on terms and conditions determined by the unit, to sell to, purchase from, exchange with, lease to, or lease from any other government unit, or enter into agreements with such unit regarding the joint use of any interest in real or personal property that one or the other unit may own. *Government unit* is defined to include cities, counties, the state, school units, and other state and local agencies. The single limitation on this broad authority is that before a county or city board of education may lease real property that it owns, it must determine that the property is unnecessary or undesirable for school purposes; and it may not lease the property for less than $1 per year.[9] Bids or published notice are not required. Thus when reaching agreements on property with another government unit, the board of commissioners has full discretion concerning procedure.

Private Negotiation and Sale: Real Property

A county may, in limited circumstances, convey real property to certain nonprofit corporations and associations by private negotiation and without monetary consideration. In addition, a county may convey real property to private companies for purposes of economic development.

Fire or Rescue Services

G.S. 160A-277 permits counties to lease or convey land to volunteer fire departments or rescue squads that is to be used for constructing or expanding their facilities. The board of commissioners must approve the transaction by adoption of a resolution at a regular meeting, on ten days' published notice. The notice should describe the property, state its value, set out the proposed monetary consideration or the lack thereof, and declare the board's intention to approve the transaction.

Nonprofit Agencies

G.S. 160A-279 permits a county to convey real or personal property to any nonprofit agency to which it is authorized by law to appropriate funds. (Property acquired through condemnation may not be so conveyed.) The same procedures must be followed as required by G.S. 160A-267 for other private sales.

Architectural and Cultural Property

G.S. 160A-266(b) permits a county to convey, after private negotiation, real or personal property that is significant for its archaeological, architectural, artistic, cultural, or historic associations; for its association with such property; or for its natural, scenic, or open condition. The conveyance must be to a nonprofit corporation or trust whose purposes include the preservation or the conservation of such property, and the deed must include covenants and other restrictions securing and promoting the property's protection. A county making a conveyance under this provision must follow the same procedures as noted earlier for the private sale of personal property.

Economic Development

G.S. 158-7.1(d) permits a county to convey interests in property suitable for economic development by private sale. Before making such a conveyance, the board of commissioners must hold a public hearing, with at least ten days' published notice of the hearing. The notice must describe the interest to be conveyed; the value of the interest; the proposed consideration the county will receive; and the board's intention to approve the conveyance. In addition, before making the conveyance the board of commissioners must determine the probable average wage that will be paid to workers at the business to be located on the property.

Finally, the statute requires the board of commissioners to determine the fair market value of the property and prohibits conveying the property for less than that value. In arriving at the amount of consideration the county receives, however, the county may count the prospective tax revenues for the next ten years from improvements on the property, prospective sales tax revenues generated by the business during that period, and any other income coming to the county during the ten years as a result of the conveyance.

Lease of Property

A county may lease any property that the board of commissioners finds will not be needed during the term of the lease (G.S. 160A-272). The procedure to be followed depends on the length of the lease. The board may, by resolution at any meeting, make leases for one year or less. It may also authorize the county manager or some other administrative officer to take similar action concerning county property for the same period.

The board of commissioners may lease county property for periods longer than one year and up to ten years by a resolution adopted at a regular meeting, after ten days' published notice of its intention to do so. The notice must also specify the annual lease payment and give the date of the meeting at which the board proposes to approve the action.

A lease for longer than ten years must be treated as a sale of property. It may be executed by following any procedure authorized for selling real property.

Grant of Easements

A county may grant easements over, through, under, or across any of its property (G.S. 160A-273). The authorization should be by resolution of the board of commissioners at a regular meeting. No special published notice is required.

Sale of Stocks, Bonds, and Other Securities

A county that owns stocks, bonds, or other securities that are traded on the stock exchanges or over the counter by brokers and securities dealers may sell them in the same way and under the same conditions as a private owner would (G.S. 160A-276). It is not limited to the competitive methods outlined earlier in the chapter in the sections "Sealed Bids," "Negotiated Offer and Upset Bids," and "Public Auction."

Warranty Deeds

G.S. 160A-275 authorizes a board of commissioners to execute and deliver deeds to any government owned real property with full covenants of warranty when the board determines that it is in the best interest of the county to do so. Commissioners are relieved of any personal liability arising from the issuance of warranty deeds if their actions are in good faith.

Additional Resources

Lawrence, David M. *Local Government Property Transactions in North Carolina.* Chapel Hill, N.C.: Institute of Government, The University of North Carolina at Chapel Hill, 1987.

Loeb, Ben F., Jr. *Eminent Domain Procedure for North Carolina Local Governments,* 2d ed. Chapel Hill, N.C.: Institute of Government, The University of North Carolina at Chapel Hill, 1997.

Notes

1. Vaughan v. Commissioners of Forsyth County, 188 N.C. 636, 125 S.E. 177 (1896).

2. Brockenbrough v. Board of Water Comm'rs, 134 N.C. 1, 46 S.E. 28 (1903).

3. Public enterprises include water supply and distribution, wastewater collection and treatment, public transportation, solid waste collection and disposal, parking, airports, and stormwater systems.

4. *Cf.* Redevelopment Comm'n v. Security Nat'l Bank, 252 N.C. 595, 114 S.E.2d 668 (1960).

5. *Id.*

6. Painter v. Wake County Bd. of Educ., 288 N.C. 165, 217 S.E.2d 650 (1975).

7. Brumley v. Baxter, 225 N.C. 691, 36 S.E.2d 281 (1945).

8. Bagwell v. Town of Brevard, 267 N.C. 604, 148 S.E.2d 635 (1966). Some county boards routinely declare as surplus any property that is to be sold. No statute

requires such a declaration, however, and it does not appear to be necessary. A county evidences its conclusion that property is surplus by selling it.

9. Although, in general, local governments may transfer property among themselves without monetary consideration, the North Carolina Supreme Court has held that a local school board must receive fair consideration whenever it conveys property for some nonschool use, including some other government use. Boney v. Board of Trustees, 229 N.C. 136, 48 S.E.2d 56 (1948). The $1 requirement for leases of school property presumably is a legislative determination that this amount is adequate consideration when title to the property remains with the school administrative unit.

16 County Planning, Land Use Regulation, and Code Enforcement

Richard D. Ducker

Contents

Richard D. Ducker is an Institute of Government faculty member whose work includes the legal aspects of local government planning, land use regulation such as zoning and land subdivision controls, and building and housing code enforcement.

The author expresses his appreciation to Phillip P. Green, a retired Institute of Government faculty member and the author of this chapter in the book's previous edition. His work was most helpful in the expansion, updating, and reorganization that this chapter represents.

North Carolina is a state characterized by small and mid-size counties, a scattered, dispersed pattern of development, and a relatively rapid rate of population growth. During the period 1990–95, the national population growth rate was about 5.6 percent, while North Carolina's population grew at a rate of 8.5 percent. Remarkably the population growth in nonmetropolitan areas in North Carolina during the period 1990–94 (4.9 percent) equaled the average rate of population growth in metropolitan areas nationwide. A significant part of this state's growth has occurred in urban fringe and formerly rural areas that are within the planning jurisdiction of counties.

What role should county government play in influencing this growth? The most critical factors in the population and economic growth of a particular North Carolina county may be economic, technological, or demographic factors or trends that are of national or international impact. Increasingly rapid technological change and diminution of job security make it difficult to see just how a county can control its own destiny. What is more, North Carolina counties are not authorized to construct and operate the road and highway systems, and often they elect not to construct and operate the water and sewerage systems that are generally regarded as the infrastructure most prominent in shaping growth. Nor are many residents of rural areas comfortable with a county government that appears to interfere with customary notions of the rights of private property.

Most counties view their primary function as simply to accommodate the growth that the private sector generates, to provide a basic level of development-review services that are commensurate with the size and the growth of the county, and to provide public facilities and services wherever and whenever they are demanded. Economic development is often a high priority, and more and more counties are engaging in strategic planning to define and accomplish their goals. In most counties (and in this chapter), county planning means land use and development planning, generally in conjunction with providing development-review services and code enforcement.

County Planning Programs and Tools

In concept, county planning looks to the future. It suggests a comprehensive approach to the county's physical and economic development. It emphasizes the coordination of the actions of various units of local and state government as they affect land development. It suggests a rational process for making decisions that are consistent, predictable, and policy based, and provides the public with opportunities to influence directly the formulation of development policy. But more than anything else, county planning can best be understood at the practical level, in terms of what county planners and code enforcement people actually do. The following programs and regulatory tools define county planning in this way.

Programs and Policy Development

The Land Use Plan and Comprehensive Planning

The centerpiece of a local planning program has traditionally been thought to be a *general comprehensive plan*. A general comprehensive plan is designed to give a county an overview of its current physical development and to serve as a guide to its future development policy. A pivotal component of a general comprehensive plan is the *land use plan*. The land use plan is based on projections of population growth and land development patterns that have implications for public facilities, transportation, and economic development, as well as housing, cultural and natural resource protection, and community appearance. In fact, many counties use the terms *general comprehensive plan* and *land use plan* interchangeably.

According to a March 1997 survey, a land use plan of some description has been adopted by sixty-three counties. In an additional eleven counties a plan has been prepared and is used as a guide by the staff or planning board, but it has not been formally adopted by the governing board. A land use plan has been prepared in still another nine counties but has not been adopted or used. In seventeen counties no county land use plan has been prepared.

Land use plans must be prepared for the twenty coastal counties subject to the Coastal Area Management Act, although the state pays 90 percent of the cost of preparing them. Counties elsewhere in the state are under no similar legal obligation.

Certain rudimentary assumptions about land use must be made if local governments are to engage in transportation planning. G.S. 136-66.2 calls for each North Carolina municipality, with the cooperation of the North Carolina Department of Transportation (NCDOT), to prepare a comprehensive street plan (thoroughfare plan). More and more counties are participating in the preparation of such plans, particularly those in metropolitan areas. In addition various state and federal aid programs require local government applicants to prepare a plan (often with land use implications) in order to qualify for assistance.

One incentive for western counties to plan grew out of the Mountain Area Planning Program. Between 1991 and 1993 the Appalachian Resources Commission (ARC) offered each of the twenty-nine western North Carolina counties the opportunity to qualify for up to $30,000 in land use planning funds. The money was intended to be used to hire a planner or to hire a consultant to complete a county land use plan. Twenty-one counties applied for and received a grant and completed land use plans. At least some of the counties have maintained a county planning program ever since.

The Mountain Area Planning Program was followed up several years later by the Year of the Mountains Planning Initiative. Building on a recommendation from the Year of the Mountains Commission, the General Assembly is expected to appropriate $300,000 in each of three fiscal years (1996–99) to be distributed primarily among ten counties (Alleghany, Avery, Cherokee, Clay, Graham, Madison, McDowell, Mitchell, Swain, and Yancey). Funds have been used to continue county planner positions and to develop and update comprehensive plans and land use plans. Funds may also be used for any planning purpose (not simply land use planning) and have been used to improve land records and to initiate a new economic development program as well.

If a comprehensive plan is to be used by the county, it must provide some guidance when important development-related decisions are made. Some jurisdictions automatically refer to the plan when considering rezoning and utility-extension decisions. The zoning statutes say that zoning must be "in accordance with a comprehensive plan" (G.S. 153A-341). This requirement has not been construed to mean that some specific consistency between the zoning ordinance and an adopted comprehensive land use plan is required. However, there is a growing tendency among the courts to look to documentation outside the land use ordinance itself in determining whether a land use regulatory power is being properly exercised. In addition, some units have bound themselves to follow their own plans.[1]

Strategic Planning

A model that serves as an alternative or a supplement to comprehensive planning is *strategic planning*. Strategic planning is a process that emphasizes focusing on a few critical issues that are important to the community's future, rather than trying to deal with everything at once. It involves looking outward at trends that may affect a community's destiny but be beyond the community's control. Strategic planning is designed to be action-oriented in order to show what steps must be taken to achieve goals, who must take them, how much it will cost, and who will pay for them. It is well adapted to the resolution of economic development and housing issues involving a number of players (government units, businesses, private individuals, and nonprofit organizations), when a distribution of responsibility is necessary and the ability to respond to opportunities is important. Strategic planning is a particularly useful process for making spending decisions. Also, its focus on setting achievable goals and setting timetables for action makes it valuable in resolving regulatory issues. Although comprehensive planning is still the primary model used in land use and development planning, it has been substantially influenced by the principles of strategic planning.

Community and Economic Development Programs

In many North Carolina counties, economic development programs enjoy a high priority on the agendas of boards of county commissioners. In some jurisdictions there is relatively little coordination between planners (who often are viewed as regulators) and economic development specialists (who often are viewed as recruiters). More progressive counties understand the relationship between good strategic and comprehensive planning and economic development. County planners can play important roles in gathering and analyzing data, maintaining inventories of land suitable for business location or expansion, helping the county establish economic development priorities, assisting in the establishment of incubator facilities and industrial parks, and developing requests for funding proposals. In some counties (Transylvania, for example) the planning and economic development activities are managed within the same department. A number of counties administer a housing or economic development program with Community Development Block Grants (CDBGs) or other program funds. (These programs are discussed in Chapter 17.)

Water and Sewer Utilities

A modest number of counties operate water and/or sewerage systems. Other counties have entered into agreements with municipalities that provide counties with opportunities to review or participate in the cost of line extensions. Planners in some counties handle this as public utilities planning—sometimes in the context of general public facilities planning, sometimes in the context of economic development projects, and sometimes in the context of land subdivision review.

Parks, Open Space, and Greenways

County planners are not as active in park land, open space, and greenway development as some city planners are. However, planners can help select locations for parks and trails and natural areas worthy of protection, develop requests for funding from the state's Parks and Recreation Trust Fund, participate in the North Carolina Public Beach and Coastal Waterfront Access Program, and arrange for the dedication of park land under a county's land subdivision ordinance (Orange and Durham counties, for example).

A project of particular note involved the development of the *Open Space Design Guidebook*. The project was funded by the Albemarle-Pamlico Estuary Study Commission in cooperation with the North Carolina Association of County Commissioners and completed in 1996. The guidebook shows how cluster development concepts can be integrated into single-family residential development without sacrificing density (even in rural areas), to preserve open space and various natural features of the land. The *Open Space Design Guidebook* illustrates these principles by showing how particular tracts of land in Orange, Craven, and Currituck counties might be designed and developed.

County Transportation Planning

The role that counties play in transportation planning is not fully appreciated. Roughly a quarter of North Carolina counties are part of a metropolitan (transportation) planning organization (MPO) that is established pursuant to federal legislation for urban areas with a population exceeding 50,000. There are seventeen MPOs in North Carolina. The policy-making board of an MPO is the Transportation Advisory Committee (TAC), which includes representatives from the local elected boards (including the boards of county commissioners). The Technical Coordinating Committee (TCC) includes county planners as well as representatives of municipal, regional, and state agencies.

An MPO must develop and update a metropolitan transportation plan (including public transportation elements) at least every five years and a companion financial plan to develop and fund transportation projects and programs. In addition, an MPO prepares a local transportation improvement program, which if approved by the state, becomes part of the state's Transportation Improvement Program (TIP). The MPO's roles provide an opportunity for a county to influence transportation programs even though counties generally have no direct responsibility for funding, operating, or maintaining roads or other forms of ground transportation. Even a county that is not included in an MPO may become a party to the preparation and adoption of a comprehensive transportation plan affecting the municipalities within that county, or play a lead role in its initiation (Greene County, for example).

Some county planners also help coordinate the process by which a county secondary road (which may or may not already be on the state system) may be upgraded to current NCDOT secondary roads standards with the help of special assessments (see G.S. 153A-205). Others may make recommendations concerning the annual NCDOT secondary road construction and paving program for each county. They may also help arrange for dedication of rights-of-way for future roads, construction of road improvements, and design of road connections through the land subdivision ordinance.

Centralized Permitting

In some counties separate regulatory systems require developers to obtain separate building permits, subdivision plat approvals, zoning permits, flood plain permits, watershed permits, well permits, certificates of occupancy, septic tank improvement permits, and soil erosion and sedimentation control permits. Better customer service demands more efficient, centralized permitting and, if possible, one-stop permitting counters. Centralized permitting provides developers with a focal point to determine the status of permits that apply to the same project. Planning departments or combined planning and inspection departments serve as obvious administrative locations for centralized permitting systems. Randolph County's award-winning system differs from many county systems by also including certain permits issued by the county health department.

Naming and Assigning Addresses to Roads

Planners in many North Carolina counties have established street address and road naming systems for public and private roads throughout their counties. The data and geographic information systems prepared have enabled counties to develop centralized emergency communications networks (911 systems) that allow county residents quick access to law enforcement, fire protection, ambulances, and other emergency services.

Regulatory Tools

Zoning, Land Subdivision Control, and Building Code Enforcement

Zoning, land subdivision regulation, and building code enforcement are discussed separately and at greater length later in this chapter.

Special-Purpose Police-Power Ordinances

Some North Carolina counties wish to regulate an activity through a special-purpose ordinance rather than through the zoning ordinance. Under a county's general police power (G.S. 153A-121), counties may adopt ordinances that deal with such matters as mobile home parks, signs and outdoor advertising, junkyards, watershed protection, telecommunications towers, and sexually oriented businesses. In some cases the adoption of various special-purpose ordinances dealing with problem land uses leads to the adoption of a comprehensive zoning ordinance later. Police-power ordinances of this type may be adopted without the notice and public hearing formalities of most planning-related ordinances. They may be enforced in all or any portion of the unincorporated area of the county and, with the permission of a city, within city limits as well.

Minimum Housing Code Enforcement

A county is authorized to adopt its own minimum housing ordinance establishing the standards that any dwelling unit must meet to be fit for human habitation (G.S. 160A-441). The standards may deal with structural dilapidation and defects, disrepair, light and sanitary facilities, fire hazards, ventilation, general cleanliness, and other conditions that may render dwellings unsafe and unsanitary. Those counties with ordinances (perhaps half of the 100 counties) try to use this authority to encourage the rehabilitation of substandard housing, typically rental housing. Although many counties are not particularly active in housing code enforcement, several counties (Halifax County, for example) have enforced the code as part of a concerted effort to increase and upgrade the housing stock for people with low and moderate incomes.

Flood Hazard Mitigation

One of the most common planning programs in North Carolina counties is a flood hazard mitigation program. Currently, ninety-three North Carolina counties participate in the National Flood Insurance Program (NFIP). The program is designed to do the following:

- Guide future development away from flood hazard areas
- Ensure that new and improved buildings are constructed to minimize or eliminate flood damage
- Provide flood plain residents and owners with financial assistance after floods
- Transfer the costs of flood losses from taxpayers to private property owners through flood insurance premiums

Federally subsidized flood insurance and most types of federal financial assistance such as mortgage loans and grants, are available only to the local units and owners of property within those jurisdictions if the local unit participates in NFIP and adopts an approved ordinance.

Soil Erosion and Sedimentation Control Program

The North Carolina Sedimentation Pollution Control Act (G.S. 113A-50 to -66) establishes state and local authority for controlling so-called "land-disturbing activities" that result in a change in the natural cover or topography and may contribute to sedimentation. With certain exceptions only land-disturbing activities that uncover more than one contiguous acre are subject to regulation. Farming, forestry, and mining activities are exempt. Regulations require a soil erosion and sedimentation control official to approve an erosion control plan and issue a grading permit before land-disturbing activities are begun.

The North Carolina Sedimentation Control Commission administers the program through the Division of Land Resources in the North Carolina Department of Environment, Health, and Natural Resources (DEHNR). A local government may administer its own program if the elements of the program (including the local soil erosion and sedimentation control ordinance) are approved by the Commission. About a dozen counties have adopted their own programs, and most administer the program for or jointly with the municipalities within the county.

Historic Preservation Program

Roughly twenty counties boast a historic preservation program. The best indicator of such a program is the existence of a historic preservation commission (formerly called a historic district commission or a historic properties commission), appointed by the governing board. Both governing boards and historic preservation commissions can have important planning and regulatory responsibilities. The governing boards of these twenty counties have designated particular structures as historic landmarks. If alterations to the exterior features of such buildings are consistent with the design guidelines adopted by the commission, the owner is issued a certificate of appropriateness by the commission. Additionally, two counties (Watauga County in the Valle Crucis area and Guilford County in the Oak Ridge area) have adopted local historic districts through their zoning power. In each case the historic preservation commission must issue a certificate of appropriateness for changes in any building in the district, not just historic landmarks. One important power wielded by any commission is that if an owner proposes to demolish a landmark or a building in a historic district, the commission may delay issuing the certificate of appropriateness for up to one year. The delay is intended to encourage the owner to explore alternative uses for the building.

Seven counties have their own commissions. An additional thirteen are partners in joint historic preservation commissions with municipalities. For example, the joint historic preservation commission formed in Wake County has representation from Wake County and all of its municipalities except one. The joint commission in Wake County conducts design review of landmarks outside of municipal historic districts. The preservation commission from each Wake County municipality with a historic district conducts the design review for properties within its district.

Historic preservation commissions also have important planning responsibilities in conducting inventories of a county's historic resources and evaluating whatever special significance each may have.

The Mountain Ridge Protection Act

The Mountain Ridge Protection Act was adopted in 1983 in reaction to the erection of a ten-story condominium project on the top of Little Sugar Mountain in Avery County. The legislation (G.S. 113A-205 to -214) authorized local governments in twenty-four western counties either to allow a state prohibition of high-rise buildings near the crest of certain mountain ridges to become effective, to reject by a referendum any development restrictions at all, or to adopt a local ordinance regulating ridgetop construction. None of the counties rejected the development restriction entirely. Roughly two-thirds of the counties elected to become subject to the state prohibitions. The remaining counties (Alleghany, Avery, Caldwell, Haywood, Jackson, Madison, Surry, and Transylvania) adopted mountain ridge protection ordinances. Several of these counties (Alleghany, Surry, and Caldwell) extended their regulatory coverage to areas beyond those subject to the state prohibition.

The Coastal Area Management Act

Some of the more integrated county planning programs in the state may be found in the twenty coastal counties that are subject to the Coastal Area Management Act (CAMA). The act, enacted in 1974 and codified in G.S. 113A-100 to -134.3, provides a state-local framework for comprehensive planning with an eye to protecting, preserving, and managing North Carolina's coastal regions. The North Carolina Coastal Resources Commission (CRC) is the primary state agency involved. The Commission adopts guidelines and standards for local land use plans; establishes areas of environmental concern; issues permits for major developments in areas of environmental concern (AECs); and supervises the enforcement of the program by local governments.

The counties affected by CAMA include Beaufort, Bertie, Brunswick, Camden, Carteret, Chowan, Craven, Currituck, Dare, Gates, Hertford, Hyde, New Hanover, Onslow, Pamlico, Pasquotank, Pender, Perquimans, Tyrrell, and Washington. Land use plans for these counties (including the municipalities within them) have been adopted in accordance with CRC guidelines, and local governments are responsible for amending and updating these plans every five years. Local governments issue minor development permits for smaller projects (typically involving less than twenty acres) that are located within an area of environmental concern. G.S. 113A-111 requires these CAMA permits to be consistent with the applicable land use plan. In addition, local ordinances such as zoning and

Figure 16-1
Organizing Planning and Land Use Regulation in North Carolina

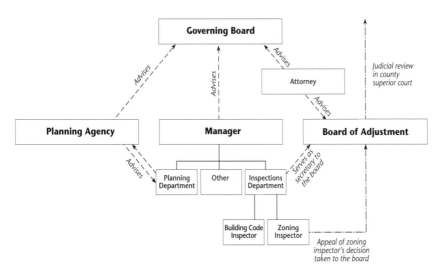

land subdivision ordinances must be consistent with the planned development of AECs.

Organization for County Planning and Development

County planning and development services programs involve a number of county functions, departments, and local boards. The organizational arrangements differ substantially among counties. Some of the most important groups in a local planning program are shown in Figure 16-1. These include the board of county commissioners, the planning agency, the zoning board of adjustment, and the county staff.

The Board of County Commissioners

The key to the success of any county land use and development services program is the board of county commissioners. More than anything else, the board establishes the climate within which a county land use and development services program operates. The board is in a position to exercise leadership, place a priority on planning matters, and establish a clear land use and development policy. The board also exercises a number of powers affecting land use and development. It approves the county budget and the financing for capital projects to be undertaken in the current fiscal year. The board allocates funds for boards, agencies, and departments that carry out planning-related responsibilities. It approves the location and design of public buildings and other public facilities. In its legislative capacity the board adopts and amends various land use and development-related ordinances. It may retain the authority to issue conditional use permits for certain land uses outlined in the zoning ordinance. The board also appoints members to the planning board, the zoning board of adjustment, and other planning-related commissions and agencies. Finally, it has the ultimate authority to enforce county ordinances, and it approves any legal action taken against violators of the various land use and development-related ordinances.

Planning Board

One of the primary citizen boards that is critical to a local planning program is the *planning board* (also called the *planning commission*). A substantial majority of North Carolina counties have established a planning board made up of lay members appointed by the board of commissioners. Often the planning board's duties and responsibilities are advisory. The planning board is generally given the responsibility for supervising the development of a county's comprehensive plan. It may arrange for and supervise the preparation of special studies, land use plans and policies, and drafts of ordinances. It may adopt plans and policies, advise the council on them, and recommend ordinances and methods of carrying out plans. The planning board also has specific duties in connection with the zoning ordinance, since a "planning agency" must prepare and "certify" the draft of a city's original zoning ordinance (G.S. 153A-344). In addition, the planning agency must be given a thirty-day opportunity in which to make a recommendation concerning any proposed amendment to the land development ordinance before the board of commissioners can adopt it.

In addition to its advisory responsibilities, a planning board may be delegated the authority to review certain development proposals. As a planning agency the planning board may be delegated the authority to approve subdivision plats (G.S. 153A-332). The planning board's potential versatility is indicated by the fact that it can take on the duties of certain other agencies if the commissioners so desire. For example, the board of commissioners may assign any or all of the duties of the zoning board of adjustment to a planning board (approval of zoning variances, issuance of conditional use permits, and hearing of appeals from decisions of the zoning official, for example) [G.S. 153A-345(a)]. Also, if at least two planning board members have demonstrated special interest, experience, or education in history or architecture, the planning board may be designated the county historic preservation commission (G.S. 160A-400.7).

North Carolina local governments also may establish a joint planning board representing two or more local units of government. The Winston-Salem/Forsyth County City-County Planning Board and the Charlotte-Mecklenburg Planning Commission are two of the better-known examples of such joint agencies.

Zoning Board of Adjustment

The zoning board of adjustment has three primary responsibilities under North Carolina law [G.S. 153A-345 (b),(c),(d)]. The board of adjustment does the following:

1. Interprets the zoning ordinance. Generally this involves hearing appeals from decisions of the zoning enforcement official when an applicant for a permit or another aggrieved party claims that the zoning official has misinterpreted the ordinance.
2. Grants variances to the zoning ordinance.
3. May be authorized by the board of commissioners to grant conditional use permits for certain land uses and types of development outlined in the ordinance.

Although it is common for a board of adjustment to be charged with some combination of these duties, it is also possible for any of these responsibilities to be delegated by the board of commissioners to the planning agency [G.S. 153A-345(a)]. Virtually all of the board of adjustment's major decisions (issuing a variance or conditional use permit or reversing a decision of the zoning enforcement officer) must be made with the concurring vote of four-fifths of its members. Board of adjustment decisions may not be appealed to the governing board; they may, however, be reviewed in county superior court.

Historic Preservation Commission

To initiate special review of development in a historic district or to designate a property as a historic landmark, a board of county commissioners must appoint a local historic preservation commission. A majority of the historic preservation commission members must have a demonstrated special interest, experience, or education in history, architecture, archaeology, or related fields. The commissioners may assign the functions of a historic preservation commission to a planning agency or to a community appearance commission.

Economic Development Commission

To promote local economic development, a board of commissioners may establish a municipal economic development commission (G.S. 158-8). This commission, with the help of any staff it hires, may engage in community promotion and business recruitment; provide advice, analysis, and assistance concerning economic and business development matters; and help form nonprofit corporations that develop industrial park sites and shell buildings for relocating businesses.

County Manager

The role of the county manager is generally unrecognized in any land use planning program. In small counties the manager or administrator may make recommendations on matters affecting the county's development, enforce planning-related ordinances, and supervise the preparation of plans. In large counties that have a staff planner, the manager may be less directly involved in planning affairs. Nevertheless, that person may coordinate the capital improvement program; administer the housing, community development, transportation, parks and recreation, and inspection programs; make recommendations on economic development proposals; and coordinate the staff review of major development projects that come before the commissioners.

Planning Staff

A county planning, development, and code enforcement program generally requires some professional planning help, which may be provided in any of the following ways:

1. The county may hire staff. Most counties with a population over 25,000 employ at least one staff planner to help administer a land use planning program. Usually planning staff are hired by and ultimately responsible to the county manager, but serve as staff to the planning board and other appointed boards with planning-related responsibilities.

2. The planning board itself may hire staff. The governing body that creates the planning board may authorize it to hire its own full-time staff with funds allocated for this purpose (G.S. 153A-322). Except for joint planning boards that represent more than one jurisdiction, however, this authority has not been used.

3. A county may contract for technical planning services provided by some other local unit of government (G.S. 153A-322).

4. Several local government units may share staff, each jurisdiction retaining its own planning board. Arrangements may be established through an interlocal agreement (G.S. Ch. 160A, Art. 20, Pt. 1).

5. A joint planning board created by two or more local governments may hire staff (G.S. 153A-321, -322). Some of the state's larger planning agencies are city-county boards with their own staff. The interlocal agreement establishing the joint planning board determines the financial contributions of each jurisdiction, the manner of appointment of board members, personnel practices affecting staff members, and the way in which work is assigned and supervised.

6. A private consultant may furnish technical assistance. Private planning consultants have been particularly active in preparing municipal zoning ordinances, economic development plans, and plans for downtown revitalization.

7. A substate regional organization may furnish technical assistance. North Carolina is divided into eighteen regions, each represented by a *lead regional organization* (LRO). LROs in North Carolina take one of three forms: a "regional planning commission" (G.S. 153A-395), a "regional planning and economic development commission" (G.S. 153-398), or a "regional council of governments" (G.S. 160A-475). Most of the LROs provide at least some municipal planning and related technical assistance.

8. The Division of Community Assistance of the North Carolina Department of Commerce may furnish technical assistance. This source provides a broad range of planning and managerial assistance through multiple field offices. The Division of Community Assistance and its predecessor agencies have prepared a number of land use plans and zoning and subdivision ordinances for communities throughout the state.

One of the key organizational questions in county government is how to organize the planning, development, and code-enforcement functions.

In many counties, planning activities and code-enforcement activities are located within the same department for administrative purposes—variously called the planning department, the planning and inspection department, planning and development, or something in that vein. In a few of the large counties (Wake and Guilford, for example) the planning and inspections activities are included within a large super-department that may include soil conservation services, county public works, flood hazard mitigation, and various other regulatory and community and economic development programs.

Code Enforcement Staff

In a large county the zoning enforcement official may be charged only with the enforcement of zoning. In small counties this person is more likely to be a building inspector, the county manager, or county clerk, and may enforce other local ordinances. The inspection department is the primary enforcement agency for a variety of development-related ordinances and codes. It typically enforces the State Building Code and sometimes also enforces the minimum housing code. In many counties, both large and small, the inspection department also enforces the zoning ordinance.

The Territorial Jurisdiction of County Planning and Development

In North Carolina, as in many other states, the areas within which a county may exercise jurisdiction in various planning-related matters are those areas in which a municipality is not exercising jurisdiction of its own. Indeed, cities may exercise jurisdiction over not only areas within their city limits; in some circumstances they may claim jurisdiction over areas located outside their respective boundaries (G.S. 160A-360). Allowing cities "extraterritorial" planning jurisdiction is justified on several grounds and North Carolina annexation laws encourage cities to annex nearby unincorporated urban areas. It is in a city's interest to ensure that areas that will ultimately be brought inside the city limits are (1) developed in a manner consistent with the city's development standards and land use objectives, and (2) served by appropriate public facilities. Otherwise, unplanned growth and substandard development may compromise municipal annexation. Even when a city has no annexation ambitions, unplanned growth and substandard development may have detrimental effects on nearby municipal areas.

In general, a city of any size may establish planning jurisdiction for one mile outside its boundaries. However, North Carolina law does not permit cities to exercise such extraterritorial jurisdiction unilaterally unless there is evidence that the county has not taken the initiative in land use planning. Specifically, a city may assume authority outside its limits on its own only if the county is not already enforcing three major types of development regulations in the target area: (1) zoning; (2) subdivision regulations; and (3) the State Building Code [G.S. 160A-360 (e)]. Where local governments work cooperatively, other jurisdictional arrangements are also possible. With the board of county commissioners' approval, a city with a population of 10,000 to 25,000 may extend its jurisdiction up to two miles outside the city limits, and a city with a population of over 25,000 may extend its jurisdiction up to three miles [G.S. 160A360(a)]. Alternatively, at the city council's request the county may exercise any of the various land use regulatory powers within the city's extraterritorial jurisdiction or even within the city limits [G.S. 160A-360(d)]. Under a third arrangement a city may not exercise extraterritorial jurisdiction unilaterally but may agree, with the county, on the area in which each will exercise the various powers [G.S. 160A-360(e)].

The package of powers that are subject to municipal extraterritorial arrangements is substantial. It includes the following:

1. Zoning
2. Subdivision regulation
3. Enforcement of the State Building Code
4. Minimum housing code regulation
5. Historic district regulation
6. Historic properties designation and regulation
7. Community development projects
8. Jurisdiction of the community appearance commission
9. Acquisition of open space
10. Floodway regulation
11. Soil erosion and sedimentation control regulation

No city may exercise any power in its extraterritorial area that it does not exercise within its city limits. Also, the boundaries of a city's extraterritorial jurisdiction are the same for all powers.

If a city intends to enforce zoning or subdivision regulations in its extraterritorial area, it must allow for the appointment of residents of the extraterritorial area to the municipal planning agency and the municipal zoning board of adjustment (G.S. 160A-362). The number of such appointees and their voting power are determined by city ordinance. However, a rule of proportional representation applies. The residents living in the extraterritorial area must be represented on the two boards in the same proportion to their population as city residents are represented on the boards. A city is directed to ask the county commissioners to appoint outside members to both the planning agency and the zoning board of adjustment. If the appointments are a result of the extension of the city's extraterritorial jurisdiction, then the board of county commissioners must hold a specially advertised public hearing to hear from the public before appointments are made. The commissioners may appoint only those individuals who apply for the position at or before the hearing. If the board of county commissioners does not make these appointments within ninety days after it receives the request, the city council may make them instead.

Zoning

Certainly one of the more controversial programs associated with county planning and development is county zoning. Interest in private property rights and the belief that landowners should be able to do as they wish with the land are views that are widely held in North Carolina, particularly in those rural areas that tend to fall under the zoning jurisdiction of counties. However, as growth and development occur in rural and suburban fringe areas, there is also a tendency for landowners to become increasingly concerned about not only what they can do with their own land but what neighboring property owners are doing with their lands. The result is that county zoning is a bit more prominent in North Carolina than one might expect. Over two-thirds of North Carolina counties have adopted zoning. Forty counties have adopted countywide zoning (zoning all of those areas outside the jurisdiction of municipalities), and twenty-seven others have adopted zoning that applies in certain portions of the areas not subject to municipal planning jurisdiction (see Figure 16-2). There is, of course, considerable variation in the nature of the zoning programs among counties. In some of the poorer and more rural counties, zoning serves only to screen the county from the most unpopular uses of land. In more affluent or more rapidly growing counties such as Currituck, Cabarrus, Orange, and New Hanover however, zoning can at times be fairly demanding and restrictive.

Figure 16-2
County Zoning and Land Subdivision Regulation in North Carolina, 1997

A. Both zoning and subdivision ordinance countywide	39
B. Countywide zoning only	1
C. Countywide subdivision regulation only	15
D. Zoning in part of county, but countywide subdivision regulation	21
E. Both zoning and subdivision regulations apply to part of county	2
F. Zoning in part of county, but no subdivision regulation	4
G. No zoning or subdivision regulations	18
Total	100

Source: Division of Community Assistance, North Carolina Department of Commerce, March 1997

One purpose of zoning is to ensure that activities with major developmental impacts are located in such a manner that they do not become nuisances for their neighbors. Zoning determines that uses as diverse as mining operations, junkyards, high-density manufactured home parks, wood chip mills, rural tourist attractions, and large-scale swine operations are not located in areas in which they would be inappropriate or established at an inappropriate scale. Matters of scale are often important in county zoning. Owners of property in rural areas often are accustomed to a mix of land uses and development activities. However, they may react strongly to activities and development projects that are out of local character because the proposed bulk, size, and scale of operations differs so much from traditional development patterns.

Second, zoning can be used to set minimum development standards for activities through lot size and shape requirements; setback standards; buffering, landscaping, and parking requirements; and road frontage and lot access standards. These standards can make new development more compatible with existing development, protect privacy, reduce development impacts, and often can improve the overall appearance of the area.

A less obvious purpose that zoning may achieve is to ensure that development activities are located in a manner consistent with the government's ability to provide the area with streets, utilities, fire protection, and other services. For example, some counties try to encourage industries to locate in concentrated areas zoned for industry along Interstate and other major highways that are served by public water and sewer and, if available, natural gas. Such a policy may discourage industries from invading rural residential areas, and may also allow public utility providers to provide services more economically than they would if they tried to serve industries at diverse locations throughout the county.

Finally, zoning is increasingly providing counties with a mechanism for comprehensively reviewing the environmental effects of proposed development projects. It is true, of course, that many environmental impacts such as stormwater runoff, ground or surface water contamination, air pollution, and even traffic congestion are the subject of state environmental programs or are otherwise subject to state control. Nonetheless, the rezoning process—even the process for considering a special use permit application—may furnish a county with the opportunity to consider such effects in determining whether certain types of development should be allowed at all, and to coordinate the development review process with state agencies if development is allowed to proceed.

There are, however, a variety of practical difficulties that tend to limit the effectiveness of county zoning. Zoning may be arbitrary, inefficient, unfair, and even confiscatory in the absence of a set of principles, policies, or values that guide zoning in accordance with the law. One problem can be the lack of analysis and guidance concerning growth and development impacts that comes when counties administer zoning without an adequate planning perspective. A related problem shows up in counties that refuse to grapple with fundamental policy questions, such as the extent to which manufactured homes and manufactured home parks in the county should be encouraged, or whether commercial and industrial growth should be concentrated or dispersed throughout the county. These questions are difficult to answer in the absence of some consensus about how and when growth will occur and what the county ought to do about it. The development and adoption of a comprehensive land use plan can help. But even in the most ideal of settings, the locational decisions that are a part of zoning are difficult to resolve. The patterns of development that tend to define urban areas and municipal jurisdictions are often absent in rural areas and county jurisdictions. Many counties are still defined by agricultural and forestry activities and low-density residential development with occasional patches and stretches of nonresidential development, often along primary state highways. In the absence of any sense as to where a county is headed and who should be protected from whom and why, it is difficult for counties to make reasoned and defensible zoning decisions. The result of a lack of clear development policy is that zoning decisions (particularly rezoning decisions) can depend more on the personalities involved than on a proposal's merits.

One unfortunate side effect of these difficulties is the heightened likelihood that a board of county commissioners will be guilty of illegal spot zoning when it makes certain rezoning decisions. Many county re-zoning petitions request the governing board to rezone small tracts of land in predominately residential or agricultural areas to districts that allow nonresidential uses. If this pattern of spot zoning is to be upheld, the county must be prepared to explain why the parcels rezoned should be treated differently from those that were not. If the decision cannot be explained in terms of land planning and zoning principles, the decision may be invalidated.

One important virtue of zoning is its ability to prevent the establishment of development activities that could amount to nuisances or result in land uses that are incompatible with existing development. However, there is also a risk that this power can be used to exclude LULUs (locally unwanted land uses) or to cater to the attitudes of NIMBYs (not in my back yard), even though the development activities and land uses involved are clearly needed by the larger community. Exclusionary zoning is a particular problem for those who care about providing a sufficient amount of good quality housing for those with low or moderate incomes. There is an unfortunate tendency, for example, for hearings that concern manufactured home parks to dwell on the characteristics of the people who are expected to live there rather than the physical characteristics of the park and the surrounding area itself. Counties must take special care to ensure that zoning is not used or viewed as an exclusionary technique.

One important limitation on county zoning is the exemption that the county zoning statutes (G.S. 153A-340) provide for bona fide farms and agricultural, horticultural, silvicultural, and aquacultural activities. These include not only the traditional family farm but many large-scale livestock operations as well. Although large-scale swine operations were made subject to county zoning in 1997, most agricultural activities remain free from regulation. As a result most farming activities may be established anywhere within a county's zoning jurisdiction. Housing developments and residential uses thus have no protection from farming activities despite the fact that the developmental impacts from these activities can, in some cases, be at least as pronounced as those from commercial or industrial activities. The bona fide farm exemption continues to undercut the integrity of county zoning.

The Territorial Extent of County Zoning

As the statistics mentioned earlier indicate, some twenty-seven counties have adopted partial zoning—zoning that applies to a subportion of a county's planning jurisdiction. Many counties establish or extend zoning by township. For example, Chatham County zones all or portions of eight of its thirteen townships. The zoned townships lie in the northern and eastern areas of the county that are undergoing the greatest growth. Others use major geographic features as boundaries. Harnett County zones only the portion of the county north of the Cape Fear River. Still other counties have begun by establishing zoning in small areas of a county to protect a historically significant residential community (such as Valle Crucis in Watauga County), to influence development along major highways (Anson and Yadkin counties), to regulate water supply watershed areas, and to protect certain coastal areas (Dare County). The governing boards in some counties (such as Buncombe County) refuse to extend zoning into unzoned areas in the absence of a petition from property owners requesting it. One disadvantage of this approach is that it can result in configurations that ignore the geographic and activity boundaries that provide integrity to a zoning scheme. The state statutes do establish minimum standards for a "zoning area." G.S. 153A-342 requires that a zoning area originally consist of at least 640 acres and include at least ten separate tracts of land in separate ownership.

Basic Elements

A zoning ordinance consists of text and a map or series of maps. The official zoning map in some counties still consists of a large display map that sets out the zoned areas of the county and indicates the zoning district designations that apply to them. Other counties use a large display map for ready reference, but the official zoning map consists of a zoning atlas made up of a series of tax maps that display zoning district boundaries at a more usable scale. Future zoning maps will be based on geographic information systems that are based on parcel identifiers that are coded in digitized fashion. The official zoning map of the future will be defined by a computer program that stores the geographic information electronically.

The text includes the substantive standards applicable to each district on the map and the procedures that govern proposals for changes in both the text and the map. The zoning ordinance divides the land subject to zoning into a number of zoning districts. The land in each district is governed by several types of regulations: (1) use regulations; (2) dimensional requirements, including setback and density standards; and (3) other, miscellaneous requirements dealing with off-street parking, landscaping and screening, property access, required public improvements, and signs.

Uses Permitted by Right

If a use is permitted by right, the zoning standards for that use are typically spelled out in specific terms. The zoning enforcement official grants a zoning compliance permit if the proposal meets the ordinance standards.

Uses Permitted by Conditional Use Permits

Some uses of land merit closer scrutiny because of their potential impact on nearby properties. These conditional uses may be permissible in a particular district but only at particular locations and then only under particular conditions. *Conditional use permits* (also known as *special use permits* or *special exceptions*) may be issued by the board of commissioners, the zoning board of adjustment, or the planning agency. Regardless of which body issues the permit, the decision to grant or deny it must be based on evidence supplied at a quasi-judicial hearing. The zoning ordinance must explicitly list the requirements that the applicant must meet and the findings that the issuing body must make in order for the permit to be issued. If these requirements are met, the board may not refuse to issue the permit. However, it may impose additional conditions and requirements on the permit that are not specifically mentioned in the ordinance. Such conditions may include specifications on the particular use to be made of the property; sign, parking, or landscaping requirements; requirements that the property owner dedicate land for and construct certain public improvements such as streets, utilities, and parks; and specifications dealing with the timing of development. Conditional use permits may be used to deal with small-scale land uses such as electric power substations and day-care centers, or with large-scale developments like shopping centers and manufactured home parks. Permission to develop or use land in accordance with a conditional use permit stays with the land and applies with equal force to future owners of the property.

Types of Zoning Districts

Most zoning ordinances include three basic types of zoning districts—residential, commercial, and industrial—and a variety of more specialized types of zones—rural, flood hazard, mobile home park, watershed protection, and perhaps planned unit development. There may be several residential districts, each based on different permissible dwelling types and required lot sizes (or densities).

Zoning districts may also be classified as *general use districts* or *conditional use districts* (also known as *special use districts*). All zoning ordinances include at least some general use districts. Various uses or activities are allowed to be located and operated in a general use district either (1) by right or (2) subject to a *conditional use permit.* Generally, any use not specifically listed as permitted is, by implication, prohibited.

The zoning ordinances of some North Carolina counties provide not only for general use districts, but for conditional use districts as well. Any use of land in a conditional use district is subject to a conditional use permit; there are no uses permitted by right. Thus all development in a conditional use district is subject to discretionary review. However, land may not be rezoned to a conditional use district except upon the petition of its owners. In counties that rely on conditional use districts, it is customary for the board of commissioners to grant the conditional use permit. This way the commissioners can consider the application for a conditional use permit at the same time that they consider a petition for the rezoning of land to the conditional use district that authorizes such a permit (see also the discussion under the section "Conditional Use Districts," later in this chapter).

Government Roles in Zoning

In most counties, zoning involves the board of commissioners, a planning board, the zoning board of adjustment, and planning and zoning staff. Collectively these groups carry out the legislative, quasi-judicial, advisory, and administrative functions of a local zoning program. The legislative and quasi-judicial roles of citizen boards in local zoning are a source of some confusion.

Legislative Role

The board of commissioners acts in its legislative role when it adopts or amends the zoning ordinance. When it makes the law, such a board has substantial discretion to make decisions as it sees fit. Although the board must hold a public hearing before it adopts or amends the ordinance, it need not explain its decision or make written findings of fact. The hearing required for legislative action is relatively free from formality. Speakers need not make sworn statements or restrict their statements to topics set forth in the ordinance. Board members may be subject to lobbying efforts before or after the hearing.

Quasi-Judicial Role

Public hearings are also required when three other important types of zoning actions are taken: (1) issuance of variances; (2) issuance of conditional use permits; and (3) the appeal of decisions of a zoning official. However, each of these types of cases must be heard in a quasi-judicial proceeding. The decision must be based on the criteria in the ordinance. Witnesses must be sworn and offer testimony according to certain rules of evidence. Board members may not discuss the case with any of the parties outside the hearing. The board must make written findings of fact. Thus quasi-judicial hearings (sometimes known as evidentiary hearings) are more formal than legislative hearings and more demanding for those who participate in them. The kinds of cases just identified are typically heard by the zoning board of adjustment. However, if the planning board is assigned the job of hearing any of these cases or if the board of commissioners grants conditional use permits itself, then these boards must also follow quasi-judicial procedures when they hear such cases.

Variances

Because no zoning ordinance can anticipate every land use or development situation that will arise, a zoning ordinance must include a procedure for varying or waiving the requirements of the ordinance when practical difficulties or unnecessary hardships would result from its strict enforcement. The permission granted by this procedure is known as a *variance*. In most North Carolina counties, granting a variance is the responsibility of the zoning board of adjustment.

Even though zoning regulations may be burdensome on individual property owners, the board of adjustment's authority to grant variances is limited under the law. The board of adjustment lacks the wide legislative discretion enjoyed by the board of commissioners. Often matters that come before it could be better handled by the planning board and the commissioners as proposals to amend the zoning ordinance. To issue a variance, the board must conclude that all of the following conditions are true:

1. If the property owner complies with the provisions of the ordinance, the owner will be unable to enjoy a reasonable return from the property or to make reasonable use of it.
2. The hardship affecting the property results from the applica-

tion of the ordinance (not from market conditions or the existence of private restrictive covenants).

3. The hardship is suffered by the applicant's property. (The
   applicant's personal, social, or economic circumstances are
   irrelevant.)

4. The hardship does not result from the applicant's own actions.

5. The hardship is peculiar to the applicant's property and does
   not affect other properties in the same neighborhood. (If a
   number of properties suffer the same problem, the council
   should consider amending the zoning ordinance.)

6. The variance is in harmony with the general purpose and intent
   of the zoning ordinance and preserves its spirit. *Use variances*,
   which purport to authorize uses of land not otherwise authorized in the district, have been held by North Carolina courts
   not to be in harmony with the purpose and the intent of a zoning ordinance and not to preserve its spirit.

7. By granting the variance, the board will ensure the public safety
   and welfare and do substantial justice.

Nonconformities and Amortization

When land is zoned or rezoned, certain legally existing uses and
structures may not conform to the new set of zoning regulations that apply. These nonconformities may take a variety of forms: nonconforming
uses, nonconforming buildings (as to height, setback, and so on), and
nonconforming lots (as to width, frontage, or area). In addition, a property may be nonconforming with respect to its provisions for off-street
parking, its landscaping and buffering features, or the position or size
of advertising signs on the property.

Most counties take a rather passive approach to the elimination of
nonconformities. Ordinance provisions are often designed to allow nonconforming uses or structures to continue. There are, of course, restrictions on their expansion or extension. Nonconforming structures may
generally not be structurally altered or replaced. Nonconforming uses
may generally not be converted to other nonconforming uses, and uses
once abandoned may not be reopened. Nonetheless, nonconformities
have proved to be very resistant to attempts to get rid of them.

A quite different method of treating nonconforming situations involves the concept of amortization. Amortization is based on the assumption that the owner of a nonconforming property may be required
to come into full compliance with new development standards if the or-

dinance provides a time period within which the owner may recover the investment made in relying on the former rules. In some cases, amortization may require the removal of a nonconforming use or structure; in other cases it may require the upgrading of a nonconforming use or structure. Amortization provisions are most often applied to nonconforming signs and certain outdoor uses of land (like junkyards) that can be moved to other locations and do not involve entrepreneurial investments of great magnitude. These regulations have been upheld both in principle and in application by the North Carolina courts, overcoming challenges that they violate the landowner's due process rights or that they amount to an unconstitutional taking of private property without just compensation.[2]

Vested Rights

Generally speaking a project that fails to comply with new ordinance standards may be accorded nonconforming status only if it lawfully exists when the new standards become effective. A major issue in zoning law involves how new standards affect construction projects that are begun but not yet completed. If the project is largely a figment of the property owner's imagination, then the project when built will be required to comply with the new standards. If the law allows the owner to complete the project without complying with the new requirements, thus making the project nonconforming, then the owner has established a *vested right.*[3]

Under North Carolina zoning law there are four ways for a property owner to qualify for protection from new ordinance standards. The first method is to establish a *common law vested right.* A common law vested right is established if an owner has made substantial expenditures to carry out a project in good faith reliance on a valid project approval or in the absence of any approval requirement.

The second method was established in 1985 by the General Assembly to provide an alternative form of protection to the property owner that was far easier to apply than the common law vested rights doctrine. G.S. 160A-385(b) simply provides that no zoning ordinance amendment may be applied to property without the owner's consent if a valid building permit for the property has been issued and remains outstanding. (If the building permit expires or is revoked, the vested right expires.) This statute does not apply, however, when the adoption of an initial zoning ordinance is involved.

The third method was established in 1990 to allow property owners to establish a vested right still earlier in the development process. The

General Assembly directed local governments to provide for a vested right when a property owner obtains approval of a *site-specific development plan,* a plan for a particular use of land as proposed for a particular site, or a *phased development plan,* a general plan for a large-scale project staged over a long period. G.S. 153A-344.1 provides that approval of a site-specific development plan establishes a vested right for between two and five years, as determined by the county. Approval of such a plan protects against zoning amendments affecting the type and intensity of use of the property, with certain exceptions. The law also authorizes but does not compel a county to provide for the approval of a phased development plan establishing a vested right for up to five years. However, this statute does not offer protection from adoption of an initial zoning ordinance.

Finally, a zoning ordinance may, without reference to the specific statutes just described, define the extent to which it applies prospectively. For example, an ordinance provision may provide that projects for which development applications are received or lots recorded before the effective date of newly adopted amendments need not meet their terms.

Special Treatment of Certain Activities

Zoning applies to virtually all uses of property. However, the treatment of certain activities under zoning is especially noteworthy because special state legislation affects the extent to which zoning requirements apply.

Manufactured Housing

Manufactured home is the term used in state and federal law for what used to be called a *mobile home.* These units must be built to special construction standards adopted by the United States Department of Housing and Urban Development. The zoning of manufactured homes is subject to legislation adopted by the General Assembly in 1987 that was designed both to counter the exclusionary tendencies of many local zoning ordinances and to clarify that some special treatment of such units was permitted. G.S. 153A-341.1 (referring to G.S. 160A-383.1) prohibits a county from adopting zoning regulations that have the effect of excluding manufactured homes from the entire zoning jurisdiction. However, it expressly authorizes counties and cities to adopt special requirements affecting the appearance and the dimensions of manufactured homes that need not also apply to site-built homes. (The law recognizes prior case law holding that a local government need not allow manufactured homes in every district in which it allows site-built residences.)

The legislation described above does not affect counties as much as it affects cities. The zoning ordinances in many counties (Orange County, for example) treat manufactured homes in essentially the same manner as site-built homes. However, the zoning treatment of manufactured homes is important because in a number of counties located on the fringes of metropolitan areas, permits for manufactured homes substantially outnumber permits for site-built single-family houses.

Modular homes are built in a factory, but meet the construction standards of the State Building Code. For zoning purposes they are usually treated in the same manner as site-built residences. The 1987 legislation does not affect modular units.

Establishments Selling Alcohol

The sale and consumption of alcohol are activities beyond the reach of zoning. The sale, consumption, and transportation of alcohol are subject to a uniform system of state regulations administered by the North Carolina Alcoholic Beverage Control (ABC) Commission, which controls the issuance of permits for such activities and preempts local zoning. State law provides that the ABC Commission "shall consider" local zoning requirements in determining whether a permit should be issued for an establishment at a particular location. However, it is clear that zoning requirements may not be used to prohibit the sale or the consumption of alcohol at a particular establishment if the ABC Commission has issued a permit for that activity.

Signs and Billboards

The erection and display of signs and billboards (outdoor advertising displays) have long been subject to county zoning and special-purpose ordinances. Certain commercial off-premise signs located along particular major federal highways are also subject to requirements imposed by the North Carolina Outdoor Advertising Control Act, which is administered by the North Carolina Department of Transportation. In areas where both sets of regulations apply, it is generally true that county sign standards for newly erected signs are more restrictive and demanding than those adopted by the state, and take precedence over state standards.

The Outdoor Advertising Control Act, however, limits the ability of a local government to require the removal of existing nonconforming signs along these federal highways. It provides that if the Department of Transportation has issued a permit for a sign along the corridors of these federal highways and if local ordinance provisions have made the sign nonconforming, the local government may not require the removal of the sign unless it provides "just compensation" (G.S. 136-131.1) to the owners of the outdoor advertising display and the land. As a result, local sign amortization regulations that require owners of signs to comply with new regulations within a certain number of years but fail to provide monetary compensation for doing so may not be applied to nonconforming signs located along certain federal highways. Amortization requirements may, however, be applied to signs located elsewhere within a county's zoning jurisdiction.

Watershed Protection

North Carolina's mandatory watershed protection legislation, initially adopted in 1989, has important implications for counties whose planning and zoning jurisdiction includes land within the watershed of a public drinking-water supply. This program is designed to protect water supplies from the impurities of runoff from land within a watershed (non-point sources of pollution). The North Carolina Environmental Management Commission has classified over 200 such watersheds into five water supply categories: WS-I, WS-II, WS-III, WS-IV, and WS-V. It has also established statewide minimum watershed protection requirements that apply to the use and development of land in both the *critical areas* of such watersheds and the remainder of the watershed. State law requires affected local governments to incorporate the appropriate land development standards into local zoning, land subdivision, and special-purpose watershed protection ordinances. No fewer than seventy-seven counties include territory within a water supply watershed area, and in most cases some part of these watersheds is located within the county's planning jurisdiction. (About 20 percent of the land in North Carolina is subject to the Water Supply Watershed Program.)

Perhaps the two primary standards established by state law are the *minimum lot size* for single-family residential lots and the *built-upon-area ratios* for multifamily and nonresidential development. For example, the minimum residential lot size in the critical area of a WS-III watershed is one acre. In such a watershed category the portion of the lot that is built upon (in other words, the area with impervious surface) may not exceed 36 percent of the total lot area. The regulations also allow a county to choose a *high-density option*, which permits a property owner to develop a lot more intensively if certain measures are taken to control stormwater. Nineteen of the counties with watershed regulations, most of them urban, have chosen this option. In addition, about a quarter of the counties (not necessarily the same quarter as have elected the high-density option, but often more urban ones) have adopted standards that exceed or are more restrictive than the state's minimum standards. In many portions of the watersheds located within county planning jurisdiction, the watershed protection development standards do not substantially impact the development that might otherwise locate there. However, in counties where watersheds coincide with areas planned for high-intensity developments such as industrial parks or mobile home parks, the standards can be rather restrictive.

Amendment of the Zoning Ordinance

Zoning Amendment Process

Unlike many county ordinances, a local zoning ordinance may be amended fairly often. Most zoning ordinance amendments are map amendments that change the zoning district classification of particular properties and are known as *rezonings*. However, important alterations may also be made in the ordinance text.

When a board of commissioners amends the zoning ordinance, it acts in its legislative capacity. Proposals to amend the zoning ordinance may typically be submitted by anyone—a planning board member, a member of the board of commissioners, a local government agency or commission, or a person in the community (whether or not they are a property owner). Before the board of commissioners may consider a proposed amendment, the planning board must have an opportunity to make recommendations on it. In some counties a zoning amendment petition is reviewed by the planning staff to ensure that the petition is complete before the commissioners decide whether to set a public hearing date to consider the proposal. In other counties the governing board refers the petition to the planning board and holds a public hearing on virtually every such petition submitted in good faith. State law requires the board of commissioners to hold a public hearing before it adopts any zoning ordinance amendment. Notice of this hearing must be published several times in a local newspaper. If property is proposed to be rezoned, notice of the hearing must generally be sent by first-class mail to the owners of the land to be rezoned and to the owners of abutting land.

Negotiating Map Amendments

Rezoning is easily one of the most controversial aspects of zoning. Rezoning procedures do not always conform to the expectations that property owners and neighbors have about how zoning should work. Part of the problem is that property owners, neighbors, and local government board members are interested in discussing the nature of the particular use that will be made of land proposed for rezoning. However, most conventional zoning districts provide for a range of permissible uses. North Carolina zoning case law has made it rather difficult for participants in rezoning hearings to focus on the specific plans of the petitioner or to give any assurance about the specific way in which the property will be used if the land is rezoned. These difficulties arise from three legal principles established by North Carolina state courts:

1. To be rezoned to a general use district, land must meet the *general suitability* criterion, which requires that the property be suitable for any use permitted in that district. Any rezoning to a general use district that cannot be justified in terms of all the possible uses permitted in the new district is considered arbitrary and capricious and may be invalidated. Just how demanding this principle can be is illustrated when a petitioner suggests to the governing board that if the land is rezoned, it will be developed in a particular way. A series of North Carolina court rulings demonstrate that a petitioning developer does so at its peril.[4]

2. Ad hoc conditions may not be attached to a zoning amendment. In other words, *conditional zoning* is unenforceable, at least in the context of rezoning to a general use district. When rezoning a particular property, many governing boards have been tempted to include in the amending ordinance, conditions on the manner of development that apply to the petitioner's land but do not apply to other lands zoned the same way. In doing so, however, boards run afoul of the zoning statute (G.S. 153A-342) that requires regulations to be uniform with respect to all properties within a particular kind of district. Under North Carolina case law, special requirements not spelled out in

the ordinance that are added as conditions to a rezoning are invalid and hence unenforceable.[5] The rezoning itself is not necessarily invalid, but the city does not gain the control that it expected over the land of the petitioning property owner.

3. A local government may not engage in *contract zoning.* Contract zoning involves a transaction in which both the landowner who seeks a rezoning and the governing board itself undertake reciprocal obligations in the form of a bilateral contract.[6] For example, a landowner might agree to subject his property to deed restrictions or make certain road improvements to enhance access to the land if the city council agrees to rezone the land when the landowner takes these steps. Contract zoning of this type is illegal because a city, by agreeing to exercise its legislative power in a particular way at a future date, abandons its duty to exercise independent judgment in making future legislative zoning decisions.[7]

Special Rezoning Methods and Issues

Conditional Use Districts

The relatively conservative legal doctrines just outlined have encouraged North Carolina cities to find more flexible ways of rezoning land. One such technique combines the discretion offered by the rezoning process with the condition-adding power of the conditional use permit. *Conditional use districts* were first expressly authorized by legislation in 1985 (codified as G.S. 160A-382 and G.S. 153A-342), but several counties and cities were using the technique in the early 1970s.[8] In ordinances that provide for conditional use districts, it is common for each such district to correspond to or "parallel" a conventional general use district. For example, an ordinance that provides for a highway business district (a general use district) may also authorize a conditional use–highway business district.

The list of uses that may be approved for a conditional use district typically corresponds to the list of uses allowed in the particular general use district that serves as its parallel. In sharp contrast to a general use district, however, a conditional use district allows no uses by right. Instead, every use allowed in it requires a conditional use permit granted by the governing board. Because of this feature, the statutes prohibit the rezoning of land to a conditional use district unless all the owners of land to be rezoned consent to the proposal.

The key feature of the conditional use district as a zoning technique is that petitions for rezoning to such a district and applications for the conditional use permit required for any development in such a district are generally considered together. The public hearing for the rezoning and the public hearing for the conditional use permit are consolidated.[9] Some counties amend the zoning map and grant the permit with the same vote. Most important, the petitioner or the applicant is encouraged to submit a development plan that indicates the proposed use of the land. If the board of commissioners is not pleased with the development proposal, it may choose not to rezone the property. If it is generally pleased with the proposal, it may restrict the use of the land (generally to that proposed by the developer) or mitigate the expected adverse impacts of the development by adding conditions to the conditional use permit, which is granted contemporaneously with the rezoning.

Spot Zoning

Another legal doctrine that limits the discretion of the board of commissioners in rezoning property involves *spot zoning*. The North Carolina Supreme Court defines spot zoning as

> [a] zoning ordinance or amendment which singles out and reclassifies a relatively small tract owned by a single person and surrounded by a much larger area uniformly zoned, so as to impose upon the small tract greater restrictions than those imposed upon the larger area, or so as to relieve the small tract from restrictions to which the rest of the area is subjected[10]

Zoning decisions that result in this spot zoning pattern are not necessarily invalid and illegal, however, unless there is no reasonable basis for treating the singled-out property differently from adjacent land. Whether there is good reason for the distinction depends, for example, on the following conditions:

1. The size of the tract
2. The compatibility of the disputed zoning action with an existing comprehensive zoning plan
3. The benefits and detriments of the rezoning for the petitioning property owner, neighbors, and surrounding community
4. The relationship between the uses envisioned under the new zoning and the uses of adjacent land[11]

Whether a specific instance of spot zoning is illegal depends to a substantial degree on the particular facts and circumstances of the case. In any case the evolving doctrine of spot zoning is consistent with the notion that any rezoning that smacks of favoritism or lacks proper justification risks invalidation.

Zoning as a Regulatory Taking

Because zoning is a potent form of land use regulation, zoning requirements may have a drastic impact on a particular property. The constitutional doctrine that comes into play most frequently in this context is the provision of the Fifth Amendment to the United States Constitution that prohibits the *taking* of private property for public use without the payment of just compensation. It has long been true that a law that severely restricts the use of property can have such a confiscatory effect as to constitute a *regulatory taking*. However, it was 1987 before the United States Supreme Court clarified that if a property owner proves such a taking, the remedy is not merely the invalidation of the regulation; the offending government may be held liable in damages for losses suffered by the property owner during the period when the unconstitutional regulation was in effect.[12]

Determining whether an unconstitutional taking has occurred typically depends on a balancing of the interests of the regulating government and the interests of the property owner. Two rules of thumb are clear: (1) If a regulation prevents the use or development of land to create a common law nuisance (for example, if a rule prevents new residences from being built in a floodway), such a prohibition is not a taking, regardless of its effect on the value of the property. (2) In contrast, if a regulation does not prevent a nuisance but does prevent an owner from making any practical use of a property or enjoying any reasonable return from it, the restriction amounts to a taking.[13]

Exclusionary Zoning

In general, the term *exclusionary zoning* describes zoning efforts designed to prohibit certain types of land use activities from the entire jurisdiction. Some local governments try to exclude completely certain less-popular land uses such as junkyards, massage parlors, hazardous waste facilities, billboards, mobile home parks, outdoor advertising displays, pawnshops, sexually oriented businesses, and nightclubs. Although the courts have not addressed constitutional challenges to exclusionary zoning, at least one North Carolina case suggests that housing types and land use-activities that are otherwise legal and do not constitute nuisances per se cannot normally be excluded from a jurisdiction where they would otherwise locate or operate.[14]

Land Subdivision Regulation

The word *subdivision* usually calls to mind a relatively large residential development of single-family homes. For regulatory purposes, however, subdivision may best be thought of as a process by which a tract of land is split into smaller parcels, lots, or building sites so that the lots or parcels may eventually be sold or developed or both.

Most subdivision ordinances are based on the premise that the division of land generally signals that the land will soon be developed and used more intensively than it was before subdivision. As a result, purchasers of the subdivided tracts or lots are likely to make more demands for community facilities and services. The platting and recording of a subdivision map offer a county the opportunity not only to review the design of the resulting lots but also to ensure that the subdivider provides streets, utilities, and other public improvements that will be required to serve the needs of those who purchase the subdivided land.

County subdivision ordinances are more common than county zoning ordinances. Seventy-seven counties have adopted subdivision ordinances; seventy-five have done so countywide (see Figure 16-2).

Subdivision Design

The most fundamental subdivision design considerations concern the arrangement of lots and streets. County ordinance provisions commonly specify minimum lot sizes and widths and require that a suitable road provide access to newly subdivided lots. Standards for street design may include width, grade, and sight distance specifications for rights-of-way and pavements, and maximum lengths for blocks and cul-de-sacs; these provisions ensure that emergency vehicles can easily reach any lot and that traffic is not overly concentrated at a particular intersection. Another design consideration ensures that the improvements in a new subdivision, such as roads, water and sewer lines, stormwater control systems, and other utilities, can be conveniently connected to public or private facilities available in the vicinity of the subdivision.

One important issue in county subdivision review concerns the minimum size of new subdivision lots that will be developed with a well and septic tank. In areas where zoning is in effect, most ordinances incorporate the minimum lot-size standards of the zoning district in which the land is located by reference. Where no zoning ordinance is in effect, separate lot-size minimums must be established in the subdivision ordinance to ensure proper design and to relieve the health department of having to establish minimum lot sizes for each lot for which a septic tank is proposed. Nevertheless, it is often helpful if the health department can conduct preliminary site evaluations to determine whether the lots proposed on a preliminary subdivision plat are likely to be adequate to support a septic tank or whether lots should be redesigned or combined. The difficulty is that health departments are understandably reluctant to "approve" proposed lots as they are being subdivided in the absence of any specific plan about the nature of the building the lot will support, particularly if approval might be construed to guarantee the developer or lot purchaser that a septic tank improvements permit will be issued in the future whenever an application for it is received.

Exactions and the Financing of Subdivision Improvements

The questions of who will finance subdivision improvements and community facilities and how they will be maintained are fundamental to subdivision regulation. It is not uncommon for a county to expect subdividers to provide certain public improvements at their own expense. The most common forms of *exactions* used by counties take the form of requirements for either the construction or installation of infrastructure improvements or the dedication of land. Table 16-1 details a county's authority to exact various types of facilities by the different means at its disposal.

Construction of Infrastructural Improvements

County subdivision regulations often require the subdivider to construct or install certain subdivision improvements. The subdivision enabling statutes (G.S. 153A-331) allow counties to require the "construction of community service facilities in accordance with county policies and standards." *Community service facilities* defies exact definition, but the most commonly required subdivision improvements include streets, drainage swales or storm sewers, and water and/or sewer lines.

Subdivision development sometimes provides an excellent opportunity to arrange for utility lines or stormwater drainage improvements that are designed not only for a particular subdivision but also for future development. If a sewer line must be extended from the end of a sewerage network to a tract being subdivided, the owners of land along the line may wish to connect to it at some future time. A 6-inch water line might adequately serve the particular subdivision, yet it might be wise to lay a 12-inch main in order to serve expected development on the far side of the subdivision in the future. Several approaches are used to allocate costs. If a developer is the first to demand service in a newly developing area, the developer may be required to furnish the line. Some local governments may impose acreage fees or other charges on later developers who use the facility, and pay over some of these funds to the original developer in partial reimbursement for all the extra costs that the original developer assumed. Alternatively, if a county requires a subdivider to provide capacity exceeding that necessary to serve the subdivision, the county may pay for the extra capacity from its general funds on the theory that the oversized facilities will benefit the community generally.

Dedication of Land

For purposes of development approval, a dedication is a form of exaction that requires the developer to donate to the public some interest in land for certain public uses. Compulsory dedication is based on the assumption that it is often desirable for a public agency to own, control, and maintain the improvements, facilities, and recreation areas in a new subdivision. In many instances, however, such government responsibility for control and maintenance is neither possible nor practical. Counties must give careful thought to whether common facilities are made public or are allowed (or required) to remain private.

North Carolina law allows counties, as a condition of subdivision plat approval, to require the dedication of sites and easements for streets, utilities, and recreation areas. One of the more important choices a county must make in its subdivision regulations is when to require a subdivider to offer subdivision roads for dedication to the public. If a subdivision road in an unincorporated area is offered for public dedication, it must be designed and constructed to the secondary road standards of the North Carolina Department of Transportation (G.S. 136-102.6). As a general rule, the only public agency that may accept and maintain such a road is NCDOT. However, NCDOT standards are rather demanding, and require the roads it accepts to be paved. Unless the road is a subdivision entrance road or the subdivision includes more than a certain number of lots (twenty-five lots, for example), most counties allow a subdivider to

Table 16-1
County Authority to Impose Exactions as a Condition of
Subdivision Plat Approval under the General Statutes

Type of Exaction	Type of Community Facility				
	Parks	Utilities	Streets	Schools	Fire Stations
Construction or installation of improvements	Yes	Yes	Yes	Probably not	Probably not
Dedication of land	Yes	Yes, for utility easements	Yes	No	No
Payment of fees in lieu	Yes	No express authority	Yes, for street construction	No	No
Payment of impact fees	Possibly	Probably, under public enterprise authority	Possibly	Possibly	Possibly

opt for private roads that are built to lesser standards. Maintenance arrangements for subdivision roads in unincorporated areas are a problem for counties, lot purchasers, and developers alike. In rare instances involving resort developments, the subdivider may agree to assume or be assigned the responsibility for the ongoing maintenance of roads. In other cases counties may require that a property owners' association be established that has been assigned road maintenance responsibility. More commonly, the subdivider is expected to draft a road maintenance agreement that is incorporated into the deed restrictions that apply to the subdivision lots. More lenient counties simply leave the resolution of subdivision road maintenance matters to the lot purchasers themselves.

Exactions and the Constitution

An important dimension of exactions is their constitutional implications. Unless exactions are flexibly applied, they can amount to an unconstitutional taking of private property for public use without just compensation. Exactions must be properly and fairly related to the need for new public facilities generated by a new development.

The United States Supreme Court recently issued a major decision on exactions, one with which North Carolina case law seems to be consistent. In *Dolan v. City of Tigard*,[15] the Court ruled that the United States Constitution requires "rough proportionality" between the impact of the development and the nature and the extent of the exaction. Although precise mathematical calculation is not required, some sort of individualized determination must be made to justify an exaction requirement as it is applied in a particular case. The Court also held that a local government bears the burden of proving that an exaction is constitutional.

Subdivision Review Process

In North Carolina, final approval of subdivision plats may be granted by (1) the board of county commissioners, (2) the board of commissioners on recommendation from a planning agency, or (3) a planning agency (G.S. 153A-332). Most counties also review a *preliminary* or *tentative plat*. Because the statutes do not say how a preliminary plat should be reviewed, local units have many choices in organizing the review process.

Some counties encourage developers first to submit a *sketch plan* or *design plan* to the planning staff or the plat approval agency. The purpose of these preliminary plans is to bring representatives of local government and the subdivider together so that the local unit can learn what the subdivider has planned and the subdivider can better understand the unit's requirements in approving the subdivision.

Usually the next important step in the review process is the submission and approval of a preliminary plat. To call a subdivision map submitted at this stage "preliminary" may be misleading because the plat will, in large measure, fix the nature, design, and scope of the subdividing activity to follow. Furthermore, it serves as a general blueprint for the installation of whatever improvements or community facilities the developer is to provide. One important aspect of preliminary plat review is the comments and recommendations obtained from various city and county departments and agencies outside local government before formal action is taken on the preliminary plat.

Generally, the final plat is submitted for approval and reviewed by various agencies in much the same manner as the preliminary plat. In counties where the developer may install improvements after final plat approval, the approval of construction plans may be delayed until the final plat approval stage.

In some circumstances a county may require no preliminary plat at all; only the final plat is reviewed. Many counties classify subdivisions as *major* or *minor* on the basis of the number and size of the lots involved. Major subdivisions are subject to the two-stage review process described earlier; minor subdivisions (those that do not involve the installation of public improvements and do not have a major impact on the community) are reviewed just once—at the final plat stage.

Once the final plat is approved, the plat must be recorded in the county register of deeds' office *before* lots may be sold. The register of deeds may not record a plat of a subdivision subject to regulation unless an authorized representative of the county has indicated on the face of the plat that it has been approved (G.S. 153A-332).

Guaranteeing Developer Performance

In general, a developer may not begin to construct subdivision improvements until the preliminary plat is approved. Once that approval is granted, the developer is obliged to arrange for certain dedications to be made and improvements to be installed or constructed before the final plat may be approved. One way to ensure that streets are properly constructed and utilities and drainage facilities properly installed is to withhold final plat approval until these improvements are completed, inspected, and, if appropriate, accepted by a government agency or unit. A more common practice is to allow final plat approval if the subdivider has provided adequate assurance to the county that improvements will be completed after the final plat is approved. The subdivider may post a letter of credit or some other form of performance guarantee (a bond or securities held in escrow, for example). Other counties require no particular performance guarantee, particularly if the subdivision improvements are to be privately maintained or operated.

Enforcing the Ordinance

In certain rural North Carolina counties the illegal subdivision of lots is a significant problem. The problem occurs most often in situations where no new roads or utility lines are required to serve the new lots, thus depriving the county of whatever leverage it may have to withhold initial service. The county register of deeds may not legally refuse to record deeds that are otherwise suitable for recordation simply because they describe lots in an illegal subdivision or because no plat for the subdivision has been approved. Furthermore, the North Carolina Supreme Court has held that a building permit may not be withheld for an illegally subdivided lot simply because the subdivision ordinance has been violated. Therefore the only courses of action available to the county include imposing a civil penalty, obtaining an injunction, or encouraging criminal prosecution against the subdivider.

Building Code Enforcement

The North Carolina State Building Code, adopted by the North Carolina Building Code Council, applies throughout the state. However, each city and county is responsible for arranging enforcement of the code within its jurisdiction. The code generally applies to new construction, but it also includes a fire code volume that applies to the use of existing buildings, a volume concerned with the alteration of existing buildings, and other provisions governing the condemnation of unsafe buildings. The code also provides for the issuance of building permits and certificates of occupancy. The building permit and certificate of occupancy are particularly important in the development and construction processes because they signify not only consistency of plans and work with the requirements of the State Building Code but also compliance with other state and local regulations applicable to the work.

The North Carolina State Building Code is really a series of eleven volumes adopted at different times and for different purposes. The code applies to all types of new buildings, structures, and their systems and facilities except farm buildings outside city building code enforcement jurisdiction and several minor classes of property. As a general rule, no local government may modify or amend the code as it applies locally. The one exception to this rule applies to proposed local amendments to the code's fire prevention regulations (volume V). These amendments must be submitted to the State Building Code Council for review. The regulations must be approved if they are more stringent than those found in the state code.

To arrange for local code enforcement services, a county may do the following:

1. Create its own inspection department
2. Form a joint inspection department with another local unit
3. Hire an inspector from another unit on a part-time basis, with the approval of the other unit's governing board

4. Contract with another unit for the other unit to furnish inspection services to it
5. Request a city within the county to provide inspection and enforcement services throughout any area within which the city may exercise such jurisdiction
6. Contract with a certified code enforcement official who is not a local government employee

Since 1979 no person may enforce the State Building Code without a certificate from the North Carolina Code Officials Qualification Board. Five categories of certified inspectors have been established: building, mechanical, electrical, plumbing, and fire. Each inspector must hold a limited, probationary, or standard certificate for one of three levels of competency (G.S. 143-151.13). All inspectors must complete certain training courses to retain their certification. The Code Officials Qualification Board may revoke an inspector's certificate for various reasons, including gross negligence.[16]

County inspection departments vary widely in their makeup and responsibilities. Several counties employ a single code-enforcement official, cross-trained to perform building, mechanical, electrical, plumbing, and fire inspections. At the other extreme Mecklenburg County employs 118 officials who are certified to enforce the State Building Code. Counties are more likely than cities to employ inspectors who are cross-trained with certifications in multiple code areas. A substantial portion of the new construction in a county's territorial jurisdiction involves single-family residential units. It is more efficient for one inspector to be able to make all of the required inspections for a house than for multiple inspectors to do so. County inspectors are also less likely to need the level two and level three certifications that may be required to inspect the high-rise buildings and complex commercial and industrial construction more commonly found within the jurisdiction of a large municipality. Nonetheless, a number of county inspection departments enforce the State Building Code for the small municipalities within their respective jurisdictions by agreement. In addition, inspection departments often enforce various local development-related ordinances as well as the State Building Code. Building inspectors in particular may also enforce the local zoning ordinance, the watershed protection ordinance, the flood hazard ordinance, the minimum housing ordinance, or even the county soil erosion and sedimentation control ordinance.

One of the notable trends of the 1990s has been the developing expectation of many counties that the inspection and code enforcement activities of county government generate sufficient revenue to recover all or a substantial portion of the costs of administering the program. As a result, development permit and inspection fees have increased dramatically in the last decade.

Additional Resources

Brough, Michael B., and Philip P. Green, Jr. *The Zoning Board of Adjustment in North Carolina,* 2d ed. Chapel Hill, N.C.: Institute of Government, The University of North Carolina at Chapel Hill, 1984.

Ducker, Richard D. "Administering Subdivision Ordinances." *Popular Government* 45 (Summer 1979): 20–28.

_____. "Community Planning, Land Use, and Development," in *Municipal Government in North Carolina,* 2d ed. (David M. Lawrence and Warren Jake Wicker, eds.) Chapel Hill, N.C.: Institute of Government, The University of North Carolina at Chapel Hill, 1996.

_____. *Dedicating and Reserving Land to Provide Access to North Carolina Beaches.* Chapel Hill, N.C.: Institute of Government, The University of North Carolina at Chapel Hill, 1982.

_____. "Federal and State Programs to Control Signs and Outdoor Advertising." *Popular Government* 52 (Spring 1987): 28–42.

_____. "Land-Use Planning in Rural Areas." *Popular Government* 46 (Summer 1980): 28–34.

_____. "Off-Street Parking in North Carolina Municipalities." *Popular Government* 46 (Summer 1980): 39–42.

_____. *Subdivision Regulations in North Carolina: An Introduction.* Chapel Hill, N.C.: Institute of Government, The University of North Carolina at Chapel Hill, 1980.

_____. "'Taking' Found for Beach Access Dedication Requirement: *Nollan v. California Coastal Commission.*" *Local Government Law Bulletin,* no. 30 (Institute of Government, Aug. 1987): 1–6.

_____. "Using Impact Fees for Public Schools: The Orange County Experiment." *School Law Bulletin* 26 (Spring 1994): 1–13.

Ducker, Richard D., and George K. Cobb. "Protecting Rights-of-Way for Future Streets and Highways." *Popular Government* 58 (Fall 1992): 32–40.

Green, Philip R, Jr. *Legal Responsibilities of the Local Zoning Administrator in North Carolina,* 2d ed. Chapel Hill, N.C.: Institute of Government, The University of North Carolina at Chapel Hill, 1987.

_____. *Organizing for Local Government Planning in North Carolina.* Chapel Hill, N.C.: Institute of Government, The University of North Carolina at Chapel Hill, 1989.

_____. "Questions I'm Most Often Asked: What Is 'Spot Zoning'?" *Popular Government* 51 (Summer 1985): 50–53.

_____. "Temporary Damages for a Regulatory 'Taking': *First English Evangelical Lutheran Church v. County of Los Angeles.*" *Local Government Law Bulletin,* no. 29 (Institute of Government, July 1987): 1–4.

_____. "Two Major Zoning Decisions: *Chrismon v. Guilford County* and *Hall v. City of Durham.*" *Local Government Law Bulletin,* no. 34 (Institute of Government, Nov. 1988): 1–7.

Owens, David W. "Amortization: An Old Land-Use Controversy Heats Up." *Popular Government* 57 (Fall 1991): 20–29.

_____. "Bias and Conflicts of Interest in Land-Use Management Decisions." *Popular Government* 55 (Winter 1990): 29–36.

_____. *Conflicts of Interest in Land-Use Management Decisions.* Chapel Hill, N.C.: Institute of Government, The University of North Carolina at Chapel Hill, 1990.

_____. *Introduction to Zoning.* Chapel Hill, N.C.: Institute of Government, The University of North Carolina at Chapel Hill, 1995.

_____. "Land-Use and Development Moratoria." *Popular Government* 56 (Fall 1990): 31–36.

_____. *Regulating Sexually Oriented Businesses.* Special Series No. 15. Chapel Hill, N.C.: Institute of Government, The University of North Carolina at Chapel Hill, 1997.

_____. *Legislative Zoning Decisions: Legal Aspects.* Chapel Hill, N.C.: Institute of Government, The University of North Carolina at Chapel Hill, 1993.

_____. "Zoning Hearings: Knowing Which Rules to Apply." *Popular Government* 58 (Spring 1993): 26–35.

Owens, David W., Richard D. Ducker, and Milton S. Heath, Jr. "Supreme Court Establishes Rule on 'Total Taking': Perspectives on the *Lucas* Case." *Planning and Zoning Bulletin*, no. 3 (Institute of Government, Sept. 1992): 1–18.

Notes

1. Although not required by state law, a local government may bind itself in its zoning ordinance to grant a special use permit or to rezone property only if the proposal is consistent with the unit's own land development plan. In addition, a subdivision ordinance may require that the dedication of land and the construction of improvements be consistent with the public facilities element of a comprehensive plan.

2. *See, e.g.,* State v. Joyner, 286 N.C. 366, 211 S.E.2d 320, *appeal dismissed,* 422 U.S. 1002 (1975) (validating the amortization of salvage yards and junkyards over three years); Naegele Outdoor Advertising v. City of Durham, 803 F. Supp. 1068 (M.D.N.C. 1992), *aff'd,* 19 F.3d 11 (1994) (validating the amortization of commercial off-premise signs over five and one-half years).

3. Technically the term *vested right* applies to a constitutionally protected property right to complete the project. However, for purposes of this discussion, the term is used also to apply to the rights of property owners to complete a project based on provisions in state statutes or local ordinances that grandfather projects and that are more liberal than required by the United States Constitution.

4. Allred v. City of Raleigh, 277 N.C. 530, 178 S.E.2d 432 (1971); Blades v. City of Raleigh, 280 N.C. 531, 187 S.E.2d 35 (1972); Hall v. City of Durham, 323 N.C. 293, 372 S.E.2d 564, *reh'g denied,* 323 N.C. 629, 374 S.E.2d 586 (1988).

5. In Decker v. Coleman, 6 N.C. App. 102, 169 S.E.2d 487 (1969), the city council rezoned a property bordering a residential area to permit a shopping center but made the rezoning subject to a proviso that the developer leave a buffer strip around the development and not cut any access road through this strip into residential neighborhoods. The regulations for the particular commercial zoning district made no mention of such requirements. When the developer ignored these condi-

tions, affected neighbors sought compliance in court. The court held that the conditions were unenforceable because they applied only to this property and not to other land with the same zoning district designation.

6. Chrismon v. Guilford County, 322 N.C. 611, 635, 370 S.E.2d 579, 593 (1988).

7. North Carolina courts have not had the occasion to rule on the validity of such a contract. However, *Chrismon* strongly implies that such contracts are void and unenforceable. *Id.* at 635, 370 S.E.2d at 593.

8. In *Chrismon*, 322 N.C. 611, 370 S.E.2d 579, the North Carolina Supreme Court approved the use of these districts even though the controversy in that case predated the adoption by the North Carolina General Assembly of express enabling legislation for all local governments.

9. It stands to reason that if a legislative hearing and a quasi-judicial hearing are combined, the more demanding requirements of quasi-judicial hearings have to be observed. Many, but not all, local governments treat such hearings as quasi-judicial.

10. *Blades,* 280 N.C. at 549, 187 S.E.2d at 45.

11. *Chrismon,* 322 N.C. at 628, 370 S.E.2d at 589.

12. First English Evangelical Lutheran Church of Glendale v. County of Los Angeles, 482 U.S. 304 (1987).

13. Lucas v. South Carolina Coastal Council, 505 U.S. 1003, 120 L. Ed. 2d 798, 112 S. Ct. 2886 (1992). *See also* Finch v. City of Durham, 325 N.C. 352, 384 S.E.2d 8 (1989), *reh'g denied,* 325 N.C. 714, 388 S.E.2d 452 (1989).

14. Town of Conover v. Jolly, 277 N.C. 439, 177 S.E.2d 879 (1971) (invalidating special "trailer" ordinance prohibiting mobile homes used as permanent residences anywhere within city limits).

15. 512 U.S. 374, 129 L. Ed. 2d 304, 114 S. Ct. 2309 (1994).

16. In a limited number of instances, the owners of new residences have been successful in convincing the board that an inspector's certificate should be revoked because of the inspector's failure to inspect adequately the house that they bought and to detect and have corrected construction mistakes made by contractors.

17 Community Development, Housing, and Economic Development

Anita R. Brown-Graham and David M. Lawrence

Contents

Anita R. Brown-Graham is an Institute of Government faculty member whose areas of
specialization include housing and community development.

David M. Lawrence is an Institute of Government faculty member whose interests
include legal aspects of economic development.

The authors express their appreciation to their colleague Kurt Jenne, whose advice and
previous work in community development are reflected in this chapter.

In one out of every four of the state's counties, 20 percent or more of the population lives in poverty. Even the more affluent counties are often plagued with pockets of severely distressed areas facing income levels significantly below the average for surrounding areas, a lack of employment opportunities, and insufficient or inadequate affordable housing. North Carolina counties have undertaken a cornucopia of programs that have combined local, state, and federal resources to improve housing, neighborhood environments, and economic conditions in these distressed areas. Although the instruments used in these efforts are variously termed *housing, neighborhood improvement,* and *economic development programs,* "community development" refers to the comprehensive and systematic efforts to balance the brick and mortar needs of a community with the economic and social development activities that improve the overall quality of life for the community's residents.

General Legal Authority for County Community Development Activities

North Carolina counties' legal authority to conduct community development programs comes from the North Carolina General Statutes, even when all the funds come from the federal government. The General Assembly has historically provided enabling legislation necessary for the state's counties to engage in federally funded activities. After the National Industrial Recovery Act was adopted in 1933, the General Assembly passed the Housing Authorities Law (1935) to enable communities to take advantage of federal grants for public housing. This law, as amended, appears as G.S. Chapter 157. In 1951, responding to the broader purposes of the Housing Act of 1949, the General Assembly passed the Urban Redevelopment Law, which, as amended, appears as G.S. Chapter 160A, Article 22. Finally, in response to the Housing and Community Development Act of 1974, the General Assembly passed and later amended G.S. 153A-376 (1975) and G.S. 153A-377 (1977) to permit counties to engage in Community Development Block Grant (CDBG) activities authorized by the federal act, subject to the provisions of other state laws.

Because these statutes were enacted at different times in response to different programs under the rubric of housing and community development, a county's authority to undertake various activities as part of a broadly defined community development effort is not laid out neatly in one place. However, the various statutes provide considerable authority for counties to undertake a wide variety of community development programs in the major categories of housing, neighborhood development, and economic development.

Major Funding Sources for Community Development

Public and Indian Housing

The United States Department of Housing and Urban Development (HUD), Office of Public Housing, operates four main programs: Section 8 Certificate, Section 8 Voucher, Section 8 Moderate Rehabilitation, and Public Housing. The Section 8 Certificate and Voucher Programs provide rental assistance to lower income families. These families can use the certificates and vouchers to select any units within the geographical areas that meet Housing Quality standards. The Moderate Rehabilitation Program subsidy provides rental assistance on behalf of lower income families for certain units that have been upgraded from the early stages of deterioration to safe, decent, and sanitary housing and made available at an affordable cost. Under the Public Housing program, HUD gives grants to local public housing agencies (PHAs) to finance capital costs of the construction, rehabilitation, or acquisition of public housing developed by the PHAs. HUD also pays operating subsidies to most PHAs to cover the shortfall between tenant rents and operating expenses. Operating subsidies are calculated on the basis of the Performance Funding System formula, which takes into account what it would cost a comparable, well-managed PHA to operate the units. In 1998, $306,200,633 was allocated to one hundred twenty-six Public Housing Agencies to enhance the housing and living environment of low-income citizens throughout the State. Public Housing Agencies serve 75,672 families in North Carolina, 29,839 of which are elderly families. To qualify for public housing, eligible families and individuals must usually have incomes no higher than 80 percent of the median income for the area.

Indian housing authorities were previously eligible to receive funds under this program. As of 1998, however, the Indian component of the Public and Indian Housing program will be removed and folded into the Native American Housing Block Grant program.

The Home Program: Home Investment Partnerships

The Home Program (HOME) is a federal program designed to increase the supply of housing for low-income persons. HOME provides funds to states and local governments to implement local housing strategies, which may include tenant-based rental assistance, assistance to homebuyers, property acquisition, new construction, rehabilitation, site improvements, demolition, relocation, and administrative costs.

After certain mandated set-asides, the balance of HOME funds is allocated by formula with 60 percent going to cities, urban counties, and consortia (contiguous units of local government) and 40 percent for states to be reallocated to remaining jurisdictions. In 1997, the federal government allocated $14,321,000 in HOME funds to North Carolina. Most North Carolina counties receive HOME funds through the state's Housing Finance Agency. These state funds are allocated regionally within the state based on each region's housing needs and are available through both competitive and open funding cycles. In fact, in 1997 nine counties received HOME funds from the Housing Finance Agency, two received HOME funding directly from HUD, and five received funds as part of consortia.

The Community Development Block Grant Program

Since 1975, the federal government has supported local government's community and economic development efforts through the Community Development Block Grant program (CDBG). HUD's Community Planning and Development Office administers and allocates these CDBG funds to states and units of general local government.

CDBG funds are divided into the two broad administrative categories of entitlement and nonentitlement funds. Seventy percent of the CDBG program's funds are designated for the nation's entitlement areas and 30 percent for its nonentitlement areas. Entitlement areas are generally cities with over 50,000 people or urban counties with more than 200,000 people. These areas receive CDBG funds directly from HUD. The entitlement counties in North Carolina are Wake and Cumberland. The entitlement cities are Asheville, Burlington, Chapel Hill, Charlotte, Concord, Durham, Fayetteville, Gastonia, Goldsboro, Greensboro, Greenville, Hickory, High Point, Jacksonville, Kannapolis, Lenoir, Morganton, Raleigh, Rocky Mount, Salisbury, Wilmington, and Winston-Salem.

CDBG funds for the remaining cities and counties ($45,165,000 in 1997) are considered nonentitlement funds and are administered by the North Carolina Department of Commerce through the Small Cities Block Grant program. Since its inception in 1982, the Small Cities program has been designed to ensure that CDBG funds primarily benefit low- and moderate-income persons or eliminate slums or blighting conditions in an area or on a spot basis. Through the use of threshold requirements and project funding selection criteria, the state's program is designed so that at least 70 percent of the funds each year will be used to benefit low- and moderate-income persons. In the CDBG program, low income is defined as 50 percent or less of the household median income of the metropolitan area or county, and moderate is defined as between 50 percent and 80 percent of the household median income of the metropolitan area or county.

The North Carolina Commerce Finance Center administers CDBG grants for economic development, while the Division of Community Assistance administers the following grants for community development: Community Revitalization, Housing Development, Community Empowerment, Urgent Needs/Contingency, and four current demonstration projects (Innovative Economic Development Demonstration, Individual Development Accounts Demonstration, Telecommunications Planning Demonstration, and Infrastructure Planning Demonstration). In 1996, twenty-five of the ninety-five grants awarded under the Small Cities program went to counties.

Community Revitalization, the largest of the community development programs administered by the Division of Community Assistance, receives no less than 66 percent of the Small Cities' annual allocation.

The Community Revitalization category, which is subdivided into Concentrated Needs, Scattered Site, and Infrastructure, provides funds for local governments to improve or develop residential areas and to rehabilitate scattered site housing. Concentrated Needs projects focus on improving, preserving, or developing residential neighborhoods. Eligible activities include housing rehabilitation, water and sewer line installation, and street and drainage improvements. Scattered Site projects are limited to the rehabilitation of substandard housing not within a defined project area, including on-site water and wastewater disposal systems or installation of on-site service connections for public facilities, and acquisition, disposition, clearance, and relocation activities. Rehabilitation, acquisition, disposition, or clearance of vacant units to the extent necessary to eliminate specific conditions detrimental to public health and safety are also eligible activities under the Scattered Site subcategory. Counties are most likely to apply for and be awarded Scattered Site grants. Infrastructure projects may only address public water and public wastewater activities that benefit homes in residential neighborhoods.

Housing Development grants support the creation of additional multi- or single-family homes for low- and moderate-income renters or owners. Community Empowerment is designed to encourage comprehensive approaches to improve distressed areas. Individual localities or a consortium of two or more localities may undertake comprehensive, community-based economic development to increase capital assets, create jobs and small business opportunities, raise incomes of local residents, and foster economic self-sufficiency among low- and moderate-income families. Urgent Needs grants are used in cases where other financial resources are not available to meet community development needs of low- and moderate-income persons that pose an immediate threat to the health and safety of the community and represent an unusual circumstance.

The most significant feature of the block grant program is its dual effect on local control over federally funded community development activities. CDBG decentralized decision making nationally. By allowing local discretion in how funds would be spent within the bounds of the eligible activities, the block grant program turns over much of the authority formerly exercised by Congress and HUD to the local government. By making the general-purpose unit of local government the grantee, the block grant program gives clear and final local authority to the county over how and where to spend its funds.

In addition, the requirement to pay specific attention to housing needs as part of a county's block grant proposal provides the means for the county commissioners to improve the coordination of subsidized housing activities in the community. Taken seriously, the required consolidated plan can guide the board's review of the quantity and the location of subsidized housing throughout the county, from public housing units proposed by housing authorities to subsidized and federally insured units proposed by general-purpose government, not-for-profit quasi-public corporations, or private-sector sponsors.

Types of Community Development Activities

Housing

The production of affordable housing is often regarded as the most direct way to achieve the general objectives of community development. The term "housing production" is used loosely here to include the creation of new units, substantial rehabilitation of units that are in such disrepair that they are no longer considered part of the housing stock, less substantial rehabilitation to preserve housing beginning to fall into disrepair, and other light rehabilitation such as weatherization assistance. In addition to construction and repair activities, counties are authorized by G.S. Chapter 157, the housing authority law, to provide other housing production–related assistance as they "prepare, carry out, and operate housing projects" (G.S. Ch. 157-9). Such assistance may include the following activities:

1. Demolition of existing unsanitary or unsafe housing
2. Direct ownership and operation of housing for low- and moderate-income persons
3. Rent subsidies to low-income persons
4. Financial assistance to low- and moderate-income persons to own or rehabilitate their homes
5. Financial assistance to public or private developers of housing for low- and moderate-income persons [G.S. 157-3(12)]

Public Housing

The construction and operation of subsidized public housing are the earliest form of involvement in housing by counties in North Carolina. In fact, until recently the housing authorities law was used primarily to build, operate, and maintain multifamily rental housing for low-income persons who were trying to get a foothold on the first rung of the economic ladder. The role of local governments in providing assisted housing was limited therefore to approving the project for federal assistance and site location, providing the municipal services spelled out in the cooperation agreement with the public housing authority, and providing an exemption to the PHA from local real estate taxes.

While most PHAs remain separate entities from local governments and the federal government remains the major provider of funds, counties have recently begun to play a more active role in the funding and management of public housing. HUD has recently developed a number of innovative programs and provided funding sources for PHAs to prepare residents to become self-sufficient and move toward financial independence. For example, the HOPE for Public Housing Ownership Program (HOPE VI) provides planning and implementation grants to enable public housing residents and other low-income families to purchase their public housing units. These programs have encouraged new partnerships with private and public entities, and local governments have been instrumental in their success.

Rent Subsidies and Homeownership

High rent burdens or owner costs are now the primary housing problem confronting low-income families in North Carolina. While the median household income in the state rose by 83.7 percent between 1980 and 1990, the median rent and owner cost rose by 110.4 and 95.1 percent, respectively. As housing prices have climbed beyond the reach of many North Carolina families, some counties have sought to facilitate the rental or purchase of existing or new homes, both through programs operated by the county itself and through development and mortgage subsidy programs run by private developers, nonprofit organizations, and lending institutions.

Housing Rehabilitation

Authorization for counties to rehabilitate deteriorated housing, found in the housing authorities law as described earlier, is also allowed under the redevelopment law (G.S. 160A-512) and under the newer community development law (G.S. 153A-376, -377). Counties, unlike cities, except those with populations in excess of 400,000 according to the most recent census, must first seek voter approval to use local tax revenues to support housing rehabilitation activities.

The county can directly rehabilitate deteriorated housing by doing the work for the owner using outside contractors or its own work crews; by itself acquiring, repairing, and disposing of the property; or by giving a grant, loan, or loan subsidy to the property owner. It can also do any of these things through a contract with the housing authority, the redevelopment authority, or a responsible private not-for-profit organization.

Both owner- and renter-occupied houses can be rehabilitated if the principal beneficiaries are low- and moderate-income persons. A county will sometimes limit its program to owner-occupied houses if the county commissioners believe that an apparent subsidy to landlords would be politically unacceptable. In such a case a county can enforce minimum housing code standards under which it can compel the repair of rental houses that do not meet such standards (G.S. 160A-411, G.S. Ch. 160A, Art. 19, Pt. 6). One problem associated with this strategy is that the intended beneficiary, the low-income tenant, can lose out. The owner, forced to make improvements, may seek to protect his or her investment and to maintain an adequate return by demanding more rent from the tenant or by seeking another tenant for the upgraded house. In either case the low-income renter might be forced to look for other housing that, unless he or she has rental assistance, will be as substandard as the rehabilitated unit was formerly. As a remedy, a county that chooses the enforcement method can use federal rental assistance to subsidize the tenant's rent, either in the newly rehabilitated house or in another higher-quality house elsewhere in the community.

Displacement and Relocation

The county is authorized to deal with other displacement problems that might arise as part of community development activities. When extensive rehabilitation is under way or when a house that is beyond repair is to be demolished, residents may have to be relocated either temporarily or permanently. G.S. 133-5 through -17—originally enacted in 1971 in accord with the federal Uniform Relocation Assistance and Real Property Acquisition Act—allows the county to help relocated residents with moving expenses, temporary or permanent rental payments, a down payment on the purchase of a house, or a lump sum to buy another house if the permanently displaced family owns the house to be demolished. The law also contains procedural requirements that give reasonable protection to a person or family displaced by the program.

Neighborhood Improvements

Affordable housing production, when coordinated with other community development activities, should result in improvements not only to the physical but also the economic and social fabric of the target community. The CDBG program continues to use the rationale that if a house is rehabilitated in a concentrated area, concurrent improvements in the public facilities that serve those houses should also be made; otherwise, the full value of improving the condition of a given house will not be realized or will not be long-lived. Consequently, the program encourages local governments to undertake neighborhood public improvements to complement housing improvements in their community development target areas. Since 1975, North Carolina counties (and cities) have tended to emphasize a balanced strategy of housing improvements supported by public facilities, while the majority of states' CDBG programs have primarily funded public facilities projects and a handful have turned to an emphasis on economic development.

Types of Neighborhood Improvements

The kinds of public improvements most commonly undertaken in a target neighborhood in conjunction with housing rehabilitation or construction include the following:

1. Sewer: usually installation or rehabilitation of collector lines; also, house connections or outfalls under certain circumstances
2. Water: installation or refurbishment of distribution lines and house connections
3. Open space: common areas, buffers between incompatible uses, and drainage areas
4. Parks: tot lots, play lots, equipped playgrounds, sitting areas, and major neighborhood parks

More recently, neighborhood improvements have included day care centers, community centers, and other activities that provide necessary resources and build a sense of community in distressed neighborhoods. These recent efforts are consistent with community developers' beliefs that the solutions to distressed areas require a comprehensive approach to interrelated community problems.

Unlike most housing activities, the kinds of improvements just listed are normal and traditional functions of counties in North Carolina, and statutory authority to undertake any of them is clear and well understood. Although the same clear authority exists for other, more general kinds of public improvements like community centers, fire stations, libraries, health centers, and off-street parking, it is usually more difficult to demonstrate that such facilities will benefit primarily low- and moderate-income persons. Consequently, block grant funds are less frequently used for the latter activities than for the former.

Economic Development

For many years counties (and cities) tended to leave economic development activities to the state and to private agencies, such as chambers of commerce, private power companies, and others. More recently, as increases in revenue bases no longer seem capable of keeping up with the cost of providing services, local governments have joined with the state and the private sector to try to actively shape local economies.

The increased local government activity in economic development has been made possible, in part, by community development funding. Since 1977 the scope of the CDBG program has embraced economic development as a legitimate activity to be undertaken with grant funds. However, such activities must meet the test of primarily benefiting low- and moderate-income persons. As a practical matter, the federal government's emphasis has usually been on job development and reversal of physical deterioration in low-income areas. Counties and private businesses are encouraged to enter into cooperative efforts to promote job-producing residential, commercial, or industrial development in their communities. Economic development, and especially job development, has become integral to counties' overall strategies to succeed in their community development programs. After all, a program that provides a safe and sanitary place for a person or a family to live, without the economic wherewithal to maintain it, is likely to fail in the long run.

Yet economic development produces widespread benefits for the community, not just to low- and moderate-income citizens. Economic development provides jobs, improves the county's tax base and other financial resources, and enhances its credit rating, thereby leading to lower borrowing costs and less pressure on the tax rate.

Counties (and cities) enjoy broad statutory and constitutional authority to engage in economic development activities, and can organize their economic development activities in a number of ways. Before describing county authority and organizational choices, however, it is first useful to set the context by summarizing state programs in economic development.

State Programs

The state's economic development activities are centered in the Department of Commerce. The department employs a number of persons who work with companies interested in North Carolina to help them locate an industrial or commercial site and to bring their executives together with local officials to discuss local incentives that might be offered to the companies. In addition, the department administers a number of grant and loan programs and large industrial projects to assist small businesses and to encourage the location and the expansion of large companies in the state. Another agency active in economic development is the Department of Community Colleges, which provides customized training for the employees of new and expanded industries through its Industrial Training Program. A third state agency that plays an important role in economic development is the Department of Transportation, which frequently makes road and highway improvements that encourage both industrial and commercial development.

The state's tax system has also been used to encourage development. The centerpiece of state efforts is a series of tax credits (codified in G.S. Ch. 105, Art. 3A), offered to companies that create jobs, invest in machinery or equipment, invest in research and development, place a central administrative facility in the state, or provide worker training. The legislation divides the state's counties into five "enterprise tiers" based on a formula that measures a county's unemployment rate, per capita income, and population growth, with the ten counties in the first tier being rated as the ten most in need of economic development. The amount of each tax credit depends on which tier the county in which company's expenditures or investments are made is in, with the amount of each credit decreasing from the lower- to the upper-number tiers. In addition to the income tax credits, a variety of property tax classifications and exclusions, such as the exclusion for manufacturers' and wholesalers' inventories, are also intended to encourage economic development, as are a number of sales tax exemptions.

Traditional County Authority for Economic Development

There are a number of traditional activities counties engage in to encourage economic development and about which there is little philosophical dispute. These include employing agents to meet and negotiate with and assist companies interested in locating or expanding in the community, undertaking surveys to identify community strengths and weaknesses, developing strategic plans for economic development, and advertising the community in industrial development publications and elsewhere. Counties have also provided public services and facilities to attract new development and to stimulate economic growth, such as by extending (or assisting in the extension of) water and sewer lines or expanding water supply and treatment facilities and sewage treatment facilities.

Industrial Revenue Bond Financing

G.S. Chapter 159C permits counties to create special authorities that issue industrial revenue bonds, subject to approval by the Department of Commerce and the Local Government Commission. These bonds finance the construction of factories and other industrial facilities and are paid for by the companies using the facilities. Use of an authority permits issuance of the bonds in tax-exempt form, thereby reducing the capital costs paid by the benefiting company.

Direct Incentives

For some years there were serious questions about the constitutionality of local governments providing direct incentives to specific industrial and commercial prospects, but those questions were resolved, in favor of constitutionality, in the 1996 case of *Maready v. City of Winston-Salem.*[1] The issue in that case was whether direct incentives benefited the public at large or only the companies receiving the incentives. The supreme court decided it was the former: the predominant benefit from incentive programs is public, running to the citizens who, as a consequence of the programs, have greater employment opportunities, and to the governments who have stronger revenue bases. Direct incentives therefore serve a public purpose.

The basic authorization to provide incentives is found in G.S. 158-7.1. Subsection (b) specifically permits a number of industrial assistance

activities, including developing industrial parks, assembling other potential industrial sites, constructing and leasing or selling shell buildings,
helping extend public and private utility lines to private facilities, and preparing sites for industrial properties or facilities. Subsection (d2) permits
a local government to convey real property to a private company, accepting as consideration for the conveyance the increased property and sales
tax revenues that will accrue to the government over the succeeding ten
years as a result of improvements by the company to the property. Finally,
subsection (a), which has been in the statute since 1925, grants broad authority to "make appropriations for the purposes of aiding and encouraging the location of manufacturing enterprises." Local governments have
relied on this last provision as support for specific incentives not included
in subsections (b) or (d2), especially the making of direct cash grants to
companies.

G.S. 158-7.1(c) requires any local government that intends to undertake activities specifically listed in subsection (b) to first hold a public
hearing on the expenditure in question. Although the statute does not
specifically require it, most local governments also hold a public hearing
if the statutory authority for the incentive is subsection (a). In the *Maready*
decision, the court clearly encouraged public hearings in that latter circumstance. If a local government intends to convey property to a private
company, whether for monetary consideration or pursuant to subsection
(d2), it must hold an additional public hearing on the conveyance. Finally, G.S. 158-7.1(f) places a limit on the total investment of a single local
government in certain economic development programs, prohibiting
them from exceeding 0.5 percent of the government's tax base.

Authority for Community Economic Development

"Community economic development" focuses on improving levels of
income to provide improved quality of life for residents of distressed communities. In addition to the authority provided for counties to engage in
traditional economic development (assisting the recruitment, growth,
and profitability of large firms), there is considerable authority for community economic development. G.S. 153A-376(a)(2) authorizes all counties to engage in programs concerned with "employment" and "economic
development," using either federal and state grants or local funds. As
stated earlier, the Department of Commerce also operates two economic
development programs under the state's CDBG Small Cities grant program: economic development and micro-enterprise programs. Economic

development projects may include a broad range of activities, but the majority of the CDBG funds must be shown to create or retain jobs for low- and moderate-income persons. Funds may be expended for public facilities related to a specific project that can be shown to produce jobs, or they may be loaned to specific businesses through a participating bank, with proceeds from repayment being used to establish and replenish a revolving loan fund used for the same purpose. In addition, the state sets aside funds each year to fund eligible micro-enterprise projects—commercial enterprises with five or fewer employees, one or more of whom own the enterprise. Project funds are used to provide loans, loan guarantees, technical assistance, and business support and training to persons trying to develop such enterprises. These grants may be made either directly to businesses or to one or more local governments that establish a program of assistance for specific projects.

Other Authority to Assist in Economic Development

A county has considerable authority to attract business development by facilitating the location, preparation, and transfer of a suitable site in the community. Besides the authority for industrial development activities under G.S. 158-7.1, a county may acquire land with or without buildings for commercial or industrial development and for public facilities to serve a major private development, under redevelopment law (G.S. 160A-512) if the redevelopment procedures are followed, and otherwise, under community development law (G.S. 153A-377). If the land to be acquired is "inappropriately developed," the county may dispose of the property to a private developer either directly or after clearing, refurbishing, or adding public improvements to make the site more attractive for development. There are limits, however, on how closely the county may work with a single developer. To dispose of the property that it acquires and improves under the two statutes cited earlier, the county must follow competitive-bidding procedures.

The redevelopment law allows a county to condemn, if necessary, in order to acquire property for any of the purposes identified in the preceding paragraph [G.S. 160A-512(6), -515)], but the community development law does not. When the county acquires land solely for public improvements, its general power of eminent domain may be used for any of the public improvements authorized by the statutes. See G.S. 40A-3 and Chapter 15 in this volume for a discussion of purposes for which counties may condemn.

Land acquisition and public improvements undertaken for economic development purposes may be financed by federal funds or by appropriation of local tax revenues without special voter approval. General obligation bonds may be used to finance any improvement authorized by G.S. 159-48, but generally only with voter approval before issuance. Revenue bonds may be used to finance public service enterprise improvements like sewer or water facilities built in conjunction with an economic development project. No vote is required for such bonds, but the facility must yield adequate revenue from operations to retire the debt. Just as with housing activities, grants, loans, interest subsidies, loan guarantees, or purchase of property for resale to and development by a private party may be financed by block grant funds without voter approval; but if local property tax revenues are used directly or for debt service related to these activities, a referendum is required as provided in G.S. 153A-149.

Tax Abatements and Cash Incentive Policies

One form of industrial or commercial development and recruitment often used in other states is not directly available in North Carolina: offering special property tax breaks to new industries or businesses. Under Article V, Section 2 of the state constitution, property tax exemptions and classifications may be made only by the General Assembly and then only on a statewide basis. A local government may not constitutionally offer a special classification to a property owner if it is not available statewide. The legislature has not enacted any special classifications for new industrial or commercial development; therefore none can be offered by local economic development officials.

Recently, however, a number of counties (and the cities in those counties) have developed a cash grant incentive policy that very much resembles tax abatements. These policies follow a common pattern: the county offers to make annual cash grants over a number of years (most often five years) to industrial companies that make investments of certain minimum amounts in the county or city. (The investment might be either a new facility or the expansion of an existing facility.) The amount of the cash grant is specifically tied to the amount of property taxes paid by the company. For example, a company that made an investment of at least $5 million might be eligible for a cash grant in an amount up to 75 percent of the property taxes it paid on the resulting facility; larger investments would make the company eligible for a grant that represented a larger percentage of the property taxes paid. These policies closely approach tax abatements, with one important difference: the company receiving the cash incentives has paid its property taxes. It is currently impossible to know whether a court would hold that the sort of policy described previously is an unconstitutional attempt to grant a tax abatement or whether it is simply a constitutionally permitted cash incentive. There is no question, however, that an increasing number of counties are adopting such policies.

Organization for Community Development

Whether a local community development program consists of only federal block grant activities or a broad range of federal, local, and private activities, it requires effective coordination and management. Meeting federal requirements and private-sector needs and expectations and conducting an effective program requires widespread community involvement on the one hand and concentrated executive control of a complex set of activities on the other. Neither the federal government nor the General Statutes mandate any specific form of organization to carry out a community development strategy in general, although there are specifications and options for the component activities discussed earlier. Each county, then, must use the options available in the General Statutes to accomplish its community development objectives in a way that satisfactorily balances community involvement and executive control, and best suits its local program and circumstances.

Board of County Commissioners

The starting point for organizing for affordable housing and community and economic development activities must be the board of county commissioners, which has the authority either to undertake directly, or to appoint an appropriate body to undertake on its behalf, all the activities discussed earlier.

Housing Authorities

Housing construction and operations are not activities with which counties have had much, if any, experience. Even though the governing boards of local housing authorities are appointed by the board, most operate quite independently of county government. With all their funding coming from the federal government (except for rental income), their operations rely primarily on federal rules and policies.

In recent years, however, especially as federal support for housing programs has decreased, a number of local governments, primarily cities, have taken a more assertive role in the operation of their housing authorities. G.S. 157-4.1 and G.S. 157-4.2 offer several alternative organizational arrangements to the traditional independent housing authority. First, under G.S. 157-4.2 a county may retain a separate housing authority, but integrate that authority's budgeting and financial administration activities into those of the county. Under this arrangement the housing authority remains a separate organization with personnel and operating responsibilities under the control of the appointed housing authority board, and the agency is treated like a county department only for purposes of budgeting, accounting, and expenditure control. Two other alternatives eliminate the housing authority altogether: under G.S. 157-4.1 the board of county commissioners may assign the powers of the housing authority to the redevelopment commission, or under G.S. 153A-376(b) the county staff may be given those powers. Brunswick, Caswell, Columbus, Harnett, Madison, Orange, and Pender counties have all assumed direct responsibility for their public housing authorities.

Community Development

County commissioners have final local authority over all CDBG activities. The board must approve the final application for federal funds and formally accept the grant funds and the responsibility for program execution. The state's community development law (G.S. 153-376, -377) authorizes the board to exercise directly any of the powers conferred on housing authorities and redevelopment commissions as needed to carry out the block grant program. The board also holds the ultimate responsibility and statutory authority for most of the locally funded activities that might be part of a community development program, especially neighborhood improvement activities that fall under its general statutory authority for planning, public works, and regulation activities related to public safety, health, and welfare.

Economic Development

The board of county commissioners may undertake economic development activities itself. When this occurs, it usually grows out of relatively small-scale, discrete programs under CDBG Small Cities economic development grants. For large-scale and long-term economic development efforts, most counties rely on an appointed commission to do the work on their behalf (see the more thorough discussion under the next section).

Citizen Boards, Commissions, and Committees

Although the board of county commissioners holds most of the ultimate authority for community development activities, it can make efficient use of citizen interest and expertise by appointing a variety of citizen boards, commissions, and committees for advice or for implementation of program mandates. To help in planning and administering the federal CDBG program, the board is required to have a citizen advisory body through which to channel public opinion. Many counties find these bodies to be extremely helpful. First, such a body can focus its full attention on the community development program, whereas the board has many other responsibilities. Second, the board can effectively delegate to the advisory group the time-consuming task of gaining widespread citizen participation in planning. Third, the professional staff can secure from this body a fairly continuous flow of informal comment and information during planning. Fourth, consultants and Councils of Governments working with the county will look to this body to provide a meaningful frame of reference on the community to be served. Finally, the advisory body can supplement professional staff advice with a lay point of view when the program is recommended to the commissioners.

Because the county's planning board and its housing authority, if one exists, usually have something to offer to community development, the board should consider what role (if any) it expects these agencies to play in planning and executing the city's housing and community development programs. The planning board's work with comprehensive planning and capital improvement planning can be very closely related to the formulation of the community development program. Also, a housing authority's deep knowledge of subsidized housing needs and problems in the community might make it a valuable resource in developing and using a Consolidated Plan to coordinate the development of all kinds of assisted housing in and around the city. The board should also consider whether to ask other boards and commissions (such as the parks and recreation commission, the streets committee, and the public works committee) for advice.

Although the board may undertake the economic development activities described earlier, using the county staff to centralize management and control, G.S. Chapter 158, Article 2, allows the governing board to appoint an economic development commission. Such a commission is a public agency, but like housing authorities, once it is created and members are appointed, it may act with some independence from the government that created it. Advantages of such a commission include the opportunity to ensure that local business leaders have an active role on the commission through their membership and the possibility of setting such a commission up cooperatively with other jurisdictions to coordinate efforts in one body. One disadvantage is that an economic development commission does not enjoy any authority to own real property and therefore cannot directly undertake some of the incentive programs authorized to cities and counties by G.S. 158-7.1(b).

Councils of Governments

Regional Councils of Governments often assist counties in the preparation and administration of community and economic development grants when there is no county staff to carry out these functions. Councils of Governments are particularly active in community development in the western region of the state. For example, in the western counties of the state Councils of Governments prepared thirty-four of the forty-five applications for the Community Revitalization grant program in 1997.

Consultants

Many counties delegate responsibility to private, for-profit consultants for completing applications for and administering community development grants. The consultant typically works closely with a member of the county's staff (perhaps the county manager) and the citizen advisory body to develop and implement the project. While the board retains ultimate responsibility for the grant, it has little involvement with the project's day-to-day activities. However, the board should be kept informed of important policy decisions such as program amendments.

Consultants are used most often in the eastern counties of the state. A primary advantage of using consultants is that the county does not have to provide gap funding for personnel costs for community development staff in between grants. A disadvantage may be that consultants are less familiar with the other aspects of county government that may bear on a community development project.

Nonprofits

Some counties delegate their economic development activities to chambers of commerce, committees of 100, or other private not-for-profit corporations, limiting the direct role of the public body to one of providing funding in some measure. These private groups share the benefits of an economic development commission in that they permit the involvement of the local business community and facilitate cooperation among several local governments. They also bear two advantages not found with economic development commissions. First, there is no bar to their owning real property; thus they can act directly as developers of industrial parks or shell buildings or can hold industrial sites for conveyance to newly locating companies. Second, because they are private organizations, they can raise private funds within the community and spend those funds without concern for the possible constitutional or statutory limitations that accompany public funds. (Any public moneys appropriated to these organizations, however, retain their public character and remain subject to such limitations.) A possible disadvantage of using these private organizations, depending on how their governing boards are selected, is that they may have considerable independence from local government, and therefore might sometimes pursue goals and strategies inconsistent with the wishes of local government officials.

Other counties delegate community development activities to a not-for-profit organization. These are typically community-based development organizations. These counties believe that organizations founded by, and grounded in, the communities they serve are more likely to be successful in building communities in the comprehensive manner necessary for sustainable community development.

Professional Staff

Most of North Carolina's counties do not have professional community development or economic development staff. Those counties that do have organized themselves using one of three major approaches: a coordinator, a department, or a task force.

A Coordinator

A coordinator may be used in counties that need few specialized staff. One person is responsible for initiating, negotiating, monitoring, and evaluating the planning and execution of development activities by several departments, usually planning, public works, and inspection departments, and sometimes the rehabilitation staff of a redevelopment authority. Where the coordinator is placed in the administration can be an important consideration. If the person is a member of the planning staff, he or she can certainly integrate the program with other planning activities, but might have little influence on operating departments that carry out the program. If the person is a member of the chief administrator's staff, he or she has more potential clout, but usually only as much as the chief administrator chooses to provide by backing him or her. To date, few counties have combined coordination of federal community development activities and economic development activities in one staff person. It is more common to find a separate coordinator for these two components of community development.

A Department

The county can form a community development department with status equal to that of the more traditional departments that might have a part in the program: public works, inspection, recreation, and so on. This arrangement is found in Orange and Forsyth counties, for example. The arrangement may originate in a county's decision to abolish a separate redevelopment authority and to bring its housing staff into the county's administration to perform housing rehabilitation work. As stated earlier, a county can also bring its housing authority operations under the county organization, either as a separate department or as part of a multifunctional department with broad responsibilities in community development. The multifunctional department might be formed from an existing planning department and from existing building inspection staff, housing inspection staff, engineering staff, housing and redevelopment staffs, economic development staff, or various combinations of all of these. Obviously the more functions that the department includes, the more powerful the community development director's influence will be over the performance of tasks that are critical to the program.

A Task Force

A county that takes the broadest possible view of community development, as an endeavor involving almost all county agencies and private-sector organizations from time to time, might adopt a task force approach to planning and managing its programs. Often, primary responsibility for the program goes to a deputy or assistant county manager who, by his or her position, clearly and often acts with the full authority of the manager. This person organizes and supervises department and agency heads who will be responsible for various aspects of program planning and implementation, and serves as a critical link to organizations outside county government. The composition of task forces might change over time as the community development program goes through different stages or changes its character. This process tends to be most successful when the county manager delegates effectively and department heads and other staff are comfortable and competent in using team-management techniques.

One of the most significant effects of the federal government's block grant programs since 1974 has been a marked improvement in the ability and the inclination of counties to bring a variety of resources to bear on problems of deteriorated housing, declining neighborhoods, and troubled local economies, in a coordinated fashion and with flexibility and sensitivity to special local needs. North Carolina law has complemented federal initiatives by providing counties with the authority they need to take full advantage of available programs. As direct federal financial support has diminished, counties have developed the ability to fashion effective strategies out of local resources, both public and private, to continue these initiatives at the local level.

Additional Resources

Publications

Dommel, Paul R. *From Nation to States: The Small Cities Community Development Block Grant Program.* Albany, N.Y.: State University of New York Press, 1986.

Green, Philip P., Jr. *North Carolina Statutes Related to Lower-Income Housing.* Chapel Hill, N.C.: Institute of Government, The University of North Carolina at Chapel Hill, 1990.

International City/County Management Association. "CDBG Funds: Resource for Innovation." *MIS Report*, vol. 27, no. 2 (February 1995).

Jenkins, Lauretta C. *CDBG: A Creative Link to Small Business Development*. Washington, D.C.: U.S. Department of Housing and Urban Development, 1987.

National Association of Housing and Redevelopment Officials. *Developing Local Housing Strategies under the Housing and Community Development Act of 1974*. Washington, D.C.: NAHRO, 1975.

Organizations (listed in order of relevance)

North Carolina Department of Commerce, Division of Community Assistance, 430 North Salisbury Street, Raleigh, NC 27611.

North Carolina Housing Finance Agency, 330 Drake Circle, Suite 200, Raleigh, NC 27607-1093.

United States Department of Housing and Urban Development, North Carolina State Office, 2306 West Meadowview Road, Greensboro, NC 27407.

National Community Development Association, 522 Twenty-First Street, N.W., Washington, D.C. 20006.

National Association of Housing and Redevelopment Officials, 1320 Eighteenth Street, N.W., Washington, D.C. 20036.

Notes

1. 342 N.C. 708, 467 S.E.2d 615 (1996).

18 Water and Sewer Enterprises

Warren Jake Wicker

Contents

Warren Jake Wicker is an Institute of Government emeritus faculty member whose work included local government law, finance, and administration with special attention to city-county relations and public enterprises.

Water and sewer services are among the most important and most widely supported enterprise services of North Carolina counties. County involvement with these services has increased steadily since they were first authorized for counties in 1955.

Cities have been the chief local governments concerned with providing water and sewer services since colonial days when they provided public wells. Urbanization and population growth of the state's economy in this century have resulted in increased state and federal efforts to protect and improve the quality of water in streams and lakes.

The state's growing urban population and the emphasis on attracting new industries have produced increased needs for water and sewer services outside municipal boundaries. For the most part, these requirements have been met by the joint efforts of cities and towns, developers, and industries, but county governments have also increasingly become involved.

The need for services outside of cities and towns has prompted the state to authorize several other types of local political subdivisions with authority to meet the needs of citizens for water and sewer services.

While the early county efforts were almost all in response to industrial needs, since the late 1960s those of residential and commercial development have received increased attention as well. Almost every county in the state has completed one or more comprehensive surveys of water and sewer needs and made preliminary projections as to where future facilities may be provided.

Federal funds that became available for planning purposes in the mid-1960s (especially those provided through the Farmers Home Administration) and the planning prerequisites for receiving other federal grants (particularly those made available through the Economic Development Administration and those authorized by the Housing and Urban Development Act of 1965) encouraged areawide and metropolitan planning by both cities and counties. In the 1970s, the regulations of the federal Environmental Protection Agency (EPA), the increase in federal grants for water-pollution control under Public Law 92-500 (the "201" program), and the funds available from state Clean Water Bonds ($300 million approved in 1972, $230 million in 1977, and $145 million in 1993) not only increased county interest in meeting water and sewer needs but also provided part of the financing. Following amendments to the federal Clean Water Act in early 1987, North Carolina's General Assembly created a Clean Water Revolving Loan and Grant Fund (G.S. Chapter 159G). Federal and state grants as well as loans to local governments for water and sewer purposes are presently channeled through this fund, with increasing emphasis on loans rather than grants. Overall, 69 percent of the grants and loans from the Fund are for sewer projects and 31 percent are for water projects.

Current Arrangements for Providing Water and Sewer Services

The 1990 census found that some 65 percent of all North Carolina housing units were served by public or private water systems; most of the remainder used private wells. The same census found that about 50 percent of the housing units were connected to a public or private sewer system.[1] Of those not connected, most used septic tanks or other on-site systems.

The Department of Environment and Natural Resources (DENR) reports that in 1998 there were some 8,500 public water systems in North Carolina.[2] This figure includes all systems that are required to report on quality tests of their water. A great majority of them are private and serve a single business, industry, campground, or other such facility.

Among local governments, cities are the principal providers of public water service. Over 400 of the state's 530 cities and towns provide water services. About half of the counties, the next most important local units, provide some water services. Water services are also provided by sanitary districts, water and sewer authorities, and county water and sewer districts, and through various interlocal arrangements.

Privately owned water systems are also providers. The state's Utilities Commission regulates the private systems that serve ten or more customers. In 1994 there were 1,127 that served some 122,000 customers (roughly 375,000 to 400,000 people).[3] Seventy-seven counties had one or more private, regulated water systems. Wake County, with 225 systems, had more systems than any other county. Their systems served 15,718 customers, also more customers than found in any other county.

The dominance of local governments in providing sewer services is even greater than their role in providing water.[4] About three of every five cities and towns provide services, as do about a fourth of the state's counties. Five other types of local governments also provide services. As with water, the state and federal governments often provide services to their own facilities and a large number of small treatment plants are owned by private parties to serve hotels, campgrounds, private schools, motels, shopping centers, country clubs, and subdivisions. In 1998, some 1,875 National Pollution Discharge Elimination System (NPDES) permits issued by the state's Division of Water Quality were outstanding.[5]

Private, investor-owned sewer systems are also in the picture, but are less numerous than in water services. In 1994 there were 200 private sewer systems subject to regulation by the state's Utilities Commission.[6] They served almost 33,000 customers (roughly 110,000–125,000 people). Private sewer systems serving ten or more customers were found in forty-five of the state's 100 counties in 1994. Wake County, with twenty-nine such systems, led the state in the number of systems. The twenty private systems in Onslow County served 5,403 customers, a larger number than found in any other county.[7]

Despite the rapid extension of services by city and county governments in recent years, the state's dispersed population has demanded that on-site wastewater disposal continue to be a major part of the picture. In 1997 some 50,000 new on-site systems, largely septic tanks, were installed in North Carolina.[8]

The Regulatory Framework

All counties are authorized to provide water and sewer services (G.S. Ch. 153A, Art. 15). When they do, they become subject to extensive federal and state regulations. See Chapter 23 for a more detailed discussion of the regulatory framework.

Water Supply and Treatment

The North Carolina DENR is chiefly responsible for administering both state and federal regulations. Its Division of Water Quality classifies the state's surface waters and designates those that are appropriate to be used as drinking water supply sources. The Division of Environmental Health of the DENR is responsible for approving public water supply plans. The same division is responsible for monitoring the safety of all public water supplies under the Safe Drinking Water Act. Finally, the state requires that all water supply systems have certified water plant operators (G.S. Ch. 90A, Art. 2). Local governments are also responsible under state legislation (G.S. 143-214.5) for watershed protection—important for protecting both public surface-water supplies and general water quality.

Wastewater Treatment and Discharge

The general structure for wastewater regulation is quite similar to that for the regulation of water supply and treatment. Federal legislation has established the long-term goals for national water quality. In short, the surface waters are to be swimmable and drinkable. The EPA is the federal actor, but most of its requirements are administered by the state. Key in this work is the Division of Environmental Management's administration of the NPDES permits. All discharges of sewage into the surface waters must meet the standards necessary for the stream classification set by the state. The division also regulates discharges of sewage to the ground surface (spray irrigation). Regulation of subsurface discharges of sewage and other wastewaters is the responsibility of the Division of Environmental Health at the state level and the county health departments at the local level. Operators in charge of wastewater treatment plants must be certified by the state (G.S. Ch. 90A, Art. 3).

Water and Sewer Services Financing

County governments have five principal sources of funds that may be used to finance water and sewer services. These are listed in Table 18-1, together with the general principle of revenue-raising involved with each of them. All water and sewer services provided by county and city governments are financed by some combination of the sources listed in the table. In fact, the list includes, directly or indirectly, almost all revenues of a county.

In accord with common practice, the term "sources" is used here to designate the different types. It would be more precise to term them revenue measures. In fact, there is only one source of funds: citizens. The different revenue measures tap that "source" in their capacity as taxpayers or as customers and beneficiaries of the utility systems. The different "sources" are simply different bases for securing funds from the body of citizens. The different revenue measures, of course, do not

Table 18-1
Sources of Funds for Financing Water and Sewerage Services
and the Revenue-Raising Principle of Each

Source of Funds	Principle
Local taxes (and non-tax revenues)	Ability to pay
Rates 1. Use 2. Availability	Benefit
Payments from property 1. Special assessments 2. Subdivision ordinance requirements 3. Payments in advance 4. Acreage charges 5. Impact fees 6. Special connection charges	Benefit
Special service charges (tap fees, hydrant rentals, etc.)	Benefit
State and federal grants	Ability to pay

fall equally on all citizens. County officials face the task of designing a system that produces adequate revenues and is fair and equitable for all users and taxpayers.

Local Taxes and Non-Tax Revenues

The property tax and the local option sales taxes are the two chief local tax measures. Proceeds of both may be used to finance water and sewer services. They are classified in economic terms as "ability to pay" taxes: the amount individual taxpayers contribute is based on the value of their property or on how much they spend, both of which are assumed to reflect ability to pay, rather than on the taxpayers' use of the utility systems and their direct benefit from them. Almost all counties have used local tax funds (or the equivalent non-tax proceeds) to finance water and sewer services.

Counties have limited amounts of non-tax general revenues (for example, interest income, ABC receipts, receipts from the sale of property) that may be used to finance water and wastewater services unless they have been earmarked for special purposes. To the extent that a county uses non-tax receipts for these purposes, it has relieved the demands on its local tax revenues and their availability for other purposes.

User Rates and Charges

User Charges

Under G.S. 153A-277 user charges are billed monthly or quarterly to utility customers on the basis of their consumption of water or use of the sewer system. In most systems, the amount of the charge reflects the amount of use and thus is related to the benefit the customer receives directly. All utility systems employ user charges, and increasingly the rates and charges are set at levels that will cover all utility costs. While proceeds from these charges are considered in the financing of all systems, in most city-county water and sewer arrangements in this state the proceeds flow through the city government and are not available directly to the county government for appropriation. (Where a county operates the system or a county and city share the proceeds, they do become directly available to the county.) The key consideration for both counties and cities is the final disposition of the proceeds. If agreement on this matter is reached in a joint enterprise involving two or more governmental units, which unit the proceeds flow through is not of much importance.

Availability Charges

Under G.S. 153A-264 counties may require owners of developed residential or commercial property to connect their premises to water and sewer lines where these are available. Counties may waive the connection requirement and permit the owners who do not wish to connect to pay an "availability" charge instead. Such an availability charge may not exceed the minimum periodic charge made for each class of properties that are connected. The charge is especially helpful in the extension of new lines where adequate financing may demand that owners connect. Providing for an availability charge assures that the financing plan continues to be satisfactory and permits the owners to continue to rely on their individual facilities where they prefer to do so.

Payments from Property

The presence of water and sewer lines provides special benefits to the properties they serve. Increasingly, cities and counties are adopting financing policies that require the owners of abutting property to bear part or all of the cost of installing the water and sewer lines to serve their property. The six devices listed in Table 18-1 under the heading "Payments from Property" are the techniques for securing payment that are most frequently used. Note that terminology is not standard; some of the devices listed in the table may have other names in some places.

Special Assessments

A special assessment is a charge against property for part or all of the cost of making an improvement benefiting that property. It is important to note that once a special assessment is made against a lot or tract, there is a lien on the property for the amount of the assessment, just as if a property tax had been levied. The major advantage to a local government in using special assessments as a financing device is that the property "stands behind" the charge. Also, the charge is not related to actual use of the utility; in theory, the presence of the water or sewer line adds value to the property because the line is available for use, so that the special assessment is seen as fair even if the owner does not connect. All counties have authority to impose special assessments for utility extensions, but only a few have done so.

Subdivision Ordinance Requirements

When subdivision regulations are used by a county or city, the developer is generally required to install utilities according to the government's specifications and dedicate them to the county or city when they are complete. The financing of the utilities is thus normally a private matter, and the funds to install the facilities do not flow through the local government's treasury. It is assumed that the cost of these installations is passed on to those who buy property in the subdivision. As with special assessments, this cost becomes a part of the cost of the developed lot or tract. This technique is widely used by cities. From an administrative standpoint, it is the simplest method of all for a local government to use.

Payment in Advance

Where a county plans to make a water or sewer line extension but does not want to use special assessments and the property to be served is already in diverse ownership, property owners may be required to pay in advance so that the county will have funds available to extend the line. Usually, the charge is based on property frontage along the line, and is set at a level that corresponds with what would be imposed if special assessments were made. This method is useful where extensions are short and the owners of the property to be served are able to make payments in advance.

Acreage Charges

Acreage charges have been made by counties and cities when they concluded that the full cost of extending utilities should be met by the properties to be served. In most cases, these charges are designed to cover each lot or tract's proportionate share of the cost of providing major trunk lines in the water and sewer systems, as opposed to the cost of the smaller distribution and collection lines to which direct connection is made. For example, in many residential areas a 6-inch water line is installed to provide direct service to abutting property. But, between such a line and the water treatment plant, there may be a network of major distribution lines of 12, 16, 24, or more inches in size, needed to bring an adequate amount of water to large areas. The reasoning is that, since each lot or tract adds to the capacity required of these larger mains, each parcel should be charged for its share of their cost. Acreage charges of about $500 to $1,000 an acre are typical. Normally, they are collected when services are first applied for. Perhaps fifty or more counties and cities in the state now use these charges or some equivalent.

Impact Fees

Impact fees—charges for a share of the cost of off-site improvements—are sometimes imposed on new connections. (The acreage charge just discussed is, in effect, an impact fee.) Some of these fees for utilities are intended to cover the cost of major distribution and collection lines; others, to cover a share of the cost of water and wastewater treatment plants. As long as these fees are reasonably related to the cost of providing services, they may be imposed under the general authority to establish utility fees and charges (G.S. 153A-277). (Impact fees for general county improvements—schools and parks, for example—are not allowed under general law and have been authorized for only a few counties by special legislation.)

Impact fees are sometimes justified as a "buy in" charge, which in theory is much like the initiation fee for membership in a private club. The assumption in this instance is that the existing capacity has been created by present and previous customers for the benefit of future ones. It is therefore proper that a new customer buy into the corporate accumulation by making a contribution: the impact fee.

In other cases, the fees are seen as a means of creating a capital reserve that will be used to enlarge the utility's capacity. The new development, it is claimed, will use some of the existing capacity and will thus hasten the day when enlargement will become necessary.

Impact fees imposed under either principle could have some negative consequences. By definition, a utility system that is operating at less than full capacity is below its optimum level. Its fixed costs—debt service on a water plant, for example—will continue at the contracted level whether it is operated at 50 or 100 percent of capacity. Existing customers of a plant that is operating at less than full capacity will thus benefit from the addition of each new customer who contributes more in additional revenues than in additional costs. And, since most utilities operate with declining marginal costs (and use average-cost pricing), an impact fee that discourages the addition of new customers results in some disadvantage to existing ones by keeping the average cost from declining. Of course, since water and sewer costs are not the principal costs of development, communities facing heavy growth will probably be able to impose impact fees and other charges with little apparent discouragement of new development.

Special Connection Charges

Special connection charges, under a variety of names, are used to recover utility extension costs from the property being served. In most cases, they are a substitute for one of the devices described above or a combination of two or more of them. For example, a county that does not impose special assessments might use a special charge at the time of connection to collect the same amount on the same basis. Or a single special-connection charge might be used that would equal the sum of a special assessment and an acreage charge.

Special Services Charges

The operation of a utility system involves a number of services that are provided directly for the benefit of particular customers: making a tap and setting a meter, turning services on and off, installing private fire hydrants or sprinkler connections, providing temporary services,

Table 18-2
Typical Pattern of Financing for a Self-Supporting Water and Sewer System

Element of Cost	Sources of Funds
Supply and treatment works	User charges (plus impact fees and grants when available)
Operation and maintenance	User charges
Major lines	Acreage charges or impact fees (plus grants when available)
Minor lines	Special assessments, subdivision ordinance requirements, payments in advance, and special connection charges
Special services	Special service charges

and the like. Usually, special charges are made for these services, often at a level to cover the actual cost.

State and Federal Grants

Funds for water and wastewater facilities are sometimes available through state and federal grants. Under the state and federal tax systems, these funds are raised largely from state and national taxpayers through the general state sales tax and individual and corporate income taxes, all of which are levied on the ability-to-pay principle.

To the extent that contributions from other governments are used to finance water and sewer services, these services are being supported on a countywide, statewide, or nationwide basis by some taxpayers who are not being served directly by any community utility system. This approach to financing water and sewer utilities is similar in principle to that used in financing education, parks and recreation, and many other general governmental functions.

As the foregoing discussion suggests, counties and cities use many different combinations of revenue measures to finance water and sewer systems (see Table 18-2). Differing views as to need and equity as well as different conditions and community traditions lead to various financing arrangements. A community actively seeking new industrial growth may be less inclined to impose high extension costs on users than one with a no-growth bent. A community that has a tradition of financing all extensions from taxes and user charges may find it difficult to change to the use of special assessments.

Table 18-3
Sample Charges for an Individual Customer

Charges	Amount
Initially	
Special assessment for line in front of property	
($12 per foot for 100 feet)	$1,200
Service connection and meter (actual cost)	400
Acreage charge (for share of major distribution	
lines serving the area: $800 per acre)	400
Total	$2,000
Monthly	
Monthly user charge for water consumed	
(includes costs of water supply and	
treatment, maintenance and repair	
of system, and administration)	$15

There has been a trend in recent years toward making water and sewer utilities self-supporting insofar as local financing is concerned. (Almost all local governments will accept state and federal grants.) Units with self-supporting utility systems have tended to adopt policies that relate elements of system cost to particular revenue measures, as shown in Table 18-2.

Most of the water and sewer utilities operated by the state's larger cities and some counties are self-supporting except for state and federal grants and a share of the local sales tax, but including all operation and maintenance, extensions, and debt service on utility bonds. Not all utilities, however, use the arrangements noted in Table 18-2. For example, those that do not use acreage charges tend to combine the costs of major lines with the cost of supply and treatment works (usually financed initially with bond proceeds), and these costs are then ultimately met through user charges.

Table 18-3 shows a hypothetical example of the meaning of the general financing plan outlined in Table 18-2 for an individual customer. It assumes that water service is being extended by special assessment to a homeowner with a half-acre lot. That person would likely face charges as indicated in the table. (The levels of charges, while typical, are given for purpose of illustration. They will obviously vary from system to system.) The flexibility granted to counties (and cities) enables them to arrange the financing in whatever manner appears most reasonable and equitable.

Public Organizational Alternatives for Providing Water and Sewer Services in North Carolina

While cities and counties are the chief local government units involved in providing water and sewer services in North Carolina, eight other organizational alternatives are also available. These have been created over the years because of local needs that could not be met by cities and counties acting alone. Including cities and counties, there are ten organizational alternatives:

1. City
2. County
3. County water and sewer district
4. County service district
5. Sanitary district
6. Water and sewer authority
7. Metropolitan water district
8. Metropolitan sewerage district
9. Interlocal agreement
10. Joint management agency

The chief features of the ten alternative arrangements are described briefly in the following paragraphs. As noted earlier, private organizations, both nonprofit and for-profit, may also provide the services, and in some cases, they do.

1, 2. *City* (G.S. Ch. 160A, Art. 16), *County* (G.S. 153A, Art. 15). Cities' and counties' authority to provide water and sewer services is very broad. They may provide services inside and outside their boundaries, issue general obligation and revenue bonds, use property tax revenues as well as rates, fees, and charges to support the services, impose special assessments, require connection to their lines, and establish availability charges. Their land use regulatory authority enables them to coordinate land use development with the provision of the services. Finally, they may join with other governments to provide the services.

3. *County water and sewer district.* A county water and sewer district may be created within any county by its board of county commissioners. Territory within a municipality may be included only with the consent of its governing board. Once established, it is a separate and independent unit of local government with the authority to provide water and sewer services. The members

of the board of county commissioners are, by law, the governing body of the district. Typically, the districts contract with the county in which they are located for administrative services. Thus they operate much like a separate fund within the county government. Districts may levy property taxes, issue general obligation and revenue bonds, establish rates and charges, and impose special assessments to recover the cost of line extensions. Districts do not have land use regulatory authority, but because the same individuals comprise the governing bodies of the county and the district, coordination of county land use polices with district utility services can be achieved.

County water and sewer districts are usually formed when services are needed in a portion of a county only and there is a need to issue general obligation bonds or to use property taxes to support part of the cost of the water and sewer services on less than a countywide basis. Those in Craven and Lincoln counties are among the ten to fifteen that have been organized in the state.

4. *County service district* (G.S. Ch. 153A, Art. 16). A county service district is established by the board of county commissioners within a county. Territory within a city or a sanitary district may be included only with the approval of its governing body. It is not a separate unit of government. It is simply a separate and defined area within which special property taxes may be levied to support services that are not provided countywide, or that are provided at a higher level within the district than in other parts of the county.

A service district has no powers separate from the county. Operations of a district are treated as a separate fund in the county's budgeting. If general obligation bonds or revenue bonds are issued to finance projects within the district, they are county obligations, even if debt service on the bonds is met entirely from rates, fees, charges, and taxes imposed only in the district. Thus general obligations for district purposes must be approved by voters in a countywide referendum when the size of the issue requires voter approval under constitutional limitations.

The administration of the services in a service district is part of the general county administration. The only reason to create a district is to enable the board of county commissioners to support part of the costs of services within the district by a property tax that is restricted to the district. The number of service districts that have been organized for water and sewer purposes is not known, but is thought to be less than a dozen. (The most common use of the county service district is for rural fire protection.)

5. *Sanitary district* (G.S. Ch. 130A, Art. 2, Part 2). A sanitary district may be formed through a petition procedure that starts with petitions from a majority of the owners of real property in a proposed district. Territory within a city or town may be included in a sanitary district only with the approval of its governing board. A district is created by the Commission on Health Services after public hearings before the board(s) of county commissioners in the county(ies) in which the proposed district is located. Its governing body is elected by the voters of the district. Sanitary districts may provide water and sewer services, fire protection, solid waste collection and disposal, mosquito control, ambulance and rescue squad services; build and maintain roads; and provide and hold property for a medical clinic.

   Sanitary districts may levy property taxes, issue general obligation and revenue bonds, impose rates and charges for utility services, and levy special assessments for the extension of water and sewer lines.

   Sanitary districts are a limited form of local government and are usually established where one or more of its authorized services are needed, incorporation of the area is not wanted, and the county government(s) is not in a position to respond to the service needs of the area. There are some thirty-five such districts in the state.

6. *Water and sewer authority* (G.S. Ch. 162A, Art. 1). A water and sewer authority may be formed by the governing body of a single county or those of two or more political subdivisions. The governing bodies that create an authority determine how large the authority board shall be and appoint the members who serve on it. Water and sewer authorities may provide water and sewer services and stormwater and drainage systems. Authorities do not have property taxation powers and their borrowing is limited to revenue bonds. They may establish rates, fees, and charges for their services, and may levy special assessments for the extension of water and sewer lines.

Water and sewer authorities have no established boundaries, although in operation they may be limited by their articles of incorporation or by the limits they establish on their service areas. There are fewer than a dozen authorities in the state. They have usually been formed where two or more cities and counties have wanted to join together to create an independent unit for water and sewer purposes and over which, by appointing its board members, the creating units continue to have influence over its operations.

7. *Metropolitan water district (MWD)* (G.S. Ch. 162A, Art. 4). These were first authorized in 1971. A metropolitan water district is created by any two or more political subdivisions within a single county. It is established by the Commission on Health Services of the DENR after public hearings. The creating units name the members of its governing body. An MWD has property taxation powers and may issue general obligation and revenue bonds. It may also establish rates, fees, and charges for its services which include water supply and distribution and sewer services, except where one overlaps a metropolitan sewerage district.

8. *Metropolitan sewerage district (MSD)* (G.S. Ch. 162A, Art. 5). MSDs were first authorized in 1961, and like the MWDs, the needs in Buncombe County gave rise to the legislation providing for them. They may be created by a petition process that starts with two or more political subdivisions or a single political subdivision and a majority of the property owners of an unincorporated area. The petition goes to the board of county commissioners, which calls a public hearing that is held jointly by the commissioners and a representative of the North Carolina Environmental Management Commission. If all is in order and the Commission finds that creation of the district would promote the public health and welfare, the Commission may adopt a resolution creating the district. MSDs may provide all types of sewage collection and disposal services, including septic tanks and other on-site facilities. They may also provide facilities for the generation and transmission of electric power and energy.

MSDs may levy property taxes; impose rates, fees, and charges for their services; levy special assessments; issue general obligation and revenue bonds; and adopt ordinances for the regulation and protection of the district's facilities. They may also require connection to the sewer lines of premises along the lines.

MSDs have usually been organized to bring together two or

more local units and unincorporated areas into an entity that has the power to levy property taxes and issue general obligation bonds. Among the few that have been organized, the Eden and Buncombe county MSDs are among the oldest in the state.

The Buncombe Metropolitan Sewerage District was originally responsible for operating wastewater treatment facilities only. Asheville and the surrounding towns and areas were responsible for the collection systems. Since that time, however, the Buncombe MSD has taken over the collection lines of the cities of Asheville, Biltmore Forest, Black Mountain, Montreat, and the Woodfin Sanitary District and now owns and operates them. Billing for the sewer services of the MSD is by the various cities that supply water to the customers. The MSD also accepts wastewater "wholesale" from the Cane Creek Water and Sewer District in Henderson County under contract.

9. *Interlocal agreement* (G.S. Ch. 160A, Art. 20). Of all the organizational alternatives for joint action by two or more local government units, the interlocal agreement is the most widely used. There are hundreds of these in North Carolina between cities and towns, between counties, and between counties and cities and towns. Counties and their partners have great flexibility in designing these cooperative arrangements to fit their specific needs. Any agreement is adopted by the respective governing boards and may cover any aspect of the management and financing of water and sewer services. (See the following section for brief descriptions of the most common arrangements.)

10. *Joint management agency (JMA)* (G.S. Ch. 160A, Art. 20). The JMA is a special form of interlocal agreement that has a free-standing management agency. This is in contrast to the typical interlocal agreement, under which the administrative and management functions are carried out by the staffs of one or more of the participating units in accord with the terms of their agreement. The JMA is designed for the situation where units may want to cooperate, but no unit is willing for the management functions to be provided by the employees of another unit.

There are no pure examples of JMAs in North Carolina. The arrangements in three counties—Buncombe County with Asheville, Forsyth County with Winston-Salem, and Mecklenburg County with Charlotte—have many of the features of a JMA, but in each case the management staffs are employees of the city involved.

Patterns of City-County Financing in Providing Services

Present Arrangements

Seven patterns of financing and action by counties have evolved as they have joined with cities to extend water and sewer services.

First, in many cases the county has simply borne part of the cost of the extension outside the city and the city has owned the lines and been completely responsible for their operation. For example, Wake County appropriated over $100,000 to extend water and sewer lines to a new industry locating outside Raleigh in 1954. The lines were built to the city's specifications, were deeded to it when completed, and are operated and maintained by it. Since that time, Wake County has financed a number of other extensions with the same arrangement. Robeson, Vance, Warren, Haywood, Lee, Cherokee, and several other counties have all made expenditures for water or sewer lines in a similar manner.

The second approach is essentially the same as the first except that ownership of the lines remains with the county. In these cases, the county bears all or part of the cost of the extension, and the lines are then leased to the city, at a nominal sum, for operation and maintenance. Catawba, Cleveland, and Lincoln counties, among others, have used this method.

The third pattern calls for reimbursement of the county for its initial outlays. Under this plan, the county and the city agree for the county to be reimbursed, in whole or in part, from fees and charges or from the sale of water. The city is uniformly responsible for system operation and maintenance, but there is a specific agreement as to the collection of user charges and the payment of part (or all) of these to the county. Sometimes the agreement also provides for the collection of an acreage charge that is remitted to the county on county-financed lines, for the county to share in the revenue from water customers, and for the city to purchase the county's interest in all county-financed lines upon municipal annexation of an area. Ownership and full responsibility for operation and maintenance are usually the city's from the beginning. Davidson, Durham, Edgecombe, Guilford, Rockingham, Rowan, and Wayne counties have all made expenditures under arrangements providing for reimbursement.

The fourth pattern involves direct county provision of services. Several counties—Anson, Dare, Durham, Forsyth, Greene, Jones, and Mecklenburg, among others—have made substantial outlays for water and sewerage systems in addition to, or in lieu of, joint financing with a city.

Anson County, for example, received a combination loan and grant of $4 million in 1966 from the Economic Development Administration (EDA). The voters then approved a $750,000 general obligation bond issue to add to the EDA funds and enable the county to establish a county-operated, countywide water supply and distribution system designed to serve all the municipalities and the areas between them. Some of the municipalities purchase water "wholesale" from the county; in others, the county serves customers directly. Anson was the first county in the state with such a system in operation. Since its establishment, Anson County has expanded its wholesale water service, and in 1998 was supplying water to Richmond and Union counties in North Carolina and to Chesterfield County in South Carolina. Anson County has more than 4,000 direct water customers. The county currently provides sewer services to fewer than 100 customers. Typical monthly residential charges for water service is in the $15 to $20 range. Sewer service charges are equal to those for water.

Durham County was the first in the state to build a full system; both a treatment facility and a collection system. It serves the Research Triangle Park area and was financed by a revenue bond issue. The county initially contracted with the City of Durham to operate and maintain the system. In recent years the county has contracted with a private firm for operating and maintenance services on the system. The monthly service fees continued to be collected for the county by the city. User rates and connection charges are set by the county commissioners. Connection charges are set to recover the full cost of all collection lines using some combination of frontage charges, subdivision improvement requirements, capital facilities charges, and acreage charges. A typical residential customer on county lines outside the city in 1998 paid monthly user charges of $15 to $20.

Early in 1968, Forsyth County voters approved a $5 million general obligation bond issue to develop a water system. Later, they approved other bond referenda, and by 1974 the county had issued $12.5 million in water bonds. After the system was constructed, mostly located in areas around the City of Winston-Salem, the county operated it directly and purchased water for distribution from Winston-Salem. In 1976 the city and county governments concluded a joint agreement under which their water and wastewater systems began operating as a single enterprise. The system, City-County Utilities Commission, now includes Clemmons, Kernersville, Lewisville, Rural Hall, and portions of other small towns in

Forsyth. The Commission has ten members and a chair. Five members are appointed by the Winston-Salem Board of Aldermen and five by the Forsyth Board of County Commissioners. The chair is appointed jointly by the mayor and the chair of the board of commissioners. All employees of the system are employees of the city. Rates and charges vary among the units and areas, reflecting agreements reached over time and the conditions under which systems were transferred to the joint city-county operation. Approximately 90 percent of the citizens of Forsyth County are served by the system.

In Greene County there was a need for improved water pressure and quality for some of the small towns and for the small, private, non-profit systems that served a number of rural communities, plus a demand for new, direct service to citizens who lived between the various communities. The system Greene County developed provided new wells, increased pressure, and distribution lines that connect the existing public and private systems. Proceeds from a general obligation bond issue, together with state and federal grants, supplied the initial financing. A special advisory committee appointed by the county commissioners initially provided policy and management guidance for the operations, and actual operations—meter-reading, billing, and the like—were carried out by the town of Snow Hill under a contract with the county.

Since that time the county has established a public works department that is responsible for the direct operation of the water system and the county's landfill. About 98 percent of the county now has water available. Typical monthly charges for residential water service are $12 to $15.

Mecklenburg County decided in 1967 to finance a large water line in the southern portion of the county to meet the demands of industrial growth. Later, the voters approved a $9.5 million water bond issue to finance a much larger water distribution system, and a $2 million bond issue to fund sewer extensions outside municipal boundaries. At first, the county operated the systems directly, but in early 1973 joined with the City of Charlotte in creating a joint department that became responsible for all water and sewer services provided through the two governments.

The Charlotte-Mecklenburg Utility Department has been expanded since its initial organization to include other municipalities within the county. Utility rates were originally higher outside Charlotte than inside, reflecting the city's policies at the time of the department's creation. Under a 1984 agreement, however, the outside rates were reduced over a period of years and now rates and extensions policies are uniform throughout the service area. (Annexation agreements among all seven of the Mecklenburg municipalities eliminated conflicts among them over annexation and paved the way for the transfer of all their utility operations to a single department.)

The fifth pattern of county action is the creation of joint city-county water and sewer departments. As noted previously, separate and independent operations in Mecklenburg and Forsyth counties were converted into joint city-county ones in 1973 and 1976, respectively. A joint operation was established by the City of Asheville and Buncombe County in 1983 following several years in which the county government had assisted in financing extensions of the municipal water and sewer systems. All three of these joint operations have advisory boards that, to a considerable extent, determine policy. (The Asheville-Buncombe agency is known locally as the "water authority," but it is organized and operates under the Interlocal Cooperation Act rather than under the Water and Sewer Authorities Act.)

A sixth county utility approach has been to create county water and sewer districts under the authority of G.S. Chapter 162A, Article 6. (See previous description, under the heading "Public Organizational Alternatives for Providing Water and Sewer Services in North Carolina," page 563.) Water and sewer districts have usually been established when the board of commissioners has found, or has concluded, that a countywide vote on bonds to finance facilities that would serve only a portion of the county could not win voter approval.

Such districts are operated, in effect, as a separate "fund" within the county government, which provides administrative and coordination advantages, while taxes and voting on bonds are limited to those citizens who are in the district and will be served. Craven, Lincoln, New Hanover, and Stanly are among the counties that have established county water and sewer districts.

The seventh approach counties have used to furnish water and sewer services has been to join with other local governments to create a new governmental agency. In each of these cases, the county government is active in creating the agency, it continues to appoint persons to the governing body, and it may have interlocal agreements with the agency relating to the financing or extension of services. Brunswick, Orange, Franklin, and Randolph counties, for example, have been parties in the establishment of water and sewer authorities; Buncombe County participated in the creation of a metropolitan sewerage district; and Harnett County was the first to take the lead in forming a metropolitan water district.

Since the MSD was organized in Harnett County, the county government has moved to create nine county and water sewer districts; six for water service and three for sewer service. General obligation bonds were issued by the districts to finance the installation of the systems. The lines are leased from the districts by the county for operation. Each district has an advisory board of local citizens. All the systems are operated by a county department. To ease the bookkeeping chores, the county expects to merge the districts in the future. The districts sell water wholesale to some towns in Harnett and to towns and associations in Wake, Moore, and Cumberland counties.

The department (acting for the districts) has some 23,000 water customers and approximately 3,500 sewer customers. Harnett County officials estimate that over 90 percent of the citizens of the county now have available water service from either the county or from one of the cities and towns in the county.

Each of these new organizations serves areas within the jurisdiction of two or more governmental units, with financing and administration independent of the creating governments. Each, in the circumstances surrounding its creation, meets the needs of the area in a manner that could not be achieved with the more common interlocal agreement.

Future Prospects

The demand for county action in providing utilities arises largely because of the rapid growth of suburban areas. For orderly and healthful development in these areas, water and sewer services need to be present before extensive development takes place. Cities are frequently reluctant and financially unable to extend services to these areas, and individuals, small developers, and industries are also often unable to do so. The county, as a general unit of government with jurisdiction over the full area, naturally comes into the picture. To date, county participation in providing water and sewer services has been primarily financial, although a number of them (through arrangements of the types noted above) are taking a larger role in utility planning and management. Whatever the county role, existing municipal systems have usually been expanded rather than new and separate systems constructed because this approach is generally the most economical.

This common approach—stressing municipal ownership and operation of facilities and county participation in financing—is in accord with the principles underlying North Carolina's municipal annexation procedures and the division of governmental powers and functions among the state, the counties, and the municipalities. These principles call for the extension of municipal boundaries and the full range of municipal types of services (such as water and sewer services and higher levels of police protection, fire protection, street construction and maintenance, and solid-waste services) to areas that become urban in character. But demands for water and sewer facilities often arise before an area has become fully urban. In these cases, if local government is to respond, the county becomes the logical unit to help provide services, at least on a transitional basis.

Some counties may also be increasingly involved in establishing water systems for small rural communities. Since 1964, the Farmers Home Administration (FmHA) has been authorized to make grants to public bodies and loans to both public bodies and private, non-profit corporations to finance water and wastewater systems for small towns, communities, and rural areas. In response, a number of non-profit corporations have been formed in North Carolina to supply water to rural communities, using loans from FmHA to finance initial installation of the necessary facilities. In some cases, the associations obtain water from a neighboring city or town; in other cases, wells are used as a source of supply. County governments also have authority to build and operate such small community water systems, and are eligible to secure loans from FmHA in the same manner as the non-profit associations. As the need for connections among small community and rural systems increases, it appears probable that more county governments will operate and manage them.

While some counties will become active in providing community water systems and others (such as Anson County) will become major suppliers of water and sewer services, recent experience suggests that most counties will probably continue to serve a financial or transitional role in providing these services, or will participate in developing areawide arrangements that bring several units of government together in a water and sewer authority, a metropolitan water district, a metropolitan sewerage district, or the like.

In this endeavor, as in most other aspects of county government, the traditional North Carolina approach of working out specific details on a county-by-county basis will undoubtedly continue, and a variety of arrangements will continue to be found around the state.

Features of City-County Financing Agreements

Because situations differ, the arrangements made between counties and municipalities for joint financing of water and sewer services will necessarily vary from county to county, and perhaps within a single county from one time to another. While there is no standard agreement that can be recommended, certain factors, listed below, should be kept in mind and, when necessary, included in all such agreements. In some circumstances, special conditions may call for consideration of other factors not listed here.

1. Responsibility for financing construction costs of the facilities should be defined. Financing costs may be borne by one governmental unit or shared by all of them, or certain portions of an improvement may be financed by one unit and other portions by the remaining units.

2. The agreement should establish the ownership of all facilities and the rights in all easements.

3. If the county is the initial owner and it does not anticipate entering into water and sewer operations directly, transfer of ownership to the entity operating the system should be provided for.

4. The agreement should specify any change in ownership that will take place upon annexation, by one of the cities involved, of areas in which the facilities are located, or should anticipate any problems that might arise if ownership does not rest with the city after the annexation.

5. The procedure and circumstances under which further extension of any facility being constructed may take place should be covered. The agreement might empower any of the participating units to extend on its own, or joint approval might be required.

6. The governmental unit responsible for prescribing the specifications for all facilities should be established. Specifications should cover the size and quality of all materials used and the location of all facilities.

7. The schedule of rates, fees, and other charges to customers should be agreed on, including water rates, sewer charges, tap fees, acreage charges, impact fees, fire-protection charges, and other miscellaneous charges. Specific rates could be stipulated, or they could be scaled to those already applicable inside the city or cities.

8. Changes, if any, in levels of rates or other fees and charges upon municipal annexation of facilities should be anticipated, taking into account both the initial cost and that of future extensions.

9. The source and amount of reimbursement, if any, to the county(ies) or city(ies) should be set forth, including the term during which reimbursement is to be made.

10. Responsibility for the operation, maintenance, and control of the facilities—including the control of connections and the collection of all charges—should be established.

Additional Resources

Howells, David H. *Historical Account of Public Water Supplies in North Carolina.* Raleigh, N.C.: Water Resources Research Institute of the University of North Carolina, 1989.

Lawrence, David M. *Local Government Finance in North Carolina,* 2d ed. Chapel Hill, N.C.: Institute of Government, The University of North Carolina at Chapel Hill, 1990.

Liner, Charles D. *State and Local Government Relations in North Carolina: Their Evolution and Current Status,* 2d ed. Chapel Hill, N.C.: Institute of Government, The University of North Carolina at Chapel Hill, 1995.

Notes

1. Bureau of the Census, *1990 Census of Population and Housing: Summary Social, Economic, and Housing Characteristics,* 1990 CPH-5-35 (Washington, DC: U.S. Government Printing Office, 1992), table 12.

2. Information provided by John McFadyen, Compliance Services Branch Head, Public Water Supply Section, Division of Environmental Health, April, 1998.

3. North Carolina Utilities Commission, *1996 Report—Volume XXVII,* (Raleigh, N.C.: The Commission, May 1997), pp. 125–62.

4. *Ibid.*

5. Information provided by Charles Weaver, Division of Water Quality, Department of Environment and Natural Resources, April 1998.

6. North Carolina Utilities Commission, *1996 Report,* p. 131.

7. Most of the people in North Carolina live in housing with complete plumbing: hot and cold piped water, a flush toilet, and either a bathtub or a shower. The 1990 census found that 98.5 percent of the housing units in the state had complete plumbing. This figure represents a major improvement in the past fifty years. In 1940 only 24 percent of the state's housing units had complete plumbing.

8. From Steve Steinbeck, Chief of Field Services, Wastewater Services Section, Division of Environmental Health, Department of Environment and Natural Resources, April 1998.

19   Other Enterprises

William A. Campbell and Warren Jake Wicker

Contents

Airports

In 1929, just over twenty-five years after the Wright Brothers made their first flights in Kitty Hawk, North Carolina's cities and counties were authorized to own and operate airports (G.S. Chapter 63). Their initial powers were broad, and have since been enlarged. Those powers appear to cover all activities that might be undertaken in connection with the establishment and operation of an airport, either directly or through contracts or leases to other operators (G.S. 63-49, -53).

William A. Campbell is an Institute of Government faculty member whose work includes state and local taxation, land records, and environmental law.

Warren Jake Wicker is an Institute of Government emeritus faculty member whose work included local government law, finance, and administration with special attention to public enterprises and city-county cooperation.

In order to protect approaches to airport runways and promote the safety of persons and property in the vicinity of airports, counties may adopt airport zoning around airports under the authority of the Model Airport Zoning Act (G.S. Ch. 63, Art. 4). The provisions of the zoning ordinance may restrict the height of both trees and buildings.

Counties may levy property taxes for airport purposes [G.S. 153A-149(c)(4)], issue general obligation bonds [G.S. 159-48(b)(2)] and revenue bonds (G.S. Ch. 159, Art. 5), condemn land for airport facilities [G.S. 40A-3(b)(2)], and join with cities and other counties in supporting and operating airports (G.S. 63-4). They may also create subordinate boards or commissions to manage airport operations, or lease airports to be operated by private persons or corporations. Counties, acting alone or jointly with other counties or cities, may establish special airport districts with authority to own and operate airports, levy property taxes, and issue general obligations bonds for airport purposes (G.S. 63, Art. 8).

A few other arrangements have been authorized by special acts. For example, Raleigh-Durham International Airport is operated by an authority created by Durham and Wake counties and the cities of Durham and Raleigh. These four units also appoint the members of the airport authority board.

Although the exact number of airports in North Carolina is not known, the Division of Aviation of the North Carolina Department of Transportation (NCDOT) estimates that there are over 400 airports and airstrips in the state.[1] The majority of these are privately owned personal-use airstrips in rural areas.

There are some 115 publicly owned airports in the state. Of these, seventy-five are open to general public use, the remaining forty landing areas are not. In the latter group are such facilities as military airports, local hospital heliports, and state airports used for forest fire fighting.

Of the seventy-five airports owned by public bodies and open to general public use, airport authorities or commissions administer thirty-one. A single-government commission operates seven of the thirty-one facilities. The other twenty-four are creations of multiple units of government, usually a city and a county, such as the Burlington-Alamance Airport Authority. Six of the twenty-four, however, reflect the joint action of more than two units. The Rocky Mount–Wilson Airport Authority, for example, is a joint operation of the cities of Rocky Mount and Wilson and the three counties—Edgecombe, Nash, and Wilson—in which they are located.

Of the remaining forty-four publicly owned airports open to general public use, one is operated directly by the federal government, three are operated directly by state agencies, eighteen are operated directly by a city, and twenty-two are operated directly by a county. Of the forty airports operated directly by a city or a county, thirty-six have some sort of advisory board or committee.

NCDOT's Division of Aviation estimates that only a small proportion of the city and county airports generate enough revenues to meet operating expenses. Only the airports served by major airlines have revenues sufficient to cover all operating expenses and most capital improvements.

Local appropriations and state and federal aid are used to meet the remaining capital outlays and, for most of the airports, to supplement operating expenses. The Division of Aviation of NCDOT administers the State Aid to Airports Program and is also the channel through which federal funds for local governments are directed. In addition, the Division provides technical assistance and information on all aspects of airport establishment and operations.

Off-Street Parking

North Carolina counties have been authorized to own and operate off-street parking facilities as a public enterprise since 1974 (G.S. Ch. 153A, Art. 15). But only a few have done so. As an enterprise, counties may establish rates and charges for the use of the facilities, and they may issue revenue bonds to finance the construction of parking facilities (G.S. Ch. 159, Art. 5).

Counties may condemn land needed to provide the facilities (G.S. 40A-3) and may join with cities in providing parking facilities (G.S. 160A, Art. 20).

Counties may also levy property taxes for parking purposes [G.S. 153A-149(c)(24)]. General obligation bond financing is authorized by G.S. 159-48(b)(12). Counties may adopt ordinances regulating the use of county-owned off-street parking facilities. The ordinances may provide for the towing of vehicles parked in violation of the ordinance (G.S. 153A-170). Such ordinances may be enforced under G.S. 153A-123 as are other county ordinances.

Counties have traditionally provided off-street parking for the convenience of employees and those using courthouses and other administrative buildings. Because of the limited parking available in many downtown areas, some counties have created card-accessed lots for employees and clients. In some cases employees and clients are charged for parking;

in other cases they are not charged and have the benefit of the controlled access to the lots.

In recent years, counties have expanded these activities to provide facilities that serve those who have business in the vicinity of county buildings as well as business with the county. Guilford, Mecklenburg, and Wake are among the counties that have provided facilities for the general public with charges for parking.

Most of the facilities that impose user fees and charges are not self-supporting and are partially financed from general county revenues.

Public Transportation

Counties have been authorized to provide public transportation as an enterprise since 1977 (G.S. 153A-274). County transportation activities, while significant, are principally related to other county functions and do not operate on a strictly enterprise basis.

Public transportation provided by local governments in North Carolina is vehicle (bus and van) transportation. The largest systems are the sixteen operated by cities that varied in 1997 populations from Hickory (32,632) to Charlotte (495,632). In 1996 eight of these city systems carried more than a million passengers. Charlotte, with 11.5 million passengers, was the largest. Hickory had the smallest number of passengers in that year—144,000.

County authority to provide transportation services is extensive. The authority includes the power to levy property taxes [G.S. 153A-149(c)(27] and to issue general obligation bonds [G.S. 159-48(b)(23)] and revenue bonds (G.S. Ch. 159, Art. 5). The authorization includes rail transportation as well as buses and other motor vehicles. [2]

Three of the state's counties—Durham, Orange, and Wake—are authorized to establish a regional public transportation authority (G.S. Ch. 160A, Art. 26). They have done so by creating the Research Triangle Regional Public Transportation Authority, known locally as the Triangle Transit Authority. The governing boards of the three counties, the cities of Chapel Hill, Cary, Durham, and Raleigh, and the state's Secretary of Transportation appoint the members of the authority's Board of Trustees. The authority's bus system's routes connect Chapel Hill, Cary, Durham, Raleigh, the Research Triangle Park, and the Raleigh-Durham Airport. [3] In 1997 it carried some 426,000 passengers. On average, there were approximately six passengers on each bus at all times. Fare-box revenue accounted for about 16 percent of operating expenses. The remainder of the operating expenses and capital costs were met from federal, state, and local appropriations. The automobile license tax on vehicles in the three counties ($5 per vehicle) produced $3,442,550.

Legislation adopted in 1997 provides for the creation of a regional transportation authority in the Piedmont Triad area (Greensboro, High Point, and Winston-Salem) (G.S. Ch. 160A, Art. 27). With the 1997 legislation, authorities created by counties under both Article 26 and Article 27 may levy motor vehicle license taxes of $5 per vehicle and privilege license taxes on vehicle rental businesses. The proceeds of both taxes may be used to support public transportation systems within their jurisdictions. The same 1997 legislation also authorized Mecklenburg County to levy a one-half percent sales and use tax, earmarked for public transportation, after approval in a voter referendum.

For most counties, involvement in providing public transportation is principally in connection with other functions: human services, education and training, recreation, and various social and human services. State and federal funds are significant in the financing of these activities.

In order to promote "improved transportation for the elderly, handicapped and residents of rural areas and small towns" the General Assembly enacted the "North Carolina Act to Remove Barriers to Coordinating Human Service and Volunteer Transportation" in 1981 (G.S. Ch. 62, Art. 12A). The act exempts charitable or governmental agencies, including county departments of social services; area mental health, developmental disabilities, and substance abuse authorities; local health departments; councils on aging; community action agencies; sheltered workshops; group homes; and state residential institutions from regulation by the state's Utilities Commission.

The state's Elderly and Disabled Transportation Assistance Program (G.S. 136-44.27) in the NCDOT administers state financial assistance to counties with such programs. Half of the funds available are distributed to counties equally; the remaining funds are distributed in accordance with a formula that takes into account the number of elderly and disabled persons in the counties and each county's population density. In 1997–98, state appropriations for the program totaled some $5,000,000. In order to receive the funds, counties must have a transportation development plan that has been approved by the board of county commissioners and NCDOT. The transportation development plans are based on a full examination of the transportation needs of all persons served by the various social and human service agencies and alternative ways of meeting those needs. The plan also designates a lead agency within the county that is responsible for making applications for state grant funds and for administering them within the county. The costs of developing the plans are shared among the levels of government: federal, 80 percent; state, 10 percent; and county, 10 percent.

Administrative arrangements for county transportation programs vary greatly. In some counties administrative responsibility may be centered in a single agency: aging or social services, for example. In other counties administrative responsibility may be contracted to a private nonprofit agency. In a like manner, services may be delivered directly by the county agency or contracted by the county, in whole or in part, to other public or private agencies. Counties in which there are city transit systems often contract for services with those systems.

Rural General Public Systems (1996) serve forty-four counties in the state. These are principally human service transportation systems. Twenty-two are single county systems. The other twenty-two counties are served by six multicounty systems. All other counties have some form of transportation, but for human services clients only.

These systems provide transportation for human services recipients: transportation to congregate meals, adult and child day care, medical and recreation services, education and training, senior and volunteer activities, and other social and human service programs.

In 1996 the county and multicounty systems had 0.25 passengers per vehicle mile. The systems provided trips for almost 3,000,000 passengers at an average cost of $4.75 per passenger.

Guilford County's 1997–98 budget illustrates the mix of financing found in some counties. Its budget for that year included an appropriation of $742,108 for transportation services in the broad human and social service areas. The county provided 51.5 percent of the appropriated funds, federal grants provided 29.9 percent, state grants provided 17.5 percent, and 1.1 percent came from miscellaneous receipts.

Administrative arrangements in Orange County illustrate the types of transportation provided.[4] In Orange County, transportation responsibility is centered in the Department on Aging. An advisory board, appointed by the county commissioners, oversees policy and procedural matters and makes recommendations to the staff and to the county commissioners.

The program uses a mix of twenty-four peak-hour vehicles: cars, mini-vans, vans, and mini-buses. There are fourteen agencies that pay for their client's transportation:

- Department of Social Services
- County Health Department
- County Recreation and Parks
- Cooperative Extension Service
- Department on Aging
- Piedmont Health Services, Inc.
- Joint Orange-Chatham Community Action
- Orange-Person-Chatham Mental Health Center
- Orange Enterprises
- Cedar Grove Day Care Center
- Wake Opportunities–Head Start
- Piedmont HIV Consortium
- Smart Start
- County Middle School After School Program

In addition, general public transportation services are provided on a space-available basis on most agency-supported routes.

In 1996–97, the Orange County program provided 103,648 passenger-trips, operated 27,960 hours, and covered 441,645 miles with an operating budget of $525,265. The cost per person per trip was $5.07. Agency contracts provided 45 percent of the necessary revenue, county funds accounted for 20 percent, and state and federal grants supplied 35 percent.

Solid Wastes

County Roles and Responsibilities in Solid Waste Management

Comprehensive state and federal laws and regulations govern solid waste management. Although cities and counties are the major providers of solid waste collection and disposal services, they must operate these services according to federal and state requirements and under the general supervision and guidance of the Department of Environment and Natural Resource's Solid Waste Division. As a general matter, a county, as a "unit of local government," must review the collection and disposal services being provided in the county and take whatever steps are necessary to see that the public health and environment are protected [G.S. 130A-309.09A(a)]. Under this general mandate, a county may undertake to provide collection and disposal services itself, contract for the provision of some or all of such services with private firms, enter into agreements for the provision of such services with other counties and with cities, and require that the providers of such services obtain a franchise from the county. To offer just one example: A county could contract with a private landfill in another county or state for the disposal of solid waste generated in the county and then could build and operate a transfer station with county funds and personnel.

State law imposes four specific requirements on counties, and these are to determine the full cost of solid waste management, to develop a ten-year management plan, to implement a waste reduction program, and to report annually on management programs and waste reduction efforts. Each county is required to determine annually the full cost of solid waste management within its service area for the preceding year [G.S. 130A-309.08(a)]. A county's service area is the portion of the county not served by municipalities. The full cost determination is to be done according to rules adopted by the Health Services Commission, and since, as of this writing, the commission has not adopted the necessary rules, this requirement is in a state of abeyance. When the rules are adopted and counties begin making the full cost determinations, they are required to publicize the information regarding costs to all users of solid waste services in the county's service area [G.S. 130A-309.08(b)].

Each county is required to develop a ten-year solid waste management plan, either on its own or in cooperation with a municipality or municipalities [G.S. 130A-309.09A(b)]. The plan must demonstrate a "good-faith effort" to achieve the state goal of a 40 percent reduction of the solid waste stream, on a per capita basis, by June 30, 2001 [G.S. 130A-309.09A(b), G.S. 130A-309.04(c)]. Among the major elements that each plan must contain are the following:

1. An evaluation of the solid waste stream in the area covered by the plan
2. A goal for the reduction of solid waste, on a per capita basis, by June 30, 2001, and a further reduction by June 30, 2006
3. An assessment of current programs
4. A description of how the solid waste reduction goals will be met

Each county must establish a waste reduction program that is designed to achieve the 2001 and 2006 goals (G.S. 130A-309.09B). In its reduction program, a county is encouraged to separate for recycling plastics, glass, metal, and paper, and to recycle yard waste.

Annually, each county must report to the Department of Environment and Natural Resources on its solid waste management activities [G.S. 130A-309.09A(d)]. Among the items that must be included in the report are the following:

1. The amount of municipal solid waste received at management facilities, by type of waste
2. The amount and type of materials from the solid waste stream that were recycled
3. The percentage of the population participating in various types of recycling activities
4. The annual reduction in municipal solid waste

The traditional role of counties in the collection of solid waste has been to do nothing, to license or franchise private haulers in areas not served by municipal collectors, or to provide collection sites at various locations around the county (sometimes called the "green box" system after the green dumpsters used to receive the waste). Under the current state planning and waste reduction requirements, doing nothing is rarely an option. Counties have ample legal authority to license or franchise private haulers, including authority to grant exclusive franchises and set the fees to be charged by private haulers (G.S. 153A-136). They may also require the separation of recyclable materials and participation in recycling programs (G.S. 153A-136). Most counties have moved away from the green box system and have instead chosen to have fewer, staffed, collection centers. At these centers, containers are provided for recyclable materials as well as for waste that is to be buried or burned.

Just as the collection of solid waste has traditionally been a municipal function, waste disposal has usually been a county function. At one time, most counties operated a county-owned landfill. This is no longer the typical pattern for two reasons: it has become more and more difficult to site a landfill for political and environmental reasons, and the federal requirements for landfills under Subtitle D of the Resource Conservation and Recovery Act (42 U.S.C. §§ 6942 through 6949a, 40 C.F.R. Part 258) have made the construction and operation of landfills more difficult (from an engineering standpoint) and much more expensive. As a consequence, there is a trend for counties to dispose of waste in large, privately-owned and operated landfills that serve several cities and counties or for several counties to operate jointly a landfill either through contractual arrangements or by creating a regional authority. Ample legal authority exists for all of these arrangements. Under G.S. 153A-299.1, a county may enter into a contract for disposal with a private firm for up to sixty years. Under G.S. 160A-461, a county may enter into an interlocal agreement with other government units for solid waste management, and under G.S. 153A-421, a county may, by acting with other local governments, create a regional solid waste management authority.

County Solid Waste Management Ordinance

Counties are authorized to adopt solid waste management ordinances (G.S. 153A-121, -132.1, -136, -274 through -278, and -291 through -293, and G.S. 130A-309A through -309D), and adoption of such an ordinance is an essential part of a county's management program. In an ordinance, a county can require that householders remove solid waste from their premises at certain intervals (every seven days is usual) and that waste be stored in watertight containers with covers. A county can prohibit certain wastes—hazardous waste, batteries, tires, used oil, white goods, and yard wastes—from being deposited in a landfill. The county can adopt rules concerning its collection centers; for example, it can prohibit the leaving of certain classes of waste at the center, require that waste be deposited in receptacles, and prohibit scavenging. In its ordinance, a county can require source separation and recycling of certain materials. It can also adopt rules against littering that are in addition to or more stringent than the state criminal statute against littering. The Institute of Government and the Department of Environment and Natural Resources have prepared a model solid waste management ordinance that may be obtained from either the Institute or the department.

Financing Solid Waste Management Services

Solid waste management activities are public enterprises within the meaning of G.S. Chapter 153A, Article 15, and therefore a county may finance these activities by levying property taxes, borrowing money, accepting grants, imposing fees and charges, or by any combination of these financing arrangements. Traditionally, counties financed solid waste management activities from general fund revenues, usually supplemented by a user fee (called a "tipping fee") if the county operated a landfill. As part of the trend toward service charges in local government—and also as a result of the escalating costs of solid waste management—more and more counties are moving toward shifting most of the financing to a fee basis.

Counties are authorized to charge collection, use, and availability fees (G.S. 153A-292). Since very few counties operate collection services, collection fees are not a significant source of funding. User fees are typically charged for the use of a landfill or other disposal facility or transfer station and set at so much per ton of waste disposed. The availability fee has gained popularity in recent years. It is not based on use of a facility, but rather it can be charged against the owners of all improved property who benefit from the existence of a solid waste management facility. The fee may be billed with property taxes and collected in the same manner as taxes. Counties have increasingly used availability fees to finance staffed collection centers and recycling facilities.

Additional Resources

Division of Aviation, N.C. Department of Transportation, *Airport Sponsor's Listing*, Raleigh, N.C., March 17, 1998.

The following issues of *Local Government Law Bulletin*, by William A. Campbell, published by the Institute of Government: No. 42, "Exclusionary Policies Regarding Municipal Solid Waste and Hazardous Waste" (June 1992); No. 46, "Legal Issues in the Financing of Solid Waste Disposal Facilities" (Oct. 1992); No. 54, "Intergovernmental and Organizational Issues in Solid Waste Management" (Jan. 1994); No. 59, "Flow-Control Ordinances Held Unconstitutional: *C & A Carbone, Inc. v. Town of Clarkstown*" (June 1994); No. 65, "Litter Control" (Feb. 1995); No. 71, "Solid Waste Management: Recent Developments in Flow Control" (Nov. 1995); No. 72, "Licensing and Franchising Solid Waste Services" (March 1996); and No. 77, "Local Government Participation in the Permitting of Sanitary Landfills" (Feb. 1997).

The Transit 2001: Executive Summary and Technical Report. Submitted by the Transit 2001 Commission to Governor James B. Hunt, Jr., prepared for the Transit 2001 Commission by the North Carolina Department of Transportation, Raleigh, N.C., January 1997.

Notes

1. Information on airports in this section was provided by Bruce Matthews and Patrice Swinten, Division of Aviation, North Carolina Department of Transportation, May 1998.

2. Information on public transportation activities cited in this section was provided by Charles Glover, Assistant Director, Division of Public Transportation, North Carolina Department of Transportation, and from the Division's "Operating Statistics Summary, July 1995–June 1996," May 1998.

3. Information on the Triangle Transit Authority operations was provided by Jim Ferrell, Operations Manager, June 1998.

4. Information on Orange County operations was provided by the Orange County Department on Aging, May 1998.

20 Parks and Recreation

Candace Goode Vick

Contents

Candace Goode Vick is a faculty member of North Carolina State University and director of its Recreation Resources Service. She specializes in management of local park recreation agencies.

    The author expresses her appreciation to J. Harold Moses and John C. Poole, authors of this chapter in the third edition of this book, whose work has been used extensively in this edition. Both have long careers in public parks and recreation services. Poole is a staff member with the state's Division of Parks and Recreation, from which Moses is retired.

Public parks and recreation are a fairly recent addition to local government functions in the United States, an outgrowth of the park and playground movement that began in large cities such as Boston and Chicago around the turn of the century. In the early years, parks and recreation were generally regarded as a municipal responsibility, and their growth in North Carolina and throughout the nation has been such that even the smaller cities and towns now provide some measure of financial support for these activities. Local county governments became active providers of parks and recreation services in 1961 with the establishment of the Person County Parks and Recreation Department. Since that time, all local government parks and recreation services have grown. In 1997, 141 municipalities and 70 counties provided year-round leisure services for their citizens. The 1996–97 Municipal and County Services Study[1] reported that the average per capita expenditure by the sixty-two reporting municipal park and recreation agencies was $64.28, while the average county per capita expenditure by the thirty-two reporting parks and recreation agencies was $12.24. The three responding city/county joint departments reported an average per capita expenditure of $16.09. In fiscal year 1996–97 the overall North Carolina per capita expenditure for parks and recreation was $45.92.

The acceptance of public parks and recreation as a county function in the state moved slowly until the mid-1960s. The reasons seem fairly obvious. In the earlier years of this century, children who lived in rural areas had less time for recreational activities. Many of them spent more time traveling to and from school than city children, and some may well have spent more time doing chores at home. Also, farm families were said to be generally less inclined to spend cash (including taxes) for goods and services than city families; and, if a farm family and a city family had the same real income, the farm family tended to provide a higher proportion of its own food, clothing, and other items—including recreation. On the face of it, there appeared to be less need for publicly provided parks and open space or for organized recreation programs in rural areas.

Without question, such attitudes toward county parks and recreation have changed. For example, in the 1960s there were only thirteen such departments in North Carolina. By 1974 the number had grown to twenty-seven. Today, sixty-four counties provide sufficient appropriations to fund a full-time department that is professionally directed. Six counties have joint agreements with municipalities to provide services. Many other counties provide financial support of varying degrees but less than required for full-time, year-round operation.

There are several reasons for this change. First, boards of county commissioners are becoming more aware of services that people want and are willing to pay for. As residents have become more affluent and more urbanized, they have demanded more services from government, including parks and recreation. In some areas, county residents who once participated in municipal recreation programs are now being discouraged from participating in programs through increases in nonresident fees, or being denied access to programs because of the lack of space in high-demand programs. Also, it is now recognized that companies consider the recreational opportunities available for their workers and families before selecting a county to move into. Parks and recreation programs are thus coming to be seen as assets to a county's economic development effort.

County Parks and Recreation in North Carolina

There is every reason to believe that, as the state becomes more urban, the number of counties offering parks and recreation programs will continue to grow and the scope and diversity of program services will multiply. As noted previously, this trend will probably be reinforced by the tendency of rural and suburban residents to demand higher levels of government services of all kinds, including a broad base of leisure services that offer program variety and diversity of facilities.

In the 1980s some predicted that public parks and recreation would eventually be regarded as a primary responsibility of the county rather than of the municipality. As urban land becomes more scarce, large parks and major recreational facilities to serve urban populations will, of necessity, be located outside cities. Cities are also feeling the strain of nonresidents enrolling in already crowded programs and facilities. However, to date, only one city and county have consolidated parks and recreation under a county system, Mecklenburg County and Charlotte. Cities like Raleigh have addressed the land issue by purchasing land outside the city limits in anticipation of growth. Many cities that incur major expenses to provide programs and services to county residents who live outside municipal boundaries charge nonresidents a higher fee than municipal residents to participate. Although public parks and recreation may be headed in the direction of many other necessary services now generally accepted as functions of county government, interest in the consolidation of parks and recreation programs has not progressed beyond the talking stages.

Scope of County Parks and Recreation Programs

The range of recreational services and activities provided by North Carolina counties is wide, and no two programs are exactly alike. Nevertheless, most of them fall within several broad categories.

Some counties own and maintain a vast network of parks and playgrounds in suburban and rural areas with little or no provision of recreation programs. A few share the responsibility for these facilities with one or more towns. The second category includes counties that operate limited summer parks and recreation programs in small towns or unincorporated communities throughout the county, using schools or other leased facilities. These programs typically focus on youth athletics and day camp activities.

A third category of county activity includes grants to towns or communities for programs and facility development. A fourth type of arrangement includes those programs that, although financed by the county, are administered by the parks and recreation department of a municipality. A final category, which stops short of the immediate full provision of parks and recreation services, is cooperative planning with municipalities for park land acquisition. Some counties may use a combination of the preceding alternatives, to benefit all their urban, suburban, and rural residents.

Only recently has a somewhat uniform pattern of county involvement in public parks and recreation surfaced. The trend is toward a full-time, full-service, autonomous department supervised by a professional administrator. Generally, appropriations by counties for parks and recreation have been relatively modest, but funding is now growing at a rapid pace.

In fiscal year 1996–97, the level of support for county parks and recreation varied greatly. Dare, Mecklenburg, and Buncombe counties were the leaders in per capita spending with $41.96, $39.17, and $27.15 respectively. At the other end of the continuum, Stokes, Harnett, and Davidson counties spent only $2.65, $3.13, and $3.38 per capita.

Legal Aspects

General Powers

The North Carolina Recreation Enabling Act, G.S. Chapter 160A, Article 18,[2] authorizes counties to provide parks and recreation services to their citizens. The act provides a broad definition of recreation:

"'Recreation' means activities that are diversionary in character and aid in promoting entertainment, pleasure, relaxation, instruction, and other physical, mental, and cultural development and leisure time experiences" (G.S. 160A-352).

This legislation (G.S. 160A-353) specifically authorizes local governments to do the following:

1. Establish and conduct a system of supervised recreation
2. Set apart land or buildings for use as parks or playgrounds or recreational centers or other facilities
3. Acquire lands or buildings by gifts, grants, purchase, lease, loan, condemnation, or any other lawful method
4. Accept any gift, grant, lease, loan, or bequest of money or other personal property or any donation for parks and recreation use
5. Provide, acquire, construct, equip, operate, and maintain parks, playgrounds, recreation centers, and recreation facilities
6. Appropriate funds for a public parks and recreation system

Counties may operate a parks and recreation system as a line department or create a policy-making parks and recreation commission. They may also join with other units of local government to operate a single system of parks and recreation.

Counties are also permitted to contract with and appropriate money to private entities to provide recreational services as long as they are provided in the nondiscriminatory fashion appropriate for a public activity and the private organization properly accounts to the county for its expenditures. G.S. 153A-449 authorizes counties "to contract with and appropriate money to any person, association, or corporation in order to carry out any public purpose that the county is authorized by law to engage in."

Financing

Before the 1973 revision of Article V of the North Carolina Constitution, recreation was not considered a "necessary expense" and could not be financed by property tax revenues without a vote of the people. Even then the limitations were severe. Under the revised constitution and the enabling legislation enacted pursuant thereto in 1973, public parks and recreation are among the purposes for which counties and cities may levy property taxes without a vote, subject to an overall property tax rate limitation of $1.50. In addition, counties may allocate to these programs any other revenue whose use is not restricted by law. There is no legal impediment to county funding of a comprehensive public parks and recreation program.

Because of the current demise of federal funding sources in this field nationally, many county departments are also exploring innovative alternative sources of funds. Examples include local foundations and trust funds, use of occupancy-tax revenues for recreational facilities as part of tourism development programs, and publication of "gift catalogs" to allow donors to give particular needed items to recreation programs.

Related Legislation

The legislative actions outlined in the two previous sections have helped North Carolina become a national leader in providing strong local government parks and recreation systems. Other legislative authority also permits both counties and municipalities to foster these activities at the local level.

Enabling statutes for subdivision regulations, for example, permit counties or municipalities to require that developers reserve or dedicate recreational areas to serve the residents in new subdivisions (see G.S. 153A-331 and 160A-372). The requirement may be imposed only as part of a subdivision ordinance adopted by the county to guide and regulate subdivision development. The subdivider ordinarily passes the economic cost on to the purchasers of subdivision lots. Once the land is dedicated, the cost of maintaining it falls on the county.

A subdivision ordinance that requires dedication or reservation of land should indicate the amount of land per subdivision that must be dedicated, its location, and some standard relating to its degree of improvement. The ordinance should include some provisions to ensure that the land is well suited and properly located for recreational purposes. Local governments may also require developers to provide funds in lieu of land so that additional recreational lands may be acquired to serve the new developments.

Counties are authorized by G.S. 160A-274 to exchange, lease, sell, purchase, or enter into agreements regarding joint use of property with other government units. In general, such arrangements may include whatever terms and conditions the units involved deem wise. This authority has permitted boards of county commissioners and school boards, for example, to work cooperatively to transfer surplus school lands and structures to parks and recreation uses.

The only significant constraint on such transfers is found in Article IX, Section 7, of the North Carolina Constitution, which prevents school systems from giving away school property. As long as the school system receives value in return, however, a transfer to another government unit is permissible. Under G.S. 115C-518(a) the school board must give the board of commissioners the first opportunity to purchase whenever it disposes of real property that is no longer suitable or necessary for public school purposes.

The 1977 Community Schools Act (G.S. Chapter 115C, Article 13) has also benefited county recreation programs. It opens schools for a variety of community uses, including recreation. A county can agree with a school board to use school gyms, playgrounds, and fields for its recreation programs and thus avoid having to construct or acquire expensive capital facilities in areas where facilities exist.

The Park and Recreation Trust Fund (PARTF) was established by the North Carolina General Assembly in 1994 (G.S. 113-44.15). Under this fund a matching parks and recreation grant program for local governments was established. Thirty percent of the funds dedicated to the Park and Recreation Trust Fund Authority will be allocated annually to local governments for the following purposes:

1. Fee-simple acquisition of real property for the preservation of natural areas and future recreation development
2. Construction, expansion, and renovation or repair of both indoor and outdoor recreation facilities
3. Construction of support facilities and improvements that support primary recreation facilities

Organization of County Programs

North Carolina's Recreation Enabling Law provides three alternatives in organizing county parks and recreation systems: (1) a line department within county government, (2) a policy-making parks and recreation commission, or (3) a joint agreement with a city.

Line Department

First, the commissioners may organize a parks and recreation department as a line department of the county. This is the system used to organize sixty-two county parks and recreation departments in North

Carolina. As in other departments with nonelected administrators, the county manager is ultimately responsible for the operation of the parks and recreation department, including staffing, accountability, fiscal control, and so on. When a department is established, it can be called a Parks Department, a Parks and Recreation Department, or a Recreation Department, depending on its mission and scope of services. In recent years, departmental titles have expanded to include such terms as cultural resources. Franklin County commissioners named their new department the Franklin County Parks, Recreation, and Cultural Resources Department.

When this line-department approach is used, it is also beneficial to appoint a parks and recreation advisory committee. Appointed by the board of commissioners, this committee interprets the needs of the citizens, works closely with the paid professional staff, and assists in providing direction for the department. The advisory group has no legal authority but, if properly directed, can greatly assist the department, the county manager, and the board of county commissioners. The committee in essence links the citizens, the department, the county administration, and the board of commissioners. Advisory board membership should ideally be representative of the population based on race, sex, interests, and geography.

Overall, citizen boards function most effectively if their members are appointed to staggered three-year terms, with all members limited to two consecutive terms.

Parks and Recreation Commission

Second, the county commissioners may establish and appoint a policy-making parks and recreation commission and charge it with the responsibility for the department's organization, personnel, fiscal matters, areas and facilities, program planning, and other functions. This commission is responsible to the county commissioners for both day-to-day operation of the department and for its long-term direction. The parks and recreation commission members answer directly to the elected board. A commission may be established and given parks and recreation responsibilities by a resolution of the county commissioners. The parks and recreation commission has not been widely used in North Carolina to establish county departments. Tanglewood in Forsyth County and the Madison County Parks and Recreation Department are the only county parks and recreation commissions that have been created in North Carolina. Forsyth County also operates its own parks and recreation department and does not contribute funds to the operation of Tanglewood.

Joint Agreement with a City or Another County

A county may also choose to enter into a joint agreement with a municipality or another county to provide services for its residents. This type of arrangement is authorized by G.S. 160A-335. A county that does not wish to hire and maintain its own staff may contract with another county or city for use of certain parks, recreation facilities, and programs by its residents, or for professional staff support from the other units, or it may agree to set up a joint parks and recreation agency with the other unit (G.S. 160A-355 and G.S. Chapter 160A, Article 20, Interlocal Cooperation). A contract must state its purpose and duration and the arrangement for handling the ownership of real property. It should also provide for its own amendment and termination. There are seven counties that have joint agreements with municipalities to provide services for their citizens, but many more have agreements with municipalities for varying levels of services.

A joint agency with its own staff may be established under G.S. Chapter 160A, Article 20. This approach can provide services that would be too expensive for any one local unit to provide with its own resources. It can take advantage of the wider population and tax base of several units. Administrative cost can be generally reduced, making more money available for programs and services. The staff can be appointed either by one unit or jointly by all participating units. Title to real property can be held jointly or can continue to be held by the individual participating units. As when services are provided by contract, the contract establishing the joint agency should specify the agency's purpose, duration, organization, appointment of personnel, financing, amendment, and termination.

Joint Programs Involving Several Units

A county choosing not to hire and maintain its own staff may find some advantages in arranging for professional services or for the use of certain parks and recreation facilities through contractual agreements with a town or city in the same county or with another county. These joint arrangements might be for a temporary summer or a year-round program. Several cities and counties have found this approach to have economic value and to be a fair way to provide leisure services for county residents who live in the fringe or suburban areas of larger cities and towns. Such a relatively simple contractual arrangement is most likely to prove satisfactory in those situations when one or two units of government are in effect "buying" the use of parks and recreation facilities and professional staff services from an existing program, and when a second full-time staff is not feasible or a second policy-making body is not needed.

If instead, a large number of local governments are involved, as might be the case when several counties (including perhaps the smaller towns within each county) band together to provide a regional parks and recreation system or facilities, a more appropriate form of organization may be an independent, jointly financed parks and recreation commission with its own staff. This latter approach is allowed by both the general wording of G.S. 160A-355 and the legislation authorizing interlocal cooperation found in G.S. Chapter 160A, Article 20.

Professional Staff

Regardless of the form of organization chosen, good professional leadership for the department's administration is probably the most essential ingredient for successful operation. The major job responsibilities for an administrator are to organize the department, train and supervise staff, select appropriate program activities, coordinate planning, manage a budget, plan for acquisition of needed park lands, and develop a variety of recreational facilities. Parks and recreation supervisors are also needed to work with the administrator, the number of supervisors depending on the scope of the department's services. Volunteers may provide some supplemental assistance but experience indicates that they should be used to enrich the program and not to substitute for paid professional leadership.

Many highly competent parks and recreation professionals are available in North Carolina. County commissioners and administrative officials should hire educated and experienced personnel to administer the program, whether the county is establishing a new department or restaffing an existing service.

The North Carolina Recreation and Park Society participated in the National Parks and Recreation Association Professional Certification Program. While voluntary, parks and recreation professionals can become credentialed as Certified Leisure Professionals and Certified Leisure Associates verifying that they have met the minimal requirements to practice as a parks and recreation professional. In July 1986, N.C. Senate Bill 249, the Therapeutic Recreation Personnel Certification Act, was passed to credential therapeutic recreation specialists.

North Carolina is fortunate to have more than twenty-one four-year colleges and universities granting bachelor's degrees in parks and recreation. Five universities confer master's degrees: North Carolina State University, The University of North Carolina at Chapel Hill, East Carolina University, The University of North Carolina at Greensboro, and The University of North Carolina at Wilmington.

Parks and Recreation Planning

Parks and recreation services and facilities, like other government activities, must be carefully planned if they are to operate efficiently and economically as well as provide an appropriate level of service. The parks and recreation program should be a part of the countywide comprehensive strategic plan.

The parks and recreation department should also have a system-wide master plan for parks and recreation as well as site specific plans for their facilities. Thus the facilities, whether consisting of many buildings and sites or of merely limited facilities, must be acquired and built with the requirements of their users in mind. Proper location and acquisition of property before land values have risen to the point that the use of land for park purposes is no longer feasible are both important. Sites and buildings should be neither too large nor too small for their intended long-term use or for the size of the geographical area to be served. Ideally, parcels of land should be of sufficient size to permit later expansion and the addition of more facilities, while retaining a spacious and uncluttered atmosphere. The adoption and enforcement of a county zoning ordinance is often required to protect major recreational facilities from possibly adverse uses of nearby property. As noted earlier, county subdivision regulations may also be helpful in acquiring public park and recreational areas as large tracts are subdivided for residential purposes.

Planning with local boards of education can also be beneficial; recreation areas can sometimes be jointly financed, constructed, maintained, and operated. As mentioned earlier the Community Schools Act has encouraged the cooperative planning and use of schools for a multitude of community purposes. Public recreational use of schools has been growing rapidly since the act's passage in 1977.

Parks and recreation planning should include the design of all areas and facilities for use by the disabled and elderly. The county must be certain that project designers are aware of and follow pertinent statutes and regulations pertaining to elderly and handicapped access.

Planning for parks and recreation facilities and services is a cooperative effort. A well-run planning program involves close coordination among the county's parks and recreation department, its planning department, the local school board(s), and other interested boards and departments.

Trends in Public Recreation

Changes in demographics, economic growth, and political arenas plus new social issues have had and will continue to have a major influence on the management and provision of public parks and recreation. In response to issues such as at-risk youth, quality day care, homelessness, an increasingly violent society, lack of general physical fitness, and other social issues, county parks and recreation departments are beginning to organize nontraditional recreation programs such as after-school child care, day care for older adults, literacy programs, and a variety of self-help classes for children and adults. As the demand for day care services increases, local parks and recreation departments are being asked to play a role in providing quality day care opportunities for working parents and their children. Summer day camps and playground programs that have traditionally been neighborhood drop-in programs are now being organized and operated as summer child care programs. Some departments operate licensed child care facilities while others provide facilities for private groups to operate needed child care programs.

Public parks and recreation professionals are also having to cope with increased government regulations. Constraints on hazardous-waste disposal, pesticide application regulations, Occupational Safety and Health Administration standards for blood-borne pathogens, guidelines for playground safety, and the Americans with Disabilities Act are just a few regulations, guidelines, and laws that impact service delivery. The challenge facing parks and recreation staff is how to implement or comply with the new regulations without additional financial resources.

Another trend in recreation is the emphasis on risk management. In an era of increasing concern about litigation, parks and recreation systems are being forced to address the issues of liability and safety. Departments must be concerned with the safety of employees, particularly those who work with toxic chemicals, and the safety of participants. Risk management plans are becoming a necessity. Larger parks and recreation departments are hiring their own risk management staff.

Right-sizing and down-sizing efforts in local governments are changing the organizational structure of parks and recreation departments. In an effort to make county services more efficient, park maintenance divisions are being moved from parks and recreation departments to public works departments. While on paper this option is a viable alternative, caution should be used when consolidating all maintenance under one department. The public works staff must understand the demands for maintenance that are caused by the scope of parks and recreation services and facilities. Recreation facilities and programs are operated beyond the traditional operating hours of county government. Maintenance services must be provided when programs are scheduled and facilities are open. Rather than losing responsibilities, other departments are expanding responsibilities beyond the traditional parks and recreation services to include care of cemeteries, roadways, civic centers, and cultural resources.

Partnerships and collaboration between local parks and recreation agencies with other government agencies and non-profit agencies are critical to addressing today's local concerns. Parks and recreation departments are working with local police departments, social service departments, schools, youth organizations, sports associations and others to help provide prevention and intervention programs for young people and low-income populations. Local parks and recreation departments can play an important role in providing services that can strengthen young people, families, and communities.

While athletics, summer playground programs, and traditional recreation classes are still important parts of a county parks and recreation program, many new programs are beginning to emerge. New programs or facilities that are beginning to appear across North Carolina include inline-skating facilities, skate board parks, high adventure elements such as climbing walls and ropes courses, shooting ranges, adventure camping, mountain bike courses, and eco-tourism experiences.

While the majority of the funds for parks and recreation services are derived primarily from the general appropriation fund, fees and charges are becoming a major revenue source for parks and recreation services. Some local governments mandate the department recover a percentage of their general fund allocation through fees and charges. While most parks and recreation authorities agree that basic services should be provided without charge to local residents, in the current focus on reducing local taxes and maximizing government efficiency few if any parks and recreation departments can provide quality services with charging user fees for most services. In addition to operating budget concerns, the most critical area of financial concern is the funding of capital improvement projects. The Parks and Recreation Trust Fund now provides a state level source for capital improvement funding, however, that money is limited. Local communities must depend on general obligation bonds, certificates of participation, or joint agreements with private and other government agencies to build multi-million dollar facilities.

As we enter the twenty-first century, the scope of recreation services will continue to broaden. Parks and recreation departments will have to offer programs to meet the needs of the aging baby boomers, the increasing Hispanic population, new family structures, and the homeless. The types of persons employed by departments will expand to include people with degrees in early childhood development, law, nutrition, computer science, and gerontology. Local parks and recreation services will change as life-styles, resources, and demographics change.

Additional Assistance

The primary source of assistance for counties that are either providing local parks and recreation services or contemplating the establishment of a parks and recreation department is the Recreation Resources Service (RRS). The Recreation Resources Service is a division of the Parks, Recreation, and Tourism Management Department of North Carolina State University, and is funded through an agreement with the Division of Parks and Recreation, North Carolina Department of Environment and Natural Resources. Services include the following:

- Educational workshops on topics such as playground safety, adventure programming, and athletic field maintenance
- Training of park and recreation advisory board members
- Publication of technical assistance manuals, directories, and a monthly job bulletin
- Applied research
- Evaluative studies of parks and recreation agencies
- Production of park conceptual maps
- Provision of individual technical assistance

The North Carolina League of Municipalities and the Institute of Government can also help with legal, budgetary, and financial aspects of parks and recreation services.

Additional Resources

Gaskill, P., ed. *Introduction to Leisure Services in North Carolina.* Dubuque, Iowa: Kendall/Hunt Publishing Co., 1997.

McKinney, W. *Introduction to Park, Recreation, and Leisure Administration.* Champaign, Ill.: Sagamore Publishing, 1998.

Mertas, J. D., and J. R. Hall. *Park, Recreation, Open Space and Greenway Guidelines.* Ashton, Va.: National Recreation and Park Association, 1995.

Notes

1. Eric Gulledge, *Municipal and County Parks and Recreation Services Study* (Raleigh, N.C.: North Carolina State University, Recreation Resources Service, 1997).

2. Recreation Enabling Act of 1945, codified as G.S. Chapter 160A, Art. 18.

IV
Functions Involving Other Boards and Agencies

21 Elections

Robert P. Joyce

Contents

Robert P. Joyce is an Institute of Government faculty member whose areas of specialization include the law related to elections.

The author expresses his appreciation to Michael Crowell, a former Institute of Government faculty member who was the author of this chapter in the third edition of this book and whose work is reflected in this edition's chapter.

County boards of elections conduct almost all elections in North Carolina. They conduct the elections for federal, state, county, and most city offices. They conduct statewide referendums and local referendums. They conduct elections for special districts, such as school administrative units, sanitary districts, and fire districts. There is one exception: in a small minority of municipalities, elections are conducted by a municipal board of elections, not the county board.

County boards maintain voter registration records (even for the municipalities that have their own municipal boards of election), determine the eligibility of applicants for registration, establish precincts and voting places, select and purchase voting equipment, publish the notices associated with an election, employ election day precinct workers, oversee election day activities, canvass the returns, declare the election results, issue certificates of election to the winners, and hold hearings on challenges to voters and on election protests.

The county board of elections must act within the regulations and directions of the State Board of Elections, and almost all of the county board's actions are subject to review by the state board.

With a few exceptions, the operating costs of elections are paid through appropriations from the county commissioners. A small portion is paid from state funds.

According to figures compiled by the State Board of Elections, as of October 1997 there were 4,398,999 registered voters in North Carolina, of whom 53.2 percent were registered as Democrats, 33.9 percent were registered as Republicans, less than 1 percent were registered as Libertarians, and the remainder were unaffiliated. Of the registered voters, 79.5 percent were white, 18.7 percent were African American, less than 1 percent were American Indian, and the remainder were other or undesignated.

Election of Candidates to Office

Elections in which the voters choose individuals to fill public offices are the most common kinds of elections. While elections for municipal offices—mayors and city councils—are held in odd-numbered years (1999, 2001, and so on), elections for all other offices are held in even-numbered years (2000, 2002, and so forth). The even-numbered years include federal offices (president and vice-president, U.S. Senate and House of Representatives), state executive offices (governor and council of state), state legislative offices (N.C. Senate and House of Representatives), judicial offices (justices and judges of the N.C. Supreme Court, N.C. Court of Appeals, superior court, and district court; clerks of superior court; and district attorneys), and, of course, county offices (county commissioners, registers of deeds, sheriffs, soil and water conservation commissioners, and, in a few places, the coroner). Most school board elections are held in even-numbered years, but a few are held in odd-numbered years.

The general election schedule is found at G.S. 163-1.

Partisan Primaries and Elections

Most elections to fill offices are conducted on a partisan basis. Candidates are nominated by political parties and run under their labels. Two parties—the Democratic and the Republican—have traditionally and consistently met the statutory definition of a political party: their candidates for governor or president have in each election polled at least 10 percent of the total vote cast in the state for governor or president. The nominees of these parties are chosen by the voters through primary elections held before the general election. The winner in the primary election is the nominee of his or her party and appears on the ballot in the general election. If no candidate for nomination receives at least 40 percent of the vote (plus one vote)—a total termed a "substantial plurality"—in a particular primary, the candidate who finishes second may request a second primary, just between those two candidates. The winner of the second primary is the nominee. Voters affiliated with a particular party are eligible to vote in that party's primary. In addition, a party may permit voting in its primary by registered voters who are not affiliated with any party. That choice is made on an election-by-election basis. Counties bear the costs of primaries, as they do for other elections. The statutes governing primary elections are found at G.S. 163-104 through -119.

A new political party may be formed through the circulation of a petition, signed by registered voters equal to at least 2 percent of the number who voted in the most recent general election for governor. For the first election after it is recognized by the State Board of Elections, the new party chooses its nominees at a party convention, not by a primary election, and is entitled to have its nominees on the ballot for state and federal offices but not for county or judicial offices. If the party fails to poll at least 10 percent of the vote for governor or president, its recognition is terminated, and it must go through the petition procedure again. The Libertarian Party went through this recognition and termination cycle a couple of times in the last decades of the twentieth century. The statutes governing political parties are found at G.S. 163-96 through -99.

An individual who wishes to run in a partisan election as an unaffiliated candidate may do so (if he or she is registered as unaffiliated) through the circulation of a petition. For state offices, the petition must be signed by registered voters equal to at least 2 percent of the number who voted in the most recent general election for governor. For county or district offices, the petition must be signed by at least 4 percent of the registered voters of the district. The statutes governing the candidacy of unaffiliated candidates are found at G.S. 163-122 and -123.

Nonpartisan Elections

While most elections to fill offices are conducted on a partisan basis, two kinds of elections to office are conducted by a nonpartisan method. The first kind includes most elections to municipal office—mayor and city council. A few North Carolina cities do, in fact, have partisan elections. These are conducted like state and county partisan elections. The overwhelming majority of municipalities, however, have nonpartisan elections. School board elections are the second kind of nonpartisan elections. Most school board elections are nonpartisan, but a few are partisan.

In a nonpartisan election, there is, of course, no nomination of candidates in a partisan primary. All candidates stand for election without party identification. Candidates are at liberty to identify themselves by party if they wish, and parties are free to endorse candidates if they wish. What is nonpartisan is the way the election officials conduct the election, not necessarily the way candidates and parties conduct the campaign.

There are three types of nonpartisan election methods. The first and most widely used is the plurality method. There is one vote on general election day, and the candidate with the most votes wins. The overwhelming majority of cities and school boards use the plurality method. The second is the election and runoff method. An initial election is held. If a candidate receives a majority of the votes, that candidate is elected and no further voting takes place. But if no candidate receives a majority, the candidate who finishes second may demand a runoff election against the first-place finisher. The third is the nonpartisan primary method. A primary vote is held to narrow the field to two candidates, and then the election is held between those two candidates.

The statutes governing municipal elections are found at G.S. 163-279 through -306. The statutory provision for school board elections is found at G.S. 115C-37.

Special Elections

Special elections are all elections other than those in which voters elect candidates to office. They may be statewide issues, such as the ratification of an amendment to the North Carolina Constitution or a statewide bond referendum. More commonly they are local ballot questions, such as local bond referendums, alcoholic beverage control (ABC) elections, fire-district and sanitary-district elections, and referendums on restructuring city or county government (such as changing the number of board members or moving from at-large to district elections).

Calling Special Elections

Special elections are called in a variety of ways, almost all of which are set by state law. Sometimes a special election comes about as a result of a petition drive (ABC elections are an example). Sometimes a city council calls the election (referendums on changing the method of electing the council are an example). Special elections that may be called by the board of county commissioners include referendums on restructuring the board of commissioners (see G.S. 153A-58), levying property taxes for purposes [such as public transportation or public housing; see G.S. 153A-149(d)] that are not among the regularly authorized ones, levying property taxes above the normal limit of $1.50 per $100 valuation [G.S. 153A-149(e)], issuing bonds or levying a tax to supplement the revenue of a bond project (G.S. 159-48, -49, -97), and ABC referendums [G.S. 18B-601(b)].

In general, special elections may be held at any time, though certain time limitations may apply. Usually, for the convenience of voters and to keep expense to a minimum, special elections are scheduled at the same time as regular elections. The county board of elections sets the election date for most elections, but the ABC election law specifies that the board of commissioners sets the date [see G.S. 18B-601(f)].

Specifying Issues for Special Elections

County officials sometimes want to have a "special referendum" or "straw vote" on a controversial issue. Generally speaking, they may not. Only elections specifically authorized by state statute or by local act of the General Assembly may be held. As then-justice Sam Ervin of the North Carolina Supreme Court said, in *Tucker v. A.B.C. Board*, "There is no inherent power in any government body to hold an election for any purpose. In consequence, an election held without affirmative constitutional or statutory authority is a nullity, no matter how fairly and honestly it may be conducted."[1] If a county wishes to have a vote on where to locate the landfill or whether to create a beautification district, it must receive authorization from the General Assembly in the form of a local act. Otherwise, county funds may not be spent on the election.

In some states, citizens may, by a petition drive, force an election on the issue of recalling an elected official from office (a recall election) or adopting or repealing a particular ordinance (initiative and referendum). There are no such provisions in the North Carolina General Statutes. A handful of cities have such provisions by virtue of local acts of the General Assembly. No North Carolina counties have them.[2]

Registration and Voting

To vote in any election in North Carolina, a person must be qualified to vote and must be registered.

Qualifications for Voting

To be qualified to vote, a person must be a United States citizen, must be at least eighteen years old by the time of the election (a person who is seventeen at the time of the primary but will be eighteen by the time of the general election may vote in the primary), must have resided for thirty days in the state and in the precinct in which he or she wishes to vote, and must not be a convicted felon (or must have had citizenship rights restored). The requirement of residence is sometimes confusing. Residence means more than living in a place. To reside in a place means to make it one's home (to plan to continue to live there, not just to stay there temporarily). For most people, it is easy to tell what place is home. For some others, however, including workers in temporary jobs and college students, what place is the residence may be more difficult. The statutes governing voter registration are found at G.S. 163-54 through -90.3.

The North Carolina Constitution contains (in Article VI) two other qualifications for voting that are no longer enforced because they have been held to violate the United States Constitution. One provides that a person must have resided in the state for one year before registering to vote. The other requires that to register, a person must "be able to read and write any section of the Constitution in the English language."

Voter Registration

North Carolina has full-time, permanent voter registration. Citizens need register only once to vote in all elections. Voters remain registered and eligible to vote unless they move out of the county, die, or are convicted of a felony. Applications to register to vote may be submitted to the county board of elections by mail or through a driver's license office or public assistance office. A person may apply to register at any time during the year but must do so by the twenty-fifth day before an election in order to vote in that particular election. An individual who registers after the deadline may not vote until the next election after the upcoming one. This provision is designed to give the board of elections time to bring its records up to date and prepare for the election. A person who moves from one county to another must reregister, but one who relocates within the county need only notify the board of elections of the change of address.

When citizens apply to register to vote, they indicate the party with which they wish to affiliate or indicate that they wish to be listed on the registration rolls as unaffiliated.

To make full-time registration available, counties with more than 14,000 registered voters must keep the elections board office open during regular business hours five days a week. In those with fewer voters, the office must be open for at least three days each week.

See the section "The Role of Federal Law in North Carolina Elections" later in the chapter for a discussion of changes in the state's voter registration practices that respond to changes in federal law.

Absentee Ballots

Absentee voting is available in almost all elections. It is not permitted in city elections conducted by municipal boards of elections. Absentee ballot statutes are found at G.S. 163-226 through -239.

The State Board of Elections

By statute, the State Board of Elections has "general supervision over the primaries and election in this State." That provision, found in G.S. 163-22, sets the framework for the administration of elections in North Carolina: the state board has general supervisory power, and the county boards conduct the elections. The statutes setting out the powers and structure of the state board are found at G.S. 163-19 through -28.

Selection and Organization

The five members of the State Board of Elections are appointed by the governor in the spring following his or her election—that is, in 2001, 2005, 2009, and so on. The appointments are made from names submitted by the state chairs of the Democratic and Republican parties. No more than three members of the state board may belong to the same party. Naturally, the three-member majority is from the governor's party.

The board's office, in Raleigh, is headed by a full-time executive secretary-director.

Duties

The State Board of Elections has overall responsibility for elections. It appoints all county board members, conducts training sessions for them and the county directors of elections, decides what kinds of voting equipment may be used, instructs county boards on what kinds of records to maintain, tells them how ballots should be printed, hears protests concerning the conduct of elections, and performs various other duties to see that elections run smoothly and properly throughout the state.

A chief duty of the state board involves challenges to the way in which particular elections have been conducted. Sometimes called *election protests* and sometimes called *election contests*, challenges are usually first heard by the county board of elections and are then appealed, if the protester is not satisfied, to the state board. The state board may also investigate the conduct of elections on its own. As part of an investigation, it may take control of local election records. When convinced that irregularities have affected the outcome, the board may invalidate an election anywhere in the state and order a new election. It may also remove any local election official who has acted improperly. Even when there is no irregularity alleged, state law provides for recounts in state and county elections in which the top two finishers are within 1 percent of each other.

County Boards of Elections

Each of the 100 counties has a three-member board of elections appointed by the state board from names submitted by the state chairs of the Democratic and Republican parties. No more than two members may belong to the same party. Because the state board is appointed by the governor, the majority on each county board is also from the governor's party. Elected officials, candidates and their close relatives, campaign managers and treasurers, and political-party officials may not serve on a county board.

County board members serve two-year terms; the appointments are made in the summer of odd-numbered years. The board chooses one of its members as its chair.

The election law requires the county board to meet at certain times for particular purposes: for example, to appoint and train precinct officials; to consider absentee ballot applications; to count absentee ballots; and to canvass the results of an election and declare the results. Other meetings are held as needed.

The statutes setting out the powers and structure of the county boards are found at G.S. 163-30 through -36.

Like other governmental bodies, boards of elections are subject to the open meetings law. They may hold closed sessions to investigate election irregularities. The open meetings law is found at G.S. 143-318.9 through -318.18.

Duties

The county boards of elections conduct all elections except some city elections (see the section "Municipal Boards of Elections," later in the chapter). Their duties fall into two categories. The first type is administrative duties. The board employs a director to manage the office, chooses other office employees, appoints precinct officials, registers voters, determines precinct boundaries, establishes voting places in the precincts, orders voting equipment, advertises elections, accepts candidates' filings, prepares and prints ballots, issues absentee ballots, supervises the counting of votes, and arranges for the many other activities that are part of registering voters and holding elections. The second type is policy-making or quasi-judicial (that is, court-like) duties. The board hears challenges to voters' registration, determines the sufficiency of petitions, declares election results, hears protests about election irregularities and complaints about election officials, and issues certificates of election (which enable winning candidates to take office). In all of its duties, the county board is subject to the state board's rules and supervision, but most responsibility for seeing that elections are conducted properly rests at the county level. The powers and duties of county boards of elections are outlined at G.S. 163-33.

Directors of Elections

Each county board has a director of elections. The county elections board chooses the person it would like to be the director and forwards that recommendation to the state board's executive secretary-director, who makes the formal appointment. The director has day-to-day responsibility for supervising board employees, ordering supplies, estimating expenses, maintaining records, and attending to the dozens of other tasks that are associated with conducting elections. In fact, only a few specific duties are spelled out in the statutes, and it is up to the county board to assign duties and responsibilities to its director. The board may delegate to the director as much of its work as it wishes other than its policy-making and quasi-judicial duties. It may not, for example, delegate its responsibility for hearing challenges to voters' registration.

The county board may not dismiss the director on its own. A majority of the board may recommend dismissal to the state board's executive secretary-director. The director must be told the reasons for a dismissal recommendation and must have an opportunity to answer those allegations. The executive secretary-director makes a decision on dismissal, which is final unless the state board chooses to consider the matter. If the state board does take the matter up, it holds a hearing and then makes a decision on the dismissal.

In counties with full-time voter registration, the director is to be paid a salary recommended by the board of elections and approved by the county board of commissioners. The salary is to be "commensurate with the salary paid to directors in counties similarly situated and similar in population and number of registered voters." In counties where the elections office is open only part-time, the director may be paid on an hourly basis. In any event, the director is to be granted the same vacation leave, sick leave, and petty leave as granted to all other county employees.

The chief statute governing the role of the director is G.S. 163-35.

Other Employees

In addition to a director, the county board of elections may approve the employment of a deputy county director and other office employees as needed. The statutes are clear that the board is responsible for hiring and firing these employees, but the law governing other aspects of employment, such as pay, working hours, and job classification, is not so clear. Because all funds for the board of elections are appropriated by the county commissioners, they effectively can control the number of employees, their pay, and other conditions of employment, if they wish to do so. In some counties, board of elections employees have been brought under the personnel ordinance; except for hiring and firing, they are listed in the county's job classifications and treated like all other employees. In other counties, personnel considerations related to election employees are negotiated between the county commissioners and the board of elections each budget period. In still other counties, the board of elections and the board of commissioners have entered into a memorandum of agreement spelling out the extent to which the personnel ordinance, the grievance procedure, the pay plan, and so on will apply to elections board employees. That agreement is, of course, subject to amendment by the parties.

The limited statutory guidance on status of elections board employees is found at G.S. 163-33(10), which provides that the county board has the power to "appoint and remove the board's clerk, assistant clerks, and other employees."

Precinct and Registration Officials

The county board of elections divides the county into precincts and establishes a voting place for each precinct. On election day, each precinct is staffed by a chief judge and two judges of election. Depending on the size of the precinct, the elections board may also appoint precinct assistants to assist the chief judge and judges.

The board of elections appoints the chief judge and two judges from names submitted by the county political-party chairs, to serve two-year terms. No more than two of these three officials may belong to the same party. For many years the law has required that these officials be residents of the precinct in which they will work. On occasion, however, party chairs and boards of elections have had difficulty locating and recruiting residents willing to serve in some precincts. The law (G.S. 163-41) now provides that when necessity dictates, the board of elections may appoint residents of the county who are not residents of the precinct to serve as chief judge and judge. A similar provision applies to precinct assistants.

The chief judge and judges must work together all day at the polls, from opening to closing through the reporting of the vote count to the elections board. The board of elections may, if it chooses, allow split shifts for precinct assistants.

The election law sets certain minimum wages for precinct officials for working at the polls and for attending the instructional meeting before each election. Otherwise, pay for precinct officials is at the discretion of the board of elections and the county commissioners. In practice, the pay varies from county to county, with the minimum pay being the state minimum wage ($5.15 per hour in 1998) and the maximum being about $120 per election day in some counties for chief judges. Precinct and registration officials may not accept payment for election-related services from anyone other than the board of elections.

Municipal Boards of Elections

A city that has nonpartisan elections—those in which the candidates are not identified by political-party affiliation—may have its own board of elections, appointed by the city council. Fewer than eighty towns, most small in size, still have municipal boards of elections. They are responsible only for the election of city officers and for special elections held within the city, such as city liquor and bond referendums. The county board conducts all other elections—such as those for federal, state, and county officers and referendums on constitutional amendments—within the city.

Because municipal boards conduct few elections and rely on part-time employees, they tend to be less careful than county boards in following correct procedures. Proportionally the State Board of Elections receives many more complaints about these boards than about county boards. Many observers favor eliminating municipal boards altogether.

The statutory provisions governing municipal boards of elections are found at G.S. 163-280 through -286.

County Boards Conducting City Elections

When a city chooses to have the county board conduct its elections, as most cities do, it must provide reimbursement for the costs involved. In such cases, the county board conducts the election and pays all the expenses; the city then pays an amount equal to the costs into the county's general fund. If the city council and the county elections board cannot agree on the amount due, the dispute is resolved by the State Board of Elections. G.S. 163-285 sets these rules.

County Board Budget

County boards of elections are subject to the Local Government Budget and Fiscal Control Act (found at G.S. 159-7 through -38). The elections board is directed by statute to "prepare and submit . . . a budget estimating the cost of elections for the ensuing fiscal year" [G.S. 163-33(11)]. Almost all county board funds come by appropriation from the county commissioners. A small amount comes from the state for help with the expenses of statewide referendums and expenses related to the statewide voter registration computer system. Sometimes civic groups and businesses wish to help pay for voter registration drives. They may do so only by donating money to the county general fund; the commissioners may then appropriate that amount to the board of elections. Election officials may not accept funds directly from anyone other than the county.

Many expenses of the elections board are controlled by state law or regulation, including the minimum pay for board members and precinct officials. The kinds of records that must be maintained, the specifications for certain supplies, the number of notices that must be published, the quantity of ballots that may be printed, the hours of operation for the polls, the days the elections board office must be open, the kinds of voting booths that may be used, the forms that must be available in the board office and at the polling place, and various other matters that affect the board's budget—all are set by statute or by regulations of the

State Board of Elections. The state board determines what kinds of voting machines may be selected by the counties; the county commissioners decide whether to purchase them; and the county board of elections chooses a particular kind.

Most of the elections board's expenses—the costs of maintaining an office and conducting the regularly scheduled elections of public officials—are predictable. Still, not all expenses can be anticipated. When it prepares its budget, the elections board may not know that citizens will petition for a liquor election, that the decision in a voting-rights lawsuit will require a change in election dates, or that the legislature will raise the pay for precinct officials. These expenses, which may be substantial, may be matters over which the elections board has no control and may require a supplemental appropriation by the county commissioners.

The appropriation needed from the commissioners is typically higher in years in which the county board of elections must administer municipal elections within the county (even though the county recoups some of the expense from the municipalities). For example, the 1997–98 appropriation in Forsyth County (with 174,000 registered voters) was approximately $1.2 million for 1997–98 (a municipal election year), but the budget request for 1998–99 (without municipal elections) was for only $700,000. In Dare County (with 17,000 registered voters), the situation is similar. The appropriation for 1997–98 was $227,000, but for the prior year (with no municipal elections), the appropriation was only $155,000.

The Role of Federal Law in North Carolina Elections

Two federal statutes passed by Congress and one provision of the United States Constitution have had major impacts on the administration of elections in North Carolina and promise to continue to do so for years to come. The statutes are the National Voter Registration Act of 1993 (NVRA)[3] and the Voting Rights Act of 1965.[4] The constitutional provision is the Equal Protection Clause found in the Fourteenth Amendment. The remaining sections of this chapter discuss these impacts.

Changes in Voter Registration

North Carolina's voter registration system is described earlier. A citizen wishing to apply to register may mail an application form to the elections board office, may bring it in or have someone else bring it in, or may fill out an application at a driver's license office, public assistance office, or employment security office. On the application form, the citizen attests that he or she meets the eligibility requirements for registering. There is no check of identity or administration of an oath. Making a false attestation is a felony.

This system was adopted by the General Assembly in 1994 in response to the passage of the NVRA in 1993. Before this system was adopted, most registration applications were taken by an elections official—elections board members, staff employees, precinct officials, and sworn officials called *special registration commissioners*—who interviewed the applicant in person, required proof of identity, and administered an oath to the applicant. Congress's purpose in passing the NVRA was to make it easier and less intimidating for citizens to register to vote. It required that states adopt the registration practices just described for federal elections. States could, if they chose, have different requirements for registering for state and local elections.

The legislature in North Carolina determined that it would be cumbersome, confusing, and expensive to have different systems for federal and for state and local elections, and thus amended the registration statutes to make the registration procedure applicable to all elections.

"Pre-Clearance" of Election Changes

The Voting Rights Act has two chief operating provisions: Section 2 and Section 5. Section 2 prohibits all forms of racial discrimination in the election process everywhere in the United States. It is discussed in the following paragraphs. Section 5, on the other hand, applies only to certain governmental units that had especially low rates of voter registration at the time the Voting Rights Act was passed. In effect, those jurisdictions were presumed to be discriminating. To prevent the introduction of new election procedures that adversely affect minority voting, governmental units subject to Section 5 must obtain approval from the U.S. Department of Justice before making any change in election procedure. The approval procedure is commonly referred to as *pre-clearance.*

Most southern states are covered statewide by Section 5, but only forty North Carolina counties are subject to it. Any change in elections procedures in any of those forty counties must be pre-cleared. Examples include a switch to or from an at-large election system, any change in the term of office for an elected position, municipal annexations, moving of polling places or precinct lines, new office hours for the board of elections, and conversion from paper ballots to voting machines. Because any state-wide election law or procedure change obviously affects those forty counties, all such changes must be pre-cleared before they can become effective.

The Justice Department reviews each such change to determine whether it places African Americans or other minorities in a worse position. Few changes are objected to, but the most likely ones to be challenged are annexations, alterations in district lines, and changes in the method of election (from district to at-large elections, for example). An objection from the Justice Department may be the start of negotiations between the governmental unit and federal officials to alter the proposed change to make it acceptable. If a change is made without Justice Department approval or without ever having been submitted for pre-clearance, the department is likely to go to court to stop its implementation.

A local government may seek pre-clearance from the federal district court for the District of Columbia rather than from the Justice Department, but that option is seldom used because it takes longer and is more expensive.

See Table 21-1 for the forty North Carolina counties subject to the pre-clearance requirement. The pre-clearance requirement also applies to all cities and other governmental units, such as school boards, within these counties.

The responsibility for submitting changes for pre-clearance is set by state law (G.S. 120-30.9A through -30.9I). The State Board of Elections is responsible for submitting statewide changes that affect all governmental units in the state, while county and city attorneys are responsible for those that apply only to their jurisdictions. Changes concerning school boards are to be submitted by the board attorneys. Once the Justice Department makes its final decision on a local pre-clearance request, the notification letter must be filed by the local attorney with the North Carolina Office of Administrative Hearings for publication in the *North Carolina Register*.

It is possible for a jurisdiction, such as a county, to "bail out," or remove itself, from the pre-clearance requirements of Section 5. Generally, to bail out, the jurisdiction must show the federal district court for the District of Columbia that for the previous ten years

1. it has not been found in violation of the Voting Rights Act,
2. it has not used a discriminatory procedure,
3. it has pre-cleared all changes that were required to be pre-cleared, and
4. it has taken positive steps to increase participation by minorities in the election process.

Table 21-1
The Forty North Carolina Counties Subject to the Pre-Clearance Requirement

Anson	Granville	Onslow
Beaufort	Greene	Pasquotank
Bertie	Guilford	Perquimans
Bladen	Halifax	Person
Camden	Harnett	Pitt
Caswell	Hertford	Robeson
Chowan	Hoke	Rockingham
Cleveland	Jackson	Scotland
Craven	Lee	Union
Cumberland	Lenoir	Vance
Edgecombe	Martin	Washington
Franklin	Nash	Wayne
Gaston	Northampton	Wilson
Gates		

The necessary showing is generally considered onerous and is seldom undertaken. The last jurisdiction in North Carolina to bail out was Wake County in the 1970s.

Shift from At-Large to District Elections

Section 2 of the Voting Rights Act prohibits all states, counties, cities, and other political units from setting voting qualifications or using election procedures that deny or abridge the voting rights of minorities. A person who believes that any governmental unit has such a qualification or procedure may sue in federal court to have it invalidated under Section 2.

The most common subject matter for these lawsuits is a challenge to the methods of conducting elections that make it harder for African Americans to be elected—especially the use of at-large elections. The two issues at the heart of such a Section 2 lawsuit are the extent to which African Americans have been elected to office under the election system being challenged and whether voting is polarized along racial lines. If, for example, 30 percent of a county's population consists of black people but none of them have ever been elected to the five-member board of commissioners, that is strong evidence that the method of election is discriminatory. If, in addition, statistical analysis shows that whites seldom vote for black candidates in that county—and this is generally the case in North Carolina—then the court will need to consider requiring an election method that provides African Americans with an opportunity to elect candidates on their own without depending on white support. The leading Supreme Court decision setting out these Section 2 requirements involved North Carolina's multimember districts for electing members of the General Assembly, *Thornburg v. Gingles*.[5]

Traditionally in North Carolina, most boards of commissioners have been elected at large; that is, all voters in the county vote for all seats. In counties that have significant African-American populations but a sparse record of electing African Americans to the board, Section 2 lawsuits—or the threat of Section 2 lawsuits—have been used to force a conversion to a different method of election. The courts' usual remedy is to require the county to switch to a system in which it is divided into several districts, and only the voters of each district vote for the seat representing that area. By creating districts with predominantly black populations, the court can give African Americans a much better opportunity to elect candidates of their own choosing than they would have with an at-large election system.

Because of the outcomes in these cases, advice commonly given to counties (and to other units of local government) typically ran like this: if you can draw a district boundary for creating a district with an African-American majority, do so. Then draw the other districts around that district to fit. If you can draw two districts with African-American majorities, do so, and draw the remaining districts to fit. Implementing this strategy, counties (and cities and school administrative units) sometimes came up with oddly shaped districts.

This common advice came into question—and the creation of the oddly shaped districts slowed down dramatically—when another North Carolina districting case came to the United States Supreme Court in the mid-1990s. That case, *Shaw v. Reno*,[6] looked at the intersection of the requirements of Section 2 of the Voting Rights Act and the Equal Protection Clause of the Fourteenth Amendment, as discussed in the following section.

Limits on the Use of Race in Drawing Districts

Following the national census of 1990, the General Assembly drew the districts for electing the state's twelve members of the United States House of Representatives, creating eleven that had white majorities and one that had an African-American majority. In so doing, the legislature was applying the advice described earlier commonly given for complying with Section 2 of the Voting Rights Act. That districting plan was submitted for pre-clearance, and the Justice Department disapproved the plan. It would have been possible, the Justice Department said, to create two districts with African-American majorities, and the failure to do so was a violation of Section 2. So in 1992 the General Assembly redrew the lines, creating two districts with African-American majorities, both with very odd shapes. In *Shaw v. Reno*, the United States Supreme Court held that the use of race in drawing district lines may constitute a violation of the Equal Protection Clause of the Fourteenth Amendment of the United States Constitution, especially when, to achieve African-American majority districts, the shape of the districts must be drawn very oddly. In a follow-up decision in 1996, *Shaw v. Hunt*,[7] the Supreme Court held that the districting plan did in fact violate the Equal Protection Clause. As a result, in 1997 the General Assembly redrew the lines, with one majority African-American district and one district nearly evenly split but majority white. The Justice Department approved the new plan, but in early 1998 a federal district court struck it down as violating the Equal Protection Clause, ordering the General Assembly to redraw the lines once again.

When the legislature drew the congressional district lines, it was applying the same principles that have been applied for years in drawing district lines for electing county commissioners, city council members, and school board members. The *Shaw v. Reno* and *Shaw v. Hunt* decisions make it likely that the movement to create districts with African-American majorities—even if the districts must be oddly shaped—will be greatly slowed.

Additional Resources

Bott, Alexander J. *Handbook of United States Election Laws and Practices: Political Rights.* New York: Greenwood Press, 1990.

Joyce, Robert P. *The Precinct Manual 1998.* Chapel Hill, N.C.: Institute of Government, The University of North Carolina at Chapel Hill, 1998.

Lawrence, David M. "Initiative, Referendum, and Recall in North Carolina," *Popular Government* 63 (Fall 1997): 8–18.

———. "Removing Local Elected Officials from Office in North Carolina," *Wake Forest Law Review* 16 (1980): 547–61.

Notes

1. 240 N.C. 177, 180 (1954).

2. For more information, see "Initiative, Referendum, and Recall in North Carolina," by David M. Lawrence, in *Popular Government* 63 (Fall 1997): 8–18.

3. 42 U.S.C. § 1973gg.
4. 42 U.S.C. § 1973.
5. 478 U.S. 30 (1986).
6. 509 U.S. 630 (1993).
7. 517 U.S. 899 (1996).

22 Public Health Services

Jill D. Moore

Contents

Jill D. Moore is an Institute of Government faculty member who works primarily in the area
of public health law.

    The author expresses her appreciation to Anne M. Dellinger, an Institute of Govern-
ment faculty member who also works in the area of public health law, and whose authorship
of this chapter in the book's previous edition is reflected in this one.

    Portions of this chapter were excerpted or adapted from Anne M. Dellinger, Jeffrey S.
Koeze, and Vicki Winslow, "Public Health," in *State and Local Government Relations in North
Carolina,* 2d ed. (Chapel Hill, N.C.: Institute of Government, The University of North
Carolina at Chapel Hill, 1995), 123–37.

History

Public health has been recognized as a proper concern of government in North Carolina since colonial times. The first public health legislation applicable to the territory that is now North Carolina was a maritime quarantine law, enacted in 1712. Throughout the colonial and antebellum eras, epidemics of typhoid fever, dysentery, malaria, and other illnesses produced demands for governmental action. Most public health efforts in those early years were undertaken by local governments, both municipal and county. Local public health initiatives were sporadic, however, and statewide legislation addressing public health concerns was rare. By the beginning of the Civil War, only three or four pages of the state statutes addressed public health, and no governmental agency had the authority to enforce public health laws.[1]

A state system for creating and enforcing public health policy began to emerge in 1877, when the General Assembly enacted a law that designated the entire membership of the North Carolina Medical Society as a state board of health with an annual state appropriation of $100. Two years later the legislature repealed that statute and enacted another that created a nine-member board of health as a regular department of state government. An 1893 statute defined the state board of health's powers to include assuring safe drinking water sources, advising managers of institutions and towns with respect to their water supply and sewage disposal systems, inspecting the sanitation of public institutions annually, and regulating the transportation of corpses on common carriers.

Local mechanisms for assuring public health began to develop in the late nineteenth century as well. The General Assembly authorized counties to form boards of health consisting of the practicing physicians in the county, the mayor of the county seat, the chairman of the county commissioners, and the city or county surveyor. The county board of health selected a physician to serve as county superintendent of health for a two-year term. The board was responsible for vaccinating citizens; quarantining, confining, and isolating citizens with dangerous diseases; gathering vital statistics; and performing postmortem medical examinations.

By the early twentieth century, North Carolina had a fledgling public health system. The state board of health's range of activities had steadily expanded, and by 1912 it had employed a full-time professional health director for the state, an office that continues to the present. In 1915, the state board had a budget of $150,000 per year and supervised a variety of activities through its bureaus: education and engineering, vital statistics, quarantine, school inspection, tuberculosis, and county health work, in addition to a laboratory of hygiene. County activity had increased as well. A 1911 statute expanded the county board's authority and membership, granting local regulatory authority to the board and adding more lay members to its composition. The first county health departments were formed shortly after the statute was enacted. Guilford County was an early leader in this area, establishing what may have been the first local health department in the nation. By 1915, seven counties were operating full-time health departments.

During these years of increasing local involvement in public health, the state's role as a provider of funding and assistance to local public health efforts began to emerge. The state contributed public health expertise, enabling legislation, and some funding to local governments that undertook organized public health efforts. The state health department also provided some services directly to citizens.

Private philanthropy also played an important role in the early development and expansion of North Carolina's public health system. Here and elsewhere in the south, the Rockefeller Sanitary Commission for the Elimination of Hookworm Disease provided funds and worked with the state board of health on health education activities, buying shoes and building privies for state residents, and creating local institutions to deal with hookworm and other public health issues. The success of those activities has been credited with spurring the formation of the first few local health departments in North Carolina.

The growth of North Carolina's public health system faltered during the Great Depression, when state and local appropriations for public health decreased drastically. By fiscal year 1932–33 the amount spent by the state was less than half that spent during 1929–30. Many local governments were defaulting on their debt. In the mid-1930s, however, for the first time federal funding became available for local public health efforts. This funding partially compensated for the loss of state and local funds. The Social Security Act of 1935 appropriated $8 million annually to assist states, counties, and other political subdivisions of states in providing public health services. By 1935 the state had recovered sufficiently for the General Assembly again to appropriate funds to its board of health to be used in establishing full-time local health services at the request of local governments. The new departments, like those already established, were required to match state financial assistance with local funds.

As the state recovered from the depression, private charity again figured prominently in the progress made in public health. In 1937 the Z. Smith Reynolds Foundation was created for the benefit of North Carolina. Its first project was dealing with syphilis, and the entire first year's budget was devoted to attacking this disease. The foundation insisted that local funds match foundation funds, on the premise that the program could not succeed without local support. After a decade the foundation's annual grant of $175,000 ended, and a combination of state, local, and federal funds replaced it.

By 1949, the services of a full-time local health department were available in every county in the state. In the 1940s and 1950s, a new source of federal funds contributed significantly to the development in North Carolina of facilities housing public health services. The federal Hospital Survey and Construction Act, commonly known as the Hill-Burton Act, provided grants of up to two dollars in federal funds for each dollar contributed to construction by state or local government. By 1960 seventy-six new local health centers had been constructed with Hill-Burton funds.

Despite help at crucial points by the federal and state governments and private charity, local public health services in North Carolina have primarily resulted from local efforts and local funds. The local share of expenditures rose steadily in the mid-twentieth century, so that local funds accounted for 79.4 percent of all funds spent for local health services in fiscal year 1959–60. Virtually all local funds came from county-wide property tax revenues. In fiscal year 1960–61 local funds rose to 81 percent of the total; state appropriations represented 15.5 percent. By 1970 the state supplied only 13.3 percent of local health departments' budgets, while local governments furnished 85.9 percent. Three years later, however, the state allocated $2 million in new funding for upgrading local health departments and encouraging counties to join together to form health districts. By fiscal year 1982–83, local governments' share of expenses for local public health had fallen to approximately two-thirds. In recent years, it has increased again, and local funds now constitute about three-fourths of total public health spending in North Carolina. Today, local funds for public health are made up of revenues from fees charged for public health services, as well as local appropriations.

As the public health service delivery structure grew, so did the legal framework authorizing public health services. Between 1911 and 1957, the General Assembly enacted a wide range of public health statutes. In 1957 and again in 1983, it completely rewrote these laws, clarifying and organizing them. Today, most of the state's public health laws are contained in G.S. Chapter 130A.

Organization and Governance of Public Health Services in North Carolina

Public health services in North Carolina are the joint effort and responsibility of the state and county governments. The Secretary of the North Carolina Department of Health and Human Services administers and enforces public health statutes and statewide regulations. At the local level, local health directors are responsible for administering local public health[2] agency programs and enforcing local public health rules.

Public Health at the State Level

Public health services at the state level have undergone two reorganizations in recent years. When the previous edition of this book was published, public health services were the responsibility of the Division of Health Services, which was part of the Department of Human Resources. In 1989, the Division of Health Services was taken out of the Department of Human Resources and combined with portions of the

Department of Natural Resources and Community Development. This resulted in a new state agency, which was named the Department of Environment, Health, and Natural Resources (DEHNR). In 1997, the non-environmental public health functions were removed from DEHNR and transferred back into the Department of Human Resources, which was renamed the Department of Health and Human Services (DHHS). At the same time, DEHNR was renamed the Department of Environment and Natural Resources (DENR).

Today, DHHS is the state agency with primary responsibility for public health. Within DHHS are the State Commission for Health Services and the programs that make up the agency's public health component. On July 1, 1998, the Division of Environmental Health, another public health agency, reported to the state health director for policy matters while remaining within DENR for administrative purposes.[3]

Commission for Health Services

In 1973, the State Board of Health was replaced by the State Commission for Health Services (G.S. Ch. 130A, Art. 1A). Today, the commission is the primary regulatory body pertaining to public health in North Carolina. The commission consists of thirteen members, four of whom are elected by the North Carolina Medical Society. The remaining nine are appointed by the governor and must include a pharmacist, a soil scientist or engineer experienced in sanitary engineering, a veterinarian, an optometrist, a dentist, and a registered nurse. The members serve four-year staggered terms.

The commission is responsible for establishing rules governing the operation of the state's public health programs. It also has general rule-making authority for the protection of the public health, and may adopt rules necessary to enable the state public health agencies to administer and enforce public health statutes. The commission is further directed by statute to adopt rules regarding specific sanitation issues. The commission's rules are codified in Title 15A of the North Carolina Administrative Code.

Department of Health and Human Services

The state agencies primarily concerned with the provision of non-environmental public health services in North Carolina are DHHS's three public health divisions:[4] the Division of Women's and Children's Health, the Division of Community Health, and the Division of Epidemiology (G.S. Ch. 143B, Art. 3).[5] The directors of these divisions report to the state health director, who is a licensed physician appointed by the state secretary of health and human services. The state health director performs duties assigned by the secretary and submits an annual report on public health to the Commission for Health Services. The only authority the statutes expressly grant the state health director is the power to issue quarantine and isolation orders under G.S. 130A-145. The duty and power to administer and enforce public health laws and rules is divided between the secretary of health and human services and the secretary of environment and natural resources (G.S. 130A-4). It is customary, however, for the secretary of health and human services to delegate administrative responsibility for all public health programs in the department to the state health director. A deputy state health director assists and reports directly to the state health director.

Each of the three public health divisions is divided into sections and offices with responsibilities for particular public health services and programs. The Division of Women's and Children's Health contains four sections: women's health, children's health, nutrition services (including the Women, Infants, and Children (WIC) supplemental nutrition program), and immunization. The five sections and offices that make up the Division of Community Health are the health promotion section, the dental health section, the chronic disease prevention and control section, the office of minority health, and the office of local health. Within the Division of Epidemiology are six sections: postmortem medicolegal examination (discussed in Chapter 31), HIV/sexually transmitted disease prevention and care, public health laboratory, occupational and environmental epidemiology, general communicable disease control, and health statistics.

The public health divisions of DHHS influence the operation of local public health agencies in several ways:

- *Training and technical assistance.* State agency staff provide training and materials for local personnel and advise them on a continuing basis. For example, the Division of Women's and Children's Health provides health education materials for use in local health departments' family planning, prenatal, and child health clinics. For another example, the Division of Community Health offers training programs for new public health nurses.
- *Monitoring enforcement of public health laws and rules.* North Carolina law requires the employees of local public health agencies

to enforce public health laws and rules. Divisions of DHHS monitor local enforcement activities. For example, the Division of Epidemiology assures that vital records information is collected by the local agency and reported to the state. DHHS personnel also provide assistance to local public health agencies' enforcement efforts. For example, the HIV/STD section provides guidelines on the enforcement of communicable disease control measures among patients with HIV or AIDS.

- *Channeling state and federal funds.* DHHS allocates federal and state money for public health projects to local public health agencies. To receive certain funds, the local board of health must enter into a contract with DHHS. The contract requires local public health agencies to comply with all public health laws and rules and it specifies how funds must be managed. This contract has a significant effect on how the local health agency operates since non-compliance with its terms will result in loss of state and federal funds.

Other State Agencies

State agencies other than DHHS also affect public health in North Carolina. The most significant public health responsibilities that are not administered by DHHS are those that remain the responsibility of DENR and the Division of Environmental Health. Those programs are discussed in Chapter 23. Other agencies with responsibilities affecting the public health are the Department of Agriculture, which regulates the labeling and purity of foods, cosmetics, and pesticides, and the Department of Labor, which is responsible for occupational health and safety.

Public Health at the Local Level

Organizational Options

Every county is required by statute to provide public health services (G.S. Ch. 130A, Art. 2, Pts. 1, 1A, and 1B). Most counties have only four ways of meeting this obligation: by forming a county health department, by joining with other counties to operate a district health department, by forming a public health authority, or by contracting for the state to provide services [G.S. 130A-34(b); 130A-45(b)]. Two additional options are available to counties with populations in excess of 425,000: the county commissioners may assume direct responsibility for providing public health (and other) services; or the county may form a consolidated human services agency that is responsible for providing public health, social services, and mental health, developmental disabilities, and substance abuse services [G.S. 130A-34(b); 153A-77].[6]

County Health Departments

On July 1, 1998, seventy-seven North Carolina counties met their obligation to provide public health services by operating a county health department. The county health department is governed by a county board of health and administered by a local health director (G.S. 130A-35; 130A-40; 130A-41).

The county board of health is composed of eleven members appointed by the county commissioners. The members must include a physician, a dentist, an optometrist, a veterinarian, a registered nurse, a pharmacist, a professional engineer, a county commissioner, and three members of the general public. All board members must be residents of the county. If no person from one of the named professions is willing to serve, a member of the general public is substituted until a member of the named profession becomes available for appointment. If there is only one county resident eligible in any of the categories of named professions, the commissioners have the option of appointing that person or substituting a member of the general public. Members serve three-year staggered terms and are limited to three consecutive full terms, unless a member is the only person residing in the county who represents one of the six named professions. The commissioner-member's position is *ex officio* and thus the commissioner must step down from the board of health if his or her term as a commissioner ends before the health board term expires. The statute requires that board members "reasonably reflect the population makeup of the county." Members of the board of health may be removed from office for cause.

The local health director is appointed by the county board of health after consultation with the county commissioners. The health director is the administrative head of the health department and also serves as secretary to the board of health.

District Health Departments

A multicounty district health department may be formed upon agreement of the county commissioners and the boards of health of two or more counties. A county may join an existing district health department upon a similar agreement, entered into by the boards of commissioners and local boards of health of each affected county (G.S. 130A-36 through 130A-38; 130A-40; 130A-41). The district may have health department offices in each component county, but it will have only one director and only one board of health.

The district health department is governed by a district board of health. Each county in the district appoints one county commissioner to the board and the commissioner members then appoint the other board members. The district board of health is composed of fifteen to eighteen members and must include a physician, a dentist, an optometrist, a veterinarian, a registered nurse, a pharmacist, and a professional engineer. As with county boards, if no person from one of the named professions is willing to serve, a member of the general public may be appointed to serve until a member of the named profession becomes available for appointment. The statutes require that the membership provide for district-wide representation and reflect the population of the district. Members serve staggered three-year terms and are limited to three consecutive full terms, unless a member is the only person residing in the district who represents one of the seven professions listed. The terms of the commissioner-members are concurrent with their tenure as county commissioners. Whenever a county joins or withdraws from an existing district health department, the district board of health is dissolved and a new board appointed.

After consultation with the boards of commissioners of each county in the district, the board of health appoints a district health director. The director serves as administrative head of the department and as secretary to the board.

Any county may withdraw from the district department when the majority of its commissioners determines that the district is not operating in the best interests of health in that county. The district may be dissolved upon a similar decision by the boards of commissioners of all the counties in the district. Withdrawal or dissolution may take place only after written notice is given to DHHS and only at the end of the fiscal year. A certified public accountant or an auditor certified by the Local Government Commission distributes surplus funds to the counties according to the percentage each of them contributed. When an entire district dissolves or when a county withdraws, the district board of health's rules remain in effect in the county or counties involved until amended or repealed by the new board or boards governing the affected counties.

On July 1, 1998, twenty counties were members of seven district health departments.[7]

Public Health Authorities

A 1997 statute permits counties to meet their obligation to provide public health services by forming public health authorities (G.S. Ch. 130A, Art. 2, Pt. 1A). A public health authority may be formed by a single county or by two or more counties jointly.

To create a single-county public health authority, the commissioners of the interested county must adopt a resolution finding that it is in the interest of the public health and welfare to create a public health authority and provide the required public health services through it. A multi-county authority is created similarly; however, the resolution establishing it must be adopted jointly by the boards of commissioners and boards of health governing each affected county. A county may join an existing public health authority upon joint resolution of the boards of commissioners and boards of health of each county involved. Before adopting any such resolution, the county commissioners must hold a public hearing with notice published at least ten days before the hearing.

After the resolution has been adopted, the county commissioners of a single-county authority or the chairs of the boards of commissioners forming a multicounty authority appoint a public health authority board. The board replaces the local board of health and becomes the rule-making, policy-making, and adjudicatory body for the authority. A single-county board is composed of seven to nine members and a multicounty board is composed of eight to eleven members. The board's membership must include a physician, a dentist, a commissioner or commissioner's designee from each county in the authority, an administrator from a hospital serving the authority's service area, a member of the general public, and at least two licensed or registered professionals from any of the following professions: optometry, veterinary science, nursing, pharmacy, engineering, or accounting. Board members serve three-year staggered terms and may be removed from their positions for cause. County commissioner members are *ex officio* and serve only during their terms as county commissioners. Whenever a county joins or withdraws from an existing public health authority, the board is dissolved and a new board appointed.

The public health authority board appoints an authority director after consultation with the appropriate county commissioners. The authority director serves as the administrative head of the authority and as secretary to the board.

Public health authorities can operate more independently of boards of commissioners than traditional local health departments can. Moreover, the public health authority board has powers that local boards of health—both county and district—do not. The powers of the local board of health and the public health authority board are compared in Table 22-1.

Despite the expanded powers of the public health authority board, county commissioners retain ultimate control. They appoint the members of the authority board and they may dissolve the authority (or withdraw from a multicounty authority) upon a finding that the authority is not operating in the best health interests of the county. Dissolution may occur only after written notification to DHHS and only at the end of a fiscal year. If the authority was a multicounty authority, a certified public accountant or an auditor certified by the Local Government Commission distributes surplus funds to the counties according to the percentage each of them contributed. All rules adopted by the authority board continue in effect until amended or repealed by the new authority board or local board of health.

On July 1, 1998, no county in North Carolina had yet decided to form a public health authority under G.S. Chapter 130A, though several counties had begun to study the matter. Since July 1, 1997, Cabarrus County has been providing public health services through the Cabarrus Health Alliance, an organization established and operated as a hospital authority under G.S. Chapter 131E, Article 2, Part B.[8] The Cabarrus Health Alliance operates very similarly to a public health authority. However, because it is a hospital authority, the Cabarrus Health Alliance has more autonomy than a public health authority, and its governing board has more powers than a public health authority board.

Consolidated Human Services Agencies

A board of commissioners in a county with a population that exceeds 425,000 may elect to establish a consolidated human services agency with the authority to carry out the functions of the local health department; the county department of social services; the area mental health, developmental disabilities, and substance abuse authority; and other human services functions [G.S. 153A-77(b)–(e)].

A consolidated human services board is the policy-making, rule-making, and administrative board of the agency. The board is composed of no more than twenty-five members appointed by the county commis-

Table 22-1
Comparison of Powers and Duties—Local Boards of Health and
Public Health Authority Boards

Powers and Duties	Local Board of Health	Public Health Authority Board
Serve as policy-making, rule-making, and adjudicatory body for public health	yes	yes
Protect and promote public health, and adopt rules necessary to that purpose	yes	yes
Appoint health director after consultation with county commissioners	yes	yes
Impose fees for services	limited[a]	yes
Employ legal counsel and staff	district–yes county–no	yes
Enter contracts for supplies, equipment, or services	no[b]	yes
Set salaries of employees and professional reimbursement policies	no	yes
Delegate powers and duties to agents or employees	no	yes
Construct, equip, operate, and maintain public health facilities	no	yes
Lease public health facilities	no	yes
Sell surplus buildings, land, and equipment	no	yes
Acquire property by purchase, grant, gift, devise, or lease, or, with permission of county commissioners, condemnation	no	yes
Establish and operate health care networks and contract for the provision of public health services[c]	no	yes

a. Fees imposed by a local board of health must be based upon a plan recommended by the health director and approved by the county commissioners. Public health authority boards have no similar limitation.

b. The local board of health has no contracting authority. The local health director is authorized to enter contracts on behalf of the local health department; however, the local health director's authority may not be construed to abrogate the authority of the county commissioners.

c. The term "network" is not defined by the statute. The statute states that this authority extends to managed health care activities, provided the public health authority board complies with the requirements of G.S. Chapter 58, Article 67 (governing health maintenance organizations) to the extent that those requirements apply.

sioners. When the agency is first established, the initial board is appointed upon the recommendations of a nominating committee comprised of the members of the preconsolidation boards of health, social services, and mental health, developmental disabilities, and substance abuse services. Subsequent appointments are made by the commissioners from nominees presented by the human services board. The composition of the board must reasonably reflect the population makeup of the county and include the following:

- Eight consumers of human services, public advocates, or family members of the agency's clients, including one person with mental illness, one person with a developmental disability, one person in recovery from substance abuse, one family member of a person with mental illness, one family member of a person with a developmental disability, one family member of a person with a substance abuse problem, and two consumers of other human services
- Eight professionals, including one psychologist, one pharmacist, one engineer, one dentist, one optometrist, one veterinarian, one social worker, and one registered nurse
- Two physicians, one of whom is a psychiatrist
- One county commissioner
- Other persons, including members of the general public representing various occupations

All members must be residents of the county. Board members serve staggered four-year terms and may be removed for cause. No member may serve more than two consecutive four-year terms. The county commissioner-member may serve in that position for only as long as he or she remains a county commissioner.

In general, consolidated human services boards assume the duties and responsibilities of a local board of health. They do not directly appoint the agency's director, but their consent is required for the appointment to be made. They are responsible for planning and recommending a consolidated human services budget to the county commissioners.

A consolidated human services agency is administered by a consolidated human services director, who is appointed by the county manager with the advice and consent of the consolidated human services board.

On July 1, 1998, only one county (Wake) offered public health services through a consolidated human services agency.

Assumption by County Commissioners of Direct Responsibility for Services

A second option that is available only to counties with populations of more than 425,000 is for the board of county commissioners to assume direct control of several county services, including public health services [G.S. 153A-77(a)]. The county board of commissioners may assume all of the statutory powers and functions of the board of health; the board of social services; the area mental health, developmental disabilities, and substance abuse board; and any other board or agency appointed by the commissioners or acting under their authority.

For the purposes of local public health, this arrangement simply means that the board of commissioners acts as the local board of health, with all its responsibilities and duties. The commissioners may then create a county health department or pursue any other arrangement that would satisfy the county's obligation to provide public health services.

As of July 1, 1998, Mecklenburg County was the only county in the state that had exercised this option. The county commissioners, acting as the local board of health, used their policy-making and contracting authority to form a unique arrangement with a local hospital authority. In 1995, Mecklenburg County and the Charlotte-Mecklenburg Hospital Authority entered into an interlocal cooperation agreement in which most of the county's public health services were transferred from the county health department to a hospital-based integrated delivery system. The county has maintained a small health department which is responsible for providing vital records registration, communicable disease control, and environmental health services. All other services have been contracted to Carolinas HealthCare System.[9] Under this arrangement, county commissioners retain the legal responsibility to protect and promote the public health in the county, and to assure that all mandated public health services are provided.

Contracting for Services to Be Provided by the State

A county or district board of health may, with the county commissioners' approval, arrange for the state to furnish public health services on contract (G.S. 130A-34). The statute limits this method to situations in which the DHHS and the local board agree that special problems or projects exist that can best be handled in this manner. The local board of health continues to be the policy-making body for the county or district. In 1998, no county in the state was operating under this type of arrangement.

Local Public Health Agency Governance

The previous section describes several types of boards that have responsibility for local public health activities: local (either county or district) boards of health, public health authority boards, consolidated human services boards, and in some cases, the board of county commissioners. Each of these boards is charged with protecting and promoting the public health, and with serving as the policy-making, rule-making, and adjudicatory body for public health in the county or counties in its jurisdiction. Each board also influences the day-to-day administration of the local health department, public health authority, or consolidated human services agency. Each of these boards has the powers and duties that are described in this section. Public health authority boards and consolidated human services boards have additional powers and duties, as described previously.

Rule-Making

Local boards of health are responsible for protecting and promoting the public health in the area they serve, and have the authority to adopt rules necessary for that purpose (G.S. 130A-39). Local rules have the force and effect of law; violation of them is a criminal misdemeanor (G.S. 130A-25).

Before adopting, amending, or repealing any local rule, the board of health must give the public notice of its intent and offer the public an opportunity to inspect its proposed action. Ten days before the proposed action is to occur, notice of the proposal must be published in a local newspaper with general circulation. The notice must contain a statement of the substance of the proposed rule or a description of the subjects and issues involved, the proposed effective date, and a statement that copies of the proposed rule are available at the local health department. At the same time, the board must make the text of the proposed rule, amendment, or rule to be repealed available for inspection by placing it in the office of each county clerk within the board's jurisdiction.

The subject matter of rules that the local board of health may adopt is constrained by the statutes and by state court decisions. G.S. 130A-39 constrains local boards' rule-making authority in two ways. First, local boards of health are forbidden from adopting rules concerning the issuing of grades and permits to food and lodging facilities, or the operation of those facilities. Second, local boards may issue their own regulations regarding wastewater management only with the approval of DHHS, which must find that the proposed rules are at least as stringent as state rules and are necessary and sufficient to safeguard the public health.

In all other public health subject areas, local boards of health may adopt rules that are more stringent than the Commission for Health Services' rules if, in the board's opinion, a more stringent rule is required to protect the public health. A local board of health may not adopt a rule that is *less* stringent than the commission's rule on the same issue.

Local boards may adopt national or state codes or standards as part of their rules. Copies of any materials so adopted must be filed with the rules. Subsequent changes in the national or state codes or standards do not become part of the local rule unless the local board expressly adopts them.

Rules adopted by the board are subject to court-imposed requirements that the rules be reasonable and that their purposes and provisions bear a substantial relationship to legitimate public health goals. Furthermore, a 1996 state court of appeals decision held that local board of health rules may not make distinctions based upon policy concerns that are unrelated to health and are traditionally reserved for legislative bodies.[10] The court used this principle to invalidate a local board of health's smoking control rules in *City of Roanoke Rapids v. Peedin*.

The rules at issue in *Peedin* banned smoking in public places in Halifax County, but made some exceptions. All bars and small restaurants—those seating thirty or fewer people—were expressly exempted from the ban. Larger restaurants were required to provide a non-smoking area that comprised an increasing proportion of the restaurant's seating capacity, beginning at one-third of the seating capacity in 1993 and rising to 80 percent by 1996, but they too were exempted from the total ban on smoking. The court of appeals reasoned that these exceptions to the smoking ban, which resulted in employees and patrons of the excepted establishments being exposed to the very health hazard the board was attempting to regulate, revealed that the board had balanced factors other than health in making the rule. The court concluded,

> the statutes cannot be held to permit the [local board of health] to consider factors other than health in promulgating its rules. While a legislative body arguably may direct that distinctions be based on factors other than public health when authorizing the promulgation of rules by health boards, such factors may not be considered *sua sponte* [i.e., of the local boards' own initiative].[11]

The implication of the *Peedin* decision for local health boards' rule-making authority is unclear. Public health traditionally concerns itself with a number of social, economic, and other factors that may contribute to a particular public health problem without being part of a specific disease process. Whether such concerns will be recognized by future courts as being sufficiently health-related to be properly within a local board's rule-making authority remains to be seen.

Adjudication

The adjudicatory function of local health boards serves as an administrative route of appeal for aggrieved parties. If a person is aggrieved by the interpretation or enforcement of the local board's rules, the person may appeal to the board. The notice of appeal must be received by the local health director within thirty days of the disputed action and contain the name and address of the aggrieved party, describe the challenged action, and state reasons why it is incorrect. The health director must then transmit the notice of appeal to the board of health within five days, which must hear the matter within the next fifteen days. The person who is appealing is entitled to a ten-day notice of the time, date, and place of the hearing. The strict rules of evidence that are enforced in courtrooms do not apply at the board hearing, but the decision must be supported by adequate evidence. The board's ruling must be written and must set out the factual findings that were relied on in making it. Otherwise, a court would return the case to the board for a rehearing. A person dissatisfied with the board's decision at the hearing may appeal to the district court within thirty days after notification of the decision.

Administration

Local boards of health have an important, though indirect, role in the administration of the local health department. First, the board appoints—and may elect to replace—the local health director, who is responsible for the day-to-day administration of the department. Second, the board makes policy decisions governing the department. Also, local boards are authorized by statute to impose fees for services to be rendered by a local health department except in certain circumstances (discussed in the following section on finance).

Local Public Health Agency Administration

The administrative functions within local public health agencies include managing operations and programs; providing in-service training for staff; preparing the budget; explaining the department's activities to the board of health, official agencies, and the public; informing the public of health laws and rules as well as enforcing them; suggesting new rules and services; and purchasing equipment and supplies. These duties generally are the local health director's responsibility, but the handling of particular functions may differ from county to county.

Local Health Directors

Local health directors serve as the administrative heads of their departments and are responsible for enforcing state and local public health regulations (G.S. 130A-41). They are authorized by statute to investigate the causes of diseases, to quarantine or isolate individuals when the public health requires it, to disseminate public health information and promote good health, to advise local officials about public health matters, to investigate cases of certain communicable diseases, to abate public health nuisances and imminent hazards, to employ and dismiss health department employees, and to enter contracts on behalf of the health department. These same duties are bestowed upon consolidated human services directors [G.S. 153A-77(e)]. Public health authority directors have all of these powers and duties except the authority to enter contracts, which is retained by the public health authority board [G.S. 130A-45.5(c); 130A-45.3(a)(12)].

Local Public Health Agency Personnel

Local public health agencies employ a wide variety of professionals (15A NCAC 25.0300). The number and types of persons employed varies greatly from county to county, depending upon the services the local department offers and the amount of resources available. All local public health agencies have a director, nurses, and environmental health specialists. Many also employ physicians, physicians' assistants, nurse practitioners, nursing assistants, health educators, and nutritionists. Additional categories of staff may include social workers, medical records specialists, epidemiologists or statisticians, and administrative staff.

The qualifications, salary, and terms of employment of health department personnel are not generally within the discretion of the county commissioners. These matters are governed by the State Personnel Commission. Counties may propose their own health department personnel regulations, which the commission may approve if it finds them to be "substantially equivalent" to the state regulations. Public health authorities have specific statutory authority to establish salary plans for the authority, but are otherwise subject to the State Personnel Commission's employment regulations.

Financing of Public Health Services

Public health activities in North Carolina are financed at the state level through federal funds, state funds, private grants, and fees. At the local level, all of the same sources of funds are important, but the bulk of local operations is funded through local revenues—income from fees and county appropriations. In fiscal year 1996–97, local revenues constituted about 76 percent of local public health agencies' total budgets. On average, North Carolina counties spent $35.48 per capita from local funds for public health. State and federal funds brought the total per capita spending that year up to $46.44.

Sources of Local Support

Federal Funds

Federal support for local public health efforts is substantial. Local agencies receive federal funds both directly and indirectly. The major source of direct federal support is reimbursement under the Medicaid program for services rendered by the local public health agency. Indirect federal support comes from federal funds that are paid to the state, and then channeled by the state to the local agencies. Federal categorical funds support maternal and child health services, the WIC program, and several other services and programs.

State Funds

The state provides general aid-to-county funds, which are distributed to local public health agencies by DHHS. Funds are allocated based on population and utilization of allocated funds (15A NCAC 25.0101). The state health director may allocate special needs funds to local public health agencies that demonstrate a critical public health need, unique to the agency's service area, that cannot be met through other funding mechanisms (15A NCAC 25.0102). Additional support comes from categorical grants, which include a combination of federal and state funds. Categorical support is typically, but not always, given out according to formulas (which can vary from program to program) that include a base amount that is the same for each county and an additional amount that varies according to population, need, and performance. The state also awards other grant or contract funds for special projects. Finally, the state reimburses some services on a fee-for-service basis.

To receive state funds, local public health agencies must sign a contract with the state. Currently, the funds are distributed under a single "consolidated contract," although no law prohibits the state from requiring a separate contract for each funding program. The contract contains a number of general provisions governing how local public health agencies must use and account for money flowing from the state, as well as provisions that set out special requirements for the use of certain funds. If a local agency fails to comply with the terms of the contract, the state may take steps to cut off state funding for the program that is out of compliance. The state would first notify the agency that it has sixty days to comply. If the problem were not corrected to the satisfaction of the state within that period, the state could temporarily suspend funding for the program that was out of compliance. If the deficiency were still not corrected within thirty days following temporary suspension of funding, program funds could be permanently suspended until the department provided evidence that the deficiencies were corrected. After all other reasonable administrative remedies have been exhausted, the state may cancel, terminate, or suspend the contract in whole or in part and the department may be declared ineligible for further state contracts or agreements. Alternatively, the state could enforce the contract by suing the county. Neither of these actions has ever been taken by the state against a county; nevertheless, the ability to withhold funds gives the state some leverage to require certain levels of services by the local public health agency.

County Appropriations

Local boards of health have no power to tax, and thus a board and its department must depend on other sources for funds. Boards of county commissioners are authorized to appropriate funds from property tax levies and to allocate other revenues whose use is not otherwise restricted by law for the local health agency's use. Commissioners may also establish a capital reserve fund to buy, construct, repair, or alter public health facilities.

For county health departments, county commissioners approve the health department budget as a regular part of their responsibility for county finance. It is common practice for a local board of health to approve the health department's budget before it is submitted to the county manager and the commissioners, but no statute requires it. For consolidated human services agencies, the budget for public health is a part of the budget planned by the consolidated human services director, recommended by the consolidated human services board, and approved by the county commissioners. Public health authorities and district health departments prepare and approve their own budgets and need not obtain county commissioners' approval. If one of these agencies were to seek county appropriations, however, the county commissioners would of course have to approve the expenditure.

The General Assembly has set no minimum level of local funding that county commissioners must provide for public health. The basic requirement is that funding must be sufficient to support the mandated services set out in the Commission for Health Services' rules (these are described in the following section on health department services). The amount set aside for mandated services varies widely from county to county, however.

Private Grants

Public health agencies often receive grants from foundations, hospitals, drug companies, and other private entities. These grants are essentially contracts between the local health department and the granting agency and usually are provided to enable the department to develop a particular project or provide a specific service.

Fees

Public health agencies may charge and collect fees for some, but not all, services. Fees can be broadly grouped into two categories. One category is regulatory fees that are charged to help cover the expenses of regulatory programs, such as well permitting and on-site wastewater treatment and disposal. These fees are typically collected at the time a permit is issued or a required inspection is conducted. The other category is payments for medical services, which includes fees for services such as family planning or prenatal care.

G.S. 130A-39(g) authorizes local boards of health to charge fees that are recommended by the health director, approved by the board of health, and approved by the board of county commissioners (or, in a district, all the boards of commissioners of the participating counties).[12]

There are, however, a number of specific restrictions on a county's power to collect fees in public health programs.

First, G.S. 130A-39(g) prohibits charging fees when a local employee serves as an agent of the state.[13] This prohibition effectively covers all environmental regulatory programs except those that are conducted under local rules. There are two significant statutory exceptions: services provided under the on-site sewage treatment and disposal program and the public swimming pools program. Second, regulatory fees must be "reasonable." A 1994 decision of the North Carolina Supreme Court strongly suggested that a fee is reasonable if it covers no more than the actual costs of the regulatory program.[14] Third, while there are no broad restrictions on fees charged for the provision of health services, in several instances state law specifically forbids charging fees. Local public health agencies must provide the following services at no cost to the client: testing and counseling for sickle cell syndrome (G.S. 130A-130), examination for and treatment of tuberculosis and sexually transmitted diseases [G.S. 130A-144(e)] and immunizations (G.S. 130A-153).

A county must use fees collected under the authority of G.S. 130A-39(g) for public health purposes. Furthermore, in most cases the consolidated contract, state statutes or rules, or federal law requires that fees be spent on the specific program that generated them. A significant exception to this general rule is the revenue generated by home health fees. That revenue is restricted to use for public health, but need not be returned to the home health program specifically.

Management of Local Funds

Local Government Budget and Fiscal Control Act

All funds received or spent at the local level must be budgeted, disbursed, and accounted for in accordance with the Local Government Budget and Fiscal Control Act (G.S. Ch. 159, Art. 3). This law mandates a standard procedure for budget operation, controls how funds are disbursed, and requires particular accounts and accounting procedures. The procedures for county health departments and consolidated human services agencies differ from those for district health departments and public health authorities. The budgeting, disbursing, and accounting for a county health department or consolidated human services agency is done by the county's budget officer and finance officer. District health departments and public health authorities (both single-county and multicounty) are responsible for performing these functions themselves.

Maintenance of Effort Provisions

When state appropriations for public health increase, or when health department receipts increase, county commissioners are sometimes interested in taking the opportunity to reduce county appropriations. This can be done, but there are several legal restrictions on counties' freedom to remove local money from public health agencies.

The consolidated contract prohibits reductions in local appropriations during the one-year term of the contract, but does not prevent the county from reducing appropriations before the contract for the next year is signed, with one exception: departments must maintain their spending on maternal health, child health, and family planning programs at no less than the level provided in fiscal year 1984–85.

Two "maintenance of effort" provisions in the statutes prohibit reductions of county appropriations when state money increases in certain circumstances. G.S. 130A-4.2 requires the state DHHS to ensure that local health departments do not reduce county appropriations for health promotion services because of state appropriations. G.S. 130A-4.1 places the same requirement on maternal and child health services.

Local Public Health Services

G.S. 130A-1.1 charges the public health system with seven tasks:

1. Preventing health risks and disease
2. Identifying and reducing health risks in the community
3. Detecting, investigating, and preventing the spread of disease
4. Promoting healthy lifestyles
5. Promoting a safe and healthful environment
6. Promoting the availability and accessibility of quality health services through the private sector
7. Providing health care services when they are not otherwise available

To accomplish these tasks, the legislature has required DHHS to assure that "essential public health services" are available to all citizens of the state.

The statute defines three categories of essential public health services:

1. *Health support services.* Assessment of health status, health needs, and environmental risks to health; patient and community health education; operation of a public health laboratory; and registration of vital events (births, deaths, fetal deaths, marriages, and divorces).
2. *Environmental health services.* Sanitation inspections and regulation of milk, restaurants, meat markets, hotels and motels, hospitals, schools, ambulances, local detention facilities, agricultural labor camps, swimming pools, and other public places.
3. *Personal health services.* Services for child health, chronic disease control, communicable disease control, dental health, family planning, health promotion and risk reduction, and maternal health.

The statute gives DHHS the responsibility for assuring that these services are available throughout the state. As a practical matter, however, many of the services must be provided at the local level. Thus the Commission for Health Services has promulgated rules giving local public health agencies the responsibility of ensuring that services are available. Services that the local public health agency must guarantee are called, appropriately, "mandated services" (15A NCAC 25.0201).

Mandated services fall into two categories. In the first category are services that the local health department must itself provide directly, under the control of the local health director and the local board of health. These are environmental health services (inspection and regulation of individual, on-site water supply; sanitary sewage collection, treatment, and disposal; food, lodging, and institutional sanitation; and public swimming pools and spa safety and sanitation), communicable disease control, and vital records registration. In the second category are services that the county may provide directly through the health department, provide by contracting with someone else to provide the services, or not provide at all, if it can certify to the state's satisfaction that the services are available in the county from other providers. These services include grade "A" milk certification, public health laboratory services, child health, maternal health, family planning, dental health, home health, and adult health.

The services provided by local public health agencies often extend far beyond these mandated services. Moreover, despite the increasing standardization required by the Commission for Health Services, the number and extent of public health agency offerings vary considerably across the state. Of the many factors that explain the variations, the most important are the availability of funds and the size of the agency's staff. It is therefore impossible to describe the precise range and scope of services that will be provided by any given public health agency. However, a typical local public health agency is likely to offer the following programs and services:

- *Vital statistics and disease reporting.* Local public health agencies collect from doctors, hospitals, and others the necessary information about all births and deaths and all instances of certain diseases that occur within the areas the departments serve and then prepare records and reports on these events. The certificates and disease reports must be forwarded to DHHS within specified time periods and in specified form. Clerical staff within the local department usually perform this function.

- *Sanitation and environmental health.* The Commission for Health Services has promulgated rules governing the sanitation of restaurants, hotels, motels, summer camps, migrant labor camps, residential-care facilities, jails, and other establishments. Registered environmental health specialists employed by local public health agencies act as agents of the state in enforcing these rules. The normal procedure calls for periodic inspections, grading, and issuing of required permits. Environmental health specialists also inspect individual water supplies and septic systems.

- *Communicable disease control.* In addition to providing clinical services for the prevention, diagnosis, and treatment of communicable diseases, local public health agencies receive reports of communicable diseases from local health care providers, schools, and others; investigate outbreaks of diseases; trace the contacts of individuals diagnosed with communicable diseases; and enforce individuals' compliance with immunization requirements and other communicable disease control efforts.

- *Clinic services.* Local public health agencies offer the communities they serve a number of screening and health-care clinics. These are usually staffed by the department's nurses and by physicians under contract. Local public health agencies are required to provide immunizations and to diagnose and treat tuberculosis and sexually transmitted diseases. Most also offer child health, maternal health, and family planning clinics. Some local public health agencies have chronic disease, adult health, or dental clinics.

- *Home health services.* Some local public health agencies provide home health visits by nurses and other professionals. The purpose of those visits is to offer skilled nursing, therapy, medical social services, and other assistance to homebound patients.
- *Nutrition services.* Many local health departments administer the federal WIC (women, infants, and children) supplemental food program. They may also offer nutrition counseling and education.
- *Health education.* Local public health agencies work to educate citizens in nutrition, healthy lifestyles and preventive health care, and health problems. Some employ full-time health educators. An agency's educational programs may be offered in its own facilities, in schools, and at public places. Local public health agencies also try to inform the community of the types and extent of services that they provide.
- *School health services.* A department's program may include giving pre- and in-school physical examinations; teaching special classes in the schools; and cooperating with educational personnel, physicians, and dentists in finding and treating health problems among pupils.
- *Services coordination.* Many local public health agencies provide case management services to coordinate the care of women with high-risk pregnancies (maternity care coordination) and children with developmental delays, chronic health problems, or other special needs (child services coordination).
- *Mosquito and vector control.* Various programs for the control of rodents, mosquitoes, and flies are conducted by local public health agencies.
- *Animal control.* Local public health agencies cooperate with veterinarians in rabies control and in testing for certain diseases in animals. Most health departments employ animal- control officers to impound strays and dangerous or vicious animals.
- *Laboratory.* The laboratory is a supportive service that enables local public health agencies to perform their work. Most public health laboratories can provide a number of services, including serologic and blood tests, water and milk analyses, and tests for communicable disease.

Additional Resources

Dellinger, Anne M., Jeffrey S. Koeze, and Vicki Winslow. "Public Health," in *State and Local Government Relations in North Carolina*, 2d ed. (Chapel Hill, N.C.: Institute of Government, The University of North Carolina at Chapel Hill, 1995), 123–37.

Koeze, Jeffrey S. "Paying for Public Health Services in North Carolina," *Popular Government* 60 (1994): 11–20.

———. "Prospects for the Future of North Carolina's Public Health System," *Health Law Bulletin*, no. 77 (Institute of Government, April 1996): 1–6.

Notes

1. Roddey M. Ligon, Jr., *Public Health in North Carolina* (Chapel Hill, N.C.: Institute of Government, The University of North Carolina at Chapel Hill, 1960), 2.

2. The term *local public health agency* is being used to mean a health department, a consolidated human services department, or another agency established by a board of commissioners or a public health authority board, that is engaged in the provision of public health services.

3. The Division of Environmental Health will remain in DENR pending a report from the Environmental Management Commission, which has been directed by the General Assembly to study environmental health's administrative placement and reporting relationships and report its recommendations to the 1999 General Assembly.

4. A reorganization of DHHS's public health programs commenced just as this book was going to press. The three public health divisions will be combined into a single Division of Public Health. The placement on the organizational chart of the various sections and offices had not been determined at press time; however, it is expected that the functions of all the existing sections and offices will all be represented in the new division.

5. There are other divisions within DHHS that are relevant to the provision of public health services in North Carolina. These include the Division of Medical Assistance, which administers the Medicaid program; the Division of Facility Services, which is responsible for licensure and certification of health care facilities; and the Division of Mental Health, Developmental Disabilities, and Substance Abuse Services, which is under the state health director's supervision but operates separately from the public health system. The mental health, developmental disabilities, and substance abuse services system is described in Chapter 26.

6. Only two North Carolina counties had populations in excess of 425,000 in 1998: Mecklenburg and Wake.

7. The districts were Appalachian (Alleghany, Ashe, and Watauga counties), Granville-Vance, Hertford-Gates, Martin-Tyrrell-Washington, Pasquotank-Perquimans-Camden-Chowan, Rutherford-Polk-McDowell, and Toe River (Avery, Mitchell, and Yancey counties).

8. Cabarrus County's power to provide public health services through a hospital authority derives from an uncodified portion of the Public Health Authorities Act, SL 1997-502. Section 12 of that act authorized counties that meet certain nar-

row, prescribed conditions and obtain the approval of the state health director to provide public health services through a hospital authority.

9. Stephen R. Keener, John W. Baker, and Glen P. Mays, "Providing Public Health Services through an Integrated Delivery System," *Quality Management in Health Care*, Vol. 5 No. 2, at 27 (1997).

10. City of Roanoke Rapids v. Peedin, 124 N.C. App. 578, 478 S.E.2d 528 (1996).

11. *Id.* at 589–90, 478 S.E.2d at 535.

12. Public health authority boards may adopt fee schedules without seeking or obtaining county commissioners' approval.

13. G.S. 130A-45.3(a)(5), which authorizes public health authorities to impose fees, contains no similar limitation. It seems reasonable, however, to assume that public health authorities would be similarly constrained.

14. Homebuilders Ass'n of Charlotte, Inc. v. City of Charlotte, 336 N.C. 37, 442 S.E.2d 45 (1994).

23 Environment, Conservation, and Agricultural Extension

Milton S. Heath, Jr.

Contents

Milton S. Heath, Jr., is an Institute of Government faculty member whose work includes environmental protection, environmental health, and natural resources law.

Counties and other local governments are involved in various ways with environmental protection and natural resource management. In some instances this takes the form of operating a local regulatory program; in others, of being regulated; in still others, of working cooperatively with other local agencies and with state agencies. This chapter seeks to give county officials a basic acquaintance with their responsibilities and opportunities in this field.

Air Pollution

Under existing federal and state legislation the federal government sets general goals and standards for air quality,[1] whereas the state governments, under close supervision from the federal Environmental Protection Agency (EPA), develop the administrative machinery, or implementation plan, for achieving these goals and standards (G.S. Chapter 143, Article 21, Part 7; Article 21B, §§ 20-128.1, -183.3). North Carolina's plan was one of the first to be approved by the EPA. The state's air and water pollution programs are governed by the Environmental Management Commission (EMC) and staffed by the Divisions of Air Quality and Water Quality (DAQ and DWQ) of the Department of Environment and Natural Resources (DENR).

Air quality regulations apply to both private and public sources of pollution. No units of government (federal, state, or local) are exempt from complying with these regulations merely because they are government agencies.

Local Programs

Local governments (cities, counties, and regional groupings of cities and counties) in North Carolina may operate local air pollution control programs but only if they can demonstrate their ability to do so to EMC's satisfaction. The powers of local programs and the procedures for obtaining state approval are spelled out in G.S. 143-215.112. A city or county that is interested in conducting or participating in an air pollution control program should review this statute carefully because it sets out the alternatives and the requirements for local programs in some detail and is the exclusive source of authority to organize a local program.

There were no active *city* air pollution control programs in North Carolina as of January 1, 1998. Forsyth and Mecklenburg counties and the western North Carolina region (Buncombe and Haywood counties) were operating local programs that had full state approval. Cumberland County previously operated a local program with partial approval, which covered such functions as open burning, dark smoke control, air quality monitoring, and investigation of complaints. The Cumberland program was returned to the state in 1997.

Land Use and Transportation Control

Several EPA requirements stress the connection between land use and air pollution controls. For example, state air quality implementation plans must include supplementary land use and transportation controls. The state must also consider the need for air quality maintenance controls in metropolitan areas, and state programs must control *complex sources* of air pollution. (A typical complex source would be a large shopping center with a high level of air contamination from motor vehicles.) On some of these matters, local planning staffs may be able to play an important part in ensuring that a reasonable balance is maintained between the need for air pollution control and the need for development opportunities.

Special mention should be made of one kind of transportation control: vehicle inspection and maintenance (I and M) for the control of pollution from vehicle emissions. When the EPA finds that an air quality control region is not attaining national standards for certain pollutants from automobile exhaust, the state that contains the offending *nonattainment area* is required to institute a vehicle I and M program for the region or risk losing major federal subsidies. Regular inspections of emission-control systems on all automobiles are the key feature of an I and M program. Federal law allows the state to decide whether these inspections are conducted by state-run, municipally run, or private inspection stations. Whatever method is chosen, motorists in a nonattainment area are required to have their auto emission controls inspected for a fee and to repair or replace defective controls at their own expense.

As of December 1997, North Carolina I and M programs were operating in Cabarrus, Durham, Forsyth, Gaston, Guilford, Mecklenburg, Orange, Union, and Wake counties. Inspectors test for emissions of hydrocarbons and carbon monoxide and enforce national standards. Violations of national standards have been detected in other counties, but no I and M programs have been initiated for those counties. The statutes concerning I and M programs are G.S. 20-128.2, 20-183.2 through -183.8G, and 143-215.107(a)(6).

Oxygenated and Reformulated Gasoline

A provision of the 1990 United States Clean Air Act Amendments requires the use of oxygenated and reformulated gasoline under some conditions. It is designed to enable the nation and the states to correct persistent nonattainment of ozone and carbon monoxide standards. (Oxygenated gasoline has oxygen-containing additives like ethanol and MTBE, a natural gas derivative. Reformulated gasoline has reduced emissions of volatile organic compounds and toxic chemicals.)

Four Research Triangle Park–area counties were required to use oxygenated gasoline because of carbon monoxide nonattainment for several years before 1997, but no counties are required to do so now. No North Carolina counties have yet been required to use reformulated gasoline.

All these arrangements to correct nonattainment conditions are in a state of flux. Continuing studies of air quality conditions showed enough improvement by 1996 to permit the EPA to redesignate the nine I and M counties from a carbon monoxide nonattainment area to an attainment area.

More recent developments, in 1997, include an EPA proposal to tighten ozone and micro-particulate standards nationally. This could result in additional responsibilities for affected local areas in North Carolina and elsewhere.

Indoor Air Pollution

The original federal and state clean air legislation focused mainly on outdoor air pollution problems. Increasing attention is now being paid to indoor air pollution—for example, problems of asbestos insulation in public buildings and of radon in homes. City and county governments may want to inquire about the current status of programs that address indoor air pollution issues. G.S. 130A-452, passed in 1994, authorizes approved local air pollution control programs to enforce asbestos standards for renovation and demolition, pursuant to EMC rules.

Consistency of Air and Water Pollution Permits with Local Land Use Ordinances

G.S. 143-215.108(f) requires every applicant for an air quality permit covering a new or expanded facility to request each local government having jurisdiction over the facility to determine whether the facility would be consistent with applicable zoning or subdivision control ordinances. If the facility is found inconsistent with a zoning or subdivision control ordinance, the EMC must attach to the air quality permit a condition that the applicant comply with this ordinance and other applicable "lawfully adopted" ordinances unless the local government or a court makes a subsequent determination of consistency. A local government must submit its determination to the EMC within fifteen days of receipt of a request from the EMC, or the EMC may consider a permit application without regard to local zoning and subdivision controls. It is not clear what scope of inquiry the EMC will or should make to determine whether a local ordinance is lawfully adopted.

This statute is similar to previous legislation that applies to nonmunicipal wastewater discharge permits, contained in G.S. 143215.1(c)(6). The water quality statute, however, allows the EMC to override the local ordinance if it finds that the application has "statewide significance and is in the best interest of the state." As originally introduced, the air quality statute would have allowed the EMC the same flexibility, but a Senate committee substitute replaced this quoted language with the requirement to attach a permit condition of compliance with the local ordinance.

Occupational Safety and Health

Some years ago Congress enacted an Occupational Safety and Health Act (OSHA),[2] which imposes standards on employers for the protection of employees' health and safety. Like most federal environmental and health protection laws, OSHA contemplates a coordinated federal-state program, with standards set nationally and administered largely by the states.

Although this chapter does not attempt to cover health legislation generally, it briefly describes OSHA for two reasons. First, OSHA provides, in one sense, the "in-plant" equivalent of the protections established by clean air laws for the outdoor environment. Thus an air quality problem in a factory is likely to be covered by OSHA rather than by clean air laws. Second, there is some overlapping and duplication between OSHA and the environmental protection laws. For example, for the protection of farm workers, OSHA administrators have imposed restrictions on applying pesticides. These restrictions are in addition to (and in some ways may even conflict with) the provisions of pesticide-control legislation (see the discussion under the section "Pesticides," later in this chapter).

North Carolina has adopted the legislation required to put it in a position to administer the OSHA program: the Occupational Safety and Health Law of North Carolina (G.S. Ch. 95, Art. 16). The legislation is administered by the state Department of Labor.

Private employers have been subject to the requirements of OSHA and related state laws since their passage. State and local governmental employers have been required to comply with standards set under these laws since July 1, 1974.

The much-publicized 1991 fire at the Imperial Foods plant in Hamlet led to a strengthening of North Carolina worker safety laws. Among the new laws that directly affect local governments are the following:

1. All employers (public and private) whose *experience rate modifier* (a calculation used in determining workers' compensation pre-

miums) equals or exceeds 1.5 are required to establish workplace safety and health programs. Every such employer must establish an employer-employee safety and health committee with employee-selected representatives. The statute spells out detailed requirements for these programs (G.S. Ch. 95, Art. 22). A committee is required at each work site where there are at least eleven permanent employees unless the workers do not report to or work at a fixed location or the labor commissioner permits a variation.

2. The previous exemption of state agencies and political subdivisions from OSHA fines has been repealed. Each local government must report each violation for which it is cited at the next public meeting of its governing board and notify its workers' compensation insurance carrier or risk pool [G.S. 95-137(b)(6)].

Water Pollution (Surface Water)

The basic system of water pollution control is generally similar to the one that operates in the air pollution control field. The federal government provides leadership in setting goals and standards; the state government is largely responsible for providing the machinery to achieve the federal objectives. The North Carolina clean water legislation is codified at G.S. Chapter 143, Parts 1 and 7, and at G.S. 143-215.77 through -215.102. Local government's role in this area has consisted largely of health department programs concerning septic tanks, but local involvement is expanding into emerging fields, such as hazardous waste management and watershed protection.

Federal legislation[3] establishes long-term national water quality goals. The standards required to meet them became increasingly stringent during the last two decades as the nation worked toward the objective of achieving recreational water quality for all its water. The EPA continues working to help the states keep their water pollution control laws and programs in compliance with federal standards.

The water pollution laws place important responsibilities on local governments to collect and treat their sewage properly. Local governments, including counties, must obtain permits to discharge their treated sewage to the waters of the United States, just as industries must obtain permits to discharge their treated wastewaters. The permit is obtained from the DWQ and is known as the *NPDES* (National Pollution Discharge Elimination System) *permit*. Failure to meet the law's requirements may result in the assessment of heavy penalties on local governments and officials.

During the 1970s and early 1980s, large-scale federal and state subsidies, ranging up to 75 percent or more of the total cost, were available to help local governments build sewage treatment plants. Although the days of this extraordinary federal and state largesse are over, some loan funds may still be available. (Financing of water and sewer projects through grants, loans, and other methods is discussed in some detail in Chapter 18 of this volume.)

The General Assembly—reflecting growing public concern over water pollution—has become increasingly proactive in recent years on water quality issues. A few examples from the 1995–97 legislative sessions are illustrative:

- It created a Clean Water Management Trust Fund in 1996 to make grants to state, local, and nonprofit agencies for the acquisition of riparian buffers and conservation easements, the repair of failing wastewater treatment systems, and the stimulation of water quality planning. The fund is financed by an earmarked percentage of unreserved annual credit balances in the General Fund, which will also help support a Wetlands Restoration Fund. The 1997 assembly created a Drinking Water Revolving Loan fund to take advantage of $20 million in annual federal grants to each state.

- It launched legislative initiatives that parallel the EMC's river basin planning program, by concentrating on perceived problems of particular basins. Special attention has been given to the Neuse River Basin by a legislative nitrogen reduction goal and atmospheric nitrogen deposition study set in 1996, expanded in 1997 by specific legislative nitrogen and phosphoric reduction limits, and aided by a 1996 grant of $2 million to help meet the nitrogen reduction goal. The 1997 assembly followed through with grants for water quality monitoring in the Cape Fear Basin ($1.5 million) and the Roanoke and Pamlico estuaries ($400,000). It also funded evaluation of septic tank use in the Neuse Basin and innovative technology to reduce nitrification ($850,000, including $150,000 targeted to Union County). Enacted alongside these river basin measures in 1997 was a law allowing the EMC to approve plans developed by coalitions of local governments for any river basin or sub-basin as an alternative way to achieve water quality standards. The 1997 assembly also directed the Department of Health and Human Resources to develop a coastal fishing waters contaminant monitoring program, and enacted a comprehensive coastal fisheries reform law directing DENR to coordinate development of critical fisheries management and habitat protection plans and reforming the coastal fisheries licensing system.

- In 1995 the assembly thoroughly overhauled the on-site wastewater (or septic tank) law, instituting a new five-year authorization concept and making improvement permits valid indefinitely. It also codified the EMC's authority to impose moratoria on wastewater systems that have reached capacity. In 1996 it funded a program aimed at eliminating "straight-piping" of domestic wastewater discharges.

Sewage Treatment, Including Septic Tanks

Local environmental health specialists (formerly called *sanitarians*) employed by county health departments have traditionally been responsible for inspecting and supervising installation of septic tanks and other on-site sewage treatment facilities. In recent years, as septic tanks have been used for larger projects and in more densely built-up areas, these wastes have become an increasing concern for the EMC (with its general mandate for water pollution control), for state health authorities, and for local health departments. As a result, jurisdiction over sewage treatment is now divided among state agencies and the local health departments in a fairly complex way. These arrangements have been changed more than once in recent years and may well change again in the future. The septic tank law is codified at G.S. Chapter 130A, Article 11.

Under 1992 legislation (1) all subsurface on-site wastewater discharge systems are regulated by state and local environmental health agencies—the Division of Environmental Health (DEH) and county health departments; and (2) all systems discharging to surface waters or to the surface of the ground (spray irrigation) are regulated by the DWQ under EMC rules. When the EMC has jurisdiction, an EMC permit is required for a sewage system: either an NPDES permit for a sewage discharge system, or a nondischarge permit for a system not covered elsewhere or for system elements such as sewer lines (G.S. 143-215.1).

The EMC may impose a moratorium on the addition of wastes to a wastewater treatment plant when it determines that the plant is incapable of treating additional wastes.

The Health Services Commission (HSC) is the rule-making body for state environmental health. Under HSC rules, local health departments are delegated routine operating responsibility for the regulatory system. Local departments may also elect to administer their own sewage rules instead of state rules, if the DEH finds that the proposed local rules are at least as stringent as the state's and are necessary to protect public health. (Fewer than five counties now have this approval.) These local rules may incorporate the state's rules together with more stringent local modifications and additions. The DEH reviews local rules for consistency with changes in state rules as they are adopted, and examines the enforcement of local rules from time to time [G.S. 130A-335(c), (d)]. The EMC may also delegate authority to local governments to approve contracts for sewage and wastewater treatment systems (G.S. 130A-317).

Persons who are subject to DEH or local health department jurisdiction must obtain authorizations and improvement permits for their sewage systems before beginning construction. They must also procure operation permits after the system is in place. Field inspection and tests are required before permits are issued. To reinforce these permit provisions, the on-site wastewater law provides that no permit for electrical or other utility or construction work on a residence or a place of business or public assembly may be issued until the necessary approvals have been obtained (G.S. 130A-338, -339).

In addition to the authority granted to local boards of health to adopt their own sewage rules with DEH approval, these boards have a more general power to adopt "a more stringent rule" in an area regulated by the EMC or the HSC [G.S. 130A-39(a), (b)]. Health officials have relied on this authority to justify a variety of local rules covering subjects such as wells, package sewage treatment plants, and odor problems from animal feedlots.

Non-Point-Source Pollution

The main thrust of traditional water pollution control programs has been to reduce pollution of streams by *point sources,* such as pipes that discharge the treated sewage of cities. There is growing recognition, however, that runoff from roads, shopping centers, farms, and forests, collectively known as *non-point-source pollution,* is a major contributor to stream pollution. This recognition is reflected in 1987 amendments to the Clean Water Act[4] at the national level that provide for states to present non-point-source water pollution control plans to the EPA for early review. These plans are likely to draw heavily on existing state and local programs, such as the North Carolina programs summarized in the following sections.

Sedimentation Pollution

Sedimentation pollution control involves preventing the silting of streams by uncontrolled stormwater runoff from construction projects, logging activities, and so on. In most states (including North Carolina), sedimentation pollution control programs are not administered by the general water pollution control agency.

The Sedimentation Pollution Control Law of 1973 (G.S. Ch. 113A, Art. 4) creates a Sedimentation Control Commission within the DENR and authorizes it to formulate and supervise a cooperative state-local program to control the pollution of streams by sediment and silt. A principal function of this commission is to review local ordinances and programs for compliance with state standards and criteria. Any city or county that wishes to adopt a sediment-control ordinance should contact the commission, which will provide assistance. About fifteen counties and twenty-four cities have established local ordinances and programs. The administrative arm of the commission is the DENR's Land Quality Division.

Developers are required to obtain approval of erosion-control plans if they engage in "land disturbing activities that result in a change of natural cover or topography and contribute to sedimentation" of streams [G.S. 113A-52(6), -54(c), -57]. G.S. 113A-57 establishes statewide standards that set buffer zones for lakes and watercourses; limit grades of graded slopes or fills to the angle that can be retained by vegetative cover, devices, or structures; and require erosion-control practices during construction, as well as permanent ground cover for tracts of land larger than one acre that are uncovered in construction.

The Sedimentation Pollution Control Law covers residential, commercial, and industrial construction activities. It exempts agriculture and applies only to forestry activities that do not comply with DENR-approved best management practices (BMPs) for water quality. It applies to local and state governmental land-disturbing activities, such as construction projects, as well as to private or commercial work. Generally, government activities are regulated directly by the Sedimentation Control Commission; only private and commercial activities can be regulated by a local program.

Agricultural Non-Point-Source Pollution

The exemption of agriculture from the Sedimentation Pollution Control Act left a gap in programs that address stream pollution caused by agricultural runoff. In theory this gap could be filled by the authority of soil and water conservation districts to adopt land use regulations concerning erosion (G.S. 139-9, -10). In practice, however, this authority has never been exercised, probably because of a combination of philosophical reasons and a requirement for referendum approval of any such regulations by a vote of two-thirds of the land occupiers of the district.

A more promising approach to controlling agricultural non-point-source pollution has been developed in recent years: the agricultural cost-share program. It provides 75 percent matching grants to encourage farmers to apply BMPs to control soil erosion and runoff from pesticides and fertilizers. The cost-share program is administered by the state Soil and Water Conservation Commission (S&WCC) under guidelines outlined in G.S. 143-215.74, with periodic review by a committee established by G.S. 142-215.74B that reports to the state legislative leadership. At the local level, soil and water conservation districts work closely with farmers in applying BMPs. The districts are responsible for reviewing and approving these practices for individual farms under the conservation compliance, "sodbuster," and "swampbuster" provisions of the 1985 federal farm bill.[5] As a result of these provisions, farmers who want to keep their commodity price supports must either apply the approved BMPs or stop farming highly erodible lands and drained wetlands. The cost-share program began in a few northeastern and Piedmont Triangle counties in the early 1980s. It was gradually extended to its present statewide coverage.

Another element of agricultural non-point-source pollution control is the so-called .0200 rules of the EMC.[6] These rules regulate a variety of water-borne wastes that do not discharge into surface waters, under *nondischarge permits.* Amendments in 1993 to the .0200 rules addressed, among other things, potential pollution from intensive livestock operations, such as large hog and poultry feedlots. They set forth a cooperative program involving local soil and water conservation districts, the S&WCC, and the EMC. In essence, the .0200 rules and related S&WCC rules contemplate these arrangements:

1. The local districts advise farmers about their need to have nondischarge pollution-control systems, to develop animal waste management plans containing approved BMPs, and to get their waste management plans properly certified. Farmers who meet all these requirements are "deemed permitted" under the .0200 rules. New or expanded systems must have certified waste management plans now, and existing systems must have been certified by December 31, 1997.

2. The S&WCC adopts rules concerning approved BMPs and certification of qualified *technical specialists* to review each farmer's animal waste management plan.[7]

3. The technical specialists are responsible for certifying animal waste management plans containing approved BMPs. (Alternatively, a farmer may comply with United States Natural Resources Conservation Service guidelines. The Natural Resources Conservation Service was formerly known as the Soil Conservation Service.) The specialist's approval may be set aside by a local district, whose decisions may be reviewed by the S&WCC.[8]

4. The EMC and its staff administer the nondischarge permit requirements, which they enforce against farmers who do not have certified animal waste management plans.

Intensive Livestock Operations

The 1995 and 1996 legislatures enacted a state swine-siting law covering swine farms larger than 250 animals, a new permit law for all intensive livestock operations, a mediation requirement as a precondition of farm nuisance suits, and substantial increases in state funding for enforcement of laws and for the agricultural cost-share program. The 1997 legislature strengthened the swine-siting law, imposed a statewide moratorium on new or expanded swine farms, and gave counties a limited authority to zone swine farms. The following rules resulted from the 1995–97 legislation:

1. On swine farms devoted to raising 250 or more swine, the swine houses and lagoons must be set back *at least 1,500 feet* from occupied residences; *at least 2,500 feet* from any school, hospital, church, outdoor recreational facility, national or state park, historic property, or childcare center; and *at least 500 feet* from any property boundary and from any public water supply well or

well supplying water for human consumption. No part of a permitted system can be constructed within a 100-year floodplain
except a land application site. The perimeter of any waste application site must be at least 75 feet from the property boundary,
from occupied residences, and from perennial streams. There
are some additional setbacks and buffers in the .0200 rules.

2. There is a two-year statewide moratorium until March 1, 1999,
    on the installation of new or expanded swine farms larger than
    250 animals and on waste lagoons at such farms. (Nominally the
    moratorium was made retroactive from its enactment on Au-
    gust 27, 1997, to March 1, 1997; the Attorney General's Office
    has advised that permits issued during the period of retroactiv-
    ity were probably valid.) There are a number of exemptions
    from the moratorium for works in progress or under permit,
    innovative systems, and the like, and the act includes a special
    moratorium without exemptions that is probably applicable
    only to Moore County.

3. As of May 1998, six county health boards had adopted local
    health rules that contained their own setbacks and other siting
    provisions for intensive livestock operations (ILOs); one of these
    counties had also readopted its health rules as a county ordi-
    nance; three county health boards had adopted health rules that
    applied public health nuisance concepts to both new and ex-
    isting ILOs; and four boards of county commissioners had
    adopted their own local moratoriums on new and expanded
    ILOs. Although the state law does not expressly preempt local
    rules or ordinances on these subjects, there is at least one
    pending lawsuit against a county that raises the preemption
    issue about the county's local health rules.

4. The long-standing exemption of agricultural operations from
    the county's zoning authority has been loosened to allow coun-
    ties to zone swine farms served by waste management systems
    with a design capacity of 600,000 pounds "steady state live
    weight" or greater. (This reportedly translates into anywhere
    from 423 sows in a "farrow-to-finish" operation to 20,000 ani-
    mals in a "weanling-to-finish" operation.) The county may
    not exclude eligible swine farms from the entire zoning juris-
    diction, prohibit the continued existence of a swine farm in
    existence when the zoning is adopted, require its amortiza-
    tion, or prohibit repair or replacement that does not in-

crease population beyond designed waste capacity. The application of this new legislation is probably limited to new and expanded operations. As of May 1998, two counties had adopted swine farm zoning, and others were considering such zoning.

Stormwater Management

Federal Requirements

A current buzzword in environmental circles is *stormwater management.* For cities this is nothing really new: it is roughly equivalent to municipal storm drainage systems, with some additions and refinements.

The 1987 amendments to the federal Clean Water Act required that large cities (those with more than 250,000 in population) and medium-size cities (those with 100,000–250,000 in population) obtain NPDES permits covering their stormwater discharges.[9] Deadlines were established for these cities to file applications and obtain permits during 1992 and 1993 and to bring the systems into compliance within the following three years.

Charlotte is the only large North Carolina city on the list; Cumberland County (including Fayetteville), Durham, Greensboro, Raleigh, and Winston-Salem are the only medium-size places on the list. As of late 1997, the EPA is considering a proposed rule to extend its stormwater regulations to stormwater systems owned by counties or by incorporated towns of any size. The exact shape and form of this proposal are not yet finalized, but county and city governments should keep in touch with these developments (Proposed 40 CFR §§ 122.30–.38).

If small cities and counties are not yet required to obtain permits for their entire storm drainage systems, they (along with large units) are already covered under another part of the federal program, curiously labeled *industrial activities.* Under this label, the EPA's stormwater regulations cover not only industrial and commercial activities literally but also municipal airports, landfills, and motorpool fleet facilities. As of June 1993, all municipal airports were covered, as were uncontrolled landfills.[10] In cities above 100,000 in population, motorpool facilities, controlled landfills, and wastewater treatment plants were covered. All local governments should watch for future rule changes concerning industrial facilities.

State Law

Prompted by the 1987 federal amendments, the 1989 North Carolina General Assembly enacted legislation broadening both the municipal and the county enterprise statutes to cover stormwater utility systems. G.S. 160A-311 and 153A-274 now define *public enterprises* to include stormwater and drainage systems. This supplements general ordinance-making and nuisance abatement powers, on which cities had sometimes relied to justify municipal drainage activities. It gives cities and counties the complete range of financing powers that go with the enterprise statutes.[11] The 1994 General Assembly authorized water and sewer authorities to adopt stormwater ordinances in G.S. 162A-6(14c). The 1997 General Assembly required the EMC to develop a model stormwater management program as a guide for local governments.

Other Non-Point-Source Pollution Control Measures

Some counties and cities have begun to include provisions in zoning and other land use ordinances aimed at reducing non-point-source pollution. Examples include buffer zones around lakes and streams, structural requirements such as silt basins, and limitations on impervious surfaces in developments. Similar provisions have been adopted in Coastal Resources Commission rules covering the twenty coastal counties under the Coastal Area Management Act.

Water Supply (Watershed) Protection

A number of state government programs combine to provide some protection for surface water supply, or *watershed*, areas. Some of these have already been noted: EMC water pollution permits, administered by the DWQ; the sewage rules administered by health departments; sedimentation pollution control standards; and the agricultural cost-share program for non-point sources of pollution.

The Drinking Water Act (G.S. Ch. 130A, Art. 10), administered by the DENR, authorizes the setting of maximum contaminant levels for physical, chemical, biological, and radiological contaminants that may affect the public health. It also authorizes watershed protection rules and disinfection rules that are graded according to the nature of the particular water *supply* source. In addition, there are statutory emergency powers and response procedures for oil or chemical spills that can be activated by the DWQ or the secretary of the DENR in response to spills and other emergencies that jeopardize public water supplies.

In 1989 the General Assembly enacted the Water Supply Watershed Protection Law, which combines minimum state standards for the protection of surface water supply watersheds with local land use powers. Since 1989 the statute has been amended, and the EMC has adopted the necessary implementing rules and has received and reviewed proposed local ordinances and programs that were required to be presented to it during 1993. The main elements of the resulting watershed protection program are as follows:

1. Streams that may be sources of water supply are placed in one of five classifications, ranging from WS-I for undeveloped watersheds to WS-IV and -V for moderately to highly developed watersheds and their upstream drainage reaches. About 20 percent of the state's land area is located in these watersheds, the majority of it in the Piedmont and mountain areas.

2. Within the WS-II, -III, and -IV classifications there are *general watershed areas* and *critical areas* (where risks associated with pollution are highest) that extend either one-half mile from the normal pool elevation of a reservoir or one-half mile upstream from a water supply intake located directly in a stream. The rules place greater restrictions on activities within critical areas than within general watershed areas.

3. The rules treat WS-I watersheds as pristine areas where no development will be allowed, nor sewer lines, sludge application, landfills, wastewater discharges, or hazardous materials storage, and where BMPs are required for agricultural, forestry, and transportation activities. (Only 0.2 percent of the state's land area lies within WS-I watersheds.) The rules regulate these activities and facilities in varying degrees within WS-II, -III, -IV, and -V watersheds.

   The heart of the rules is the standard for allowable density of development in WS-II, -III, and -IV watersheds. For each of these classifications, local governments may select a low-density option without stormwater controls or a high-density option with stormwater controls. The *most restrictive* low-density option without stormwater controls (for WS-II watershed critical areas) are the 2-acre-minimum lots or 6-percent built-upon areas. The *least restrictive* high-density option with stormwater controls (for WS-IV *protected areas*) is development up to a 74-percent built-upon area that controls runoff from a 1-inch rainstorm. For the WS-V watersheds (the upper drainage reaches of WS-IV watersheds), there are no restrictions other than in-stream water quality standards that apply to all water supply sources.

4. Cities and counties that contain WS-I water *supply* watersheds are essentially bound to maintain these areas in an undeveloped state. Cities and counties containing WS-V watersheds are not bound to restrict development at all in these watersheds.

5. Cities and counties containing WS-II, -III, or -IV watersheds may choose to go with the applicable low-density option or the high-density option with stormwater controls. They may apply the relevant development options either through their zoning, subdivision control, and sediment control ordinances, or through police power ordinances. The EMC has approved a model ordinance as a guide for cities and counties in meeting their requirements for local watershed protection planning under the statute.

The ultimate sanction available to the state if a city or a county fails to adopt a satisfactory program or to enforce it adequately is a civil penalty of up to $10,000 per month. After notice, the EMC may assume responsibility for the program in the affected area and assess the civil penalty to recoup its administrative and enforcement costs.

6. The rules allow expansion of existing single-family residences without any restrictions, and they allowed development to continue in watershed areas until the applicable deadlines for submission of local watershed plans (from July 1, 1993, to January 1, 1994). The rules also protect vested rights under the 1989 vested rights legislation.

7. The state standards set by this legislation require cities and counties to protect water *supply* watersheds located within their boundaries whether these watersheds serve their own residents or the residents of other units. That is, County A may be required to protect watershed areas within the county that serve the residents of City X located in neighboring County B.

8. The General Assembly has begun to chip away at the statutory scheme by exempting the Ivy River, located in Buncombe and Madison counties (1993 N.C. Sess. Laws ch. 5), and by setting a lower classification (WS-IV rather than -III) for the North Toe River, located in Avery and Mitchell counties (1995 N.C. Sess.

Laws ch. 301). It is too soon to tell whether these exceptions will be isolated or will set a pattern for further erosion of the program.

9. The North Carolina Supreme Court upheld the constitutionality of the act against a claim that it lacked adequate standards for the powers that it delegated to the EMC.[12]

Hazardous Wastes and Low-Level Radioactive Wastes

There is a growing body of federal and state legislation that regulates hazardous waste management, another pollution control field in which the federal government sets the basic goals, standards, and procedures, and state governments provide much of the machinery to achieve federal objectives. One of the principal federal statutes is the Resources Conservation and Recovery Act (RCRA).[13] It regulates the generation, transportation, treatment, and storage of hazardous wastes under a so-called cradle-to-grave system, which monitors the wastes from the time they are generated through ultimate disposal, relying on a manifest that follows the materials and is filed with regulatory agencies. The 1984 amendments to the RCRA contain special regulations concerning underground storage tanks.

Another major federal statute is the Comprehensive Environmental Response Compensation and Liability Act (CERCLA, or *Superfund*).[14] It establishes two funds to help finance removal and disposal of hazardous substances released to the environment, especially substances disposed of to the ground through dumps or otherwise. It also makes those responsible for these releases strictly liable for all costs of removal or remedial action and for damages to natural resources.

North Carolina has statutes that parallel the RCRA and the CERCLA (G.S. 130A-294 through -309, and 130A-310 through -310.23). Other legislation has made the state a party to the Southeast Interstate Low-Level Radioactive Waste Compact and has established state boards to seek sites for disposal of hazardous wastes and low-level radioactive wastes. These boards also have general responsibility for state hazardous waste management policy. As of late 1997 the only remaining active boards were the Low-Level Radioactive Waste Management Authority and the Pollution Prevention Advisory Council, and lack of continuing funding threatens to end the work of the Low-Level Authority (G.S. Chs. 104F, 104G; G.S. 143B-285.23, note).

One unintended result of hazardous waste programs such as the Superfund has been to deter the reuse of many properties that are stigmatized because of known or suspected contamination, properties sometimes known as *brownfields*. National and state policy is now encouraging a new look at this subject, with a view to encouraging productive reuse of some brownfields properties. North Carolina has joined the ranks of states that are participating in this reappraisal, by enactment of two brownfields statutes in 1997. G.S. 130A-310.30 promotes the reuse of brownfields by developers under procedures overseen by the DENR. The basic idea is that the state gives property owners protection from liability in exchange for the owners' agreement to take some measures to make the property safe. G.S. 130A-310.3 and 143-215.84 establish procedures by which an owner who does not want contaminated property to be used may place enforceable restrictions on current and future use of the property. The county may be interested in the policy implications of these new laws, and the registers of deeds must be familiar with the recording requirements spelled out in G.S. 130A-310.8 and G.S. 143-215.85A.

Federal legislation goes beyond the regulation of hazardous wastes to the regulation of useful but toxic chemicals that have not reached the waste stream. The lead federal statute on this subject is the Toxic Substances Control Act (TSCA),[15] which establishes a system for regulatory review and clearance of new chemicals that are proposed to be placed on the market, and review of existing chemicals, as well as special regulations concerning PCBs (polychlorinated biphenyls). In addition, the 1986 amendments to the CERCLA (which are designated by the acronym SARA) contain complex chemical right-to-know and emergency planning provisions. This subject was already addressed by state legislation in some states, including North Carolina (G.S. Ch. 95, Art. 18).

Some cities and counties have adopted ordinances that add local controls on hazardous wastes to the complex set of federal and state laws. These ordinances range from those that merely supplement state inspections and monitoring, to those that regulate small waste-producing sites below the minimum size for state regulation, to those that establish comprehensive procedures for reviewing proposed sites for hazardous waste or low-level radioactive waste treatment and disposal. At least one county has adopted an underground storage tank ordinance.

Any county that is considering a local ordinance on these subjects should closely examine the underlying statutory authority, the possibility of state or federal preemption of the field in question, and the constitutionality of the proposed ordinance. Unless the ordinance takes the form of zoning, the only source of local authority may be the general ordinance-making power (G.S. 153A-121). It may or may not be a legally adequate basis for this kind of local regulation. The general tests for preemption of local ordinances by state or federal laws are set forth in G.S. 160A-174, but several of the state regulatory statutes concerning hazardous waste management contain specific preemption or override provisions of their own that should be considered (see, e.g., G.S. 130A-293).

Solid Waste Regulation

The subject of solid waste management is addressed in detail by Chapter 19. A brief summary of the subject follows here for general information.

Federal Law

The RCRA regulates hazardous wastes from cradle to grave, as already noted. It also regulates management of nonhazardous solid waste in some important ways. The RCRA itself prohibits the establishment of new open dumps, requires that existing open dumps be closed, and requires that all solid waste be disposed of in sanitary landfills, be used for resource recovery, or otherwise be disposed of in an environmentally sound manner.

The EPA's landfill rules under the RCRA go beyond these statutory provisions by requiring monitoring, leachate collection, effective liners, financial responsibility, and closure and postclosure care. They require states to exclude household hazardous wastes from landfills. EPA rules also contain restrictions, such as a ban on receiving sewage sludge in landfills. Collectively these restrictions and requirements are estimated to cost $10 or more per household annually.

State Law

In 1989 the General Assembly began to enact legislation that comprehensively regulates solid waste management by local governments. (The 1989 act is often identified by its original bill number, Senate Bill 111.) County governments are primarily responsible for the disposal of solid wastes, but cities are also involved, some more than others. Most cities are responsible for day-to-day collection. Counties are responsible for planning to meet the state goal of 40 percent reduction of the solid waste stream by June 30, 2001. Counties can (and some do) license or franchise private haulers of solid waste. See Chapter 19 for the details.

Counties can adopt solid waste management ordinances, and the ordinance is an essential part of the county's management program. A model ordinance is available from the Institute of Government or from the DENR.

Groundwater Quality

There is growing concern about protection of groundwater quality, especially in states like North Carolina where many people depend on wells for drinking water. This concern is also reflected nationally. Congress recently enacted legislation concerning underground storage tanks, and in 1986 it amended the federal Safe Drinking Water Act[16] to mandate new federal-state programs for the protection of public water supply well fields and well heads.

In North Carolina there is no comprehensive state law on groundwater quality, only a number of separate laws on the subject that neither collectively nor individually cover most significant groundwater pollution problems. The most nearly comprehensive approach is the North Carolina groundwater classification system administered by the DENR, which adapts the concepts of an earlier surface water classification system to groundwater conditions and serves as a checkpoint for other decisions (such as landfill siting) that may affect groundwater quality. In addition, wells are to some extent regulated by the Well Construction Standards Act (G.S. 87-83 through -96), by some county well ordinances or health board rules, and by the Capacity Use Areas Law (G.S. 143-215.11 through -215.22). The 1997 General Assembly enacted a statute that requires individuals in the business of constructing, installing, repairing, altering, or abandoning wells to be certified by a new Water Well Contracting Certification Commission, a unit of the DENR (G.S. 87-98.1). In some specific situations, groundwater quality may also be protected by state solid and hazardous waste regulations (including underground storage tank regulations), septic tank regulations, or radiation protection regulations, or the federal or state oil and hazardous substances spill-control acts.[17] Some of these topics are covered elsewhere in this chapter.[18]

Pesticides

Federal laws and programs set general standards for pesticide control, which must be met by state laws and programs if a state is to retain control over its permit system for the use of pesticides. In 1971, North Carolina enacted a comprehensive law that clearly meets minimum federal standards (G.S. Ch. 143, Art. 52). Principal elements of the state's program are regulation of the sale and the use of restricted-use pesticides, licensing of dealers who sell restricted-use pesticides, licensing of commercial pesticide applicators and consultants, and registration of pesticides. The North Carolina Pesticide Board is the policy-making agency for the state program, and the commissioner of agriculture has administrative responsibility. The EPA is responsible for the federal program.

Local governments are subject to the licensing requirements and regulations of the North Carolina Pesticide Board. Local and state government agencies that use or apply pesticides, as well as commercial operators, must obtain licenses unless they are specifically exempted by law.

Chapter 445 of the 1995 Session Laws preempts local ordinances regulating the sale, use, or application of pesticides. (The United States Supreme Court had previously held that the federal pesticide law did not preempt local spraying ordinances.[19] The 1995 state law, however, makes it clear that North Carolina local governments do not have the authority under state law to regulate pesticide sale, use, or application.)

Floodway and Floodplain Management

The *floodway* of a stream is essentially the channel, banks, and adjoining areas that carry normal stream flow and moderate flooding. The floodway is defined by G.S. 143-215.52(b) as "that portion of the channel and floodplain of a stream designated to provide passage for the 100-year flood, without increasing the elevation of that flood by more than one foot." The *floodplain* is the broader area receiving and carrying large floods that overflow the banks of a stream and spread out extensively into surrounding areas. It is widely believed that construction and related activities within floodplains, and especially within floodways, should be limited to protect life, property, and the environment.

The state's counties and cities have long had the legal authority under their general zoning powers to adopt floodplain zoning ordinances (for counties, G.S. Ch. 153A, Art. 18, Pt. 3). Special zones or districts may be established to regulate land use in floodplains, or floodplain management provisions may be added to existing zones. A number of local governments have used the zoning approach to regulate floodplain land uses.

State legislation passed in 1971 specifies in detail the procedure for adopting and administering controls over the use of floodways, as opposed to floodplains (G.S. 143-215.51 through -215.61). Counties and cities may adopt floodway ordinances under this legislation whether or not they have zoning ordinances, or they may adopt floodway ordinances that supplement floodplain zoning. Once a floodway has been officially delineated, construction is prohibited there without a permit from the appropriate county or city government, except for certain uses of the land that may be made as a matter of right; these include farming, parking areas, recreational areas, streets, utility and railroad facilities, dams, docks, ramps, and temporary accommodations such as those for circuses. Counties and cities must adopt ordinances providing for floodway permits in order to allow any construction within an officially delineated floodway other than construction for the exempted uses.

The EMC may trigger local adoption of a floodway permit system by delineating a floodway if a local government does not do so. Except for this authority, however, the state government's role in floodplain and floodway management is generally limited to providing technical assistance to local governments.

The North Carolina Supreme Court upheld Asheville's flood hazard district ordinance in 1983.[20] The court found that it was a valid exercise of the police power and that there was no regulatory taking of affected commercial properties because the plaintiffs were left with adequate "practical uses" of their land. The Asheville ordinance was a free-standing regulation; it was not part of another ordinance. It established floodway and flood-fringe areas, and it set standards for some construction and prohibited other new or improved construction in these areas.

Any floodway or floodplain ordinance that is adopted by a county or a city should take into consideration the Federal Flood Insurance Program, administered by the Federal Insurance Administration (a branch of the Department of Housing and Urban Development—HUD).[21] Under this program, federal mortgage guarantees and other housing assistance programs are not available to communities with flood hazards unless they have adopted approved floodway or floodplain controls. Information on this subject can be obtained from the EMC or from HUD.

Environmental Impact Statements

The North Carolina Environmental Policy Act of 1971, G.S. Chapter 113A, Article 1, requires that state agencies file an EIS (environmental impact statement) in connection with all "actions involving expenditure of public moneys or use of public lands for projects and programs significantly affecting the quality of the environment." (A similar requirement applies to federal projects and programs under federal law.) As defined in G.S. 113A-9(9), a "state agency" does not include local governments except when their programs, projects, and actions are subject by law to review, approval, or licensing by a state agency.

A provision in the North Carolina statutes, G.S. 113A-108, authorizes counties and cities by ordinance to require EISs in connection with "major development projects" (those larger than 2 acres) of private developers and special-purpose governments. The authorization could cover such projects as shopping centers, residential subdivisions, and industrial or commercial developments. A few counties and cities have made use of this authority. A 1986 revision of the state guidelines under the Environmental Policy Act stimulated further local interest; it provides that "state [permitting] agencies shall consider any information generated by" local governments under the act.[22] A 1991 amendment codified this provision at G.S. 113A-4(2a). Note that G.S. 113A-8 allows a local EIS to be required of a private developer, whereas G.S. 113A-4 only provides for an EIS to be required of a state agency.

G.S. 113A-8 places certain restrictions on local EIS processes:

1. They must be adopted by ordinance.
2. They may not be designed to apply only to one particular project, and they must be applied consistently.
3. They must exempt projects for which a state or federal EIS or functionally equivalent permit is required.
4. The ordinance must establish minimum criteria to determine whether an EIS is required and may not require an EIS for a project that does not exceed the minimum criteria. (The state guidelines in 25 NCAC 25.0801 *et seq.* set forth examples of minimum criteria.)

The Institute of Government has examples of local EIS ordinances.

A good starting point for a county considering the adoption of a local EIS ordinance would be to limit the ordinance to projects that require (1) any listed state environmental permit, such as a mining permit or a water quality NPDES permit, or (2) any listed local land use permit, such as a subdivision approval or zoning conditional use permit. (The county should compile its own list of these state and local permits, subject to the exemptions noted in the previous paragraph.) These limitations would keep the ordinance focused on specific "actions" within the purview of G.S. 113A-4(2).

In a case involving Cane Creek Reservoir in Orange County, the North Carolina Court of Appeals held that the state Environmental Policy Act also required preparation of an EIS for certain local government projects—in particular, for a local water supply reservoir that needed a state permit.[23] The logic of this decision probably extends to, and requires that impact statements be prepared for, other state-licensed local government projects. (After the Cane Creek decision the legislature specifically exempted sanitary landfills operated by local governments from the act, as well as the siting of a superconducting supercollider and the siting of certain prison units and law enforcement training facilities. It also exempted applications for hazardous waste facility permits "to the extent that the review thereof provides the functional equivalent" of an EIS.)[24] The Cane Creek case also illustrates the fact that partially overlapping federal, state, and local EISs may be required for some projects. In that case, separate but similar federal and state impact statements were necessary.

Environmental impact analysis provides an opportunity for a thorough (and sometimes very lengthy) ventilation of the possible environmental consequences of major developments. A county that wants to act to take advantage of this opportunity can either adopt a separate environmental impact ordinance under G.S. 113A-108 or insert similar provisions into its local zoning ordinance or subdivision control ordinance. Which approach is preferable will depend on the county's objectives.

Soil and Water Conservation, Small Watersheds, and Drainage Districts

North Carolina has a soil and water conservation district in each county (except for one multicounty district covering five counties in the Albemarle Sound region). Each district is governed locally by a board of supervisors that is partly elected by the voters of the district and partly appointed by the State Soil and Water Conservation Commission. A majority of the local board is elected. District activities include the following:

1. The basic soil erosion control and land treatment programs that date from the dust bowl era.
2. The agricultural cost-share program for non-point-source water pollution control, and related animal waste control responsibilities, described in the section "Agricultural Non-Point-Source Pollution," earlier in this chapter.
3. Assistance to farmers in preparing farm plans required by the 1985 and 1990 federal farm bills to retain crop price supports.
4. Educational programs for adults and schoolchildren.
5. The small watershed (or watershed improvement) program, which assists farmers and other local residents with flooding, farmland drainage, and related water conservation problems. Individual small watershed projects are usually carried out either by counties acting under G.S. 139-41 or by drainage districts acting under G.S. Chapter 156, Subchapter III. Federal and state aid may be available for small watershed projects.[25]

A typical piedmont or mountain small watershed project in North Carolina may involve one or more small impondments that provide for water storage to prevent flooding, a sedimentation pool, and downstream channel clearance. It may also include limited storage for water-supply and recreational use, as well as areas for conservation of fish and wildlife habitat. Eastern Carolina projects usually emphasize drainage improvements rather than flood prevention.

Cities or counties sometimes serve as cosponsors of small watershed or drainage projects. Cities and counties are *authorized* to assist small watershed programs in any or all of the following ways:

1. By levying property taxes to undertake watershed improvement projects, pursuant to G.S. 160A-209(c) (34) and 153A-149 (35)
2. By participating in small watershed projects and contributing funds to projects that provide (or protect) city or county water supply sources, flood damage protection, or drainage benefits to the city or the county, pursuant to G.S. 139-37
3. By issuing bonds to finance water supply storage in small watershed projects, pursuant to G.S. 139-37.1
4. By installing and maintaining recreation facilities or fish and wildlife habitat features in small watershed projects, pursuant to G.S. 139-46.28
5. By levying (county) special assessments under G.S. Chapter 153A, Article 9, and by borrowing funds with voter approval under G.S. 159-48, the Local Government Bond Act

The federal government aids small watershed projects under Public Law 83-566 by paying all costs of construction for flood prevention, contributing to costs for recreational features and fish and wildlife enhancement, providing planning services, and making loans to help pay for water-supply features of projects. Local sponsors must initiate and maintain the projects, obtain easements, and secure agreements with landowners to carry out needed soil conservation measures. In North Carolina, the legislature has usually appropriated funds annually in recent years to help plan, organize, and coordinate small watershed work, as well as varying amounts to help pay capital costs of watershed projects. The legislature has also appropriated matching funds annually for soil and water conservation district programs and travel and subsistence for soil and water conservation supervisors.

Drainage Districts

While drainage districts can and do serve as sponsors of federally aided small watershed projects, programs of farm drainage and land reclamation in North Carolina, especially in the coastal plain region, long antedate Public Law 83-566.

Under G.S. Chapter 156, Subchapter III, drainage districts may be organized with the approval of the clerk of superior court following an engineering survey by a board of viewers. The procedures to be followed by the clerk—beginning with the filing of a landowner petition to create a district and ending with the clerk's adjudication on the final report of the board of viewers and appointment or election of a board of drainage commissioners—are spelled out in G.S. 156-54 through -78. (The appointment authority for multicounty districts was held invalid by a supreme court decision in 1990, but this defect was remedied by the General Assembly.)[26]

No county participation is required in organizing or operating drainage districts, except that district assessments are collected by the county tax collector. The procedures to be followed in levying and collecting these assessments are set out in detail in G.S. Chapter 156, Article 8.

County Involvement in Soil and Water Conservation District Programs

Counties are not involved in creating or operating soil and water conservation districts. However, G.S. 153A-440 authorizes them to cooperate with and support soil and water conservation work and to appropriate for this purpose revenues not limited as to specific use by law. Acting under this authority, a number of counties have assisted the districts in such ways as funding or supporting particular projects or activities, furnishing office space, and helping to pay staff salaries.

In recent years local staffs serving the districts have grown to meet expanding program needs. In some counties these personnel are treated as county employees, and the districts function essentially as divisions of county government under the guidance of their independent boards of supervisors. In other counties some or all of those personnel are clearly district employees rather than county employees, and there are shades of gray between these extremes. A variety of hiring, firing, and supervision arrangements have evolved from county to county. The situation is further complicated by the status of *district conservationists*, who are employees of the United States Natural Resources Conservation Service, often functioning as supervisors of the local staff in some respects.

The State Division of Soil and Water Conservation and the State Soil and Water Conservation Commission (both units of the DENR) are coordinating efforts to clarify and standardize these staffing and supervisory arrangements. They are also working to resolve some important incidental issues, such as whether counties have the legal authority to represent some or all local soil and water conservation staff and board members in civil litigation and to pay any civil judgments against such persons. (So far, these issues have been largely academic, but the growth of program responsibilities makes it likely they will not remain so indefinitely.)

The Environment and Land Use

Coastal Area Management

The 1974 General Assembly enacted a Coastal Area Management Act (CAMA) (G.S. Ch. 113A, Art. 7). Its basic objective is to establish a comprehensive plan for protection, preservation, orderly development, and management of the coastal area of North Carolina. Twenty counties are covered by the CAMA: Beaufort, Bertie, Brunswick, Camden, Carteret, Chowan, Craven, Currituck, Dare, Gates, Hertford, Hyde, New Hanover, Onslow, Pamlico, Pasquotank, Pender, Perquimans, Tyrrell, and Washington.

The three main features of the act provide as follows:

1. That each of the twenty coastal area counties be covered by a land use plan, preferably prepared by local government and in basic harmony with the plans adopted for the other nineteen coastal area counties. (All the counties have plans.)
2. That all critical areas that need to be considered for protection and possible preservation in each county be designated as *areas of environmental concern.*
3. That any proposed development, change, or other use of land within a designated area of environmental concern be subject to review by means of a development permit procedure. Generally, counties and cities handle permits for minor developments (in most cases those under 20 acres), and the state Coastal Resources Commission handles permits for major developments.

The thrust of this act is to establish a cooperative state-local program of coastal land management. It is the responsibility of counties and cities to establish local land use plans and to issue permits for minor development in areas of environmental concern. It is the state government's responsibility to adopt guidelines and standards for the local land use plans; to establish areas of environmental concern; to issue permits for major developments in areas of environmental concern; and to assume the responsibilities of the local governments if and when they do not exercise their powers under the act. Enforcement is a concurrent state-local responsibility. Amendments to the CAMA in the 1980s added two land acquisition elements, the coastal reserve and beach access programs (G.S. Ch. 113A, Art. 7, Pts. 5, 6).

Directly participating in the CAMA program at the state level are the Coastal Resources Commission, the Coastal Resources Advisory Council, and the secretary of the DENR. The local agencies most involved are the counties, the cities, and the multicounty planning agencies in the twenty coastal area counties.

Coastal cities and counties play an important role in the coastal area management program. Each coastal area city nominates one person to the Coastal Resources Commission, and each county nominates four. Eight representatives of coastal cities and one representative of each coastal county serve on the Coastal Resources Advisory Council. If they wish, coastal area cities and counties may play a role in the planning process, in enforcement, and in beach access programs.

Mountain Ridge Protection

In 1983 the General Assembly enacted a Mountain Ridge Protection Act (G.S. Ch. 113A, Art. 14), which regulates construction of tall buildings along the tops of high mountain ridges. The legislature gave local governments in mountain counties the option of either regulating ridgetop construction through permit systems or allowing the act's prohibitions on this type of construction to go into effect. About two-thirds of the affected counties accepted the state prohibitions. Only one city, Beech Mountain, adopted a city ordinance; one other, Banner Elk, asked its county (Watauga) to enforce the county ordinance inside the city. (The act also allowed mountain counties and cities the opportunity to reject its coverage, but none chose to do so by the statutory deadline.) State government's role under this act is limited to providing technical assistance in identifying and mapping protected mountain ridges.

Consent of Counties to Land Acquisition

G.S. 153A-15, which as of December 1997 applies to seventy-two counties, requires the consent of the board of county commissioners before land in the county may be condemned or voluntarily acquired by a unit of local government outside the county. The motive behind the original legislation (enacted in 1981) was to give a small group of southeastern counties control over the acquisition of landfill sites by a large neighboring county. The number of covered counties has been gradually increased from the handful of original counties to the current seventy-two. Motives for the post-1981 amendments have addressed other resource acquisitions, such as water supply sites; but the literal scope of the statute is not limited by any of these motives. See Chapter 15 of this volume for more information.

The "Contract with America"

The "Contract with America" that was presented to the 103rd Congress in 1994 sought major changes in the philosophy and the process of environmental regulation at both the federal and the state level. At this writing, more has been said than done so far in the Congress and the state legislatures on key elements of the contract, such as imposing risk-based or benefit-cost tests on environmental rules, expediting permit issuance, reducing unfunded mandates, and giving landowners additional protection against regulatory takings.

The 1995 North Carolina General Assembly took several steps toward meeting the objectives of the contract:

1. It required *risk-based analysis* in one program area, the cleanup of discharge from leaking underground storage tanks, to determine whether a discharge from a tank poses risks to human health or the environment that are greater than acceptable levels of risk established by the EMC. The objective is to avoid unproductive cleanup efforts that have threatened the stability of the underground storage tank cleanup fund (1995 N.C. Sess. Laws ch. 377). [A cost-benefit analysis had previously been required under G.S. 143-215(c) and -215.107(f) for new water and air pollution control rules that were more stringent than federal rules.] A similar risk-based analysis was also required in 1997 legislation concerning cleanup of contamination from dry cleaning solvents (G.S. 143-215.104A).

2. It required *expedited review* of air pollution permit applications prepared by engineers (1995 N.C. Sess. Laws ch. 484).

3. It addressed the *unfunded mandates* issue by imposing a comprehensive set of obligations on the governor's office and state agencies to flag and publicize new federal and state mandates and to minimize their impact on local governments (1995 N.C. Sess. Laws ch. 415). [This reinforced the existing requirements in G.S. 150B-21.4(b) for fiscal notes on proposed state rules that affect local government.]

To date, Congress has enacted only an unfunded mandate act that relies on the rules of each house to require "full consideration" of unfunded mandate proposals.[27] The act makes it not in order for either house to consider a bill or a committee report proposing an unfunded mandate without an attached Congressional Budget Office statement on the cost of the mandate, or to consider increasing federal mandates to state, local, or tribal government of more than $50 million annually without full federal funding. Congress also adopted a rider allowing logging in ancient forests and put temporary restrictions on new Superfund sites and endangered species listings.

Cooperative Extension Service

The North Carolina Cooperative Extension Service is headquartered at North Carolina State University, in partnership with North Carolina A&T State University. The Extension Service helps people put research-based knowledge to work to improve their lives, primarily through improved agricultural production. It originated with the Morrill Acts of 1862 and 1890, which established the land grant college system.

Extension focuses on five program areas: sustaining agriculture and forestry; protecting the environment; maintaining viable communities; developing families; and developing youth. Its local constituent units are familiar household words: county extension agents (or chairs), 4H Clubs, Extension Homemakers, and Master Gardeners. Allied with the agricultural experiment stations, the Cooperative Extension Service has helped farmers improve productivity of the traditional row crops (tobacco, corn, and soybeans) and helped them diversify to livestock and poultry, vegetables, Christmas trees, wood processing, and turfgrass. The service has also been a leader in promoting programs like integrated pest management, reduced tillage, and controlled drainage.

There is a county extension agent and center in each of North Carolina's 100 counties and on the Cherokee Reservation. The agent serves as the bridge from the universities to the county government and to county citizens. Extension researchers at North Carolina State and North Carolina A&T State universities furnish technical training and support to the county agents. Thousands of lay advisers keep extension professionals and researchers informed of local concerns and help set extension priorities.

A memorandum of understanding (MOU) between the Cooperative Extension Service and each board of county commissioners sets the terms under which extension personnel function in the county. Under a standard MOU the county and the Extension Service would jointly determine the share of the salaries of extension personnel to be paid by each. The county commissioners would appoint and determine salaries of local extension personnel on recommendation of the Extension Service; would provide offices, equipment, supplies, and utilities for the county extension center; and would provide the county's share of salaries for extension personnel. The Extension Service would submit an annual budget request to the county commissioners and provide available funds for travel and to purchase publications.

Additional Resources

Environmental Law Reporter. Environmental Law Institute, Washington, D.C. Monthly news and analysis and other materials on cases, statutes, etc.

Findley, Roger, and Daniel Farber. *Environmental Law in a Nutshell.* St. Paul, Minn.: West Publishing Co., 1988.

Mandelker, Dan. *NEPA Law and Litigation.* Deerfield, Ill.: Callaghan Press, 1985, with supplements.

Rodgers, William H., Jr. *Environmental Law.* St. Paul, Minn.: West Publishing Co., 1992. 4 vols. with supplements.

Selected Environmental Law Statutes. St. Paul, Minn.: West Publishing Co., 1997–98 edition.

Notes

1. The federal Clean Air Act is codified at 42 U.S.C. §§ 7401–7671q (1983 & Supp. 1995).

2. 29 U.S.C. §§ 651–673 (1985 & Supp. 1995).

3. The primary federal legislation for water pollution control is the Water Pollution Control Act, codified at 33 U.S.C. §§ 1251–1387 (1986 & Pocket Pt. 1995).

4. 33 U.S.C. § 1329 (Pocket Pt. 1995).

5. Food Security Act of 1985, 16 U.S.C. §§ 3811–3836 (1985 & Pocket Pt. 1995).

6. 15A NCAC 02H.0200 (Feb.1, 1976–Feb. 1, 1994).

7. 15A NCAC 06F.0001 through .0005 (effective March 1, 1994).

8. 15A NCAC 06F.0003 (effective March 1, 1994).

9. 33 U.S.C. § 1342(p) (1986 & Pocket Pt. 1995).

10. *Uncontrolled* landfills are those that do not meet the runoff requirements of the Resources Conservation and Recovery Act, Subtitle D, 42 U.S.C. §§ 6941–6949a (1983 & Supp. 1995).

11. For further details on stormwater, see J. Mark Payne, "Stormwater Management: Municipalities' New Requirements under the Clean Water Act," *Popular Government* 58 (Summer 1992): 29–33. Also, contact the League of Municipalities or the Association of County Commissioners, both of which have counseled local governments extensively about stormwater.

12. Town of Spruce Pine v. Avery County, 346 N.C. 787, 488 S.E.2d 144 (1997).

13. 42 U.S.C. §§ 6901–6992k (1983 & Supp. 1995).

14. 42 U.S.C. §§ 9601–9675 (1983 & Supp. 1995).

15. 15 U.S.C. §§ 2601–2629 (1982 & Supp. 1995).

16. 42 U.S.C. §§ 300f through 300j-26 (1991 & Pocket Pt. 1995).

17. The federal and state oil and hazardous substances spill-control acts are codified at 33 U.S.C. § 1321 (1986 & Pocket Pt. 1995) and G.S. 143-215.75 through -215.104, respectively.

18. *See also* Milton S. Heath, Jr., "Ground Water Quality Law in North Carolina," *Popular Government* 52 (Winter 1987): 39–49. This article addresses the subject of groundwater quality law in greater detail. Because of the rapidly changing nature of

the groundwater protection field, counties that have concerns about groundwater quality may wish to consult with federal, state, or private experts before addressing those concerns.

19. Wisconsin Public Intervenor v. Mortier, 501 U.S. 597, 111 S. Ct. 2476, 115 L. Ed. 2d 532 (1991).

20. Responsible Citizens in Opposition to the Floodplain Ordinance v. City of Asheville, 308 N.C. 255, 302 S.E.2d 204 (1983).

21. The statutes governing the Federal Flood Insurance Program are codified at 42 U.S.C. §§ 4001–4129 (1994).

22. 15A NCAC 25.0802 (amended effective May 3, 1993).

23. *In re* Environmental Management Comm'n, 53 N.C. App. 135, 280 S.E.2d 520 (1981).

24. *See* G.S. 113A-1, note; 1987 N.C. Sess. Laws ch. 3, §§ 4, 5; G.S. 130B-9.

25. The federal statutes pertaining to small watershed programs are codified at 16 U.S.C. §§ 1001–1009 (1985 & Pocket Pt. 1995). In addition to this NRCS–assisted program, a comparable activity known as the "tributary areas development program" is sponsored by the Tennessee Valley Authority in the Tennessee Valley section of western North Carolina. Localized flood control and navigation improvement projects are also sponsored by the U.S. Army Corps of Engineers with county or municipal cooperation, sometimes assisted by state cost-sharing.

26. Northampton County Drainage District Number One v. Bailey, 326 N.C. 742, 392 S.E.2d 352 (1990). G.S. 156-81 (1996 Cum. Supp.).

27. Pub. L. No. 104-4., 109 Stat. 48 (1995).

24 Social Services

Janet Mason

Contents

Janet Mason is an Institute of Government faculty member who works in the areas of social services law and juvenile law.

The author expresses her appreciation to Mason Thomas, a former Institute of Government faculty member, and to John Saxon, a current faculty member, whose work is reflected in this chapter on county social services.

"Social services" refers to a complicated system of programs that can be divided into three main categories: public assistance, services, and child support enforcement. The first of these provides money payments for eligible low-income people. The second assists citizens, including many who are at risk of abuse or neglect, in a variety of ways and often without regard to income. Employment-related services overlap these two categories, as participation in employment programs is often a condition for receiving public assistance. The third category, child support enforcement, assists all citizens who apply for help in establishing and enforcing child support obligations; it also recoups some public assistance costs and collects child support payments that enable some families to end or avoid dependence on public assistance.

In most states, the state, rather than local government, administers social services programs. By contrast, in North Carolina most social services programs are administered by counties under the state's supervision. North Carolina's county-administered, state-supervised social services system reflects the state's long history of local (county) responsibility for public social services, the strength of county government in the state, and the role of North Carolina's counties as the primary vehicle for the delivery of basic services to citizens. The county's role in relation to social services is the subject of more misunderstanding and criticism than most other functions of local government. Many people view social services programs as being too costly; many are unaware of what the programs actually involve and accomplish. In addition, the complexity of the social services system and of individual programs contributes to public misunderstanding.

The major social services programs are based in federal law, are funded in part by the federal government, and involve complicated relationships among the federal, state, and county governments. In addition, each branch of the state and federal governments—legislative, executive, and judicial—plays an important part. Of course, the social services system is also affected by shifts in the availability of private and charitable resources, economic conditions, and the prevailing political climate.

This chapter will describe the roles of the federal, state, and county governments in relation to social services, with an emphasis on the specific responsibilities of county officials. It will also briefly describe the major programs and the financing of social services.

Historical Background

Historically, public social services were known as public welfare, and, earlier still, as public charity or poor relief.[1] Early poor relief in North Carolina had its roots in the English Poor Laws. North Carolina's colonial Assembly passed laws to authorize the vestrymen of each parish to levy a poll tax for the support and relief of the poor. The colonial response to dependent children often involved apprenticeship—placing poor or neglected children with families to work or learn a trade without pay.

The North Carolina Constitution of 1776 made no provision for care of the poor. Nonetheless, the duties and powers of the vestry were assumed by elected overseers of the poor in each county. Eventually county courts were authorized to appoint wardens of the poor. The state legislature passed numerous local acts, and statewide laws in 1793 and 1831, that authorized counties to build almshouses or poorhouses for the housing and employment of the poor. The use of public tax funds to care for the poor became accepted as a function of county government.

The present social services system began to take shape after the Civil War. In 1868 the General Assembly made it the duty of county commissioners to provide for the poor and authorized counties to employ an overseer of the poor. The precise means of providing poor relief, however, were left to local discretion. The North Carolina Constitution of 1868 established, for the first time, a role for the state government with respect to social services:

> Beneficent provision for the poor, the unfortunate and orphan[s] being one of the first duties of a civilized and a christian state, the General Assembly shall, at its first session, appoint and define the duties of a Board of Public Charities, to whom shall be entrusted the supervision of all charitable and penal State institutions, and who shall annually report to the Governor upon their condition, with suggestions for their improvement.[2]

The first substantial state action in the welfare field tended to complement rather than impinge on local welfare activity. The state established residential schools for young people who were deaf or blind, a hospital for the insane, and other state institutions. At the same time, orphanages for dependent children were being developed through private and religious groups, with some state support. These institutions relieved the counties of some, though by no means all, of the responsibility for the care and support of these groups.

Many features of today's social services system were created by North Carolina's first statewide public welfare law, enacted in 1917 and supplemented in 1919, which marked the beginning of an organized system of state supervision and local administration of social services. The law provided for a State Board of Charities and Public Welfare and a state Commissioner of Public Welfare. It also provided for three-member local boards of charity and public welfare and for County Superintendents of Public Welfare.

In 1923 the state enacted a Mother's Aid law to provide financial assistance to indigent mothers with children under the age of fourteen. The program, which was state supervised and county administered, was optional to counties. The cost of the program was divided equally between the state and the counties that chose to participate. In the 1930s North Carolina was becoming a leader in the national trend toward centralized, or state, financial responsibility for governmental services. The state's role in social services increased, but much more modestly than it did in relation to schools, roads, corrections, and other areas. Both the funding and administration of social services remained primarily county responsibilities.

During and following the Great Depression, public welfare activities by state and local governments expanded. The federal government, which had previously resisted involvement in most public welfare efforts, seriously tackled unemployment and its effects. The Social Security Act of 1935 became, and remains, the "cornerstone of the American welfare state."[3] It marked the beginning of a drastic redefinition of the role of government at every level in the social services field. The Social Security Act included public assistance or "relief" programs for low-income people in specified categories, including children in single-parent families. Funding for these programs came from the federal and state governments, and federal funding was conditioned on states' complying with federal standards. Needy persons who did not qualify for these categorical programs continued to be dependent on completely county-funded programs.

In 1937 the Social Security Act triggered the enactment of state leg-islation to qualify North Carolina for federal funds, and led to a shift in responsibility from the local to the state level. The federal act required that state public assistance plans be in effect in all political subdivisions of the state, and that a single state agency administer or supervise the administration of the state plan. As a result, state legislation made partici-pation by counties mandatory. The burden of providing matching funds to attract federal dollars fell largely on the counties.

The development of the social services system in North Carolina since 1937 has largely reflected initiatives and funding criteria at the fed-eral level. From World War II through the 1960s the social services sys-tem grew tremendously at the federal, state, and local levels. The late 1970s and the 1980s, however, witnessed a period of decreased federal funding for social programs and of substantial talk about welfare reform. The 1988 federal Family Support Act, although labeled a welfare reform measure, failed to make fundamental changes in the welfare system. Not until 1996 did Congress truly revamp some aspects of the public welfare system.

The General Assembly rewrote the laws structuring North Carolina's welfare program in 1969. The state board's name was changed from the State Board of Public Welfare to the State Board of Social Services, reflect-ing both a change in philosophy and the fact that the program's scope was much broader than just financial aid. The General Assembly rewrote the social services laws again in 1981 and, in response to federal welfare reform, amended them substantially in 1997.

The Federal Role: Congress and Federal Agencies

The legal basis for most federally supported social services programs is the Social Security Act of 1935, as amended (codified in various parts of Title 42 of the United States Code). Federal law does not require any state to operate particular programs. Rather, Congress enacts laws that establish a variety of programs and appropriates funds that are available to states that agree to operate them in accordance with applicable fed-eral laws and regulations. The level of federal financial participation varies from program to program. For state fiscal year 1998–99, the state estimated that for programs involving federal and/or state financial par-ticipation (that is, excluding those funded only by counties), federal funds would provide about 66 percent of public assistance payments (those paid to or for clients), about 59 percent of associated administrative costs (staff, overhead, and other expenses), as well as about 46 percent of the costs of service programs.[4] Thus for states that want to provide certain kinds of financial assistance and services for their citizens, there are significant financial incentives to participate in the federally supported programs.

The federal executive agency with primary responsibility for overseeing social services programs is the Department of Health and Human Services. The Department of Agriculture supervises the Food Stamp program and the Temporary Emergency Food Assistance (surplus commodities) program. These agencies promulgate regulations to carry out the federal laws, issue policies to the states, and monitor states' compliance with federal requirements. They can impose financial sanctions on states for failing to meet these requirements, including failing to stay within the prescribed error rate limits—that is, limits on payments to ineligible individuals and overpayments to eligible recipients.

Federal laws and regulations define basic characteristics of federally assisted public assistance programs, but leave a number of decisions to the states. In the Medicaid program, for example, federal law defines categories of people who may be eligible for assistance, while states have leeway in determining which medical services are covered, how much the providers are paid, and what the income limits are for eligibility.

Federal requirements and restrictions apply to federally-funded service programs as well as public assistance programs. Very specific conditions apply to the state's receipt of funds under the federal Adoption Assistance and Child Welfare Act of 1980 (Public Law 96-272) and the Adoption and Safe Families Act of 1997 (Public Law 105-89), relevant portions of which are codified as parts of Titles IV-B and IV-E of the Social Security Act. For example, any court order placing a child in the custody of a county department of social services for foster-care services must contain a finding that reasonable efforts were made to prevent the need for placement or that special circumstances justified not making those efforts. The court must conduct a permanency planning hearing—to determine a permanent plan for the child—within twelve months after the child enters foster care. State law reflects these requirements, and the origin of many other state social services laws can be traced to similar federal funding criteria.

State Government's Role

General Assembly

In 1937 the General Assembly adopted legislation to enable the state to participate in federal social services programs and qualify for federal assistance in funding them. It has amended or rewritten the legislation many times to establish new programs, conform state law to federal changes, modify program features that federal law leaves to the state, and establish or modify programs based solely on state law. Chapter 108A of the General Statutes contains most of the state's social services legislation. G.S. 108A-25 establishes the following public assistance programs:

1. Work First
2. State-County Special Assistance for Adults
3. Food Stamps
4. Foster Care and Adoption Assistance
5. Low-Income Energy Assistance
6. Medical Assistance (Medicaid)

In addition, G.S. 108A-71 authorizes the state Department of Health and Human Services (DHHS) to accept all grants-in-aid for social services programs that may be available under the Social Security Act, other federal laws or regulations, and non-federal sources.

Chapter 108A also addresses confidentiality, appeal rights, and other subjects, to assure the state's compliance with federal requirements. Many program details do not appear in the General Statutes. Some are addressed by administrative rules and policies pursuant to authority the General Assembly has delegated to DHHS and the state Social Services Commission (described later in the chapter). Others are decided by the legislature when it appropriates funds for public assistance and social services programs.

The General Assembly determines how the state and the counties will share responsibility for the non-federal portion of the cost of federally supported programs. For example, in the Current Operations and Capital Improvements Appropriations Act of 1997 [SL 1997-352, § 11.11(b)] the legislature provided that the state would pay 85 percent and the counties 15 percent of the nonfederal share of the cost of Medicaid services—the same proportional shares as in a number of preceding years.

In addition to appropriating state funds to pay the state's share of the cost of certain social services programs, the legislature allocates lump-sum federal funds that the state receives under federal block grants for social services programs and approves plans for the expenditure of these funds. The General Assembly also decides issues that federal law leaves to the states' discretion, such as income eligibility limits and the designation of covered medical services for Medicaid. It determines what other, non-federally-based, public assistance and service programs counties must provide; decides whether to provide state funding for services for which federal funds are not available; and defines counties' responsibilities in such areas as child and adult protective services, adoptions, guardianships, and child support enforcement.

Department of Health and Human Services

DHHS is the state executive department that is responsible for most public human services programs. The secretary of DHHS, who is appointed by the governor, appoints the directors of various departmental divisions that issue policies and program manuals for use by county departments of social services in interpreting and carrying out the various laws and regulations. DHHS divisions that supervise programs administered by the county departments of social services, or with which county departments must interact regularly, include those described in the following sections.

Division of Social Services

The Division of Social Services oversees the counties' administration of the Work First program, the Food Stamp program, and other public assistance programs except Medicaid. The division is directly responsible for administering child support enforcement programs that serve almost a third of the counties, and for supervising county-administered child support programs in the remaining counties. Other county-administered programs that the division supervises include foster care services, adoption services, child and adult protective services, and family preservation services.

The division provides consultation and technical assistance to counties, develops policy, and conducts some training for county staff. The division's program sections include Economic Independence, Child Support, Children's Services, and Adult and Family Services. In addition to its state office, the division has four field offices—in Black Mountain, Winston-Salem, Fayetteville, and Greenville. Most of the division's work with counties is directly carried out through ten teams, each headed by a local support manager. Each team includes specialists in adult services, children's services, business and financial matters, Work First, and program integrity. In addition to providing support in these areas, the teams broker other services from the division and from DHHS and help coordinate with other divisions in DHHS.

Division of Medical Assistance

The Medicaid program is the responsibility of a separate Division of Medical Assistance in DHHS. The division supervises county social services departments' administration of Medicaid eligibility determination, establishes policies and procedures, and oversees the payment of medical providers—such as hospitals, physicians, and nursing homes—that deliver services to eligible clients. It includes a third-party recovery section, which pursues claims for reimbursement of Medicaid expenses. The division also manages the Community Alternatives program, which provides health and personal care services to enable elderly and disabled people to remain in their homes; the Baby Love program, which focuses on women's access to early prenatal care and preventive health care for low birth-weight infants; Carolina Access, which connects people with primary care doctors; and Health Check, an outreach program aimed at improving health care for low-income children.

Division of Facility Services

This division licenses residential child care facilities, domiciliary homes for aged and disabled adults, maternity homes, and other care providing facilities. Staff members do on-site inspection and monitoring in collaboration with the staff of the county departments of social services and the Division of Social Services. The division also has a substantial role in relation to health facilities.

Division of Child Development

The Division of Child Development licenses, monitors, and regulates child care facilities. It also provides technical assistance to help child care programs accommodate children with special needs, assists home child care providers in meeting safety standards, and helps communities establish child care resource and referral agencies. The division administers funds to help low-income families pay for child care so that parents can work. One-stop Family Resource Centers provide information and referrals to promote self-sufficiency and enhance child development and education.

Division of Aging

The Division of Aging supervises and coordinates programs for older citizens, through area agencies on aging (AAAs) and local service providers (G.S. 143B-181.1). (For additional information about the division, see Chapter 25 in this volume.)

Division of Services for the Blind

The Division of Services for the Blind provides treatment, rehabilitation, education, and independent living alternatives for persons who are blind or visually impaired. The division also oversees the operation of the Governor Morehead School, a residential school in Raleigh, which serves blind persons from birth to age twenty-one.

Division of Services for the Deaf and Hard of Hearing

The Division of Services for the Deaf and Hard of Hearing provides information and services for children and adults who are deaf or hard of hearing, their families, and the professionals who serve them. More than 770 children attend the North Carolina Schools for the Deaf. The division also provides interpreter services, advocacy, access to technology, and coordination of human services for people who are deaf or hard of hearing.

Division of Mental Health, Developmental Disabilities, and Substance Abuse Services

This division provides or oversees a variety of services for people who suffer from mental illness, have substance abuse problems, or have a developmental disability, as well as for the families of those people. (For additional information about the division and mental health, developmental disabilities, and substance abuse services, see Chapter 26 in this volume.)

Office of Economic Opportunity

The Office of Economic Opportunity in DHHS, among other things, funds and supports emergency facilities that provide shelter and support services to homeless individuals and families.

Social Services Commission

Three state commissions play a significant role in relation to the state's social services programs. The Social Services Commission, a semi-independent state body, has rule-making authority for most of the state's social services programs (G.S. Ch. 143B, Art. 3, Part 6). (The secretary of DHHS, rather than the Social Services Commission, has rule-making authority for the Medical Assistance program.) The commission also is authorized by statute to establish standards for inspecting and licensing maternity homes, domiciliary homes for aged or disabled persons, and residential child-care facilities. The governor appoints the commission's twelve members, one from each congressional district, for four-year terms.

The Social Services Commission's rule-making authority, defined in G.S. 143B-153, is quite broad. The commission's rules and regulations, when properly adopted pursuant to the Administrative Procedure Act (G.S. Ch. 150B), have the force and effect of law. The commission may authorize investigations of social problems, subpoena witnesses, and compel the production of documents. It appoints either one or two members (depending on whether the county has a three- or five-member board) of each county social services board. It also may assign responsibilities to the county social services boards and directors.

Child Care Commission

This commission, formerly called the Child Day-Care Commission, in DHHS, adopts standards and rules for the licensing and operation of child care facilities (G.S. Ch. 143B, Art. 3, Part 10A). It also is charged with making rules for responding to child abuse or neglect in child care facilities. The commission has fifteen members—seven appointed by the governor and eight by the General Assembly, all for two-year terms.

State Personnel Commission and Office of State Personnel

The State Personnel Commission and the Office of State Personnel regulate and administer the state personnel system, including the merit system under which most county social services personnel are appointed (G.S. Ch. 126). The State Personnel Act applies to all county social services employees, unless the county's personnel system, or a portion of it, has been approved by the State Personnel Commission as being "substantially equivalent" to that of the state. (For additional information on personnel, see Chapter 13 in this volume.)

The County's Role

County Social Services Board

Composition and Appointments

Every county except Mecklenburg and Wake counties, whose unique systems are described in the section "Mecklenburg County and Wake County," has a three- or five-member social services board (G.S. Ch. 108A, Art. 1, Part 1). In these ninety-eight counties, the board of commissioners decides whether the county's social services board will have three or five members. Most counties have five-member boards.

Members are appointed as follows: two (or one, for a three-member board) by the state Social Services Commission; two (or one) by the board of county commissioners; and one (the fifth or third member) by the first four (or two) members. On a five-member board, the selection of the fifth member is by majority vote of the other four members. If a majority do not agree on a fifth member (or if the two appointed members of a three-member board do not agree on a third member), then the senior regular resident superior court judge of the county makes the selection. A county board of commissioners may select one of its members as its appointee to the social services board, and many boards of commissioners do this as a means of enhancing communication between the two bodies. At its July meeting each year, the board elects one of its members as the chair, to serve for one year or until a new chair is elected.

A social services board member must be a resident of the county to whose board he or she is appointed. The statutes specify no other required qualification for serving on the board. The fact that a person is related to someone who is employed by the department of social services does not preclude that person's appointment to the board. However, once a person is on the board, the department may be prohibited from hiring someone who is related to that board member. A rule of the Social Services Commission (10 NCAC 24A.0302) provides that no person may be considered for employment in a county department of social services during the time a member of that person's immediate family is serving on the county board of social services or the board of county commissioners in the same county.

Terms

Social services board members are appointed for staggered three-year terms that end on June 30. If the board of commissioners appoints one of its members to the social services board, that person's term is three years even if his or her term as commissioner ends earlier. A member might resign voluntarily in this circumstance to enable the board of commissioners to appoint another of its members to the social services board, but the member is not required to do so.

Social services board members may not serve more than two consecutive terms, with two exceptions. First, this limitation does not apply to those who were county commissioners at any time during the first two consecutive terms and are serving in that capacity at the time of reappointment. Second, when a person is appointed during a term to fill a vacancy, service on the board for the remainder of the former member's term does not count as a term for purposes of determining whether the new member has served two consecutive terms.

Change in Size of Board

The board of county commissioners may change the size of the county social services board from three to five members or from five to three members. The chairman of the board of commissioners must report to DHHS the board's decision to take either action. An increase in a board's size becomes effective as soon as the two new members are appointed—one by the board of commissioners and one by the state Social Services Commission. A decrease in a board's size is effective on the first day of July following the decision. Determination of which two members leave the board is made according to the dates on which the members' terms are set to expire, as provided in G.S. 108A-5(c).

Meetings

County social services boards must meet at least once a month, and more often at the call of the chair. The boards are subject to the open meetings law (G.S. Ch. 143, Art. 33C), and all meetings must be open to the public. During a public meeting, however, a board may go into a closed session from which the public is excluded, upon adoption of a motion to do so for one of the reasons specified in G.S. 143-318.11. The board would go into closed session, for example, for any discussion that involved identifying a particular client, to conduct the performance evaluation of the director, or to evaluate a case of possible welfare fraud. Among the things the board may do only in an open session are consider candidates for or fill a vacancy on the board and appoint or discharge the director. (For a detailed description of the open meetings law, see the "Meetings" section in Chapter 1 of this volume.)

Compensation

Social services board members may receive per diem compensation in an amount established by the board of county commissioners. They also may be reimbursed for subsistence and travel in accordance with a policy set by the commissioners. Many board members attend the annual Social Services Institute or other events sponsored by the North Carolina Association of County Directors of Social Services, the North Carolina Association of County Boards of Social Services, or others. Reimbursement for approved expenses of attendance should be paid from the budget of the county department of social services, according to the policy established by the board of commissioners.

Removal of Board Members

Social services board members do not serve at the pleasure of the appointing authority and cannot be removed from office for political reasons. In fact, the social services law makes no provision for removal except as a consequence of decreasing the size of a board from five to three members. In that circumstance the statute determines which two members leave the board. Moving out of the county in which the member was appointed almost certainly is grounds for removing a board member, and one would expect a member who moves out of the county to resign from the board. Aside from these narrow circumstances, the removal of social services board members "for cause" is probably an option under the common law. Such a removal can be effected only by the appointing authority and only through procedures that protect the board member's due process rights.[5]

To help avoid issues of removal as well as to maximize the board's effectiveness, a county social services board should consider adopting policies or a resolution that defines expectations of board members. These might include a statement of conditions under which the board would consider a member's resignation appropriate. Such a document would aid prospective board members in understanding the obligations entailed in serving on the board, and could remind all members of the problems that chronic non-attendance or uncooperativeness can create for the board.

Mecklenburg County and Wake County

Pursuant to a special provision in G.S. 153A-77, the Mecklenburg County Board of Commissioners abolished the county social services board and assumed its powers, duties, and responsibilities. The county took this step as part of its total reorganization of human services. Under another provision of the same statute, Wake County implemented a different form of reorganization, consolidating its human services programs and departments, including social services, into a consolidated county human services agency. The powers and authority of the county's consolidated human services board, appointed by the board of county commissioners, include most of the powers and authority of a county social services board. The statute authorizing these reorganizations applies only to counties with populations in excess of 425,000. Through 1998, proposals to extend these or similar options to other counties had not been successful.

Powers and Duties

County social services boards, unlike many other local boards, are primarily advisory. The statute that deals with their creation, G.S. 108A-1, states that social services boards are to establish policies for programs established by G.S. Chapter 108A. These policies, however, must conform with state and federal rules and regulations, which leaves little room for county boards to engage in programmatic policy making. When the General Assembly expanded counties' local policy-making authority for the Work First Program in 1997, that authority was assigned to boards of county commissioners (in electing counties) or to county departments of social services (in standard counties), not to county boards of social services.

G.S. 108A-9 specifies the following duties and responsibilities of the county social services boards:

1. To select the county social services director in accordance with the merit system rules of the State Personnel Commission.

   The county social services board has sole responsibility for recruiting and selecting the director of the county department of social services. (Two or more county social services boards may employ one director jointly, but none have done so.) Board members may have little training or experience in personnel matters. A board that needs to hire a director (or to take other personnel action in relation to the director) should seek whatever help it needs to ensure that its procedures are effective and legally sound. Sources of assistance include the local support manager, who heads the local support team of Division of Social Services personnel serving that county; the county's personnel department; the county attorney or county social services attorney; one of the four regional personnel directors of DHHS; and social services board members in other counties.

   The social services board, with the approval of the board of commissioners, determines the director's salary in accordance with the State Personnel Commission's (or, in a few cases, the county's) pay and classification plan. Implicit in the board's authority to hire the director are the authority to discipline or fire a director if necessary, also in accordance with state personnel rules, and a responsibility to evaluate the director's performance. The board should develop, and ideally, the board and director should agree on, the purposes of and the procedures for performance evaluation. (For additional information on personnel matters, see Chapter 13 in this volume.)

   In Mecklenburg County, the board of county commissioners, which acts as the social services board for the county, hires the social services director. In Wake County, the county manager, with the advice and consent of the consolidated human services board, hires and may fire the human services director, who reports directly to the county manager.

2. To advise county and municipal authorities in establishing policies and plans to improve the community's social conditions.

This broad advisory authority indicates that the county social
services board has a legitimate function that extends beyond
the programs and activities of the county department of social
services. Some social services boards are represented on local
human services advisory committees or similar bodies that address social problems and conditions in the community. The
law requires that the board be represented on the county's
Work First planning committee, which is appointed by the
board of commissioners to identify the needs of the population
to be served by the Work First program and to review and assist
in developing the county plan to respond to those needs.

3. To consult with the county social services director about problems relating to the director's office.

The director is the administrator of the county department of
social services, with authority to hire or discharge staff. The board's
role includes advising the director about administrative matters
in the department or problems of program administration.

4. To assist the director in planning budgets for the department
and to transmit or present the budget to the board of county
commissioners.

The extent to which social services boards are actively involved in planning and presenting the department's budget varies from county to county. The department's position in the
county's budgeting process is strengthened if the board understands the proposed budget, endorses it, and can advocate it
knowledgeably. Some county social services directors routinely
ask the board to approve the budget, although that is not legally
required. (See the "Financing Social Services" section, later in
this chapter, and Chapter 10 in this volume.)

5. To carry out whatever other duties and responsibilities the General Assembly, DHHS, the state Social Services Commission, or
the board of commissioners assigns to the board.

The state Social Services Commission, through its rules, has
given county social services boards responsibility for reviewing
cases involving suspected public assistance fraud. The boards
may either review each case individually or adopt a fraud policy
and delegate its enforcement to the county social services director and staff.

The General Assembly has assigned several other duties and responsibilities to social services boards. Under G.S. 108A-10, boards may enter into contracts to provide services for a fee. The fees may not exceed the cost of furnishing the services and must be based on a plan recommended by the county social services director and approved by both the social services board and the board of commissioners. The social services board should report annually to the board of commissioners on the receipt of such fees. A function for which a number of counties have adopted fee policies is the social services department's preparation of home studies for the district court's use in child-custody disputes between private parties, a service that departments are not required to provide and for which they receive no federal or state funding.

Under G.S. 108A-16 and -18, the board of commissioners must have the approval of the social services board in order to appoint a special county attorney for social services matters. If such an attorney is appointed, the commissioners determine the attorney's compensation. (This authority is discussed more fully in the section "County Commissioners," later in this chapter.)

The duties and authority discussed previously apply to the social services board acting as a board, not to its individual members. Another law, G.S. 108A-11, gives board members the right to inspect confidential county social services records relating to public assistance and services. The statute prohibits members' disclosing or making public any information they acquire from the records. Obviously, individuals should exercise this authority only for purposes related to their responsibilities as board members, not for personal reasons.

County Social Services Department and Its Director

Except for the special arrangements in Mecklenburg County and Wake County described previously, each county has a social services department headed by a director selected by the county social services board. The director administers the public assistance and service programs directly, and through the social services staff. In many counties, the department also is the local agency responsible for administering the child support enforcement program.

General Duties of the Director

G.S. 108A-14 specifies fourteen principal duties and responsibilities of a county social services director. The first five are general duties:

1. *To serve as executive officer of the county social services board and act as its secretary.* The director must provide clerical services to the board and, as its executive officer, implement its policies and decisions. The director is not a member of the board, however, and does not have a right to attend closed sessions of board meetings except at the board's invitation.

2. *To appoint departmental staff under the state merit system rules.* It is the director's responsibility to hire staff and make personnel decisions regarding them. County social services staff are covered by the State Personnel Act unless the county's personnel system (or a portion of it) has been judged by the State Personnel Commission to be substantially equivalent to that of the state. In Wake County, the county human services director hires the staff of the consolidated human services agency with the county manager's approval.

3. *To administer public assistance and social services programs under applicable regulations.* Program administration is the director's responsibility, though much of it is accomplished through delegation of duties to and supervision of the staff. Most programs are administered according to federal and state laws and regulations; those funded solely with county funds are subject only to county policies. As described later, in some counties the board of county commissioners or the board's delegate is responsible for administering the county's Work First program.

4. *To administer funds provided by the board of commissioners for the care of indigent persons in the county under policies approved by the social services board.* Counties are authorized to operate social services programs that are neither mandated nor funded by the federal or state government. A county might choose to provide financial or other aid to persons who do not qualify for federally- or state-funded public assistance programs. The director is responsible for administering these programs under policies adopted by the social services board, subject to the direction of the board of commissioners in establishing and funding the programs.

5. *To act as the agent of the state Social Services Commission and the state DHHS in relation to work they require in the county.* The county so-

cial services director is a county employee who, as noted earlier, is hired and may be fired only by the county social services board. He or she oversees the expenditure of substantial federal, state, and county funds. The director also is required by statute to act as the agent of the state Social Services Commission and DHHS in relation to their programs in the county.

In the context of a director's possible liability for alleged negligence, several court decisions have addressed the question of whose "agent" the social services director is when he or she is carrying out various statutory responsibilities. In *Vaughn v. North Carolina Department of Human Resources*,[6] the North Carolina Supreme Court held that a county director of social services acts as an agent of the state when engaged in administering the county's foster-care program for children. (Consequently, foster parents who claimed to have been injured by the county social services department's negligent placement of a foster child in their home were allowed to pursue their claim against the state.) In reaching its conclusion, the court pointed to the extent of state regulation and funding of the foster-care program and the fact that the county social services director is hired by a board that has equal numbers of state and county appointees. In *Coleman v. Cooper*,[7] relying on *Vaughn*, the court of appeals held that the county director also acts as an agent of the state when engaged in administering the county's child protective services program. In *Myer v. Walls*,[8] both the court of appeals and the supreme court appeared to accept the county's assertion that the director acted as an agent of the state for purposes of adult protective services and guardianship responsibilities. (Questions concerning "agency" generally arise in the context of liability issues, which are discussed in Chapter 4 in this volume.)

Programmatic Duties of the Director

Other parts of G.S. 108A-14 describe specific programmatic duties of the county director of social services or refer to duties that are the subject of other, more detailed, statutes:

1. *To investigate adoption cases and supervise adoptive placements.* Under the state adoption law (G.S. Ch. 48), county departments of social services have many responsibilities in relation to the adoption of children. They arrange for and supervise adoptive

placements; recruit, screen, and supervise adoptive parents; and investigate and report to the court on adoption cases.

2. *To issue youth employment certificates.* A state labor law, G.S. 95-25.5, provides for county social services directors to issue the youth employment certificates that persons under age eighteen must have before being employed in most occupations. With the approval of the Commissioner of Labor, a director may delegate this authority to personnel on or outside the director's staff.

3. *To supervise domiciliary homes for aged or disabled persons.* Under G.S. Chapter 131D, domiciliary homes must be licensed by DHHS. The county social services director's responsibilities include monitoring implementation of the Domiciliary Home Residents' Bill of Rights (G.S. Ch. 131D, Art. 3) and investigating complaints relating to violations of these rights.

4. *To assist and cooperate with the Department of Correction.* G.S. 148-33.1(f) authorizes the Department of Correction to make payments out of prisoners' work-release earnings for the support of their dependents. If no court order provides for support, payments are to be made according to the county social services department's determination of dependency status and need. Under G.S. 148-4(7), which covers maternity leave for female prisoners, county departments of social services "are expected to cooperate" with prison officials to coordinate prenatal care, financial services, and placement of prisoners' children.

5. *To make certain sterilization decisions or recommendations.* Chapter 35 of the General Statutes authorizes county directors of social services to petition the court for the sterilization of non-institutionalized mentally ill or developmentally disabled persons. It also requires directors to investigate and make recommendations to the court about cases in which someone else petitions for a person's sterilization.

6. *To investigate and respond to reports of child abuse and neglect.* The state Juvenile Code includes the child abuse reporting law, which requires anyone who suspects that a child is abused, neglected, or dependent, or has died as a result of maltreatment, to make a report to the county department of social services. The law requires the department to make a prompt and thorough investigation of each report, to evaluate the level of risk to the child or to other children in the home, and to take appropriate protective action.

7. *To arrange and supervise children's placements in foster care.* Under the Juvenile Code, a district court judge may place abused, ne-

glected, dependent, undisciplined, or delinquent children in the custody of the county department of social services. Many of these children are placed in state-licensed foster homes. Some county social services departments also place and supervise children in foster care pursuant to voluntary placement agreements with parents.

8. *To investigate proposed adoptive placements of children.* Under the adoption law, G.S. Chapter 48, county departments of social services may be required to conduct pre-placement assessments of prospective adoptive parents and their homes and to make reports to the court regarding actual adoptive placements.

9. *To receive and respond to reports of abuse, neglect, or exploitation of disabled adults.* Under G.S. Chapter 108A, Article 6, anyone with reasonable cause to believe that a disabled adult needs protective services must make a report to the county director of social services, who must evaluate each report promptly and thoroughly. This law gives the director a number of other specific duties in relation to disabled adults who are abused, neglected, or exploited.

Other Duties of the Director

This list is not exhaustive. Other statutes address the county social services director's duties or authority in such areas as guardianship of incompetent adults (G.S. Ch. 35A); services to the blind (G.S. Ch. 111); consent for a pregnant minor to marry (G.S. 51-2); and unclaimed dead bodies (G.S. 130A-415).

Boards of County Commissioners

Duties and Authority of All Boards of Commissioners

A primary role of the board of commissioners in relation to social services is ensuring the adequacy of funds for these programs in the county budget. That role is discussed in the section "Financing Social Services," later in this chapter. The commissioners' other powers and responsibilities include the following:

1. *To determine whether the county has a three- or five-member social services board, and to appoint one or two, respectively, of the members (G.S. 108A-2, -3).* Many boards of commissioners appoint one of their

own members to serve on the social services board to foster communication and understanding between the two bodies. The procedure for changing the size of a board from three to five members or from five to three members is described in the previous section, "Change in Size of Board."

2. *To establish per diem rates and policies for subsistence and travel reimbursement for county social services board members (G.S. 108A-8).* The commissioners need to establish these policies in addition to including in the budget funds to cover these expenses.

3. *To approve, along with the county social services board, fees to cover the cost of certain non-mandated services that the social services board contracts to provide (G.S. 108A-10).* The board of commissioners should receive an annual report from the social services board concerning the receipt of such fees.

4. *To approve the county social services director's salary (G.S. 108A-13).* The social services board appoints the director and determines the director's salary based on the State Personnel Commission's pay classification plan, but the salary must be approved by the board of commissioners. Although the two boards should make every effort to reach agreement, the commissioners, having control over the budget, probably have the final say in accepting or rejecting the social services board's recommendation.

5. *To appoint, with the approval of the county social services board, a special attorney for social services matters, and to determine the attorney's compensation (G.S. 108A-16, -17, and -18).* A county is not required to have an attorney designated under this section as a special county attorney for social services. If it does, the attorney's duties include serving as legal adviser to and performing duties assigned by the board of commissioners, the director of social services, and the social services board. (If a case arises involving a serious dispute between two of these entities, the attorney is likely to have a conflict of interest that would prevent his or her advising or representing any of them in regard to that matter.) It is not clear whether the section requires the social services board's approval only of having the designated position or also of the individual chosen to hold that position. County departments of social services have substantial, and growing, needs for legal resources, which counties address in a variety of ways—one or more contract attorneys, in-house social services staff attorneys, a full-time county attorney, or one or more assistant county attorneys. The board of commissioners and the social services board should ex-

amine together which approach is most effective and cost efficient for a particular county, but the final decision rests with the
board of commissioners.

6. *To determine whether financial assistance for certain disabled persons will be provided under the State-County Special Assistance for Adults program (G.S. 108A-45).* State law requires counties to operate this state- and county-funded program, which is designed primarily to subsidize needy aged or disabled persons who live in residential-care facilities. The board of commissioners has the option of including in the program certain needy disabled persons who live in their own homes.

7. *To be responsible, through the county department of social services, for the administration and operation of the Food Stamp program in the county (G.S. 108A-51).* As with most other statewide federally funded programs, the Division of Social Services, in DHHS, is responsible for supervising the counties' operation of the Food Stamp program.

8. *To decide which non-mandated public assistance programs or services the county will provide (G.S. 153A-255).* State law requires counties to participate in a number of social services programs but also authorizes counties to "undertake, sponsor, organize, engage in, and support other social service programs intended to further the health, welfare, education, safety, comfort, and convenience of its citizens."

9. *To determine which agency or entity will operate the Child Support Enforcement program in the county (G.S. 110-141).* About two-thirds of the counties are responsible for administering a Child Support Enforcement program in the county. In the other counties, the state operates the program pursuant to an option counties were given when the program was established in 1975. Counties that administer the program no longer have the option of turning it over to the state; however, a county in which the state administers it may elect to administer the program itself. Most county-administered child support programs are operated by the county department of social services. The board of commissioners has the option, though, of creating an independent county department for child support enforcement, locating the program in another county department or office, or contracting with a private entity to operate the program.

10. *To plan for, or to both plan for and administer, the Work First program in the county.* State welfare reform legislation enacted in 1997

implemented the federal law that established the Temporary Assistance to Needy Families (TANF) program, replacing the former Aid to Families with Dependent Children (AFDC) program. In North Carolina the program is called Work First (described in the "Work First" section later in this chapter). The state law required each board of county commissioners to indicate by October 31, 1997, whether it wanted to be a "standard" or "electing" county for purposes of the Work First program. A board's request to be an electing county had to be supported by a three-fifths vote by the commissioners. The General Assembly, which is responsible for deciding counties' Work First status, made the first designations in October 1998.

In electing counties, the boards of county commissioners are responsible for the development, administration, and implementation of the Work First program. In standard counties, the state retains more control over the program, which is administered by the county departments of social services. In both types of counties, however, boards of commissioners have substantially greater responsibilities and authority than they had previously in relation to federally-funded programs. State law requires each board of county commissioners, regardless of the county's designation, to appoint a committee to identify the needs of the population to be served by Work First and to review and assist in developing a county plan to respond to those needs.

Duties and Authority of Boards of Commissioners in Standard Counties

Boards of county commissioners in standard counties are authorized and required to perform the following duties:

- Review and approve the county Work First plan, developed by the county department of social services, for submission to the state DHHS
- Consult (along with the county department of social services) with DHHS in relation to that department's establishment of county performance levels for Work First, measured by outcome and performance goals contained in the State Plan
- Consult (along with DHHS) with the county department of social services in relation to the county department's establishment of county Work First outcome and performance goals

Duties and Authority of Boards of Commissioners in Electing Counties

In relation to Work First, boards of county commissioners in electing counties are authorized and required to perform the following duties:

- Establish county outcome and performance goals
- Establish eligibility criteria, prescribe the method of calculating benefits, and determine individuals' and families' eligibility
- Develop and enter into mutual responsibility agreements with Work First recipients, ensure that services and resources are available to help participants comply with the agreements, and monitor compliance with and enforce those agreements
- Ensure that participants engage in the required hours of work activities
- Consider providing community service work for recipients who cannot find employment
- Make benefit payments to eligible recipients
- Monitor and evaluate the impact of the Work First program on children and families
- Ensure compliance with applicable state and federal laws, rules, and regulations
- Develop, adopt, and submit to DHHS a biennial county Work First plan
- Provide monthly progress reports to DHHS
- Develop and implement an appeals process for the county's Work First program that substantially complies with G.S. 108A-79

A board of commissioners may delegate most of these responsibilities to other public or private entities; however, the board remains accountable for all of them.

Allocation of Responsibility among Counties

The legal residence of a person who is eligible for public assistance or who needs social services determines which county is responsible for providing them. G.S. 153A-257 establishes the rules for determining an adult's or child's legal residence for social services purposes. In most cases, legal residence is the county in which a person resides. The fact that a person is in an institution or residential facility located in a county, however, is not sufficient, by itself, to establish legal residence in that county. Counties routinely cooperate in providing public assistance and services to people who are in the county but legally are residents of other counties. A child may need a foster home or other special placement that is not available in the county of legal residence. An adult who has left his or her county of residence to receive care in a nursing home may need to apply for Medicaid. In cases such as these, the county in which the child or adult is located can provide the needed services or assistance, but the county of legal residence is responsible for the cost of the services and benefits.

Social Services Programs

Public Assistance Programs

Public assistance programs provide financial assistance in the form of direct money payments to recipients; cash-like benefits, such as food stamps; or payments on behalf of recipients to vendors or providers, such as physicians participating in the Medicaid program. The granting of public assistance is governed by financial eligibility rules, which vary from program to program but usually take into account an applicant's income and resources. "Categorical" programs require, in addition to financial eligibility, that the recipient belong to a defined population, such as the aged, the disabled, or dependent children.

State law requires counties to administer certain public assistance programs that involve a mix of federal, state, and county funding. Occasionally programs are optional or are operated as pilot programs in only some counties. As explained earlier, counties may provide non-mandated financial assistance programs with county funds. Laws, policies, and regulations governing public assistance programs change frequently. General descriptions of the major public assistance programs and directly related service programs follow. Detailed provisions relating to these programs may be found in the policy manuals issued by the appropriate divisions of DHHS.

Work First

In 1996, Congress enacted federal welfare reform legislation (Public Law 104-193) that replaced the former basic welfare program, Aid to Families with Dependent Children (AFDC), with a federal block grant to states for Temporary Assistance to Needy Families (TANF). North Carolina implemented the TANF program administratively in October 1996, when the state submitted a plan to the (U.S.) DHHS converting the state's AFDC program to a new Work First program for needy families with children.

In 1997, the North Carolina General Assembly enacted state welfare reform legislation (Part XII of S.L. 1997-443, the Current Operations and Capital Improvements Appropriations Act of 1997), establishing the Work First program statutorily and making changes to it (G.S. 108A-27 through 108A-39). Major characteristics of this legislation that impact counties include the following:

1. The shift from open-ended to capped, or block grant, funding
2. Increased flexibility, especially in the area of services
3. The ability of a limited number of counties to be "electing" counties, with local authority to set eligibility criteria, payment levels, and other program features
4. Expanded involvement of other state and local agencies in both planning and implementing programs
5. A strong emphasis on, as well as reporting requirements for, measuring program results

The Work First program is a public assistance and social services program that provides temporary assistance to help needy families with children to become self-sufficient through employment. Work First consists of six components: Work First family assistance (time-limited financial assistance); Work First diversion assistance (short-term cash payments to reduce the likelihood of a family's receiving Work First family assistance); Work First services (services designed to help families become self-sufficient); First Stop employment registration; First Stop employment services; and Work First administration.

Every two years the state DHHS must prepare a two-year state Work First plan that includes provisions applicable to all counties, provisions applicable to the standard (nonelecting) counties, and approved county plans from the electing counties. DHHS must submit the state plan to the Director of the Budget who, by May 15 of each even-numbered calendar year, must approve the plan and recommend its adoption by the General Assembly. Before submitting the plan to the General Assembly for approval, DHHS must submit the plan to the Joint Legislative Public Assistance Commission for review, consult with local governments and private sector organizations, and allow local governments and private sector organizations forty-five days to comment on the plan. The plan must then be approved by the General Assembly, enacted into law, signed by the Governor, and submitted to the U.S. Department of Health and Human Services.

In regard to the standard Work First program, the state Work First plan includes eligibility criteria (including income and asset limits); benefit levels, limitations, and payments; methods of calculating benefit levels and payments; exceptions or exemptions from work requirements or from time limits on assistance; sanctions for failure to comply with program requirements; and allocation of federal, state, and county funds for Work First. Standard counties must administer the Work First program through the county department of social services (or, in Wake County, the consolidated human services agency). The county department of social services, in consultation with DHHS, may delegate any or all of its duties with respect to the county Work First program to another public agency or to a private contractor but remains accountable to the state with respect to these duties.

The 1997 legislation authorized the General Assembly to designate one or more counties as electing counties as long as the aggregate Work First caseload in those counties does not exceed 15.5 percent of the statewide Work First caseload. The first designations were to be effective for state fiscal years 1998–99 and 1999–2000; however, the General Assembly did not make the initial designations until October 1998. That delay was due in part to debate over whether to raise the 15.5 percent cap, a step the General Assembly did not take but may reconsider in subsequent sessions. Counties initially designated as electing counties—by random drawing—were Alamance, Caldwell, Caswell, Chatham, Cherokee, Davie, Forsyth, Henderson, Iredell, Lincoln, Macon, McDowell, New Hanover, Polk, Randolph, Rutherford, Sampson, Stokes, Surry, Transylvania, and Wilkes. Counties that had applied for electing county status but were not selected were Catawba, Craven, Davidson, Mitchell, and Moore. A county may apply to change its designation for subsequent biennia.

While the state plan governs some aspects of the Work First program in electing counties, many details of the program are left to the discretion of the board of county commissioners, which may designate the county department of social services or some other entity to administer the program in the county.

Both standard and electing counties must develop biennial Work First plans and submit them to DHHS for approval. In standard counties, the plan is developed by the county department of social services (or consolidated human services agency) and must describe the Work First diversion assistance and Work First services that the county will provide. The county board of commissioners must appoint a committee to identify the needs of the population to be served and to assist the county department of social services in developing the plan. By January 15 of each even-numbered year, the board of county commissioners must approve the county Work First plan and submit it to DHHS for approval.

In electing counties, the board of county commissioners develops the county's Work First plan but must also appoint a committee to identify the needs of the population to be served and to assist in developing the plan. The plan must describe conditions in the county, outcomes and goals for the county, plans to achieve and measure the outcomes and goals, how the Work First program will be administered, and funding requirements. An electing county's plan also must describe county policies relating to benefit levels, eligibility for assistance, asset and income requirements, time limits and extensions, rewards, and sanctions; a list of community service programs equivalent to full-time employment that are offered to Work First recipients who are unable to find full-time employment; and the number of "mutual responsibility agreements" entered into between the county and Work First families.

Some of the key components of Work First include the following:

- Recipients of Work First cash assistance who are able to work must become employed or participate in short-term job training within a specified time period.
- Recipients must move off welfare within two years (or, in electing counties, the time established by the county but not more than five years). Extensions can be granted in hardship cases.
- Each recipient must sign a personal responsibility contract that describes the recipient's plan for moving off welfare and for carrying out family responsibilities.
- Recipients must be provided help with child care, transportation, job search, and short-term job training, and can receive Medicaid for up to a year after they stop receiving assistance.
- Teen parents must stay in school and live at home or under other approved adult supervision.
- No additional cash payments may be made for children born after a family has been in Work First longer than ten months.
- Sanctions apply to families that do not meet their Work First obligations.

Food Stamps

State law requires every county to operate the federally funded Food Stamp program, which issues to eligible recipients coupons that are redeemable for food products at most retail food stores (G.S. 108A-51 to -53). A shift from the use of paper coupons to the use of electronic benefit transfer (debit cards) is expected to be implemented statewide by June 1999. Basic policies for eligibility are based on income and resource guidelines issued by the U.S. Department of Agriculture. The federal government pays the full cost of food-stamp benefits—estimated to be almost $382 million in North Carolina in fiscal year 1998–99.[9] The federal government pays half of the program administration costs; the counties pay most of the other half. Recipients age eighteen to fifty-nine who are not disabled or otherwise exempt must register for work and participate in job search or education and training activities. In fiscal year 1997, an average of almost 262,000 households (over 621,000 individuals) per month received food-stamp benefits that averaged $173.49 per household.[10]

Medical Assistance Program (Medicaid)

Medicaid is a public assistance program that covers most of the cost of medical care and services for several categories of people who cannot afford the costs of health care (G.S. 108A-54 to -70.16). (Medicaid is completely separate from Medicare, which is a federal health-insurance program administered by the federal Social Security Administration.) Those who may receive Medicaid include low-income aged, disabled, or blind persons; needy children and pregnant women; individuals who receive federal Supplemental Security Income (SSI) benefits; and other low-income people who meet eligibility requirements. Once people are certified as being eligible for Medicaid, direct payments are made on their behalf to medical providers, such as doctors, hospitals, and pharmacists.

The eligibility determination aspect of the Medical Assistance Program is administered by every county social services department and is supervised by the Division of Medical Assistance, in DHHS, pursuant to complex federal and state regulations. The General Assembly, in its appropriations acts, sets eligibility standards and lists the medical services that are covered by Medicaid. Recipients are deemed to have assigned to the state any right they have to health-insurance benefits.

County departments of social services are responsible for assuring that transportation to needed medical services is available to Medicaid recipients. While federal Medicaid funds pay a portion of the cost of this transportation, counties must pay the total non-federal share. Counties may choose to pay for Medicaid transportation with Social Services Block Grant funds, which have a matching rate that is more favorable to counties than the Medicaid reimbursement rate.

State-County Special Assistance for Adults

Counties are required to participate in this program of financial assistance for people who (1) are either age sixty-five or older or permanently and totally disabled, (2) need rest-home care, and (3) are financially eligible (G.S. 108A-40 to -47). Counties have the option of providing assistance, with state financial participation, to "certain disabled persons" from eighteen to sixty-five years of age who come within a state definition of "disabled," are in private living arrangements, and meet other eligibility requirements.

Low-Income Home Energy Assistance Block Grant Programs

The federal Low-Income Home Energy Assistance Block Grant provides funds to the state for two energy programs that are administered by county departments of social services. The Low-Income Energy Assistance Program (LIEAP) provides one-time cash payments to help eligible families pay their heating bills. In fiscal year 1996, the program served over 186,000 cases, representing over 460,000 recipients.[11] In fiscal year 1997, eligibility requirements were changed due to Congressional reductions in energy funding. Fewer than 40,000 cases and individuals received assistance, which averaged $147.41 per case, and payments were targeted toward households with persons age 65 or older who were receiving food stamps.[12]

The Crisis Intervention Program is a year-round heating and cooling assistance program that provides cash payments to help eligible families. In fiscal year 1997, average benefits of $224.43 were paid to 28,527 households, representing over 89,000 individuals.[13]

Commodity Distribution

The U.S. Department of Agriculture makes surplus foods available to emergency feeding organizations, including county departments of social services. Those who are eligible for this food include food-stamp recipients as well as families with incomes less than 130 percent of the federally-established poverty level. Surplus foods usually are distributed quarterly, often by volunteers. The state Department of Agriculture and the Division of Social Services, in DHHS, cooperate in planning for distribution through county departments of social services, but the state does not pay any of the administrative costs that counties incur in handling food distribution. In fiscal year 1997, an average of almost 80,000 people per month received food distributions under this program.[14]

Foster-Care and Adoption Assistance Payments

All counties administer and contribute to the funding of programs to pay for room and board (as well as provide a modest special-needs allowance) for children placed in foster care and to subsidize the cost of caring for some adopted children (G.S. 108A-48 to -50). In fiscal year 1997, the average monthly number of children for whom federal foster care payments were made was over 4,500; the state foster home fund made payments for another 1,600 children; and monthly adoption subsidy payments were made on behalf of more than 3,700 children.[15]

Welfare Fraud

It is a crime in North Carolina to obtain public assistance by making a false statement or concealing a material fact. (The amount of money involved determines whether welfare fraud is a misdemeanor or a felony.) Each county social services department is responsible for dealing with welfare fraud. State policy requires the county social services director to consult with the county social services board about fraud cases. In some counties, the director brings each case of suspected fraud to the board for review and advice on how to proceed. Other boards adopt fraud policies that are carried out by the director and staff. Some departments have specialized fraud units.

At the state level, the Office of Inspector General in the Department of Justice is responsible for coordinating activities related to the detection, prosecution, and prevention of fraud, abuse, and waste in public assistance programs. Among other things, that office can receive and investigate complaints; review the fraud-related activities of state and local agencies; and provide training for law-enforcement agencies and others with responsibilities relating to public assistance fraud.

Service Programs Not Involving Financial Assistance

Many services are provided by county departments of social services. The availability and adequacy of some of these vary among counties, depending on local priorities and funding, community support, and other factors. Pursuant to a state plan adopted as a condition of receiving federal Social Services Block Grant funds, each county must provide certain mandated services: adoption, child care, family planning, foster care, protective services for children and adults, and either chore or homemaker services. Some of these services are also required by state law. Counties may also use these funds, which require local matching money, to help provide a number of optional services, such as delinquency prevention, day-care services for adults, and transportation. Counties may provide any other social services programs they choose with county funds. Only the major service programs are described in the following sections.

Protective Services for Children and Adults

State laws require that cases of suspected child abuse, neglect, dependency, and death from maltreatment, and cases involving disabled adults who may be abused, neglected, or exploited, be reported to the county department of social services. The North Carolina Juvenile Code, which includes the child abuse, neglect, and dependency reporting law, is designed to protect children under age eighteen from neglect and abuse by parents or other caretakers. The Juvenile Code also requires that protective services be provided for children who either have no parent or caretaker or whose parent is not able to care for the child or to make suitable alternative arrangements. The disabled-adult reporting law, which is part of the Protection of the Abused, Neglected, or Exploited Disabled Adult Act (G.S. Ch. 108A, Art. 6), is meant to protect persons who are age eighteen or older, are physically or mentally incapacitated, and are vulnerable to abuse, neglect, or exploitation. These laws are aimed at identifying children and disabled adults who are being harmed or are at risk and ensuring that they receive protective services. When a county department of social services receives a report under either law, it must investigate promptly and take appropriate action to protect the child or disabled adult.

In cases of child abuse, neglect, or dependency the department provides a wide range of treatment and supportive services to children and their families, often while the children remain at home, since one purpose of the law is to keep families intact unless the risk of harm to a child requires the child's removal from the home. Under the Juvenile Code, the department may file a petition in district court seeking either legal custody of a child or some other court order to protect the child.

When a department finds that a disabled adult needs protective services, it must provide or arrange for services if the disabled adult consents. If the individual lacks the capacity to consent, the department may seek a court order authorizing it to provide services. The broad range of services covered by this law includes social, medical, psychiatric, psychological, and legal services. In appropriate cases, the department may petition to have the disabled adult declared incompetent and to have a guardian appointed for the person.

Child Placement Services

Children needing placement services come into the custody of county departments of social services in several ways. The district court may order that an abused, neglected, dependent, undisciplined, or delinquent juvenile be placed in the department's custody. Sometimes a parent facing a crisis, such as a single parent's hospitalization, enters into an agreement with the department for the child's placement in foster care. The department may also have custody of children whose parents have relinquished them for adoption, whose parents' rights a court has terminated, or whose adoptive placements have failed. The county departments and the Division of Social Services, in DHHS, also cooperate with other states to arrange placements when children from other states need placement here or children from North Carolina need placement elsewhere.

Many children who are in the custody of a county department of social services are placed in state-licensed foster homes that are supervised by the county department. Federal and state funds pay a portion of the monthly foster-care board rate. State policies allow counties to receive additional reimbursements for payments to qualified foster parents who provide services to children who are developmentally disabled or physically handicapped or who have other special needs.

Permanency Planning Services

Social services policies emphasize the prevention of unnecessary or unduly long foster-care placements, viewing them as costly in terms of both money and children's well-being. A permanency planning program that operates in every county aims to provide all children with permanent homes, preferably with their own parents, as early as possible. While the emphasis is on keeping children in or returning them to their own homes, there is a complementary emphasis on moving children into long-term plans like adoption if returning them to their homes is unlikely. County departments provide preventive services to help families deal with their problems so that children can remain in their own homes, as well as reunification services aimed at reuniting children with their families as soon as possible when removal is necessary. Much of the success of these approaches depends on whether the county has adequate specialized staff and resources to make needed services available to families. The state provides some special funding to help counties pay for the required staff and resources.

Child Care

Child care is an important service at the county level, given the number of single-parent families and the high percentage of mothers of young children in the work force in the state. The Work First program, discussed earlier, provides child care services to eligible participants who are working or receiving job training. All child care facilities must be licensed by the state. The General Assembly establishes standards for licensing (G.S. Ch. 110, Art. 7) and the state Child Care Commission issues related rules.

Adoptions

Every county department of social services has an adoption program that includes accepting children for placement, recruiting and screening adoptive parents, and arranging and supervising placements. State adoption law (G.S. Ch. 48) requires that either the county department of social services or a licensed child-placing agency conduct a preplacement assessment of every prospective adoptive home and a report to the court on every adoptive placement. (Some exceptions exist for relative and stepparent adoptions.) The state Division of Social Services supervises county adoption programs. State support includes legal guidance to ensure sound adoptions; guidelines for services to biological parents, children in need of adoption, and adoptive parents; a central registry for indexing and filing adoption proceedings and protecting adoption records; and an adoption resource exchange.

Family Planning and Problem Pregnancy

Services offered by county departments of social services may include counseling in human sexuality, information about family planning, medical services, contraceptive services (through local health departments), and funds for sterilization by private medical providers. County departments also offer counseling to help prospective parents consider the legal, emotional, and social implications of choices for dealing with a pregnancy; and help in locating housing, employment, and health care. The State Maternity Home Fund assists with the cost of maternity care for women who need placement outside their own homes during pregnancy. The State Abortion Fund provides limited funding for poor women who meet strict abortion eligibility criteria established by the General Assembly.

Services to Aged or Disabled Adults

In addition to, and sometimes in conjunction with, the protective services described previously, county departments of social services provide a number of services to aged and disabled adults that range from those furnished in the client's own home, to community-based services, to institutional care. The focus is on helping people remain in their own homes and avoiding unnecessary and expensive institutional care, although people may be helped in obtaining appropriate care outside the home when it is needed. Under the state guardianship law (G.S. Ch. 35A), county social services directors are among the "disinterested public agents" that a clerk of superior court may appoint as guardians for incompetent adults when there is no suitable family member, other individual, or corporation to serve in that capacity. (For more information about services for older adults, see Chapter 25 in this volume.)

Supportive Services

County departments of social services provide supportive services to help individuals and families cope with a variety of problems. Many of these services relate to programs that have been described earlier. Problem areas addressed include employment, household management, consumer affairs, family life, teenage pregnancy, and health- and school-related problems. Paraprofessional staff may work with clients in their own homes to help avoid the need to remove children from the home or to place other family members in substitute-care arrangements. The departments also facilitate referrals to other community resources and the coordination of services among community agencies.

Child Support Enforcement ("IV-D") Program

The Child Support Enforcement program operates statewide and is supervised by the Division of Social Services, in DHHS (G.S. Ch. 110, Art. 9). Often referred to as the "IV-D" program because it is based on Title IV-D of the Social Security Act, it is administered by the social services department or some other county office designated by the board of commissioners in seventy counties. The state administers the program in thirty counties, sometimes through multicounty child support programs. As noted earlier, when the program was established in 1975, state law gave each county the option of administering it or having the state do so. After an increasing number of boards of commissioners voted to turn the program over to the state, the General Assembly adopted legislation providing that counties that administer the child support program no longer may turn it over to the state. Counties that want to resume administration of a state-run child support program, however, still may do so. Most county-administered programs are located in the social services department, but a few are operated elsewhere in county government.

Child support enforcement agencies help locate absent parents for the purpose of obtaining child support, and they assist in establishing paternity and establishing and enforcing child support obligations. The agencies are authorized to use a variety of methods, including the interception of state or federal tax refunds, to collect child support. IV-D agencies are required to seek support on behalf of children who receive Work First cash assistance, and the adult recipients are required to cooperate in agencies' efforts to obtain child support. Child support enforcement agencies also must provide services to anyone else who applies and pays a modest application fee.

Compared to many social services programs, child support services tend to have broad public and political support. But problems for counties that administer this program include complex and changing child support laws and procedures; large caseloads; the need for increased automation in order for the local programs to operate more efficiently; and the need for coordination among child support agencies and the courts, the Work First program, and agencies and officials in other states. A few counties contract with private entities to operate their child support enforcement programs.

In fiscal year 1997, child support enforcement programs statewide were responsible for the collection of almost $324 million in child support (up from $281 million the year before).[16] Still, the "default rate" for public assistance cases was 47 percent and for non-public assistance cases was 33 percent.[17] Administrative costs, as a percent of collections, were 13 percent for state-administered programs and 16 percent for county-administered programs.[18] Also in 1997, the programs established over 79,700 new support obligations, established paternity of 24,488 children, and located more than 145,600 absent parents.[19]

Financing Public Assistance and Social Services Programs

More than any other area of local government finance, social services financing is complicated by intricate patterns of federal, state, and county funding. Since the mid-1930s, the federal government has assumed a major role in the financing of social services programs. Those programs contribute many federal and state dollars to local economies; they also require the expenditure of substantial county funds. Some county expenditures are required by the General Assembly's assignment of responsibility to the counties for a portion of the nonfederal cost of certain programs. Some are required as a condition of receiving other federal and state funds for social services. Others are required in order to provide needed, and sometimes mandated, services and programs for which state and federal funds are either unavailable or insufficient.

The Federal Role in Funding Social Services

Federal laws—such as the Social Security Act, the Food Stamp Act, and Congressional budget acts—determine how much money the federal government will provide for each program, how the money will be distributed among the states, the purposes for which the federal funds may be used, conditions with which states must comply to receive the federal funding, and whether the states will be required to pay part of the costs of the program. The share of costs funded by the federal government is called the federal share or the rate of federal financial participation. The share of costs that must be paid by the state (or by the counties) is called the nonfederal share or, sometimes, the required state match.

Open-Ended Funding

Some federally funded public assistance programs, such as Food Stamps and Medicaid, are entitlement programs, meaning benefits must be provided to every person who applies and meets the program's eligibility requirements. The federal government's financial obligation is open-ended. Regardless of how many people qualify for benefits, the federal government must provide funds sufficient to pay the federal share of benefits for everyone who is entitled to assistance. In the Food Stamp program, the federal government pays the full cost of the benefits (but only half of the administrative costs). In the Medicaid program, the state's (and counties') financial obligation also is open-ended, as the state must provide funds sufficient to pay the nonfederal share of the cost of the benefits.

Capped Funding

In other programs, such as Work First (Temporary Assistance for Needy Families), the Low-Income Energy Assistance Program, and most service programs, the amount of federal funding is capped. Federal appropriations provide a fixed amount of funding, often called a block grant. State or local funds must provide either a specified percentage match or an amount representing a "maintenance of effort" tied to amounts expended or budgeted for the program in a designated prior period.[20] If the federal funds and the required state and local contributions are insufficient to provide benefits or services to everyone who is eligible, the state must limit the number of people served by the program, limit the amount of benefits or the level of services provided, or provide additional state or local funding for the program.

The newest and most significant federal block grant, for Work First (see the "Public Assistance Programs" section, earlier in the chapter), replaced what had been open-ended federal funding for the former Aid to Families with Dependent Children (AFDC) program. (See the following "Work First Funding" section.)

The Social Services Block Grant provides funds for services directed at the following goals:

- To help people become or remain economically self-supporting
- To help people become or remain able to take care of themselves
- To protect children and adults who cannot protect themselves from abuse, neglect, and exploitation, and to keep families together, preserve family life, or rehabilitate families
- To prevent or reduce inappropriate institutional care by making home and community services available
- To help place people in appropriate institutions when placement is in their best interest, and to strengthen services in institutions

County social services departments also administer capped federal funds the state receives under the Low-Income Home Energy Assistance Block Grant (see the "Public Assistance Programs" section, earlier in the chapter) and from several sources for child welfare services. The state must develop comprehensive plans, such as the Work First plan and the Social Services Block Grant plan, describing the proposed use of the federal block grant funds and related state and local funds. The General Assembly is responsible for approving the distribution of federal block grant funds to counties.

State and County Roles in Financing Social Services

In most states the nonfederal share of the cost of public assistance and social services programs is paid entirely by the state government from state revenues. Under North Carolina's county-administered, state-supervised system, the nonfederal share of social services costs is divided between the state government and the counties. Under G.S. 108A-87 the General Assembly has the authority to decide whether, and how, to divide the nonfederal share of costs for social services programs between the state and counties. North Carolina generally requires counties to pay the bulk of the nonfederal share of administrative costs, as well as a significant portion of the cost of social services provided to county residents. For the most expensive public assistance program, Medicaid, state appropriations pay 85 percent of the nonfederal share of the cost of benefits. The General Assembly appropriates several million dollars each year to reimburse counties for part of the nonfederal share of the cost of administering public assistance programs, for additional eligibility workers to support the expansion of public assistance programs, and for additional social workers to provide protective services to abused, neglected, and dependent children.

G.S. 108A-90 requires all boards of county commissioners to levy and collect taxes sufficient to meet the county's share of social services expenses. If a county does not pay or arrange for payment of its full share of the costs, the governor is authorized under G.S. 108A-93 to withhold from it any state appropriations for public assistance and related administrative costs or to direct the secretary of revenue and the state treasurer to withhold specified tax revenues owed to the county. Before withholding funds, the governor must notify the chairman of the board of commissioners of the proposed action. While the commissioners must provide funds sufficient to pay a county's formula-determined share of the cost of mandated programs, they have total discretion as to what, if any, county money to budget for non-mandated social services programs.

Work First Funding

Work First funding, which is governed by G.S. 108A-27.11, operates somewhat differently in standard counties and electing counties. (See the "Public Assistance Programs" section, earlier in the chapter.) For all counties, Work First funds other than those for Work First Family Assistance are computed as block grants to the counties. To determine the amount of a county's block grant, first a percentage is determined representing the relationship of the county's total AFDC and JOBS (Job Opportunities and Basic Skills) expenditures, other than expenditures for cash assistance, to statewide actual expenditures for those programs in fiscal year 1995–96. Then that percentage is applied to the state's total budgeted funds for county-level Work First expenditures, other than for Work First Family Assistance.

For standard counties, in which Work First eligibility criteria and payment levels are set at the state level, the state DHHS makes the cash assistance payments to recipients. Other Work First payments are made to the counties as reimbursements for county expenditures. (In both instances, the state's obligation is subject to the availability of federal, state, and county funds.)

An electing county's allocation for Work First Family Assistance is a block grant computed by (1) determining a percentage representing the relationship of the county's total expenditures for cash assistance in 1995–96 to statewide actual expenditures for cash assistance in that year, and (2) applying that percentage to the total budgeted funds for Work First Family Assistance. DHHS is required to transmit the federal funds in an electing county's block grant to the county as soon as practicable after the funds become available to the state and "in accordance with federal cash management laws and regulations." The state must transmit one-fourth of the state funds in a county's block grant to the county at the beginning of each quarter. Once paid, those state funds do not revert.

G.S. 108A-27.9(c) sets out provisions the state Work First plan must include that apply to all one hundred counties. They include the following:

- Incentives for high-performing counties
- Contingency plans for counties that are unable to meet their financial commitments
- Sanctions against counties that fail to meet performance expectations, including allocations of any federal penalties that may be assessed against the state as a result of a county's failure to perform

The Budgeting Process

G.S. 108A-88 requires the state DHHS, by February 15 of each year, to notify all county social services directors of the amount of state and federal funds estimated to be available to their counties for public assistance and social services programs and related administrative costs for the next fiscal year—July 1 through June 30. (For examples of these estimates, see Table 24-1.) The estimates include funding for programs, such as Medicaid eligibility, that are supervised by DHHS divisions other than the Division of Social Services but are administered by county departments of social services. The notice states the percentage of county financial participation that is expected to be required for each program. Periodically, the state revises these estimates to reflect new state budget figures and actions taken by the General Assembly, Congress, and federal agencies. The budget process in the counties must proceed with some

Table 24-1
Estimated Funds Available for Selected Programs—State Fiscal Year 1998–1999

Program	Total ($ in millions)	Federal	State	County	Federal	State	County
		($ in millions)			(%)		
Medicaid Benefits	4,570	2,927	1,389	255	64	30	6
Medicaid Administration	101	51	72	107	60	16	24
Food Stamp Benefits	382	382	0	0	100	0	0
Food Stamp Administration	80	40	0	40	50	0.1	49.9
Social Services Block Grant	40	30	0	10	75	0	25
Work First Family Assistance	203	203	0	0	100	0	0
Work First County Block Grant	178	50	30	97	28	17	55
Day Care Subsidy Payments	214	155	59	0	73	27	0

Source: N.C. Department of Health and Human Services, Division of Social Services, *Estimated Funds Available—State Fiscal Year 1998–1999* (3 February 1998).

uncertainty as to the exact amount of county funds that will be required to fund the counties' share of the cost of mandated programs.

In providing estimates to the counties in odd-numbered years, the state must include notification of any changes in public assistance funding levels, formulas, or programs that the governor has proposed to the General Assembly under the Executive Budget Act. Counties also must be notified of changes in the proposed budget of the governor and the Advisory Budget Commission that result from action by the General Assembly or Congress subsequent to the February 15 estimates. Often, the initial estimates that counties receive are revised several times.

Every county's social services budget contains more than the amounts indicated in the state's estimates for mandated programs. In the services area, for example, federal and state funds available to the county, along with any county match required to receive those funds, are not likely to be sufficient to hire the number of social workers necessary to carry out the county's legal responsibility to provide protective services to abused and neglected children and disabled adults. Some state mandates, such as the requirement that a county social services director serve as guardian for incompetent adults when appointed by the court to do so, are not accompanied by state funding. In addition, to meet local needs, county social services departments may operate programs and provide services that are not mandated and that are funded with only county funds.

Directors of county departments of social services are responsible for preparing an annual budget for the county department of social services. G.S. 108A-9 states that the county board of social services should assist the director in planning budgets for the department and transmit or present the department's budget to the board of commissioners. County social services directors consult with the county social services board on budget matters, and some directors submit the department's proposed budget to the social services board for a formal vote of approval. Some boards actively help the director develop and advocate the budget, a practice that no doubt strengthens the department's position in the county budgeting process.

Local Budgeting Procedures

Budgeting for social services departments, like that for other parts of county government, is controlled by the Local Government Budget and Fiscal Control Act (G.S. Ch. 159, Art. 3). The act requires that before April 30 of each fiscal year (or an earlier date fixed by the county's budget officer) each department head transmit to the budget officer the budget request and revenue estimates for the budget year. (The county manager, if the county has one, is the budget officer.) Not later than June 1, the budget officer submits a proposed budget to the board of commissioners, which of course is responsible for adopting the county's budget ordinance.

For those programs for which the Division of Social Services allocates specific amounts to counties, each county is provided with funding authorizations for disbursements up to those amounts. By accepting these authorizations, a county certifies that the required local matching funds are available in its current budget. State and federal funds for other programs flow to the county in the form of reimbursements for program expenditures. The Division of Social Services provides budget forms for counties to use in allocating administrative costs among programs.

Conclusion

Unlike most states, North Carolina continues to call on counties to be the primary deliverers of public social services. North Carolina's arrangement of county administration and state supervision, and the intergovernmental cooperation it requires, generates some special frustrations and problems. But it also results in a statewide social services system that combines general uniformity with the maintenance of some measure of local flexibility and control.

Given the extent of federal involvement in establishing, regulating, and funding social services programs, the system is perhaps the most complex example of federal-state-county interaction. Social services programs in North Carolina will continue to be greatly influenced by changes at the federal level and by federal funding conditions for the many programs for which federal funding is critical. Even apart from federal influences, however, the state and counties must address serious issues regarding how best to meet the needs of children, families, and disadvantaged adults within the limited resources available.

North Carolina's social services system strikes a balance of state and county responsibilities for funding and administering a complex group of public assistance and social service programs. The adequacy of that balance is, and will continue to be, the subject of debate.

Additional Resources

Liner, Charles D., ed. *State and Local Government Relations in North Carolina*, 2d ed. Chapel Hill, N.C.: Institute of Government, The University of North Carolina at Chapel Hill, 1995, Chapter 12.

Mason, Janet. *Reporting Child Abuse and Neglect in North Carolina*. Chapel Hill, N.C.: Institute of Government, The University of North Carolina at Chapel Hill, 1996.

North Carolina Department of Health and Human Services, Division of Social Services. *County Budget Estimates*, issued each year by February 15, setting out both budget estimates and explanatory narrative.

———. *Annual Statistical Reports*.

Saxon, John L. "Removal of Members of County Social Services Boards from Office during Their Terms," *Social Services Law Bulletin*, no. 17 (Institute of Government, February 1993).

———. "Welfare Reform: Legislation Enacted by the 1997 General Assembly," *Social Services Law Bulletin*, no. 26 (Institute of Government, October 1997).

———. "Welfare Reform: What Will It Mean for North Carolina?" *Social Services Law Bulletin*, no. 24 (Institute of Government, March 1997).

Trattner, Walter I. *From Poor Law to Welfare State: A History of Social Welfare in America*, 5th ed. New York: The Free Press, 1994.

Notes

1. For a more thorough discussion of the history of social services in North Carolina, see Chapter 12 in Charles D. Liner, ed., *State and Local Government Relations in North Carolina*, 2d ed. (Chapel Hill, N.C.: Institute of Government, The University of North Carolina at Chapel Hill, 1995).

2. N.C. Const. of 1868, Art. XI, § 7.

3. Edward D. Berkowitz, *America's Welfare State from Roosevelt to Reagan* (Baltimore, Md.: Johns Hopkins University Press, 1991), 13.

4. North Carolina Department of Health and Human Services, *Estimated Funds Available—State Fiscal year 1998–1999* (3 February 1998) (hereafter, *DHHS, Estimated Funds Available, SFY 1998–99*). Federal funds for administration of the Work First program are included in counties' Work First block grants and for purposes of these state estimates are included in the services category rather than the public assistance administration category. For that and other reasons, while these figures give some picture of the extent of federal funding, they are not precise.

5. For a thorough discussion of issues relating to the removal of board members, see John L. Saxon, "Removal of Members of County Social Services Boards from Office during Their Terms," *Social Services Law Bulletin*, no. 17 (Institute of Government, February 1993).

6. 296 N.C. 683, 252 S.E.2d 792 (1979).

7. 102 N.C. App. 650, 403 S.E.2d 577, *cert. denied*, 329 N.C. 786, 408 S.E.2d 517 (1991).

8. Meyer v. Walls, 347 N.C. 97, 489 S.E.2d 880 (1997), rev'g 122 N.C. App. 507, 471 S.E.2d 422 (1996).

9. *DHHS, Estimated Funds Available, SFY 1998–99.*

10. North Carolina Division of Social Services, *Annual Statistical Report, State Fiscal Year 1997.*

11. *Id.*

12. *Id.*

13. *Id.*

14. *Id.*

15. *Id.*

16. *Id.*

17. *Id.*

18. *Id.*

19. *Id.*

20. G.S. 108A-27.12, for example, sets out the maintenance of effort requirements for the Work First program.

25 Government Programs for Senior Citizens

John L. Saxon

Contents

John L. Saxon is an Institute of Government faculty member whose fields of interest
include the organization and legal aspects of programs for the elderly.

Significant increases in the number of older Americans, their grow-ing proportion in the total population, and the political strength of se-nior citizens over the past sixty years have helped forge the now generally accepted conviction that the federal government, states, and local gov-ernments have a shared responsibility, along with community and private organizations, employers, and families, to provide programs, services, and assistance that address the economic, health, housing, and social needs of America's 34 million senior citizens.

Although the federal government has assumed the lion's share of responsibility for the elderly through the Social Security (OASDI), Supplemental Security Income (SSI), Medicare, Medicaid, and Older Americans Act programs, state governments—and, in North Carolina, county governments—also play important roles in delivering programs and services for senior citizens.

The role of North Carolina counties with respect to government ag-ing programs, however, cannot be understood in isolation or out of con-text. This chapter, therefore, discusses some of the economic, health, and social characteristics of senior citizens in North Carolina and the United States[1] and the roles of the federal and state governments in ad-dressing the economic, health, and social needs of the elderly, as well as the authority and responsibility of North Carolina counties, in the con-text of their relationship to the federal and state governments, with re-spect to government programs for senior citizens.

In addition, discussing government programs for the elderly neces-sarily requires consideration of three threshold questions:

1. Who are the "elderly"?
2. What are the economic, health, and social needs of the elderly that government aging programs seek to address?
3. What distinguishes a government aging program from other pro-grams and services that a government provides for its citizens?

Defining the Elderly

An answer to the question, "who are the elderly?" depends on how one defines the term elderly. How old must one be to be considered elderly? There is no universal definition of elderly, aging, or senior citizen. For example, under the SSI, Medicare, Medicaid, and State-County Special Assistance programs, "elderly" is defined as sixty-five years or older. The Social Security retirement age for "old age" insurance also is sixty-five, but partial retirement benefits may be paid to retirees who are at least sixty-two years old, and the minimum age for full retirement benefits will gradually increase to sixty-seven between 2003 and 2027. By contrast, the federal Older Americans Act and some state laws relating to senior citizens define "older" adults as anyone who is at least sixty years old.

Nonetheless, unless otherwise noted, this chapter uses the terms elderly, older adults, older Americans, senior citizens, the aging population, and similar terms interchangeably to describe all persons who are at least sixty-five years old (or, when used in relation to aging programs under the federal Older Americans Act, the state Home and Community Care Block Grant, or G.S. 160A-497, to persons age sixty or older).

Size and Growth of the Aging Population

In 1996, more than 1.2 million North Carolinians (about one-sixth of the state's population) were at least 60 years old, almost 920,000 state residents (one of every eight North Carolinians) were at least 65 years old, and about 92,000 of the state's senior citizens were 85 or older. In five North Carolina counties (Clay, Henderson, Macon, Moore, and Polk), more than one of every five citizens is at least 65 years old (see Figure 25-1).

The aging population in North Carolina has grown significantly during this century and will continue to increase, in absolute numbers and as a percentage of the total population, over the next thirty years. Demographic studies estimate that North Carolina's aging population will double between 1996 and 2025, rising to more than 2 million senior citizens (more than one-fifth of the total population) and including more than a quarter million senior citizens age eighty-five or older. More importantly, the number and proportion of older North Carolinians (especially, older women) age eighty-five or older (the "oldest old"), whose economic, health, and social needs are often greater, will

Figure 25-1
Percentage of North Carolina Population Age Sixty-Five or Older, 1990

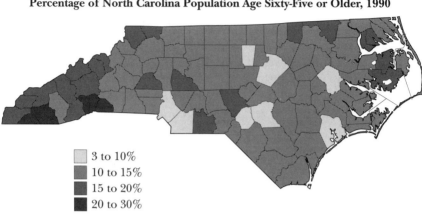

☐ 3 to 10%
■ 10 to 15%
■ 15 to 20%
■ 20 to 30%

Source: U.S. Bureau of the Census, 1990

almost certainly continue to increase as the result of increases in average life expectancy, decreases in mortality rates, and differences between men and women with respect to life expectancy and mortality.

Economic, Health, and Social Needs of the Elderly

With respect to the second question, "what are the economic, health, and social needs of the elderly that government aging programs seek to address?" research indicates that, although many people think of senior citizens as a homogenous group or make certain assumptions about the elderly as a class (for example, that all, or at least the great majority of all, elderly people are poor, vulnerable, incapacitated, or unable to care for themselves), older Americans are extremely diverse with respect to their economic needs, health status, and social characteristics, and that common stereotypes of the elderly are seldom accurate.

Economic Characteristics of Senior Citizens

Although a number of government aging programs—such as Social Security, SSI, State-County Special Assistance, food stamps, energy assistance, and the homestead property tax exemption—provide economic assistance to senior citizens, it would be incorrect to assume that the elderly, as a class, are poor.

Figure 25-2
Poverty Rates of the Elderly in North Carolina Counties, 1990

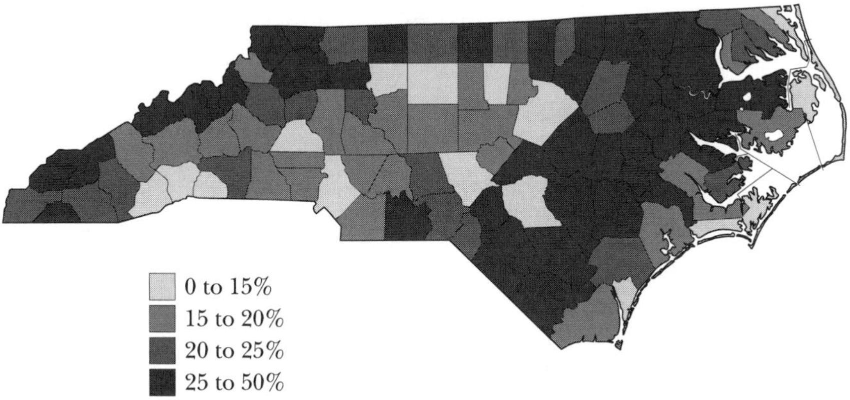

☐ 0 to 15%
■ 15 to 20%
■ 20 to 25%
■ 25 to 50%

Source: U.S. Bureau of the Census, 1990

Over the past forty years, the economic well-being of the elderly has improved dramatically, due in large part to financial assistance provided by government aging programs such as Social Security and SSI. Between 1957 and 1992, the median income (adjusted for inflation) of senior citizens more than doubled (from $6,537 to $14,548 per year for elderly men, and from $3,409 to $8,189 for elderly women), while the poverty rate of senior citizens was cut by more than half (from 24.6 percent to 10.8 percent) between 1970 and 1996. The elderly, as a class, also own substantial assets; the median per capita net worth of senior citizens is more than $88,000 (including the value of their homes).

On the other hand, more than one of every four older Americans (and more than one of every three persons age seventy-five or older) is poor or near poor (that is, has income less than 150 percent of the federal poverty level). Within the aging population, poverty is more prevalent among African Americans, elderly women, the "oldest old," elderly persons with functional impairments, and senior citizens who live alone.

North Carolina's elderly poverty rate is significantly higher than the national poverty rate for older Americans. In 1990 almost one of every five elderly North Carolinians lived in poverty, over 40 percent of senior citizens in North Carolina were either poor or near poor, the elderly poverty rate exceeded 30 percent in ten counties, and only five counties (Carteret, Catawba, Dare, Henderson, and Moore) had elderly poverty rates below the national average (see Figure 25-2). Almost a quarter of all elderly women in North Carolina are poor (almost twice the poverty rate for elderly men). In 1990, the poverty rate for elderly African Americans in North Carolina was twice that of elderly whites (37.8 percent compared to 15.6 percent); over half of elderly blacks in North Carolina had incomes of less than $10,000 per year (compared to 34.2 percent of elderly whites).

Health Status of the Elderly

Poor health among the elderly (especially among the "younger old") is not as prevalent as many people assume. The prevalence of chronic or severe health problems (such as heart disease, stroke, hypertension, arthritis, and hearing loss), cognitive impairments (such as Alzheimer's disease or dementia), and functional limitations (impaired abilities to perform daily activities such as eating, dressing, bathing, going to the toilet, doing housework, preparing meals, shopping, and traveling) due to physical or mental impairments, however, increases with age.

Research indicates that only one out of every four to five senior citizens has a physical or mental impairment that significantly limits his or her ability to engage in at least one essential activity of daily living. About half of senior citizens age eighty-five or older, however, have physical or mental impairments that significantly limit their ability to care for themselves. Functional limitations are more prevalent among elderly women than among elderly men, and among elderly African Americans than elderly whites.

Functional limitations due to physical and mental impairments contribute greatly to the need of many senior citizens—especially the "older old," those with multiple impairments, and senior citizens who live alone—for long-term care. Approximately 1.6 million older Americans (including about a quarter of all functionally-impaired senior citizens, and three of every five elderly persons with five or more functional impairments) live in nursing or adult care homes. Almost a quarter of all senior citizens age eighty-five or older live in nursing or adult care homes, and over 70 percent of all nursing or adult care home residents are women age seventy-five or older. Research also estimates that over half of all women who reached age sixty-five in 1990 (and about one-third of all men who reached age sixty-five) will be admitted as patients in nursing homes at some time during their lives. The average length of nursing home care is twenty-six months for elderly women and nineteen months for elderly men.

The cost of institutional long-term care has a significant impact on the elderly, their families, and government aging programs. In 1995 the average cost of nursing home care in the United States was about $3,400 per month ($41,000 per year). In 1993 the total cost of nursing home care was $75 billion; government programs (primarily Medicaid) paid about 60 percent of the cost of nursing home care for the elderly and disabled, and patients or their families paid almost all of the remainder.

Nursing and adult care homes, however, care for only a fraction of older Americans. Only 5 percent of all senior citizens live in nursing homes or other institutional facilities. The vast majority of senior citizens live in the community, often in their own homes, and most live with their spouses or other relatives. More than one of every four senior citizens (more than 40 percent of all elderly women and almost half of all senior citizens age eighty-five or older), however, live alone. Senior citizens who live alone are not necessarily socially isolated or vulnerable, but they often are more dependent on public or private social services than elderly persons who live with spouses or other relatives.

Because about three of every four senior citizens with functional limitations live in their own homes, in the homes of relatives, or in other community based settings, government aging programs increasingly have focused on providing long-term care through home and community based services (such as home health services under the Medicare, Medicaid, and Older Americans programs) that enable senior citizens to remain in their own homes or in the community rather than moving to a nursing or adult care home. (In 1993 government aging programs provided more than $20 billion in home health services for the elderly and disabled and accounted for more than three-quarters of total spending for home health care.)

In 1987, health care for the elderly cost about $162 billion (an average of more than $5,000 per year per elderly person and nearly $9,200 per year for those age 85 or older). Almost all senior citizens are covered by Medicare and over 60 percent of the cost of health care for senior citizens is paid by Medicare, Medicaid, or other government aging programs. Medicaid and Medicare, however, do not completely cover the health care needs of senior citizens. Medicaid covers only the poorest senior citizens and elderly nursing home patients. Medicare provides only limited coverage for nursing home care, does not pay the cost of most prescription drugs, and requires elderly beneficiaries to pay part of the cost of covered medical care through annual deductibles, monthly premiums, and copayments. As a result, senior citizens spend, on average, about one-eighth of their personal income for health care.

Government Responsibility for Senior Citizens

Today, few people would deny that government has at least some responsibility for the care and support of senior citizens. Nonetheless, it is important to note that the welfare of senior citizens is not the exclusive responsibility of government. Government aging programs do not, and cannot, meet all of the economic, health, and social needs of senior citizens. Indeed, studies indicate that family caregivers provide more than 80 percent of all personal care and in-home services for the elderly.

The real questions, instead, are what is (or should be) the scope of government's responsibility for senior citizens, and how is (or should) that responsibility be allocated among the federal government, state governments, and local governments?

The short answers to these questions are that the scope of government's responsibility for addressing the economic, health, and social needs of senior citizens has expanded dramatically during the past sixty years, and that the burden of meeting that responsibility is shared, though not necessarily equally, by the federal government, by each state government, and to at least some extent by local county and city governments.

Although the primary focus of this chapter is the authority and responsibility of county governments with respect to government aging programs, the role of North Carolina counties in providing services to senior citizens can be fully understood only in the context of the authority and responsibility exercised by the federal and state governments with respect to the care and support of senior citizens. The following sections of this chapter therefore describe some of the federal and state aging programs that provide services to senior citizens in North Carolina and some of the federal and state agencies that comprise the aging network.

Government Aging Programs

Answering the question posed previously, "what distinguishes government aging programs from other government programs and services?" is not as easy as it might appear.

Some government aging programs, such as Social Security, Medicare, and the Older Americans Act, are targeted (primarily, if not exclusively) to the elderly and provide assistance to virtually all senior citizens regardless of economic or social need. In many cases, however, government aging programs (such as SSI and Medicaid) provide assistance only to a particular subgroup of senior citizens—those senior citizens who are poor or financially needy. In addition, government programs that are targeted to the elderly or a subgroup of needy senior citizens (such as Medicaid) often provide assistance to needy, nonelderly individuals (such as the blind, disabled, or children) as well, and nonelderly beneficiaries of these programs sometimes outnumber elderly beneficiaries. In some cases, age may not even be a factor in determining eligibility for programs that are considered government aging programs. For example, although senior citizens comprise about 70 percent of the persons served by the adult protective services program, the program is targeted to all disabled adults—not just elderly adults—who have been abused, neglected, or exploited. Similarly, other government programs (such as food stamps and energy assistance) are broadly targeted to persons who are financially needy regardless of their age, but nonetheless provide needed assistance to large numbers of senior citizens.

Thus although government aging programs provide some type of assistance, service, or benefit to persons who, by at least some definition, are elderly and directly or indirectly address their economic, health, or social needs as senior citizens, it is not always clear whether or to what extent a particular government program or service should be considered a government aging program.

The "Aging Network"

Senior citizens receive assistance from a large number of public (federal, state, and local government) and private (nonprofit and for-profit) agencies that provide a wide range of services (economic, health, housing, nutrition, employment, transportation, social) to several distinct categories of older adults (well, at-risk, frail, poor, nonpoor).

This multitude of public agencies and private organizations that provide economic, health, social, and other services to senior citizens is sometimes referred to as the "aging network." The term "network," however, may imply that public and private services for senior citizens are provided in a much more organized, seamless, and coordinated manner than they really are. Nonetheless, the term is accurate to the extent that it conveys the fact that the system of aging services is an amalgamation of many distinct programs separately administered by different public and private agencies; that the welfare of senior citizens is a shared responsibility of the federal government, states, local governments, private agencies, families, and senior citizens themselves; and that to understand how

America cares for its senior citizens, one must look at the big picture rather than focusing on only one or two particular government programs or services.

Federal Programs for Senior Citizens

History and Overview

The enactment of the Social Security Act in 1935 marked the first time that the federal government assumed significant responsibility for ensuring the economic security of the nation's elderly.

Title II of the Social Security Act created the Old Age Insurance program [now known as the Old Age, Survivors, and Disability Insurance (OASDI) program and commonly referred to as Social Security]. Title I of the Social Security Act authorized the Old Age Assistance (OAA) program, which was administered by state or local welfare agencies, was funded by federal and state or local tax revenues, and provided financial assistance to the elderly poor. [The OAA program was replaced in 1974 by the federally administered Supplemental Security Income (SSI) program.]

The federal government's responsibility for the nation's senior citizens expanded dramatically in 1965 when Congress amended the Social Security Act to establish the Medicare and Medicaid programs, which provide health insurance for the elderly, and enacted the Older Americans Act, the only federal social services statute targeted specifically for the elderly.

The extent of the federal government's responsibility for senior citizens is reflected by the fact that almost one-third of the federal budget (about $522 billion in 1995) is spent for retirement, welfare, health care, housing, and social programs for the elderly. Indeed, over the past sixty years, the federal government, rather than state or local governments, has assumed primary responsibility for meeting many of the economic, health, and social needs of senior citizens, and today federal aging programs for the elderly, such as Social Security, SSI, Medicare, Medicaid, and the Older Americans Act, are undoubtedly the most important government programs for North Carolina's senior citizens.

Federal aging programs affect the responsibility of state and local governments for senior citizens in two ways. First, by assuming responsibility for creating, administering, and financing a number of important government programs for senior citizens (such as Social Security, SSI, and Medicare), the federal government, in effect, has relieved state and local governments of at least some of the responsibility for providing financial assistance and health care to senior citizens that they might otherwise have been called upon to assume, leaving them free to use state and local resources to supplement or complement federal aging programs or provide services to other segments of the population. Second, state and local governments sometimes have a direct role in administering or financing some federal aging programs. For example, although both Medicaid and the Older Americans Act are federal aging programs in the sense that they were created by federal law, are governed in large part by federal laws and regulations, and are financed primarily by federal tax revenues, both of these federal aging programs are administered by state and local aging, health, or social services agencies and are financed in part by state or local funds. Thus even with respect to so-called federal aging programs, there may be at least some degree of shared responsibility among the federal government, states, and local governments.

Social Security

Social Security is the largest and most important government program that provides financial assistance to senior citizens. In 1995 the Social Security program paid more than $250 billion in benefits to 31.5 million older Americans (including approximately $6.67 billion to almost 850,000 elderly North Carolinians). Almost nine out of every ten Americans between the ages of sixty-five and seventy-one, and virtually all senior citizens age seventy-two or older, receive monthly Social Security benefits, which constitute the primary, and often the sole, source of income for many senior citizens.

The federal government, rather than state or local governments, is responsible for establishing policies, financing, and administering all aspects of the Social Security program (except the disability determination process which is administered by state agencies under contracts with the Social Security Administration). Policies regarding coverage of workers under the Social Security program, eligibility for Social Security benefits, the Social Security retirement age, the amount of monthly Social Security benefits, cost-of-living increases, and other matters are established by Congress through legislation amending the Social Security Act. Social Security benefits for elderly, retired workers and their families are financed by the federal FICA payroll tax on employers, employees, and self-employed persons. At the local level, Social Security is administered by employees of the federal Social Security Administration through a system of district offices, including forty Social Security district offices in North Carolina.

Supplemental Security Income

The federal Supplemental Security Income (SSI) program provides financial assistance to the elderly (and to blind or disabled adults and children) whose Social Security benefits and other income are insufficient to provide them with a minimal (below poverty) standard of living. In 1996 almost 2.1 million older Americans (about 6 percent of all older Americans and more than 55 percent of the elderly poor) received more than $6.5 billion in SSI benefits. In North Carolina, about 67,000 senior citizens received more than $125 million annually in SSI benefits.

The SSI program was established in 1974 to replace the Old Age Assistance, Aid to the Blind, and Aid to the Totally and Permanently Disabled programs. These programs were funded jointly by the federal government and states and were administered by state or local welfare agencies subject to federal and state rules and policies. By contrast, the federal government, rather than state or local governments, exercises complete responsibility for the SSI program (except for payment of federally mandated supplemental benefits in some states).

Like Social Security, SSI is administered by the federal government through the Social Security Administration. Eligibility requirements and benefit levels are established by federal law and regulations, and SSI benefits are financed primarily by federal tax revenues.

Medicare

Medicare is a federal health insurance program for the elderly. It is administered by the federal government through the U.S. Department of Health and Human Services' Health Care Financing Administration and through private insurance companies (known as Medicare intermediaries and carriers) that contract with the federal government to process claims and make payments to beneficiaries within each state. State and local governments have no responsibility or authority with respect to the administration or financing of Medicare.

The Medicare program consists of two parts. Part A provides insurance for hospital care, skilled nursing care, home health care, and hospice care, and is financed by a portion of the FICA payroll tax and other federal tax revenues. Part B covers medical services provided by doctors, outpatient care, and laboratory and diagnostic tests. The cost of Medicare Part B is financed by monthly premiums paid by enrolled beneficiaries and by federal tax revenues.

Most elderly people are covered by the Medicare. Anyone who is at least sixty-five years old and insured under the Social Security system is eligible for coverage under Medicare Part A. In 1995 approximately 32.7 million senior citizens (about 95 percent of all older Americans) were covered by Medicare Part A, and Medicare Part A covered approximately 890,000 elderly North Carolinians. Enrollment in Medicare Part B is voluntary; anyone who is at least sixty-five years old, regardless of whether he or she is insured under Social Security or is eligible for Medicare Part A, may purchase health insurance through Medicare Part B by paying a monthly premium ($43.80 in 1997). In 1995 approximately 31.3 older Americans (including more than 870,000 elderly North Carolinians) were enrolled in Medicare Part B.

In 1995 the Medicare program paid almost $155 billion for health care for senior citizens. As noted earlier, however, Medicare does not pay the entire cost of providing health care to senior citizens. In 1995, elderly and disabled Medicare beneficiaries paid approximately $37 billion (an average of $1,385 per enrollee per year and 7.2 percent of per capita income) for Medicare deductibles, premiums, copayments, and other charges for covered Medicare services. In addition, Medicare does not cover the cost of prescription drugs and provides only limited coverage for long-term care in a nursing home. Many senior citizens therefore rely on supplemental health insurance or other government programs to help meet their health care needs.

Medicaid

The Medicaid program provides health care to elderly persons (and to disabled persons, children, and pregnant women) who are too poor to pay for medical care. Elderly people who receive SSI benefits generally are eligible for Medicaid as well. Senior citizens also may qualify for Medicaid if they cannot afford the cost of nursing home care or if their income minus the cost of their medical care is less than the Medicaid eligibility limit.

Medicaid is a significant source of health care for the elderly poor. In 1995 Medicaid paid almost $40 billion for medical care for the elderly poor, and approximately 4.4 million older Americans (about one of every eight senior citizens and most, but not all, of the elderly poor) were covered by Medicaid. In North Carolina, Medicaid provides almost $1.2 billion per year in medical care to more than 168,000 elderly North Carolinians. The elderly, however, constitute only a small minority of eligible Medicaid recipients. In North Carolina, about one of every seven Medicaid recipients is sixty-five or older. Medicaid benefits for the elderly, however, account for about one-third of total Medicaid spending (an average of more than $7,000 per year per elderly Medicaid recipient).

The federal government pays more than half the cost of the Medicaid program and establishes many of the policies, rules, and regulations governing the program. The federal Medicaid law, however, gives each state some flexibility in designing and administering its own Medicaid program, resulting in significant differences among the states with respect to eligibility standards, the amount and scope of medical services provided to eligible recipients, and the amount of reimbursement paid to hospitals, doctors, and other health care providers. Unlike Social Security, SSI, and Medicare, Medicaid is administered at the state and local levels by state or local health or social services agencies, rather than a federal agency.

The roles of the state and counties with respect to financing and administering North Carolina's Medicaid program are discussed in the following sections of this chapter.

Older Americans Act

The Older Americans Act (OAA), enacted in 1965, provides federal funding to states for a wide range of services for older Americans, including information and referral, case management, transportation, in-home services (chore, homemaker, and personal care), home-delivered meals, congregate meals, senior centers, adult day care, nursing home ombudsman and elder abuse programs, legal services, and other home- and community-based supportive services.

Anyone who is age sixty or older is eligible to receive nutrition and supportive services under Title III of the OAA. (Individuals age fifty-five or older are eligible for the community employment services program under Title V of the act.) Federal law, however, requires that aging programs funded under Title III give priority to older persons with the greatest economic and social need, particularly low-income minority older persons. There are no mandatory fees for services under the Older Americans Act. Older persons, however, are encouraged to make contributions to help defray the costs of services, and these contributions (about $200 million per year) are used to expand services for the elderly. In 1995 almost 7.5 million senior citizens age sixty or older (16 percent of all older Americans) received OAA-funded services; about 40 percent of the older Americans served under the OAA had incomes below the federal poverty level.

Federal funds under Title III of the OAA are distributed to each state based on the number of senior citizens (age sixty or older) who live in the state. State and area agencies on aging may use federal OAA funds to pay up to 85 percent of the cost of nutrition services, social and supportive services, and senior centers for older Americans, and must provide matching state or local funds to pay the remaining cost of services. In 1995 Congress appropriated $831 million for services for older Americans under Title III of the OAA; total spending (including other federal funding, state and local funding, and fees paid by persons using the programs) for aging programs funded under Title III of the OAA was about $1.7 billion. Congregate and home delivered meals and transportation services for the elderly accounted for almost two-thirds of total Title III OAA service expenditures.

In order to receive federal funding under the Older Americans Act, a state must establish a state aging agency (in North Carolina, the Division of Aging in the state Department of Health and Human Services), submit a state aging plan for approval by the federal Administration on Aging, adopt a funding formula for distribution of federal OAA funding within the state, divide the state into one or more aging planning and service areas, and designate an area agency on aging (AAA) for each planning and service area.

Under the OAA, a state may designate as a planning and service area (1) any city, county, or other general purpose unit of local government that has a population of at least 100,000 persons (and any adjacent area that the state determines is necessary and desirable for the effective administration of federally funded aging programs), or (2) any multicity or multicounty region within the state that is recognized for purposes of areawide planning (and any adjacent area that the state determines is necessary and desirable for the effective administration of federally funded aging programs).

North Carolina has established eighteen aging planning and service areas that are coextensive with the state's eighteen, multicounty planning

Table 25-1
North Carolina Area Agencies on Aging (AAAs) and Planning and Service Areas

Region	AAAs and Counties Served
Region A	*Southwestern NC Planning and Economic Development Commission (Bryson City):* Cherokee, Clay, Graham, Haywood, Jackson, Macon, Swain
Region B	*Land-of-Sky Regional Council (Asheville):* Buncombe, Henderson, Madison, Transylvania
Region C	*Isothermal Planning and Economic Development Commission (Rutherfordton):* Cleveland, McDowell, Polk, Rutherford
Region D	*Region D Council of Government (Boone):* Alleghany, Ashe, Avery, Mitchell, Watauga, Wilkes, Yancey
Region E	*Western Piedmont Council of Government (Hickory):* Alexander, Burke, Caldwell, Catawba
Region F	*Centralina Council of Government (Charlotte):* Cabarrus, Gaston, Iredell, Lincoln, Mecklenburg, Rowan, Stanly, Union
Region G	*Piedmont Triad Council of Government (Greensboro):* Alamance, Caswell, Davidson, Guilford, Randolph, Rockingham
Region H	*Pee Dee Council of Governments (Rockingham):* Anson, Montgomery, Moore, Richmond
Region I	*Northwest Piedmont Council of Governments (Winston-Salem):* Davie, Forsyth, Stokes, Surry, Yadkin
Region J	*Triangle J Council of Government (Research Triangle Park):* Chatham, Durham, Johnston, Lee, Orange, Wake
Region K	*Kerr-Tar Regional Council of Governments (Henderson):* Franklin, Granville, Person, Vance, Warren
Region L	*Region L Council of Government (Rocky Mount):* Edgecombe, Halifax, Nash, Northampton, Wilson
Region M	*Mid-Carolina Council of Government (Fayetteville):* Cumberland, Harnett, Sampson
Region N	*Lumber River Council of Governments (Lumberton):* Bladen, Hoke, Robeson, Scotland
Region O	*Cape Fear Council of Governments (Wilmington):* Brunswick, Columbus, New Hanover, Pender
Region P	*Neuse River Council of Governments (New Bern):* Carteret, Craven, Duplin, Green, Jones, Lenoir, Onslow, Pamlico, Wayne
Region Q	*Mid East Commission (Washington):* Beaufort, Bertie, Hertford, Martin, Pitt
Region R	*Albemarle Commission (Hertford):* Camden, Chowan, Currituck, Dare, Gates, Hyde, Pasquotank, Perquimans, Tyrrell, Washington

and development regions (established in 1970) (see Table 25-1). The OAA, however, allows the state to designate additional planning and service areas, establish different planning and service areas, or redraw the boundaries of planning and service areas, and any city or county with a population of more than 100,000 or any multicity or multicounty region may request the state Division of Aging to designate it as an aging planning and service area. (None of the six North Carolina cities or twenty-two North Carolina counties with populations of at least 100,000 has done so.)

The state aging agency must designate for each aging planning and service area an area agency on aging (AAA), which is responsible for administering OAA funds at the local level. Under the Older Americans Act, an AAA may be any of the following:

1. An established office on aging that is operating with a planning and service area
2. A city or county office or agency that is designated to function solely as an area agency on aging
3. An office or agency that is designated by a combination of cities or counties to function solely as an area agency on aging
4. Any public or nonprofit private agency that is designated by the state aging agency as the area agency on aging for a planning and service area

In North Carolina, the state Division of Aging has designated aging offices within regional councils of government, regional economic development commissions, or lead regional organizations as AAAs (see Table 25-1).

Federal OAA funds for nutrition and other home and community based supportive services received by the state must be distributed to each AAA within the state based on an intrastate funding formula that is developed by the state aging agency and approved by the federal Administration on Aging. The intrastate funding formula must take into account (1) the geographic distribution of older Americans (age sixty or older) within the state, and (2) the distribution among planning and service areas of older individuals who have the greatest economic and social needs, particularly low-income minority older Americans.

Each AAA, with the advice of an advisory council (comprised of senior citizens, service providers, local elected officials, and others) and input from the public and senior citizens within the area, is required to develop an area aging plan that does the following:

1. Determines the extent of need for aging programs and services within the area
2. Evaluates the availability and effectiveness of other resources for meeting the need for aging programs and services

3. Designates a focal point for comprehensive delivery of aging services in each community
4. Determines, within the limits of federal and state rules, the supportive services that will be provided to older Americans within the planning and service area and the amount of funding allocated for each service
5. Provides for the delivery of aging programs and service to older Americans through public or private providers
6. Ensures that OAA funds will be administered consistent with applicable federal laws and regulations

AAAs may provide some aging services (such as long-term care ombudsman, information and referral, and case management) directly to older Americans within the planning and service area. An AAA, however, may not directly provide nutrition services, in-home services, or other supportive services unless the state aging agency determines that direct provision of aging services by an AAA is necessary to ensure adequate provision of the service or that the service may be provided more economically by the AAA than by a service provider. Therefore, AAA's generally must enter into contracts (subject to federal procurement regulations governing federal grantees) with public agencies, private nonprofit organizations, and for-profit companies to provide nutrition, supportive, and social services to senior citizens within the area, paying the contractor on a per unit basis for meals or other services provided to senior citizens.

The responsibilities of the state Division of Aging, AAAs, and counties under the Older Americans Act and the state's Home and Community Care Block Grant are discussed in more detail later.

The State's Responsibility for Senior Citizens

Despite the federal government's extensive involvement in providing services for senior citizens, North Carolina and other states play an important role in administering or funding several joint federal-state aging programs (including Medicaid and the Older Americans Act) as well as establishing, administering, and funding a wide variety of programs and services for the elderly that supplement or complement the federal aging programs discussed previously.

State Programs for Senior Citizens

Like other states, North Carolina provides a wide array of economic, health, transportation, education, employment, social, and other services for the state's senior citizens. Although a complete listing and description of every state aging program is almost impossible and beyond the scope of this chapter, Table 25-2 lists some of the government aging programs that are established or authorized by state law, administered by or through state agencies, or funded in whole or in part by state appropriations.

As discussed previously, some state aging programs are, in fact, joint federal-state aging programs (such as the Medicaid, food stamp, energy assistance, and Older Americans programs) that are established by federal law and financed in large part by federal grants to the state, but administered by state or local agencies and partially funded by the state or local governments. A few state programs for senior citizens (for example, the state university tuition waiver for senior citizens) are created, administered, and funded entirely by the state.

In many cases, however, state aging programs are created by state law, governed by state law, rules, and policies, and supported in part by state tax revenues, but locally administered and partially financed by counties or other local agencies. For example, although the State-County Special Assistance program (which provides financial assistance to elderly residents of adult care homes) is a state aging program, state law requires counties to pay half of the cost of providing financial assistance to elderly adult care home residents and to administer the program through county departments of social services.

Thus North Carolina counties often share administrative or financial responsibility for state and joint federal-state aging programs.

The State "Aging Budget"

Examining the state's "aging budget" (the total amount of federal, state, and local government spending for all of the different types of services provided to North Carolina's senior citizens through federal, state, and local government aging programs) illustrates the types of services provided to senior citizens by government aging programs, the scope of government's responsibility for senior citizens, and the allocation of this responsibility among the federal government, the state, and local governments. Compiling the state's aging budget, however, is complicated

Table 25-2
State Aging Programs

Agency	Program
Department of Commerce	JTPA Older Workers Training Program
Department of Insurance	Seniors' Health Insurance Information Program
	Licensing and Regulation of Continuing Care Retirement Communities
	Regulation of Medicare Supplement Insurance
	Regulation of Long-Term Care Insurance
Department of Revenue	"Homestead" Property Tax Exemption
Department of Transportation	Elderly and Handicapped Transportation Assistance Program
Division of Aging (DHHS)	Older Americans Programs
	Home and Community-Based Services
	Long-Term Care Ombudsman
	Senior Tar Heel Legislature
	Community Service Employment Program
Division of Facility Services (DHHS)	Licensure, Inspection, and Regulation of Nursing Homes and Adult Care Homes
Division of Health Services (DHHS)	Older Adult Health Program
	Arthritis Program
	Home Health Services Program
	Hypertension Program
	Kidney Program
	Cancer Control Program
	Diabetes Control Program
	Heart Disease and Stroke Prevention Task Force
Division of Medical Assistance (DHHS)	Medicaid
	Medicaid Community Alternatives Program
Division of Mental Health, Developmental Disabilities, and Substance Abuse Services (DHHS)	Psychiatric Hospitals
	Alzheimer's Unit
	Mental Retardation Centers
	Alcohol and Substance Abuse Treatment Centers
	Area Mental Health Authorities
Division of Parks and Recreation (DENR)	Technical Assistance for Senior Centers
Division of Social Services (DHHS)	Adult Protective Services
	Public Guardianship for Incompetent Adults
	State-County Special Assistance
	Food Stamps
	Low-Income Energy Assistance

Continued

Table 25-2 (*continued*)

Agency	Program
Housing Finance Agency	Financing and Tax Credits for Construction of Low-Income Rental Housing
	Loans for Predevelopment Costs for Assisted Living Projects
	Home Equity Conversion Mortgage Program
Local Government Employees' Retirement System	Retirement Benefits for Retired Local Government Employees
Office of State Personnel	Older Workers Recruitment and Retention Program
	PREPARE Pre-Retirement Planning Program
Teachers and State Employees' Retirement System	Retirement Benefits for Retired Teachers and State Employees
University of North Carolina	Free Tuition for Senior Citizens
	Elderhostel
	Institute of Aging
	NC Center for Creative Retirement
	Encore Program for Lifelong Enrichment

by the number of federal, state, and local government aging programs, the number of federal, state, and local agencies responsible for administering these programs, the number of funding sources for these programs, differing definitions of elderly among these programs, differing tracking and reporting requirements, and other factors.

Nonetheless, in recent years the state DHHS Division of Aging has compiled a state aging budget that reports the total amount (including federal funds received by the state and some locally funded spending as well as appropriations from the state's General Fund) spent by or through eight state agencies (the Department of Transportation and the DHHS Divisions of Aging, Services for the Blind, Health Services, Medical Assistance, Mental Health, Social Services, and Vocational Rehabilitation) for institutional care (nursing and adult care homes); home health and in-home services; hospitals, physicians, and other health care; economic support; and other social and supportive services for the elderly (age sixty and older).

According to the state Division of Aging, North Carolina's state aging budget for SFY 1995–96 was approximately $1.67 billion. The Division of Aging's state aging budget, however, does not include more than $10 billion in spending by the federal government for Social Security,

SSI, Medicare, veterans benefits, or retirement benefits for older North Carolinians, nor spending by the state or local governments for retirement benefits, the "homestead" property tax exemption, or a number of other state aging programs listed in Table 25-2. The state aging budget therefore would look quite different—with respect to its size, source of funding, and allocation of funding for various categories of services for senior citizens—if one considered the total amount of spending for elderly North Carolinians through all federal, state, and local government aging programs.

In terms of the scope of government responsibility for senior citizens, the total amount of spending for aging programs included in the state aging budget ($1.67 billion) is certainly not insignificant, providing about $1,800 in assistance and services for every senior citizen and constituting about 9 percent of total state government expenditures.

With respect to the allocation of government responsibility for senior citizens, the state aging budget clearly indicates the extent to which federally-funded spending for aging programs exceeds state and local spending. First, the $1.67 billion in spending for state aging programs included in the state aging budget is completely overshadowed by the $10 billion annual spending for North Carolina's senior citizens through federal aging programs such as Social Security, SSI, and Medicare. In addition, federal funds received by North Carolina under Medicaid, the Older Americans Act, and other federal aging programs ($1.05 billion in SFY 1995–96) pay about 63 percent of the cost of state aging programs included in the state aging budget. State-funded appropriations for aging programs ($483 million in 1995–96) constitute only 29 percent of the total state aging budget and less than 5 percent of total state General Fund spending; local funding (from local taxes, private agencies, and fees) pays about 8 percent of the total cost of state aging programs.

Only 2 percent ($33.8 million) of the state aging budget is administered by or under the supervision of the state Division of Aging. Medicaid spending for the elderly (almost $1.4 billion in 1995–96) administered through the DHHS Division of Medical Assistance accounts for more than 82 percent of spending included in the state aging budget, far exceeding spending for mental health ($133.2 million), Special Assistance ($57.5 million), food stamps ($51.2 million), and home and community care ($32.6 million).

Spending for health care accounts for about 95 percent of the state aging budget. Medicaid and Special Assistance payments for the care of elderly residents in nursing and adult care homes (over $800 million in 1995–96) constitute almost half of the state aging budget, compared to about 10 percent ($170 million) in spending for home health and in-home care for the elderly. (The ratio of spending for institutional care compared to home and community based care would be considerably smaller, however, if Medicare spending for home health care was included in the state aging budget.)

Economic support of the elderly (primarily food stamps and energy assistance payments) constitutes about 3 percent ($53 million in 1995–96) of the state aging budget. (Again, however, the amount of spending for economic support of the elderly and the ratio of economic support to health care spending would be dramatically different if the state aging budget included spending under the federal Social Security, SSI, and Medicare programs.) Spending for other social and supportive services (about $26 million) accounts for only 1.5 percent of spending for state aging programs.

The Role of Counties in Providing Services for Senior Citizens

History and Overview

Historically, North Carolina counties have always exercised some degree of responsibility for the care and support of their senior citizens. The scope of government responsibility for the elderly, however, and the allocation of this responsibility among local governments, states, and the federal government has changed greatly over the past two centuries, and especially over the past sixty years.

During the 1800s, average life expectancies were much shorter than today; there were far fewer older Americans and the elderly comprised a much smaller proportion of the total population. More importantly, the care and support of the elderly was generally considered a family respon-sibility, and older Americans for the most part were not recognized as a distinct demographic, socioeconomic, or political group for whom gov-ernment had any significant responsibility.

Before 1935, the role of North Carolina counties in providing assis-tance for the elderly was fairly limited, but nonetheless significant in comparison with the roles of the state and federal governments. Since 1935, county responsibility for senior citizens has decreased significantly in relation to the roles of the federal and state governments, but has in-creased in absolute terms as counties have been called upon, by the state and their own senior citizens, to administer and support a number of federal, state, and local aging programs to address the needs of their growing aging population.

Until 1935, the only significant program of government assistance for the elderly (other than federal and state pensions for elderly or disabled veterans and their widows) was the system of "poor relief" for "aged and infirm" adults who were too old or sick to work, who could not support themselves financially, and whose families were unable or unwilling to care for them. In North Carolina, state law required counties (rather than the state government) to administer and pay the cost of poor relief for poor, dependent, disabled, or elderly citizens, and counties often discharged their obligation (in at least some minimal fashion) by building and operating county "homes for the aged and infirm." By 1922, counties operated ninety-two county homes that provided care for some 1,800 elderly and disabled residents. During the 1940s and 1950s, county homes for the aged gradually were replaced by privately-owned board and care homes (or rest homes) for the elderly, nursing homes, and other federal and state programs (such as the federal-state Old Age Assistance program and the state Boarding Care Fund for the Aged and Infirm) that provided assistance and care for the elderly. By 1968, only nine counties continued to operate county homes for the aged, and today only Beaufort County continues to do so.

More than anything else, however, the 1935 enactment of the federal Social Security Act marked not only a dramatic increase in the scope of government responsibility for the elderly but also a shift of government responsibility for the elderly from state and local governments to the federal government—changes that were amplified by the creation of the federal Medicare, Medicaid, and Older Americans programs in 1965, the federalization of the Old Age Assistance through the SSI program in 1974, and the creation or expansion of other federal aging programs over the past sixty years. This expansion of federal (and, to a lesser extent, state) responsibility for senior citizens has decreased local government responsibility for the elderly *vis a vis* the federal government. It has not, however, completely eliminated the role of counties in providing assistance and services for senior citizens, and by contrast may have served as a catalyst for increased county involvement in administering, supporting, and supplementing federal and state aging programs.

Perhaps the primary reason for the continued involvement of North Carolina counties in providing assistance to senior citizens in the face of increased federal and state responsibility for the elderly is North Carolina's long tradition of providing public assistance and social services to the poor, disabled, and elderly through a state human services system that requires counties to administer and pay part of the cost of these programs. Thus when North Carolina established the new federal-state Old Age Assistance (OAA) program in 1937, state law required counties to administer OAA through their county boards of public welfare and to pay half of the nonfederal share of cash assistance payments to elderly county residents. Today, the state continues to require counties to assume or share responsibility for administering and financing a number of federal and state aging programs, including Medicaid, State-County Special Assistance, adult protective services, and the homestead property tax exemption.

Thus today, as in the past, the scope of the responsibility of North Carolina counties for their senior citizens depends in part on the extent to which the federal or state governments have assumed responsibility for creating, administering, and financing government programs and services that meet the economic, health, and social needs of their senior citizens. In addition, however, because counties are political subdivisions of the state, they *may* exercise only those government functions that state law authorizes them to perform and *must* exercise those government functions that state law directs them to perform. Thus the scope of a county's legal *obligation* or legal *authority* to provide services to senior citizens is determined by state law and policies that allow or require counties, as political subdivisions of the state, to administer or financially support government aging programs.

General Statutory Authority to Provide and Fund Services for Senior Citizens

State law gives local governments broad, discretionary authority to provide and fund services for senior citizens. Under G.S. 160A-497, both counties and cities may "undertake programs for the assistance and care of senior citizens [age sixty or older], including but not limited to programs for in-home services, food service, counseling, recreation, and transportation, and [may] appropriate funds for such programs."

G.S. 160A-497 allows counties to establish county departments of aging, construct senior citizens centers, establish or fund new programs and services for the elderly, or provide funding to expand or supplement aging programs or services provided by other government agencies or public or private organizations. The law, however, does not require any city or county to provide or fund services for senior citizens.

Under G.S. 160A-497, counties may provide programs and services for senior citizens directly through a county department on aging or another county office, by contract with any other government agency or public or private organization, or by appropriating county funds to any government agency or public or private organization. Although services may be provided to any county resident age sixty or older, the county may establish additional requirements that limit the number of senior citizens eligible for assistance or target assistance to particular categories of senior citizens (provided that the additional restrictions are reasonable, fair, and nondiscriminatory).

The Role of Counties under the Older Americans Act and the Home and Community Care Block Grant Program

One of the ways that counties provide services to senior citizens is by acting, through the county department on aging, the county department of social services, or another county agency, as an aging service provider under a contract with an area agency on aging (AAA) to provide congregate or home-delivered meals, in-home services, transportation, or other social or supportive services to senior citizens under the federal Older Americans Act (OAA). But while federal law allows counties to receive federal OAA funding and provide services to senior citizens under the OAA, it does not give counties the authority to administer federal OAA funds (that is, to plan how federal OAA funds will be used, to allocate federal OAA funds, to decide what agencies will receive OAA funds, or to contract with community aging services providers to provide aging services under the OAA) unless the state has designated the county as an area agency on aging. Rules adopted by the state Division of Aging, however, appear to give counties greater authority with respect to federal OAA funds, OAA programs, and state funding for home and community based services for senior citizens.

In 1991 the General Assembly enacted legislation [G.S. 143B-181.1(a)(11)] creating a new Home and Community Care Block Grant (HCCBG). The HCCBG is comprised of federal funding under the Older Americans Act, federal funding under the Social Services Block Grant for the state's respite care program, state funds for home and community care services administered by the state Division of Aging, state funds for in-home services and adult day care for older adults formerly administered by the state Division of Social Services, and other appropriated state funds. Federal grants for congregate meals, home delivered meals, and other social and supportive services under Title III of the Older Americans Act, however, comprise the majority of funds (about $29.4 million in SFY 1995–96) included in the HCCBG. In 1995–96, aging programs funded through the HCCBG provided home-delivered meals to almost 16,000 elderly North Carolinians, congregate meals to over 32,000 senior citizens, transportation to over 20,000 elderly persons, and in-home aide services to more than 8,000 senior citizens.

Although the 1991 legislation establishing the HCCBG does not specify what services may be funded under the HCCBG, describe how or to whom block grant funds will be distributed, or discuss what role counties play with respect to the HCCBG (other than providing that allocations of block grant funds to counties may not be less than the resources made available to support older adults during SFY 1990–91), DHHS rules (10 NCAC 22R.0101 through 22R.0301) implementing the HCCBG provide that HCCBG funds will be allocated to each of North Carolina's 100 counties and expended pursuant to a county funding plan for home and community care services for senior citizens developed by a county-designated lead agency on aging.

The DHHS rules authorize the board of commissioners of each county to designate, on an annual basis, a public or private agency as the county's "lead agency for planning and coordination" of aging programs and services. (In 1992 thirty-eight counties designated the AAA as the county's lead agency for the HCCBG, over thirty counties named the county departments of social services or aging as the lead agency for the county, and twelve counties authorized the county manager to act as the lead agency with respect to the HCCBG.) Under the state's HCCBG rules, the county-designated lead agency for aging is responsible for developing, with input from a county block grant advisory committee appointed by the board of county commissioners, a county HCCBG funding plan that identifies (1) the HCCBG-funded services that will be provided to older adults within the county, (2) the portion of the county's HCCBG funding that will be expended for each type of service, and (3) the agencies or organizations that will receive HCCBG funds to provide nutrition, social, and supportive services to older adults within the county. A copy of the county's preliminary HCCBG funding plan for the following state fiscal year, including the amounts of the county's HCCBG allocation and required local matching funds, must be provided to the county finance officer by April 30.

The state HCCBG rules do not explicitly address the manner in which a county determines which agency or organization will be designated by the county funding plan to provide a particular home and community care service to the county's senior citizens. Thus counties, acting through their designated lead aging agencies and boards of county commissioners, apparently have broad discretion to designate any public or private agency as an aging services provider. A county's HCCBG funding plan may provide that a particular service, such as home-delivered meals, in-home care, or transportation, will be provided by an established county department on aging, the county department of social services, another county agency, a city or other local government agency, a non-profit council on aging, a community action agency, another private nonprofit organization, a public or private hospital, a home health agency, or a for-profit business. A county funding plan also may designate one aging service provider to provide all home and community care services within the county, may designate different service providers to provide particular services, or may designate more than one service provider to provide a particular service. In addition, the county funding plan developed by the lead agency apparently may designate the lead agency itself (other than AAAs which generally are prohibited by the federal OAA law and regulations from directly providing certain types of aging services) as a local aging service provider.

Unlike the federal OAA regulations (which appear to require AAAs to expend federal OAA funds for nutrition, social, and supportive services through contracts with aging service providers pursuant to federal procurement regulations that generally require competitive bidding), the state HCCBG rules do not expressly require that contracts between the county and aging services providers be awarded pursuant to a competitive bid process. State law (G.S. 143-129) requires counties to use a formal procurement process with respect to certain construction or repair contracts, contracts for certain professional services, and certain contracts for the purchase of property or equipment, but does not require competitive bidding for most types of services provided to or on behalf of a county. Counties and lead aging agencies therefore are not required by state law to use formal procurement or competitive bidding procedures in selecting agencies to provide aging services under the county's HCCBG funding plan. They may, however, be required to do so under federal procurement regulations that apply to federal OAA funds, and may choose to adopt local procurement policies that will ensure the selection of aging service providers that will provide quality services at the most reasonable cost.

After the lead agency holds a public hearing on the county HCCBG funding plan, the plan must be submitted first to the chair of the board of county commissioners for approval, and then to the appropriate AAA. The AAA is required to approve the county HCCBG funding plan if the amount of funding allocated for aging services meets the minimum funding levels required by the Division of Aging, the county's HCCBG is completely utilized but not exceeded, and the funding plan documents are accurate and complete. Upon approval of a county's HCCBG funding plan, the AAA must enter into a grant agreement with the county incorporating the county's funding plan.

Each county's share of HCCBG funds is determined based upon the state's Older Americans Act intrastate funding formula (which provides an equal share of base funding for each county plus additional funding based on the number of senior citizens living in the county, the number of poor, minority, and rural elderly county residents) and the legislatively mandated formula for distributing state funds for respite care. The state Division of Aging distributes HCCBG funds to counties through AAAs on a monthly basis by making interim payments based on estimated expenditures for home and community care services provided by public and private agencies under the county's HCCBG funding plan and final settlements based on monthly reports from aging service providers indicating the amount and type of services actually provided to senior citizens.

Payments to counties for HCCBG services may not exceed 90 percent of the net allowable cost (allowable cost minus program income from fees or other sources) of services actually provided to eligible senior citizens. Counties therefore must provide local funding (from county revenues or matching funds provided by aging services providers) equal to at least 10 percent of the county's HCCBG allocation. Upon receipt of HCCBG funds from the state, the county finance officer must promptly reimburse public or private aging service providers for services provided to senior citizens under the county's HCCBG plan.

The state HCCBG rules therefore significantly increase the role of counties—through the board of county commissioners, the lead agency designated by the board of county commissioners, and the advisory committee appointed by the board of county commissioners—with respect to aging programs funded by the state Home and Community Care Block Grant. According to the state Division of Aging, the state HCCBG

> gives County Commissioners maximum discretion in deciding how aging funds will be administered and budgeted in the county. By endorsing a local Funding Plan, Boards of County Commissioners will define the services to be provided, determine funding levels for services, and identify the community service providers to be involved in providing Home and Community Care Block Grant services.

Counties, however, do not have unlimited freedom, flexibility, or authority under the HCCBG. First, federal law and regulations, as well as state rules and policies, specify the types of aging services that may be funded by the HCCBG. Second, although HCCBG funds are designated as a block grant, portions of the federal and state funds included in the HCCBG are earmarked for specific types of aging services (for example, congregate and home delivered meals) and may not be used for other purposes. Third, state rules specify, sometimes in great detail, the standards governing the provision of aging services funded by the HCCBG.

Nonetheless, the primary intent and effect of the HCCBG rules is to transfer from AAAs to boards of county commissioners and county-designated lead agencies much, if not all, of the authority and responsibility for determining how federal OAA funds will be used and what agencies will receive federal OAA funds. This expanded authority of counties with respect to programs for senior citizens under the state's HCCBG is clearly consistent with North Carolina's long tradition of local government responsibility for administering social services, health, and other human services programs, as well as the 1991 recommendations by the DHR Advisory Committee on Home and Community Care. But transferring authority from AAAs to counties with respect to administration of federal OAA funds may be inconsistent with a number of explicit requirements contained in the federal OAA law and regulations and raises questions regarding the role of counties with respect to federal OAA funds included in the state's HCCBG.

The role of counties under the OAA is quite limited. As discussed previously, the federal Older Americans Act provides that AAAs, rather than counties or the state agency on aging, are responsible for administering federal funds that are provided to states under Title III of the OAA. Unless a county agency has been designated as an AAA, counties have *no* explicit authority or responsibility under the Older Americans Act with respect to planning for the needs of senior citizens, allocating OAA funds and other resources to meet those needs (except to the extent that elected county officials are represented on the AAA's aging advisory council), selecting the public or private agencies that will receive OAA funds or provide OAA services to senior citizens in the county (except to the extent that a county agency may be selected by the AAA as an aging services provider), or administering or distributing OAA funds to aging services providers.

Instead, the Older Americans Act expressly provides that AAAs are responsible for (1) developing an area aging plan (with input from the aging advisory council and the public) that evaluates the need for aging services within the planning and service area, assesses the public and private resources available to meet those needs, determines (within federal limitations) the types of services that will be provided through OAA-funded contracts with aging services providers and that amount of OAA funds that will be allocated for each service, and designates focal points for the delivery of aging services within the area, and (2) selecting and entering into contracts with aging services providers, pursuant to federal procurement regulations that apply to federal grantees and subgrantees, to provide OAA funded services to senior citizens (see 42 U.S.C. 3026). By contrast, the state HCCBG rules transfer, directly or indirectly, all of these responsibilities from AAAs to counties.

Federal regulations issued by the Administration on Aging (45 C.F.R. 1321.25) expressly prohibit AAAs from delegating to another public or private agency (such as a board of county commissioners or a county-designated lead agency) their "authority to award or administer" federal OAA funds. Yet, by requiring AAAs to enter into grant agreements with counties that allocate and award federal OAA funds on the basis of the counties' HCCBG funding plans, the state HCCBG rules, in effect, mandate the delegation of authority from AAAs to counties with respect to the administration of federal OAA funds included in the HCCBG. And although county HCCBG funding plans must be approved by AAAs and may be incorporated within an area aging plan adopted by the AAA, it seems clear that "rubber stamp" approval by the AAA of county funding plans or county contracts with aging services providers selected by the county through the county funding plan does not change the fact that the actual authority with respect to the award and administration of federal OAA funds has been delegated or transferred from the AAA to counties.

Federal regulations [45 C.F.R. 1321.63(b)] also prohibit AAAs from awarding federal OAA funds by grant or contract to any entity unless the entity is a "community services provider agency or organization" (that is, an agency or organization that provides aging services to senior citizens under the area aging services plan adopted by the AAA). The HCCBG rules, however, require AAAs to enter into grant agreements with counties and distribute federal OAA funds to counties regardless of whether the county provides aging services or serves only as a funding conduit for the community services provider agencies that actually provide aging services to county residents.

Finally, federal OAA regulations [45 C.F.R. 1321.5(g)] provide that the federal procurement rules applicable to federal grantees and subgrantees (45 C.F.R. Part 92) apply to contracts between AAAs and aging services providers for OAA funded services provided to senior citizens under the area aging plan. The federal procurement rules, in turn, require that AAAs follow federal procurement procedures that ensure "full and open competition," allow procurement of services through noncompetitive procedures only when competitive procurement is not feasible, solicit price or rate quotations from "an adequate number of qualified sources," and require formal advertising and sealed bidding under certain circumstances. The HCCBG rules, on the other hand, include no provisions addressing the procurement of aging services by AAAs or counties or requiring competition in the procurement of HCCBG funded services.

The state HCCBG rules therefore appear to be inconsistent with the federal OAA law and regulations in several respects—but most notably the transfer of authority from AAAs to counties with respect to the allocation of federal OAA funding and the selection of aging services providers. State laws, rules, and policies, however, cannot override or supersede federal requirements and limitations that are attached to federal funds received by the state. Instead, state laws, rules, and policies affecting the administration of federal funds received by the state are legally invalid to the extent they are inconsistent with applicable federal laws and regulations. Thus to the extent that the state HCCBG rules are inconsistent with the federal OAA law and regulations with respect to the expanded role, responsibility, and authority of counties with respect to the administration of federal OAA funds, they may be invalid.

Medicaid

As discussed earlier, Medicaid is a joint federal-state public assistance program that reimburses hospitals, doctors, nursing homes, and other health care providers for medical services provided to the poor, and is an important source of health care (and, in particular, nursing home care) for the elderly. While senior citizens comprise only a small fraction (about one-seventh) of the total number of poor people covered by Medicaid, Medicaid spending for the elderly accounts for about one-third of total Medicaid spending. North Carolina's Medicaid program accounts for over four-fifths of spending under the state's aging budget, providing almost $1.2 billion per year in medical care (including over $600 million for nursing home care) to approximately 168,000 elderly North Carolinians (an average of over $7,000 in Medicaid spending per elderly recipient).

In North Carolina, the federal government, the state, and counties share responsibility for providing health care to the elderly poor through the Medicaid program. The federal government pays most of the cost of North Carolina's Medicaid program (about 64.5 percent of the cost of providing health care to eligible Medicaid recipients and half of the cost of administering the program), and establishes many of the policies and rules governing eligibility for Medicaid and the services provided to eligible Medicaid recipients.

In most states, Medicaid is administered by a state social services, health, or welfare agency and the nonfederal share of Medicaid costs is paid by state tax revenues. North Carolina, however, is one of a handful of states that require county social services agencies to administer some aspects of the state Medicaid program and require counties to pay part of the cost of providing Medicaid benefits to county residents.

North Carolina's Medicaid program is administered jointly by the DHHS Division of Medical Assistance (which contracts with a private company to issue payments to hospitals, doctors, nursing homes, and other health care providers who provide medical services to elderly, disabled, or poor persons who are eligible for Medicaid) and county departments of social services (which are responsible for processing applications and determining eligibility for Medicaid). State law also requires counties to pay half of the cost of administering the Medicaid program at the local level and 15 percent of the nonfederal share (approximately 5 percent of the total cost) of Medicaid services provided to county residents. In 1995–96, North Carolina counties paid more than $60 million for health care for elderly Medicaid recipients.

State-County Special Assistance for Elderly Adult Care Home Residents

State-County Special Assistance is a state public assistance program that provides financial assistance to elderly or disabled persons who need to live in an adult care home but cannot afford the cost of this care. In 1995–96, the State-County Special Assistance program provided more than $91 million in financial assistance to some 20,000 elderly or disabled North Carolinians who lived in adult care homes.

Policies with respect to eligibility and the amount of benefits payable under the State-County Special Assistance program are established by state law and rules adopted by the state Social Services Commission. State law, however, requires each county to administer the State-County Special Assistance program through the county's department of social services. State appropriations pay half of the cost of providing Special

Assistance benefits to elderly or disabled residents of adult care homes. Counties must pay, from county tax revenues, half of the cost of Special Assistance payments to county residents (about $45.5 million in 1995–96) as well as the entire cost of administering the program at the local level (about $2.9 million in 1995–96).

Adult Protective Services

The adult protective services program is a state social services program that attempts to protect disabled adults from abuse, neglect, and exploitation. State law requires county departments of social services to investigate reports involving the abuse, neglect, or exploitation of disabled adults and to provide protective services to disabled adults who have been abused, neglected, or exploited (G.S. 108A-99 through 108A-111). State law also requires counties to pay for essential medical or social services to protect a disabled adult from abuse, neglect, or exploitation if the disabled adult is not financially capable of paying for the services (G.S. 108A-108).

Funding for adult protective services is provided from county tax revenues and unearmarked federal or state social services funding (such as the Social Services Block Grant) that may be available to the county. Aging services providers who are funded under the state Home and Community Care Block Grant are required to give preference to elderly or disabled adults who need protective services.

In 1995–96, county departments of social services investigated almost 6,500 reports of alleged abuse, neglect, or exploitation of disabled adults and provided adult protective services for more than 8,000 disabled adults (at a cost of about $3.5 million). About three-quarters of these reports involved disabled adults who were age sixty or older. Abuse, neglect, or exploitation was confirmed in about one-third of the reported cases.

Nursing and Adult Care Homes

There are about 400 nursing homes and 1,400 adult care homes in North Carolina. Together, these facilities provide long-term care for more than 40,000 elderly North Carolinians.

Although the licensing and regulation of nursing homes and adult care homes is primarily a state responsibility, counties exercise two specific responsibilities with respect to the monitoring and regulation of nursing and adult care homes within the county.

First, although adult care homes are licensed by the DHHS Division of Facility Services, county departments of social services are responsible for routine inspection and monitoring of adult care homes with respect to their continuing compliance with state licensing requirements and other state laws and regulations concerning the care and treatment of elderly or disabled residents of adult care homes [G.S. 131D-2(b)(1a)]. If a county department of social services finds that an adult care home has violated state laws or rules, it must report the alleged violation to the state DHHS, which is responsible for determining whether the facility violated state requirements and taking action to punish or remedy violations of the state's licensing requirements or other applicable laws and regulations.

Second, state law requires the establishment of a nursing home advisory committee in each county in which a licensed nursing home is located, and an adult home advisory committee in each county in which a licensed adult care home is located or, with the approval of the state DHHS assistant secretary for aging, a joint nursing and adult home advisory committee (G.S. 131D-31, 131E-128). Members of the county's nursing and adult home advisory committees are appointed by the board of county commissioners, or by the state DHHS assistant secretary for aging if the board of county commissioners fails to make appointments to the committees. County nursing and adult home advisory committees are required to visit on a quarterly basis each nursing home and each adult care home that has more than nine beds, monitor the care and treatment of nursing home patients and adult care home residents, work to protect the legal rights of elderly or disabled residents of nursing or adult care homes under G.S. 131D-21 and 131E-117, advise the board of county commissioners, the county department of social services, and the state Division of Aging with respect to problems in adult care homes and issues with respect to long-term care, assist elderly or disabled nursing and adult care home residents who have grievances against nursing or adult care homes, and facilitate the resolution of these grievances at the local level.

Property Tax Exemption for Elderly Home Owners

Although elderly home owners are not completely exempt from county or city property taxes, state law (G.S. 105-277.1) provides property tax relief for certain low-income elderly or disabled home owners.

Under G.S. 105-277.1, the first $20,000 of the appraised value of a permanent residence owned and occupied by an elderly county resident is excluded from the county or city property tax if the elderly home owner meets all of the following criteria:

1. Is a North Carolina resident
2. Is at least 65 years old (or totally and permanently disabled) on January 1 of the preceding tax year
3. Has an income for the preceding tax year of not more than $15,000
4. Files an application with the county tax assessor for exemption from property tax by April 15 of the preceding tax year

The cost of providing property tax relief for elderly and disabled home owners falls primarily on county (and city) governments. Although the exact cost of property tax relief for the elderly and disabled is not known, it has been estimated that at least 155,000 elderly and disabled taxpayers qualify for the homestead property tax exemption and that counties lose at least $19.5 million per year in property tax revenues due to the homestead property tax exemption. The state Department of Revenue makes annual payments to reimburse counties for half of the local property tax revenues they lost in 1990 due to the homestead property tax exemption (approximately $6 million per year) and will make additional payments in 1998 and 1999 to reimburse counties for half of the local property tax revenues they lost in 1997 due to expansion of the homestead property tax exemption.

Additional Resources

Aging Services Guide for Legislators. Raleigh, N.C.: North Carolina Study Commission on Aging, 1996.

American Association of Retired Persons. *A Profile of Older Americans: 1997.* Washington, D.C.: American Association of Retired Persons, 1997.

Center for Aging Research and Educational Services for the N.C. Division of Aging. *North Carolina Comes of Age: County Profiles in Aging.* Chapel Hill, N.C.: School of Social Work, The University of North Carolina at Chapel Hill, 1990.

Hobbs, Frank B. (with Bonnie L. Damon). *Sixty-Five Plus in the United States.* Bureau of the Census, U.S. Department of Commerce, Current Population Reports, Special Series, P23-190. Washington, D.C.: U.S. Government Printing Office, 1996.

McCann, Michael J., and John L. Saxon, eds. *The Law and the Elderly in North Carolina.* Chapel Hill, N.C.: Institute of Government, The University of North Carolina at Chapel Hill, 1995.

North Carolina Division of Aging. *North Carolina Aging Services Plan [1991–93].* Raleigh, N.C.: Division of Aging, N.C. Department of Human Resources, 1991.

————. *North Carolina Aging Services Plan [1993–95]*. Raleigh, N.C.: Division of Aging, N.C. Department of Human Resources, 1993.

————. *North Carolina Aging Services Plan [1995–97]*. Raleigh, N.C.: Division of Aging, N.C. Department of Human Resources, 1995.

Saxon, John L. "Aging Programs," *State and Local Government Relations in North Carolina: Their Evolution and Current Status*, 2d ed., Chapter 13. Charles D. Liner, ed. Chapel Hill, N.C.: Institute of Government, The University of North Carolina at Chapel Hill, 1995.

Streets, Dennis W., and Margaret L. Morse. "Aging: Challenges and Opportunities for North Carolina," *Popular Government* 56 (Spring 1991): 2–8.

Notes

1. Demographic, statistical, fiscal, and other data cited in this chapter are derived from a number of sources, including: Frank B. Hobbs (with Bonnie L. Damon), *Sixty-Five Plus in the United States* (Bureau of the Census, U.S. Department of Commerce, Current Population Reports, Special Series, P23-190) (Washington, D.C.: U.S. Government Printing Office, 1996); Committee on Ways and Means (U.S. House of Representatives), *Overview of Entitlement Programs* (1994 Green Book) (Washington, D.C.: U.S. Government Printing Office, 1994); and information published or provided by the U.S. Bureau of the Census, the U.S. Social Security Administration, the U.S. Health Care Financing Administration, the U.S. Administration on Aging, the N.C. Division of Aging, the N.C. Division of Facility Services, the N.C. Division of Medical Assistance, and the N.C. Division of Social Services.

26 Mental Health Services

Mark F. Botts

Contents

Mark F. Botts is an Institute of Government faculty member who specializes in mental health law.

The author expresses his appreciation to Joan G. Brannon, an Institute of Government faculty member, mentor, and author of this chapter in the book's previous edition. Her past work in the mental health field is reflected in this edition's chapter and has facilitated the author's professional development.

Services for the treatment of mental illness, developmental disabilities, and alcohol and drug abuse—known collectively as *mental health services*—are provided through a state and local government system that involves county governments, state government, and agencies known as *area authorities* (the short term used for area mental health, developmental disabilities, and substance abuse authorities). Some people receive services directly from state-operated facilities such as Dorothea Dix Hospital in Raleigh or Broughton Hospital in Morganton, which provide inpatient psychiatric services. But most public mental health services are planned, coordinated, and delivered on the local level by area authorities. These agencies operate under state supervision, are bound by state policy, and spend state funds. Although they receive county funds and are governed by boards appointed by the boards of county commissioners, they are separate local government agencies with independent authority and responsibility for providing community-based mental health services.

This chapter discusses the governing structure of the area authority, the legal responsibilities of its governing board, and the area authority's relationship to county and state government. The chapter also addresses the types of services provided by area authorities and the primary sources of revenue used to pay for these services.

Historical Development

Only in recent history has local government in North Carolina adopted a significant treatment role in mental health care. In the eighteenth and nineteenth centuries, county governments sometimes confined persons with mental disabilities in poorhouses or jails, but this was solely a custodial function undertaken to protect property or public safety from the dangers, real or perceived, posed by persons believed to be possessed by demons. Confinement for curative or treatment purposes did not begin until 1856, when the General Assembly, concerned about the abuse and neglect endured by persons indefinitely confined in local facilities and influenced by the emerging belief that mental disabilities could be cured if treated in the right environment, opened the first "State Hospital for the Insane," now Dorothea Dix Hospital in Raleigh. By 1914, North Carolina had opened two more state hospitals and a state facility for persons with mental retardation. Due to the limited capacity of state institutions, however, many people with mental disabilities remained confined to local poorhouses and jails.

During the first half of the twentieth century state government continued to take primary responsibility for mental health services. There was a growing interest in the development of local mental health care facilities that could intervene with preventive treatment before confinement in a state institution was necessary, and Charlotte and Winston-Salem each established a local mental health clinic in the 1930s. But most counties did not have the financial resources or substantive expertise sufficient to develop mental health clinics. Federal funding spurred some development of community-based services when Congress passed the National Mental Health Act in 1946.[1] By 1959, North Carolina had utilized this funding to establish eleven community mental health clinics and psychiatric services in eight county departments of health.

Despite the federal incentives to develop community mental health care, North Carolina continued to focus on state-operated institutions, spending money to improve existing state facilities and adding a fourth mental hospital in 1947 and three more mental retardation centers between 1958 and 1963. Ironically, this expansion occurred during a period of increasing dissatisfaction—both in North Carolina and in the rest of the nation—with the institutional model of mental health care, one that relied on prolonged or permanent confinement of the mentally ill in huge, crowded hospitals. Revelations of inhumane treatment at some state institutions, advocacy for community services by parents of mentally retarded children, and new drug therapies for mental illness contributed to a national movement to reduce the traditional emphasis on state institutions in favor of community-based services intended to fulfill the institutional functions of mental health treatment, medical care, nutrition, recreation, social contact, and social control, without excessive restrictions on personal liberty.

The watershed event in the movement to reform mental health care came in 1963, when President Kennedy proposed,[2] and Congress passed, the Community Mental Health Centers Act (CMHCA),[3] which authorized federal funding for the construction of community mental health clinics. The level of funding available provided a powerful incentive to states to implement federal mental health policy, a policy that emphasized the responsibility of communities and local governments. The North Carolina General Assembly responded immediately by authorizing local communities to establish and operate mental health clinics as a joint undertaking with the state, which would develop a plan for establishing community outpatient clinics, administer federal grants, set standards for clinic operations, and appropriate state funds for community services.[4]

In the two decades that followed the passage of the CMHCA, Congress enacted a series of laws that expanded federal support to include funding for clinic staff and operations, ensuring that federal appropriations would continue to influence the development of mental health care at the state and local level. In North Carolina, as in other states, federal policy achieved the twin goals of reducing the proportion of mental health clients receiving treatment in state hospitals while expanding the number of persons receiving mental health services in the community. By 1980, 740 federally-funded community mental health centers were serving areas comprising roughly one-half of the nation, and approximately 3 million persons received services annually. The number of inpatients in state mental hospitals, which had peaked at 560,000 in 1955, decreased to 160,000 by 1977, and to about 120,000 in 1986, a decline of almost 80 percent since 1955.[5]

North Carolina's experience matched the national trend as the percentage of public-sector mental health clients served by state institutions declined dramatically between 1961 and 1981, from 74 to 13 percent of total persons served. (This includes institutional care for persons with developmental disabilities and substance abuse, as well as those with mental illness.) By fiscal year 1996–97, state-operated institutions would account for only 7 percent of all persons receiving treatment from the public-sector mental health system, with the remainder served by community-based facilities. The relative decline in institutional care, however, appears related more to the dramatic increase in the number of persons served by community programs—from 31,523 in 1961 to 298,022 by 1997—than to any significant decrease in the actual number of persons served at state institutions (see Table 26-1). State institutions served 23,327 persons in 1961 compared to 20,979 in fiscal year 1996–97, a modest decline, while the number of persons receiving community-based care continues to grow, increasing by more than 50,000 between 1994 and 1997. The greatest legacy of the develop-

Table 26-1
Number and Percentage of Persons Served by
Community Mental Health Programs and State Institutions in North Carolina,
Fiscal Years 1960–61 to 1996–97

Fiscal Year	Persons Receiving Institutional Care		Persons Receiving Community-Based Care		Total Persons Served
	Number	Percentage of total	Number	Percentage of total	Number
1960–61	23,327	74	8,196	26	31,523
1970–71	30,019	32	63,791	68	93,810
1980–81	25,658	13	171,712	87	197,370
1993–94	21,825	9	225,167	91	246,992
1996–97	20,979	7	277,043	93	298,022

Note: The figures for state-operated institutions include psychiatric hospitals, mental retardation centers, alcoholic rehabilitation centers, and other special care institutions.

Sources: Data for fiscal years 1960–61, 1970–71, and 1980–81 derived from the *Strategic Plan 1983–1989*, Vol. I, Quality Assurance Section, N.C. Division of Mental Health, Mental Retardation, and Substance Abuse Services (Raleigh, N.C.: NCDMHMRSAS, 1981), 39. Fiscal year 1993–94 figures from Deborah Merrill, Data Support Branch, N.C. Division of Mental Health, Developmental Disabilities, and Substance Abuse Services, memorandum to author, 8 December 1994. Data for fiscal year 1996–97 from *North Carolina Area Programs Annual Statistical Report*, Management Support Section, N.C. Division of Mental Health, Developmental Disabilities, and Substance Abuse Services (Raleigh, N.C.: NCDMHDDSAS, 1997).

ment of community-based services, therefore, is not so much the deinstitutionalization of mental health clients as it is the expansion of services to persons not previously served, including those with less severe disabilities.

The Area Authority

Although the federal government repealed the CMHCA in 1981,[6] North Carolina's current mental health system—local governmental entities created specifically for the purpose of coordinating and delivering mental health services with state supervision and financial support—is founded squarely upon a vision of the community as the locus of care, the original goal of the CMHCA and its legislative progeny. In its last major response to changes in federal law, the General Assembly revised and consolidated the statutes related to community mental health programs in 1977, requiring counties to establish, either singly or jointly with other counties, local agencies (area authorities) responsible for managing community-based mental health services and accountable to a locally-appointed governing board.[7] The structure of today's community mental health system, as provided in the Mental Health, Developmental Disabilities, and Substance Abuse Act of 1985, differs minimally from the system established by the 1977 legislation.

There are forty area authorities, each serving a designated geographic portion of the state called a "catchment area." Twenty-four serve multicounty catchment areas ranging from two to seven counties in size. The remaining sixteen each serve a single county (see Figure 26-1).

Catchment areas vary widely in geographic size and population. Some area authorities cover relatively small populations spread over large rural areas of the state, while others serve large urban populations concentrated in smaller geographic areas. The Mecklenburg and Wake programs, for example, each serve single-county catchment areas with populations of 584,856 and 528,405, respectively. Tideland Area Authority, on the other hand, serves five eastern counties—Martin, Beaufort, Washington, Tyrrell, and Hyde—with a combined population of 94,171; while the Smoky Mountain Area Authority serves a population of 154,168 spread over seven of the state's westernmost counties: Cherokee, Clay, Macon, Jackson, Haywood, Swain, and Graham.

In addition to differences in catchment size and population (and sometimes because of them) area authorities vary in other ways. For example, area authorities vary in terms of the amount of local tax revenue committed to mental health services and the number of persons served. These characteristics, as well as general distinctions between multicounty and single-county area authorities, are discussed in following sections of this chapter.

Services

Disabilities Served

Area authorities provide care and treatment for mental illness, developmental disabilities, and substance abuse.

Mental illness covers a group of illnesses, including both mental and cognitive disorders, that may be evidenced by disordered thinking, perceptual difficulties, delusions, visual and auditory hallucinations, mood

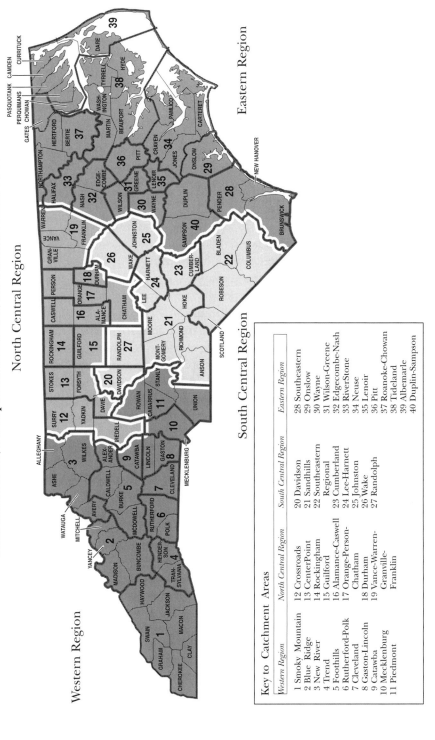

Figure 26-1
Area Mental Health, Developmental Disabilities, and Substance Abuse Services

Eastern Region

North Central Region

South Central Region

Western Region

Key to Catchment Areas

Western Region	North Central Region	South Central Region	Eastern Region
1 Smoky Mountain	12 Crossroads	20 Davidson	28 Southeastern
2 Blue Ridge	13 CenterPoint	21 Sandhills	29 Onslow
3 New River	14 Rockingham	22 Southeastern	30 Wayne
4 Trend	15 Guilford	Regional	31 Wilson-Greene
5 Foothills	16 Alamance-Caswell	23 Cumberland	32 Edgecombe-Nash
6 Rutherford-Polk	17 Orange-Person-	24 Lee-Harnett	33 RiverStone
7 Cleveland	Chatham	25 Johnston	34 Neuse
8 Gaston-Lincoln	18 Durham	26 Wake	35 Lenoir
9 Catawba	19 Vance-Warren-	27 Randolph	36 Pitt
10 Mecklenburg	Granville-		37 Roanoke-Chowan
11 Piedmont	Franklin		38 Tideland
			39 Albemarle
			40 Duplin-Sampson

disturbances, and impairments in personal, social, and occupational functioning. For children, the common term is "emotional disturbance." Schizophrenia, affecting a small percentage of the population, is the most expensive and debilitating of the mental illnesses. Depression, on the other hand, is quite common; a major cause of suicide, it frequently goes unrecognized and untreated, particularly in elderly populations.

The term *developmental disabilities* includes severe physical, cognitive, and mental impairments that appear before age twenty-two, are likely to continue indefinitely, and produce substantial functional limitations in three or more of the following major areas of life activities: self-care, learning, mobility, language, independent living, self-direction, or economic self-sufficiency. Depending on severity, developmental disabilities may include mental retardation, epilepsy, autism, and cerebral palsy. The term also includes delayed cognitive, physical, or communication and social-emotional development in children.

Substance abuse is the pathological use or abuse of alcohol or other drugs in a way or to a degree that produces an impairment in personal, social, or occupational functioning.

Anyone in need of care or treatment for mental illness, developmental disabilities, or substance abuse may come to an area facility for evaluation and make a written application for services. Whether an area authority will serve a particular individual depends on the individual's needs, the purpose of the services applied for, the resources available to the area authority, and whether the individual is from the geographic area served by the area authority. Services cannot be denied due to an individual's inability to pay, although clients are required to pay what they can (G.S. 122C-146).

In fiscal year 1996–97, all area authorities combined served 277,043 people, with 65 percent of clients (180,192) receiving mental health services, 6 percent (16,837) receiving services for developmental disabilities, and 29 percent (80,014) receiving treatment for substance abuse. The number of persons served by each area authority varies considerably. Mecklenburg, a single-county area authority, served 23,555 clients in 1996–97. In comparison, Guilford and Wake, also single-county programs, served 14,798, and 9,513 persons, respectively. Some of the rural multicounty area authorities may serve less people, but they provide services over a larger geographic area. For example, in fiscal year 1996–97, the Smoky Mountain Area Authority provided services to 11,953 people in a seven county catchment area, while the Tideland Area Authority served 5,526 clients residing in five counties.

Required Services

Each area authority is required by state law to offer the following services (10 NCAC 14V.0501):

- *Outpatient services* (short, recurring visits) for individuals of all disability groups, available through at least one clinic that is open no less than forty hours per week
- *Emergency services* for individuals of all disability groups, available on a twenty-four-hour, non-scheduled basis, for immediate screening or assessment of presenting problems
- *Consultation and education services* for clients and the general public to help them understand mental disabilities and the treatment resources available in the community
- *Case management* for individuals of all disability groups: a support service designed to coordinate services from the area authority and other agencies to assist clients in meeting total needs (including treatment, educational, vocational, residential, health, financial, social, and other needs)
- *Inpatient hospital services* for individuals with mental illness or substance abuse disorders (twenty-four-hour treatment and supervision)
- *A psychosocial rehabilitation program* to help chronically mentally ill persons achieve and maintain independent living (a day program providing a broad range of services, including skills development, educational and prevocational training, and supported employment services), or *a partial hospitalization service* intended to prevent psychiatric hospitalization or to serve as an interim step for those leaving an inpatient hospital (a day program providing intensive treatment)
- *Developmental day services* for preschool children with developmental disabilities or delays or who are at high risk for developmental disabilities, in a specialized child care center (eight-hour day programming to meet development needs in self-help, physical, language, cognitive, and psychosocial skills)
- *Adult developmental and vocational programs* for individuals with developmental disabilities to prepare them to live and work as independently as possible (vocational evaluation, remunerative employment, personal and community living skill development, and adult basic education)

- *Alcohol and drug education traffic schools* designed primarily for first offenders convicted of driving while impaired
- *Drug education schools* designed primarily for court-referred drug users who are not drug dependent or engaged in drug dealing
- *Residential or outpatient detoxification services* for individuals with substance abuse disorders experiencing physical withdrawal from alcohol or other drugs
- *Forensic screening and evaluation* for all disability groups for the purpose of assessing a criminal offender's capacity to proceed to trial
- *Early childhood intervention services* for infants and toddlers who are mentally retarded, are otherwise developmentally disabled or delayed, have atypical development, or are at risk of the preceding conditions (support and information to families on child-rearing skills and available services, and assessment and programming in cognitive, language, physical, self-help, and psychosocial development).

In addition to the required services, many area authorities also offer a range of other services, including employee assistance programs for individuals with personal problems affecting job performance, specialized foster care services provided in conjunction with the local department of social services, supervised community-based alternatives to incarceration for substance abusers involved in crimes of a nonviolent nature, and group homes or supervised apartment living programs for persons with mental retardation or other developmental disabilities.

Contracting for Services

In fulfilling its duty to provide services to clients in the catchment area, the area authority may either provide services directly using area employees and facilities or contract with other public or private agencies for the provision of client services (G.S. 122C-141). For example, in meeting its requirement to provide inpatient psychiatric services for children, adolescents, and adults with mental illness, the area authority may use an inpatient facility operated by the area authority or enter into a written agreement with a private psychiatric hospital for the provision of inpatient psychiatric services to area authority clients.

The area authority is responsible for assuring that all area authority services, whether provided directly or under contract, meet the standards for services specified in state statutes and regulations (G.S. 122C-141, -142). Toward this end, the area authority must distribute copies of laws and regulations applicable to the service being provided to each of its contract providers. In addition, contracts must contain a provision requiring the area authority to monitor contracted services for compliance with applicable service standards. The minimum requirements for all written service contracts are stated in title 10, chapter 14C, rule .1010 of the North Carolina Administrative Code.

The area authority also may enter into a written agreement requiring it to provide services to governmental or private entities [G.S. 122C-117(a1)]. For example, the area authority may contract with a public or private employer to provide an "employee assistance program" designed to serve employees who have family, marital, psychological, or substance abuse problems that affect or could affect their job performance. In addition, the area authority may contract with health maintenance organizations to provide mental health, developmental disabilities, or substance abuse services to enrollees in health care plans provided by the health maintenance organizations [G.S. 122C-141(c)].

Governance

Area Board Composition and Appointment

Each area authority is governed by an area board that exercises specific powers and duties enumerated in the General Statutes of North Carolina. According to G.S. 122C-118, area boards must have between fifteen and twenty-five members, with the size determined by the boards of county commissioners of the counties served by the area authority. In a single-county area, the board of county commissioners appoints the members of the area board. In a multicounty area authority, each board of county commissioners within the catchment area is authorized to appoint one commissioner as a member of the area board. These commissioner members then appoint the remaining area board members.

Area board membership must include a county commissioner; a physician (who should be a psychiatrist, if possible); a professional from the field of either psychology, social work, nursing, or religion; a person representing the interests of individuals with mental illness; a person representing the interests of individuals with developmental disabilities; a client of the area authority who is recovering from alcoholism or other drug abuse; a family member of a client with mental illness; a family member of a client with developmental disabilities; a family member of a client suffering from alcoholism or other drug abuse; an attorney; and someone with experience in finance who can understand and interpret audits and other financial reports. In a single-county area authority, the county commissioners may appoint any resident of the county instead of a county commissioner.

The terms of commissioner members on the area board are concurrent with their terms as county commissioners. Other area board members serve four-year terms. Area board members may be removed for any or no reason by the group of commissioners authorized to make the initial appointment. If a vacancy occurs on the area board, the group who filled the seat must choose a replacement to complete the remaining term within 120 days. In addition, the group authorized to make appointments must declare vacant the office of a board member who does not attend three scheduled meetings within a twelve-month period without justifiable excuse.

Area board members elect the area board chair, who may be a commissioner member of the area board, to serve a one-year term (G.S. 122C-119). The area board must meet at least six times per year. Meetings are called either by the board chair or by three or more members who have given written notice to the chair.

Alternative Governing Bodies

In the special case of a county with at least 425,000 people, the board of county commissioners may choose a governing body different from the area board. For these counties, the relevant statute, G.S. 153A-77, provides two alternatives. Under the first option, the board of county commissioners, by a resolution adopted after a public hearing, may become the governing body for the area authority. In this event, the powers and duties of the area board become the responsibility of the board of county commissioners. Under this law, the board of county commissioners for Mecklenburg County has abolished the area board, board of health, and board of social services, and assumed governing authority over these human service agencies.

The second option applies to counties that operate under the county-manager form of government. The board of county commissioners for these counties may consolidate the administration and delivery of health services, social services, and area authority services under the control of the county manager and a consolidated human services board. In broad outline, this consolidated human services option, which Wake County has chosen, has four main features. It permits the board of county commissioners to do the following:

1. Consolidate human services in the county (mental health services, social services, and public health services) under the direct control of a human services director appointed and supervised by the county manager
2. Create a consolidated human services board that includes representatives of professional and constituent groups specified by statute
3. Create a consolidated county human services agency having the authority to carry out the functions of the local health department, the county department of social services, and the area authority
4. Assign other county human services functions to be performed by the consolidated human services agency, under the direction of the human services director, with policy-making authority granted to the consolidated human services board as determined by the board of county commissioners

The primary differences between a consolidated human services agency and an independent area authority concern these agencies' respective authority to make decisions regarding personnel matters and client services. Unlike the area authority, a consolidated human services board may recommend, but not establish, client services. Further, a consolidated agency has no independent authority to enter into contracts for the provision of client services (a power held by single and multicounty area authorities). Only if specifically authorized by the county board of commissioners may a consolidated human services agency enter into contracts.

As for personnel, the director of a consolidated agency is appointed, dismissed, and supervised by the county manager, whereas the director of the area authority (area director) serves at the pleasure (and is an employee) of the area board. Further, the personnel of a consolidated agency are subject to county personnel policies and may be appointed only upon approval of the county manager. In contrast, employees of the area authority are appointed by the area director and are subject to the State Personnel Act.

Powers and Duties of the Area Board

The General Statutes confer many powers and duties upon the area authority. Of course, the area board must rely on the area director and staff to carry out many of the tasks associated with these legal responsibilities, thus limiting the level of direct board involvement in the operation of the area authority. But some legal responsibilities, including the adoption of certain policies mandated by law, require direct action by the board. And as the governing body for the area authority, the area board bears ultimate responsibility for the execution of all powers and duties conferred by law on the area authority.

While many board duties are specified by statute and regulation, two of these are so fundamental and broad that they can be viewed as encompassing the remainder. First, the area board is legally responsible for providing mental health, developmental disabilities, and substance abuse services to clients in the catchment area. This is, after all, the area authority's reason for existing. Second, statutory law requires the area board to do what is necessary to meet the first responsibility: to engage in comprehensive planning, budgeting, implementing, and monitoring of community-based services (G.S. 122C-117). Other responsibilities specified by statute or regulation require the area board to fulfill the following duties:

1. Determine the needs of the area authority's clients and coordinate with the state the provision of services to clients through area and state facilities (G.S. 122C-117).
2. Assure that services meet state standards and are of the highest possible quality, and develop internal procedures for monitoring and evaluating the level of quality obtained by all programs and services (G.S. 122C-117, -191). Most area authorities establish a "quality assurance committee" staffed by area employees that submits an annual report to the area board with recommendations regarding the quality of services provided by the area authority and its contract agencies.
3. Develop local service implementation plans that set forth service philosophy and priorities concerning the types of persons to be served, the kinds of services to be provided, and strategies for meeting service priorities (G.S. 122C-143.1).
4. Develop and secure state approval for a single-portal-of-entry-and-exit policy (an admission and discharge policy for coordi-

nating services between area, state, and private facilities) for public and private services for individuals with developmental disabilities (G.S. 122C-132.1).

5. Establish a client rights committee that monitors services for compliance with client rights, reports annually to the area board, and establishes review procedures for client grievances. The area board client rights committee must be comprised of a majority of non–area board members, with a reasonable effort made to have all disabilities represented (10 NCAC 14V.0504).

6. Appoint an area director who serves at the pleasure of the area board. The area director appoints and supervises area authority employees, implements area board programs and policies, and administers services in compliance with state law (G.S. 122C-117, -121).

7. Appoint a budget officer (multicounty programs only) to serve at the pleasure of the governing board (G.S. 159-9). The finance officer may be appointed by either the area board or the area director to serve at the pleasure of the appointing board or director. The *county* budget and finance officers serve the *single-county* area authority.

8. Establish a salary plan that sets the salaries for area authority employees in conformance with the State Personnel Act. Approval of the plan by the county commissioners is not required unless the salary plan for a single-county area authority exceeds the county's salary plan, or the salary plan for a multicounty area authority exceeds the highest paying salary plan of any county in that area (G.S. 122C-156).

9. Adopt and enforce a professional reimbursement policy that (1) requires fees for services provided directly by the area authority be paid to the area authority (not to its employees); (2) prohibits area employees from providing on a private basis services that require the use of area program resources and facilities; and (3) allows area employees to accept dual compensation and dual employment only if they first obtain the written permission of the area authority (G.S. 122C-157).

10. Establish a finance committee that meets at least six times a year to review the financial strength of the area authority. This committee must have a minimum of three members, two of whom must have expertise in budgeting and fiscal control. The entire area board may function as the finance committee if it chooses,

but the meetings of the committee must be distinct from meetings of the area board (G.S. 122C-119).

11. Prepare annual financial statements that set out the financial position of the area authority as of the end of the fiscal year and the financial results of operations during the course of the year (G.S. 159-34). This annual financial report gives the board information necessary to making budgetary and program decisions, determining whether those decisions are being implemented, and generally assessing the area authority's performance.

12. Have an independent certified public accountant complete an annual audit for submission to the Local Government Commission in conformance with the Local Government Budget and Fiscal Control Act (G.S. 122C-144.1).

13. Develop and maintain an annual budget as required by the Local Government Budget and Fiscal Control Act (G.S. 122C-117, -144.1).

14. Prepare and enter into an Annual Memorandum of Agreement (MOA) with the state that establishes how the area authority will use state-allocated funds (G.S. 122C-143.2). The MOA establishes the kinds of services the area authority will provide using state-allocated funds, the levels of state funding available for these services (by category of service), and the procedures for reporting the amounts of services actually provided—or the amount of state money expended or earned—by the area authority.

15. Prepare fee schedules for services and make reasonable efforts to collect reimbursement for the costs of services from individuals or entities able to pay, including insurance companies or other third parties who cover patient costs (G.S. 122C-146).

16. Establish informal dispute resolution procedures for (1) persons who claim the area authority's failure to comply with state laws adversely affected their ability to participate in planning or budgeting processes, and (2) clients or contractors who claim the area authority acted arbitrarily and capriciously in reducing funding for services (G.S. 122C-151.3, -151.4).

In addition to these powers and duties, the area board has the authority to enter into contracts on behalf of the area authority for a variety of purposes. As noted earlier, the area board has the authority to enter into contracts for the provision of services to area program clients (G.S.

122C-141). The area board also may contract for the purchase, lease, or lease-purchase of personal property, including equipment necessary for the operation of the area authority, and it has authority to lease real property (G.S. 122C-147). The area board may purchase life insurance, health insurance, or both for the benefit of all or any class of area authority officers or employees as part of their compensation (G.S. 122C-156). In addition, the area board may enter into a contract to insure the area authority, board members, and employees against civil liability for damages caused by the actions of agents, board members, or employees of the area authority when acting within the course of their duties or employment (G.S. 122C-152, -153, -142).

The board also has implicit authority to enter into other contracts necessary to carry out its duty to provide services. Other contracts that might be necessary to area authority functions include contracts for the construction and repair of facilities and contracts for professional or other services not directly related to client services.

Client Rights

Under state law, every client of area authority services enjoys certain rights, including the right to receive an explanation and written summary of those rights (10 NCAC 14Q.0201). Some client rights are specified by state statutes, and others are set forth in state regulations. According to G.S. 122C, Article 3, every area authority client enjoys the following rights:

- The right to receive age-appropriate treatment according to an individualized written treatment or habilitation plan
- The right that no client information be disclosed except where authorized by law
- The right to be informed of treatment choices
- The right to refuse treatment unless involuntary treatment is legally authorized
- The right to be free from unnecessary or excessive medication, physical restraint, and seclusion

The area board bears ultimate responsibility for the assurance of client rights (10 NCAC 14V.0504), and specific policies must be developed and implemented toward that end. Client rights policies must specifically address such matters as the procedures for informing staff of client rights; the reporting of suspected abuse, neglect, or exploitation of clients; the procedures and safeguards relating to the use of medications that are known to represent serious risks; the use of restrictive interventions (physical restraint and seclusion); the suspension and expulsion of clients from services; and the conditions under which searches of the client or his or her living area may occur and the procedures for seizure of client property or possessions (10 NCAC 14Q).

In addition to establishing a client rights committee to monitor the area authority's compliance with client rights, the area board also must develop and implement policy that sets the following guidelines for the committee:

1. The composition, size, appointment, and training of the committee
2. Rules of conduct for and frequency of meetings
3. Procedures for monitoring the effectiveness of methods for protecting client rights
4. Requirements for routine reporting to the board (10 NCAC 14V.0504)

The board may require that the governing body of a contract agency also establish a client rights committee to perform for the contracted services the same functions as the area board's client rights committee. Finally, the area board must see that a compliance review is conducted at least every three years to assure that all area authority facilities and services comply with state and federal law regarding client rights (10 NCAC 14Q .0104).

Personnel Administration

Under G.S. 122C-121, the area director, appointed by the area board, is responsible for staff appointment, supervision, and discipline.

Personnel administration for area authority employees must be conducted in accordance with the State Personnel Act and the rules and policies of the North Carolina State Personnel Commission (G.S. 122C-154). These rules and policies govern position classification, qualifications, recruitment, promotion, dismissal, compensation, personnel records, and nepotism (employment of relatives). For example, area authorities must use a competitive recruitment process that selects employees based on a relative consideration of the applicants' skills, knowledge, and abilities. In addition, with the exception of board-appointed personnel, employees who have satisfactorily completed a probationary and/or trainee appointment may not be demoted, suspended, or dismissed except for "just cause" or reduction in force. These and other rules applicable to area authority employees are found in title 25, subchapter 1I of the North Carolina Administrative Code.

The area board is authorized, but not required, to purchase life insurance and health insurance for the benefit of all or any class of area authority officers or employees as part of their compensation. Other fringe benefits for officers and employees may also be provided (G.S. 122C-156).

Budgeting and Fiscal Management

Like all other local governments and public authorities, the area authority's budgeting and fiscal management must be administered according to the Local Government Budget and Fiscal Control Act (G.S. 159), which prescribes a general system for adopting and administering a budget. This means that area authorities must operate under a balanced annual budget ordinance. Except for funds used for certain purposes, all moneys received or expended by the area authority—whether federal, state, local, or private in origin—must be spent in accordance with the budget ordinance. Multicounty area authorities operate under a budget ordinance adopted by the area board, whereas single-county area authorities operate under the county budget ordinance. The single-county budget process is explained later in the section "The County's Role in Mental Health Services."

Each area authority also must complete and submit an annual independent audit to the Local Government Commission. Under the audit requirement, an independent certified public accountant examines the area authority's accounting records and other evidence supporting its financial statements to provide independent verification that the financial statements are credible and can be relied upon. This is called a *financial audit*. The accountant also conducts a *compliance audit* to determine whether the area authority has complied with requirements for receiving federal or state financial assistance.

Multicounty area programs are responsible for contracting for their own auditing. However, because a single-county area program is considered a department of the county for purposes of budget and fiscal control, the county is responsible for including the single-county area program in the county's audit process. The area boards for both single and multicounty areas, however, have a need for the information produced by the audit and a duty to follow up on the auditor's findings and recommendations.

The County's Role in Mental Health Services

The area authority is a local political subdivision of the state, except that a single-county area authority is considered a department of the county in which it is located for purposes of budget and fiscal control (G.S. 122C-116). Thus for most purposes the area authority is a separate, local unit of government, not a mere agency or lesser department of a particular county or city. When governing the area program and exercising the powers and duties conferred by the state, the area board has the authority and responsibility to act independently of the board of county commissioners on many matters.

This does not mean, however, that area authorities have no relationship with county government or that the administration of the area authority is not sometimes linked to county governance. Rather, the state has granted a limited but significant role to county government by providing for county responsibility and involvement in certain area authority matters. As noted earlier, the board or boards of county commissioners appoint, and may remove, area board members within their catchment area. County commissioners must serve on the multicounty area board and may serve on the single-county area board. In addition, counties may appropriate funds for the support of programs that serve their catchment area, even if the county does not own or operate the facilities housing the programs or the programs are not physically located within a single county (G.S. 122C-115; G.S. 153A-248). County appropriations for mental health services are discussed later in this chapter in the section "Financing Community Services."

Property

Generally the authority to purchase and hold title to real property used by an area authority is vested in the county where the property is located. However, this authority may be delegated to the area authority by the board or boards of county commissioners of all the counties within the area authority's catchment area (G.S. 122C-147). Further, an area authority may not finance or acquire real or personal property by means of an installment contract under G.S. 160A-20 without the approval of the board or boards of county commissioners for the counties constituting the catchment area. The area board for both single-county and multicounty areas, however, has the authority to purchase personal property, including equipment necessary to the operations of the area authority, and to lease personal and real property (G.S. 122C-147).

Budget and Fiscal Control

Because a single-county area authority is considered a department of the county for purposes of the Local Government Budget and Fiscal Control Act (G.S. 159), its administration is linked to county administration in ways not characteristic of the more independent multicounty authorities. The single-county area authority must present its budget for approval of the county commissioners in the manner requested by the county budget officer, and the area authority's financial operations must follow the budget set by the county commissioners in the county's budget ordinance. Further, the county has responsibility for fiscal management and may require all disbursements, receipts, and financial management of the area authority to be handled by the county's finance officer. The county, however, may designate a deputy finance officer for the area authority to disburse money (sign checks) and to preaudit obligations, such as contracts and purchase orders, to ensure that the budget ordinance for the county contains an appropriation authorizing the obligation and that a sufficient amount remains in the appropriation to meet the obligation. This officer could be an employee of the area authority.

As part of the county budget preparation for each year, the single-county area authority must transmit to the county budget officer an estimate of the financial requirements of the area program (expenditure requests and revenue estimates) in a form prescribed by the county budget officer. In addition, a report on the revenues and expenditures for the previous and current years must be prepared, a task sometimes completed by the county finance officer. Although not required by law, budget requests may include program goals or objectives that address anticipated concerns of the county budget officer and the board of county commissioners. Local policy may also require or advise that single-county program officials, like heads of county departments, meet with the county budget officer to review departmental or program requests and attend governing board meetings to review the proposed budget.

By contrast, multicounty area authorities—considered *public authorities* for purposes of the Local Government Budget and Fiscal Control

Act—are not a part of the budgeting and accounting system of any county. They are responsible for their own budgeting, disbursing, accounting, and financial management, and must appoint a budget officer and a finance officer to assume the duties of those offices as set forth in the budget and fiscal control law.

Notwithstanding these distinctions, the statutory obligation of the area board to consider and approve a budget for the area authority does not vary according to the authority's single- or multicounty status. All area boards have the power and duty to engage in budgeting. Even though the county has ultimate authority over the budget decisions for a single-county area authority, the single-county area board should set whatever policy is necessary for the preparation of the area program's budget request, as well as consider and approve the budget to be submitted to the county.

Personnel

Employees under the direct supervision of the area authority are area employees, not county employees. Nonetheless, county personnel policies may apply to area employees in certain circumstances, and counties may pursue statutory options to bring the personnel administration of a single-county authority within the county personnel system. The degree to which county personnel policies may regulate area employees depends, in part, on whether the area authority is a single-county or multicounty authority and, in part, on whether a county affirmatively acts to exert authority over area employees.

In the case of a *single-county* area authority, the board of county commissioners may prescribe for area employees rules governing annual leave, sick leave, hours of work, holidays, and the administration of the pay plan, if these rules are adopted for county employees generally [G.S. 126-9(a); G.S. 153A-94]. The State Personnel Act also appears to grant the same authority to counties that comprise the catchment area of a *multicounty* authority, but the respective boards of county commissioners would have to jointly exercise this authority and apply the rules to their respective county employees. The county rules must be filed with the state personnel director in order to supersede any rules adopted by the State Personnel Commission.

The county served by a *single-county* area authority has the option of bringing area employees within the county system of personnel administration. If the board of county commissioners establishes and maintains a personnel system for all county employees and that system is approved by the State Personnel Commission as being substantially equivalent to the state's personnel system for area authority employees, then the county personnel system will cover employees of the area authority (G.S. 126-11). In this case, employees covered by the county system would be exempt from the State Personnel Act, but the provisions on equal opportunity for employment and compensation would continue to apply. In order for the county personnel system to be deemed substantially equivalent, it would have to meet the State Personnel Commission's basic requirements for recruitment, selection, advancement, classification, compensation, suspension, dismissal, and affirmative action.

As for multicounty area authorities, county governments have no independent authority to substitute a substantially equivalent personnel system for the state rules of personnel administration.

The State's Role in Community Services

Rulemaking

The Commission for Mental Health, Developmental Disabilities, and Substance Abuse Services is the state body authorized to adopt, amend, and repeal rules governing the delivery of mental health, developmental disabilities, and substance abuse services (G.S. 143B-147 through -150). Appointed by the governor and the General Assembly, the twenty-six-member commission is made up of persons with a special interest in these services, including representatives of area authorities, professionals in the field, and representatives of clients of services. Commission rules set standards for the management and operation of area authorities and their contract agencies, the use of federal funds according to federal requirements, and the licensing of public and private facilities that provide mental health, developmental disabilities, and substance abuse services. The rules that pertain specifically to area authorities are intended to ensure that area authorities and their contract agencies provide adequate and appropriate services, and each area authority must demonstrate compliance with the rules by periodically being reviewed and accredited by the state or an accrediting body acting under the auspices of the state.

Administration

The Division of Mental Health, Developmental Disabilities, and Substance Abuse Services, in the Department of Health and Human Services, is the state agency responsible for enforcing state regulations and statutes governing the operation of area authorities (G.S. Ch. 143B; G.S. 122C-111 and -112). The Division also allocates and administers federal and state funds designated by the General Assembly for area authority services, enforces requirements for federal and state aid, and adopts rules governing the accreditation of area authority programs and the expenditure of all area authority funds. Moreover, the Division is directly responsible for operating sixteen state facilities for persons in need of twenty-four-hour treatment or residential services: four psychiatric hospitals, five mental retardation centers, three alcohol and drug abuse treatment centers, three specialized facilities for children and adolescents, and a special care center for adults in need of mental health and nursing care services.

To facilitate planning and coordination between the Division and area authorities, the state is divided into four regions—the Western, North Central, South Central, and Eastern regions (see Figure 26-1). Each region is served by a state psychiatric hospital and a state mental retardation center, and three regions are each served by a state alcohol and drug abuse treatment center. The specialized state facilities (special care center and schools for adolescents and children) provide services to persons from throughout the state. The area authorities in each region use the regional facilities to provide services that are unavailable as yet in the community or cannot practically be carried out in each individual community.

Policymaking

In 1973, the General Assembly established the Mental Health Study Commission (MHSC) to study mental health, developmental disabilities, and substance abuse services and recommend to the legislature changes in the law. Since then, many of the improvements made to the public-sector service system, and most legislation adopted by the General Assembly related to mental disabilities, have evolved from the work of the MHSC.

For example, the state's funding priorities are guided by long-range plans developed by the MHSC and adopted by the General Assembly. Since 1987 the MHSC has developed and recommended five comprehensive plans for services to persons grouped according to age and disability: the child mental health plan, the child and adolescent substance abuse plan, the plan for adults with severe and persistent mental illness, the adult substance abuse treatment plan, and the plan for persons with developmental disability. Each plan identifies unmet service needs, sets service goals and strategies, outlines specific service improvements, and targets services to particular clients within each age and disability group. The area authority's local service implementation plan must be consistent with the state's long-range plans.

In 1996 the General Assembly repealed the legislation authorizing the MHSC and created in its place a similar body called the Legislative Study Commission on Mental Health, Developmental Disabilities, and Substance Abuse Services. Comprised of legislators, a county commissioner, and others appointed by the governor and the General Assembly, this twenty-two member commission is charged with studying the development, administration, and delivery of mental health services and reporting its recommendations to the General Assembly.

Financing Community Services

Sources of Revenue

Funding for area authorities comes from a variety of sources, including state appropriations, federal block grants, special purpose grants from the federal government and private foundations, county appropriations, client fees, Medicaid receipts, and other third party receipts such as private insurance.

Area authority revenues totaled approximately $776 million for fiscal year 1996–97. State funds appropriated directly to area authorities are the largest single source of revenue, amounting to roughly $304 million in 1996–97, or 39 percent of all area authority revenues (see Table 26-2). Medicaid receipts, the next largest source of revenue, accounted for $257 million, or roughly one-third of area revenues. This figure includes the federal share and a portion of the state share of Medicaid. Federal block grants and other receipts allocated by the Division provided approximately $86 million in statewide area authority revenues.

County appropriations funded through property tax proceeds or other local revenues contributed $81 million, or roughly 10 percent of area authority revenues. This figure includes a portion of the state's rev-

Table 26-2
Area Authority Revenues by Source:
Amount and as a Percentage of Total Revenues, Fiscal Year 1996–97

Type of Revenue	Amount in Millions ($)	Percentage of Total
State General Fund	304	39
Medicaid	257	33
Federal Block Grant/Other	86	11
County	81	10
Other	48	6
Total	776	99

Note: Percentages do not add up to 100 due to rounding.
Source: N.C. Division of Mental Health, Developmental Disabilities, and Substance Abuse Services, Management Support Section, Memo, *Community Program Revenues by Source* (Raleigh, N.C.: NC DMHDDSAS, December 1997).

enue from the sale of alcoholic beverages, which is allocated to counties for the treatment of alcoholism or for research or education on alcohol abuse pursuant to G.S. 18B-805. While there is no statutory provision expressly stating that counties must appropriate county general funds to support area authority services (G.S. 122C-155 says that counties "may" appropriate funds), G.S. 122C-2 provides that the furnishing of services through a public system centered in area authorities "requires the cooperation and financial assistance of counties, the State, and the federal government." Further, counties are not permitted to reduce county appropriations and expenditures to area authorities because of revenue available to area authorities from state-allocated funds (including capitated funding), client fees, or fund balances [G.S. 122C-115(d)].

Because area authorities do not have the power to levy taxes, their ability to generate revenue is limited. Client receipts other than Medicaid provide some revenue, but this, too, is limited, as no person may be refused services because of an inability to pay (G.S. 122C-146). Yet the law also requires area authorities to collect reimbursement for services to the extent that clients are able to pay, and in Table 26-2, the category designated "other" includes fees from clients and private insurance. The revenue generated through the collection of fees may be used only for the operation or capital improvement of area authority programs and may not be used as a justification for reducing or replacing the budgeted commitment of county tax revenue (G.S. 122C-146).

Client fees for services, while not a large source of revenue, are nevertheless important. For example, in fiscal year 1996–97 the $20.6 million in revenue received by the Durham Area Authority included $181,469 in client fees. Similarly, when planning for 1997–98, the Piedmont Area Authority anticipated that its $26.2 million in total revenues would include $354,862 in client fees.

Revenue Trends

In the last five years, combined revenues for all area authorities have more than doubled, growing from $339 million in fiscal year 1991–92 to approximately $776 million in 1996–97. The growth in Medicaid receipts is the primary reason for the overall growth in area authority revenues. Medicaid dollars grew at a faster rate than any other source of revenue during the five-year period—from about $29 million to $257 million, a 786 percent increase. The increase is a direct result of state policy requiring area authorities to more fully utilize Medicaid as a source of revenue to fund a growing demand for services, including services previously supported by only state or local funds.

State appropriations rose from $182 million in 1991–92 to $304 million in 1996–97, an increase of 67 percent. County funding showed a slower rate of growth, rising from $57 million to $81 million (a 42 percent increase) between 1992 and 1997. Revenue from federal block grants and other Division receipts increased by 160 percent during the same period, from $33 million to about $85 million.

While each source of revenue has contributed to the overall increase in area authority revenues, the varying rates of growth among revenue sources have resulted in a notable shift in the proportionate financial responsibility of the federal, state, and local governments for community mental health services. The portion of area authority revenues coming from the state general fund has slipped from roughly 59 percent in 1988–89 to 39 percent in 1996–97, while Medicaid funding has grown from 2 to 33 percent of total area revenues during the same period (see Figure 26-2, which separates state funding into two categories). While the increased utilization of Medicaid has enabled the state to dramatically expand revenues and meet increasing demands for services without relying heavily on state and local resources, some service providers are concerned that the percentage of money available to serve indigent clients *not* eligible for Medicaid is growing ever smaller.

By separating state appropriations for court-ordered services from other state funds received by area authorities, Figure 26-2 reveals that a growing percentage of the state funding for community-based services is going to specific court-ordered programs such as the Thomas S. and

Figure 26-2
Change in Funding as a Percentage of Total Area Authority Revenues,
Selected Fiscal Years 1989–97

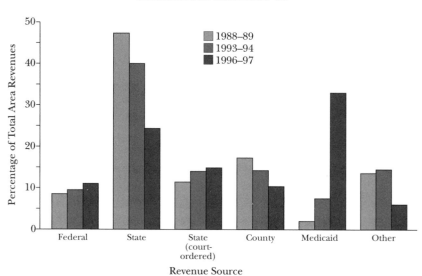

Source: N.C. Division of Mental Health, Developmental Disabilities, and Substance Abuse Services, Management Support Section, Memo, *Community Program Revenues by Source* (Raleigh, N.C.: NCDMHDDSAS, December 1997).

Willie M. programs (services to two disability-specific client groups that the state is obligated to provide without regard to budgetary restraints).[8] This leaves a lesser portion of state dollars for other community services, as state funding not dedicated to court-ordered programs makes up only 24 percent of area revenues in 1996–97 compared to 47 percent in 1988–89. This funding trend, according to some who work in the local service system, constrains the area authority's ability to meet the needs of clients not eligible for court-ordered services.

Distribution of Revenues

Because the percentage of area revenues from each source in Table 26-2 are based on the combined revenues of all area authorities, the percentages depicted do not represent the experience of a particular area program. Rather, the percentage of revenues from each source varies among the area authorities. For example, state-allocated funds (General Fund appropriations and federal block grants) for mental

Table 26-3
State and Federal Funding to Area Programs, 1996–97

Rank	Area Program	State and Federal Funding ($)	Per Capita ($)	Rank	Area Program	State and Federal Funding ($)	Per Capita ($)
1	Tideland	4,034,475	42.84	22	Blue Ridge	7,103,923	29.67
2	Rutherford-Polk	3,107,733	41.46	23	Trend	3,100,639	29.40
3	RiverStone	2,290,847	39.56	24	Crossroads	2,886,365	29.28
4	New River	5,794,053	38.60	25	Southeastern		
5	Alamance-Caswell	5,284,243	38.55		Regional	6,352,732	27.83
6	Smoky Mountain	5,593,090	36.28	26	Piedmont	7,071,136	26.74
7	Roanoke-Chowan	2,630,873	35.85	27	Guilford	9,913,695	26.54
8	Lenoir	2,110,045	35.72	28	Neuse	4,408,625	26.50
9	Lee-Harnett	4,314,973	34.82	29	Gaston-Lincoln	6,231,353	26.36
10	Orange-Person-Chatham	6,255,525	34.06	30	Edgecombe-Nash	3,730,966	26.34
				31	Wayne	2,899,360	26.15
11	Sandhills	6,341,684	33.72	32	CenterPoint	8,403,023	26.09
12	Randolph	3,737,654	32.25	33	Foothills	5,815,263	26.05
13	Vance-Granville-Franklin-Warren	4,548,415	32.04	34	Mecklenburg	15,058,610	25.75
14	Pitt	3,832,349	32.03	35	Catawba	3,153,401	24.90
15	Wilson-Greene	2,707,871	32.00	36	Davidson	3,425,802	24.70
16	Duplin-Sampson	2,971,695	31.95	37	Tri-County	5,799,276	22.90
17	Rockingham	2,803,599	31.72	38	Southeastern	5,317,579	22.33
18	Albemarle	3,311,768	30.86	39	Cumberland	6,361,934	21.14
19	Cleveland	2,721,219	30.60	40	Onslow	3,154,350	21.09
20	Durham	5,988,205	30.44	41	Wake	10,576,383	20.02
21	Johnston	2,854,761	29.87		Total/State per capita	203,999,492	28.10

Note: Excludes Willie M., Thomas S., one-time and carryover funds, cross area service program funds, and Carolina Alternatives funds. The table lists forty-one area authorities rather than the current forty because data was collected prior to the dissolution of Tri-County in 1997.

Source: N.C. Division of Mental Health, Developmental Disabilities, and Substance Abuse Services, Memorandum, *1996–97 Area MHDDSAS Per Capita Calculations*, Budget Office tables (Raleigh, N.C.: NCDMHDDSAS, 9 May 1997).

health services are unevenly distributed among the area authorities. As shown in Table 26-3, while state allocations for community-based mental health services amounted to $28.10 for each person in North Carolina in 1996–97, the distribution of allocations to area authorities ranged from $20.02 per capita for Wake County to $42.84 per capita for the Tideland Area Authority.

Table 26-4
County General Funds Budgeted to Area Programs in 1996–97

Rank	Area Program	County General Funds ($)	Per Capita ($)	Rank	Area Program	County General Funds ($)	Per Capita ($)
1	Mecklenburg	23,333,658	39.90	24	Wilson-Greene	319,229	3.77
2	Durham	6,514,441	33.12	25	Piedmont	970,871	3.67
3	Guilford	8,202,068	21.96	26	Tideland	329,069	3.49
4	Cumberland	5,608,839	18.64	27	Smoky Mountain	495,261	3.21
5	Wake	8,701,279	16.47	28	Crossroads	305,844	3.10
6	Lenoir	863,392	14.62	29	Blue Ridge	662,000	2.76
7	Pitt	1,698,422	14.19	30	Roanoke-Chowan	201,250	2.74
8	Alamance-Caswell	1,798,717	13.12	31	Tri-County	674,731	2.66
9	CenterPoint	4,119,236	12.79	32	Lee-Harnett	317,040	2.56
10	Johnston	1,116,525	11.68	33	Neuse	403,629	2.43
11	Rockingham	944,868	10.69	34	Vance-Granville-		
12	Orange-Person-				Franklin-Warren	339,808	2.39
	Chatham	1,764,557	9.61	35	Duplin-Sampson	221,480	2.38
13	Cleveland	835,000	9.39	36	Davidson	323,153	2.33
14	Catawba	1,122,937	8.87	37	Onslow	346,987	2.32
15	Edgecombe-Nash	1,057,661	7.47	38	Sandhills	391,764	2.08
16	RiverStone	398,258	6.88	39	Foothills	415,011	1.86
17	Southeastern	1,500,764	6.30	40	Albemarle	177,915	1.66
18	Trend	570,073	5.40	41	Southeastern		
19	Gaston-Lincoln	1,202,391	5.09		Regional	353,240	1.55
20	Wayne	546,938	4.93				
21	Randolph	563,343	4.86		Total	80,713,604	
22	New River	685,893	4.57		Average of 41 Areas		8.09
23	Rutherford-Polk	316,062	4.22		Statewide per Capita		11.12

Note: The table lists forty-one area authorities rather than the current forty because data was collected prior to the dissolution of Tri-County in 1997.

Source: N.C. Division of Mental Health, Developmental Disabilities, and Substance Abuse Services, Memorandum, *County General Funds Comparison Report, Comparison Report for 1995–96 and 1996–97,* Budget Office Tables (Raleigh, N.C.: NCDMHDDSAS, 15 April 1997).

Similarly, the level of county support for community mental health services varies from area to area authority. As depicted in Table 26-4, county funds budgeted for mental health services in fiscal year 1996–97 ranged from $39.90 per capita for the Mecklenburg Area Authority to $1.55 per capita for the four-county Southeastern Regional Area Authority. When viewed on a state per capita basis, county funds budgeted for mental health services amounted to $11.12 per person.

It must be noted that Table 26-4 represents county funds budgeted, not actually spent, in 1996–97. Area authorities do not always receive and expend all of the funds budgeted to them by their respective counties, although most do. Mecklenburg County spent roughly $16 million from its county general fund on mental health services in fiscal year 1995–96. In the same year, Wake County spent about $9.5 million on mental health services, and the Guilford Area Authority, which serves a population of 374,000, received approximately $8.3 million in county revenues. In 1995–96 the Smoky Mountain Area Authority received $456,000 in revenue from the seven counties it serves: $25,000 from Cherokee; $28,000 from Clay; $10,000 from Graham; $198,000 from Haywood; $123,000 from Jackson; $57,000 from Macon; and $15,000 from Swain. In the same year, Tideland Area Authority received $328,000 in revenue from the counties it serves: $120,000 from Beaufort; $34,000 from Hyde; $113,000 from Martin; $17,400 from Tyrrell, and $43,478 from Washington.

Additional Resources

Botts, Mark F. *A Legal Manual for Area Mental Health, Developmental Disabilities, and Substance Abuse Boards in North Carolina.* Chapel Hill, N.C.: Institute of Government, The University of North Carolina at Chapel Hill, 1995.

————. "Community Mental Health Services in North Carolina: Yesterday, Today, and Tomorrow." *Popular Government* 61 (Summer 1995): 18–42.

Botts, Mark F., and Ingrid M. Johansen. "Mental Health, Developmental Disabilities, and Substance Abuse Services." In *State and Local Government Relations in North Carolina*, 2d ed. Liner, Charles D., ed. Chapel Hill, N.C.: Institute of Government, The University of North Carolina at Chapel Hill, 1995.

Lawrence, David M. *Local Government Finance in North Carolina*, 2d ed.. Chapel Hill, N.C.: Institute of Government, The University of North Carolina at Chapel Hill, 1990, especially chapter 5.

Notes

1. Pub. L. No. 487, 60 Stat. 421 (1946).

2. John F. Kennedy, *President's Messages: Mental Illness and Mental Retardation*, H.R. Doc. No. 58, at 1468 (1963). 109 Cong. Rec. 1744.

3. Title II of Pub. L. No. 88-164 (1963).

4. 1963 N.C. Sess. Laws ch. 1166; former G.S. 122-35.1 through -35.12.

5. Rebecca T. Craig and Barbara Wright, *Mental Health Financing and Programming* (National Conference of State Legislatures, 1988): 7. Other factors contributing to the deinstitutionalization included legal decisions restricting the involuntary commitment of persons to psychiatric hospitals and federal funding policies that motivated the transfer of some patients to Medicaid-supported nursing homes.

6. The Omnibus Budget and Reconciliation Act of 1981, Pub. L. No. 97-35, Title IX § 901, 42 U.S.C. § 300x.

7. 1977 N.C. Sess. Laws ch. 568; former G.S. 122-35.35 to -35.57.

8. In January 1998 court jurisdiction over the Thomas S. and Willie M. programs was terminated, providing the state greater flexibility in running the programs. As a result of these legal developments, there is some uncertainty as to whether state appropriations for these programs will be sustained at past levels.

27 Elementary and Secondary Education

Laurie L. Mesibov

Contents

Laurie L. Mesibov is an Institute of Government faculty member who specializes in public school law.

    The author expresses her appreciation to Robert E. Phay, whose authorship of this chapter in previous editions of this book is reflected here.

Education is one of government's most important responsibilities. It is both the foundation for a viable democratic society and a service the state is obligated to foster and protect. The North Carolina Constitution provides: "Religion, morality, and knowledge being necessary to good government and the happiness of mankind, schools, libraries, and the means of education shall forever be encouraged" (Article IX, Section 1). The constitution also states: "The people have a right to the privilege of education, and it is the duty of the State to guard and maintain that right" (Article I, Section 15). To carry out these constitutional mandates, the State of North Carolina maintains a system of elementary and secondary schools, a system of fifty-eight community colleges, and The University of North Carolina, which is comprised of sixteen institutions of higher education.

In 1839, the first year that North Carolina's public schools began to function as a statewide system, the General Assembly made $40 available to each school district that raised $20 locally (1839 N.C. Pub. Laws ch. 8). That was the legislature's first stab at dividing the fiscal burden of public education between the state and local governments. The struggle to find a proper division while ensuring fairness in the financial burden, equity in educational opportunities, and quality in education has continued for the ensuing 156 years and stands as one of the state's liveliest political topics in 1998.

Today's intricate division of responsibilities and control among the state, county governments, and local school administrative units is largely a result of the cumulative efforts over time to resolve the struggle. This chapter traces those efforts and describes current issues of financial responsibility, equity, and education reform. The relationship between the local board of education and the board of county commissioners is discussed in detail. Post-secondary education is not discussed in this chapter. (Community colleges are discussed in Chapter 28, and statutes relating to the university are codified as G.S. Ch. 116.)

Table 27-1 provides a statistical profile of the state's public school system. Information about any particular school system is available from the local board of education and school officials. Many school administrative units and individual schools have Internet sites; the Department of Public Instruction's home page can be found at http://www.dpi.state.nc.us.

The Educational System from 1776 to the 1930s

1776 through the Civil War

The North Carolina Constitution of 1776 (Article XLI) required the General Assembly to establish schools staffed by teachers who were paid by public funds. The legislature took its first step to carry out that mandate in 1825 by creating the Literary Fund as a source of revenue for public schools (1825 N.C. Pub. Laws ch. 1).

The public schools began to function as a statewide system in 1839. That year the General Assembly created the first formal local government bodies to supervise public education, ordering the justices of the peace in each county to appoint a body known as the board of county superintendents to administer that county's public schools. The General Assembly further required the superintendents to divide their counties into school districts and to appoint school committees to manage the schools in each district.[1] By the mid-1840s all counties had established a public school system.[2]

In 1852 the General Assembly created the appointive post of state Superintendent of Public Instruction,[3] and required for the first time that all teachers be certified by local committees of examination.[4] Local officials had full control over the curriculum and textbook selection.[5]

But North Carolina's new public school system, growing and improving under the leadership of Superintendent Calvin H. Wiley, became a casualty of the Civil War. When the war ended, Wiley was removed as state superintendent and the Literary Fund collapsed because the North Carolina and Confederate securities that supported the fund's endowment were worthless.[6]

1868 to 1900

With the adoption of the constitution of 1868, the state began the task of reviving the public school system. The constitution directed the General Assembly to maintain, through taxation or otherwise, a general and uniform system of free public schools for a minimum four-month term. The state is still bound by that provision, although the length of the minimum term has increased to nine months.

The constitution of 1868 also changed the form of governance for the school system. To replace the old Literary Board the constitution created a new state agency, the State Board of Education, composed of designated state officials empowered to manage state school funds and issue rules to govern the public schools. The office of state Superintendent of Public Instruction became elective. Boards of county superintendents were abolished, and local supervision of schools was transferred to the boards of county commissioners. Commissioners were required to divide their counties into districts and to maintain from county resources one or more schools in each district for at least four months a year. The constitution authorized the General Assembly to require at least sixteen months of compulsory education for children between the ages of six and eighteen.

The General Assembly implemented the provisions of the constitution of 1868 (1868–69 N.C. Pub. Laws ch. 184). The new statute (ch. 184) set the framework for the school system that prevailed until 1900, establishing a State Board of Education and vesting county commissioners with local control over public schools. It also created, for all townships, popularly elected school committees with duties similar to the duties of today's local school boards: to maintain schools for the minimum term with free tuition for all children, to hire and fire teachers, and to provide schoolhouses and furnishings.

The statute earmarked 75 percent of total state and county poll tax proceeds as school revenue, in addition to the General Assembly's appropriation of $100,000 to the schools from the state's general fund.[7] Chapter 184 required that all state-appropriated school money be apportioned according to local school-age populations. The law further required county commissioners to levy local school taxes sufficient to raise revenue to operate schools for a four-month term.

Chapter 184 contained a legislatively prescribed course of study for the first time: reading, writing, spelling, arithmetic, geography, and grammar. It also began the practice of state adoption of textbooks. The State

Table 27-1
Statistical Summary of North Carolina Public Schools

Item	Number	Percent
SCHOOLS (1997–98)		
Local Administrative Units		
County units	100	85.5
City units	17	14.5
Total	117	100.0
Public Schools		
Elementary (PK–8)	1,570	78.4
Secondary (9–12)	308	15.4
Combined	124	6.2
Total	2,002	100.0
STUDENTS		
Membership (First month, 1996–97)		
Grades K–8	877,004	73.1
Grades 9–12	322,958	26.9
Total	1,199,962	100.0
Ethnic Distribution (Fall 1996)		
American Indian	18,092	1.5
Asian	17,520	1.4
Black	368,478	30.7
Hispanic	27,300	2.3
White	769,065	64.1
High School Graduates' Intentions (1995–96)		
Enroll in four-year institutions	25,449	44.8
Enroll in two-year institutions	18,087	31.9
Enroll in other schools	1,349	2.4
Military service	2,630	4.6
Employment	7,169	12.6
All others	2,086	3.7
Total	56,770	100.0
PERSONNEL		
Public School Full-Time Personnel (Fall 1996)		
State funded	112,192	78.9
Federal funded	7,577	5.3
Local funded	22,429	15.8
Total	142,198	100.0
Highest Degree Held by Instructional Personnel (1996–97)		
Less than a bachelor's	955	1.1
Bachelor's degree	51,851	61.9
Master's degree	28,294	33.8
Sixth year level	2,089	2.5
Doctorate	617	2.5
Total	83,806	100.0

Continued on next page

Table 27-1 (*continued*)

EXPENDITURES (1995–96)
Per Pupil Expenditure in Average Daily Membership
(current expenses only) $4,930

Administrative Units by Size and Per Pupil Expenditure (PPE)

	1995–96 Final Avg. Daily Membership	1995–96 PPE (State Sources Only)
Largest: Mecklenburg County	87,597	$3,240
Medium: Pender County	5,653	$3,404
Smallest: Hyde County	762	$5,884

AUXILIARY SERVICES
Transportation (1995–96)

Number of buses operated	12,913
Number of pupils transported daily (includes contract transportation)	711,391
Average bus mileage per day	58
State cost (includes contract transportation and bus replacement)	$203,001,947
Annual state cost per pupil transported on buses	$227

Textbooks (1995–96)

Total textbook sales	$50,650,621
Cost of textbooks per pupil	$44
Average cost of textbook/kit:	
Elementary	$21
High school	$32

Child Nutrition (1995–96)

Schools serving breakfast	1,832
Average breakfasts served daily	199,628
Average cost (includes indirect cost)	$1.14
Schools serving lunch	1,931
Average lunches served daily	699,868
Average cost (includes indirect cost)	$1.82

Item	1997–98 Preliminary Estimates

ESTIMATED AVERAGE TEACHERS' SALARIES

North Carolina average	$31,286
U.S. Average	$38,516

Source: State Board of Education, *North Carolina Education Directory, 1997–98,* pp. 276–78.

Board of Education was to adopt particular texts, and all schools were required to use these books exclusively.

The system established in 1868 and 1869 evolved during the rest of the century. In 1872 the General Assembly directed the boards of county commissioners to serve as boards of education (1872–73 N.C. Pub. Laws ch. 90). The 1881 legislature created the post of county superintendent, identical to today's local superintendent; the superintendent was elected by joint action of the county board of education and the county justices of the peace (1881 N.C. Pub. Laws ch. 200). In creating the new executive position, the legislature brought local operation of public education under consolidated, countywide management. In 1885 the General Assembly created three-member county boards of education as separate agencies, with members chosen biennially by the board of county commissioners and the county justices of the peace (1885 N.C. Pub. Laws ch. 174).

In 1885 the state supreme court dealt a serious blow to the rehabilitation of public education. In *Barksdale v. Commissioners of Sampson County* in 1885,[8] the court declared that local school expenses were not "necessary expenses," and therefore the constitution required a vote of the people before local taxes could be levied for schools.

1900 through 1930

The first years of the twentieth century marked a turning point for North Carolina's public school system. They ushered in a period of heightened public support for education, spurred by the efforts and enthusiasm of Governor Charles B. Aycock, governor from 1901 through 1905. The state also adopted a new approach to its funding of education: direct financing from the state's tax revenue. The state renewed its commitment of $100,000 as an ongoing element of public school finance.[9] In 1901 the legislature appropriated an additional $100,000 to bring those counties unable to afford the minimum term, even if they levied the maximum property tax allowed by the state constitution, up to the four-month term.[10] In 1903 the legislature reestablished the Literary Fund to serve as a loan fund for school construction (1903 N.C. Pub. Laws ch. 567).

A major breakthrough occurred in 1907, when the state supreme court reversed the *Barksdale* decision in *Collie v. Commissioners*[11] and ruled that spending for public schools was a "necessary" expense. This decision made it possible for counties to levy local taxes to raise the revenue needed to support the minimum four-month school term without a vote of the people.

The General Assembly increased the state-levied property tax in 1913 (1913 N.C. Pub. Laws ch. 33) to fund appropriations to the counties that enabled local school boards to lengthen school terms, and in 1918 the constitution was amended to make the minimum term six months statewide. To provide more financial support for the longer term, the General Assembly instituted a system in 1919 under which the state and counties shared the burden of paying for the six-month term; it also established an equalization fund to help poorer counties meet this obligation.[12]

Equity was a chief financial concern in public education in the 1920s. In 1919 the General Assembly had ordered a statewide revaluation of all property to prevent counties from minimizing the amount their citizens owed in state property taxes by underassessing property values.[13] But after a constitutional amendment that authorized the income tax in 1920, the legislature began levying a state income tax as a chief source of state revenue and abandoned the property tax, leaving its levy entirely to local governments.[14]

The appropriation of state revenue to public schools in Chapter 146 of the Public Laws of 1921 included a new equalization procedure, known today as power equalization. The statute directed the State Board of Education to distribute to each county the amount needed to make up any deficit in financing a six-month term if a county local property tax levy of 30 cents on every $100 valuation did not produce enough money.[15] Despite the 1920 revaluation of property, the problem of fair and accurate valuation continued to spark controversy throughout the 1920s. To ensure the uniformity of property assessment required for effective power equalization, the General Assembly established a State Board of Equalization in 1927. The legislature directed the board to standardize local property values and to distribute to the respective counties the money necessary to finance a six-month term after they had levied a local property tax of 40 cents on every $100 valuation.[16]

The period from 1900 through 1930 saw major changes in other facets of public education as well. The General Assembly enacted statewide compulsory education in 1913, requiring all children between the ages of eight and twelve to attend school for four months each year (1913 N.C. Pub. Laws ch. 173). To facilitate attendance, the legislature passed child labor laws limiting the hours in which children could work in factories.[17]

In 1901 the General Assembly designated the State Board of Education as a textbook commission responsible for adopting texts for elementary schools on the basis of recommendations from a subcommission (1901 N.C. Pub. Laws ch. 1). In 1923 the legislature created a separate textbook commission to recommend elementary school books to the State Board of Education; the board then selected books for adoption. High school texts were selected differently: the State Board of Education approved a list of books, and the local school boards made final choices on the basis of recommendations by the county commissioners (1923 N.C. Pub. Laws ch. 136). The General Assembly made the state board responsible for adopting high school textbooks in 1931 (1931 N.C. Pub. Laws ch. 359). The 1923 legislation also directed the textbook commission to prepare a course of study, subject to approval by the superintendent of public instruction.

Fiscal Reforms of 1931 and 1933

The fiscal chaos of the Great Depression led directly to the creation of the fiscal framework for public education that North Carolina has today (1998). By 1931 the problems faced by taxpayers in paying property taxes had thrown the public school finance system into disarray. Many counties were defaulting on debts, and many teachers were not paid.[18] The General Assembly responded by enacting the School Machinery Act, which radically changed the structure of public school finance.[19] For the first time the state was made responsible for paying all current expenses necessary to finance a minimum six-month school term, leaving the counties responsible for constructing and maintaining school buildings. State responsibility for financing a uniform statewide basic level of education for a minimum term remains the framework of public school finance in North Carolina.

In 1933 the legislature completed the reform of 1931 by extending the minimum term financed by state funds to eight months; abolishing all existing local school taxes; and authorizing counties, with the approval of county voters, to levy new supplemental school taxes to support schools at standards higher than minimum state requirements.[20] Counties, as the basic governmental unit for operating schools, remained responsible for providing and maintaining school buildings.

By providing a basic level of state support for education throughout North Carolina, the state acted decisively and dramatically to rescue public schools from economic collapse. The legislation of 1931 and 1933 shifted responsibility for financing schools to the state, which meant that achieving the constitutionally mandated minimum standard no longer depended on the ability or willingness of local taxpayers to pay for schools. In addition to avoiding economic disaster, these fiscal reforms moved North Carolina in the direction of equal opportunity for all children and put in place the structure for financing schools that remained largely unchanged until the adoption of the Basic Education Program in 1985.

Current Governance of Public Schools

State Level

General Assembly

The state constitution sets out the basic structure of public school governance. The General Assembly is responsible for "a general and uniform system of free public schools" [Article IX, Section 2(1)] and must ensure that children have a basic education of at least minimum duration, content, and quality made available to them. The General Assembly obviously cannot attend to the day-to-day operation of more than 2,000 schools, although from time to time it prescribes in a very specific way what should happen in schools.[21] As a general rule, the General Assembly carries out its duty to provide a system of free public schools primarily by appropriating money and by delegating major decision-making authority to the State Board of Education, to local boards of education, and, beginning in the 1990s, to individual schools.

State Board of Education

The North Carolina Constitution provides for the State Board of Education in Article IX, Section 4(1). The state board has thirteen members. The lieutenant governor and the state treasurer are *ex officio* members, and the remaining eleven are appointed by the governor, subject to confirmation by the General Assembly in joint session. G.S. 115C-10 permits one member to be a public school employee. Appointments are for eight-year terms and are staggered. In addition, G.S. 115C-11 authorizes the governor to appoint two high school students to serve as advisers and non-voting participants in board deliberations. The State Teacher of the Year, as designated by the Department of Public Instruction, serves *ex officio* for a two-year term as advisor to the board. The state constitution makes the Superintendent of Public Instruction the board's secretary and chief administrative officer [Article IX, Section 4(2)].

The state constitution makes the state board responsible for supervising and administering the free public school system and all funds provided for it except local school funds (Article IX, Section 5). The board determines education policy for the state and has the power to make all rules and regulations necessary to carry out this responsibility, subject to laws enacted by the General Assembly. The board regulates the grade and salary of school employees, adopts a standard course of study, and develops accountability measures for individual schools. The board's statutory powers and duties are listed in G.S. 115C-12 and include apportioning all state school funds, certifying teachers, and adopting and supplying textbooks.

Superintendent of Public Instruction

In most states, the state school superintendent is appointed by the governor or selected by the state school board. In North Carolina, the Superintendent of Public Instruction is a constitutional officer, popularly elected for a four-year term. Although not a voting member of the state board, the state constitution makes the superintendent the board's secretary and chief administrative officer [Article IX, Section 4(2)]. As such, the state superintendent is responsible for administering board policies and organizing and administering the Department of Public Instruction as the state board directs. G.S. 115C-19 defines the superintendent's responsibilities as managing the day-to-day administration of the public school system and carrying out the duties specified in G.S. 115C-21, subject to the "direction, control, and approval" of the state board. The superintendent also has an important voice in explaining the needs of the school system to various constituencies and recommending changes to improve public schools.

Efforts to fundamentally change the complicated relationship between the state board and the superintendent by making the superintendent an appointive office have been a standard feature of recent sessions of the General Assembly, but these efforts have not been successful.

Department of Public Instruction

G.S. 143A-44.1 creates the Department of Public Instruction (DPI), headed by the State Board of Education. Ths Superintendent of Public Instruction organizes and administers the Department of Public Instruction. All appointments of administrative and supervisory personnel in the DPI are subject to the state board's approval. In spite of reorganization and downsizing in 1995, the DPI continues to provide important leadership and assistance to local boards in areas such as instructional support, media and technology, research and testing, and personnel.

Other State Agencies Involved in Public Education

The Department of Health and Human Services is responsible for administering the state's special schools for children who are hearing- and sight-impaired (G.S. 143B-216.40 through -216.44 and G.S. 143B-164.14 through -164.17).

The Board of Governors of The University of North Carolina administers two schools that include instruction at the high school level. The North Carolina School of the Arts, one of the University's constituent institutions, was established to provide professional training to students from North Carolina and other states who are exceptionally talented in the performing arts (G.S. 116-63). It offers both high school and college-level training at its campus in Winston-Salem. The North Carolina School of Science and Mathematics, located in Durham, is an affiliated school of the University. It was created to foster the education of state high school students who are academically talented in science and mathematics and who would benefit from a residential program (G.S. 116-230.1). The school also serves other schools in North Carolina through its research and outreach activities.

Local Level

School Administrative Units

The local school administrative unit is the legal entity that operates directly below the state board in the public school organizational hierarchy. The school administrative unit is called the "school district" in most states, and that term frequently is used informally in North Carolina as well. By statute, each North Carolina county is classified as a school administrative unit, and schools in it are under the general supervision and control of a county board of education. "City" administrative units are school systems, established within a county or adjacent parts of two or more contiguous counties, that have been approved to operate as separate school units by the General Assembly. The schools of a city unit are under the control of a board of education established by the special legislative act that created the unit. In most cases, the administration of a city unit is not connected with a municipal governing body; the unit merely draws its name from the municipality with which it is geographically associated. Although city units may also serve as special taxing districts in which supplemental property taxes may be levied for school support, for fiscal purposes city units are the responsibility of county boards of commissioners. Any countywide revenues appropriated for school operating expenses (but not for capital outlay) must be distributed to all units in the county equally, in proportion to average daily membership.

Merger of School Units

In the 1997–98 school year the state was divided into 117 school units, 100 county units and 17 city units, each administered by its own school board. Enrollment in these units ranged from under 1,000 to over 85,000 students. In each unit, the board of education is responsible for directing, supervising, and planning for the public schools.

Although the General Assembly could mandate the merger of all city units with county units, it has not done so. Instead, the General Assembly has provided three other methods for merger where all involved school units are in one county.

1. The school systems themselves may bring about the merger (G.S. 115C-67). The merging units adopt a plan of merger, which becomes effective if the board of county commissioners and the State Board of Education approve it. The plan may make the merger contingent on approval of the voters in the affected areas.

2. The board of county commissioners may compel a merger by adopting a merger plan for all school units in the county (G.S. 115C-68.1). Under this type of merger, the county must provide local funding per average daily membership to the merged school unit for subsequent years of at least the highest level of any school unit in the county during the five fiscal years that preceded the merger. The boards of education do not participate in preparing the plan and need not agree to it. A merger plan developed by a board of county commissioners cannot be made subject to voter approval.

3. A city board may force a merger by dissolving itself (G.S. 115C-68.2). In that case the State Board of Education must adopt a

merger plan. Plans developed in this way cannot be subject to voter approval. Boards of education and boards of county commissioners do not participate in preparing such a plan and need not agree to it.

Through these various methods, the number of school units has been steadily declining. In 1960 the state had 174 separate school units; in 1987–88, 140 units; in 1997–98, 117 units. Reducing the number of administrative units to one per county continues to be a focus of discussion and study in counties with more than one school unit.

Local Boards of Education

The board is a corporate body with the power to sue and be sued (G.S. 115C-40), and G.S. 115C-36 gives it "[a]ll powers and duties conferred and imposed by law respecting public schools, which are not expressly conferred and imposed upon some other official." G.S. 115C-47 requires the school board to provide an adequate school system. In doing this, local boards have five major types of duties to perform:

1. Hire and fire school employees
2. Set education policy within the guidelines of state education policy
3. Preserve the assets of the school unit and manage the local school budget
4. Inform the county commissioners of the school unit's fiscal needs
5. Serve as a hearing board for local education disputes

School boards in most other states have the authority to levy taxes to help finance the schools they administer; North Carolina boards do not have this authority. The tax levying authority for school administrative units is the board of county commissioners.

Membership

The general law for selecting county school board members requires non-partisan election of board members. G.S. 115C-35 provides that "[t]he county board of education in each county shall consist of five members elected by the voters of the county at large for terms of four years." Local legislation has created many exceptions to this general requirement. Similarly, although G.S. 115C-37 specifies that county boards of education shall be elected on a non-partisan basis at the time of the primary election, some board elections are held at the time of the general election and some are on a partisan basis. G.S. 115C-37 also provides that terms of office shall be staggered so that only half (or as nearly equal to half as possible) of the terms expire every two years.

The general law does not apply to any city school administrative unit with a local act providing for a different selection procedure. Many methods of selecting city boards of education are used; a majority of city units elect members to the board on a non-partisan basis.

Individual boards of education and county boards of election should be consulted for information about elections for a particular school board.

G.S. 115C-39 sets out the statutory procedure for removal of a school board member. If the State Board of Education has sufficient evidence that any school board member is "not capable of discharging, or is not discharging, the duties of his office as required by law, or is guilty of immoral or disreputable conduct," and then, after proper notification, if the board investigates the charges and finds them to be true, it can declare the office vacant. Recall elections to remove a school board member are permissible only if specifically authorized by the General Assembly. In 1998 only one such local act, which applies to the Chapel Hill-Carrboro City Board of Education, has been enacted [1993 N.C. Sess. Laws (Reg. Sess. 1994) ch. 660].

Organization and Meetings

The General Statutes give little guidance for organizing school boards. G.S. 115C-41 provides that a board must hold an organizational meeting and elect a chairman no later than sixty days after the swearing-in of members following election or appointment.

The board must meet on the first Monday of each quarter or as soon thereafter as possible. It may hold regular meetings and meet in special sessions on the call of the chair or secretary as often as school business requires. Local acts may depart from general law requirements and must be checked when a question concerning board organization arises.

Boards of education and their committees must comply with the open meetings law, Article 33C of G.S. Chapter 143, which requires public notice of meetings, defines the purposes for which a board may meet in closed session, and controls the method of voting. As secretary to the board, the superintendent keeps a record of all its proceedings and issues all its notices and orders. Each meeting's minutes are available for public inspection according to the open meetings law.

The General Statutes do not define a quorum for school board meetings; the law in this area has been made by the courts. In *Edwards v. Board of Education* the state supreme court ruled that a quorum is a majority of the whole membership of the board.[22]

Compensation

Using the procedures in G.S. 153A-92, a school unit's tax-levying authority may set the compensation and expense allowances for members of the local school boards (G.S. 115C-38). Funds for the per diem, subsistence, and mileage for all meetings of county and city boards of education must be provided from the current expense fund budget of the particular county or city.

School Superintendents

The superintendent is the chief local school administrator as well as the system's executive officer. The superintendent serves *ex officio* as secretary for the board of education; recommends personnel to the board for employment; carries out state and local policies and rules; monitors the condition of school buildings; and prepares the budget. G.S. 115C-276 list many of a superintendent's duties, including the duty to carry out the local board's rules and regulations.

The superintendent is employed under a contract with the board of education (G.S. 115C-271). The board is free to choose the superintendent as long as the individual meets certain state board requirements concerning education, credentials, and experience. A board may elect a superintendent at any time for a term of one to four years, ending on June 30 of the final twelve months of the contract. The board may extend or renew the term of the contract at any time after its first twelve months; a contract may not be extended for more than four years. However, if new board members have been elected or appointed but not yet sworn in, the board may not extend or renew the current superintendent's contract until after the new members have been sworn in. Superintendents' contracts for a period of less than one year are governed by G.S. 115C-275.

Individual Schools

Before the 1990s an individual school had no independent authority except the authority specifically delegated to the school by the local board of education. As part of the state's decision to increase accountability of school personnel for their students' achievement, this situation has changed. Individual school improvement teams must develop a school improvement plan (G.S. 115C-105.27), and a school may participate in a dispute resolution process with the local board of education if the board refuses to approve the plan. These plans may include requests for waivers of certain state laws, rules, and policies (G.S. 115C-105.26). The school board must distribute 75 percent of staff development funds to individual schools to be used in accordance with their improvement plans (G.S. 115C-105.30). In a broader direction, local boards are instructed to provide maximum flexibility to schools in the use of funds to enable the schools to accomplish their goals (G.S. 115C-105.25). Each individual school principal, in consultation with the school improvement team, has the authority to schedule some days in the annual school calendar (G.S. 115C-84.2).

Boards of County Commissioners

The board of county commissioners is an integral part of the legal structure of public education. Although county commissioners are not typically thought of as educational policy makers, they do influence and at times determine policy though the budget process. The board of commissioners is the tax-levying authority for the schools, except in a very few situations in which the governing body of a municipality levies a supplemental tax for a city administrative unit. Because commissioners provide the local tax money, they influence and at times even substitute their judgment for that of the school board on some educational issues. There are, however, limits on the authority of the boards of commissioners; they may not interfere with the control of the schools vested in the board of education.

In addition to its funding responsibilities, the board of commissioners has statutory authority or responsibility to approve certain school board budget amendments; levy and collect supplementary taxes for the school board; transfer the proceeds of fines, penalties, and forfeitures to school boards; approve certain school board contracts; conduct special school elections; approve the amount the school board proposes to spend to purchase a school site; mandate the merger of all school units in the county; issue bonds for school construction; and in some counties, construct schools. Each of these is discussed in greater detail later in this chapter.

Counties also provide essential services independent of public schools that affect education significantly. The health of citizens, the economic well-being of a community, the strength of its families, and the safety of its streets affect students and school staff. Although the notion of schools as safe havens devoted to learning is an appealing idea, schools cannot avoid being affected by the problems that students and staff bring to school.

Current System of School Finance

State and Local Responsibilities

Public schools are a responsibility of both state government and local government. As noted above, the basic structure of school finance has not changed since the 1930s. The state is responsible for current expenses necessary to maintain the minimum nine-month term. Counties are responsible for financing construction and maintenance of school facilities and may supplement state funding for current expenditures. However, the state has frequently appropriated funds for school construction, and school boards continue to rely on counties to provide funds for current expenses.

The state's fiscal responsibility has two dimensions: financing a school term of minimum length, and providing a level of support that will maintain an educational program of basic content and quality throughout the state. From the 1930s into the 1980s, the state had no established standard for determining the level of funding it would provide for the minimum term—that level was set simply by the amount appropriated by the General Assembly and distributed through various allocation formulas. The appropriations and formulas gave the only definition of the state-provided educational program.

This situation changed in the 1980s. In 1984 the General Assembly reaffirmed the traditional state-local government split in funding responsibilities by announcing that "it is the policy of the State of North Carolina to provide from State revenue sources the instructional expenses for current operation of the public school system as defined in the standard course of study" [G.S. 115C-408(b)]. Accompanying this sweeping statement was a direction to the State Board of Education to develop a standard course of study to be offered to every public school student.

In response, the state board proposed, and the General Assembly adopted, the Basic Education Program. In addition to describing the educational program that should be available to every child in North Carolina, the Basic Education Program adds a new feature to the school finance system—a standard for the program of education the state should finance. The essential difference between North Carolina's current system of finance and the system established in 1933 is that the level of state support is now being set according to the Basic Education Program's requirements.

Although the General Assembly has not provided full funding for the Basic Education Program, it has provided substantial funding for its key components with the effect of raising the level of state support. The state allocates money to school units through formulas intended to measure the need for resources required to offer the standard course of study, as defined by the Basic Education Program. The effect of the program's allotment formulas is to allocate more money per student in the smallest counties, which tend to be relatively poor, rural counties.[23] Although the state funds are intended to provide a uniform statewide program, school units receive different dollar amounts per student because of variations in state spending for salaries, transportation, and certain other costs.

The most important feature of North Carolina's school financing system is that the state takes income, sales, and other tax revenue from all residents and allocates it for teachers and other school resources statewide, without regard to the ability or willingness of local residents to support schools through local taxes. In many other states the state government helps poor units through grants designed to help the units provide a basic level of funding, but in North Carolina the state government itself provides the basic level of support. Taxpayers in the highest-income counties contribute more than others toward financing schools across the state. As a result, North Carolina does not have funding disparities between poor and wealthy units that are as large as the disparities in most other states.

North Carolina's approach to financing its public schools differs in three respects from that of most other states.

1. The basic financial backing for public schools comes from state rather than local revenues. Thus state income and sales taxes rather than the locally levied *ad valorem* property tax are the primary revenue sources for financing schools.
2. State funds are basically a flat grant to a school system based on the number of students enrolled and the general cost of operation. North Carolina differs from most other states in that it does not allocate state money on the basis of the local unit's financial ability to operate schools.
3. The local board of education has no authority to levy taxes for the schools in its unit; it must rely upon the board of commissioners for the tax levy.

The state contribution for current operating expenses of the public schools comes from several sources. The primary one is the State Public School Fund, which supplies over 90 percent of the state money. This fund supports various recurring expenses of the regular school program—primarily the salaries and benefits of most teachers and other school employees.

Each school administrative unit's share of the state appropriations is determined by the state board. The two most significant standards the state board uses are the number of pupils in average daily membership and the salary schedules for various classes of personnel employed by the local school board to fill state-allocated positions. State salary schedules for professional staff are based primarily on level of education and years of experience.

Most of the state financing for public schools is provided through the State Public School Fund. These funds are released only on warrants issued by the school finance officer and drawn on the state treasurer. Deposits in the state treasury are made to the credit of local school units at least monthly. Some other state funds are released directly to the school unit.

The state-financed basic support of schools is supplemented by local governments and the federal government. In recent years, approximately 65 percent of the total public school costs (current expense, capital outlay, and debt service costs) has been paid by state appropriations; local governments have contributed about 25 percent and the federal government about 10 percent. Table 27-2 shows the sources of funds for the public schools in 1995–96. Table 27-3 shows the sources of funds for

Table 27-2
Sources of Funds for Current and Capital Expenditures,
North Carolina Public Schools, 1995–96

	Current Operating Expenditures		Capital Expenditures		Totals	
	Amount ($)	%	Amount ($)	%	Amount ($)	%
State	3,951,627,335	68.6	13,971,215	2.3	3,965,598,550	62.3
Federal	443,660,694	7.7	173,929	>0.1	443,834,623	7.0
Local	1,369,159,208	23.7	589,164,976	97.7	1,958,324,184	30.7
Total	5,764,447,237	100.0	603,310,120	100.0	6,367,757,357	100.0

Source: State Board of Education, *North Carolina Public Schools: Statistical Profile 1997* (Raleigh, N.C.: SBE, 1997): 58–62, 63.

public schools by purpose. The exact proportions of state, local, and federal aid in the various school units differ.

Funding Disparities and Equal Educational Opportunities

Although the state provides funds in a way intended to meet operating expenses of the basic program, the state constitution [Art. IX, Sec. 2(2)] guarantees local governments with financial responsibility for public education the right to supplement the basic level of state support. Thus because some counties are more able or more willing than others to use local tax money to supplement what the state provides, funding disparities between school units exist. Table 27-4 shows the average salary expense per pupil and average pupil ratios in school units classified by per capita income of counties.

This variation in financial support takes place within a finance system that tends to equalize expenditures in several ways. First, the basic program financed by the state is provided equally to all school units without regard to the resources of the respective units. Second, because the state support is provided at a relatively high level, the effect is to reduce the relative differences in local spending. Third, by financing a large proportion of school expenditures from statewide taxes, the state redistributes tax revenues from high-income to low-income units. In addition, federal funds are distributed in ways that tend to equalize expenditures because more federal funds go to low-income units. Although North Carolina's equity problems are less serious than those in many other states, legislators, school officials, parents, and taxpayers have long been concerned about them.

Table 27-3
Sources of Funds for Public Schools by Purpose, 1995–96

	State		Federal		Local	
	Amount ($)	%	Amount ($)	%	Amount ($)	%
Instruction[a]	2,944,546,404	83.1	195,149,803	5.5	403,463,054	11.4
Support[b]	276,363,776	70.8	40,557,196	10.4	73,414,466	18.8
Administration	440,491,370	59.7	19,863,982	2.7	277,470,022	37.6
Food	10,746,691	2.9	178,137,272	48.7	176,819,496	48.4
Transportation	203,001,947	84.8	1,261,010	0.5	35,197,949	14.7
Plant Operation	67,261,094	23.0	2,636,797	0.9	222,530,270	76.1
Plant Maintenance	5,884,031	4.3	1,731,602	1.3	130,023,557	94.4
Community Services[c]	3,331,021	8.3	362,203	0.9	36,595,919	90.8
Non-Program Charges[d]	1,001	>.01	3,960,829	22.5	13,644,475	77.5
Total Current Expense	3,951,627,335	68.6	443,660,694	7.7	1,369,159,208	23.7
Total Current Expense (less food)	3,940,880,644	73.0	265,523,442	4.9	1,192,339,712	22.1
Capital Outlay[e]	13,971,215	2.3	173,929	>0.1	589,164,976	97.7
Total Capital and Current Expenditures (with food)	3,965,598,550	62.3	443,834,623	7.0	1,958,324,184	30.7

Source: State Board of Education, *North Carolina Public Schools: Statistical Profile 1997* (Raleigh, N.C.: 1997): 58–62.

a. *Instructional programs* are activities dealing directly with the teaching of pupils, or the interaction between teacher and pupils, and include: regular instruction; special instruction; adult instruction; co-curricular programs; math/science computer programs; vocational education school technology program; employee benefits; and additional pay.

b. *Support services* are those services that provide administrative, technical, personal, and logistical support to facilitate and enhance instruction for both pupil and teacher and include: direction of pupil support; attendance and social service work services; guidance services; health services; psychological services; speech, pathology, and audiology services; industry education and sex equity coordination; special populations coordination; other pupil support services; improvement of instructional services; educational media; and curriculum development.

c. *Community services* are activities not directly related to the provision of education for pupils in the local school administrative unit.

d. *Non-programmed charges* are conduit-type (outgoing) payments to other local school administrative units or other administrative units in the state or in another state.

e. *Capital outlay* covers expenditures for acquisition of property, construction, renovation, and other similar activities.

Table 27-4
Average Salary Expense Per Pupil and Average Pupil-Teacher Ratios
in School Units Classified by Per Capita Income of
Counties in North Carolina 1995–96 or 1996–97

1994 Per Capita Income of County ($)	No. of Units	Avg. per Capita Income ($)	Avg. Current Expend- iture per ADM ($)	Avg. Salary Expense per ADM ($)	ADM per Teacher, Professional, and Teacher's Assistant		
					Teachers	Other Profes- sionals	Teach- ers' Assists
Less than 12,000	1	11,938	4,781	2,942	16.8	13.6	42.0
12,000–12,999	3	12,629	5,917	3,705	14.4	11.9	39.5
13,000–13,999	2	13,492	4,691	3,013	16.2	13.7	52.1
14,000–14,999	5	14,500	5,059	3,304	15.3	12.6	50.1
15,000–15,999	20	15,491	5,195	3,384	15.2	12.5	49.1
16,000–16,999	22	16,485	5,329	3,498	15.0	12.3	47.3
17,000–17,999	16	17,505	4,858	3,226	15.4	13.0	48.5
18,000–18,999	9	18,316	4,846	3,210	15.4	13.0	51.5
19,000–19,999	8	19,571	4,994	3,288	15.3	12.8	47.7
20,000–20,999	4	20,490	5,335	3,483	15.2	12.4	50.9
21,000–21,999	1	21,710	5,002	3,350	15.9	13.1	46.1
22,000–22,999	3	22,512	5,131	3,416	14.9	12.6	50.5
23,000–23,999	3	23,363	5,551	3,674	14.2	11.6	51.6
24,000–24,999	2	24,704	5,072	3,450	15.4	13.1	63.7
25,000–25,999	1	25,993	5,272	3,485	16.0	13.1	49.8

Source: State Board of Education, *North Carolina Public Schools: Statistical Profile 1997* (Raleigh, N.C.: SBE, 1997): 48, 82–319.

Note: Figures from the individual school units for pupil-teacher ratios are from 1996–97, while figures on average operating expense and average salary expense are from 1995–96. It's not clear exactly how, or from what school year, the final ADM (as given under the current expense expenditure tables for each county) is derived.

In 1987, plaintiffs from Robeson County challenged North Carolina's system of school finance, alleging that it creates unequal educational programs and facilities and that these inequities violate the constitutional mandate that "equal opportunities shall be provided for all students" [N.C. Const. Art. IX, Sec. 2(1)]. In *Britt v. North Carolina State Board of Education*, the North Carolina Court of Appeals ruled that the fundamental right guaranteed by the constitution is only the right to equal access to the public schools—that is, every child has a fundamental right to receive an education in the public schools.[24] This right of access may not differ according to a child's race.

Even though the court ruled in the Robeson County case that the finance system does not violate the state constitution, in 1991 the General Assembly began providing funds to low-wealth and small school units, independent of the Basic Education Program (1991 N.C. Sess. Laws ch. 689, secs. 201.2, 201.2). These two programs distribute additional state funds to school units that, because of relatively low property tax bases or enrollments, have difficulty supporting schools. The money is intended to allow school units to enhance the instructional program and student achievement and must be used to supplement, not supplant, county appropriations.

In addition to providing funds through the Basic Education Program and the low-wealth and small-system formulas, the General Assembly appropriates funds for special challenges faced by school systems. For example, in 1994 the General Assembly created the State School Technology Fund, a nonreverting special revenue fund under the control and direction of the State Board of Education [1993 N.C. Sess. Laws (Reg. Sess. 1994) ch. 769, sec. 8.5]. These funds must be used to help local school boards implement the technology plans developed to improve student performance through the use of learning and instructional management technologies.[25]

In 1998 the state faces the prospect of major changes in its system for financing schools because of a 1997 decision of the North Carolina Supreme Court in *Leandro v. State of North Carolina*.[26] In 1994 plaintiffs from five poor counties, later joined by school boards from the state's largest school units, claimed that the state's system of financing schools violates the North Carolina Constitution. The state supreme court ruled that the constitution guarantees to every school child a right to access a "sound basic education." Elements of that education include the following:

1. Sufficient ability to read, write, and speak the English language, and a knowledge of fundamental mathematics and physical science to enable the student to function in a complex and rapidly changing society

2. Sufficient fundamental knowledge of geography, history, and basic economic and political systems to enable the student to make informed choices with regard to issues that affect the student personally or affect the student's community, state, and nation

3. Sufficient academic and vocational skills to enable the student to successfully engage in post-secondary education or vocational training

4. Sufficient academic and vocational skills to enable the student to compete on an equal basis with others in formal education or gainful employment in contemporary society

The decision's immediate effect is to direct the trial court to rule on the merits of the lawsuit, that is, to determine whether some school units are not meeting the obligation of offering students a sound basic education. According to the state supreme court, factors the trial court should consider in making this determination include, but are not limited to, educational goals and standards adopted by the legislature, performance levels on standard achievement tests, and the state's general educational expenditures and per-pupil expenditures. The supreme court cautioned the trial court not to intrude on areas of judgment best left to the legislature, but the court did not identify these areas. There is no way to predict the outcome of the lawsuit and its future impact on North Carolina's schools.

In a second aspect of the *Leandro* case, the state supreme court was asked to interpret Article IX, Section 2(1) of the state constitution, which requires a "general and uniform system" of schools in which "equal opportunities shall be provided for all students." Do the county-by-county funding inequalities produced by the state's current public school finance system violate that provision? The supreme court said no.

Because this aspect of the *Leandro* decision held that the finance system is not constitutionally deficient, the General Assembly is not immediately compelled to change that system. But, of course, it remains free to change the system on its own initiative.

Financing Construction

Local governments have been responsible for financing school construction in North Carolina since the state's public school system was established in 1839. Even the dramatic structural changes of the 1930s, when the state assumed the duty of financing current expenses of local school units, did not change this basic responsibility. It was reaffirmed by the General Assembly in 1984 in G.S. 115C-408(b), which says "It is the policy of the State of North Carolina that the facilities requirements for a public education system will be met by county governments."

However, over the years the state has repeatedly, and increasingly, offered direct and indirect assistance for construction costs in response to the need for new and improved school facilities across the state. Since 1903, for example, the state has made relatively modest loans from the

State Literary Fund to counties for construction.[27] Several times since 1949 the state has issued bonds to finance grants to local school boards for school construction. Those bond issues were $25 million in 1949 (combined with $25 million from the postwar reserve fund), $50 million in 1953, $100 million in 1963, and $300 million in 1973. Proceeds of the 1963 and 1973 bond issues were distributed solely on the basis of school enrollment.

As the funding wells created by the 1963 and 1973 state bond issues ran dry, many local school units found it increasingly difficult to pay for school construction with local funds. In 1979 the Governor's Commission on Public School Finance recommended additional bond issues to aid local school construction.[28]

The General Assembly did not adopt that recommendation. Instead, it provided alternative relief in 1983 by authorizing counties to levy an additional one-half cent sales and use tax, with a specified percentage of the resulting revenue earmarked for school capital outlay, including retirement of existing school indebtedness (G.S. Ch. 105, Art. 40). In the first five years after the tax is imposed, 40 percent of the proceeds must be used for school capital outlay or to retire indebtedness incurred by the county for school capital outlay purposes; in the next twenty-three years, 30 percent (G.S. 115C-487). In 1986 the General Assembly authorized another local retail sales tax with the same half-cent rate (G.S. Ch. 105, Art. 42). In the first twenty-five years of the tax, counties must use 60 percent of the revenues received for public school capital outlay purposes or to service school debt incurred during the five years before the tax became effective (G.S. 115C-502). The county may hold these moneys in a capital reserve fund for future projects; any interest earned on the earmarked revenue must also be used for school capital outlay.

Both the 1983 and 1986 laws include a provision that allows a county to petition the North Carolina Local Government Commission for authorization to use part or all of the earmarked revenues for other purposes. The Local Government Commission will approve a petition only if the county demonstrates that it can provide for school capital needs without the earmarked revenue. A local board of education may petition the Local Government Commission if it believes that the county has not complied with the intent of these sales and use tax laws.

Although the local responsibility for financing school capital outlay is still in place, these local sales taxes may reasonably be viewed as a form of state revenue sharing because the state is collecting and using a traditional state revenue source—the retail sales tax—to provide funds to local units to meet school construction needs. In addition, the General

Assembly changed the distribution of the sales tax proceeds to favor poorer counties; the proceeds of the 1983 and 1986 local sales taxes are distributed to counties according to their population, rather than the point of collection.

The School Facilities Finance Act of 1987 (G.S. 115C-546.1 and -546.2; G.S. 115C-489 through -489.4), financed mainly by an increase in the corporate income tax, provided additional state funds for school construction. The act established two new funds, the Public School Capital Building Fund and the Critical School Facility Needs Fund.

The Public School Capital Building Fund provides aid to all county governments. Moneys may be used for school building capital needs and school technology needs (these moneys are transferred to the State School Technology Fund and allocated by that fund to the school unit). Moneys are distributed to all counties according to their school enrollment. Funds used for capital projects must be matched by $1 of local funds for each $3 of state funds; earmarked local sales tax revenues can be used as local matching funds. This match is not required for funds used for technology.

The Critical School Facility Needs Fund aids counties and school units that have the most critical needs in relation to their resources. The commission determines which counties have the greatest critical needs. Once the priorities set in 1988 by the commission have been funded, the Critical School Facility Needs Fund statutes will be repealed and any remaining funds transferred to the Public School Building Capital Fund [1995 Sess. Laws (Reg. Sess. 1996) ch. 631, sec. 14]. This repeal is not expected to occur until after 2000.

This fund, like the method of distributing proceeds of the 1983 and 1986 additional sales taxes, reflects the General Assembly's concern for the needs of counties with the least ability to pay for school construction. As a result of these provisions, poorer counties have received more state aid per student for construction than have larger, high-income counties.[29]

From 1984 to 1993 the new state aid measures (the earmarked portion of sales tax revenues and money from the two funds established in 1987) provided local units nearly $1.5 billion in additional funds for school construction.[30] While this additional state aid was substantial, it was only one-half of the total spending of $3 billion on school construction during this period. Counties provided the other half by using local revenue sources and debt financing for school construction. Debt financing has become increasingly popular, in part because the most effective way for a county to take advantage of state aid is to leverage it by issuing bonds and using earmarked sales tax proceeds to pay debt service payments.

In 1996, when school construction needs were estimated at over $6 billion, the General Assembly turned back to state general obligation bonds as a way to meet these needs. The legislature authorized and the voters approved the issuance of up to $1.8 billion in state general obligation bonds for school capital outlay purposes in the Public School Building Bond Act of 1996 [1995 N.C. Sess. Laws (Reg. Sess. 1996) ch. 631]. Of this total, $1.77 billion is to be divided among the school administrative units in amounts specified for each school unit. Overall, 40 percent of the total is allocated on the basis of average daily membership, 35 percent on the basis of ability to pay, and 25 percent on the basis of the unit's growth. All school units participate in the allocation based on average daily membership, but not in allocations based on the other two factors. A match, derived through a formula, is required for every dollar of bond proceeds allocated on the basis of average daily membership and high growth. A county may meet the match requirement through non-state expenditures made on or after January 1, 1992, for public school facilities. The remaining $30 million (of the $1.8 billion) will be distributed among small school systems; no local match is required for these funds. Counties must report annually to the state board on the match requirement and on the impact of the bond proceeds on the property tax rate for that year.

A minor source of state aid for school capital outlay is the State Literary Fund. Established in 1825 as an endowment for education, it became, early in this century, a permanent loan fund available to local school units for constructing and equipping their plants. The fund is maintained by the state board, which makes loans for ten years at a rate of interest not to exceed 8 percent per year. The borrowing procedure is outlined in Article 32 of Chapter 115C of the General Statutes and the State Board of Education rules.

Local Funds

Although the public school system is primarily financed by the state, the average county allocates nearly a third of its funds for the operation of the public schools. In 1995–96 county expenditures for education were nearly 30 percent of total county spending, on average, for all 100 counties. These locally raised revenues are used in two major ways: to provide, equip, and maintain the physical plants for the schools and to supplement the state's support for operating the schools.

Local administrative units, and thus county commissioners, are required by statute to finance some areas of school operation. The General Statutes specify several categories that must be provided for mainly from local revenues:

1. Buildings, furniture, and apparatus [G.S. 115C-521(b)]
2. Garage and maintenance equipment for school buses [G.S. 115C-249(e)]
3. Liability insurance [G.S. 115C-47(25)]
4. Maintenance of plant [G.S. 115C-521(c) and (d) to 115C-524]
5. Sites (G.S. 115C-517)
6. Proper furnishings for the superintendent's office (G.S. 115C-277)
7. Supplies for school buildings [G.S. 115C-522(c)]
8. Water supply and sewerage facilities [G.S. 115C-522(c)]

Counties may raise money for school construction through a general obligation school bond issue; school administrative units have no authority to issue bonds. Projects may also be paid for from current revenue, including county property taxes, local sales and use taxes, voted supplemental property taxes, proceeds of the sale of capital assets, and proceeds of claims against fire and casualty insurance policies, and other sources [G.S. 115C-426(f)].

Federal Funds

Although public education is a state and local responsibility, since the 1950s the federal government has assumed a significant role in public education primarily by providing funds to states. Congress generally conditions a state's receipt of federal funds on the state's compliance with federally-defined conditions.

Most federal moneys are categorical funds, which means they are appropriated by Congress to the states for specific educational purposes such as vocational education, school lunch programs, instruction and guidance services, school library resources, and special programs for disadvantaged children. These funds are channeled through the state board for distribution to the local units, but the board has little control over the programs for which they may be spent. In general, poorer school units receive more federal dollars relative to their enrollment than wealthier units do.

The School Budget and Fiscal Control Act

The legal responsibility for public education is shared by state government, local boards of education, and boards of county commissioners. The primary responsibility, both for policy making and for financing, rests at the state level with the General Assembly and the state board. Local responsibility is divided between boards of education and boards of county commissioners. Broadly speaking, the school board formulates educational policy, while the commissioners control the county's financial policy and determine the amount of the county funds that go the schools.

In practice, of course, the division of responsibility is not that simple. In appropriating funds for schools, the commissioners cannot help but influence educational policy. And school boards, dissatisfied with the share of county resources allocated to them, are entitled to take their case beyond the commissioners to the courts. Recognizing that it has created a framework for local school funding that has the potential for conflict built into it, the General Assembly also enacted legislation encouraging local boards of education and boards of county commissioners to conduct periodic joint meetings to promote "greater mutual understanding of immediate and long-term budgetary issues and constraints affecting public schools and county governments." In particular, the boards are encouraged to assess school capital outlay needs and develop a joint plan to meet those needs (G.S. 115C-426.2).

Because the relationship between the two boards is fundamentally financial and because some local government budgeting procedures are inappropriate for school operations, the General Assembly has provided a separate budgeting procedure for school boards. They do not operate under the Local Government Budget and Fiscal Control Act (G.S. Ch. 159, Art. 3), which applies to units of local government. Budgeting procedures for school boards are established in the School Budget and Fiscal Control Act (hereafter, the School Budget Act), codified at G.S. 115C-422 through -452. This act outlines a uniform budgeting, accounting, and fiscal-control procedure that every school board must follow. The act also establishes a budgetary relationship between school units and their local tax-levying authorities that dovetails with the provisions of the Local Government Budget and Fiscal Control Act.

Major features of the School Budget Act include the following:

1. Each school administrative unit must operate under a balanced annual budget resolution that authorizes all expenditures, regardless of the revenue source.
2. Each administrative unit's superintendent acts as its budget officer, and each unit also must have a finance officer.
3. The state's substantial financial role in public education is reflected in special reporting requirements, in special provisions for disbursing state moneys, and in a state-designed, mandatory uniform budget format.
4. The role of local governments in supporting schools and in the school budgetary process is described.
5. A special dispute-resolution procedure is available when a school board is dissatisfied with the county's appropriations to the school unit.

Uniform Budget Format

G.S. 115C-426 charges the state board with preparing and promulgating, in cooperation with the Local Government Commission, a uniform budget format for school administrative units. This format mandates the fund structure and chart of accounts, thereby establishing the framework within which financial information is presented and budgetary decisions made. Administrative units prepare their budgets in conformity with the uniform format, and this is the format in which proposed school budgets should be transmitted to the county commissioners.

In addition to creating a framework for decisions, the uniform format facilitates the fiscal management of each local school unit and facilitates gathering accurate and reliable data on the operation of the public school system. The format allows comparisons among school units.

Each administrative unit must maintain at least four funds (a fund is an independent accounting and fiscal entity): a state public school fund, a local current expense fund, a capital outlay fund, and a school food services fund. The state public school fund accounts for current operations funded by state moneys made available to the local unit by the state board. The local current expense fund accounts for current operations. It is funded by county revenues; supplemental taxes; fines, penalties, and forfeitures received from the court system; state money disbursed directly to the administrative unit; and other moneys available for current operations. The capital outlay fund accounts for land acquisition; construction, reconstruction or renovation, acquisition, and equipping of buildings; acquisition or replacement of furniture, furnishings, instructional apparatus, and similar equipment; and acquisition of school and activity buses. It is funded by both state and county capital outlay appropriations, local supplemental school taxes, if any, and minor sources such as proceeds from insurance and the sale of capital assets. The school food services fund's purpose is described by its name. The uniform budget format sets out in detail the project, program, and function breakdown within each fund.

The uniform format also permits other funds for federal grant moneys, special tax areas, and trust and agency accounts. A school unit's decision to establish additional funds will depend on its programs, revenue sources, and accounting practices.

Budget Preparation and Adoption

The Budget Calendar

The superintendent submits a proposed budget and budget message to the school board no later than May 1 and makes the proposed budget and budget message available for public inspection in the superintendent's office. The budget message "should contain a concise explanation of the educational goals fixed by the budget for the budget year, should set forth the reasons for stated changes from the previous year in program goals, programs, and appropriation levels, and should explain any major changes in educational or fiscal policy" [G.S. 115C-427(c)].

The board considers the superintendent's proposed budget, holds a public hearing if it chooses to, makes changes it decides are advisable, and submits the entire budget to the board of county commissioners no later than May 15, unless that board sets a later date.

By July 1 the county commissioners make appropriations to the school administrative unit, unless the school board agrees to extend this deadline. (Note that in many years the board of commissioners must act before the General Assembly has adopted the state budget, which may make budgeting decisions difficult.) Shortly after the county acts, the school board adopts its budget resolution. The following sections discuss this process in more detail.

Submission to the Board of County Commissioners

The school board normally transmits the administrative unit's budget to the county commissioners in mid-May. Although the board of commissioners may extend the May 15 deadline, it may be reluctant to do so. Education is a substantial part of a county's budget, and the county's budget officer needs time to review the school board's requests before submitting the entire county budget to the board of commissioners around June 1.

Although the county budget officer is free to recommend funding levels for programs different from those requested by the school board, the budget officer must present the school board's actual requests to the county commissioners because G.S. 115C-429 directs the school board to submit its budget to the board of county commissioners.

The superintendent must make the proposed budget available for public inspection in the superintendent's office, but there is no requirement that the school board publish any notice of the fact of submission or that the board hold a public hearing on its budget request before transmitting it to the county commissioners. While it does not explicitly say so, the School Budget Act relies on the open meetings law, the public records law, and procedures in the Local Government Budget and Fiscal Control Act to provide opportunities for public knowledge, inspection, and comment on the school budget. The school board's proposed budget often is available along with the county's budget in the office of the clerk to the board of county commissioners, and funding for schools is likely to be a topic at the county's budget hearing.

School Financial Information

In light of their funding responsibilities, commissioners have an interest in the total financial operations of their county's school unit(s) and need information to make informed decisions. The School Budget Act recognizes the validity of this interest and of the need for information by entitling the board of county commissioners to a broad range of information on the full financial operations of public schools.

First, the school board must submit its entire budget to the county commissioners, not just that part for which county funding is requested [G.S. 115C-429(a)]. Second, the person who conducts the annual audit of school operations must file a copy of the report with the commissioners (G.S. 115C-447). Third, at the commissioners' request, the school board must make available to them all books, records, audit reports, and other information bearing on the financial operation of the local administrative unit [G.S. 115C-429(c)]. And, finally, the school finance officer must make periodic reports to the county commissioners, if they so request in writing [G.S. 115C-436(a)(4)]. In addition, of course, school board records are subject to the public records law (G.S. Ch. 132).

County Appropriation

The county commissioners review the school board's proposed budget as part of the county's regular budget process. Although the commissioners have the entire proposed budget and may examine it line-by-line, they appropriate only county revenues and may prescribe their use only within statutory limits.

A county's budget ordinance should include at least two appropriations to each administrative unit in the county: one to local current expense fund and one to the capital outlay fund. The current expense fund includes instructional, support, and other operating expenditures of the school system. The capital outlay fund includes appropriations for site acquisition, new buildings, renovations of existing buildings, furnishings and equipment, new school buses, and activity buses and other vehicles.

The board of county commissioners may make lump-sum appropriations to these funds, or it may allocate all or part of its appropriations to particular purposes or functions, as defined in a chart of accounts promulgated by the state board, in the current expense funds or to specific projects in the capital outlay fund [G.S. 115C-429(b)]. The purpose categories are instructional programs, supporting services, community services, and non-programmed charges. Each purpose has from two to seven functions in it. The uniform chart of accounts identifies three categories of capital outlay projects:

1. Category I projects include acquisition of real estate and construction and renovation of buildings.
2. Category II projects include acquisition or replacement of furnishings and equipment.
3. Category III projects include acquisition of school buses, activity buses, and other motor vehicles.

Capital outlay appropriations for Category I may be allocated by specific acquisition, construction, or renovation project. Category II and Category III appropriations are allocated by the entire category rather than by individual items of equipment or furniture or by individual vehicles. These allocations serve, in effect, as a maximum authorization for the use of county money for each of the projects, purposes, and functions specified, and the board of education must observe them when it adopts its own budget resolution.

The commissioners may not control the school board budget for current expenses at the line-item level. They may not direct the school board to limit expenditures within a given function to specified line items, nor may they in any other way limit the school board's line-item discretion; for example, they may not direct that funds be spent on the band or athletic teams or set a principal's salary. Nor may commissioners bypass the budget process and contribute county funds directly to individual schools for purposes they favor.

The board of county commissioners is limited in its authority to amend the county's budget ordinance with respect to the school board budget. G.S. 159-13(9) prohibits the board from reducing school appropriations after it adopts the county budget ordinance unless the school board consents to the reduction or economic conditions require a general reduction in county spending. The board of county commissioners may unilaterally add money to the school board budget.

G.S. 115C-437 permits the county and each school unit within it to set procedures by which county appropriations are transferred to the unit. If a school unit and county cannot agree on a transfer procedure, the county must remit the moneys to the school unit in monthly installments sufficient to meet the unit's needs for the coming month.

Apportionment

If a county has only one administrative unit, the board of commissioners may divide its school appropriations between current expense and capital outlay as it sees fit, subject only to the school board's ability to challenge this division under the dispute-resolution procedure. In counties with more than one administrative unit, the School Budget Act requires that county appropriations to local current expense funds be apportioned among the school units according to each unit's average daily membership. On the basis of those figures, the "dollar amount obtained by dividing the amount . . . appropriated to each unit by the total membership of the unit" must be the same for each unit (G.S. 115C-430).

The apportionment requirement is designed to promote equity and prevent favoritism in current operations appropriations among school units in the same county. Capital outlay needs of units may differ, however, and so the apportionment requirement does not apply to county appropriations for capital outlay.

Budget Disputes

The board of county commissioners appropriates funds to many departments and agencies, and commissioners generally exercise sole discretion as to the amounts. County departments and agencies must accept their decision, but school boards have a statutory right to challenge the board of commissioners' school funding decisions.

G.S. 115C-431 establishes a procedure for resolving disputes when a school board is dissatisfied with the county appropriation. The process begins with a formal determination by the school board that the amount of the county appropriation to the local current expense fund, or the capital outlay fund, or both, is "not sufficient to support a system of free public schools." After such a determination, the two boards must meet and attempt to resolve their differences. A mediator, selected by the two boards or by the senior resident superior court judge, conducts this initial meeting.

If the dispute is not resolved at the joint meeting, mediation is available at the request of either board. Unless the boards agree otherwise, each board will be represented in the mediation by a working group. Working group members are the chair of each board or the chair's designee, the superintendent and county manager or their designees, each board's finance officer, and each board's attorney. Mediation sessions are closed to the public.

Mediation must end no later than August 1, unless both boards agree to continue. If the mediation continues beyond August 1, the board of county commissioners must appropriate the same amount to the school unit's current expense fund as it appropriated the previous year.

If the working groups reach a proposed agreement, each board must approve it. If no agreement is reached, the mediator announces that fact but may not disclose any other information about the mediation or make any recommendations or public statement of findings or conclusions.

If no agreement is reached, the mediator announces that fact, and within five days of that announcement the board of education may file an action in superior court. The court "shall find the facts as to the amount of money necessary to maintain a system of free public schools, and the amount of money needed from the county to make up this total" [G.S. 115C-431(c)]. A judge will hear the case unless either board requests a jury trial. Under the rule set in *Kinston City Board of Education v. Board of Commissioners,* the trial court judge may summon a jury from another county if necessary in order to provide a fair trial.[31] The issue submitted to the jury "shall be what amount of money is needed from sources under the control of the board of county commissioners to maintain a system of free public schools" [G.S. 115C-431(c)].

The court orders the board of county commissioners to appropriate a specific sum to the school board (which may be the amount the county originally appropriated) and to levy property taxes as necessary. The court's findings of fact are conclusive and will not be overturned on appeal unless the "findings were made arbitrarily or in abuse of statutory duty" according to *Board of Education v. Board of Commissioners.*[32]

Special Appropriation to Local Current Expense Fund

A court order to the board of county commissioners to increase the funding for the school unit may create a significant disruption in the county's budget. The dispute procedure recognizes this urgency through short deadlines and through accelerated scheduling for a case to be heard in court.

Despite the accelerated procedure, disputes sometimes are not resolved until mid-fall or even later in the budget year. If the superior court's decision is appealed and the judge feels that the appeal cannot be resolved in time for additional taxes to be levied that year, the judge will order the board of county commissioners to appropriate to the school unit's local current expense fund "a sum of money sufficient when added to all moneys available to that fund to equal the amount of this fund for the previous year" [G.S. 115C-431(d)]. (Presumably "amount" in this context refers to the amount budgeted for the fund, not the amount actually spent.)

This provision is intended to establish a reserve in case the final decision goes against the county. The school board should look on the difference between the court-ordered appropriation and the actual county appropriation as a kind of trust fund. If the final decision favors the county, the difference will revert to the county.

This provision has only a limited effect. First, it applies only to the local current expense fund, not to the capital outlay fund. Second, the provision is useful only if the local current expense fund appropriation is lower for the disputed budget year than in the previous year. If the county's current expense appropriation is the same or higher than that of the previous year, the provision has no effect.

Appeals

Despite a losing party's right to appeal the trial court's decision, the state court of appeals effectively blocked almost all appeals from superior court in its 1993 decision in *Cumberland County Board of Education v. Cumberland County Board of Commissioners.*[33] In that case the board of education and board of county commissioners disputed the amount of county funding for the 1992–93 school year. The boards followed dispute resolution procedures then in effect, and ultimately the board of commissioners appealed the superior court's ruling in favor of the school board to the state court of appeals. The appeals court did not hear the case until October 1993—five months after the 1992–93 school year had ended.

The court dismissed the appeal, ruling that the matter was moot because the school year at issue was over. The court recognized that its decision created a barrier to almost all appeals to the appellate court because any dispute would likely be moot by the time it reached the appellate level. Nevertheless, the court stated that the General Assembly was the appropriate body to solve this problem.

Additional Taxes

If the final judgment demands further appropriations from the county that are greater than its available resources, the board of county commissioners is authorized to levy supplemental property taxes in addition to those already levied in the county budget ordinance [G.S. 115C-431(e)]. If the court's order is entered before September 1, the second levy should be collected as a part of the original one. If the order comes after September 1, the new taxes become due on the date levied, and interest begins to accrue 120 days later.

Budget Execution by the School Board

After the commissioners have made their appropriations to the board of education, or after the dispute-resolution procedure has concluded, the school board must adopt a budget resolution. If the school board does not act by July 1, it must make interim appropriations for salaries and the usual ordinary expenses of the administrative unit.

The budget resolution must account for all expenditures of the school administrative unit, regardless of the revenue source. G.S. 115C-

432(b) subjects the school board to several budget directions and limitations. The budget must be balanced and contain sufficient appropriations to fund continuing contracts and past deficits. Estimated revenues from any supplemental taxes must be realistic; the estimated percentage of collections may not exceed the percentage of those from the previous year.

G.S. 115C-432(b) requires the school budget resolution to observe any allocations that the county made in its appropriations to the school unit. For example, if the county allocates $75,000 of its local current expense fund appropriation to Adult Education, the school board must appropriate $75,000 of county money for that function. If the school board has other funds available, it may increase the total funds spent on that (or any other) function.

School Budget Amendments

Once adopted, the school board may need to amend its school budget resolution in response to changing circumstances. The amended budget must remain balanced, and the county commissioners must approve certain changes.

Amendments to Capital Outlay Projects

G.S. 115-426(f) groups capital outlay expenditures into six categories:

1. Acquisition of land
2. Acquisition and construction of buildings
3. Acquisition or replacement of furnishings and equipment
4. Acquisition of school buses
5. Acquisition of activity buses and other motor vehicles
6. Other items assigned to capital outlay by the uniform budget format

G.S. 115C-433(b) governs amendments to appropriations for capital outlay projects, and it may be interpreted two ways. Under the first interpretation, a proposal to amend the school budget resolution to increase or decrease funding for projects in categories (1) and (2) must be approved by the board of commissioners only if the school board is considering an amendment to a project that has been itself the subject of an allocation. A second view is that commissioner approval is required for any change in the school budget resolution affecting a project in category (1) or category (2), if the commissioners have allocated *any* portion of their appropriation. The second interpretation rests on a very literal reading of the statute and seems unnecessarily harsh. If the commissioners want to maintain some control over county appropriations for school capital outlay, they may do so by allocating their capital outlay appropriation among projects.

Because the statute is silent about changes in allocations in the other four categories of capital outlay expenditures, the school board may change these allocations as it sees fit.

Amendments within the Current Expense Fund

If the commissioners make a lump-sum appropriation to current expense, the school board may amend the current expense budget on its own. If the commissioners have allocated all or part of the county's appropriation to the local current expense fund, the school board acting alone may modify an allocation only to a limited extent. If the commissioners have made an allocation, the school board may amend its budget to increase or decrease the allocation up to 25 percent. Any amendment that results in a larger change must be approved by the commissioners.

This 25-percent rule applies unless the board of commissioners reduces the percentage change that will invoke commissioner review at the time the county budget is adopted. The commissioners may select a percentage anywhere from 10 to 25 percent and may apply different percentages to different allocations. The school board always has discretion over amendments that change an allocation by less than 10 percent [G.S. 115C-433(b)].

Transfers to or from the Capital Outlay and Current Expense Funds

Out of respect for the board of commissioners' allocation decisions and the requirement of apportionment, transfers of county moneys from the capital outlay fund to the local current expense fund, or vice versa, are permitted but tightly restricted [G.S. 115C-433(d)]. First, they may be made only to meet emergencies that were both "unforeseen and unforeseeable" when the school budget resolution was adopted; for example, if a hurricane lifts the roof off of a school building. Second, a proposed transfer must be approved by the board of commissioners.

The school board initiates a transfer between the capital outlay and current expense funds by adopting a resolution that states the following:

1. The amount of the proposed transfer
2. The nature of the emergency
3. Why the emergency was unforeseen and could not have been foreseen
4. What objects of expenditure will be added or increased
5. What objects of expenditure will be reduced or eliminated

The school board sends copies of the resolution to the board of commissioners and to other school boards (if any) in the county. Within thirty days, the commissioners must offer those school boards an opportunity to comment on the transfer and then act on the request. If the commissioners do not act within thirty days, approval is assumed, although the school board may agree to an extension of the thirty-day deadline. Once the commissioners act, the county must notify the requesting school board and any other board that commented on the request.

School Finance Officer

Each school unit must have a school finance officer, appointed by the superintendent with the approval of the school board and serving at the superintendent's pleasure (G.S. 115C-435). Although the statute permits the superintendent, with the approval of the school board and the county commissioners, to designate the county finance officer as school finance officer, this is rarely, if ever, done. In counties where there is more than one school unit, the statute also permits one person to serve as school finance officer for all units in the county, if the arrangement is approved by the affected superintendents and school boards as well as the board of commissioners. This, too, is an unusual arrangement.

G.S. 115C-436 describes the major duties of the school finance officer. The school finance officer is responsible for keeping the accounts of the school unit; receiving and depositing moneys; investing idle cash; signing and issuing checks, drafts, and state warrants; and providing the preaudit certificate required on all contracts, agreements, and purchase orders. The finance officer must make any periodic financial reports that the superintendent or the school board requests and periodic financial reports to the county commissioners if they so request in writing. G.S. 115C-446 requires semiannual reports to the Local Government Commission.

The state pays for one school finance officer for each county as part of the Basic Education Program, and every finance officer paid in whole or in part with state funds must meet standards set by the state board. In counties with more than one school unit, the amount for each unit is determined by applying its percentage of the total county average daily membership to the schedule for the appropriate finance officer certification level.

Management of Funds

Incurring Obligations

The School Budget Act requires an annual balanced budget, and a school unit may not incur an obligation unless (1) the budget resolution adopted by the school board includes an appropriation authorizing the obligation and (2) the appropriation contains an unencumbered balance sufficient to pay the sums that will become due during the current fiscal year. In addition, a preaudit certificate signed by the school finance officer is necessary if the obligation is evidenced by a contract, agreement, or purchase order. An obligation incurred without meeting these conditions is invalid and unenforceable (G.S. 115C-441).

Disbursements

Claims against a school unit may be paid only if they have been approved by the school finance officer or the school board. Finance officers may approve claims if (1) they determine the amount to be payable, (2) the budget resolution includes an appropriation authorizing the expenditure, and (3) either an encumbrance has been created for the transaction or an unencumbered balance remains in the appropriation sufficient to pay the amount to be disbursed [G.S. 115C-441(b)].

The board of education may approve a bill, invoice, or other claim that has been disapproved by the finance officer, only if an appropriation appears in the budget resolution and the school board has an unencumbered balance in the appropriate fund that is more than the amount to be paid. If the board authorizes payment, it must do so by formal resolution, stating the reasons for the action. The resolution must be put in the minutes along with the names of members who voted for it. The board chair or some other member designated for this purpose signs the certificate (see the next paragraph) on the check or draft given in payment. If payment results in a violation of law, all members who voted to allow payment are jointly and severally liable for the full amount of the payment.

With the exception of payroll checks, all payments made by the school unit by check must bear a certificate signed by the school finance officer, or by a school board member as described above, indicating that the payment has been approved as required by the School Budget Act.

Special Funds of Individual Schools

Individual schools often handle cash, which may include gate receipts from athletic events, dues of student organizations, or yearbook money. The board of education must appoint a treasurer for each school that handles $300 or more in cash during the school year. The treasurer keeps appropriate records and reports to the superintendent and finance officer of the administrative unit as they or the board of education prescribe (G.S. 115C-448).

The board of education has two options for handling these special funds. It may require that all funds of individual schools be deposited with and accounted for by the school finance officer, or it may permit the treasurer at the school to be responsible for the funds.

Investment of Idle Cash

When there is a cash balance in any fund held by the school unit, the cash may be either deposited at interest or invested (G.S. 115C-443). The finance officer is responsible for managing the unit's investments. The unit may invest only moneys it has actually received, so that investment of county funds allocated to the school unit is the responsibility of the county finance officer until the county has actually transferred them to the school finance officer.

Annual Audit

To ensure compliance with the School Budget Act and to permit monitoring the financial status of local school units, each unit must have an annual audit of its accounts and the accounts of the individual schools (G.S. 115C-447). The school board selects the auditor, who must be a certified public accountant or an accountant certified by the Local Government Commission as qualified to audit local government accounts. The auditor reports directly to the school board, and copies of the audit report are filed with the secretary of the Local Government Commission, the State Board of Education, the local board of education, and the board of commissioners.

Other County Responsibilities

Special School Elections

Special school elections may be held to vote on proposals to do the following (G.S. 115C-501):

1. Authorize a local supplemental tax
2. Increase the supplemental tax rate in an area that already has a supplemental tax of less than the maximum rate set by statute
3. Enlarge a city administrative unit by consolidating areas of a county unit into the city school unit
4. Supplement and equalize educational advantages by levying a special tax in an area of a county administrative unit enclosed in one common boundary line
5. Abolish a supplemental school tax
6. Authorize the county to issue school bonds
7. Provide a supplemental tax on a county-wide basis pursuant to merger of all administrative units within a county
8. Annex or consolidate school areas from contiguous counties and provide a supplemental school tax in such annexed or consolidated areas

If an election is held on any of these issues and the proposition rejected, another election on the same issue in the same area may not be called until at least six months after the preceding election. An election on whether to abolish a local tax district may not be held sooner than one year after the election establishing a district or after an election on the issue of dismantling the local tax district. If a local tax district is in debt or has unmet obligations, no election may be held on the issue of abolishing that tax district (G.S. 115C-502).

The board of county commissioners' role in the election procedure begins when it receives a petition from a county or city school board requesting a special school election. The petition, which must be approved by the school board and submitted to the board of commissioners, need not originate with the school board itself. A majority of qualified voters who have resided for the preceding year in an area adjacent to a city administrative unit may petition the county board of education for an election on the question of annexing that area to the city unit. For other types of special elections, 25 percent of the qualified voters in a school area may initiate a petition and submit it to the board of education. The school board must consider the petition and decide whether or not to approve it.

If a petition is approved by the school board and submitted to the county commissioners, G.S. 115C-506 requires the commissioners "to call an election and fix the date for the same." In *Yancey County Board of Education v. Board of County Commissioners*,[34] the North Carolina Supreme Court held that, if a petition for an election on authorizing a special supplemental tax is properly presented, the duty of the board of commissioners is ministerial and not discretionary; it is obliged to call the election. This rule probably does not apply to petitions for school bond elections because of inconsistent provisions in the laws regulating local government debt, but it seems to apply to all of the other kinds of special elections listed above. The school board may withdraw a petition at any time before the election is called. All school elections, whether for county or for city school administrative units, are held and conducted by the appropriate board of elections.

Voted Supplemental Taxes

Under G.S. Chapter 115C, Article 36, the voters within a school unit may approve the levy of supplemental taxes for any item of expenditure in the school budget. The maximum supplemental tax rate that voters may approve under general law is $0.50 per $100 value ($0.60 for a school administrative unit or school area with a total population of no less than 100,000). Some school units have higher rates authorized by local legislation. The maximum rate of the tax and the uses to which the proceeds may be put are established by the terms of the ballot used in the referendum approving the tax.

In almost all cases the special tax is levied by the county commissioners; in a very few units, by a city council. G.S. 115C-511 establishes the procedure for levying a supplemental tax approved under the general law procedures. (The levy of a supplemental tax approved pursuant to a local act is subject to that act.) Based on an estimate of the appraised valuation of the unit from the county tax assessor, the school board, in the proposed budget it submits to the commissioners, requests a specific rate for the supplemental tax. The board's request, which may not exceed the maximum approved by the voters, establishes the maximum that may be levied by the board of county commissioners for that year. The commissioners, however, have discretion in setting the rate as long as they do not exceed the rate requested by the school board.

A supplemental tax is not part of a county's appropriation to the school unit. Both G.S. 115C-511 and G.S. 159-26(b) anticipate that the tax-levying authority acts simply as agent for the school unit or tax district in collecting the tax. Two practical effects arise from this. First, while commissioners may consider the availability of supplemental tax proceeds when setting the county's appropriation to the school board, they may not specify how the proceeds of the tax are to be used by the school board. This decision is the school board's, subject only to the terms of the ballot measure under which the tax was approved. Second, the school unit is entitled to the proceeds of the tax remitted monthly, less the actual cost of levying, computing, and collecting the tax if the board of commissioners decides to deduct it (G.S. 115C-437). If collections exceed budget estimates, the school board receives the excess; if actual collections are less than the estimates, the school board must adjust expenditures to account for the shortfall.

Fines, Penalties, and Forfeitures

Article IX, Section 7, of the state constitution provides that "clear proceeds of all penalties and forfeitures and of all fines collected in the several counties for any breach of the penal laws of the State, shall belong to and remain in the several counties and used exclusively for maintaining free public schools." G.S. 115C-437 defines "clear proceeds" as the full amount collected, diminished only by the actual costs of collection, not to exceed 10 percent of the amount collected.

The county acts as agent for the school board with regard to these revenues, collecting them from the clerk of superior court (to whom the fines, penalties, and forfeitures are paid) and apportioning and transmitting them monthly to the county's school unit or units. If the county has more than one school unit, the proceeds are apportioned according to the same formula that is used for apportioning current expense fund appropriations (G.S. 115C-452).

These revenues are comparable to the proceeds of a voted school supplemental tax. They are not part of the county's appropriation, and the school board, not the board of county commissioners, decides how they will be used. Commissioners may consider the availability of fines, penalties, and forfeitures in determining how much county money to appropriate to the school unit.

In 1996 the state supreme court in *Craven County Board of Education v. Boyles*[35] made it clear that this constitutional provision covers penalties paid to a state agency. After the decision, all proceeds at issue in the case were paid to the local board of education. Apparently in response, the

General Assembly created the Civil Penalty and Forfeiture Fund (G.S. 115C-457.1 through 115C-457.3). The fund consists of the clear proceeds of all civil penalties and civil forfeitures collected by a state agency and payable to the county school fund pursuant to Section 7 of Article IX of the state constitution. These proceeds will be put in the State School Technology Fund and allocated to local school units on the basis of average daily membership.

Approval of Purchase Price for School Sites

A school board may not execute a contract to purchase a site or make any expenditures for it without the county commissioners' approval "as to the amount to be spent for the site" [G.S. 115C-426(f)]. The requirement applies whether the county has made a blanket capital outlay appropriation or has allocated moneys for this particular project. In 1975 in *Painter v. Wake County Board of Education,* the state supreme court considered an earlier version of this statutory provision; its ruling indicates that this approval requirement applies only when the school board is using funds from the county.[36]

If the two boards disagree over this matter, they may resolve the dispute through the same judicial procedure used to resolve budgetary disputes. If that procedure is used, the issue is the amount to be spent for the site, not its location. The school board has the authority to choose school sites, and, if the amount it proposes to spend is found to be reasonable, presumably the school board will prevail.

Continuing Contracts for Capital Outlay

School administrative units may enter into continuing contracts for multiyear capital improvement projects or outlays even when the school unit's budget resolution for the current year does not include an appropriation for the entire obligation [G.S. 115C-441(c)]. Three conditions for these continuing contracts must be met: (1) the budget resolution includes an appropriation authorizing the current fiscal year's portion of the obligation; (2) an unencumbered balance remains in the appropriation sufficient to pay in the current fiscal year the sums obligated by the transaction for the current fiscal year; and (3) the board of county commissioners have approved the contract by a resolution binding the board to appropriate sufficient funds in future fiscal years to pay the amounts falling due under the contract.

Lease Purchase Contracts

Local boards of education may use lease purchase or installment purchase contracts to finance the acquisition of certain kinds of equipment: automobiles, school buses, mobile classroom units, photocopiers and computers, computer hardware and software, and related support services (G.S. 115C-528). The contract term may not exceed the useful life of the property being acquired. The school unit may give the seller a security interest in property being financed under an installment purchase contract as security for payment. The school board need not obtain commissioner approval of a contract as long as the contract term is less than three years and the total amount financed under the contract is below the lesser of $250,000 or an amount equal to three times the local school system's annual allocation from the state for classroom materials and equipment. Commissioners must approve other contracts. In addition the Local Government Commission must approve a contract that has a term of five years or more and obligates the school board to pay $500,000 or more over the term of the contract. The school board must submit information concerning these contracts as part of the annual budget it submits to the board of county commissioners.

Guaranteed Energy Savings Contracts

G.S. 115C-47(28a) authorizes local school boards to purchase energy conservation measures (a facility alteration or training related to a facility's operation that reduces energy consumption or operating costs) by using guaranteed energy savings contracts (G.S. 143-64.17 through -64.17E). These are contracts for the valuation, recommendation, or implementation of energy conservation measures in school facilities, in which payments are to be made over time and energy savings are guaranteed to exceed costs. Local boards of education may finance energy conservation measures by using installment contracts or lease-purchase contracts.

Operational Leases

An operational lease is a lease in which the lessor obtains no ownership interest or option to obtain an ownership interest in the leased property. G.S. 115C-530 authorizes local boards of education to enter into operational leases of real or personal property for use as school buildings or school facilities. Leases for terms of three years or longer, including optional renewal periods, must be approved by the board of county commissioners. Approval obligates the commissioners to appropriate sufficient funds to meet the payments due in each year of the lease. In addition the school board's budget resolution must include an appropriation for the current fiscal year's portion of the obligation and an unencumbered balance to pay that obligation.

Under G.S. 115C-530 and G.S. 115C-521(d), school boards may make improvements to leased property. Contracts for repair and renovation must comply with the energy guidelines in G.S. 115C-521(c), and must be approved by the board of county commissioners if they are subject to the competitive bidding requirement in G.S. 143-129(a) (the current threshold for which is $100,000) and do not otherwise constitute continuing contracts for capital outlay [see G.S. 115C-441(c1) and -426(f)].

Merger

Merger of school administrative units by a board of county commissioners is one of the ways merger of school units may be achieved. This process is described earlier in the chapter.

Bonds for School Facilities

Counties, not local boards of education, have the authority to issue bonds for school capital outlay purposes. For a more detailed discussion of this subject, see Chapter 11 in this volume.

Construction of School Facilities

A number of local acts amend G.S. 153A-157 to permit specified counties to construct, equip, expand, improve, renovate, or otherwise make available property for use by a school administrative unit within the county.

School Reform Efforts

Beginning in the mid-1980s the General Assembly embarked on an ambitious program of school reform. Reform efforts have been designed to achieve better student learning through more stringent educational standards and increased accountability on the part of school personnel for their students' performance. At the same time, school boards and individual schools have been given both new authority to determine how to improve student performance and new flexibility in determining how to deliver the educational program.

Even as the General Assembly has offered school boards new flexibility, it has constructed a safety net for schools in trouble. Schools that are "low-performing," that do not follow appropriate fiscal management practices, or that have serious safety problems not appropriately addressed by local officials are subject to state intervention.

Several key school reforms measures are described briefly in the next section.

Basic Education Program

As discussed previously, the Basic Education Program describes the educational program that should be available to every public school student. Its primary goal is to ensure that public school students have access to a basic, adequate program, no matter where they attend school. Reflecting the state board's concern with quality as well as equity, it adopted a comprehensive definition of a "basic education program." The Basic Education Program includes not only curriculum (including instruction in arts, communication skills, physical education and personal health and safety, mathematics, media and computer skills, science, second language, social studies, and vocational education), but also staffing, libraries, technology, support services, and facilities. Local school boards are responsible for implementing the Basic Education Program, and they also are free to supplement it.

The ABCs of Public Education

For years the General Assembly has enacted programs designed to improve student learning and achievement. In 1996 the General Assembly passed the School-Based Management and Accountability Program (G.S. 115C-105.20 through 105.40). In response to the legislature's directives in this act, the State Board of Education developed the ABCs of Public Education, which focuses on individual school *A*ccountability, student achievement in *B*asic subjects, and local *C*ontrol and flexibility over school operations and use of state funds. The program is based on a model of state recognition, reward, assistance, and intervention.

The ABCs represent a substantial shift in authority and accountability, not just from the state to local school boards but also from local boards to individual schools. Each school, through a school improvement team, must develop a school improvement plan designed to improve student performance and to identify strategies for improving student performance. Individual schools have new authority over the use of staff development funds and the development of the school calendar. In a broad direction, local boards of education are required to provide "maximum flexibility to schools in the use of funds to enable the schools to accomplish their goals" [G.S. 115C-105.25(a)].

If a local board accepts a school improvement plan that requests waivers of certain state laws, rules, or policies, the board must submit the request to the state board for its approval. The local board must explain the circumstances under which the waiver will be used and explain how it will contribute to improved student performance. A local board also may request waivers of laws, rules, or policies that affect the central office. G.S. 115C-105.26 sets out the laws, rules, and polices that are subject to waiver.

The most visible part of the ABCs is its accountability model. Under this program, the state board sets a minimum student performance growth standard for each school. Schools that perform much better than expected on state achievement tests in reading, writing, and mathematics will receive recognition and financial rewards that may be used for bonuses for individual employees or, if those employees support the idea, for some other school purpose. Schools that fare poorly may be identified as low-performing and thereby become eligible for state assistance and possible intervention through a state assistance team. If an assistance team is assigned to a school, testing of certain staff members may occur and jobs of teachers and administrators are at risk. Statewide implementation of the program began in 1996–97 in elementary and middle schools; implementation in high schools began in 1997–98.

Budget Flexibility and Accountability

In recent years the General Assembly has granted local school boards increased flexibility in how they use state school funds (G.S. 115C-105.12A). State funds come to school boards with fewer restrictions than in the past, and boards also may request waivers of some of the restrictions still in place. With this flexibility comes increased accountability. Under G.S. 115C-451(b), the state board must issue a warning and require remedial action when a local school board willfully or negligently fails or refuses to comply with state laws and regulations regarding budgeting, management, and expenditure of funds. The state board also has authority to suspend the local board's budget flexibility described above. During the suspension, the state board may require the local board to use funds only for the purposes for which they were allotted or for other purposes with the state board's specific approval.

Excellent Schools Act

The Excellent Schools Act (SL 1997-21) was passed in 1997 to address problems in attracting and retaining good teachers in our public schools. It raises the standards of teacher education and performance through changes in teachers' preparation in schools of education, certification, professional performance and evaluation, acquisition of tenure, demotion and suspension, dismissal, and salaries.

Administrator Contracts

Beginning in 1995 individuals hired as principals, assistant principals, supervisors, and directors are employed under contracts of from two to four years (G.S. 115C-287.1), not under the tenure system that applies to teachers (G.S. 115C-325). This change allows school boards to 'non-renew' an administrator's contract, subject to statutory restrictions and procedures, rather than go through the dismissal process required by the tenure statute, which both limits the grounds for dismissal and often requires a costly and prolonged process.

Safe Schools

In 1997 the General Assembly said, "If students are to aim for academic excellence, it is imperative that there is a climate of respect in every school and that every school is free of disruption, drugs, violence, and weapons" (Safe Schools Act, SL 1997-443). Many efforts are underway to make schools safe and orderly so that students and staff can focus on education. Among the actions taken are the following:

- Creation of the North Carolina Center for the Prevention of School Violence
- Enactment of more serious disciplinary consequences for students who bring a weapon to school or who physically assault and seriously injure others
- Expansion of situations in which expulsion (permanent separation from school) is possible

- A requirement that principals report specific illegal acts on school property to law enforcement
- Restrictions on admission to school for disruptive students
- Widespread use of school resource officers
- Authority for school boards to conduct criminal record checks of job applicants
- Creation of safe school unit plans by each local board
- Availability of state assistance teams to promote or restore a safe and orderly learning environment
- Inclusion of conflict resolution in the curriculum; use of peer mediation programs
- Expansion of situations in which school employees may use reasonable force, including corporal punishment
- Growth of alternative schools
- Improvements in school security systems

Even with all these measures, it is unfortunately impossible to guarantee safety at school.

Charter Schools

As part of its educational reform efforts, in 1996 the General Assembly authorized the establishment of charter schools, which are public schools that operate under a charter from the state board and are free from many of the restrictions that affect other public schools (G.S. 115C-238.29A through -239.29K). There is a statewide cap of 100 set on the number of charter schools. In 1997–98 thirty-four charter schools began operation.

As long as the school meets the terms of its charter, it is not bound by most of the state statutes and regulations that apply to other public schools. However, unlike other public schools, the state board may close a charter school by revoking its charter if the school fails to live up to the charter's terms.

North Carolina's first charter schools began operating in the 1997–98 school year. Any child qualified for admission to a North Carolina public school is qualified for admission to a charter school, but no child may be required to enroll in a charter school. Teachers already employed by a local board of education may take a leave of absence from their regular position to teach at charter schools.

State and local current expense funds follow students to charter schools. This means that local school units and charter schools participate on an equal footing in the allocation of state and local current expense funds distributed on the basis of average daily membership. At the local level, the school administrative unit must transfer to a charter school an amount equal to the per pupil local current expense appropriation to the local school unit for every child who resides in the unit and attends a charter school.

Counties are not required to appropriate capital funds to charter schools.

Conclusion

Complex challenges face North Carolina's public schools. Equity remains a serious concern, along with many new questions about the state's duty to offer all students access to a "sound basic education." School boards must educate increasing numbers of students with limited English proficiency and students with disabilities. Costly school security efforts continue, but can never guarantee safety. Construction and renovation of facilities must keep pace with increasing enrollments, possible reductions in class size, and new teaching methods. Increasing access to technology and deciding how best to use it are ongoing challenges for schools. In addition to questions directly related to education, schools also continue to be asked to take on functions traditionally the responsibility of other institutions, including health care, nutrition, and before- and after-school care. The challenge to school boards—working with the board of county commissioners, other community agencies, and concerned parents and other citizens—is to find a way to meet the goal set by the General Assembly: "the mission of the public school community is to challenge with high expectations each child to learn, to achieve, and to fulfill his or her potential" [G.S. 115C-105.20(a)].

Additional Resources

Murphy, Janine M., ed., and Robert E. Phay, ed. emeritus. *Education Law in North Carolina.* Chapel Hill, N.C.: Principals' Executive Program, The University of North Carolina at Chapel Hill, 1997. This comprehensive school law treatise is updated regularly. It currently is available in a two-volume set; it will be available on CD-ROM in 1999. Individual chapters are also available for purchase.

North Carolina Public Schools Statistical Profile 1997. Raleigh, N.C.: State Board of Education, 1997. This book provides general statistical data about public schools and includes information on pupils, personnel, and finances. It contains both statewide data and data for each local school administrative unit. A new statistical profile is published annually.

School Law Bulletin. Chapel Hill, N.C.: Institute of Government, The University of North Carolina at Chapel Hill. This Institute of Government quarterly publication is available by subscription. Each issue contains articles about current school law topics, short summaries of new school law court decisions, and a summary of new legislation affecting public elementary and secondary schools is published annually.

Notes

1. Edgar E. Knight, *Public School Education in North Carolina* (Boston: Houghton-Mifflin Co., 1916) (hereinafter Knight, *Public School Education*), 140–47.
2. *Id.*, 148–49.
3. *Id.*, 156–57. Calvin H. Wiley, an ardent supporter of public education, was selected as the first state superintendent.
4. M. C. S. Noble, *A History of the Public Schools of North Carolina* (Chapel Hill, N.C.: The University of North Carolina Press, 1930), 204–5.
5. *Id.*, 199.
6. *Id.*, 233–49; Hugh T. Lefler and Albert R. Newsome, *North Carolina, The History of a Southern State*, rev. ed. (Chapel Hill, N.C.: The University of North Carolina Press, 1963) (hereinafter Lefler and Newsome, *Southern State*), 380–81.
7. This $100,000 was never actually spent due to insufficient funds in the state treasury following the Civil War. Reference to this appropriation was deleted from the school code in the Public Laws from 1887–88 and did not reappear until 1899, when the $100,000 became an annual appropriation.
8. 93 N.C. 472 (1885).
9. 1899 N.C. Pub. Laws ch. 637; Paul V. Betters, ed., *State Centralization in North Carolina* (Washington, DC: The Brookings Institution, 1932) (hereinafter Betters, *State Centralization*), 23.
10. 1901 N.C. Pub. Laws ch. 543; Betters, *State Centralization*, 23.
11. 145 N.C. 170 (1907).
12. 1919 N.C. Pub. Laws ch. 102; Betters, *State Centralization*, 30–31.
13. 1919 N.C. Pub. Laws ch. 84; Betters, *State Centralization*, 31.
14. Lefler and Newsome, *Southern State*, 541–42.
15. 1921 N.C. Pub. Laws ch. 146; Betters, *State Centralization*, 32.
16. 1927 N.C. Pub. Laws ch. 256; Betters, *State Centralization*, 37–39, 54–56; Charles D. Liner, "Public School Finance," *Popular Government* 42 (Spring 1977): 13–19.
17. 1913 N.C. Pub. Laws ch. 64; Knight, *Public School Education*, 347–48; Lefler and Newsome, *Southern State*, 558.
18. By November, 1933, 61 counties and 146 municipalities had defaulted on debts. See *Report of the Local Government Commission* (Raleigh, N.C.: Local Government Commission, 1934), 8.
19. 1931 N.C. Pub. Laws ch. 728; Betters, *State Centralization*, 48–54.
20. 1933 N.C. Pub. Laws ch. 562. The requirement of voter approval was repealed in 1943. 1943 N.C. Sess. Laws ch. 255.
21. *See, e.g.*, G.S. 115C-81(e) (school health education program) and G.S. 115C-81(g) (civic literacy).
22. *See* Edwards v. Board of Education, 235 N.C. 345, 70 S.E.2d 170 (1952).

23. Charles D. Liner, "Distribution of State Funds to Poor and Small School Units: An Analysis," *School Law Bulletin* 23 (Spring 1992): 12–13.

24. 86 N.C. App. 282, 357 S.E.2d 432 (1987). *See also* Guilford County Bd. of Educ. v. Guilford County Bd. of Elections, 110 N.C. App. 506, 430 S.E.2d 681 (1993), upholding the funding level set by the General Assembly for the merger of the Guilford County Schools. The court noted that "Nothing in the Constitution requires that funding of public schools in all counties in the State be identical or addressed through a single uniform law." *Guilford,* at 517, 430 S.E.2d at 688.

25. The technology fund began with an appropriation from the General Assembly. G.S. 115C-457.1 through -457.3 provide that clear proceeds of civil penalties and civil forfeitures that are collected by a state agency and are payable to the county school fund under the state constitution will go to the Civil Penalty and Forfeiture Fund. These funds will be transferred to the State School Technology Fund and distributed to school units on the basis of average daily membership.

26. 346 N.C. 336, 488 S.E.2d 249 (1997). For a more complete discussion of the case, see John C. Boger, "*Leandro v. State*—A New Era in Educational Reform," *Popular Government* 63 (Spring 1998): 2–12.

27. Benjamin B. Sendor, "Financing School Construction: A Primer," *School Law Bulletin* 16 (Winter 1985): 1–8.

28. Governor's Commission on Public School Finance, *Access to Equal Educational Opportunity in North Carolina* (Raleigh, N.C.: GCPSF, 1979).

29. Charles D. Liner, "Twelve Years and $3 Billion Later: School Construction in North Carolina," *Popular Government* 60 (Fall 1994): 30–43.

30. *Id.*

31. 29 N.C. App. 554, 225 S.E.2d 145 (1976).

32. 240 N.C. 118, 121, 81 S.E.2d 256, 258 (1954).

33. 113 N.C. App. 164, 438 S.E.2d 424 (1993).

34. 189 N.C. 650, 127 S.E.2d 692 (1925).

35. 343 N.C. 87, 468 S.E.2d 50 (1996).

36. 288 N.C. 165, 217 S.E.2d 650 (1975).

28 Community Colleges

Robert P. Joyce

Contents

Robert P. Joyce is an Institute of Government faculty member whose areas of specialization include the law related to higher education.

Each year, one North Carolinian in ten goes to school in the state's community college system. The fifty-eight campuses serve 800,000 students at an annual cost exceeding $800 million dollars.[1] That cost is shared by the state and counties in much the same way that the costs of running the public elementary and secondary schools are shared. Similarly, the operating authority and decision making power are shared by the state (chiefly through the State Board of Community Colleges) and local government (chiefly through the local community college board of trustees).

Brief History

Both The University of North Carolina and the system of free public schools are provided for by the North Carolina Constitution and both have roots that reach back to the nineteenth century and earlier. The community college system, by contrast, is not mentioned in the constitution and is strictly a creation of the General Assembly in the twentieth century.

In 1927, Buncombe County Junior College opened as the state's first tuition-free public junior college. Shortly afterward, the Asheville board of education started the College of the City of Asheville, also tuition-free, open to any high school graduate in the city. Because of the financial difficulties faced after the Great Depression, the two colleges merged, in effect, into Biltmore Junior College. Under the names Biltmore College and then Asheville-Biltmore College, the institution remained the sole public junior college in North Carolina until 1946.

With the end of World War II, North Carolina was flooded with former GIs eager for higher education, along with the regular complement of new eighteen- and nineteen-year-olds. Existing campuses, such as the one at Chapel Hill, were filled past overflowing. In response, the extension division of The University of North Carolina opened twelve off-campus freshman centers around the state in the fall of 1946. Most of the centers closed when the wave of students passed, but local taxpayers took up responsibility for two: Wilmington College (destined to become The University of North Carolina at Wilmington) and Charlotte College (later The University of North Carolina at Charlotte) joined Asheville-Biltmore College (later The University of North Carolina at Asheville) as public junior colleges.

About this time, the notion of "community college" was gaining its first acceptance nationally through the 1947 report of the Truman Commission, more formally known as the President's Commission on Higher Education. In 1950 the state superintendent of public instruction authorized a study of North Carolina's need for community colleges. In 1952 the resulting report, adopting the philosophy of the Truman Commission report, called for the creation of a system of tuition-free institutions designed to meet all the post-secondary-school needs of the community, including both academic preparation and practical vocational and technical training.

In 1957, the General Assembly passed the state's first Community College Act, but it did not create the community college that was envisioned by the Truman Commission or by the North Carolina study at all. Instead, the act provided funds for public junior colleges—that is, the institutions at Asheville, Wilmington, and Charlotte—to offer a freshman and sophomore curriculum in liberal arts and sciences. The vocational, technical, and adult education aspects of their curricula faded away.

As the public junior colleges moved away from vocational training, the General Assembly appropriated half a million dollars to create industrial education centers devoted entirely to vocational training, under the auspices of the State Board of Education. Soon the Burlington center enrolled 2,400 students, and by 1963 a total of twenty centers enrolled 34,000 students statewide. To serve the needs of their vocational students, the industrial education centers began offering liberal arts courses in English, mathematics, and the like.

The duplication of effort between the public junior colleges and the industrial education centers motivated Governor Terry Sanford to set up the Governor's Commission on Education beyond the High School in 1961, which called for the creation of "community colleges" offering not only freshman and sophomore college-level courses, like the public junior colleges, but also technical, vocational, and adult education courses for both college and non-college students. Instead of expanding the

1957 version of public junior colleges into true "community colleges," North Carolina started from a base of non-college, industrial education centers and, in effect, transformed them into a community college system. The General Assembly's Omnibus Higher Education Act of 1963— codified at G.S. Chapter 115A, and since replaced by Chapter 115D— authorized the community college system that exists today. Within five years the system comprised fifty institutions. Through the 1970s eight more were added, with the last, now known as Brunswick Community College, joining the system in 1978.

Education Philosophy

The education philosophy of the community college system embraces four elements that distinguish it from more traditional academic institutions of higher education: the 'open door,' low tuition, convenience of location, and a comprehensive curriculum.

- **The 'open door.'** The notion is that the institution is available to anyone who wishes to take advantage of the opportunities it presents, without rigorous entrance obstacles. The North Carolina Administrative Code provides that "[e]ach college shall maintain an open-door admission policy to all applicants who are high school graduates or who are at least 18 years of age" (24 NCAC 2C.0301). To carry out this mission, the community college system offers three types of instruction. In technical programs, the colleges offer two-year degree programs specializing in subject matters such as nursing and computer technology. In vocational programs, one-year programs specialize in plumbing, automobile mechanics, and similar practical training. And in college transfer programs, many institutions offer liberal arts and science courses at the freshman and sophomore levels. (In addition, the system offers a variety of programs such as adult literacy and high school diploma equivalency programs under the rubric of general education.) In any particular program— nursing, for example—a community college may impose entrance requirements. The general philosophy, however, is that the college will offer educational opportunities for all adults who wish to pursue them.

- **Low tuition.** Expense should, to the fullest extent possible, provide no barrier to a community college education. In 1997, in-state tuition for North Carolina residents was $280 per semester.
- **Convenience of location.** North Carolina's community colleges are not residence colleges like the campuses of The University of North Carolina. The vast majority of students live at home—many of them working to support families. Today's community college system has the goal of having a school within thirty miles of nearly all potential students.
- **A comprehensive curriculum.** These colleges provide educational opportunities for all adults, at whatever educational level the adults may be. Course offerings range from rigorous health technology programs to basic literacy training. Academics and technical and vocation training coexist in the same broadly based institution.

Relationship with the Public Schools and The University of North Carolina

Of particular concern to a community college are (1) its relationship with the public schools in its area and (2) its relationship to The University of North Carolina.

Relationship with the Public Schools

Community colleges have deep and historical links to the public schools. The vocational education centers from which the community colleges grew were established as parts of the public school system under the State Board of Education. As described in the following pages, the community college system operated under the State Board of Education from its creation until 1980. Also, local boards of education elect members to the board of trustees for each community college.

Generally speaking, however, the community colleges do not exist to serve public school students; high school students are encouraged to stay in their high schools until graduation. Nonetheless, there are two distinct ways in which high school students may enroll in courses in a community college.

The first is termed "dual enrollment" (see 23 NCAC 2C.0305). A particular high school student—at least sixteen years of age—may be admitted to courses at the community college, to be taken concurrently with courses at the high school, upon the approval of the president of the college and the superintendent of schools. Admission is on a space-available basis and must not displace adult students. Once admitted, the student earns credit at the community college like any other student. Dual enrollment is an individualized case-by-case matter and requires no approval at the state level.

The second involves a more formalized program of cooperation between a community college and the local public school system to offer enhanced educational opportunities for high school students that would not otherwise be available to them. Such programs of cooperation are commonly known as "Huskins Bill" programs, after the statutory provision authorizing them [see G.S. 115D-20(4)]. A Huskins Bill program, in contrast to individualized dual enrollment, will involve the enrollment of a number of local high school students in one or more courses offered by the community college. It requires a formal agreement between the school system and the college and approval by the State Board of Community Colleges.

Relationship with the University

Most of today's community colleges offer college transfer programs in the liberal arts and sciences, but the General Assembly has required (in G.S. 115D-4.1) that "[a]ddition of the college transfer program shall not decrease [the community college's] ability to provide programs within its basic mission of vocational and technical training and basic academic education." Nonetheless, community colleges with college transfer programs are quite reasonably concerned about the ability of their college transfer students to gain admission to four-year institutions and to gain credit for the work undertaken at the community college.

To address that concern, community colleges over the years worked out agreements—termed "articulation agreements"—with four-year colleges that spelled out how course credits would transfer when a community college student gained admission to the four-year college. In time, the welter of such agreements exceeded 300. In 1993 the General Assembly created the Education Cabinet (consisting of the governor, the president of The University of North Carolina, the state superintendent of public instruction, and the president of the North Carolina Community College System) and directed it, among other things, to design a program for better cooperation among the public schools, the community colleges, and the university. That impetus resulted in the Comprehensive Articulation Agreement between the community college system and the university in 1997, detailing how credits will transfer from community college transfer programs to any of the sixteen campuses of the university—Asheville, Boone, Chapel Hill, Charlotte, Cullowhee, Durham, Elizabeth City, Fayetteville, two in Greensboro, Greenville, Pembroke, Raleigh, Wilmington, and two in Winston-Salem. In general, no community college transfer student is guaranteed admission to any UNC institution; the admission decision is made by the UNC institution on a student-by-student basis. Once admitted, however, the Comprehensive Articulation Agreement governs the transfer of course and grade credit.

The individual community colleges are still free to enter into individual agreements with private four-year colleges to spell out how course and grade credits will transfer between the community college and the private college.

State Governance Structure

The Omnibus Higher Education Act of 1963, creating the community college system, placed the Department of Community Colleges and the individual institutions under the State Board of Education. The community colleges were an adjunct of the state's public schools, providing thirteenth and fourteenth grades, in a sense. But in 1979 the General Assembly established the State Board of Community Colleges and transferred the department under its control. This transfer was made with the enactment of Chapter 115D of the General Statutes to replace Chapter 115A. The transfer to the new State Board of Community Colleges became effective July 1, 1980.

State Board of Community Colleges

The State Board of Community Colleges has broad authority over the operations of the community college system and the individual institutions. Since its creation, however, it has exercised its powers with restraint, granting flexibility to the colleges.

Appointment

The State Board of Community Colleges consists of twenty members. The lieutenant governor and the state treasurer are *ex officio* members. The remaining members serve six-year terms. The governor appoints ten members, four from the state at large and one each from the six regions of the community college trustees' association. The General Assembly elects eight members, four each by the House of Representatives and the Senate (see G.S. 115D-2.1).

Powers and Duties

The General Assembly has by statute granted power over the community college system very broadly to the State Board, providing in G.S. 115D-5(a) that

> [t]he State Board of Community Colleges may adopt and execute such policies, regulations and standards concerning the establishment, administration, and operation of institutions as the State Board may deem necessary to insure the quality of educational programs, to promote the systematic meeting of educational needs of the State, and to provide for the equitable distribution of State and federal funds to the several institutions.

In addition to this broad and general grant of authority, the State Board is authorized to approve the budget of individual colleges, approve building sites, approve building plans, approve the selection of the president for a college, establish and enforce financial accounting procedures, approve a college's adoption of a college transfer program, set pay scales for community college employee salaries, remove local community college trustees, set tuition and fees, and, if necessary, withdraw state financial support from a college if the local county or counties fail to provide adequate support.

The State Board has been reserved in exercising the broad authority over individual colleges granted to it by the General Assembly. It has, in fact, adopted a rule (found in 23 NCAC 1A.0003) specifying that "[a]ll power and authority vested by law in the State Board which related to the internal administration, regulation, and governance of any individual college . . . are hereby delegated to the board of trustees of such college." At the same time, mindful of its ultimate responsibility, the State Board has also adopted a rule [found in 23 NCAC 1A.0003(b)(3)] stating that "[t]he State Board reserves the right to rescind any power or authority as it deems necessary."

Creation of New Community Colleges

By 1978, the community college system had grown to fifty-eight institutions, its current number. A fifty-ninth institution, the North Carolina Center for Applied Textile Technology (in Gaston County), is also under the authority of the State Board of Community Colleges. Establishment of new colleges is subject to the approval of the General Assembly upon the recommendation of the State Board.

Department of Community Colleges and the State President

The Department of Community Colleges is defined by the statutes as a principal administrative department of state government under the direction of the State Board of Community Colleges. Chief among its duties are the allocation of state funds to the individual colleges on an equitable and lawful basis and the financial accounting oversight.

The State Board elects a president of the North Carolina System of Community Colleges to act as chief administrative officer of the Department of Community Colleges. The president's salary is fixed by the State Board from funds appropriated by the General Assembly. Neither the statutes nor the administrative code provisions spell out specific duties of the president.

Local Governance Structure

Each community college is governed—under the authority of the State Board of Community Colleges—by a local board of trustees and is administered by a president, employed by the board of trustees.

Local Board of Trustees

Appointment

Each community college board of trustees is composed of four different sets of members. In the first group are four trustees elected by the board of education of the public school administrative unit located in the administrative area of the college. If there are two or more school units in the administrative area, the four trustees are elected jointly by all the local boards, with each board having one vote. In the second group are four trustees elected by the county commissioners of the county in which the college is located. If the administrative area of the college consists of two or more counties, the trustees are to be elected jointly by all the boards, with each board having one vote. (If a community college has established a satellite campus in another county, the commissioners of that county may elect two members to the board of trustees, if the board of trustees agrees.) Only one trustee elected in this group may himself or herself be a county commissioner. In the third group are four trustees appointed by the governor. In the fourth group is the president of the student government, as an *ex officio*, nonvoting member. All trustees except the student government president serve four-year terms and must be residents of the administrative area of the college (see G.S. 115D-12).

A trustee may be removed from office in one of two ways. First, the board of trustees may declare a seat vacant if a member misses three consecutive scheduled meetings without excuse or fails to participate in the trustee orientation program sponsored by the trustees' association. Second, if the State Board has reason to believe that a trustee is not capable of discharging the duties of the office, or is not discharging them, or is guilty of immoral or disreputable conduct, the State Board may bring the matter to the attention of the local board of trustees. The trustees may then investigate and hold a hearing and, by two-thirds vote, find the charges to be true and declare the seat vacant (see G.S. 115D-19).

Powers and Duties

The broadest grant of authority to the local community college board of trustees comes from the State Board, which has provided by rule (found in 23 NCAC 1A.0003) that "[a]ll power and authority vested by law in the State Board which related to the internal administration, regulation, and governance of any individual college . . . are hereby delegated to the board of trustees of such college." In addition, specific statutory grants of authority empower the board of trustees to do the following things:

- Purchase and hold title to land, easements, and rights-of-way
- Sell, exchange, or lease real and personal property
- Acquire land by condemnation
- Elect a president (subject to the approval of the State Board)
- Employ employees (or delegate the employment authority to the President)
- Adopt rules and regulations for the disciplining of students

- Enter into contracts
- Sue and be sued
- Adopt rules for the use of campus streets, alleys, and driveways, including setting speed limits
- Purchase liability insurance and thereby waive sovereign immunity

These grants of authority are found variously in G.S. 115D-14, -15, -20, and -21. In addition, the trustees are authorized by statute to "exercise such other rights and privileges as may be necessary for the management and administration of the institution," and to "perform such other acts and do such other things as may be necessary or proper for the exercise of the foregoing specific powers, including the adoption and enforcement of all reasonable rules, regulations, and bylaws for the government and operation of the institution" (G.S. 115D-14).

Service Areas, Administrative Areas, and Alternative Trustee Selection

The State Board assigns to each community college a "service area" for providing educational and training services (see NCAC 2C.0107). A college may offer services in an area assigned to another college only by written agreement between the colleges.

The college's service area may be exactly coterminous with its "administrative area"—the county or counties that are directly responsible for providing financial support for the college. Or the service area may be broader. A college may establish a satellite campus in a county that is not in the administrative area—with the approval of the commissioners of that county—and that county must accept the maintenance and utility costs of the satellite campus [by G.S. 115D-32(d)].

If a college's administrative area includes two or more counties, the boards of commissioners of all the counties may establish the terms for providing the financial support of the college by contract, and they may provide for an alternative structure for the selection of trustees. The contract is subject to approval by the State Board.

College President

The president of the community college is selected by the board of trustees "for such term and under such conditions as the trustees may fix" [G.S. 115D-20(1)]. The selection is subject to the approval of the State Board. The trustees may delegate as much administrative authority to the president as they deem prudent. Two statutory provisions provide explicitly for significant delegation. The first one authorizes the board of trustees to delegate to the President the authority to make hiring decisions for all college personnel [G.S. 115D-20(2)]. The second one authorizes the board of trustees to delegate to the president the authority to transfer moneys from one appropriation to another within the same fund [G.S. 115D-58(c)].

Financial Responsibility for Community Colleges

The state and the counties served by a community college share the duty of paying for the college. By statute, the state pays for salaries and other costs of administration, instructional services, and support services (called current operations expenses). The state pays for furniture, equipment, and library books, and, when the appropriations are made by the General Assembly, provides matching funds (to be paired with local funds) to buy land and to construct buildings (collectively called the plant fund). The counties served by community colleges must pay for maintenance and repairs to buildings and equipment, rent, utilities, costs of custodians, insurance, and legal fees. In addition, acquisition of land, erection and alteration of buildings, purchase and maintenance of vehicles, and maintenance of grounds are local responsibilities (see G.S. 115D-31 and -32). Total spending for investment in land and buildings for the community college system since July 1, 1963 just slightly exceeds $1 billion. Of that total, counties have provided nearly $550 million and the state, through the proceeds of bond sales and direct appropriations, has provided about $425 million. The remainder has come primarily from the federal government.

The State Appropriation

The total state appropriation for the operations of the Department of Community Colleges and the individual institutions for 1997–98 was $518 million (SL 1997-443). The General Assembly bases its appropriation (in part) and the Department of Community Colleges bases its allocation of the appropriation to the individual colleges (in part) on the concept of the FTE, which stands for "full-time equivalent." An FTE is a statistical picture of a "typical" student. This hypothetical student spends sixteen hours in class each week of each semester, totaling 256 hours per semester and 512 hours for a full school year [see 23 NCAC 1A.0001(4)].

Two students who attend eight hours each over the forty-four weeks of the school year together count as one FTE. If a college should offer a one-hour course that was attended by 512 people, that crowd together would generate one FTE.

Calculating FTEs is not simple. The community college system's open door policy makes counting students difficult. To a much greater extent than is typical in noncomprehensive, selective colleges, students drop courses before the end of a term. The system deals with this problem through the "ten percent report date," established for 1997–98 by SL 1997-443, section 9.4. On the date that a class has met one tenth of the times that it will meet for the semester, the instructor counts the students who have not withdrawn or been dropped from the course and who have attended at least once. That number multiplied by the number of hours the class meets is the figure used to calculate the course's contribution to the college's FTE total.

Once the college's FTE grand total is calculated, the budgeting process begins. First the State Board calculates the FTE total for all colleges in the system and presents that total to the General Assembly with a request for a certain amount of money per FTE as the state's appropriation for operating expenses. For 1997–98 the appropriation was $3,585 per curriculum FTE. In the spring of each year, the State Board notifies each college of the FTE expectation for the coming fiscal year and the college's corresponding state appropriation.

The County Appropriation

While the state, through appropriations by the General Assembly disbursed by the Department of Community Colleges, provides the overwhelming majority of the funds needed by community colleges for operating expenses, the counties in the administrative area of a community college provide the appropriations that permit the college to do the following:

- Acquire land
- Erect and alter buildings
- Maintain buildings and grounds
- Purchase and maintain vehicles
- Acquire and maintain equipment necessary for the upkeep of buildings and grounds
- Purchase furniture and equipment that is not provided by state funds for administrative and instructional purposes

- Pay the salaries of custodians and maintenance workers; pay for fuel, water, power, and telephones
- Rent land and buildings
- Pay for insurance for buildings and their contents, motor vehicles, workers' compensation for employees paid by county funds, and other necessary insurance
- Pay tort claims that result from the negligence of employees
- Pay the cost of bonding employees for the protection of local funds and property
- Pay legal fees in connection with local administration and operation of the college

Two statutory provisions make state funds available in particular circumstances to assist counties with these expenses. The first applies to community colleges whose service areas include three or more counties [G.S. 115D-31(a)(3)]. A formula found in the statute provides matching state funds to help the host county, in recognition of the fact that students from other counties are benefiting from expenses borne by the host county. The second, similarly, provides that state funds for the operation of physical facilities is to be made available to colleges with more than 50 percent of the enrollment at the main campus being composed of out-of-county students (G.S. 115D-31.2).

The Role of the Commissioners

The college board of trustees is required by statute to submit its proposed budget for the upcoming year to the county commissioners by May 15 each year, or a later date to which the commissioners may agree. By July 1 (or a later date agreeable to the board of trustees, but in no event later than September 1), the commissioners determine the amount of county revenue to be appropriated to the community college for the budget year. The statute permits—but does not require—the commissioners to allocate all or part of an appropriation by purpose, function, or project, within guidelines provided by the State Board of Community Colleges through its uniform budget manual. Some counties combine all their appropriations into one lump, while others make one appropriation for current operations and one for plant maintenance and operation. If the commissioners allocate their appropriation by purpose, the board of trustees is bound by the allocation (see G.S. 115D-55).

The Role of the State Board

The State Board of Community Colleges, through its staff in the Department of Community Colleges, sets budgetary and accounting guidelines for the community colleges. As an example, the format for the budget request which the trustees submit to the commissioners is set by the State Board.

Once the college receives notification of the commissioners' appropriation, it must submit its entire budget to the State Board within ten days for that board to approve the budget's provisions with respect to the spending of state funds (see G.S. 115D-55).

If the State Board should determine that the appropriations made by the county commissioners are not sufficient to provide the required local financial support of a college, the State Board may withdraw or withhold state financial or administrative support (see G.S. 115D-6).

Adoption of the Budget and Amendments

Once the State Board has approved the budget, the trustees adopt a budget resolution, authorizing expenditure of the money available to it. The resolution must comply with the approvals of the State Board and the allocation of the county commissioners.

Consistent with rules adopted by the State Board, the trustees may amend the budget resolution during the year, or they may authorize the President to transfer moneys from one appropriation to another within the same budget fund.

The chief limitation on budget amendments concerns funds allocated by the county commissioners to certain purposes. To change the budget resolution concerning such funds, the trustees must obtain the commissioners' approval, if the amendment increases or decreases the amount of the appropriation allocated to the purpose by 25 percent or more. (The commissioners may reduce this threshold to as low as 10 percent.)

Transferring County Funds to the College

By statute, the county finance officer is to make the county budgeted funds available to the college on a monthly basis by the fifteenth day of the month. Most colleges meet this schedule, but some turn moneys over more frequently. Typically, capital outlay funds are transferred when needed, often on the basis of invoices presented by the college.[2]

Additional Resources

Dowdy, Helen B. *A Manual for Trustees: Role, Responsibilities, Relationships.* Cary, N.C.: North Carolina Association of Community College Trustees, 1996.

Fountain, Ben E., and E. Michael Latta. *The Community College System in North Carolina: A Brief History.* Raleigh, N.C.: State Advisory Council on Vocational Education, 1990.

N.C. Department of Community Colleges, "Annual Financial Report," FY 1996–97. Raleigh, N.C.: The Department, 1997.

Wiggs, Jon Lee. *The Community College System in North Carolina: A Silver Anniversary History, 1963–1988.* Raleigh, N.C.: Department of Community Colleges, 1989.

Notes

1. N.C. Department of Community Colleges, "Annual Financial Report" (Raleigh, N.C.: The Department, 1997).

2. *See generally* David M. Lawrence, *Local Government Finance in North Carolina,* 2d ed. (Chapel Hill, N.C.: Institute of Government, The University of North Carolina at Chapel Hill, 1990), pp. 277–82.

29 Public Library Services

Alex Hess and Rebecca S. Ballentine

Contents

Alex Hess is the Institute of Government's librarian.
   This chapter is a modification of the public library services chapter in the third edition of *County Government in North Carolina* that was written by Rebecca Ballentine, Institute of Government librarian from 1965 to 1989.

The public library is an educational institution whose purpose is to help people of all ages and interests continue to learn. Its function is to help individuals to educate themselves, keep better informed about public affairs, and enjoy the pleasure of reading by acquiring, assembling, organizing, and making freely available the printed materials and other resources in its collection, and by providing access to remote information sources. Automation of local public library operations, the creation of systems of shared resources, and technological advances that give access to international networks of information and databases have combined to allow a tremendous increase in the speed and breadth of service delivery to library users.

Library Establishment and Operation

Statutory Authority

The public library—whether municipal, county, or multicounty (regional)—traditionally has been primarily the responsibility of local government. The legislature may grant authority to a local unit of government to establish library services by a general enabling law or by a special local act. Although most public libraries in the state have been established and are supported by local governments under the general law (G.S. Chapter 153A, Article 14), some operate under local acts with provisions different from the statewide statutes. The law also authorizes counties to appropriate funds to support libraries that provide free services to all [G.S. 153A-263(6); 153A-264]. The local governing body should be familiar with all the laws that created and govern its library.

Library Board of Trustees

The governing body of a city or county (board of county commissioners or city council) may appoint a library board of trustees (G.S. 153A-265). Appointments to the board are made at the discretion of the local governing body, which is authorized to determine the number of trustees (not to exceed twelve), their terms of office, rules for their removal from office, and any compensation they might receive. Powers that may be delegated to a library board by a governing body are listed in G.S. 153A-266. The board is required to make an annual report on library operations to the local governing body and also to the Department of Cultural Resources as required by G.S. 125-5. (If a board of trustees has not been established, the local governing board itself would have to submit the report.)

Library Employees

To serve as the chief administrator of any public library system in North Carolina, G.S. 153A-267 requires that a person have a professional librarian certificate issued by the Secretary of Cultural Resources, pursuant to G.S. 125-9 and 125-10 under regulations for certification established by the Public Librarian Certification Commission (G.S. 143B-67). All employees of a public library are "for all purposes" bona fide employees of the county or city that supports it (G.S. 153A-267). They are covered by workers' compensation insurance and are eligible for membership in the local retirement system and other fringe benefits. G.S. 160A-463 provides that employees of regional libraries (G.S. 153A-270) are entitled to the same rights and privileges as employees of the individual governments that participate in these libraries.

Area Served by the Library

The earliest public libraries in the state were municipal libraries, serving the immediate community. Local initiative and interest were instrumental in their organization and support. By the mid-1920s, however, the county library had been recognized as a more efficient unit of library service. Primarily for this reason, more libraries that provide countywide service have been established than have purely municipal ones. The fact that until 1979 state aid was given only to libraries that served entire counties also partly accounts for the preponderance of this type.[1]

The American Library Association (ALA) has stressed the importance of cooperation and joint action among libraries in reaching and sustaining adequate service, pointing out that only those bound together formally or informally in systems, sharing their services and materials, can meet the full needs of their clientele. The trend toward such broader-based library systems has proved practical not only because the per capita cost is less if the library serves a large area but also because the quality of services and resources can be improved through cooperation.[2]

The position of the North Carolina Library Association has also been to encourage public libraries to share resources and services. In 1987, it stated as follows:

> Since on a per capita basis it takes more to run a small library than a large one, many communities cannot raise sufficient tax funds to support public libraries that will meet . . . minimum standards. Whenever inadequate support makes it impossible to meet these standards, libraries should find an alternative method of providing library service, either by combining [libraries in] small localities into a large library unit or by contracting for local services with an existing, strong library unit. In this way, effective library services can be made available to any community, no matter how small.[3]

Toward this end, the law enables two or more units of local government to operate libraries and other undertakings jointly (G.S. Ch. 160A, Art. 20, Pt. 1) and to acquire or construct public buildings together (G.S. 153A-164). The units may acquire the necessary land for such purposes, or they may use that already belonging to one of the participating governments. In 1996, fifty-one counties and nine municipalities maintained their own individual units, while forty-nine counties had formed fifteen regional library systems, making larger book collections and more varied services possible.[4] These systems are defined as "public authorities" and are subject to the Local Government Budget and Fiscal Control Act (LGBFCA).[5]

The importance of examining local needs in determining the best way to provide library services is an increasing concern. For example, the Public Library Association, a division of the ALA, now recommends that national standards for library performance be abandoned in favor of formulating local goals and objectives based on the needs of particular communities. In *A Planning Process for Public Libraries*,[6] a report of the recommendations from a study commissioned by the association, differences in communities are recognized. The report emphasizes the needs of individual citizens as the basis for analyzing the area to be served, and it urges libraries to seek active participation from every segment of the locality in conducting a community survey.

Following the ALA's recommendation, community analyses were conducted by most of the public library systems in North Carolina, and now, as a requirement for eligibility to receive state aid, each library is required to compile an assessment of the needs of the library community, prepare and annually revise a long-range plan of service, and submit copies each year of the needs assessment and long-range plan to the North Carolina State Library.[7]

Financing the Public Library

Local Financial Support

Since library service to the general public has been considered chiefly a function of local government, financial backing has come predominantly from the locality served. Both counties and cities have authority to support libraries from any available source of funds [G.S. 153A-263(6); 153A-268], including, most importantly, the property tax (G.S. 153A-149 for counties; 160A-209 for cities). Since both types of governments may finance libraries, cities may contribute to the operation of county or regional libraries. Also, counties may make appropriations to municipal libraries that are used by county residents who live outside the municipality. In a few places, libraries are legally entitled to share in the profits of the local alcoholic beverage control (ABC) system,[8] and some of them have their own endowment funds.

Federal Aid

There was a major change in 1996 in federal funding for public libraries. The act that has served as the basis for federal allocations for over thirty years was replaced with new federal legislation effective October 1, 1997, after a transition period of one year.

The Library Services and Construction Act

Federal aid began when Congress passed the Library Services Act[9] in 1956 to help states improve and extend public library services in rural areas. This act was replaced in 1964 by the Library Services and Construction Act (LSCA),[10] which broadened and increased federal assistance to the states for public library services and specified that urban areas could share in those funds on the same basis as rural areas. The 1964 act extended the use of federal allocations to library construction and gave the library agency of each state (the State Library of North Carolina in this state) full authority to plan for the use of LSCA funds.

The act was divided into titles to achieve its objectives. The three main titles to be administered by the State Library of North Carolina were established in the first two years of the LSCA's existence: Title I for Library Services, Title II for construction and improvements, and Title III to encourage interlibrary cooperation.[11] Five further titles were added over the next thirty years, extending the use of funding to include foreign language materials, literacy programs, services for Indian tribes, library learning centers, and provision for evaluation and assessment.[12] Aid for the physically handicapped was initially added as a separate title in 1966, but was later transferred to Title I as a part of public services.[13] The LSCA was reauthorized several times between 1964 and 1996 with new directives and requirements for the use of funds as well as extensions for new purposes. During that period, the State Library of North Carolina submitted annual plans and reports to the federal oversight agency (the U.S. Department of Education) for grants awarded under the LSCA, except for those under Title IV in which qualifying Indian tribes applied directly to the federal government.

Titles I and II required matching local public or private funds.[14] The federal share of the "match" was set according to the ratio of a state's per capita income to the average per capita income in the United States. Under that formula, the federal share varied from 58.82 percent for fiscal years 1986 and 1987 to 55.64 percent in fiscal 1996 and 1997.[15] By the end of 1973, some fifty-four public libraries had received Title II construction funding. There followed a ten year hiatus in appropriations which finally ended with a renewed commitment to construction funding with the reauthorization of the LSCA in 1984.[16] The initial appropriation for North Carolina amounted to $590,913 for federal fiscal year 1985 (to be spent in state fiscal year 1986).[17] In recent years, Title II construction funding has averaged just over $400,000 per year, with $421,993 being allocated for state fiscal year 1996.[18]

LSCA funding for Titles I and III has been distributed in the form of direct grants to enrich collections and services, to support special demonstration projects such as community information and referral systems, and to encourage interlibrary cooperation in collection development, planning, and resource sharing. North Carolina public libraries have been aided in improving their facilities and resources, automating services, and participating in a statewide network of shared information and services. Public Services grant awards for state fiscal years 1996–97 and 1997–98 included projects for data systems upgrades and transfers, public access, youth and student collections, video services, large print and books-on-tape collections, and Internet and local area network services.[19]

LSCA funds were also used to serve people across the state who need materials in a language other than English (the Cumberland County Public Library has been the headquarters for the foreign languages program). Some LSCA funding helped support workshops and conferences that provided information and continuing education for librarians and library trustees, and a part of the appropriation was used by the Division of State Library for research and publications as well as to foster and strengthen cooperative efforts among libraries.[20]

After 1977 the LSCA also addressed the financial problems of libraries in large metropolitan areas by requiring that in any year when total federal funding under Title I exceeded $60 million, a state must reserve a percentage of its allocated share for libraries in cities with over 100,000 in population. The exact percentage of urban funds for each state was determined by comparing its aggregate urban population with its total population. For example, in a state with 30 percent of its population in urban areas, 30 percent of its allocation of federal funds must have been earmarked for urban libraries. The maximum amount of the excess that could have been allocated to large cities on this basis was 50 percent.[21]

The Library Services and Technology Act

In 1996 Congress enacted the new Library Services and Technology Act (LSTA).[22] It continues the LSCA approach of using a state agency (again, the North Carolina State Library in our state) as the conduit for federal funds to local libraries, but transfers federal oversight from the U.S. Department of Education to the Institute of Museum and Library Services and expands the definition of which libraries are to be funded.[23] The LSCA serves as a successor to the library programs found in the Higher Education Act (HEA) as well as those of the LSTA, and will include appropriations for programs for library education and academic libraries as well as for local public libraries. The focus of the act is upon two key priorities: (1) information access through technology and (2) improving access to library services for those having difficulty using a library or those who have been underserved for whatever reason. Specifically, the act requires that 96 percent of the funds provided to a state library administrative agency be expended directly, through subgrants, or cooperative agreements to be used for the following:

(1) (A) establishing or enhancing electronic linkages among or between libraries;

(B) electronically linking libraries with educational, social, or information services;

(C) assisting libraries in accessing information through electronic networks;

(D) encouraging libraries in different areas, and encouraging different types of libraries, to establish consortia and share resources; or

(E) paying costs for libraries to acquire or share computer systems and telecommunications technologies; and

(2) targeting library and information services to persons having difficulty using a library and to underserved urban and rural communities, including children (from birth through age 17) from families with incomes below the poverty line . . . (20 U.S.C. § 9141)

The new LSTA provides greater flexibility and reduces the administrative burden on the state administering agency. There are no separate titles with individual purposes and no mandated set-asides for institutional library services and services for the blind and handicapped or for major urban resource libraries. There is also no provision for a continuation of the old LSCA Title II construction and facilities funds. Continuity is found instead with the old Title I and III allocations for library services and cooperation, with an emphasis on technological innovation. The LSTA also requires the state library agency to file a five-year implementation plan and includes strong requirements for increased accountability and evaluation, including an independent evaluation prior to the end of the five-year plan.

The plan filed by the North Carolina State Library includes criteria for eligibility and policies for evaluating proposals in the grant-awarding process established for future fund distribution to public, academic, school, and special libraries. The chief goals listed are to (1) enable all North Carolina libraries to serve as gateways to information by providing access for users to all available electronic and print resources; (2) achieve equity in public library service for all North Carolinians; and (3) have the State Library serve as a leader and model in the development and delivery of library services. Libraries should have a basic automated system and the physical infrastructure to support access to networked information, and library staff members should be provided with the needed skills and knowledge to make use of the technology involved. Public access to the Internet and programs to meet the needs of North Carolina's children are listed as priorities. The State Library will offer training for library staff and models for integrating technology into library management and services.

To implement its plan under the LSTA, the State Library expects to have about the same $3 million annually that was available for LSCA Titles I, II, and III. General directions for policy decisions in awarding grants include an intention to require some form of matching funds from local governments, strategies to make funding accessible and attractive to libraries of all sizes, and four different categories of grants to be awarded. The grant categories include the following:

1. Statewide Leadership Grants to support programs with a broad, statewide impact that serve as change-oriented initiatives
2. Mini-Grants (EZ-LSTA Grants) to allocate money for specified purposes based on annual priorities and with a simplified application process
3. Innovation Grants to fund projects at one or more libraries that are designed to test or demonstrate new concepts or approaches
4. Grants for Local Projects for allocations that aid in implementing annual plans that support the overall strategic plan.

Libraries are to submit letters of intent briefly outlining the projects they intend to propose for funding. The State Library staff and an LSTA Advisory Committee will evaluate the letters of intent according to the state's priorities, the goals of the LSTA, and grant eligibility guidelines, and will advise applicants whether or not to submit full proposals based upon the completed review. Final proposals will undergo a second review process to determine which projects will be actually funded. The streamlined process proposed for the Mini-Grants will skip the letter of intent phase and proposals will go straight to final review by the State Library staff, subject to a right of appeal to the LSTA Advisory Committee.

This initial plan for implementation of the LSTA focuses on the first two years (1997–99) of the five-year program required by the act. The State Library intends to continue soliciting feedback from libraries and users during the initial period to help evaluate the program it has developed, and to be ready to prepare a strategic plan for the final three years that will best serve the needs of libraries in North Carolina while achieving the objectives mandated by the LSTA.

State Aid

History

State financial aid to county and regional public libraries usually takes the form of cash grants and/or services. The state aid fund for public libraries was established in 1941. The first appropriation of $100,000 per annum for "payment to counties" was increased during each successive session of the General Assembly until 1957, when the figure reached $425,000. It remained at that level until an increase was approved in 1965.[24]

In 1964 the Governor's Commission on Library Resources was appointed to study the overall status of libraries in the state and to suggest ways to meet steadily increasing needs for educational and informational materials as well as services. The commission recommended that "continued study be given to the development of a plan for joint local-state-federal responsibility for public library financing."[25]

In 1967 the General Assembly created the Commission to Study Library Support in the State of North Carolina by joint resolution. Concluding that sources of public revenue for local governments are more limited than other sources of public revenue, this commission recommended that the state gradually assume equal responsibility with local government for public library support. It proposed that this goal be accomplished over a period of several years, during which time annual increases in state grants to public libraries would amount to approximately 20 cents per capita.[26]

The Present System

State funds are intended to stimulate the improvement and expansion of public library services. They are allocated among qualifying library systems on the basis of the rules and regulations formulated by the secretary of the Department of Cultural Resources in accordance with G.S. 125-7 and G.S. 143B-10.

The present formula for distributing state aid for public libraries was adopted in 1983 after a four-year study of the financial needs of library systems. Under this formula, 50 percent of the state aid appropriation is distributed among qualifying county and regional libraries in equal block grants. Regional libraries receive one overall grant in addition to the ones that are received for each county in the region. The remaining 50 percent of the appropriation is awarded to county, regional, and municipal library systems in amounts that vary inversely with the per capita income of the area served. The formula thus directs more aid to the counties and municipalities that are less able to support libraries from local treasuries.[27]

General Assembly appropriations for the state aid fund for public libraries increased rapidly from 1983 to 1987, with the annual total moving from $4.8 million in fiscal year 1982–83 to $11.3 million in fiscal year 1987–88.[28] The annual appropriation declined to below $11 million from 1990 to 1996 but started rising again to $12.9 million for fiscal year 1996–97, and $14.9 million for fiscal year 1997–98.[29] In addition, the

Table 29-1
Sources of Income for Public Library Services (in dollars)

Year	Municipal Funds $	County Funds $	State Aid $	Federal Aid (LSCA) $	Other Income $
1942–43	194,741	201,377	95,380	—	120,168
1952–53	612,138	717,319	350,000	—	214,868
1956–57	822,816	1,019,072	390,000	14,031	266,184
1966–67	1,649,781	3,041,989	686,250	717,713	550,587
1976–77	4,454,919	10,859,461	3,514,635	1,262,289	1,969,069
1986–87	8,026,586	36,347,438	10,789,462	1,335,700	4,911,091
1995–96	14,176,384	73,551,036	10,949,669	1,819,449	6,283,978

Sources: Biennial Reports of the North Carolina State Library; N.C. Department of Cultural Resources, Division of State Library, *Statistics & Directory of North Carolina Public Libraries* (annual).
Note: Capital expenditures are not shown in this table.

General Assembly made separate appropriations for library construction from 1987–90 and again in fiscal year 1995–96. The $2 million in non-recurring funding for 1995–96 was to be used as grants for construction or for the purchase of books for public libraries and public school libraries. The State Library administered $1.5 million according to the state aid formula, with the remainder being distributed by the Department of Cultural Resources.[30]

The rules for the allocation of state aid to public libraries are compiled by the Department of Cultural Resources and specify application procedures for receiving state aid (7 NCAC 2E.0301). If a library system receives an appropriation from local government sources less than that of the previous year, a state grant will not be terminated, but instead reduced in proportion to the decrease; state aid is designed to supplement local funds rather than to replace them [7 NCAC 2E.0301(4)]. Tables 29-1 and 29-2 provide an overview of support for public library services.

Interlibrary Cooperation

Besides formal organizations such as regional libraries, other cooperative efforts are being made to help libraries meet increasing demands for a variety of services and materials. The systems in the areas served by several of North Carolina's regional councils of governments

Table 29-2
Percentage Contribution and Per Capita Income for Libraries by Source,
1966–67, 1986–87, and 1995–96

Year	County and Municipal Funds		State Aid		Federal Aid (LSCA)		Other Support (Private Donations, etc.)	
	% Contri- bution	Per Capita ($)	% Contri- bution	Per Capita ($)	% Contri- bution	Per Capita) ($)	% Contri- bution	Per Capita ($)
1966–67	73	1.02	10	0.16	8	0.11	9	0.12
1986–87	72	7.09	18	1.73	2	0.21	8	0.79
1995–96	82	12.19	10	1.52	2	0.25	6	1.14

Sources: Biennial Reports of the North Carolina State Library; N.C. Department of Cultural Resources, Division of State Library, *Statistics & Directory of North Carolina Public Libraries* (annual).

have conducted feasibility studies and have found that they can stretch their tax resources further by sharing materials, information, and specialized personnel.

On a broader scale, G.S. 125-12, the Interstate Library Compact, authorizes local and state library agencies of those states that are parties to the agreement (North Carolina is one) to engage in joint and cooperative library programs and services.

In 1977 the General Assembly designated the Department of Cultural Resources as the agency to administer and coordinate state participation in regional and national cooperative library programs and "to plan and coordinate cooperative programs between the various types of libraries within the State of North Carolina" (1977 N.S. Sess. Laws ch. 645, § 1). An outgrowth of this responsibility was the State Library Division's appointment of an ad hoc committee to study multi-type library cooperation[31] and to employ King Research, Inc., to conduct a study to determine whether the establishment of a statewide information network would be feasible.

The King Report recommended the creation of a machine-readable bibliographic database of holdings of all libraries in the state, and specified that it should be maintained through the Online Computer Library Center, Inc. (OCLC), a national service already being used by major libraries in North Carolina for cataloging and interlibrary loans. The study also recommended the creation of zones of cooperation (ZOCs) in areas where different types of libraries could share information at the local and regional levels.[32]

By late 1986, a number of ZOCs had been organized and were operating successfully. The North Carolina Online Union Catalog, the North Carolina Union List of Serials, and a statewide electronic mail/bulletin-board system had become accessible, and a number of public library systems were continuing or starting up automated union lists of their holdings. These new projects were coordinated by the State Library through the North Carolina Information Network (NCIN), which served as a base for information dissemination and interlibrary cooperation. The NCIN itself migrated to a new Internet base starting in the winter of 1994–1995 and provides information updates, a help desk, Internet guidance, and e-mail accounts for public library staff statewide.[33]

The desire for further steps toward interlibrary cooperation remain strong. In December 1994, the North Carolina Library Association, the North Carolina State Library Commission, and the State Library of North Carolina chose JNR Associates to conduct a needs assessment and evaluation study. The single greatest need identified by public librarians was networking. Public librarians wanted the State Library to take the lead in developing and managing a statewide automated network for librarians. Progress in this has been rapid: by 1997, sixty-four of the seventy-five public library systems had automated their local operations, and four more were beginning automation projects.[34] All public libraries are members of the North Carolina Library and Information Network (NCLIN), the former NCIN, and have been provided Internet access for library staff. Forty of the systems now offer Internet access to the public.

The existence of the Online Union Catalog (now a subset of the OCLC WorldCat database) and the Union List of Serials has made resource sharing an increasingly popular option. Requests for articles now constitute nearly half of all items requested by patrons, so constant maintenance and expansion will be required to adequately serve library users. The wider scope of the new LSTA in embracing all libraries serves as a good blueprint for future cooperation in this sphere and in other areas of shared resource cooperation. The North Carolina Libraries and Virtual Education (NC LIVE) project aims to provide North Carolinians with universal electronic access to the full text of standard reference works, indexes, and core academic journals, and to improve access to library holdings and archives through an expanded program of resource sharing and electronic delivery of information.[35] The links already established between the State Library–supported NCLIN and other networks such as the Triangle Research Libraries Network (TRLN), which consolidates the holdings of Duke University, The University of North Carolina at Chapel Hill, North Carolina Central University, and North Carolina State University, have already proved invaluable in making huge quantities of information available to the people of North Carolina.[36]

The State Library

General Information

The reorganization of state government enacted by the General Assembly in 1971 brought the State Library under a new Department of Art, Culture, and History (1971 N.C. Sess. Laws ch. 864, §19). The Executive Organization Act of 1973 renamed the latter the Department of Cultural Resources and assigned the Division of State Library to it (1973 N.C. Sess. Laws ch. 476, §31).

Besides administering state and federal financial-aid programs, the division provides a program of reference services for state and local government agencies, businesses, other libraries, and the general public. It offers research assistance and training for electronic census products as a participant in the State Data Center, and collects and provides access to federal documents, state documents, genealogical materials, periodicals, newspapers, and maps. The State Library operates a processing center that orders and catalogs books for public libraries; maintains and circulates a large film collection; and coordinates public library activities on a statewide basis. It also provides reading materials in alternative format and specialized playback equipment via Free Matter for the Blind postal privileges to over 10,000 citizens with disabilities.[37]

The powers and duties of the State Library were further expanded by the 1987 General Assembly, which designated the Department of Cultural Resources to serve as an information center for the people of the state and state government [G.S. 125-2(4)] and to assist non-profit corporations in establishing and maintaining cooperative information exchange programs [G.S. 125-2(10)]. Through the use of computerized databases and the more traditional kinds of library resources and services, the Division of State Library became instrumental in fostering commerce and business in the state as well as educating and informing the general public. Services already provided through the NCLIN will form one of the major components of the North Carolina Information Highway, the advanced digital broadband network that is being developed for high speed transmission of data and video communications. The State Library will also be one of the agencies involved in establishing the North Carolina Network Information Center (NC NIC), to make accessing and using the Internet easier and more attractive to users.

The State Library, in promoting better public libraries throughout North Carolina, has sought to establish standards and guidelines to help them attain their greatest potential in service to their communities and, ultimately, to all citizens of the state. Libraries are one of the basic educational resources available to the public. The continued development and implementation of cost-effective services and modern technology for sharing knowledge have become even more essential in the current environment of rapidly changing methods for compiling, sending, and receiving information.

State Documents Depository System

In 1987 the General Assembly enacted the Documents Depository Act to improve public access to publications of state agencies and to provide a better system for preserving them (G.S. Ch. 125, Art. 1A). The law named the State Library as the official depository of all these publications and created a State Publications Clearinghouse in the Department of Cultural Resources to receive and distribute publications to depository libraries. The clearinghouse advises state agencies of the number of their publications needed for distribution. It also prepares microfiche copies for reference and interlibrary loans and publishes a checklist of state publications. The Checklist of Official North Carolina State Publications is distributed without charge to all North Carolina libraries that request it and is also available electronically via the State Library's Internet site.

Taking into account regional distribution patterns and persons served so that the publications will be conveniently accessible to all residents of the state, the State Library may designate at least one library in each congressional district to serve as a depository. The State Library is responsible for formulating standards of operation and rules under which the depository system will be administered. The law also allows the Secretary of the Department of Cultural Resources to appoint a committee of depository librarians and state officials to advise the department in carrying out the provisions of the act.

In 1991 the General Assembly amended the Documents Depository Act to require that state publications of historical or enduring value and importance be printed on alkaline (acid-free) paper. Such publications are to be designated on an annual basis by the State Librarian and the university librarian at The University of North Carolina at Chapel Hill. The coordinator of the North Carolina State Publications Clearinghouse monitors compliance by state agencies with this requirement. The State Librarian and the librarian at The University of North Carolina at Chapel Hill are required to report annually to the Joint Legislative Commission on Governmental Operations regarding the titles designated, and are to include a compliance report from the coordinator of the North Carolina State Publications Clearinghouse.

Additional Resources

Bremer, Suzanne W. *Long Range Planning: A How-to-Do-It Manual for Public Libraries.* New York: Neal-Schuman Publishers, 1994.

Childers, Thomas, and Nancy A. Van House. *What's Good?: Describing Your Public Library's Effectiveness.* Chicago: American Library Association, 1993.

Himmel, Ethel E., and William James Wilson with the ReVision Committee of the Public Library Association. *Planning for Results: A Public Library Transformation Process.* 2 vols. Chicago: American Library Association, 1998.

Statistics and Directory of North Carolina Public Libraries. Raleigh, N.C.: North Carolina Department of Cultural Resources, Division of State Library, Library Development Section, published annually.

Young, Virginia G., ed. *The Library Trustee: A Practical Guidebook.* 5th ed. Chicago: American Library Association, 1995.

Notes

1. In 1979 G.S. 125-7(c) was amended to allow municipal and regional libraries to share in state-provided library equalization funds.

2. American Library Association, *Minimum Standards for Public Library Systems, 1966* (Chicago: The Association, 1967), 10–11.

3. North Carolina Library Association, Public Libraries Section, Standards and Measures Committee, *Standards for North Carolina Public Libraries* (Raleigh, N.C.: Division of State Library, 1987), 7.

4. North Carolina Department of Cultural Resources, Division of State Library, Library Development Section, *Statistics and Directory of North Carolina Public Libraries, July 1, 1995–June 30, 1996* (Raleigh, N.C.: The Section, 1996), 30.

5. Letter, Harlan Boyles, Secretary, N.C. Local Government Commission, to Elaine von Oesen, Assistant State Librarian, October 2, 1973.

6. Vernon E. Palmour, Marcia C. Bellassai, and Nancy V. DeWath, *A Planning Process for Public Libraries* (Chicago: Public Library Association, ALA, 1980), xi–xii.

7. 10 NCAC 2E .0301; G.S. 125–5.

8. *See, e.g.,* 1947 N.C. Sess. Laws ch. 835 for a specific grant of 5 percent of net ABC profits to the Public Library of Charlotte and Mecklenburg County.

9. Pub. L. No. 84-597, 70 Stat. 293 (1956).

10. Pub. L. No. 88-269, 78 Stat. 11 (1964). Before its repeal in 1996, the LSCA was codified at 20 U.S.C. § 351 *et seq.*

11. Pub. L. No. 88-269, 78 Stat. 11 (1964); Pub. L. No. 89-511, 80 Stat. 313 (1966).

12. Pub. L. No. 98-480, 98 Stat. 2236 (1984) (Titles IV, V, VI); Pub. L. No. 101-254, 104 Stat. 107 (1990) (Titles VII, VIII).

13. Pub. L. No. 91-600, 84 Stat. 1660 (1970).

14. Before repeal, these provisions were found at 20 U.S.C. §§ 351e(b); 353a; 355b(a), (b).

15. 49 Fed. Reg. 42,777 (October 24, 1984); 59 Fed. Reg. 61,310 (November 30, 1994).

16. Pub. L. No. 98-480, 98 Stat. 2236 (1984).

17. *Tar Heel Libraries* 7 (November/December 1984): 1.

18. *Tar Heel Libraries* 17 (November/December 1994): 8.

19. North Carolina Department of Cultural Resources, Division of State Library, *North Carolina Public Library Services Grant Awards, 1996–97* (Raleigh, N.C.: Division of State Library, 24 April 1997), ⟨http://hal.dcr.state.nc.us/ld/pubaward.htm⟩; North Carolina Department of Cultural Resources, Division of State Library, *LSCA Title I Public Library Services Grants FY 1997–98* (Raleigh, N.C.: Division of State Library, 19 Sept. 1997), ⟨http://hal.dcr.state.nc.us/ld/lsca97.htm⟩.

20. David M. McKay, "Epilog," in Thornton W. Mitchell, *The State Library and Library Development in North Carolina* (Raleigh, N.C.: Division of State Library, 1983), 138–39.

21. Pub. L. No. 95-123, 91 Stat. 1095 (1977).

22. Pub. L. No. 104-208, 110 Stat. 3009 (1996). The LSTA is codified at 20 U.S.C. § 9121 *et seq.*

23. The description of the LSTA in this section is based on that found in two publications from the North Carolina State Library: North Carolina Department of Cultural Resources, Division of State Library, *Discussion Paper: Implementing the Library Services & Technology Act in North Carolina June 1997* (Raleigh, N.C.: Division of State Library, 23 June 1997) ⟨http://hal.dcr.state.nc.us/hottopic/lsta/discuss.htm⟩, and North Carolina Department of Cultural Resources, Division of State Library, *Library Services and Technology Act: Plan for Implementation in North Carolina August 1997* (Raleigh, N.C.: Division of State Library, 25 Aug. 1997), ⟨http://hal.dcr.state.nc.us/hottopic/lsta/plan9708.htm⟩.

24. Financial records on file in the N.C. Department of Cultural Resources, Division of State Library, Raleigh.

25. North Carolina Governor's Commission on Library Resources, *Resources of North Carolina Libraries*, ed. Robert B. Downs (Raleigh, N.C.: The Commission, 1965).

26. North Carolina Legislative Commission to Study Library Support in the State of North Carolina, *Report* (Raleigh, N.C.: August 1968).

27. "Keeping Up," *North Carolina Libraries* 41 (Fall 1983): 162.

28. *Tar Heel Libraries* 6 (July/August 1983): 2; *Tar Heel Libraries* 8 (July/August 1985): 1; *Tar Heel Libraries* 11 (July/August 1987): 2.

29. North Carolina Department of Cultural Resources, Division of State Library, Library Development Section, *Statistics and Directory of North Carolina Public Libraries July 1, 1994–June 30, 1995* (Raleigh, N.C.: Library Development Section, 1995), 2; North Carolina Department of Cultural Resources, Division of State Library, *Five-Year Statewide Summary: FY 1992–1997, North Carolina Public Library Statistics, FY 1996/97* (Raleigh, N.C.: Division of State Library, 29 May 1997), 1 (http:// www.dcr.state.nc.us/ld/plstats9697/5yrsumm.htm); SL 1997-443, §§ 2 and 35.1, and *Conference Report on the Continuation, Expansion and Capital Budgets*, dated 27 Aug. 1997, p. b7.

30. *Tar Heel Libraries* 18 (July/August 1995): 1; 1995 N.C. Sess. Laws ch. 507, § 12.4; Grace-Ellen McCrann, North Carolina Department of Cultural Resources, Division of State Library, telephone conversation with author, 30 Dec. 1997.

31. Alberta S. Smith, "Access to Information for North Carolinians: Multitype Library Cooperation," Working Paper no. 1 (Raleigh, N.C.: Division of State Library, 1981).

32. *North Carolina Library Networking Feasibility Study* (Rockville, Md.: King Research, Inc., August 1982), 132–33.

33. *Tar Heel Libraries* 19 (March/April 1996): 3; *Tar Heel Libraries* 19 (May/June 1995): 2.

34. For these statistics and further information on library systems, see North Carolina Department of Cultural Resources, Division of State Library, *Libraries in North Carolina: A Snapshot* (Raleigh, N.C.: Division of State Library, 29 May 1997), 1 (http://hal.dcr.state.nc.us/hottopic/lsta/snapshot.htm).

35. North Carolina Department of Cultural Resources, Division of State Library, *Working Together for Excellence: A Vision for North Carolina LIVE—An Electronic Library Project* (Raleigh, N.C.: Division of State Library, 9 Oct. 1996), 1–2 (http:// www.ncccs.cc.nc.us/~blackmun/ncvisn.html).

36. Howard F. McGinn, Jr., "Foreword," *North Carolina Libraries* 44 (Fall 1986): 133–34.

37. North Carolina Department of Cultural Resources, Division of State Library, *More About the State Library: Library Services* (Raleigh, N.C.: Division of State Library, January 1997), 1 (http://hal.dcr.state.nc.us/about.htm).

30 The Courts

James C. Drennan

Contents

James C. Drennan is an Institute of Government faculty member whose fields of work include judicial administration, judicial education, legal aspects of impaired driving, and sentencing of criminal offenders.

The framework of North Carolina's court system is established in Article IV, the judicial article, of the state constitution, which was substantially revised in 1962. This article calls for a unified statewide and state-operated General Court of Justice, which is comprised of three divisions: the Appellate Division (which includes the Supreme Court and the Appellate Division), the Superior Court Division, and the District Court Division.

Virtually all current operating costs of the General Court of Justice are borne by the state, and it employs all those assigned to the judicial system. (Some local personnel, such as bailiffs, assist the courts, but are not, strictly speaking, court employees.) However, local governments—primarily the counties—must provide appropriate and adequate space as well as furniture for those functions of the court system that are carried out at the local level. These include practically all operations of the system, except its central administration and the work of the appellate courts. Thus the court system is a major governmental function carried on largely at the level of the county and housed at its expense. For more information about the county's responsibility for court operations, see the discussion of that subject at the end of this chapter.

History

The current structure of the court system, in its most important organizational principles, dates back to the 1950s and 1960s. During a fifteen year period beginning around 1955, the organizational structure of that period was studied, the resulting new recommended structure was approved by the people as they approved a series of constitutional amendments, and the new structure was implemented across the state. The final counties came under the new system in December 1970, fifteen years after the initial studies began.

What were the organizational principles that directed that reform effort? There are several that were important.

- The trial court system of the 1950s was largely a local system, with almost every county having a slightly different structure. The reformed court structure eliminated all those local courts and replaced them with a system that was state-funded in almost all respects.

- The trial court system of the 1950s had unique jurisdictional rules for each local court, the costs charged were different and the methods of selection varied from county to county. The reformed court structure had uniform jurisdictions, cost structures, and methods of selection.

- The court system of the 1950s compensated lots of officials from the fees they collected, and in criminal cases, only those found guilty were assessed fees. The reformed court structure made all court officials state employees, paid only by salaries.

- The court system of the 1950s had no central administration, since counties and cities provided most of the funding. The reformed court structure is administered by a state agency, the Administrative Office of the Courts.

The result of that sustained reform effort is a system that has as its guiding principle the notion that a person who seeks justice from the courts should find that the matter is heard by a person who has the same powers, is selected in the same way, and who has no financial stake in the outcome, regardless of where that person may live in North Carolina. In short, the goal is equal justice for all, in small towns and large cities; in the east and the west; in mountains and on the coast. The remainder of this chapter is a brief description of that organizational structure, as it was suggested by the court reform efforts of the 1950s and 60s, and as it has been modified since then.

Appellate Division

Supreme Court

The supreme court has seven justices (G.S. Chapter 7A, Subchapter II). Justices (and all judges) must be lawyers and may not practice law while serving as a judge. They are elected in statewide partisan elections for eight-year terms. Meeting as a body in Raleigh, the court hears oral arguments by attorneys representing the various parties in cases appealed from the lower courts. It is also authorized to meet in up to two sessions per year in the Old Chowan County Courthouse in the Town of Edenton. The supreme court does not have a jury, and it makes no determinations of fact; it considers cases on the written record of the trial only, and it decides questions of law. Its opinions (decisions) are printed in bound volumes and become state law to the same extent as enactments of the General Assembly.

The supreme court primarily decides cases involving questions of constitutional law, legal questions of major significance to the state as a whole, or murder cases including a sentence of death. These cases may already have been decided in the court of appeals or may have come to the supreme court directly from the trial court. The supreme court also must hear cases heard by the court of appeals in which one of the judges hearing the case dissents from the position taken by the majority.

Court of Appeals

The court of appeals is composed of twelve judges who are elected in the same manner and for the same number of years as the justices of the supreme court. Court of appeals judges, however, sit and render decisions in panels of three. Panels are authorized to convene in various localities throughout the state, although they usually do so in Raleigh. Like the supreme court, this court decides only questions of law, including whether the trial procedure was free of error that was prejudicial to the appellant.

The court of appeals was created in 1967 to relieve the supreme court of a portion of its case load, which had become more than it could reasonably handle. As noted earlier, the court of appeals hears and decides all appealed cases, except those that go directly to the supreme court. No matter what the issue, every appellant has a right to be heard by at least one of these appellate courts, except in one instance: a defendant who pleads guilty to a criminal charge in the superior court may have his conviction reviewed only by petitioning the court of appeals for a *writ of certiorari*. It is up to that court to decide whether to issue the writ and hear the case.

Operation of the Appellate Courts

The supreme court is housed in the Justice Building, across the street from the southeast corner of the capitol. The court of appeals is located in the Ruffin Building, similarly situated, but on the southwest corner. Both courts are supported by the Supreme Court Library, housed primarily in the Justice Building, and each has a clerk, who is that court's administrative officer. The opinions of each court are prepared for publication by an appellate division reporter. Each justice or judge has two research assistants, who must be law school graduates.

When a vacancy arises in the membership of the supreme court or the court of appeals other than at the end of a judge's term—usually through death or mid-term retirement—the governor may fill the vacancy by an appointment effective until the next general election. Vacancies often occur in this fashion. At the general election, the incumbent appointee almost always runs for the office, and is elected most of the time. Thus while the state constitution provides for election of appellate judges, a majority of them attain office originally by appointment; the same is true with respect to trial court judges.

Appellate judges may be removed by impeachment or by the appellate courts (the supreme court in the case of a court of appeals judge and the court of appeals for a supreme court justice) on recommendation of the Judicial Standards Commission, which is discussed later in this chapter.

Justices of the supreme court and judges of the court of appeals are required to retire by age seventy-two, but they may do so earlier. A retiring judge can become an "emergency" judge, and may be recalled to active service for temporary duty on the court from which he or she retired (a retired supreme court justice can also serve in a similar capacity on the court of appeals). The governor issues commissions to emergency justices and judges that are valid until the holder reaches age seventy-two. After that age, a judge may continue to serve temporarily as a "recalled retired" judge. The compensation and jurisdiction are the same for both kinds of temporary service.

Superior Court Division

Organization

The Superior Court Division is comprised of the superior court, which is the trial court for most cases involving a jury. At least two sessions of superior court for the trial of cases involving a jury are held each year in each county of the state; in the busiest counties, several judges conduct sessions each week. The state is currently divided into judicial districts (G.S. Ch. 7A, Subchapter III).

The district structure for superior courts is complicated. There are sixty-two districts, and in each of those districts a specified number of judges must reside in and be elected from that district (the number ranges from one to three). Districts are generally established based on geographical considerations, caseload, and population, but the "one person, one vote" rules that govern the establishment of legislative districts do not apply to judicial districts. Some of those districts are composed of part of one county, others are composed of a single county, a few are composed of parts of two counties, and a few are composed of several counties. (The 1st Judicial District, in the northeastern part of the state, has seven counties.) Some of the districts serve only as units for election and are grouped with other districts to form a single administrative unit. Those grouped districts are called "sets of districts." Of the sixty-two districts, thirty-eight are also single administrative units. The remaining twenty-four districts (primarily in urban areas) are grouped into seven sets of districts for administrative purposes. Thus there are forty-five districts or sets of districts used for administrative purposes. The largest of those units, District 26A–C (in Mecklenburg County) elects six judges. Many of the districts have only one resident judge. The forty-five administrative judicial districts are grouped into four divisions, each of which represents roughly one-quarter of the state (see Figure 30-1).

Judges

The regular resident superior court judges (in January 1998 there were ninety) are nominated in nonpartisan primaries by the voters of the district in which they live. They are elected in nonpartisan elections by those same voters for eight-year terms. In addition, there are nine special superior court judges (eight of whom are appointed by the gov-

Figure 30-1
North Carolina Superior Court Districts and Divisions as of September 1, 1997

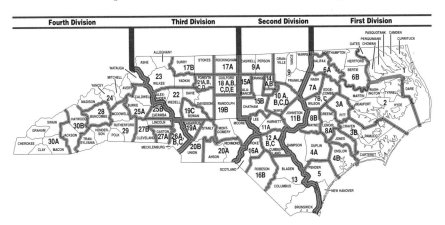

ernor, and one who serves pursuant to a legislative provision extending his original term). One of those special judges is designated by rule of the supreme court as a Special Superior Court for Complex Business Cases, and his or her caseload is composed almost exclusively of such cases assigned to him or her by the chief justice. The terms of special judges are dependent on the act of the legislature establishing the judgeship, but most are for four or five years. Special judges may reside anywhere in the state. The number of judges at a particular time is specified by the General Assembly on the basis of the volume of judicial business.

All superior court judges, whether resident judges or special judges, serve full-time, and may not practice law. Vacancies in resident judgeships are filled by appointment of the governor until the next general election.

North Carolina's constitution requires regular resident superior court judges to rotate, or "ride circuit," from one district to another within their divisions. In a rotation cycle, each regular resident judge holds court for six months in each district for each judgeship authorized for the district. Thus when a judge rotates to a district that has two, three, four, or five resident judges, the rotation period in that district is lengthened accordingly: to twelve, eighteen, twenty-four, or thirty months served in six-month segments, although those six-month segments may not be served in continuous order. Many regular resident judges thus spend months or years holding court as far as 200 miles or more away from their homes, commuting on weekends or, in some instances, establishing a second home in the district to which they are temporarily assigned. The extent to which North Carolina rotates the judges of its major trial courts is unique among the states.

Special superior court judges are assigned by the Chief Justice of the supreme court to hold court in any county where they may be needed, without regard to district of residence or rotation requirements. Theoretically, a special judge could sit in each of the 100 counties of the state over the years. In practice, special judges are usually appointed so that they come from all parts of the state; and, insofar as possible, they are assigned to counties reasonably close to their residences.

Retirement rules for superior court judges are similar to those for Appellate Division justices and judges. Those who retire before reaching the mandatory retirement age of seventy-two can become "emergency" judges and as such may be assigned by the Chief Justice to temporary service on the superior court bench until age seventy-two. A judge who is older may continue to serve temporarily as a "recalled retired" judge. The compensation and jurisdiction are the same for both kinds of temporary service. A retired judge who engages in private legal practice is not eligible for this temporary service, although many retired judges do serve as mediators or arbitrators and still serve as judges on a temporary basis.

Superior court judges may be removed by impeachment, or by the Supreme Court upon recommendation of the Judicial Standards Commission (see the section "Judicial Standards Commission," later in this chapter).

Jurisdiction

Civil

Civil jurisdiction is concurrent between the two trial divisions (superior and district) of the General Court of Justice (G.S. Ch. 7A, Art. 20, 22). The "proper" division, however, for cases that involve $10,000 or less in controversy is the District Court Division; for cases over that amount, the Superior Court Division. Normally this $10,000 dividing line is followed, but by consent of the parties and for reasons of speed or convenience, cases may be filed and tried in the "improper" division. No such case is ever "thrown out of court" for lack of jurisdiction, but on request a superior court judge may transfer it to the proper division.

Exceptions to the general rule that the amount in controversy determines the proper forum arise in certain specific subject-matter categories. For example, civil domestic relations matters (divorce and custody/support of children) are properly the business of the district court, while the superior court is the proper forum for constitutional issues, special proceedings, corporate receiverships, and reviews of certain administrative agency rulings. The clerk of superior court (rather than a superior or district court judge) handles probate of wills and appointment of guardians. Civil cases involving amounts not over $3,000 may, under certain conditions, be assigned to a magistrate for trial. (Clerks of court and magistrates are discussed later in this chapter.)

Criminal

The superior court hears cases involving felonies (serious crimes), misdemeanors (less serious crimes), and infractions (non-criminal law violations such as minor traffic cases). Misdemeanor and infraction cases must first be heard by the district court, but trials by jury of those matters, and all dispositions of felony cases, occur only in the superior court. Defendants are tried by a jury of twelve. If the charge is a felony, the process is usually begun by an indictment issued by a grand jury, composed of eighteen members. A defendant may waive the indictment process, except in capital (potential death sentence) cases. The trial by jury cannot be waived, unless the defendant chooses to dispense with trial altogether and plead guilty. Trial of misdemeanors and infractions that are appealed from district court is *de novo*—that is, the case is tried anew, without regard to the proceedings in the original trial court. About 40 percent of the superior court's criminal caseload consists of such appeals from the district court.

District Court Division

Organization

The District Court Division is divided into forty judicial districts (see Figure 30-2) (G.S. Ch. 7A, Subchapter IV). Thirty-eight of those districts are used as units for elections and for administration of the courts. Two districts (9 and 9B) are used as units of election, but are combined into a set of districts for administrative purposes. Like the superior court, the district court sits in the county seats. It may also convene in certain other cities and towns specifically authorized by the General Assembly. Most counties have no additional seats of court, but a few have several; the

Figure 30-2
North Carolina District Court and Prosecutorial Districts
as of September 1, 1997

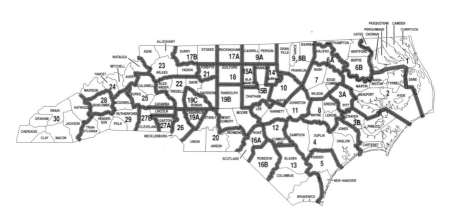

present total number is forty-one (a table in G.S. 7A-133 lists all the additional seats).

District court judges serve an entire district. Unlike judges in the superior court, they do not hold court out of their district of residence, unless specially assigned by the Chief Justice of the supreme court for a particular session of court.

Judges

District court judges, in the number authorized by the General Assembly (204 in January 1998), are elected in partisan, district elections for four-year terms. They must be lawyers, serve full-time, and may not practice law. Each district has from two to fourteen judges, depending on population and geography. Specialization by subject matter (for example, juvenile or domestic relations cases) is encouraged by law, but can be achieved to a significant degree only in those districts with several judges; in less populous counties, district court judges must be generalists.

The Chief Justice of the supreme court appoints one judge in each district as chief district judge. Their responsibilities include assigning themselves and the other judges in their districts to sessions of court, prescribing the times and places at which magistrates will discharge their duties, and assigning civil ("small claims") cases to magistrates for trial. Chief district judges are required to meet at least once a year to discuss mutual problems, make recommendations concerning improvement of the administration of justice, and promulgate a schedule of minor traffic, alcohol, boating, littering, fish, game, and parks offenses for which clerks of court and magistrates may accept guilty pleas.

Vacancies in the office of district court judge are filled by the governor for the remaining unexpired term from nominations submitted by the district bar (if submitted within four weeks after the vacancy occurs). Retirement and removal of district judges are governed by the same principles that pertain to superior court judges.

Magistrates

Magistrates for each county are appointed for two-year terms by the senior regular resident superior court judge, based on nominations of the clerk of superior court (G.S. Ch. 7A, Art. 16). Magistrates are officers of the district court and they are subject to supervision by the chief district court judge in non-discretionary judicial matters and by the clerk in clerical matters. Magistrates serve only in their county of residence, subject to special assignments. They are full-time or part-time officials, as determined by the chief district judge and the Administrative Office of the Courts (the state agency responsible for court administration), and their salaries—paid by the state—vary with their educational levels and length of service. Very few are lawyers. All magistrates appointed after July 1, 1994, must either be college graduates or must have an associate degree and four years of experience in a related field. New magistrates must also complete a two-week training course during their first two-year term.

The minimum and maximum numbers of magistrates allowed for a county are fixed by law. If the minimum quota is inadequate and if funds are available, additional ones within a maximum quota per county may be authorized by the Administrative Office of the Courts on recommendation of the chief district judge. A vacancy in the office of magistrate is filled for the remaining unexpired term in the same manner as the original appointment was made. A magistrate may be removed from office for cause, after a hearing before a superior court judge, with right of appeal to the court of appeals.

914   PART IV: FUNCTIONS INVOLVING OTHER BOARDS AND AGENCIES

Jurisdiction

Civil

As noted in the discussion of the superior court's civil jurisdiction, most jurisdiction of this type is held concurrently by the superior and district courts (G.S. Ch. 7A, Art. 20, 22). Domestic relations cases are an exception, however. They are heard in the district court regardless of the amount of money involved. When large monthly child-support awards are entered or large amounts of marital assets are distributed on divorce, a district court's orders can involve millions of dollars.

Juvenile

The district court also has jurisdiction over juvenile matters. These cases concern children under the age of eighteen (sixteen for delinquent children) who are delinquent, undisciplined, dependent, neglected, or abused. Delinquents are children who have committed acts that, if committed by adults, would be crimes or infractions. Undisciplined children are primarily those who are beyond parental control, or truant from school, or both. The dependent, neglected, and abused groups are self-explanatory. (All these categories are defined in G.S. 7A-517.)

There are really two kinds of juvenile cases: those in which children have committed an offense, an act of truancy, or something similar (delinquent and undisciplined cases); and those in which children have been, or are threatened with being, harmed, and the court is seeking to protect them (abuse, neglect, and dependency cases).

Proceedings in juvenile court are begun by petition (warrants or indictments in criminal cases, and complaints in civil cases). The hearing conducted by the judge on the petition is less formal than in other kinds of cases. Before a hearing to determine either the child's status or what disposition should be made of the case, a court counselor (juvenile probation officer) or social services official may investigate both the matter alleged in the petition and the child's background, and make findings for the judge's consideration. The judge's authority in delinquency cases ranges from placing children on probation to confining them in state institutions. In abuse, neglect, and dependency cases, the judge has wide latitude in deciding how to protect children. No juvenile cases are heard by a jury.

Involuntary Commitment

The district court has jurisdiction over the involuntary commitment of mentally ill persons, inebriated individuals, and alcoholics to mental health and alcoholic treatment facilities.

Criminal

The criminal jurisdiction of the district court is limited in felony cases. Since they must be tried or otherwise disposed of in the superior court, the district court only has the authority to conduct preliminary hearings to determine whether there is probable cause (that is, a good reason exists for believing that the defendant is probably guilty) to bind the defendant over to the superior court for trial. If all parties (and the judges) consent, a district court judge may accept a guilty plea to the two lowest levels of felonies (Classes H and I) and enter a judgment in the case. In misdemeanor and infraction cases, the district court has exclusive original jurisdiction that, with respect to very minor offenses, it shares with the magistrate.

Magistrate

The magistrate's jurisdiction is both civil and criminal. This official's authority in criminal matters is limited to the following:

- Trying worthless-check cases, or accepting guilty pleas in cases involving $2,000 or less
- Accepting guilty pleas to other minor misdemeanors for which the maximum punishment is thirty days' confinement or a $50 fine
- In cases involving minor traffic, alcohol, boating, and fish and game offenses, accepting guilty pleas and imposing a fine fixed by a uniform statewide schedule promulgated by the Conference of Chief District Judges

In addition, magistrates have the important duties of issuing arrest and search warrants and setting conditions for release on bail.

The magistrate is also authorized to try small civil claims that involve up to $3,000 in money value, including summary ejectment (landlord's action to oust a tenant) cases, on assignment of the chief district judge. The plaintiff must request that the claim be assigned to a magistrate and at least one defendant must reside in the county in which the action is filed. (If the chief district judge does not assign a small claim to a magistrate within five days after the plaintiff so requests, the claim is tried in district court as a regular civil case.)

The typical small claim is for recovery of personal property, for money for goods sold or services rendered, or for summary ejectment, and the parties are not usually represented by attorneys. Often the claim is uncontested. Simplified trial procedures are followed. The magistrate's judgment has the same effect as a judge's, and it is recorded by the clerk of superior court.

The magistrate is also authorized to perform various quasi-judicial or administrative functions. Of these, performance of the marriage ceremony is the most common; magistrates are the only judicial officials in the state who can officiate at weddings. Other authorized functions include administering oaths, verifying pleadings, and taking acknowledgments (notarizing) of instruments.

Judicial Standards Commission

The historical methods of removing judges—impeachment and joint resolution by the legislature—have not been used in North Carolina in this century (G.S. Ch. 7A, Art. 30). These procedures are still authorized by Article IV of the state constitution, but that article has also been amended to require the General Assembly to provide another procedure. In 1973 the legislature created a Judicial Standards Commission, composed of judges, lawyers, and non-lawyers. If a judge is charged with willful misconduct in office, failure to perform the duties of the office, habitual intemperance, conviction of a crime involving moral turpitude, or conduct prejudicial to the administration of justice that brings the judicial office into disrepute, the commission is authorized to conduct a public hearing to investigate that charge. If the commission decides that the evidence warrants such action, it may recommend to the supreme court that the judge be removed. The court may actually do so. The commission may also recommend removal for physical or mental incapacity, and in any case can recommend lesser sanctions, such as public censure. This procedure for disciplining, removing, and retiring judges is fairly recent, but a similar one is now used by all states.

Through January 1998 the North Carolina Supreme Court has censured sixteen district court judges for professional misconduct and has removed three from office. Two superior court judges have been removed from office and four others have been censured, and several others have vacated their offices while under investigation.

The grounds for removing a magistrate are the same as for a judge, but the removal proceeding is conducted by a superior court judge rather than by the supreme court.

Court-Related Personnel

District Attorneys

In criminal matters, the district attorney represents the state in the superior and district courts (G.S. Ch. 7A, Art. 9). This official is elected in partisan, district elections for a four-year term. In each prosecutorial district, full-time assistant district attorneys, paid by the state, serve at the district attorney's pleasure. The state also provides part-time assistant district attorneys and compensates them at a daily rate in those districts where, because of case load or geography, they are needed. With one exception, the prosecutorial district lines are identical to the district court lines.

A district attorney may be removed from office for misconduct after a hearing before a superior court judge.

Clerks of Superior Court

The clerk of superior court is elected in partisan, county elections for a four-year term (G.S. Ch. 7A, Art. 12). Unlike trial and appellate judges, clerks need not be lawyers, and relatively few are. Paid by the state on the basis of the county's population and his or her years of service, the clerk is responsible for all clerical and record-keeping functions of the superior and district courts for both civil and criminal cases. Thus in each county there is only one clerk's office for the two trial courts.

The clerk is also *ex officio* judge of probate and is thus the first to hear matters relating to the probate of wills and the administration of decedents' estates. In addition, the clerk has jurisdiction over the estates of minors and incompetents, and is authorized to hear a variety of special proceedings, such as adoptions, condemnation of private lands for public use, and sales of land for partition or to create cash assets. Depending on the volume of business, the clerk employs a number of assistants and deputies, who are paid by the state in accordance with a schedule fixed by the General Assembly [see G.S. 7A-102(c)].

The clerk's books and accounts are subject to annual audit by the state auditor, and the clerk is bonded by a blanket state bond. The senior regular resident superior court judge who serves the clerk's county may, after a hearing, remove a clerk for misconduct or mental or physical incompetence.

Court Reporters

Court reporters are appointed for the superior court by the senior regular resident superior court judge in each judicial district. Compensation is set by the appointing judge, within limits fixed by the Administrative Office of the Courts. Reporters are required to record verbatim such courtroom proceedings as testimony of witnesses and orders, judgments, and jury instructions by the judge. Transcripts of courtroom proceedings are required when an appeal is taken, and reporters receive a per-page fee in addition to their salaries for preparing transcripts for appellants. The reporter's original notes are state property and are preserved by the clerk of superior court.

If a reporter is not available, the state will furnish electronic recording equipment on request of the senior regular resident superior court judge. The clerk of superior court is responsible for operating such equipment and for preserving the record produced, and the Administrative Office of the Courts is responsible for transcribing the record if that becomes necessary. In several counties, video recordings of proceedings are used instead of court reporters.

All recording of civil and juvenile proceedings in district court is by audio recording equipment. There is no verbatim record kept of district court criminal proceedings, since they may be appealed for a trial *de novo* (anew) in superior court where such a record is kept. In 1995, the General Assembly eliminated all court reporter positions assigned to the district courts.

Juvenile Court Counselors

A statewide system of court counselors provides probation and after-care services to juveniles in the jurisdiction of the district court (G.S. Ch. 7A, Art. 24). Each judicial district is assigned one or more counselors. In addition to acting as probation officers, they conduct prehearing studies of children alleged to be delinquent or undisciplined. This program, called intake counseling, attempts to direct the handling of juveniles from the courts to appropriate community-based agencies in those situations in which it is possible to do so. Counselors also help the court handle cases in which children require detention before or after a hearing.

Office space for court counselors is provided by the county.

Probation and Parole Officers

North Carolina also has a statewide system of adult probation and parole officers (G.S. Ch. 15, Art. 20). These officers, who supervise adults placed on probation or released on parole, are employees of the state Department of Correction. Their salaries and operating costs are paid by the state, but office space for local offices must be furnished by the county.

Guardians *Ad Litem*

In child abuse, neglect, and dependency cases, the parents are entitled to the services of an attorney and the department of social services represents the state's interest. In 1983, the General Assembly recognized the need for the children affected to have the benefit of an advocate who represents only their interests. In establishing a statewide program to meet that need, the legislature utilized the results of some privately funded pilot programs that provided that service with volunteer guardians *ad litem*, who were themselves supported by an attorney and a volunteer coordinator (G.S. Ch. 7A, Art. 39). That program is now in place statewide and provides representation to children who are abused, dependent, or neglected. In doing so, it recognizes that while social services departments are seeking the best interests of children in their representation to the courts, the issues involved are so important and difficult that judges would benefit from having another perspective that is independent of the agency that has to implement the court's decision. In some districts (usually smaller rural ones), the program does not use volunteers, but instead contracts with lawyers who are interested in juvenile law to provide these services. In the majority of districts, the program is run by coordinators, who recruit volunteers to work with the children; and, in cases in which lawyers are needed in court, hire them.

The county is responsible for providing office space for the coordinator and any other employees of the guardian *ad litem* program.

Community Service Coordinators

In some criminal cases, judges require convicted defendants to perform community service work for public or non-profit agencies. The state Department of Crime Control and Public Safety is responsible for administering this program; it assigns a community service coordinator and a supporting staff to each judicial district (G.S. 20-179.4; 143B-475.1). These persons are state employees, but their office space must be provided by the county.

Representation of Indigents/Public Defenders

Defendants who are accused of crimes for which confinement is likely and who are financially unable to employ counsel to represent them are entitled to such services at state expense (G.S. Ch. 7A, Subchapter IX). In seven judicial districts (including District 3A—Pitt; District 3B—Carteret County only; District 12—Cumberland and Hoke counties; District 15-B—Orange and Chatham counties; District 18—Guilford County; District 26—Mecklenburg County; District 27-A—Gaston County; and District 28—Buncombe County), most of those who are indigent are represented by the public defender's office, a staff of full-time, state-paid attorneys whose sole function is to represent indigents.

Indigents who are not handled by the public defender's office in these counties are assigned to private attorneys, whose fees are paid by the state on a per-case or per-day basis; they are used when the public defender has a conflict of interest or an overload of cases. In districts not served by a public defender, legal representation of indigents is provided solely by state-paid private attorneys.

Each public defender is appointed by the senior resident superior court judge in the judicial district on the written nomination of the district bar. Public defenders serve four-year terms and select their own attorney-assistants. The county must provide office space for the public defender staff.

Since this system began, cost studies have suggested that it would be more cost-effective than the assigned-counsel system in several other urban districts where it is not currently being used. In recent years, however, the General Assembly has created new public defenders' offices only upon a request of local legislative delegations. Because rural districts have greater travel times and fewer cases per county, the defender system is not as likely to be as cost-effective in them as in urban areas.

Additionally, there is an appellate defender's office. Its function is to provide representation for indigents whose cases are appealed, when it is appointed to do so by the trial judge. It is a relatively small office and handles comparatively few cases, but they are usually among the most difficult. The appellate defender is appointed by the Chief Justice.

The costs of indigent representation (public defenders, appellate defenders, and privately assigned counsel) in fiscal year 1996–97 were $45,218,877—or around 14 percent of all Judicial Department expenditures. Defendants are often ordered to repay the state for their lawyers' fees, in one of three ways—as a condition of probation, in lieu of any future state tax refunds, or as a civil money judgment. Even though most defendants never become financially able to pay the entire amount of their fees, each year the state does recover about 10 percent of its costs.

Selection of Jurors

The law provides for selection of prospective jurors in each county by a jury commission (G.S. Ch. 9). Each commission draws from the Division of Motor Vehicles' driver's license list and the voter-registration list for that county in compiling jury lists. Selection is by a random process, with no opportunity for favoritism or discrimination because of race, sex, or any other constitutionally prohibited reason. No one is exempt from jury duty; all qualified citizens, if summoned, are expected to serve. (Inability to hear or understand English, physical or mental incompetence, or conviction of a felony are common grounds for disqualification.) Excuses can be granted only by a trial judge, or, if the responsibility is delegated by the chief district court judge, by a trial court administrator (a non-judicial official in certain counties whose function is to expedite the work of the courts in that county)—and then only for reasons of compelling personal hardship or because service would be contrary to the public health, safety, or welfare.

Some counties use computers in putting together the master jury list and in keeping records of those who have already served. When more than one jury session of court is sitting at a time, jurors may be "pooled" (jurors for more than one court session are selected from the same panel); this is done in the interest of saving both money and jurors' time.

Prospective jurors who are not selected for grand jury service usually serve only one week. In some counties (typically the more urban counties), instead of week-long service, jurors serve for only one trial or one day, whichever is longer. A certain number of jurors (generally nine each six months) are selected to serve on the grand jury. These jurors (whose main duty is to decide whether to charge persons accused of felonies by indicting them) usually serve for a year (six months in some large counties), but are usually "on duty" for no more than the first day of a session of superior court for the trial of criminal cases. Where criminal sessions occur weekly, the grand jury is not needed each week but is convened every few weeks.

The superior court uses a twelve-person jury in both civil and criminal cases. The district court uses the same-sized jury in civil cases only; criminal cases are tried by the judge without a jury.

Administrative Office of the Courts

The Administrative Office of the Courts, with its central office in Raleigh, handles the administrative details of the court system (G.S. Ch. 7A, Art. 29). Its director is appointed by the Chief Justice of the supreme court. The director is a non-judicial officer, responsible for a variety of administrative functions of the Judicial Department. The major duties include preparing the Judicial Department's budget; fixing the number of employees in the respective clerks of court's offices; supervising a statewide system of court counselors; prescribing uniform forms, records, and business methods for the clerks' offices; keeping statistics; and helping the Chief Justice in assigning superior court judges and the supreme court in scheduling sessions of superior court.

The Judicial Department budget for fiscal year 1997–98 was approximately $334,000,000. Less than half of this amount is offset annually by court costs and fees that accrue to the state.

Allocation of Financial Responsibility for the Court System

All operating expenses of the Judicial Department are borne by the state (G.S. Ch. 7A, Subchapter VI). These include salaries and travel expenses of all judges, district attorneys, clerks and their assistants, magistrates, court counselors, court reporters, public defenders, and guardians *ad litem.* Also included are the books, supplies, records, and equipment in all these officials' offices, and the fees of all jurors and witnesses for whom the government is responsible. This is a direct result of court reform efforts in the 1950s and 60s. Before court reform, salaries and other operating expenses for most trial court officials (clerks, lower court judges, justices of the peace, and so forth) were the responsibility of local governments. Correspondingly, most fees collected went to local governments or directly to court officials as their compensation. The current arrangement reflects the fundamental policy decisions made during this court reform effort that all court officials should have the same duties and be paid the same salaries. As a result, citizens should receive roughly the same services from the courts wherever they live.

After the court reform of the 1960s, the primary responsibilities counties (and a few cities) retain for the court system is to provide "adequate" physical facilities for the courts. The most obvious such facilities are courtrooms, but this duty also extends to the need for office and storage facilities, parking, and so forth for judges, the clerk of superior court and the clerk's staff, district attorneys, and magistrates. In addition, most of the ancillary personnel listed in this chapter are entitled to county office space, either by specific statute or because they are part of the court system. The obligation to provide facilities includes the responsibility for furniture (but not equipment) and the cleaning and maintenance of the courthouse.

Questions often arise about whether particular expenses should be covered by the county or by the state. Often the issue is whether a particular item is an operating expense or part of a facility. What is the cable to connect the state's mainframe computer to the courthouse? (probably equipment). What about cable inside the courthouse? (generally thought to be part of the courthouse infrastructure, and thus facilities). Is a sound system for use in courtrooms an operating expense or part of the facility? (an infrastructure item, and thus part of the facility). What about court security equipment like metal detectors? (security is the sheriff's responsibility, and if the equipment is permanent, is part of the infrastructure). Sometimes the line is clear—furniture, drapes, and fixtures are part of the facility, and computers and specialized court equipment are operating expenses. But often the distinction is not clear, and is usually resolved through negotiation.

Sometimes the issue is a different one—is the facility or the furnishing of the facility "adequate"? In such cases, the initial determination is made by the county when it allocates and maintains the space allocated to the courts, pursuant to its general authority to control the use of its property. When court officials or users question the adequacy, they almost always do so informally, and usually the issue can be settled there. But if court officials or users of the courts believe that the county's decision about allocation of facilities does not result in "adequate" facilities, the North Carolina Supreme Court has indicated that it is possible for the county to be sued to force it to provide adequate facilities. If that litigation results in a decision that a complained-of facility is inadequate, the court may order the county to provide an adequate facility. The county generally has the discretion to decide how to remedy the inadequacy. If it fails to take action, or if its action is found to be inadequate, the court could then hold the appropriate officials in contempt of court, although as of January 1998, no case had ever reached that stage. Negotiated settlements are almost always reached before that stage of litigation results.

If the facility is a municipal district court, the same process described previously for counties would be applicable, but the courts have additional options for dealing with the issue. The statutes authorize the director of the Administrative Office of the Courts to forbid the use of a municipal facility if he or she determines it to be inadequate (GS 7A-302). Additionally, a chief district court judge may simply direct that no cases be scheduled in a municipal facility if he or she finds it to be inadequate.

A "facilities fee" is collected in each court case as part of the court costs paid by the litigants. This fee is distributed to the counties (and a proportionate share goes to municipalities for the cases heard in municipally-owned district court facilities) and must be spent exclusively for providing, maintaining, and constructing court facilities for court officials and court-related personnel, as well as for some related functions. Court-related personnel are generally thought to be the other employees administratively housed in the Judicial Department, such as juvenile court counselors, trial court administrators, custody mediation personnel, and so on. Those other related functions, as listed in G.S. 7A-304, include jail and juvenile detention facilities, free parking for jurors, and a law library, including books. Sometimes court officials or others ask for an accounting of the use of the facilities fee, and under the public records law, they are entitled to that information. When the state assumed the costs of operating the trial courts in the 1960s, this fee was preserved as a local government source of revenue to help offset the continuing costs retained by the county for court operations. It is rarely sufficient to cover the entire cost of operating a court facility, and almost never can support the cost of construction of facilities. In 1996–97, the facilities fee collections paid to counties totaled over $11 million.

Uniform Costs and Fees

The system the state uses for billing court costs and fees is based on a lump-sum averaging of costs (per type of case and court) (G.S. Ch. 7A, Art. 28). In civil actions, special proceedings, and administration of estates, there are only two cost items: a General Court of Justice fee (ranging from $28 to $55 in 1998, depending on the court hearing the matter), which accrues to the state for financing the courts generally; and a facilities fee, discussed previously. The amount of the fee in each case may vary with the nature of the action or proceeding and with the court in which it is tried. Over time, the amount of total fees collected amounts to about one-third of the cost of operating the courts, and reflects the policy decision (often debated by the legislature) that courts, like most other governmental functions, should not be supported solely by user fees.

In criminal actions, there are four items in the uniform bill of costs. In addition to the General Court of Justice fee (ranging from $61 to $68 in 1998) and the facilities fee (ranging from $6 to $24 in 1998), a law enforcement officers' fee of $5 is chargeable for each arrest or personal service of criminal process; it is payable to the county or city whose officer performed the service. (Fees for arrests made by state officials accrue to the county where the arrest was made.) The fourth item is a Law Enforcement Officers' Benefit and Retirement Fund fee of $8.

Besides these four basic costs items, in any particular case additional expenses—such as fees of witnesses, charges for those who fail to appear, court-appointed guardians, referees, interpreters, or commissioners—may be incurred. These charges are assessed against the party that is liable for them along with the basic costs.

Witness fees are fixed at $5 per day, plus mileage if the witness comes from outside the county; juror fees—paid by the state—are generally set at $12 per day, with no mileage allowance. A charge for the miscellaneous services rendered by magistrates and clerks is also authorized, and the charges assessed by the sheriff for serving civil process (legal documents in civil cases) and for related costs are lumped into five all-inclusive, uniform categories. No charges of any kind other than those specified in the law may be imposed for the use of court-related facilities and services. All costs charged by clerks, magistrates, and sheriffs accrue to the governmental unit concerned; none accrue to individuals. The only fees assessed by court employees which accrue to the person assessing the fee are transcript fees collected by court reporters.

In all 100 counties during fiscal year 1996–97, facilities fees totaled $11,233,624, with an additional $456,598 paid to municipalities; officers' arrest fees totaled $6,088,599 ($1,915,441 to municipalities); jail fees (paid to counties by prisoners awaiting trial if they are convicted) totaled $1,675,595 ($2,250 to municipalities); and impaired driving driver's-license civil revocation fees (paid by persons whose driving privileges were revoked upon being charged with driving while impaired) totaled $1,178,461.

Fines, Penalties, and Forfeitures

Fines, penalties, and forfeitures are to be distinguished from costs and fees. A fine is the monetary penalty imposed by the sentencing judge as part or all of the punishment when a defendant is convicted of a crime. Penalties include the monetary penalty ordered for commission of an infraction (the most common infractions are minor traffic violations). A forfeiture occurs when a defendant, at liberty under bond, fails to meet the conditions it specifies (usually a court appearance), and the bond is forfeited. Forfeitures also may be vehicles, seized and sold when driven by persons convicted of alcohol, impaired driving, or drug offenses. Fines, infraction penalties, and forfeitures, by state constitutional mandate (Article IX, Section 7), accrue to the public schools in the county involved, and may not be used for any other purpose. In fiscal year 1996–97, fines, penalties, and forfeitures throughout the state totaled $55,631,503.

Additional Resources

Annual Reports of the Administrative Office of the Courts.

Brannon, Joan. *The Judicial System in North Carolina.* North Carolina Administrative Office of the Courts, 1998.

Brannon, Joan, et al. "Law Enforcement, Courts and Corrections." Chapter 6 of *State and Local Government Relations in North Carolina*, Charles Liner, ed. Chapel Hill, N.C.: Institute of Government, The University of North Carolina at Chapel Hill, 1995.

Rothman, David B., et al. *State Court Organization 1993.* United States Department of Justice, Bureau of Justice Statistics. Washington, D.C.: USGPO, 1995.

"Without Favor, Denial, or Delay: A Court System for the 21st Century." Report of the Commission for the Future of Justice and the Courts in North Carolina. December 1996.

31 The Criminal Justice System: Sheriff, Jails and Corrections, and the Medical Examiner

Joan G. Brannon, Stevens H. Clarke, Anne M. Dellinger, and Robert L. Farb

Contents

Joan G. Brannon is an Institute of Government faculty member whose interests include sheriffs' civil process duties, small claims law and procedure for magistrates, and civil matters affecting the clerks of superior court.

Stevens H. Clarke is an Institute of Government faculty member whose work includes the law of sentencing, probation, and parole, as well as research on crime and crime prevention programs.

Anne M. Dellinger is an Institute of Government faculty member whose interests include legal aspects of public hospitals and public health.

Robert L. Farb is an Institute of Government faculty member whose specialization is criminal law and procedure.

The office of sheriff is one of the oldest offices known to the common law system of jurisprudence. It has been in existence in England since the Norman Conquest and has been an office in North Carolina since its very founding. The term "sheriff" evolved from the Saxon word "Scyre" meaning shire and the word "Reve" meaning keeper.[1] Today the sheriff is a constitutional officer, which means that the office is named in the North Carolina Constitution (N.C. CONST. ART. VII, Sec. 2) and its duties are not enumerated in the General Statutes but are those that existed at common law.

The Sheriff and County Law Enforcement

One principal means by which government influences citizen behavior is by enacting and enforcing criminal law. Other ways include subjecting those who violate laws to a civil penalty (similar to a fine in a criminal case but collectible only by a civil suit), or giving others a right to sue those who act in a manner they are not supposed to (for example, negligently causing an automobile accident).

The criminal law has historically been reserved largely for use against behavior that carries a moral stigma, although some violations of merely regulatory provisions now appear in criminal statutes. For example, although the General Assembly changed most traffic misdemeanors to non-criminal infractions, some regulatory types of traffic violations, such as driving without proper registration, are still treated as misdemeanors. Thus not everything called a *crime* carries the possibility of social disgrace and the loss of personal freedom for the offender.

As a practical matter, the use of the criminal law as a means of regulating behavior is distinguished from civil remedies by the various special procedures defendants can claim before any criminal sanction can be imposed on them. These include provision of counsel to indigent defendants, trial by jury, a heavy burden of proof on the state, and so on.

The apparatus for enforcing criminal law in the United States has three main components. Law enforcement agencies comprise the first component: sheriffs, police departments, and others who investigate reported crimes and undertake to apprehend those believed to have committed them. The courts—charged with determining whether arrested people are guilty as charged and then, if they are convicted, pronouncing the punishment to be imposed on them—make up the second component. The third component is composed of correctional agencies, which execute whatever sentence the court has imposed on a convicted defendant.

This apparatus, commonly referred to collectively as the criminal justice system, is intended to serve several purposes. First, it makes defendants "pay for their crimes"—that is, it permits society to exact some kind of retribution from offenders for their offenses. Second, it aims to prevent further crimes through deterrence—persuading potential criminals not to commit crime by apprehending and convicting offenders—and through the reinforcement of citizens' notions of right and wrong. A third goal is the rehabilitation of convicted criminals—that is, treating convicted criminals in such a way that they will be less likely to commit further criminal acts in the future. A fourth objective of the system is to put offenders out of harm's way; convicted offenders who might otherwise repeat their criminal activities may be locked up or supervised so closely that they are unable to do so.

The county's principal roles in criminal justice are to do the following:

- Investigate crimes and apprehend criminals (traditional activities of sheriffs' and police departments)
- Provide custody or control of arrested defendants during the interval between the arrest and trial
- Incarcerate convicted defendants who are serving short active sentences

The county also has other minor responsibilities with respect to most other parts of the criminal justice system.

Sheriffs, Policing, and Law Enforcement

General Information

County government's involvement with the criminal justice system has traditionally focused on law enforcement which is carried out through the sheriff's department, or occasionally, through a county police department. Although a law enforcement agency's work is usually thought to consist mainly of investigating crimes and apprehending offenders, most officers spend a majority of their time on matters that are not intended to lead to an arrest, and often are not even associated with crimes. For example, deputy sheriffs are expected to intervene in domestic fights, disperse trouble-making youths, subdue and transport those who are dangerous and mentally ill, and help in emergencies around citizens' homes. They may also spend a great deal of time serving civil process (court documents associated with non-criminal legal proceedings) on individuals and organizations. Despite these activities, however, investigating crimes and arresting suspects is the deputy's or officer's basic and most widely recognized job duty.

Specific demands of the law shape the activities of a sheriff's department or county police department. Not only are officers limited in their enforcement role to focusing on activities that are precisely defined as illegal, but the methods they may use to detect offenses are also closely regulated by both federal and state constitutions and laws. Thus an activity that is generally regarded as undesirable may sometimes be beyond the law enforcement agency's reach because the law does not make that activity a crime. Or an agency may be unable to make an arrest for a crime that "everybody knows" is happening because there is no lawful way to obtain evidence that would justify the arrest.

Local Law Enforcement Organization

In most North Carolina counties, sheriffs are the principal law enforcement officers. The state constitution requires each county to have a sheriff who is elected to a four-year term (N.C. CONST. ART. VII, Sec. 2). Although sheriffs have jurisdiction to enforce the criminal law throughout their counties, as a practical matter, they generally confine their activities to territory outside the boundaries of municipalities that have their own police departments. Sheriffs are charged with general enforcement of the criminal law and have general legal powers of arrest, search, and seizure.

County police departments have been established in Gaston and Mecklenburg counties by local acts of the legislature, although the Mecklenburg County Police Department has since merged with the Charlotte Police Department to form the Charlotte-Mecklenburg Police Department. Officers of county police departments have the same powers as sheriffs and their deputies; they assume much of the general responsibility for enforcing the criminal law traditionally associated with the sheriff. In counties that establish police departments, responsibility for executing court-issued civil process remains with the sheriff.

Under G.S. 160A-288, counties may also seek cooperative arrangements with other jurisdictions for the shared use of law enforcement officers. That statute permits city and county law enforcement agencies to assist each other, on written request from the head of one local law enforcement agency to the head of another. The assistance may involve lending officers, equipment, or supplies. The governing body of the lending agency must adopt guidelines under which any loaned officers are used. If a county considers this type of arrangement, the commissioners should be careful to resolve issues of insurance coverage and the like before the agreement is completed.

G.S. 160A-288.2 permits city and county law enforcement agencies to assist state law enforcement agencies in a manner similar to that described earlier. Also, G.S. 160A-288.1 allows the governor, on request of a city or county, to assign state law enforcement officers temporarily to a locality in an emergency.

State Involvement in Local Law Enforcement

Education and Training

Although the state generally exercises little control over local law enforcement operations (except by legislative enactment of criminal laws themselves), it does try to control the quantity and quality of training that local officers undergo. The North Carolina Sheriffs' Education and Training Commission sets minimum entry-level education and training standards for deputy sheriffs and county jailers. (The commission has seventeen members, at least twelve of whom are sheriffs. The attorney general provides staff assistance to the commission through the Sheriffs' Training and Standards Section of the North Carolina Department of Justice.) Deputies may be appointed on a probationary basis without completing the required training program, but they must complete the program within a year of the date of taking their oath of office.

To meet the training needs of their law enforcement officers, counties may take advantage of certain state-provided criminal justice educational programs. These programs are offered through the North Carolina Justice Academy (an agency of the Department of Justice), in Salemburg and Edneyville; the Department of Community Colleges; and the Institute of Government.

General Law Enforcement Assistance

Certain state-level agencies are in a position to aid a county's law enforcement effort. The State Bureau of Investigation (SBI) investigates crimes and has specialized equipment and facilities for scientific analysis of evidence. In most cases, the SBI investigates or assists in investigating a crime only when specifically requested to do so by the local enforcement agency with jurisdiction over the case.

The state Department of Crime Control and Public Safety can also help local law enforcement. Its Division of Victim and Justice Services provides technical assistance to local agencies on request. The Governor's Crime Commission is also within that department, and includes local law enforcement executives and public officials. It is the primary planning arm of the state executive branch for the criminal justice system.

The state also plays a part in returning defendants from outside North Carolina. Article 37 of Chapter 15A of the General Statutes authorizes the governor to extradite defendants and have them returned to the county in which they are charged, on application by the district attorney representing that county. The state pays the costs of extraditing defendants who are charged with a felony; the county does so if they are charged with a misdemeanor. (Local law enforcement officers may be sent to pick up a defendant in either case.)

Finally, the state provides assistance through its medical examiner program, discussed in greater detail later under the heading, "Medical Examiners."

The Sheriff and the Civil Justice System

Although most citizens think of the sheriff as the chief law enforcement officer of the county, the sheriff has always had other substantial duties. The sheriff is responsible for operating the jail, maintaining security in the courtroom and acting as the bailiff in court, and serving civil process. This section of the chapter explains the sheriff's role in serving civil process. Civil process is a term that covers the service of pleadings, motions, orders, and other papers on parties in civil cases, and the service of orders to enforce judgments entered by the courts. In North Carolina for the most part only the sheriff and the sheriff's deputies may perform civil process duties; other law enforcement officers are not given that authority, and only in limited situations are private process servers allowed to serve civil process. Serving civil process requires a significant commitment of the time and resources of the sheriff's department. Each order must be carried out in strict compliance with the law, otherwise a deputy subjects the sheriff to liability.

Procedures for Serving Civil Process

The sheriff must use due diligence in carrying out any civil process properly given to the sheriff for service. The difficulty in serving process depends sometimes on the kind of process to be served, and at other times on the behavior of the person to be served. It is instructive to list the most frequently issued types of process and what each process requires for proper service.

Summons

To initiate a civil lawsuit, the party bringing the lawsuit (the plaintiff) must file a complaint with the clerk of superior court. The complaint indicates who is being sued (the defendant), why that person is being sued, and for what. The clerk then issues a summons, which is a court process that indicates what steps the defendant must take in response to the complaint. G.S. 1A-1, Rule 4 specifies how the sheriff must serve the summons. It allows the plaintiff to serve the summons by certified mail or to have the sheriff serve it. For an individual defendant, the sheriff or deputy sheriff must find the defendant and give a copy of the documents to the defendant personally, or must leave copies at the defendant's dwelling with a person of suitable age and discretion who resides with the defendant. If the defendant is a corporation, the sheriff must give a copy to the registered agent of the corporation, to an officer of the corporation, or must leave a copy at the office of an officer of the corporation with a person apparently in charge. For government units, other legal entities, or persons with special disabilities, the statute specifies how service must be accomplished. Service of the process puts the defendant on notice that he or she is being sued and gives the court jurisdiction over the defendant. Without proper service of the summons, the court cannot proceed in the case.

In 1995–96, 513,543 civil actions (including special proceedings, juvenile actions, and small claims) were filed in North Carolina, many of which had more than one defendant. Although in some cases the defendant was served by certified mail, in the great majority of them a deputy sheriff had to make at least one visit to the defendant's dwelling or business to try to serve the process. In some instances a deputy might have to make numerous attempts to try to locate the defendant.

Subpoenas

Another very common process that the sheriff must serve is a subpoena—an order from the court requiring a person to appear at a court proceeding to testify or to bring documents to the proceeding. In some cases, the attorney for the party will serve the subpoenas in the case; frequently, however, the party seeking to subpoena a person will give the subpoena to the sheriff for service. If the subpoena requires a person to testify, the sheriff may give a copy to the person personally, or may tell the person about the subpoena by telephone. Most departments try to serve the subpoena by telephone, because it is less costly and time-consuming. Also, because the sheriff may designate someone other than a deputy to serve subpoenas by telephone, in many departments an office secretary serves the subpoenas by telephone rather than using the deputy's time. The sheriff or deputy must serve a subpoena to produce documents by delivery of a copy to the person named in the subpoena.

Other Orders, Motions, and Notices

In addition to serving summonses and subpoenas, there are numerous orders that the sheriff must serve. Examples include child support orders, child custody orders, domestic violence civil protective orders, notices of hearings, various motions, and involuntary commitment custody orders. In most of these cases, the sheriff must deliver a copy of the order or notice to the person. However, sometimes the sheriff's duties are more significant. A child custody order might require the sheriff to take a child from one parent and deliver the child to the other parent, while an involuntary commitment custody order requires the sheriff to take a mentally ill person into custody and transport the person to a local physician for an evaluation and then to a state psychiatric hospital for a second evaluation.

Serving Writs

The sheriff also must serve orders (called *writs*) commanding the sheriff to enforce judgments entered in the civil courts of North Carolina. Most writs are issued after a judgment is entered, but sometimes enforcement is ordered before the judgment is entered and these are called *prejudgment remedies*.

Executions and Attachments

The most common enforcement order that the sheriff must serve is a *writ of execution*. If a civil judgment orders the defendant to pay money to the plaintiff and the defendant does not comply with the judgment, the clerk issues a writ of execution directing the sheriff to seize a sufficient amount of the defendant's property to satisfy the judgment. The sheriff must discover what real and personal property the defendant owns in the sheriff's county, locate that property, seize it, and then, after advertisement, offer it for sale at a public auction. Obviously, this is a very complicated and time-consuming process.

In some situations the clerk will issue a *writ of attachment*, which is similar to a writ of execution except that it is issued after a lawsuit has been filed but before a judgment is entered. It orders the sheriff to seize the defendant's property and store it until the case is tried and a judgment is rendered.

Writs of Possession for Personal Property and Claim and Delivery Orders of Seizure

Sometimes a judgment orders the defendant to turn over specific personal property to the plaintiff; for example, a living room suite of furniture, motor vehicle, or mobile home. In that situation the clerk issues a *writ of possession for personal property* requiring the sheriff to locate the personal property, take it from the defendant, and turn it over to the plaintiff. The clerk may enter a similar order, called a *claim and delivery order of seizure*, before a judgment is entered. In that case the sheriff is ordered to seize the property, hold it for three days to give the defendant the opportunity to reclaim it, and then turn it over to the plaintiff.

Writs of Possession for Real Property

The clerk issues a *writ of possession for real property* to enforce a judgment that orders the defendant to give possession of real property (land and anything permanently attached to it) to the plaintiff. The most prevalent reason for issuing this writ is when a landlord has received a judgment evicting the tenant from the landlord's premises. The writ requires the sheriff to remove the defendant from and put the plaintiff in possession of the premises. The sheriff must notify the defendant when the eviction will occur, must remove the tenant and other persons from the premises, and must either remove the tenant's personal property and store it in a warehouse, or at the plaintiff's request, leave the tenant's property on the premises and padlock the premises.

Department Procedures for Delivering Services

There are three models for how departments are organized to discharge the civil process duties of the office. One organizational framework, found most often in counties with small populations, has the patrol deputies performing both criminal and civil functions. Patrol deputies serve all civil processes, as well as handle law enforcement responsibilities. A second model, found primarily in the most populous counties, separates criminal and civil duties by setting up a special civil process division. The deputies in the civil division serve all civil processes. Under the third—and probably most prevalent model in North Carolina—road deputies serve civil summonses and notices in addition to their regular law enforcement responsibilities, and one or more civil deputies serve writs that are more complicated and require the officer to seize property, sell property, or remove the defendant from property.

Collection of Fees and Costs

The sheriff does recoup some of the costs of carrying out these civil duties through fees imposed by G.S. 7A-311. The sheriff receives $5 for each item of civil process served, in other words, for each summons served on a defendant, each subpoena served, each notice, motion, order, or writ served on a party. The civil process service fee must be paid in advance by the party seeking the service. Although no statewide information is available on the amount collected, in 1996 there were 513,543 civil filings in the state and in most of those cases at least one $5 service fee was paid; however, that amount does not reflect fees for service of subpoenas, motions, orders, and writs.

When a sheriff enforces a civil judgment, the statute provides that the sheriff is entitled to collect all expenses of carrying out the writ. Many sheriffs demand that the expenses be paid in advance by the plaintiff before the sheriff will carry out the writ in order to avoid the possibility that the sheriff's office will be responsible for paying expenses of seizing, selling, or storing property when the property does not sell for a sufficient amount to recoup the costs. For example, a sheriff will not do the following:

1. Seize a motor vehicle until the plaintiff pays the costs of towing the vehicle and storing it until sale
2. Levy on real property until the plaintiff pays the expenses of advertising the sale in the newspaper
3. Evict a tenant until the landlord pays the costs of removing the tenant's property and storing it for one month

When carrying out a writ of execution, the sheriff also receives a commission of 5 percent on the first five hundred dollars of the money collected or property sold, and $2\frac{1}{2}$ percent on all sums over five hundred dollars. Again, there are no data on the amount that is collected by sheriffs under this provision.

All of the fees and commissions collected by the sheriff must be remitted to the county fund; the sheriff is not entitled to keep any of these funds.

Department Costs of Civil Functions

Data from one county that attempted to determine its 1996 costs of performing its civil duties are informative. This department has 140 employees and a total budget of $6,537,795. Twenty positions (14.29 percent) are allocated to serving civil process. The department processed 40,952 civil papers for the year; 14,452 were ejectment summons (which can be posted), and 3,908 were writs of possession for real property (which must be carried out within seven days and require a great deal of effort). The costs (personnel and operations costs and capital outlay) for carrying out civil duties was $927,159 (14.18 percent) of the total departmental budget.

As mentioned previously, the county receives some revenue for carrying out civil process—$5 for each process served, and a commission on money collected under writs of execution. The county collected $215,500 from these fees, which means that the county general fund had to support $711,659 (76.76 percent) of the costs. The department determined that the cost of serving civil process was $22.64 per process. This figure was derived by dividing the total personnel costs by the number of processes served. The county also attempted to come up with a figure that would indicate the true costs to the county based on the assumption that it takes deputies an average of three attempts to serve process.

Not surprisingly, the analysis by this one county indicates that the costs to the county of serving civil process are significant and that the county recovers only a small portion of the costs through fees from the parties seeking the service.

County Jails

Responsibility

Counties are responsible for providing jails, also known as local confinement facilities, for the incarceration of criminal defendants awaiting trial and for convicted offenders serving short sentences. County jails should not be confused with state prisons, operated by the Department of Correction (DOC), which house offenders serving longer sentences.

State laws require commitment of arrested criminal defendants to jail if they fail to meet conditions of pretrial release, and also require or allow convicted offenders to be sentenced to jail under certain circumstances (G.S. 15-6, 15A-521, 15A-1352). No law actually says that counties must provide or arrange for jail space, but the obligation is strongly implied from a multitude of statutes. Some counties allow some space in their jails to be used to house prisoners from the state prison system or from other jurisdictions such as the federal court system, under contracts that reimburse the counties for their costs. If a jail is filled to capacity or cannot handle prisoners who have unusual needs or present security risks that the jail cannot control, the jail administrator can apply to a judge for an order transferring prisoners to another jail within the judicial district or to state prison [G.S. 148-32.1(b),

162-38, 162-39]. If the county's prisoner is transferred to state prison, the county must pay the DOC for the cost of maintaining its prisoner, including any extraordinary medical care.

Responsibility for the operation of county jails is divided among the board of county commissioners, the sheriff, the courts, and state government. The commissioners build, maintain, and pay for the jail (G.S. 153A-218), and the sheriff administers it (G.S. 162-22), often by appointing a jail administrator who reports to the sheriff. Two or more counties or other units of local government may jointly operate a district jail (G.S. 153A-219), as do Camden, Pasquotank, and Perquimans counties. The courts control admissions to and releases from the jail by setting conditions of pretrial release for arrested defendants and by sentencing convicted offenders.

The DOC reimburses counties at the rate of $18 per day toward the cost of housing prisoners serving sentences in their jails for terms of thirty days or more, as well as their medical costs (G.S. 148-32.1). Also, if a convicted offender is held for more than five days in jail awaiting transportation to state prison to serve a prison sentence, beginning on the sixth day of such confinement the DOC must reimburse the county at a rate set by the General Assembly, currently set at $40 per day (G.S. 148-29), and pay the offender's medical costs as well. These payments by the DOC do not cover the full cost of housing the inmates, which a 1994 North Carolina Sheriffs' Association survey estimated at $50 per day per bed, including operation, construction, and equipment. More importantly, DOC reimbursement does not cover the great majority of jail prisoners who either are unsentenced awaiting trial or are serving terms of less than thirty days.

The state Department of Health and Human Services (DHHS) issues standards concerning the construction and operation of jails (G.S. 153A-221). In 1990, the department issued standards applicable to all jails (10 NCAC 3J) that cover construction, operation, classification and housing of inmates, fire safety, supervision of inmates, sanitation and personal hygiene, food, health care and exercise, and enforcement of the standards by the secretary of DHHS. A jail inspection service within the DHHS inspects every jail twice a year to see that the standards are met (G.S. 153A-222). If a jail does not meet the standards and the secretary of DHHS finds that the conditions in the jail jeopardize the safe custody, safety, health, or welfare of the persons confined, the secretary may either order corrective action or close the jail (G.S. 153A-223). The county commissioners must comply with the secretary's order or ask for a hearing to contest it. Also, the commissioners may appeal the order to the senior resident superior court judge of the judicial district that includes the county.

Management and Planning

Although courts, not county governments, control admissions to and releases from jails, county governments pay most jail costs. This gives counties an incentive to manage the jail population and plan for expansion of the jail or for alternatives to it. Because of the divided responsibility for jails, managing and planning for them requires an inter-agency planning approach. Many counties have formed planning committees or task forces for this purpose, each usually including judges, magistrates, prosecutors, defense attorneys, the clerk of court, the sheriff, the jail administrator, and county commissioners or other county officers. Often, these committees have relied on professional facilitators to help them work together effectively.

Care of Jail Inmates

State law makes special provision for the health and safety of jail inmates (G.S. 153A-220 *et seq.*). The county commissioners must provide sufficient jail personnel who must be present continuously and available to supervise prisoners. Also, the commissioners must develop a plan for providing medical care. The local health director reviews the commissioners' plan and approves it if it adequately protects inmates' health and welfare (G.S. 153A-225). The jail must provide emergency medical care from a licensed physician according to its medical care plan. The county must pay the cost of emergency medical services unless the inmate has third-party insurance. If the inmate has insurance, the health care provider bills the insurer, and the county is liable for costs not covered by insurance. With regard to non-emergency medical care, the jail may set and collect fees not exceeding $10 per incident of such care, but must also establish a procedure for waiving the fee where the inmate is indigent.

Jail Population: Composition, Growth, and Costs

Most North Carolina jail prisoners are not serving sentences; rather, they are defendants awaiting trial (pretrial detainees), held in jail because they are unable to post an appearance bond set by the court. Since 1975, the percentage of the statewide jail population who are not serving sentences has ranged from 68 to 84 percent, and currently is about 77 percent. Compared with most states, North Carolina houses fewer of its sentenced offenders in county jails. In 1996, about 49 percent of jail prisoners in the United States were serving sentences, compared with about 23 percent in North Carolina. The difference stems from the Great Depression of the 1930s, when North Carolina incorporated what were formerly county prison farms into the state prison system to relieve counties of that financial burden.

In the near future, counties' responsibility for sentenced offenders may increase. There are recent indications that the structured sentencing laws effective in 1994 may be lengthening the average time served by sentenced jail prisoners; if this trend continues, it will increase the sentenced jail population.

During the last two decades, the county jail population has increased much faster than the state prison population. The average statewide jail population rose 401 percent from June 1975 (2,337 prisoners) to June 1996 (11,704 prisoners). In comparison, the state prison population grew by 145 percent (from 12,572 to 30,775) over the same period.

Most of the jail population increase has been in the pretrial detainee segment. Two factors have contributed to the enlargement of the number of detainees: the average time that prisoners stay in jail lengthened; and admissions to jail grew. Growth in admissions results from increased arrests by police; the lengthening of detention time is probably a consequence of increasing criminal case disposition times.

Jail capacity may be an important factor in continued jail population growth. Starting in 1987 there was a surge in new construction, raising the total capacity of the jails from about 6,200 in 1987 to about 12,000 currently. To some extent, counties were merely reacting to the growth in arrests and consequent court delays. But after 1990, when the number of arrests by police (which had been increasing) leveled off, the expansion of jail facilities continued. To protect public safety, counties may have decided to spend more money so that more criminal suspects may be locked up. In any event, the availability of new jail space has made it easier to detain arrested defendants—at least, until the new space is filled, which has already happened in some counties.

The rapid increase in the county jail population since the 1970s has meant increasing costs to county government. Jail construction costs are considerably higher than those for state prisons—an average of about $56,000 per bed for twenty jail building projects in 1991 and

1992, compared to an average of $25,000 to $30,000 per bed for prison construction. The operating costs of jails, over the life of a typical facility, are much greater than the initial construction costs. The 1994 survey mentioned earlier estimated the daily cost per bed at $33 for operation plus $17 for construction and equipment. Costs today are probably higher. Of special concern are health costs, which, in many jails, have increased by several orders of magnitude since the 1980s. Serious illnesses among jail inmates are unpredictable and, for the most part, unavoidable; their high cost makes them fiscally disruptive, especially for small counties.[2]

Pretrial Services Programs

As an approach to controlling the size and cost of the county jail population, some counties conduct a pretrial services program, either as a direct service of county government or through a private nonprofit organization. These programs, which essentially are locally operated adjuncts to the criminal courts, are an exception to the general rule that court operations are funded and administered by the state. The first pretrial services program was undertaken by Mecklenburg County in 1971. Technical assistance and grant funds available under the Criminal Justice Partnership Act, discussed later in this section, have recently spurred the development of pretrial services programs, which now serve twenty-six counties.

Pretrial services programs generally perform three functions: (1) obtaining information about pretrial detainees; (2) reporting to the court; and (3) supervising released defendants. The first function includes determining the status of each pretrial prisoner (to determine the legal basis for the detention and how the prisoner's case could be expedited), and collecting information such as the criminal record (to measure the risk of releasing the prisoner prior to trial). The second function entails reporting to the court information such as the prisoner's criminal record, employment, and residence, for the judge or magistrate to use in setting or modifying conditions of pretrial release. The third function involves supervising defendants as a court-ordered condition of their release prior to trial, to make sure that they appear in court as required and to reduce their chance of repeated involvement in crime.

Pretrial services programs, if operated effectively, offer several advantages. They can reduce jail expenditures by identifying defendants who can be released at acceptable risk. They can reduce the hardship of incarceration for defendants who are unable to post a secured bond. Finally, supervision of defendants can help to control the risks of pre-trial release.

Other Correctional Functions of Counties

North Carolina counties' role in the correctional system—the incarceration, supervision, and treatment of convicted offenders—has been much less than that of state government. Examples of state dominance in the correctional system are the state's takeover of county prisons in the 1930s; the creation of a statewide, centrally-administered court system in the 1960s; and the state's administration of prisons, probation, and parole. But the county's role may grow because of two factors: the rise of community corrections, and the recent enactment of structured sentencing legislation.

In North Carolina, the term "community corrections" is used in two senses. The phrase is sometimes used to refer to sanctions that keep a convicted offender "in the community"—that is, sanctions such as probation supervision or payment of restitution to crime victims, that do not involve long-term imprisonment. Another use of the term is to refer to correctional programs operated with a substantial degree of local influence, control, or participation, rather than being the exclusive concern of state government. The local control or influence may be by local governments or by local nongovernmental organizations. Community corrections in the locally operated sense has often involved an emphasis on non-incarcerative sanctions. Community corrections programs generally have been created through state and local cooperation rather than through purely local efforts.

The Community Service Work Program (CSWP), begun in 1981, was a first step toward the adoption of community corrections. In this program, offenders are sentenced to perform unpaid work for public purposes, usually as a condition of probation [G.S. 15A-1343(b1)(6); 143B-475.1]. State government administers the CSWP in the sense that state courts order it, state community service coordinators arrange and monitor it, and state probation officers enforce it. However, local involvement is a major component of the program in three respects:

- The program keeps offenders in their home communities rather than sending them off to state prisons.
- The program relies heavily on the cooperation of local organizations' personnel to supervise the work.

- The major beneficiaries of the work it produces are local organizations.

In 1996–97, 73,474 offenders were enrolled in the CSWP program. They performed a total of nearly 2.4 million hours of work that year, the bulk of which (89 percent) was for recipients other than state government agencies—mostly local public or nonprofit agencies.

The community penalties programs are a second example of community corrections (G.S. 7A-770 *et seq.*). Under legislation originally effective in 1983, these programs, most of which are operated by local nonprofit organizations, conduct pre-sentence investigations of certain defendants concerning their prospects for intermediate punishment rather than incarceration, and prepare sentencing recommendations considered by the court if the defendant is convicted. Another function of some community penalty programs has been to help develop programs in their areas for sentenced offenders, most of which qualify as "intermediate punishments" (explained in the following section) for purposes of the new structured sentencing law. Most community penalties programs, while operated locally, obtain the bulk of their operating funds through contracts with the state Administrative Office of the Courts. Currently, community penalties programs throughout the state serve eighty-eight counties, forty-four of which contribute to the programs' support.

A third community corrections initiative is the Criminal Justice Partnership Act, which accompanied the structured sentencing legislation effective in 1994. This legislation prescribes "intermediate punishments"—stricter punishments and treatments of offenders than routine probation supervision but less severe than long-term imprisonment—for many offenders. Some programs that constitute intermediate punishments are well-suited for local administration, for example: residential treatment programs, day reporting centers, restitution centers, and employment services for offenders on probation.

The Partnership Act is intended to assist local organizations to implement structured sentencing by developing intermediate punishment programs. The act's goals are to reduce offenders' recidivism, alcoholism, and drug dependency; to reduce probation revocations; and to reduce the cost of incarceration to the state and the counties (G.S. 143B-273 *et seq.*). The DOC provides planning assistance and offers some initial funding for partnership programs, with a current annual budget of $9.6 million. Currently, some eighty-seven counties have applied for technical assistance under the program, and many of these have gone on to initiate programs partially supported by state funds under the act. Eighty-five programs are currently in operation, and as of November 1997, approximately 1,800 offenders were participating in intermediate punishment programs across the state.

Medical Examiners

Background

In 1955 the General Assembly enacted legislation allowing counties to appoint local physicians as medical examiners. Like the coroners who originally had this responsibility, they were to investigate any death that apparently occurred, in the words of today's law, "under any suspicious, unusual or unnatural circumstance." Only a few counties appointed medical examiners before 1967, when the Assembly created the present statewide system which requires medical examiners. The system was funded a year later.

Several counties continue to preserve the office of coroner, though they may not fill it. This elected official's historical duty was to determine whether a death was caused by a criminal act or omission. However, in most of the state, medical-legal investigations are conducted by county medical examiners. In the counties where a coroner is still active, the coroner either serves as "acting medical examiner" and functions under the medical examiner system or serves as an investigator working in cooperation with local medical examiners.

Organization of the System

North Carolina is among the minority of states with a centralized, state-administered medical examiner system. The chief medical examiner (CME) is an employee of the Division of Epidemiology within the Department of Health and Human Services. The CME, aided by a staff of forensic pathologists, appoints and supervises county medical examiners. The CME's office is located in Chapel Hill within the University Hospital complex, to ensure proximity to a medical school and its pathology department for the sharing of resources and for teaching purposes. The CME appoints at least one medical examiner for each county, and usually more. Currently, there are between five and six hundred county medical examiners. Their term of office is three years. Autopsies are performed by a network of pathologists designated by the CME or the CME's office.

Most medical examiners are physicians licensed to practice in North Carolina. By statute, the CME selects county medical examiners from nominees of the county medical society or, if there are none, names any local physician willing to accept appointment. If none is willing, the CME may appoint any other state-licensed physician or a non-physician. The latter serves as "acting medical examiner." A non-physician examiner may be the coroner if there is one, or another responsible person. At this time, nurses and physicians' assistants are serving in this capacity in a number of counties.

The Chief Medical Examiner

The CME must be a board-certified forensic pathologist, licensed to practice medicine in North Carolina. This official is appointed by the secretary of health and human services. At present, the CME has a staff of thirty, including four other pathologists. They review each case investigated by local medical examiners and pathologists.

Legal responsibility for investigations of deaths in the state rests with county medical examiners. Although this responsibility is exercised locally, the CME can assume jurisdiction over any case or assign it to a medical examiner (or acting medical examiner) other than the one in whose jurisdiction the death occurred. The CME is also authorized to amend a death certificate filed by a local medical examiner.

Investigations

The county medical examiner must be notified of deaths that occur in these circumstances: those "resulting from violence, poisoning, accident, suicide or homicide; occurring suddenly when the deceased had been in apparent good health or when unattended by a physician; occurring in a jail, prison, correctional institution or in police custody; [executions]; or [deaths] occurring under any suspicious, unusual or unnatural circumstance." The obligation to report such deaths falls on certain categories of people—attending physicians, hospital employees, and police, for example—but also on anyone who suspects that a death may fall into one of the previous categories. Also, anyone who discovers what may be part of a human body must report it.

To aid their inquiries, medical examiners can rely on subpoena power and on statutory prohibitions against disturbing a body at the scene of a reportable death, or embalming, burial, or cremation of a body when the death requires investigation. Medical examiners may also inspect physical evidence and documents including the deceased's medical records, which normally are confidential.

If a medical examiner thinks that an autopsy would be "advisable and in the public interest," he or she may order one. A district attorney or superior court judge may also authorize performance of an autopsy in a medical examiner case. The CME issues guidelines to define which deaths require autopsy. Sometimes questions arise about a death after the body has been buried. In that case, after the CME authorizes an investigation and the district attorney with jurisdiction petitions the judge, a court may order the body exhumed so that it can be autopsied by the CME.

In all cases, following the investigation the county medical examiner files a report with the CME and completes a certificate stating the cause of death (disease, or other means). If the death resulted from external causes, the certificate states whether from accident, homicide, suicide, or in an undetermined manner.

In 1996, approximately 14 percent of all deaths in the state were investigated and certified by the medical examiner system. Of these, half were ruled unnatural (homicide, suicide or accident). In forty percent of the investigations an autopsy was performed. The CME staff performed approximately one-third of the autopsies.

Other Services of the CME's Office

The CME's office maintains a toxicology laboratory to analyze alcohol, drug, and other toxic substances that may be significant in a medical examiner's case. The office also pays transportation costs necessary for a medical examiner to examine a body or a pathologist to perform an autopsy. The office is the repository of all records of investigations and autopsies and generally issues copies of the records without charge.

Financing the System

The medical examiner system costs about $4 million annually. The state pays 60 percent of the cost through the CME office; the counties, 40 percent, almost entirely in the form of fees to medical examiners and regional pathologists for investigations and autopsies.

Notes

1. Walter Anderson, *Treatise on the Law of Sheriffs, Coroners and Constables*, Vol. 1 (Buffalo, N.Y.: Dennis & Co., Inc., 1941), 2, §§ 1, 2.

2. John Manuel, "County Jails Struggle with Rising Costs of Health Care," *Popular Government* 59 (1993): 1, 2–9.

32 Fire Protection

Ben F. Loeb, Jr.

Contents

Rural fire protection as a function of county government in North Carolina dates almost entirely from the period following World War II. Historically, fire protection was a most important activity of early cities and towns, whose compact development with largely wooden buildings presented a constant danger of a community-wide conflagration. But in rural areas, characterized by widely separated farm buildings, fire protection was regarded as a matter of concern to the individual property

Ben F. Loeb, Jr., is an Institute of Government faculty member whose interests include eminent domain, alcoholic beverage control, fire protection, and animal control law.

owner rather than to the community. Only in recent times, since rural areas became subject to an urban type of development and their citizens began demanding the same kinds of governmental services as those enjoyed by city dwellers, have county governments been called on to furnish fire protection.

Counties first became concerned with fire problems around 1900, when the sheriff was authorized to investigate the possibility of arson when fires occurred outside municipal corporate limits. The concept of a county fire-fighting service emerged only in 1939, when counties were authorized to contract with municipal fire departments to provide service beyond town limits. Not until 1945 were counties empowered to establish and maintain departments of their own. Another approach was made possible by a statute enacted in 1951 that authorized the creation of rural fire-protection districts supported by special taxes levied within them, if the residents voted for such an arrangement. The 1973 General Assembly, in an effort to make municipal types of services more available to county residents, enacted the County Service District Act (G.S. Chapter 153A, Article 16), which permits the establishment of districts for fire protection, as well as for certain other designated purposes, without a popular vote.

Many counties pay specific amounts to municipal fire departments or to incorporated non-profit volunteer departments to furnish fire protection in rural areas. Also, groups of county residents have occasionally formed associations for the purpose of contracting for such protection with various public and private agencies without the benefit of specific legislation. In 1959 statewide legislation authorizing the appointment of county fire marshals was passed, and in 1989 a statewide fire prevention code was mandated. Both of these measures have further strengthened county fire-protection.

Alternative Approaches

County fire protection may be provided by several methods or by a combination of them, including the following:

1. Creating a county fire department.
2. Contracting with one or more municipalities or volunteer fire departments to furnish fire protection in rural areas.
3. Creating one or more rural fire-protection tax districts.
4. Establishing a county service district or districts.

5. Forming associations of groups of citizens to contract for fire-protection services.

County Fire Departments

G.S. 153A-233 provides in part that "a county may establish, organize, equip, support, and maintain a fire department; may prescribe the duties of the fire department; [and] may provide financial assistance to incorporated volunteer fire departments."

Most counties have not established fire departments as such. Past practice has been to enter into agreements with volunteer fire departments to furnish the protection in designated rural areas for a fixed fee (financial assistance). These volunteer departments then function as county fire departments for all intents and purposes. The area protected by an individual volunteer department is usually referred to as a fire-response district (or insurance district). County governments, in fixing fire-district boundaries, often ask for help from the Insurance Services Office (ISO), in Raleigh, or the State Department of Insurance. Such a cooperative effort means that these districts can receive an improved rating for fire-insurance purposes. Such a rating, of course, means savings for property owners because of reduced costs for homeowner's or fire insurance.

Contracts with Municipalities

G.S. 153A-233 expressly authorizes counties to contract for fire-fighting or fire-prevention services with cities or other units of local government, and also to pay for rural fire protection from tax funds. Fire fighters who answer calls outside the cities that employ them have the same authority, rights, privileges, and immunities that they have while responding to calls within their home municipalities. A municipality that dispatches its fire department to an emergency outside its boundaries is deemed to be exercising a governmental function and thus has all the privileges and immunities it enjoys when it exercises that function within its corporate limits (G.S. 160A-293, -58-82-1, -58-83-1).

Tax-Supported Rural Fire Districts

Countywide fire protection is the exception, and the inhabitants of most rural areas must rely on the services of a volunteer department and/or a tax-supported fire-protection district (G.S. Ch. 69, Art. 3A).

The first step in establishing a tax district is to present the county commissioners with a petition signed by at least 35 percent of the resident freeholders of an area outside the corporate limits of a city or town (to be a freeholder, one must own an estate in land or other realty; a lease is not sufficient). The area to be included in the district must be described in the petition, and the proposed district must be given a name (G.S. 69-25.1).

The question of levying a special tax for the purpose of providing fire protection is submitted to the "qualified voters" of the proposed district. Those who own realty in it but do not reside therein are not "qualified voters" and may not vote in the election. If approved, this special tax is collected on all taxable property in the district, real and personal, but may not exceed 15 cents per $100 assessed valuation. A method is also provided whereby an existing district that has previously authorized a tax of 10 cents per $100 valuation may vote on whether to increase the tax to 15 cents per $100. The fact that a 15-cent tax is authorized does not require that the full amount be levied, and most districts that have authorized the 15-cent levy actually tax at a lower rate (G.S. 69-25.1).

The board of county commissioners (after consulting with the board of elections) sets the date for the election, which is then conducted by the county board of elections (G.S. 69-25.2). The form of the ballot is prescribed by statute. If a majority of those casting ballots vote "in favor of tax for fire protection in _____ Fire Protection District," the county commissioners then select the means of providing such protection. The statutes provide several alternative methods of doing so, including the following:

1. Contracting with an incorporated city or town
2. Contracting with an incorporated nonprofit volunteer or community fire department
3. Contracting with the state Department of Environment and Natural Resources
4. Using the county's fire department if it has one
5. Establishing a fire department within the district
6. Using a combination of the above (G.S. 69-25.5)

The taxes collected for fire-protection purposes go into a special fund administered by the board of county commissioners or by a three-member "fire protection district commission" appointed by the county commissioners. Fire-protection district commissioners must be qualified voters who reside in the district; they serve for two-year terms and are subject to the county commissioners' supervision (G.S. 69-25.7).

The statutes also authorize an election to determine whether an existing fire district should be abolished. This election is called on the petition of 15 percent of the resident freeholders within the district (G.S. 69-25.10). Fire-district boundaries may be increased or decreased; such a change may be accomplished by petition, so that another election is not necessary. Even territory within a city can be added, if the city so desires (G.S. 69-25.11). When all or any part of a district is annexed by a municipality that furnishes fire protection, the annexed territory ceases to be a fire district (or part of a fire district), and fire-district taxes may no longer be collected in the annexed area. The procedure for prorating fire-district taxes in the event of annexation during a fiscal year is specified by statute (G.S. 69-25.15).

County Service Districts

The County Service District Act of 1973, codified as Article 16 of G.S. Chapter 153A, empowers boards of county commissioners to create special districts to furnish several urban services, including fire protection.

The county commissioners must hold a public hearing, after giving statutory notice, before they adopt a resolution defining a new district. To justify a district, they must find that all of the following criteria have been met:

1. There is a demonstrable need for one or more of the authorized services.
2. The proposed services cannot practically be provided on a countywide basis.
3. The proposed services can be provided to the district without unreasonable or burdensome tax levies.
4. There is a demonstrable demand for the proposed services by those who live in the district.

No territory that lies within a municipality or a sanitary district may be included within a service district without the approval of that unit's governing body. It should be noted that, contrary to the requirement for a rural fire-protection tax district, no election need be held to establish a county service district. The county commissioners' resolution that defines and in effect creates one becomes effective at the beginning of the fiscal year following its adoption (G.S. 153A-302).

The county service district shares one important characteristic with the rural fire-protection district: those who own property within the district are required to pay additional taxes to support the services provided within the district. Counties are expressly authorized to levy property taxes within a service district in addition to those levied throughout the county, and to finance services within the district at a higher level than other county residents receive. A county may also allocate any other revenues to a district that are not restricted in use by law (G.S. 153A-307, -309.2).

Associations that Contract for Fire Protection

Occasionally, individuals or associations of persons who live outside a municipality contract with a city or a volunteer fire department so that they receive the protection of a municipal or other accredited department for a fixed fee. This type of contract is expressly authorized by G.S. 160A-293.

Selection of an Approach

Each of the alternatives outlined earlier for furnishing county fire protection has both advantages and disadvantages. A paid professional countywide department, for example, would provide municipal-quality fire protection to county residents, but would also be prohibitively expensive for most counties. The customary practice of contracting with volunteer departments to furnish protection in rural areas is relatively inexpensive since no salaries need be paid, but this system leaves the county government without any real control over the fire-protection services, other than what the contract provides.

Contracting with a city for fire protection to be furnished by its department has the advantage of relieving the county of the responsibility for organizing, training, administering, and maintaining its own department. Also, many city departments are staffed by highly trained personnel and have excellent equipment. But not all cities will agree to furnish protection to outlying rural areas, and in any event, a city department's first duty and highest priority is to protect life and property within the municipal corporate limits. To maintain the city's fire-insurance rating, the Insurance Services Office may require that certain equipment and personnel remain within its boundaries at all times, and thus the full resources of the department are never available to all county residents.

A tax-supported rural fire-protection district is attractive because it can be established without increasing the tax burden on county residents who do not own property within the district. If this alternative is chosen, the cost of the protection is placed entirely on those who will receive the service. This approach has the disadvantage of requiring a successful district-wide election before the district can be created. If an election is not feasible, the county commissioners may be asked to establish a county service district for the provision of fire protection. Either a rural fire-protection district or a service district will probably operate under contract with one or more rural volunteer or city fire departments, with the advantages and disadvantages mentioned earlier in this chapter.

The final alternative, encouraging groups of rural residents to contract with a city or volunteer department for fire protection, creates few if any problems for the county government. Unfortunately, most residents lack the initiative and expertise to organize and contract for such an arrangement.

Organizing Volunteer Fire Departments

Whatever approach is used to furnish rural fire protection, probably one or more volunteer departments will be used. For example, no county in this state has a fully paid fire department, and counties usually contract with volunteer departments to furnish protection to rural residents. Similarly, when a tax-supported fire district is established, fire-protection services are usually provided by a volunteer department. Such departments may be incorporated pursuant to the Nonprofit Corporation Act, as contained in G.S. Chapter 55A. The corporation is legally created when one or more incorporators sign the articles of incorporation, have them notarized, and then file them in the office of the secretary of state, in Raleigh.

Requirements in this state for creating a non-profit corporation are simple. Any person or persons at least eighteen years of age may act as the incorporator, and they need not even be residents of North Carolina. The initial board of directors is usually named in the articles of incorporation, and bylaws are adopted and officers are elected at the organizational meeting. Corporate officers usually consist of a president, at least one vice-president, a secretary, a treasurer, and any other officers deemed necessary (G.S. Ch. 55A, Art. 2).

Fire District Finance and Insurance Rates

For decades—perhaps generations—rural volunteer fire departments were supported by contributions and fund-raising events, supplemented in more recent times by appropriations from the county general fund. However, by the 1950s additional sources of revenue were needed, primarily because of the rapidly increasing cost of fire department equipment. (Currently fire trucks can cost in excess of $150,000 each.) By 1997, there were over 1,100 fire districts in North Carolina, and most were supported at least in part by fire district taxes levied pursuant to G.S. Chapter 69 (Fire Tax District) or G.S. Chapter 153A (County Service District). The tax rates in these districts range from a low of about 3 cents per $100 valuation to a high of 15 cents per $100 valuation—the average being in the 5 cent to 7 cent range. Tax rates vary somewhat with the nature of the district. For example, a rate of 5 cents per $100 will bring in much more revenue in an area composed of homes and businesses than it will in a district consisting mostly of farmland. The need of departments for new and high-priced equipment is also a factor.

The amount a property owner pays for fire, or homeowners insurance depends in part on the insurance classification assigned to the fire department that protects the fire district. An area with no fire protection receives a rating of Class 10, while a paid and well-equipped city department can be rated as high as Class 1. Most areas protected by a rural volunteer department have a rating of Class 9 (or 9S), although some rural departments have received much better ratings, occasionally comparable to those received by professionally-staffed city departments. The savings from being within the boundaries of an insurance-rated district are substantial. A homeowner who is located in a Class 9 (or 9S) district will pay at least 25 percent less for his insurance than if he were in a Class 10 (unrated area). An additional 25 percent can be saved if the insurance rating is a Class 6 or below. However, to have a Class 6 (or better) requires an adequate water supply (by fire plugs or otherwise), and only about 137 districts have this rating. Any county interested in acquiring or improving a fire insurance rating should contact the Fire and Rescue Services Division of the North Carolina Department of Insurance in Raleigh.

The diversity of tax rates and insurance classifications is illustrated by Table 32-1. The districts (fire departments) are listed by area, from the mountains to the sea.

Table 32-1
Fire Departments Listed by Area

Fire Dep't (or District)	Size (in sq. mi.)	Type	Tax Rate (per $100)	Tax Revenue (1997–98) ($)	Insur- ance Class	Assessed Value of Property ($ in millions)
Broad River (Buncombe)	70	G.S. Ch. 153A	.10	40,000	9S	39
Skyland (Buncombe)	52	G.S. Ch. 69	.06	952,000	5	1,200
Martins Creek (Cherokee)	11	G.S. Ch. 69	.05	22,000	9S	45
Saint Stephens (Catawba)	64	G.S. Ch. 153A	.05	42,000	6	446
Erwin (Harnett)	60	G.S. Ch. 69	.05	145,000	Part 3/ Part 9S	64
Sea Gate (New Hanover)	11	G.S. Ch. 153A	.025	152,000	9	No figures available[a]
Ogden (New Hanover)	41	G.S. Ch. 153A	.025	200,000	9S	No figures available[a]

a. New Hanover has one tax district, which is serviced by numerous fire departments, each of which has a response district.

County Fire Marshals

G.S. 153A-234 authorizes counties to appoint a fire marshal and to employ whatever assistants may be required. However, a county need not appoint a marshal and it may even assign the duties involved to another qualified county officer or employee. The county commissioners set the duties for fire marshals, which may include the following:

1. To keep the county manager and the board of commissioners informed of the progress and development of rural fire departments

2. To inform the manager and the commissioners about any matters pertaining to the present and future expansion of these departments

3. To act as a liaison between fire departments and the manager or the board of commissioners

4. To help organize and develop new fire departments
5. To be the county manager's and commissioners' adviser concerning requirements of the Insurance Services Office
6. To help develop a comprehensive training program for all rural fire departments
7. To advise fire departments on equipment purchases and problems
8. To make fire prevention inspections of both schools (as required by G.S. Ch. 115C) and day-care facilities (as required by G.S. Ch. 110)
9. To help fire departments develop a fire-prevention program in their respective districts
10. To help school authorities develop a fire-prevention program for each school
11. To coordinate all fire departments within the county in a mutual aid program

Fire-Prevention Codes

Prior to 1991, G.S. Chapter 160A and G.S. Chapter 153A authorized cities and counties to adopt fire-prevention codes, and many did so. In 1989, the General Assembly enacted Chapter 681, which provides that the state building code could regulate "activities and conditions in buildings, structures, and premises that pose dangers of fire, explosion, or related hazards." This provision, which is contained in G.S. 143-138(b), resulted in the addition of a fire-prevention code to the North Carolina State Building Code, effective July 1, 1991. The state fire-prevention code is a minimum standard and counties (as well as cities) may adopt more stringent provisions, subject to the approval of the building code council.

Additional Resources

Fire Chiefs Reference Manual. Published by the N.C. Fire Chiefs Association in Raleigh, North Carolina.

Loeb, Ben F., Jr. *Fire Protection Law in North Carolina*, 5th ed. Chapel Hill, N.C.: Institute of Government, The University of North Carolina at Chapel Hill, 1993.

Minimum Rating Requirements for Fire Districts in North Carolina. Published by the Fire & Rescue Service Division of the State Department of Insurance in Raleigh, North Carolina.

33 Alcoholic Beverage Control

Ben F. Loeb, Jr.

Contents

Ben F. Loeb, Jr., is an Institute of Government faculty member whose interests include eminent domain, alcoholic beverage control, fire protection, and animal control law.

North Carolina regulates the sale and consumption of alcoholic beverages through a complex but comprehensive and integrated set of laws, codified in Chapter 18B of the General Statutes. These statutes assumed their present form in 1981, when they were reorganized and clarified in order to make them easier for permit holders, law enforcement officers, and local government officials to understand. The current alcoholic beverage control (ABC) law gives local officials the power to decide some local matters previously under state control, such as whether an ABC board should contract with a local law enforcement agency to enforce the ABC law rather than hire its own officers. Local authority with respect to consumption and display of alcoholic beverages remains quite limited, but G.S. 18B-300 does allow a city or county to prohibit the consumption of beer and some wines on government property, as well as on public streets.

Certain basic statutory definitions are crucial to understanding North Carolina's alcoholic beverage laws. This is how the statutes (G.S. 18B-101) categorize the different kinds of beverages:

- Alcoholic beverage—a beverage containing one-half of 1 percent or more of alcohol by volume, including beer, wine, and hard liquor.
- Malt beverage—beer, ale, or other brewed or fermented beverages containing between one-half of 1 percent and 6 percent alcohol by volume.
- Unfortified wine—wine produced only by natural fermentation or by the addition of sugar.
- Fortified wine—wine made by fermentation that contains not more than 24 percent alcohol by volume, the natural alcoholic content being supplemented by brandy.
- Spirituous liquor—whiskey, gin, rum, brandy, and other distilled spirits.
- Mixed beverage—a drink containing spirituous liquor and served in a quantity that is less than the amount in a closed package.

ABC Stores

Local Option

Alcoholic beverages, as a general rule, may be sold in a county only with the approval of the voters. State law provides the procedure for a county to determine whether it wants to establish ABC stores for the sale of spirituous liquor and fortified wine. If a county does not have ABC stores, a municipality within the county may establish a city ABC system by following a separate but similar procedure (G.S. 18B-600).[1]

ABC stores sell only spirituous liquor and fortified wine, and only they may sell "hard liquor" for off-premises consumption. Malt beverages and wine (unfortified and fortified), on the other hand, may be sold by restaurants, grocery stores, and other businesses. The procedure for approval of beer and unfortified wine sales is described in a later section.

Election Procedures

An election on establishing county ABC stores may be requested by the board of commissioners or by petition of 35 percent of the registered voters at the time the petition is initiated. The election is conducted by the county board of elections, which must hold it within 120 days from the date on which the request was received from the governing board or on which the petition was verified. The provisions of G.S. Chapter 163 (the general election law) are to be followed in conducting the election, except as otherwise specified in the ABC law. City alcoholic beverage elections also fall under the general law and use procedures that generally parallel those of the counties set out previously (G.S. 18B-601).

Operating a County ABC System

If the voters approve county ABC stores, the stores are managed by a county ABC board, which is usually comprised of three members appointed by the board of commissioners. Typically, the initial three appointments are for one, two, and three years, respectively, and all subsequent appointees serve three-year staggered terms. Chapter 18B provides that a county ABC board member may be removed "for cause" at any time. Also, any local board member or employee who is convicted of violating Chapter 18B or committing any felony may be removed from office by the state ABC Commission or by a judge. Salaries of county board members are set by the board of commissioners. Each local ABC board member must be bonded in an amount of at least $5,000. A person who handles no funds may be exempted from this requirement, but one who does handle funds may have to be bonded for more than $5,000 (G.S. 18B-700).

The local ABC board operates its system subject to the provisions of state law, as summarized later in this section. Salaries and other expenses are paid from store profits. The board hires and fires employees, provides for local enforcement of the ABC laws, buys and sells alcoholic beverages, issues purchase-transportation permits, purchases or leases the necessary real and personal property, and otherwise manages the system (G.S. 18B-701).

The state ABC Commission, composed of a full-time chairman and two other members serving at the governor's pleasure, sets the price for all alcoholic beverages sold in local ABC stores, and must approve the location of the stores (G.S. 18B-200). It is the state ABC Commission, and not the local boards, that determines which brands of liquor may be sold in this state, but a local board need not stock all approved brands (G.S. 18B-203). Under state law, ABC stores may not be open before 9:00 a.m. or after 9:00 p.m. on weekdays or at any time on Sundays, New Year's Day, the Fourth of July, Labor Day, Thanksgiving, or Christmas Day. Within these guidelines, hours and days of operation are left to local ABC board discretion (G.S. 18B-802).

Revenue

Generally, the state receives the tax revenue from alcoholic beverages and local governments keep the ABC stores' profits from sales. Some of those profits must be spent in specific ways. For example, local boards must spend at least 5 percent of profits on liquor-law enforcement. This mandate means hiring one or more local ABC officers or contracting with the sheriff or city police (or other local law enforcement agency) to perform this service. Local ABC officers' main responsibility is to enforce the ABC laws and the North Carolina Controlled Substances Act (G.S. Chapter 90, Article 5). They may, however, make arrests for any crime committed anywhere in the county (G.S. 18B-501).

Another limitation on how profits are distributed is the requirement in G.S. 18B-805(c)(3) that at least 7 percent be spent on alcoholism programs. This requirement does not apply, however, to a number of boards that have a different distribution set by local act. All undesignated county ABC profits must be paid to the county general fund unless a local act provides otherwise. Local acts on this subject differ. Often they call for distribution to named schools, hospitals, and similar activities; it is not uncommon for some profits from a city ABC system to go to the county general fund as part of a political compromise that helped pass the local act establishing the system. Chapter 18B allows cities and counties that receive store profits to change their distribution without any need for a local act of authorization (G.S. 18B-805).

During the last fiscal year for which figures are available (1996–97), local ABC stores had a net profit of over $28 million, $25 million of which went to county and city governments. The Mecklenburg ABC system alone had profits of over $5 million. In contrast, some of the small systems actually lost money, apparently because their population base was too small to support an ABC store.

Fortified Wines

Although many voters do not realize it—and although the election ballot does not so indicate—approving ABC stores also means approving the sale of fortified wine (not only in ABC stores if they choose to carry it but also in other locations). If ABC stores are approved, fortified wine may also be sold in grocery stores, as well as in restaurants and private clubs for on-premises consumption. As noted above, fortified wine can have an alcoholic content of up to 24 percent and in general is treated under state law more like spirituous liquor than like unfortified wine (G.S. 18B-603, -800).

Use of Spirituous Liquor and Fortified Wine

Spirituous liquor and fortified wine may be bought, sold, possessed, and transported by persons aged twenty-one and older, but only as expressly authorized by G.S. Chapter 18B. One may buy and transport 8 liters at one time or 40 liters with a purchase-transportation permit issued by the local ABC board. The 8-liter limit on transportation in a single vehicle applies regardless of the number of its passengers, except in the case of taxicabs. The law allows 8 liters per passenger in taxis, but they may not haul alcoholic beverages without a passenger. While a vehicle could in times past be confiscated if more than the legal amount were carried, this now can occur only if non-tax-paid liquor is being transported. Fortified wine or spirituous liquor may be transported in the passenger area of a motor vehicle only in the manufacturer's unopened original container. Possession of more than 8 liters of spirituous liquor (except with a permit) creates a presumption that it is for sale. There is no comparable presumption concerning fortified wine, but it is illegal to sell or purchase more than 8 liters at one time without a permit (G.S. 18B-302, -303, -304, -400, 401, -504).

A person may possess and consume fortified wine and spirituous liquor without a permit from the local ABC board in the following places:

1. A home or a temporary residence like a motel room
2. Any other property not primarily used for commercial purposes and not open to the public when the beverage is possessed (with the property owner's consent)
3. A private club or restaurant with a brown-bagging[2] permit from the state ABC Commission
4. A residence or establishment where a "special occasion" is being held (G.S. 18B-301).

Some other restrictions on consumption and display of alcoholic beverages should be briefly noted. State law prohibits consumption of any kind of alcoholic beverages at locations licensed for on-premises consumption between 2:30 a.m. and 7:00 a.m. daily, and before noon on Sunday (G.S. 18B-1004). Drinking or offering a drink of fortified wine, spirituous liquor, or mixed beverages on a public street or on ABC store premises is also unlawful, as is displaying these beverages at any athletic contest [G.S. 18B-301(f)]. Also, counties (and cities) may prohibit Sunday sales of beer and wine by establishments not having a brown-bagging or mixed-beverage permit [G.S. 18B-1004(d)].

Mixed Beverages

Local Option

Counties and cities with ABC stores may choose to allow the sale of mixed drinks within their boundaries. A mixed-drink election may be called by the unit of government that operates the ABC system; that is, if there is a county system, an election on mixed drinks must be countywide; for a municipal system, the vote must be in the city only. A county may hold a mixed-drink election only if it already operates an ABC store or is conducting a store election on the same day. The provisions for elections on selling mixed drinks essentially parallel those for elections on establishing ABC stores: the elections are requested by the county commissioners or by petition of 35 percent of the voters (G.S. 18B-600, -601).

Permits

Once the voters approve the sale of mixed drinks in a county or city, several kinds of places are eligible to receive permits from the state ABC Commission, including restaurants, hotels, private clubs, convention centers, and community theaters. A private club (a country club or Elks' club, for example) is eligible for both a brown-bagging permit and a mixed-beverage permit, but, once a city or county approves mixed drinks, a restaurant or hotel may have only a mixed-beverage permit— brown-bagging is no longer permitted there. Local approval of mixed-beverage sales also allows the state ABC Commission to issue permits for sales of malt beverages, unfortified wine, and fortified wine for on-premises consumption to places holding mixed-beverage permits, regardless of any other election or any local act concerning sales of those kinds of alcoholic beverages (G.S. 18B-603(d), -1001).

Purchase and Taxation of Mixed-Beverage Liquor

Holders of mixed-beverage permits must purchase their liquor at a designated local ABC store. Before each purchase, they must obtain from the local ABC board a purchase-transportation permit that states how much they are allowed to buy and carry. When permit holders purchase the liquor, they pay an additional charge of $20 per four liters (just over a gallon); one half of this extra charge is paid to the state Department of Revenue. Each bottle bought for resale as mixed drinks must carry a special stamp to indicate that this additional tax has been paid. Once permit holders carry the liquor to their premises, they must store it separately from all other liquor and keep detailed records of their purchases and sales (G.S. 18B-404, -804, -805, -1007).

Sale and Consumption of Mixed Beverages

Mixed drinks are subject to essentially the same rules as spirituous liquor and fortified wine. A person must be at least twenty-one to buy a mixed drink. Sales are allowed on licensed premises from 7:00 a.m. until 2:00 a.m. on weekdays and may not begin until noon on Sunday. Drinks may be consumed on the premises for a half-hour after sales must stop (G.S. 18B-302, -1004). A local government may not pass an ordinance setting additional restrictions on the sale or consumption of mixed beverages, and any local act of the legislature concerning mixed drinks is unconstitutional under the North Carolina prohibition against local acts regulating trade.[3]

Malt Beverages and Unfortified Wine

Local Option

Malt beverages (beer) and unfortified wine may be sold in grocery stores, hotels, restaurants, and various other places after the sale has been approved in a local election and after the proper permits and licenses have been issued by the state and local governments (G.S. 18B-1001).[4] The county board of elections calls the election when it receives a written request from the county governing body or a petition signed by 35 percent of the registered voters. The election must be held within 120 days of the request. No election on the sale of beer and wine may be held within three years of the last one. A city may not hold an election until sale has been rejected in a county election, and a city may not vote out beer or unfortified wine after the county has approved their sale (G.S. 18B-600, -601, -604).

G.S. 18B-603(c) provides that unfortified and fortified wine may be sold in any city or county where ABC stores have been established. This provision allows the sale even if a referendum on unfortified wine was to the contrary. However, G.S. 18B-603 does not allow such sale without an election in any jurisdiction that approved ABC stores before January 1, 1982 and held an unfortified wine election before that date at which neither on- nor off-premises sales were approved.

One or more of the following propositions may be placed on the same ballot in a malt beverage election:

1. Whether both on- and off-premises sales shall be allowed
2. Whether on-premises sales only shall be permitted
3. Whether off-premises sales only shall be permitted
4. Whether both off- and on-premises sales shall be allowed, the latter to be limited to Class A restaurants and hotels. (Class "A," as used here, apparently means a health or sanitary rating.) Similar choices are allowed in elections on the sale of unfortified wine (G.S. 18B-602).

Because beer and unfortified wines are sold by private businesses, a local act that sets election provisions or other procedures different from those found in the General Statutes would probably be void as a local act regulating trade.[5]

Permits

Once a city or county approves the sale of beer or unfortified wine, the state ABC Commission may issue permits for selling these beverages in that jurisdiction. Permits for the on-premises sale of beer may be issued to restaurants, convention centers, hotels, private clubs, retail businesses, and similar places. An establishment with an on-premises permit may also sell beer in original containers for consumption off the premises. Unfortified wine may be sold for on-premises consumption in hotels, restaurants, eating establishments, private clubs, convention centers, cooking schools, wineries, and community theaters. As a general rule, beer and wine permits may not be issued for public schools or colleges, but may be for private educational institutions (G.S. 18B-1001, -1006). Before issuing a permit, the state ABC Commission must give notice to the county or city governing body and allow fifteen days for the filing of written objections (G.S. 18B-901).[6]

Use of Beer and Unfortified Wine

Beer and unfortified wine may be purchased and possessed only by persons aged twenty-one or older. Twenty liters (just over five gallons) of unfortified wine may be bought without a permit, and 100 liters with a purchase-transportation permit from the local ABC board. A customer may not purchase more than 80 liters of beer at a time; but this limitation does not apply to draft beverages in kegs. Possession of more than 80 liters of beer (except in kegs) raises a presumption that it is possessed for sale in violation of law. There is no comparable presumption with respect to unfortified wine (G.S. 18B-302, -303, -304, -403).

G.S. 18B-300(c) authorizes cities and counties to adopt local ordinances regulating the consumption (and possession) of beer and unfortified wine, but the ordinances may deal only with public streets and property "owned or occupied" by the local government. Thus consumption of beer and wine in the parking lot of a local nightclub may not be restricted, but possession of an open container in a city-owned parking lot can be made illegal. Since beer and unfortified wine are *not* subject to the same restrictions as spirituous liquor, fortified wine, and mixed beverages, the various state prohibitions on the use of the latter beverages—

such as a display at an athletic contest—do not apply to malt beverages and unfortified wine.

Public/Local Acts

Over the past decade numerous provisions have been added to the General Statutes, which really relate to only one or two localities—the purpose being to circumvent the constitutional provision against local acts regulating trade. For example, G.S. 18B-600(g) authorizes ABC elections in "beautification districts." At least a dozen similar provisions are now in state law.

Additional Resources

Loeb, Jr., Ben F. "ABC Law: The Rise and Fall of Local Option." *Popular Government* 58 (Spring 1993): 36–42.
State ABC Commission. *Alcoholic Beverage Legal Sales Areas.* Raleigh, North Carolina. Published periodically.
———. *Annual Revenues from Spirituous Liquors.* Raleigh, North Carolina. Published yearly.

Notes

1. Before 1981 no general state law authorized cities to hold ABC elections; as a result, all city ABC systems put in place before that year were established by separate local acts of the legislature. These acts usually provided essentially the same procedure for city elections (and for operating city ABC systems) as state law provided for counties. Because ABC stores are operated by the government as a means of regulating liquor and not by private entrepreneurs for profit, these local acts do not violate the state constitutional provision against local acts regulating trade. Gardner v. Reidsville, 269 N.C. 581, 153 S.E.2d 139 (1967).

2. The term "brown-bagging" means taking a bottle containing an alcoholic beverage to a club or restaurant and serving drinks from it. It need not be carried in a bag of any kind.

3. Smith v. Mecklenburg, 280 N.C. 497, 187 S.E.2d 67 (1972).

4. Counties, as well as cities, issue on-premises and off-premises malt beverage and wine retail licenses. Usually the local government must issue the license if the applicant holds the corresponding ABC permit from the state. Thus these local licenses are more a matter of revenue than of control (G.S. 105-113.70).

5. Nelson v. Board of Alcohol Control, 26 N.C. App. 303, 217 S.E.2d 666 (1975).

6. G.S. 18B-901(c) lists the factors that the state ABC Commission may consider in deciding whether to issue a permit. It is not clear whether a local government may raise additional objections. In any event, the factors that the commission may consider are very broad and include whether the applicant is a suitable person to hold an ABC permit and whether the operation of the business at that location would be detrimental to the surrounding neighborhood.

34   Other County Services

Ben F. Loeb, Jr., Jill D. Moore, and Warren Jake Wicker

Contents

Ben F. Loeb, Jr., is an Institute of Government faculty member whose interests include eminent domain, alcoholic beverage control, fire protection, and animal control law.

Jill D. Moore is an Institute of Government faculty member who works primarily in the area of public health law.

Warren Jake Wicker is an Institute of Government emeritus faculty member whose work included local government law, finance, and administration.

Emergency Medical Services and Rescue Squads

In 1971 the General Assembly directed the Legislative Research Commission to study emergency medical care in North Carolina. The commission's study resulted in the Emergency Medical Services Act of 1973 (G.S. Chapter 143, Article 56). The Act established the state's emergency medical services (EMS) program within the state Department of Human Resources (now the Department of Health and Human Services).

The Office of Emergency Medical Services (OEMS) administers the state EMS program, which is located in the Division of Facility Services in the Department of Health and Human Services (G.S. 143-508). Two state agencies regulate the program. The North Carolina Medical Care Commission adopts the rules and standards that govern ambulance licensure and basic life support services, and the North Carolina Medical Board adopts rules and standards governing advanced life support services. The Emergency Medical Services Advisory Council is, as its name suggests, an advisory body that considers matters pertaining to EMS and makes recommendations about regulations or programs to the Medical Care Commission and the secretary of health and human services. The twenty-one-member council is composed of four legislators, plus seventeen members appointed by the secretary of health and human services. The secretary's appointees must include physicians versed in emergency medicine, emergency room nurses, ambulance service providers, representatives of hospitals, local government officials, and members of the general public (G.S. 143-510).

The OEMS is responsible for ensuring that emergency treatment centers are available throughout the state, inspecting and permitting ambulances, licensing ambulance service providers, certifying ambulance personnel, designating trauma centers and a state poison control center, and assisting in the development of a statewide EMS communications system. This work is accomplished through a central office in Raleigh, and through three regional offices in Black Mountain, Raleigh, and Greenville. The central office is staffed by a director and specialists in the areas of transportation, public education, hospitals, EMS staff education and training, and communications. The primary role of the central office staff is to develop programs and provide expertise and assistance in each of those areas. A physician serves as part-time medical advisor to the state EMS program.

Each of the three regions is staffed by a regional supervisor and regional coordinators who work closely with local EMS providers. Regional staff inspect ambulances, administer certification examinations to ambulance personnel, coordinate services in the area they serve, and provide technical assistance and advice to local EMS providers and the regional EMS council. They also serve as part of the state's emergency response team. In addition to the OEMS regional offices, each region has a regional EMS council, composed of representatives of local government, rescue squads, hospitals, the medical community, and the general public. Each regional council is affiliated with a lead regional organization (LRO)—a multipurpose organization responsible for planning and administering a variety of programs. The LRO is usually a council of governments or a planning and development commission designated by the state secretary of administration as a lead regional organization.

Neither the state nor the regional EMS offices are engaged in the actual delivery of emergency medical services in North Carolina. That responsibility is shouldered by agencies and organizations at the local level. County governments are the key players in assuring and overseeing EMS programs at the local level.

G.S. 153A-250 authorizes counties to adopt ordinances franchising ambulance services provided in the county. Sixty-five counties had adopted such ordinances by June 1, 1997.[1] An *ambulance* is a vehicle that is designed to transport persons who are "sick, injured, wounded, or otherwise incapacitated or helpless" and may need medical care while being transported (G.S. 131E-55). A county ordinance may perform the following functions:

- Grant franchises to ambulance operators on terms set by the commissioners
- Make it unlawful to provide ambulance services or operate an ambulance in the county without a franchise
- Limit the number of ambulances that may be operated within the county
- Limit the number of ambulances that may be operated by each operator
- Determine which areas of the county each franchised operator may serve
- Establish and from time to time revise rate, fee, and charge schedules
- Set minimum amounts of liability insurance for franchise operators
- Establish other necessary regulations consistent with state statutes and regulations [G.S. 153A-250(a)]

Before adopting an ordinance, commissioners must hold a public hearing on the need for ambulance services. Notice of the hearing must be published once a week for two weeks. After the hearing, the board of commissioners may adopt an ordinance if it finds that an ordinance is necessary to assure adequate and continuing ambulance services in the county and to protect the public health [G.S. 153A-250(a)].

In lieu of or in addition to adopting an ordinance, a county may operate or contract for ambulance services in all or a portion of the county. A county may operate its ambulance services directly, or it may create an ambulance commission and authorize it to operate the services [G.S. 153A-250(b)].

A city may adopt an ambulance franchising ordinance and may operate or contract for ambulance services in only two circumstances: when (1) the county in which the city is located has adopted a resolution authorizing the city to do so; or (2) the county has not provided for ambulance services within the city within 180 days after being requested by the city to do so. The county may subsequently preempt the city's authority to operate or franchise ambulance services after giving the city 180 days' notice of its intention to take action [G.S. 153A-250(c)]. Thus a city's operation of services must initially be approved (explicitly or implicitly) by a county and the county may end the operation in its discretion.

Emergency medical services in North Carolina are supported primarily by local funds. The state OEMS receives both state and federal funds. In 1996, the OEMS received approximately $3.2 million in state funds and $193,000 in federal funds.[2] Some of those funds are used to provide grants to regional EMS councils and the LROs with which they are affiliated. LROs write grant proposals that may include requests for funds to support regional EMS administration and programs or local EMS equipment purchases. The LRO must match 30 percent of state grant funds used on administration or programs. A 50 percent match is required for state grant funds that are used on equipment purchases. That match is usually paid by the local service provider for whom the equipment is purchased.

The actual operation of local services is financed entirely at the local level. If the county operates an ambulance service as a line department, it may establish rates, fees, and charges to be collected by the service, and it may appropriate county funds to the service (G.S. 153A-250). Counties may also levy property taxes to support ambulance services within the county [G.S. 153A-149(c)].

By statute, all ambulance service providers that operate in North Carolina must be licensed by the state (G.S. 131E-155.1), each vehicle that is operated as an ambulance must be permitted by the state (G.S. 131E-156), and ambulance personnel must be certified by the state (G.S. 131E-158). In 1997, 673 providers operated more than 1,700 ambulances in North Carolina.[3]

Ambulance services offering at least basic life support services were available in all counties, and ninety-seven counties had advanced life support programs. Persons who are certified to perform advanced life support are called emergency medical technicians (EMTs) and are certified at one of four levels. The level of certification determines which treatments the EMT may administer in the out-of-hospital setting. The lowest level of advanced life support certification is EMT-defibrillation (EMT-D). In ascending order, the remaining levels are EMT-intermediate (EMT-I), EMT-advanced intermediate (EMT-AI), and EMT-paramedic (EMT-P). In 1997, eleven counties had advanced life support programs at the EMT-D level, twelve had programs at the EMT-I level, three had programs at the EMT-AI level, and seventy-one had programs at the EMT-P level.[4]

Rescue squads traditionally have been nonprofit volunteer organizations that rescue persons at the sites of accidents and disasters, but do not transport sick patients or provide medical treatment beyond first aid. Today, some organizations in North Carolina that are called "rescue squads" are actually EMS providers that operate ambulance services. Moreover, it is common for a single county department to provide more than one of the three chief emergency functions: EMS, rescue services, and fire protection. Any service provider that operates EMS vehicles (ambulances) is subject to the licensing and permitting requirements described previously. Traditional rescue squad vehicles (a rescue truck with extrication equipment, for example) do not engage in the transportation and treatment of patients and thus are not subject to those requirements.

Counties typically do not operate traditional rescue squads but they may support them financially. G.S. 160A-487 authorizes counties to appropriate funds to rescue squads. Counties may also levy property taxes to support rescue squads [G.S. 153A-149(c)]; lease, sell, or convey land to volunteer rescue squads to build or expand facilities (G.S. 153A-176 and 160A-277); and appropriate property to rescue squads providing services within the county (G.S. 153A-176 and 160A-279).[5]

Animal Control

Animal control in North Carolina is largely discretionary at the local level. The only mandated activities are in the fields of rabies control and dangerous dogs. Hunting, fishing, and other activities involving wildlife fall under the jurisdiction of the State Wildlife Commission, and for the most part their officers enforce statewide laws. Farm and other animals raised to be commercially processed as food fall under the jurisdiction of the North Carolina (and federal) Department of Agriculture. Thus animal control at the local level deals largely with dogs, cats, and other animals which are generally considered pets.

Rabies Control Law

The North Carolina Rabies Control Law, which is contained in Part 6, Article 6 of G.S. Chapter 130A, requires the owner of every dog and cat over four months of age to have the animal vaccinated against rabies (G.S. 130A-185). The local health director must organize (or assist other county departments to organize) at least one countywide rabies vaccination clinic per year (G.S. 130A-187). Licensed veterinarians usually administer these vaccines. However, a local health director may appoint one or more "certified rabies vaccinators" to administer the vaccine, even if licensed veterinarians are available. Those appointed to administer the vaccine must be provided four hours of training and then be certified by the State Public Health Veterinarian (G.S. 130A-186).

Boards of county commissioners are authorized to establish a fee for the rabies vaccine, which may include an administrative charge not to exceed $4. The veterinarian or certified rabies vaccinator who administers the vaccine to the dog or cat must complete a three-copy rabies vaccination certificate, with the original being given to the pet owner. A rabies vaccination tag is also furnished to the owner; dogs are required to wear the tag at all times, but cats may be exempted by local ordinance (G.S. 130A-188, -189, -190).

There is no statewide law authorizing stray dogs to be impounded. However, G.S. 130A-192 provides that if a dog or cat is not wearing the required vaccination tag and the ownership of the animal cannot be determined, the animal control officer may impound the animal. The duration of impoundment is established by the board of county commissioners, but may not be less than seventy-two hours. (Many communities keep impounded animals for a much longer period. Raleigh, for example, keeps dogs for at least a week.) During the impoundment period a reasonable effort must be made to locate the animal's owner. In those cases where the animal is not reclaimed during the impoundment period, it must be disposed of in one of the following manners: put up for adoption, sold to an institution within the state registered by the U.S. Dept. of Agriculture pursuant to the Federal Animal Welfare Act, or put to death by a procedure approved by the American Veterinary Medical Association, the Humane Society of the United States, or the American Humane Association.

G.S. 130A-194 authorizes local health directors to declare an area under quarantine in cases where rabies exists, to the extent that lives are endangered. A dog or cat in a quarantined area must be confined on its owner's premises or in a veterinary hospital. Any dog or cat continuing to run uncontrolled in the area may be destroyed by an animal control officer after reasonable effort has been made to apprehend the offending animal (G.S. 130A-195).

A person bitten by a dog or cat (and any person owning or having control of the animal) must notify the local health director immediately. The offending animal is then immediately confined for ten days in a place designated by the local health director. (After reviewing the circumstances of the case, the health director "may" allow the owner to confine the animal on the owner's property.) An owner failing to confine an animal in accordance with instructions of the health director is guilty of a Class 2 misdemeanor. Any physician who attends a person bitten by an animal known to be a potential carrier of rabies must notify the local health director within twenty-four hours (G.S. 130A-196).

G.S. 130A-197 provides that a dog or cat bitten by a proven rabid animal or any animal suspected of having rabies (and not available for laboratory diagnosis) must be immediately destroyed by its owner, the county animal control officer, or a peace officer, *unless the dog or cat has had the required vaccination*. Any person owning or in possession of an animal which is suspected of having rabies must immediately notify the local health director or county animal control officer and securely confine it in a place designated by the health director. This confinement must be for a period of at least ten days (G.S. 130A-198). An animal diagnosed as having rabies by a licensed veterinarian must be destroyed and its head sent to the State Public Health Laboratory. Also, the heads of all dogs and cats that die during the ten-day confinement period shall immediately be sent to the laboratory for rabies diagnosis (G.S. 130A-199).

During 1997 North Carolina was in the midst of the worst rabies epidemic in its history, and thus the previously discussed laws received stricter enforcement than in past decades.

Dangerous Dog Law

Biting dogs are a real and growing problem in North Carolina; and as the state becomes more urban and crowded the problem is likely to worsen. The first comprehensive statute to deal with this problem is contained in Article 1A of G.S. Chapter 67 (as enacted in 1990 by the General Assembly). G.S. 67-4.1 defines "dangerous dog" to mean a dog with any of the following characteristics:

1. it has killed or inflicted severe injury on a person without provocation; or
2. it is owned or harbored primarily or in part for the purpose of dog fighting, as well as any dog trained for fighting; or
3. it is determined to be potentially dangerous by a city or county board designated for that purpose.

A "potentially dangerous dog" is one so designated by a duly appointed person or board because the dog has committed any of the following acts:

1. Inflicted a bite on a person that resulted in broken bones, disfiguring lacerations, or hospitalization
2. Killed or inflicted severe injury on a domestic animal *when not on its owner's premises*
3. Approached a person *when not on its owner's premises* in a vicious or terrorizing manner

The city or county authority responsible for animal control designates a person or board to be responsible for determining when a dog is a "potentially dangerous dog." It also designates a separate board to hear any appeal—typically a city council or board of county commissioners makes this designation. The dog owner must receive written notice before his or her dog may be considered potentially dangerous and he or she may then appeal by filing written objections with the appellate board within three days. An appeal from a final decision of the appellate board can be taken to the superior court, where it will be heard *de novo* [G.S. 67-4.1(c)].

Apparently *de novo*, as used in this statute, requires that the superior court hear the case on its merits from beginning to end (as if the appellate board had held no hearing). In other words, a *de novo* review of the existing record is *not* sufficient[6] (this case also upheld the constitutionality of the North Carolina Dangerous Dog Law). A dog found to be potentially dangerous pursuant to the previously cited section is thereafter treated under the law as a dangerous dog.

G.S. 67-4.2 makes it unlawful for the owner of a dangerous dog to do the following:

1. Leave the dog unattended on the owner's premises unless it is confined indoors, or is in a securely enclosed and locked pen, or put in another structure designed to restrain the dog. *There is nothing in the wording of this statute that would indicate that chaining the dog on the owner's premises meets the requirements of this section.*

2. Permit the dog to go beyond the owner's premises unless it is leashed and muzzled or otherwise securely restrained and muzzled.

Also, notice requirements are imposed in the event that the owner of the dog transfers its ownership or possession to another person. Violation of G.S. 67-4.2 is a Class 3 misdemeanor.

The owner of a dangerous dog that attacks a person and causes physical injuries requiring medical treatment in excess of $100 is guilty of a Class 1 misdemeanor (G.S. 67-4.3). In addition, the owner of a dangerous dog is "strictly liable" in civil damages for any injuries or property damage the dog inflicts upon a person, his or her property, or another animal (G.S. 67-4.4).

An unusual feature of the North Carolina Dangerous Dog Law is that it apparently permits a city or county to adopt and enforce its own program for the control of dangerous dogs (G.S. 67-4.5). Local government action in this regard has taken several forms. In some cases a city or county has adopted its own definition of "dangerous or potentially dangerous dog" that differs somewhat from state law. In other cases local ordinances have added detail that goes beyond state law, such as designating who should make the original determination that a dog is potentially dangerous, and the composition of the board that hears the appeal. (In one instance, the animal control officer was designated to make the original determination, with health department employees constituting the appellate board.)

Vicious Animals

The North Carolina Rabies Control Law (as contained in Article 6 of G.S. Chapter 130A) contains a provision authorizing a local health director to declare *any* animal (not just a dog) to be vicious and a menace to public health. To be awarded this designation the animal must have attacked a person causing bodily harm without being teased, molested, provoked, beaten, tortured, or otherwise harmed. When an animal has been declared vicious or a menace to public health, the local health director must order the animal confined to its owner's property (G.S. 130A-200). Most communities now use the dangerous dog law, rather than this statute, when the offending animal is a dog.

Killer Dogs

In rare cases the misdeeds of an animal can result in serious criminal charges. Thus in *State v. Powell*,[7] the owner of two Rottweilers was convicted of involuntary manslaughter after his unattended dogs attacked and killed a jogger.

County Discretionary Powers

Counties have the following ordinance-making powers (similar to cities) with respect to animals, as follows:

1. To define and prohibit the abuse of animals (G.S. 153A-127). (State law in G.S. 14-360 also defines animal abuse, but the wording of that statute is somewhat antiquated.)
2. To regulate, restrict, or prohibit the possession or harboring of animals that are dangerous to persons or property G.S. 153A-131). (As is the case with cities, primary jurisdiction with respect to wildlife is vested in the N.C. Wildlife Resources Commission.)
3. To levy an annual license tax on the privilege of keeping dogs and other pets within the county (G.S. 153A-153).
4. To establish, equip, operate, and maintain an animal shelter or to contribute to the support of an animal shelter (G.S. 153A-442).

Unlike cities, counties do not have specific authority to adopt a leash law. However, like cities, they do have the general ordinance-making power to define, regulate, prohibit, or abate acts, omissions, or conditions detrimental to the health, safety, or welfare of their citizens, as well as to define and abate nuisances. A leash law could probably be adopted under the authority of this statute (G.S. 153A-121).

The above listing omits G.S. 67-31, which sets forth the powers and duties of a county dog warden, because that section is essentially obsolete. First, the section, which was enacted in 1951, gives the dog warden the "power of arrest." Subsequent legislation limits the power of arrest to law enforcement officers who have successfully completed the basic law enforcement officers' training program. Second, a dog warden is by definition responsible only for the enforcement of laws pertaining to the ownership and control of dogs; most counties now prefer an official with broader authority. Thus the prevailing practice is to appoint one or more animal control officers pursuant to the provisions of G.S. 67-30.

Although the rabies law and dangerous dog law each contain mandatory provisions, in general the North Carolina animal control laws are permissive, giving cities and counties the authority to determine how much animal control they wish to undertake. Thus any county or city that wishes to have a comprehensive set of laws on animal control will have to adopt them by ordinance.

What counties actually do with regard to these discretionary powers varies a great deal from county to county. Almost all counties now have an animal shelter or access to an animal shelter. Sometimes these are shared with other units of government. The city of Chapel Hill and Orange County, for example, utilize the same animal shelter, which is actually operated by the local Humane Society. On the other hand, leash laws, which require pets to be under the control of an adult when off the owner's premises, are usually limited to the more populous and urban counties. Thus Mecklenburg and Cumberland counties have such laws, but Mitchell County does not.

At least a third of North Carolina counties require some sort of dog tag for which a fee is charged. (The fee is occasionally reduced if the animal is neutered.) A typical tax would be in the $5 to $10 range per animal.

As is the case with some cities, a few counties have contracted out their animal control functions as authorized by G.S. 153A-449. In Buncombe County all animal control functions (including the animal shelter) are now performed by the Buncombe County Friends of Animals, Inc., while in Orange County the local humane society runs the animal shelter, while other functions (such as rabies control and stray dogs) are still performed by the county.

Animal Cruelty Investigators

In addition to animal control officers, boards of county commissioners are authorized to appoint one or more animal cruelty investigators to serve without compensation or other employee benefits (G.S. 19A-45). In making these appointments, the board may consider nominees of an animal cruelty society.

Animal cruelty investigators serve one-year terms subject to removal for cause by the county commissioners. While in the performance of their official duties, the investigators must wear a badge of a design approved by the board, identifying them as cruelty investigators. These investigators take and subscribe to the oath of office required of public officials and are not required to post bond. While animal cruelty investigators do not receive salary or benefits, they may be reimbursed for necessary and actual expenses associated with performing their duties (G.S. 19A-45).

Whenever any animal is being treated cruelly the cruelty investigator may file a sworn complaint with a magistrate requesting an order "allowing the investigator to provide suitable care for and take immediate custody of the animal." A magistrate issues the order only when he or she finds probable cause to believe that the animal is being treated cruelly and that it is necessary for the cruelty investigator to take custody immediately. The magistrate's order is valid for only twenty-four hours after its issuance, and the cruelty investigator must return it, with a written inventory of the animals seized, to the clerk of court in the county where the order was issued [G.S. 19A-46(a)].

G.S. 19A-46(b) provides that an animal cruelty investigator may request a law enforcement officer or an animal control officer to accompany him or her and assist in seizing the animal. A cruelty investigator may forcibly enter premises or a vehicle when necessary to execute the order, but only if he or she reasonably believes that the premises or vehicle is unoccupied by a person and that the animal is on the premises or in the vehicle. Forcible entry may be used only when the cruelty investigator is accompanied by a law enforcement officer, and even then only during daylight hours. While the assistance of a law enforcement officer is required only in the case of forcible entry, animal cruelty investigators would be well-advised to have the assistance of an officer whenever *any* type of confrontation with the animal owner is anticipated.

Once he or she has taken custody of a cruelly treated animal, the investigator must file a complaint in district court pursuant to G.S. 19A-3 as soon as possible. When an animal is seized, the owner must be given a copy of the magistrate's order and such other information as required by G.S. 19A-46(c). Any seized animal must be taken directly to a safe and secure place where suitable care will be provided for it. Necessary expenses of caring for seized animals, including necessary veterinary care, are a charge against the animal's owner and a lien on the animal, which can be enforced pursuant to G.S. 44A-4 (G.S. 19A-47).

Administrative Organization

Counties and municipalities usually handle their animal control activities separately. (Certainly this is the case in the more urban counties.) Thus Chapel Hill and Orange County each have their own animal control ordinance and animal control officers, although they do share one animal shelter which is operated by the local humane society under contract with both governments. The general rule in North Carolina is that a county ordinance is not effective inside cities unless the city approves it by resolution (G.S. 153A-122). Thus for the most part, animal control functions remain separate.

Administratively, animal control has to be placed somewhere and a variety of approaches have been tried over the years. Since the county health department has statutory responsibility for rabies control, that is one obvious agency to assume responsibility for all animal control activities. Randolph, Craven, and numerous other counties have assigned this responsibility to the health department. A few counties place this function with a law enforcement agency. In Burke County, for example, the sheriff's department has responsibility for animal control. Obviously, having law enforcement officers available to enforce animal control law has some advantages when it becomes necessary to make a search and seizure or arrest. Some counties have put their animal control function under the county manager. In Cumberland County there is an animal control department under the supervision of an animal control warden who is appointed by and reports to the county manager. Finally, some counties are experimenting with contracting the animal control function out to private agencies. Buncombe County, for instance, has contracted with a local humane society to run its shelter and provide other animal control services.

Level of Activity

Animal control is a major activity for many North Carolina local governments. According to the office of the State Public Health Veterinarian, over 400,000 dogs and cats were vaccinated for rabies in 1996 (the last year for which figures are available), and several counties did not report their number of vaccinations. The number of animal control officers per North Carolinian is not known, but is estimated to be about one animal control officer for every 16,000 to 18,000 citizens nationwide. North Carolina is probably somewhere close to this range. Craven County, for example, has five persons working in animal control who serve a population of approximately 66,000. (This does not count the city of New Bern [21,000 population], which has its own animal control employees.) Craven County vaccinates approximately 17,000 animals annually and answers over 1,400 complaints per year. The cost of keeping an animal at the shelter is thought to be about $1 per animal per day. The annual cost of the animal control program in Craven County is approximately $200,000.

Guilford, a much larger county, has an animal control budget of over $1 million a year. Their animal shelter is indeed a busy one. During financial year 1996 the number of animals seized in the shelter was 14,500. Less than a third of these were reclaimed or adopted, and the remaining two-thirds were euthanized. During the year approximately 160 animals were held for rabies observation. As is the case with most animal control operations, the largest single item was "personnel services," with a total expenditure of about half a million dollars.

Cabarrus County is one of the few in the state where the animal control function comes under the sheriff. During financial year 1996–97 approximately $370,000 was spent on animal control. This sum financed a very busy animal control division, which received over 16,000 complaints; some 5,500 of these were actually investigated, and over 4,000 dogs and cats were picked up. Reported dog bites for 1996–97 were 145 and cat bites a mere fifty. There were approximately 130 investigations of animals other than dogs and cats, and a total of 300 civil citations were issued. Approximately twenty animals were identified as having rabies. Almost 4,000 dogs and cats were destroyed, indicating a rather low rate of adoption or reclaiming of the animals.

Arts Programs and Museums

North Carolina counties have broad authority to provide arts programs, historic preservation programs, and museums or similar facilities (G.S. 153A-445 with reference to G.S. 160A-488). Counties may establish and support museums, art galleries, and art centers as long as the facilities are open to the public. As used in G.S. 160A-488, *arts* refers to ". . . the performing arts, visual arts, and literary arts and includes dance, drama, music, painting, drawing, sculpture, print-making, crafts, photography, film, video, architecture, design and literature, when part of a performing, visual or literary arts program."

Financial support may include purchasing works of art as well as providing buildings and meeting operating and maintenance expenses. Counties may levy property taxes to support arts programs [(G.S. 153A-149(c)(6a) and (14)] and issue general obligation bonds to finance the construction of museums or other facilities [G.S. 159-48(11)].

Counties may operate the various programs directly or contract with any public or private, nonprofit organization to establish and operate the programs. They may also appropriate funds to such organizations to carry out museum, historic preservation, and arts programs and activities.

Most counties provide some support for historic preservation programs and arts and cultural activities. A number of counties—Orange, Onslow, and Granville, for example—have constructed county history museums that also include space for displaying art. A few counties—including Carteret, Edgecombe, Person, and Union—have county libraries that include galleries that regularly offer exhibitions. Others support local arts councils that also receive state support. County outlays are significant, but do not begin to match the appropriations for the major county programs for education, health, and welfare.

Auditoriums, Coliseums, and Civic and Convention Centers

Counties, under the authority of G.S. 153A-445, may establish and support public auditoriums, coliseums, and convention centers. Support includes the acquisition and construction of these facilities and their operation, maintenance, and improvement. Counties may use any funds they have available for these purposes unless their use is otherwise limited by law. Support includes the levy of property taxes for these purposes [G.S. 153A-149(c)(6b)]. Counties may also issue general obligation bonds [G.S. 159-48(b)(3)] and revenue bonds (G.S. 159, Art. 5).

Local officials agree that outlays for auditoriums, coliseums, and convention centers are investments in economic development, cultural opportunities, and tourism. Rarely are such facilities fully self-supporting from the revenues of the activities and events presented in them.

A facility is usually considered financially successful if it produces enough revenue to cover operating and maintenance costs.

Most of these facilities are built and operated by cities. County governments have been involved in only a few cases, sometimes as the sole owner, and at other times in partnership with a city or town. Cumberland and Wake are among the counties that own and operate a coliseum, civic or convention center, or an auditorium. Several other counties have joined with a city or town to finance a facility that is owned and operated by the municipality. Only Cumberland County had outstanding indebtedness on auditoriums, coliseums, or convention centers in 1998.

All counties have meeting rooms and facilities that are available to some extent to community groups. These are found in agricultural extension offices, courthouse or county administrative buildings, and libraries, for example. A few are known as community service buildings and are large enough to handle small conventions, although not designed primarily for that purpose. Community colleges also have auditoriums and meeting facilities. Some are designated as civic centers and cater to small conventions and exhibitions.

Cemeteries

Concern for the proper burial of the deceased has been almost universal throughout history. Well-maintained cemeteries evidence respect for the dead, are often significant in connection with religious burial rituals, and are important in safeguarding the public health.

State officials in North Carolina estimate that there are more than 35,000 active, inactive, and abandoned cemeteries in North Carolina.[8] This tabulation includes family, church, private, and public cemeteries. A recently completed survey for Robeson County, for example, found over 600 cemeteries within its boundaries. In 1981 the General Assembly established the North Carolina Cemetery Survey within the Division of Archives and History of the Department of Cultural Resources. The goal of the survey is to identify and locate all existing cemeteries in North Carolina. Counties are primarily responsible for the work, but it is often carried out with the assistance of volunteers and historical, genealogical, and other interested organizations. Robeson is one of the seventeen counties that had submitted reports by 1998.

State law generally regulates the operation of cemeteries. The North Carolina Cemetery Act (G.S. 65, Art. 9) governs the operations of cemeteries and applies to all cemeteries except those operated and maintained by government units and churches. G.S. 65-13 prescribes the procedures to be followed in the disinterment, removal, and reinterment of graves. These procedures are carried out under the direction of the board of commissioners, or by the health director or other appropriate officials appointed by the board of commissioners.

County governments have important, but limited, duties and responsibilities with respect to cemeteries. A primary duty is set forth in G.S. 65-1. This statute makes it the duty of boards of county commissioners ". . . to prepare and keep on record in the office of the register of deeds a list of all public cemeteries in the counties outside [cities and towns] and not established and maintained [for a city or town], together with the names and addresses of the persons in possession and control of the [cemeteries]." The lists prepared by the commissioners must also include a list of ". . . public cemeteries [in each county] that have been abandoned." The commissioners are directed to supply a copy of these lists to the office of the secretary of state. At the end of 1997 the secretary of state's office had received a list from only one county.[9]

G.S. 65-2 authorizes boards of commissioners to appropriate up to $50 as one-third of the cost of beautifying cemeteries if the operators provide the other two-thirds of the cost.

Boards of commissioners are required by G.S. 65-3 to take over abandoned cemeteries in their respective counties, and may appropriate funds to protect them and to establish their boundaries. The boards may appoint a board of trustees to carry out the duties of the commissioners under the law. Commissioners may levy property taxes to support cemetery outlays [G.S. 153A-149(c)(8)].

Counties, under the authority of G.S. Chapter 153A, Article 16, may establish county service districts for the purpose of operating and maintaining cemeteries. Once such a service district is established, the commissioners may levy a special property tax within the district for cemetery purposes. They may also issue general obligation bonds for cemetery purposes.

There has been no recent survey of the level of county government expenditures for cemetery purposes. Officials familiar with county government in the state believe the outlays by most counties to be quite small.

Additional Resources

Bailey, Bob, and Cary McDonald. "The Status of Emergency Medical Services in North Carolina," *North Carolina Medical Journal* 58 (1997): 238.

Loeb, Ben F., Jr. *Animal Control Law for North Carolina Local Governments*, 3d ed. Chapel Hill, N.C., Institute of Government, The University of North Carolina at Chapel Hill, 1997.

Notes

1. Unpublished data, Office of Emergency Medical Services, Division of Facility Services, North Carolina Department of Health and Human Services.

2. Bob Bailey and Cary McDonald, "The Status of Emergency Medical Services in North Carolina," *North Carolina Medical Journal* 58 (1997): 238, 239. Federal funding for EMS services has declined significantly in recent years. In 1981, the federal Omnibus Budget Reconciliation Act allocated federal funds for EMS through the Preventive Health Services Block Grant and the Social Services Block Grant. In 1982, North Carolina received more than $1.4 million in federal funds. EMS still receives some funds from the Social Services Block Grant, but it has not received Preventive Health Services Block Grant funds since 1992. In 1995, the OEMS received approximately $450,000 in federal funds. In 1996, that figure dropped to $193,000. From time to time, OEMS receives federal funds from other sources in the form of limited-term grants. *Id.*

3. *Id.*

4. *Id.* at 240.

5. The author is indebted to Bob Bailey, director of the North Carolina Office of Emergency Medical Services, who provided invaluable information through interviews and written materials. Portions of this section were excerpted or adapted from Warren Jake Wicker, "Other Services and Functions," in *Municipal Government in North Carolina*, 2d ed. (Chapel Hill, N.C.: Institute of Government, The University of North Carolina at Chapel Hill, 1996), 747–50.

6. Caswell County v. Hanks, 120 N.C. App. 489, 462 S.E.2d 841 (1995).

7. 336 N.C. 762, 446 S.E.2d 26 (1994).

8. Debra A. Blake, Special Projects Archivist, Archives and History, Department of Cultural Resources, May 1998.

9. Sheila Pope, General Counsel, Office of the Secretary of State, May 1998.

Where to Obtain Further Assistance

Contents

Additional resources are available to readers of this volume who need more detailed information concerning the subjects that it covers. This section discusses some of the consultation-advisory services and other aids that may be helpful. In addition, a list of additional resources may be found at the end of each chapter.

Detailed listings of local government resources in North Carolina may be found in the Fall 1996 issue of *Popular Government,* an Institute of Government magazine available from the Institute's Publications Office,

CB# 3330, Knapp Building, The University of North Carolina at Chapel Hill, Chapel Hill, NC 27599-3330. Telephone (919) 966-4119. References to a variety of resources, including a complete catalog of Institute publications, may also be found on NCINFO, the Institute of Government's Internet home page, at http://ncinfo.iog.unc.edu.

Institute of Government

A primary resource is the Institute of Government, a unit of The University of North Carolina at Chapel Hill. Founded in 1931 to help state, county, and local officials improve government administration and policymaking in North Carolina, the Institute is the largest and most diversified of the university-based governmental training and research organizations in the country. Not only does it enjoy a national reputation, but it also plays a significant role in the governmental life of the state.

Engaging in research, teaching, writing, and consultation in public law and government, for nearly seventy years the Institute's faculty members have served public officials throughout North Carolina by teaching courses, preparing publications, and providing advice on a broad variety of topics. These services are extended without regard to political considerations and recognize that policy determinations are the province of elected and appointed officials.

The Institute's professional staff are on the faculty of The University of North Carolina at Chapel Hill and are based in the Institute rather than in university departments or schools. Twenty-seven of the current faculty of forty hold law degrees; other fields represented include accounting, business administration, city and regional planning, conflict analysis and resolution, economics, library science, political science, psychology, public administration, and public finance. Each faculty member specializes in certain subject-matter fields but sometimes joins colleagues on special teams that address broader problems that call on several disciplines. Institute lawyers concentrate in one or more areas of public law that concern North Carolina officials—such as health, city and county government, finance, taxation, the administration of criminal justice, land use regulations, and the environment.

Nearly 60 percent of the Institute's financial support is provided by state appropriations to the university; the remainder comes from revenues the Institute receives from city and county membership dues, fees for special consulting services, sales of publications, and reimbursement for direct costs incurred in serving particular governments. The percentage of the Institute's budget from state appropriations has declined in recent years.

Readers of this book who wish to obtain further information about the general activities of the Institute, including a list of faculty members and their fields of work, may write to the Director, Institute of Government, CB# 3330, Knapp Building, The University of North Carolina at Chapel Hill, Chapel Hill, NC 27599-3330. The Institute's telephone number is (919) 966-5381. Readers may also contact the Institute Publications Office or its home page, at http:// ncinfo.iog.unc.edu.

Consultation/Advisory Assistance

One of the many services provided by the Institute is consultation/ advisory assistance, available on request to state and local government officials and agencies, legislative committees, associations of public officials, and, to some extent, citizens' groups.

Readers needing individual assistance concerning any of the subjects covered in County Government in North Carolina *are invited to contact the appropriate chapter author at the Institute of Government's address. A list of faculty members with their fields of expertise may be obtained free of charge from the Institute's Publications Office at the same address.*

Classes

Teaching activities of the Institute provide in-service training for elected and appointed officials—municipal, county, and state. Some courses introduce new personnel to the responsibilities of their posts; others help experienced officials increase and update their knowledge of both the laws and programs they administer as well as methods of administration.

During 1996–97, the Institute sponsored or cosponsored 184 sessions of courses, conferences, and schools. Faculty participated in an additional 114 sessions sponsored by other organizations. Those attending include county commissioners; mayors and city council members; county and city managers and attorneys; public school administrators; public health, social services, and mental health officials; planners; tax assessors and collectors; finance officers; county and municipal clerks; law enforcement personnel; school board members; correctional agency staff;

judges; district attorneys; and many others. More than 6,000 people a year come to Chapel Hill for training that lasts from half a day to sixteen weeks; another 6,000 attend conferences and classes held by the Institute at other North Carolina sites. The Institute is also home to the university's Master of Public Administration program, which involves a two-year course of study.

Inquiries about classes in particular subjects related to county government should be addressed to the appropriate faculty member in care of the Institute. A Selected List of Schools for County Officials *may be obtained free of charge from the Institute's Publications Office at the same address.*

Publications

Research and writing are essential activities of the Institute's faculty. Many of the research projects are undertaken on staff initiative; others are conducted at the request of government agencies or governmental clients.

The Institute publishes about twenty volumes a year, nearly all of which are written by the faculty. Many are basic reference works that assist particular groups of officials in performing their jobs, such as guidebooks for board of health members, election officials, magistrates, and tax collectors. Other volumes cover topics of interest to a variety of officials—for example, general governmental administration, health affairs, financial-budgetary matters, and the criminal justice system. These books are supplemented by two quarterly magazines, *Popular Government* and *School Law Bulletin,* and by many specialized bulletins in such areas of law as health, local government, the administration of justice, finance, and social services. The Institute also produces the *Daily Bulletin* on legislative activity while the North Carolina General Assembly is in session.

A free copy of the Institute's publications catalog may be obtained by contacting the Publications Office, Institute of Government, at the address listed previously. As noted, the complete catalog is also available on the Institute's Internet home page, at http://ncinfo.iog.unc.

Many Institute publications amplify or supplement the material in this volume. Some pertinent ones are listed in the "Additional Resources" section at the end of most chapters.

Library and Online Assistance

The Institute Library provides assistance to inquirers with questions concerning public law, public administration, management, and government. The library staff helps in locating information and answers through the use of its print collection and databases or by referrals to members of the Institute's faculty, separate government agencies, or other reference resources as necessary. *The library may be reached at (919) 966-4139.*

NCINFO is an Internet site (found at http://ncinfo.iog.unc.edu) sponsored by the Institute of Government in conjunction with the North Carolina League of Municipalities and the North Carolina Association of County Commissioners. It serves as an electronic information resource to individuals interested in local government in North Carolina. The site seeks to use Internet technology effectively to increase efficiency and enhance services to those involved in the administration and governance of local government in North Carolina.

For more information on NCINFO, contact NCINFO Director at (919) 962-0592.

North Carolina Association of County Commissioners

The North Carolina Association of County Commissioners represents county governments as essential partners with state government in providing services to more than seven million citizens. Since 1908, the Association has served as the counties' advocate before the executive, legislative and judicial branches of state government. All 100 counties have been voluntary members for several decades and pay annual dues to fund the Association. Collectively, the organization strives to protect and preserve the authority and ability of county governments to carry out their responsibilities.

County commissioners serve on the Association's Board of Directors, who are primarily selected by their colleagues from across the state. Six steering committees, comprised of elected and appointed county officials, review issues and make recommendations to the board.

The professional staff members, housed in the Albert Coates Local Government Center in Raleigh, carry out the directions of the board and represent a wide range of expertise.

County Government Advocacy

A Legislative Goals Committee, appointed by the current president every two years, reviews legislative goals submitted by counties and develops a package of proposed goals for consideration by the full membership prior to each long session of the General Assembly. Using these adopted goals for direction, the Association advocates the counties' interest before the legislative bodies. The Association keeps county officials updated and involved through its weekly *Legislative Bulletin* and through its home page on the Internet.

The Association represents counties' interests before state administrative bodies, such as the Governor's Office, state departments and regulatory commissions, and before judicial bodies through the filing of "friend of the court" briefs. One increasingly critical example is providing a strong county voice on technology issues through several councils and commissions.

The Association also works closely with the National Association of Counties in advocating the county viewpoint to federal officials.

Research and Special Services

The Association provides detailed comparative data on county finances, including results of the annual survey of county property tax rates and the annual *Fiscal Summary Databook* of each county's revenues and expenditures. The staff also researches county ordinances, practices, county election results, and policy issues as needed.

The Association also tries to reduce counties' costs through guidance on technology issues, pooled purchasing contracts, and through its three self-insurance programs.

The annual publication of the *Directory of County Officials* includes county demographic information, a listing of major county officials, an Association Staff Contact list, and a summary of election methods in each county. Individuals can purchase mailing lists or labels from the Association.

Communications

The Association sponsors and supports several conferences and district meetings each year to further educate and involve county officials in discussions about important issues.

Periodic publications include a twice-monthly tabloid newspaper, *CountyLines,* and *Legislative Bulletin,* which is printed weekly during legislative sessions. The Association also sells an educational brochure for adults describing the basics of county government, *County Government: Public Service in the Public Interest.* The Association's homepage on the Internet (located at http://ncinfo.iog.unc.edu/NCACC/) also provides a wide range of information on county-related issues and Association activities.

The Association's field representative visits every county at least once a year to provide on-site assistance and to keep staff informed about emerging county issues.

For more information, please contact the North Carolina Association of County Commissioners at P.O. Box 1488, Raleigh, NC 27602-1488, phone (919) 715-2893, or send e-mail to: ncacc@ncacc.org.

State Government

Consultation/Advisory Assistance

State government officials are another source of assistance for readers of this volume. On request, chapter authors and other faculty members of the Institute of Government can provide referrals to state (or federal) agencies that deal with a reader's areas of concern. *Contact the appropriate individual in care of the Institute.*

Publications

Various state publications also provide information concerning subjects discussed in this book. *Some recommended by chapter authors are listed in the "Additional Resources" sections at the end of numerous chapters.*

State and National Organizations

Various state and national organizations may also be able to assist readers of this volume. Some of those generally concerned with local government include the following:

International City/County Management Association, 777 North Capitol Street, NE, Suite 500, Washington, DC 20002-4201; phone (202) 289-4262; fax (202) 962-3500. http://www.icma.org

International Municipal Lawyers Association, 1110 Vermont Avenue, NW, Washington, DC 20005; phone (202) 466-5424; fax (202) 785-0152. http://www.imla.org

National Association of Counties, 440 First Street, NW, Washington, DC 20001; phone (202) 393-6226; fax (202) 737-0480. http://www.naco.org/naco.htm

National Civic League (including Alliance for National Renewal), 1445 Market Street, Suite 300, Denver, CO 80202-1728; phone (303) 571-4343; fax (303) 571-4404. http://www.ncl.org

National League of Cities, 1301 Pennsylvania Avenue, NW, Washington, DC 20004; phone (202) 626-3000; fax (202) 626-3043. http://www.nlc.org

North Carolina Association of County Commissioners, P.O. Box 1488, Raleigh, NC 27602; phone (919) 715-2893; fax (919) 733-1065. http://ncinfo.iog.unc.edu/ncacc/ (See description earlier in this section.)

North Carolina League of Municipalities, P.O. Box 3069, Raleigh, NC 27602; phone (919) 715-4000; fax (919) 733-9519. http://ncinfo.iog.unc.edu/nclm/

Specialized professional associations of public officials may also be helpful. *Contact chapter authors, the North Carolina Association of County Commissioners, or the North Carolina League of Municipalities for more information about professional associations of officials serving in local government.*

For Reference

Not to be taken from this room

NORTH CAROLINA ROOM
NEW HANOVER COUNTY PUBLIC LIBRARY

NCR